53

Cutting Propagation

Cutting Propagation

Propagation

A Guide to Propagating
and Producing Floriculture Crops

John M. Dole and James L. Gibson

Ball Publishing | Batavia, Illinois

Ball Publishing
335 N. River Street
P.O. Box 9
Batavia, IL 60510
www.ballpublishing.com

Library of Congress Cataloging-in-Publication Data

Cutting propagation : a guide to propagating and producing floriculture
    crops / John M. Dole and James L. Gibson, editors.
      p. cm.
    Includes index.
    ISBN-13: 978-1-883052-48-5 (hardcover : alk. paper)
    ISBN-10: 1-883052-48-3 (hardcover : alk. paper)
    1. Plant cuttings. 2. Plants, Ornamental--Propagation.   I. Dole,
John M. II. Gibson, James L.
    SB123.75.C87 2006
    635.9'1535--dc22
                                                    2006007486

Printed by InnerWorkings in Peru.

12 11 10 09 08 07 06   1 2 3 4 5 6 7 8 9

Contents

■■ ■ ■

Part 1

Part 2

Part 3 Crop-by-Crop Cutting Propagation

John M. Dole, James L. Gibson, and Harold F. Wilkins

Preface

Audience

Cutting Propagation: A Guide to Propagating and Producing Floriculture Crops is designed for both industry professionals and horticulture students and teachers. As the young plant industry continues to increase, more growers and students will work in it and need to know about cutting propagation. We trust that this book will provide what they need to get started.

Coverage

This book focuses on terminal, stem, and leaf/stem cuttings. We start with stock plant establishment and management, continue with cutting harvest and propagation environment, and finish with the shipping of unrooted, callused, and rooted cuttings and plugs.

Highlights

This book covers the major floriculture crop species that are cutting propagated. The book is organized into three sections to allow easy use of the information.

Part 1

This part consists of twelve chapters providing an introduction to the floriculture cutting propagation and young plant industry. It contains general propagation information and basic plant physiology principles. In addition, we profiled examples of how several floriculture businesses evolved in the propagation industry.

Part 2

The second part contains information on hundreds of minor crop species and basic production information organized into four chapters on bedding plants, herbaceous perennials, field-grown cut flowers, and foliage plants. We did not include general chapters on potted flowering plants or greenhouse-grown cut flowers because most species grown commercially are covered in individual genera chapters in Part 3.

Part 3

This part covers sixty-one of the major crop species being commercially grown in the floriculture industry. These chapters are laid out in a consistent manner to allow easy retrieval of information. Each chapter will provide enough information for a professional grower or a student to propagate and start a crop of each species.

The most important bedding plants, potted flowering plants, and greenhouse-grown cut flowers are included. The large number of specialty bedding plants, specialty cut flowers, potted foliage plants, and perennials precludes us from covering them all individually. For those segments of floriculture, we have included overview chapters in Part 2. The species included in Part 3 were chosen due to their current commercial importance or, in a few cases, their uniqueness or estimated importance in the future.

Nomenclature follows *The New Royal Horticultural Society Dictionary of Gardening* whenever possible. Dozens to hundreds of cultivars are available for many of the species, the most popular of which sometimes change annually. We did not attempt to list cultivars unless propagation techniques varied with specific cultivar groups.

The Future

As the cliché states, "The buck stops here." Despite the careful attention of both editors, numerous assistants, reviewers, and the Ball Publishing staff, there are no doubt errors. Please send any corrections, suggestions, and additional information to John Dole and James Gibson. Also keep in mind that a book like this represents only a snapshot of what is current in the industry at the time the book was written. New species, cultivars, techniques, materials, and production methods are constantly being introduced and accepted by the industry. Use this book as the beginning of your research; new information may be available from trade publications, scientific journals, industry suppliers, conferences, and fellow propagators and producers.

Acknowledgements

■ ■

We live in one of the golden eras of floriculture. This complicated and diverse industry is awash in wonderful, interesting plants. Some have been recently brought into cultivation from the wilds of countries all around the world. Others have been the result of painstaking, decades-long breeding programs. Each year entirely new species are introduced, and the currently available species are made longer flowering, more heat tolerant, more vigorous, less vigorous . . . you name the characteristic, and it probably has been enhanced. An increasingly large portion of this diversity is now dependent on cutting propagation, which takes place everywhere around the world and includes practitioners ranging from local garden centers overwintering a few favorite species to large-scale commercial propagators producing millions of cuttings. It has been a delight to learn more about this dynamic industry and to pass it along to you; we hope you will enjoy and benefit from this book.

Many of the chapters have been reviewed by or contributed to by producers and academicians who have specific expertise. Without a doubt, this book is much stronger because of their contributions. In particular, we would like to thank Jim Faust, Clemson University, for providing additional information on a number of species in Part 3.

Finally, the most important acknowledgments are for those who provided moral support, encouragement, and specific information. A great number of colleagues both within our departments and around the world are gratefully acknowledged.

John Dole dedicates this book . . .
To my partner, John Buettner, for his love, support, energy, humor, and encouragement.

To my father, mother, brother, and sister.

To my friends for their support and for listening to me talk about this project.

To the ever-changing, ever-exciting world of plants and the floriculture industry, which keeps me forever motivated.

James Gibson dedicates this book . . .
To my wife, Suzi, for her glowing optimism and endless love and support.

To a propagation industry icon, John Waldrep; as a young propagator I was inspired by him to achieve great things, and I will always remember him as a champion of growers.

To my mentor, Brian Whipker, an inspiring colleague—past, present and future.

To my family and friends in Maryland who are separated by distance but are always close to my heart.

About the Editors

Dr. John M. Dole

A professor in the Department of Horticultural Science at North Carolina State University, John Dole is a native of western Michigan who received his B.S. from Michigan State University. After obtaining his Ph.D. from the University of Minnesota, he served on the Oklahoma State University faculty for eleven years before moving to North Carolina State University. Dr. Dole has written hundreds of trade journal articles, scientific journal articles, and book chapters. His research program has focused on such crops as bedding plants, specialty cuts, bulbs, and poinsettias, and on such topics as flowering physiology and water and mineral nutrition. As an active member of the Association of Specialty Cut Flower Growers (ASCFG), Dr. Dole has served on the board of directors as southern region director, treasurer, and executive advisor and coordinates the National ASCFG Trial Programs. In addition, he teaches greenhouse management and commercial floriculture crop production. Dr. Dole has visited floriculture operations in Colombia, Costa Rica, Ecuador, Israel, Japan, Korea, Mexico, Ukraine, and most western European countries. He received the Kenneth Post Award for the outstanding graduate student paper in 1992, the ASCFG's Outstanding Service Award in 1995, and the ASCFG's Allan Armitage Award in 2000.

Dr. James L. "Jamie" Gibson

An assistant professor at the West Florida Research and Education Center, University of Florida–Milton Campus, James Gibson received his B.S. in plant and soil sciences in 1996 from West Virginia University, Morgantown. He later earned his M.S. and Ph.D. in 2000 and 2003, respectively, from North Carolina State University, Raleigh. He teaches introductory nursery management, greenhouse and nursery crop culture, advanced nursery management, principles of irrigation and water quality in horticulture, and retail management and marketing in horticulture. His research program in Florida serves to develop production and management solutions for the ornamental plant industry, with special emphasis on trialing winter annuals and tropical perennials, stock plant management, plant growth regulators, and plant nutrition. Dr. Gibson also conducts retail and marketing research at local garden centers to generate greater awareness of the increasing demand for local plant products in Florida. He is a member of the Florida Nursery, Growers and Landscape Association (FNGLA) and serves as the educational representative for Florida for the FNGLA Panhandle Chapter and the Southeast Greenhouse Conference. Dr. Gibson is also a member of OFA and the International Plant Propagators' Society, Southern Region of North America.

Contributors

Ted E. Bilderback
North Carolina State University
Department of Horticultural Science
164 Kilgore Hall, Campus Box 7609
Raleigh, NC 27695-7609
919-515-1201
fax: 919-515-7747
ted_bilderback@ncsu.edu

Matthew G. Blanchard
Michigan State University
Department of Horticulture
A224 Plant and Soil Science Building
East Lansing, MI 48824-1325
517-355-5191, ext. 1435
fax: 517-353-0890
mgblanch@msu.edu

Sylvia M. Blankenship
North Carolina State University
College of Agriculture and Life Sciences
110 Patterson Hall, Campus Box 7601
Raleigh, NC 27695-7601
919-515-6213
fax: 919-515-6980
sylvia_blankenship@ncsu.edu

Christine A. Casey
North Carolina State University
Entomology
124 Kilgore Hall, Campus Box 7613
Raleigh, NC 27695-7613
919-515-7746
fax: 919-515-7746
chris_casey@ncsu.edu

Christopher B. Cerveny
University of Florida
Institute of Food and Agricultural Sciences
1545 Fifield Hall, P.O. Box 110670
Gainesville, FL 32611-0670
352-392-1831
cervenyc@yahoo.com

Jianjun Chen
University of Florida
Mid-Florida Research and Education Center
Institute of Food and Agricultural Sciences
2725 Binion Rd.
Apopka, FL 32703-8504
407-884-2034, ext. 161
fax: 407-814-6186
jjchen@mail.ifas.ufl.edu

Joaquin A. Chong
Qntas de Monserrate
C9 Calle 4
Ponce, PR 00730
787-307-3653
fax: 408-668-1700
jachong@gmail.com

Raymond A. Cloyd
University of Illinois
Department of Natural Resources
    and Environmental Science
384 NSRL
1101 W. Peabody Dr.
Urbana, IL 61801
217-244-7218
fax: 217-333-4777
rcloyd@uiuc.edu

John M. Dole
North Carolina State University
Department of Horticultural Science
158 Kilgore Hall, Campus Box 7609
Raleigh, NC 27695-7609
919-515-3537
fax: 919-515-7747
john_dole@ncsu.edu

Amy L. Enfield
Clemson University
Department of Horticulture
E-143 Poole Agricultural Center
Clemson, SC 29634-0375
864-656-4972
fax: 864-656-4960
aenfiel@clemson.edu

James E. Faust
Clemson University
Department of Horticulture
D-136 Poole Agricultural Center
Clemson, SC 29634-0375
864-656-4966
fax: 864-656-4960
jfaust@clemson.edu

William C. Fonteno
North Carolina State University
Department of Horticultural Science
152 Kilgore Hall, Campus Box 7609
Raleigh, NC 27695-7609
919-515-5368
fax: 919-515-3192
bill_fonteno@ncsu.edu

James L. Gibson
University of Florida
West Florida Research and Education Center
Institute of Food and Agricultural Sciences
5988 Highway 90, Building 4900
Milton, FL 32583
850-983-5216, ext. 103
fax: 850-983-5774
jlgibson@ifas.ufl.edu

Lane Greer
D6282 Davenport
West Linn, OR 97068-2723
503-723-9906
lanegreer@msn.com

Debbie J. Hamrick
North Carolina Farm Bureau Federation, Inc.
P.O. Box 27766
5301 Glenwood Ave.
Raleigh, NC 27611-7766
919-782-1705
fax: 919-783-3593
dhamrick@ncfb.net

Gary W. Moorman
Pennsylvania State University
Department of Plant Pathology
111 Buckhout Laboratory
University Park, PA 16802
814-863-7401
fax: 814-863-7217
g1m@psu.edu

Erik S. Runkle
Michigan State University
Department of Horticulture
A240-C Plant and Soil Science Building
East Lansing, MI 48824-1325
517-353-3761
fax: 517-353-0890
runkleer@msu.edu

Holly L. Scoggins
VPI & SU
Department of Horticulture
301C Saunders–0327
Blacksburg, VA 24061-0327
540-231-5783
fax: 540-231-3083
hollysco@vt.edu

Robert H. Stamps
University of Florida
Mid-Florida Research and Education Center
Institute of Food and Agricultural Sciences
2725 Binion Rd.
Apopka, FL 32703-8504
407-884-2034, ext. 164
fax: 407-814-6186
rhs@gnv.ifas.ufl.edu

Brian E. Whipker
North Carolina State University
Department of Horticultural Science
51 Kilgore Hall, Campus Box 7609
Raleigh, NC 27695-7609
919-515-5374
fax: 919-515-7747
brian_whipker@ncsu.edu

Harold F. Wilkins
3701 S. Bryant Ave., Apt. 719
Minneapolis, MN 55409-1050
612-824-0589
fax: 612-824-0589

Kimberly A. Williams
Kansas State University
Department of Horticulture, Forestry,
    and Recreation Resources
2021 Throckmorton Plant Sciences Center
Manhattan, KS 66505-5506
785-532-1434
fax: 785/532-6949
kwilliam@oznet.ksu.edu

Part 1

Propagation Basics

John M. Dole and Debbie J. Hamrick

The American floriculture industry has never before experienced a boom in breeding and new plant introductions such as the one that has occurred in the past ten years. Each year hundreds of new hybrids and cultivars are brought to market. A retail greenhouse or garden center may sell thousands of different species and cultivars (fig. 1.1). A typical perennial catalog lists countless species and cultivars. Cut flower wholesalers and foliage plant brokers handle and distribute hundreds of additional cut flower and foliage plant species produced around the world. These numbers do not include the many new plant species being brought into cultivation each day or the thousands of new cultivars waiting to be released from breeding and research facilities worldwide. A visit to a growers' conference, large production facility, or Dutch flower auction can leave a person numb with excitement over the great diversity of plant material. In the floriculture industry, most of us are "plant people" at heart, and we revel at the beauty of floriculture plants.

Each one of these plant materials has been propagated by someone. The various propagation methods can be separated into sexual methods (seeds and spores) and asexual methods (cuttings, layers, divisions, natural reproductive structures such as bulbs, grafts, and micropropagation). Many bedding plants and a significant number of cut flower, potted flowering plant, and foliage plant species are propagated from seeds. In a number of species, however, sexual reproduction produces plants that are too variable for commercial production or do not reliably replicate desirable traits.

In such cases, asexual methods are used to produce clones (individual plants propagated from one original plant) that have the same traits as the original plant. Asexual propagation is also used in situations where seed propagation is either too lengthy or too expensive. However, the potential for disease spread is much greater with asexual propagation. To reduce diseases, commercial propagators have developed a process called disease indexing, which allows for the production of disease-free cuttings (see chapter 9). It is wise to always work with cuttings that originated from certified disease-free mother stock. Another important consideration is that plants selected for propagation must have the characteristics of the cultivar being propagated, which is known as being *"true-to-type."*

Figure 1.1. Garden center filled with dozens of plant species and hundreds of cultivars.

Asexual Propagation

Cutting propagation is the most common form of asexual propagation and is the dominant method for many important floriculture species including poinsettias, chrysanthemums, carnations, roses, and numerous foliage and bedding plant species. Cutting propagation involving terminal and subterminal stem sections is the focus of this book. A variety of other asexual propagation methods can also be used; they are briefly described below and in various other chapters, but are not the focus of this book.

Micropropagation

Micropropagation, or *in vitro* propagation, is also an important method for reproducing many foliage plants, cut flowers, and potted plants. This form of propagation offers the potential to produce a virtually unlimited number of identical plants from one original plant using very small pieces of plant shoots, roots, or reproductive structures (fig. 1.2). In practice, however, *in vitro* propagation is elaborate, time consuming, economically risky, and expensive. Occasionally the resulting plants are not identical to

Figure 1.2. Micropropagation culture tube.

the parent due to somaclonal variation. Due to the intense labor requirements of micropropagation, most of it for the floriculture industry is performed offshore in places such as Thailand, Taiwan, and Poland. There are some American laboratories, most of which specialize in foliage plants.

Regardless of the difficulties, numerous plant species including alstroemeria, hybrid lilies, gerbera, orchids, and many foliage plant species are commercially propagated by this method. Micropropagation is especially important in the production of disease-free stock plants, as is done with geraniums (*Pelargonium*) and carnations, and in new cultivar development and research. Micropropagation techniques have been well described in other books and are outside the scope of most floriculture businesses.

Some plants are offered for sale as Stage 2 or Stage 3 microcuttings, which are shoots harvested directly from tissue culture. These plants must be acclimated to the greenhouse environment using cultural techniques and environmental conditions similar to those used for cutting propagation outlined later in this chapter. Growers acclimate the microcuttings to the greenhouse production environment by providing shade and placing them under mist once they have been planted. Special attention must be made to maintaining high humidity, since the microcuttings are quite soft and susceptible to drying out. The substrate should be kept moist, but not wet. Light levels should slowly be increased over a four-week period and mist reduced as plants become established. Day temperatures should be maintained between 80° to 85° F (27° to 29° C).

Geophytes

Geophytes include any species that form modified plant organs for storage such as bulbs, corms, tubers, tuberous roots, rhizomes, and pseudobulbs (fig. 1.3). Many geophytic species reproduce through the natural replication of these storage organs. Some genera such as gladiolus produce numerous small cormlets. Propagation can be commercially hastened with corms, tubers, tuberous roots, and rhizomes by cutting these structures into pieces, each containing at least one vegetative meristem (axillary bud or eye),

Figure 1.3. Various bulbs and corms. (International Flower Bulb Centre)

and replanting the pieces. The flesh storage organs of caladium, dahlia, iris, and narcissus can be handled in such a manner. Nontunicate lily bulbs can be propagated by removing individual scales for propagation. Although tunicate bulbs are generally more difficult to propagate, hyacinth and scilla bulbs can be propagated by "scooping" or "scoring" the basal plate (the basal "stem" of the bulb from which the roots develop). In scooping, the entire basal plate is removed, and new bulblets form at the base of the scales. In scoring, three crossing knife cuts forming a star shape are made through the basal plate, and bulblets form along these cuts. With a few exceptions, natural reproduction of geophytes is a relatively slow process. Mechanical propagation of geophytes generally produces many more propagules, plant parts used for propagation, than natural division of geophytes.

Division

Division is the process of separating individual shoots clustered in a clump. The clumps are dug up and cut into sections with a sharp knife or saw. Each section should have a few roots and one or more growing points (sometimes referred to as "eyes") to allow for shoot regeneration. Spring- and summer-flowering species, such as coneflower (*Echinacea*) and astilbe, which produce new growth after flowering, should be divided in fall. Summer- and fall-flowering plants, such as perennial aster and goldenrod, which produce little growth after flowering, should be divided in the spring. Hosta, probably the plant most often divided by American growers, may be propagated in the spring or fall. Daylily is also a frequently divided crop; it too may be separated in the spring or fall. Indoor plants, which grow year-round, can be divided at any time; division during the spring and early summer, however, may allow quickest regeneration due to longer days and greater light intensity. Commercially, division is limited in use because of high labor requirements and slow rate of replication, but it can be used with many outdoor perennial and indoor foliage plant species.

Layering

Layering induces adventitious roots to form on stems while they are still attached to the parent plant. Adventitious refers to newly formed growing points. The process of layering can be thought of as rooting a terminal stem cutting while the cutting is still attached to the parent plant. Layering can occur naturally when low-growing branches root when in contact with the soil, such as occurs with forsythia, or it can be induced artificially by burying stems under soil or by mounding soil around the base of a multistemmed plant.

In *tip layering*, shoot apices are bent into the ground, root, and finally grow upward. *Simple layering* occurs when the stems are bent to the ground, and part of the stem is covered with soil, but the shoot tip remains uncovered. *Mound layering* involves mounding the soil around the base of a multistemmed plant to induce root development at the base of the stems. In *trench layering*, the entire plant is bent over and laid flat on the bottom of a trench 3 to 9 in. (8 to 23 cm) deep; the plant is then covered with soil, and axillary shoots grow upward through the soil and root. In *air layering*, a moistened substrate such as sphagnum moss peat is wrapped around a wounded area on the stem and covered with plastic or some other type of water-retentive wrap.

In simple, mound, and air layering, rooting can be promoted by wounding the stem, which involves cutting part of the way through the stem, girdling the stem, or sharply bending the stem. Air layering, in particular, generally requires stem wounding. Rooting powders may be used to increase rooting of difficult-to-root species. In trench layering, the etiolation of the shoots growing through the substrate promotes rooting. Due to the labor-intensive nature of layering and the large amount of space needed for both the stock plant and the layers, layering is rarely done on a large commercial scale in floriculture.

Runners and other modified stems

Many plant species produce elongated or modified stems terminating in a vegetative meristem, which can be easily propagated. *Runners*, which arise from leaf axils, grow horizontally above and along the ground and produce new plants at each node or at the tip (fig. 1.4). The new plants can be removed and propagated or allowed to form roots while still attached to the original plant. Spider plant (*Chlorophytum*) and strawberry geranium (*Saxifraga stolonifera*), for example, form runners. Redosier dogwood and mint form *stolons*, which are stems that grow at or just below the surface of the soil and produce plants at the nodes. *Offsets* and *suckers* are shoots that develop from adventitious or axillary buds at the base of the plant and are removed to form individual plants. Traditionally, offsets refer to those shoots formed at the base of a stems, and suckers are defined as those shoots that arise from an adventitious bud on a root. However, the meaning of the terms have been blurred in popular usage, and offsets and suckers are often considered synonymous. Runners and stolons are often used in commercial propagation, but offsets and suckers are generally limited to small-scale propagation.

Figure 1.4. Runners produced by spider plant.

Grafting and budding

Grafting is the process of uniting two plants or plant parts in such a way that they become one plant after cell division and union occur. Grafting is used to propagate species or cultivars that cannot be propagated by other methods, enhance vigor, create a unique plant with improved characteristics compared with the individual plants from which it was created, and study physiological processes or plant diseases. For example, hybrid tea roses often grow poorly on their own roots but grow better when grafted onto the roots of a vigorous rootstock that may have inferior flowers. Most cut rose production in developing countries is from grafted roses. However, for production on artificial substrates such as rock wool or coco fiber, many growers in developed countries such as the Netherlands or the United States prefer to produce their crop on the rose's own roots. In floriculture, the standard topiary or tree forms of plants such as roses and azaleas are created by grafting the top cultivar onto an elongated stem and rootstock. Breeding may also involve grafting seedlings to a rootstock to accelerate maturation and flowering and to shorten the time between breeding cycles for species such as crabapple.

Grafting is most successful when both plants are the same species. Grafting between different species of the same genus is also likely to be successful but not guaranteed. Grafting between different genera of the same family and between different families has been successful in some cases, but has rare commercial significance. Grafting requires that a part of the cambium of both plant parts be in contact. The graft union is wrapped with grafting rubber, plastic, or paraffin to prevent separation and drying. Cell division subsequently occurs, uniting the pieces.

The different types of grafting techniques include whip (tongue), splice, side, side-tongue, side-veneer, cleft, bark, and approach grafting. Stenting is a technique used to simultaneously graft and root a rootstock for cut rose production. A cutting is taken from the desired variety and grafted onto a cutting of the rootstock (fig. 1.5). With the aid of a clothespin, the two cuttings are held together and fuse while simultaneously the rootstock develops roots. Budding is a type of grafting that uses one axillary bud and an associated piece of bark, which is inserted under the bark of a second plant. Budding techniques include

Figure 1.5. Stented rose plant showing graft union.

T-budding (shield budding), inverted T-budding, patch budding, flute budding, ring budding (annular budding), I-budding, and chip budding. Grafting and budding are often described as easy to learn but difficult to master. Detailed procedures can be obtained from Hartmann et al. (2002).

Cutting propagation

The majority of asexually propagated floral crops are commercially propagated by cuttings. Of the leading thirty cut flower, pot plant, and bedding plant crops, more than half (55%) are propagated via cuttings.

Companies specializing in producing cuttings have become a subindustry within the floriculture industry. Most use offshore locations or cooperators that maintain and produce stock plants, shipping the unrooted cuttings to the United States or other countries for rooting at a rooting station or a finished grower. Rooting stations root and ship the cuttings to growers that finish the plants for sale. In addition, some finished growers also produce cuttings from stock plants maintained onsite.

Stem cuttings

Various types of stem cuttings can be taken depending on the species and desired crop time. *Terminal* or *tip cuttings*, which include the stem apex, young leaves, and one or more mature leaves, generally produce a finished crop the quickest (fig. 1.6). *Basal cuttings* are a type of terminal cutting that is harvested

Figure 1.7. Adventitious roots on pothos stem.

Figure 1.8. Salvia subterminal stem cuttings with either one or two nodes.

Figure 1.6. Salvia terminal stem cutting with lower leaves removed and ready to insert in propagation substrate.

from the crown of the plant, that part of the plant where new stems are produced each growing season, and may include stem tissue or unelongated crown tissue. While old stem tissue is frequently slower to root than young tissue, in practice cutting size often depends on the species being propagated, the size of the stock plant from which the cuttings are harvested, and the expected time to produce a liner or finished plant. In some species such as poinsettias, larger cuttings can be taken later in the season to produce larger plants more quickly. Generally, cuttings with thick stems and short internodes produce the best plants. The stems of some species such as pothos produce adventitious roots at the nodes (fig. 1.7), hastening establishment of the cutting after propagation. Normally, only the lowermost leaves that interfere with inserting the cuttings into the substrate are removed, and at least one fully mature leaf should remain on the cutting. Rooting will be slow if no mature leaves remain on the cuttings to serve as a source of photosynthates.

Stem cuttings with one or more axillary buds and leaves, but without the terminal apex, are also used with such species as pothos, hydrangea (*Hydrangea macrophylla*), tradescantia, and some perennials (fig. 1.8). These stem cuttings, which are also known as *subterminal* or *butt cuttings*, often have two or more

nodes. *Single bud (eye) cuttings* are those pieces of stems with only one axillary bud (eye), and *double eye cuttings* have two axillary buds or eyes. *Leaf-bud cuttings* are examples of single

Figure 1.9. Single eye hydrangea stem cuttings consisting of a leaf, bud, and associated stem tissue. Note that the leaf has been trimmed to reduce surface area and transpiration.

eye cuttings in which a small amount of stem, including one node and axillary bud, is used; the stem and bud are both inserted below the substrate surface (fig. 1.9). The term "eye cut-

Figure 1.10. Different lengths of dracaena cane cuttings are used to produce finished potted foliage plants of various heights.

ting" is usually associated with vining plants, and leaf-bud cuttings with upright plants. Single eye or leaf-bud cuttings are often used when propagation material is limited.

Figure 1.11. Close-up of a dracaena cane cutting showing new foliage growth.

Cane cuttings

Cane sections without foliage are used to propagate dracaena and other foliage plants (see chapter 16). Mature stems are harvested from stock plants that are most commonly grown in Central America, sawed into sections of varying length, shipped to the finished plant producer, and inserted into the rooting substrate (figs. 1.10 and 1.11). Care must be taken to ensure that the end of the cutting inserted into the substrate is the basal end of the stem closest to the roots (when previously attached to the stock plant). Canes require misting to root, and they will root faster when dipped in a rooting hormone. Fungicides can also be used for disease prevention.

Root cuttings

Root cuttings are created by harvesting roots, cutting them into sections, and then planting the sections vertically in the substrate. When root cuttings, such as those of butterfly weed (*Asclepias tuberosa*), are inserted, be sure they are oriented correctly. To avoid confusion, cut the proximal end (previously closest to the crown) of the cutting straight across, and the distal end (farthest from the crown) at an angle. Plant the cuttings with the proximal end up. The root cutting of many species such as of Oriental poppy can also be planted horizontally 1 to 2 in. (2.5 to 5 cm) below the surface of the substrate, eliminating the problem of orientation.

Leaf cuttings

Leaf cuttings are used with a variety of common floriculture crops including African violet, rex begonia, sansevieria, peperomia, streptocarpus, and numerous succulent species. In

Figure 1.12.
Sansevieria leaf cuttings.

some cases, such as with sansevieria, the leaves are cut into segments and inserted with the basipetal (previously closest to the crown) end down into the substrate (fig. 1.12). Each segment regenerates shoots and roots. The extreme form of this method is to use a cork borer to cut out dozens of begonia leaf disks from a single leaf. The disks are treated with IBA and kinetin and placed on moist filter paper in a petri dish. Other species, such as peperomia, require that both the leaf blade and the petiole be present for shoot and root regeneration.

Physiological Process of Cutting Propagation

Depending on the type of cutting, the roots and/or shoots must be regenerated after the cutting is harvested to produce a functioning plant. These newly generated roots and shoots are termed *adventitious*. With stem and cane cuttings, roots are regenerated to support the shoot system. With root cuttings, both root and shoot systems must develop. Two types of adventitious roots occur: *preformed roots*, which are already on the stem prior to harvesting the cutting, and *wound-induced roots*, which arise after the cutting is harvested.

Preformed roots are common on a number of plant genera including coleus, pothos, and philodendron. The preformed roots may be outwardly visible, such as on pothos, or they may be below the outer epidermis or bark and not visible, in which case they are known as *latent root initials*. Not surprisingly, most species with preformed roots root rapidly.

Most species, however, produce wound-induced roots after cutting harvest. As soon as the cutting is severed, the outer cells die, forming a protective layer of necrotic cells and suberin, a corky substance. The living cells underneath the protective layer begin to divide to form *callus*. Callus formation occurs in four steps: tissue swells without any color change, the swollen area begins to turn white or tan, white or tan areas begin to crack open (the epidermis ruptures), and root initials begin differentiating within the callus. Roots develop from the root initials. Roots usually emerge from the callus, but rooting and callus formation are two independent processes. The presence of callus does not always mean that rooting will occur, but it is often a sign that the propagation process is proceeding and that the cutting is beginning to develop roots.

Cutting Propagation Stages

The propagation process starts with the harvest of the cuttings. If cuttings are purchased, the commercial propagators will harvest and ship the cuttings directly to you. See chapter 12 for information on handling cuttings after you receive them. If you are harvesting your own cuttings, choose ones with the following characteristics.

Healthy. Cuttings must be insect, mite, and disease free.

True-to-type. This is especially important with variegated cultivars, which tend to vary greatly in the amount of variegation.

Nutritionally sound. Generally, cuttings should not have a deficient or excessive amount of nutrients, but exceptions are described in chapter 7 and in the individual species descriptions in Part 3.

Proper maturity. Cuttings that are too immature or too old may not root rapidly and uniformly.

Proper size. The optimum size will vary with the species, cultivar, time of year, desired crop time, and other factors. For example, larger cuttings may allow a shorter crop time,while smaller cuttings will take longer to produce a specific plant size. For many species, the cuttings must have one mature leaf that can provide the photosynthates necessary to support the cutting during propagation.

In addition to having quality cuttings, a successful commercial propagator requires proper grading and sorting. A high-quality crop begins with uniform, properly sorted cuttings. Typically, cuttings are sorted by stem length, node and leaf number, and axillary leaf or flower development. Criteria will vary with the species and cultivar. If propagation material is limited, keep the blocks of similar cuttings together so they can be handled as a group. For example, if some of the cuttings are too old but are still required for production, sort them and stick (plant) them as a group. If the older cuttings root more slowly, they can be held back without reducing the quality of the rest of the cuttings that are developing properly. Remember, however, that sometimes it is better to be short a few cuttings than to spend a lot of time trying to grow substandard cuttings into a quality product.

Finally, all aspects of propagation are dependent on employee training and retraining. For many species, the manner in which the cuttings are harvested, sorted, graded, and stuck will greatly influence the quality of the final product. Employees need to know how to do each step. Because even experienced employees can drift off the mark on occasion, periodic training sessions are advisable for both new and long-standing employees.

The cutting propagation process is divided into five stages.

Stage 0: Prior to arrival or harvest of cuttings

- Clean, weed, and disinfect the handling and propagation areas.
- Check the environmental controls to make sure they are functioning correctly.
- Select flats. Size can vary, but those with 72 to 105 cells per flat are generally used for cuttings.
- Fill sanitized flats with a moist, pathogen-free substrate. Do not pack it in; a well-aerated substrate will produce a better root system.
- Ensure that sufficient labor will be available to stick all the cuttings, generally within twenty-four hours (table 1.1).

Stage 1: Cutting arrival or harvest and sticking

- When ordering cuttings, open and check the boxes for turgid, high-quality, properly labeled cuttings. High-quality cuttings should be of uniform size: the stem length and caliper as well as the leaf number and size should be appropriate. The cuttings should not be wilted or show any

Figure 1.13. Stage 1 unrooted cuttings ready for insertion in the propagation substrate. (J. Faust)

evidence of disease. They may be stored in the cooler overnight to rehydrate if they arrive wilted. Keep the shipping tags with each batch of cuttings; the tags can be used by suppliers to troubleshoot problems if they occur.

- When harvesting your own cuttings, choose material with uniform stem caliper, leaf count, and cutting length to ensure uniform rooting: The more consistent the cuttings, the more consistent the finished crop (fig. 1-13).
- Make multiple passes over the stock to collect uniform-diameter cuttings.
- Harvest cuttings at the correct stage of maturity; be certain stem cuttings are not woody.

- Harvest cuttings in the early morning or late afternoon, depending on the species, when ambient temperatures are below 90° F (32° C). Be careful about holding cuttings in boxes or bags in the greenhouse since internal temperatures can rapidly rise, damaging the cuttings.
- Place all cuttings in carriers either base up or base down.
- Avoid crushing the cuttings when harvesting to decrease botrytis problems.
- Cover the carrier with a damp towel to prevent desiccation of the cuttings.
- Store the cuttings for at least two hours at 48° F (9° C) to reduce their temperature. Determine how many cuttings can be stuck in one to two hours, and store the remainder in a cool location or a cooler until they can be planted.
- Maintain 75 to 90% relative humidity in the cooler to prevent desiccation of the cuttings.
- For transport from the cooler to the potting bench, place all cuttings in carriers either base up or base down.
- Stick cuttings of high-priority species first (table 1.1).
- Begin misting, or close the propagation tent immediately. Misting may need to begin before all cuttings are planted to prevent wilting of the first cuttings planted. However, use the minimum amount of mist possible to reduce future disease problems.
- Store cuttings at 40° to 60° F (4° to 16° C), depending on the species, for up to twenty-four hours, if planting is going to be delayed. To prevent quality problems at the liner stage, or in the finished crop, do not store cuttings any longer than necessary.

Stage 2: Callusing

- Maintain the substrate temperature at 70° to 74° F (21° to 23° C) for most species.
- Maintain air temperatures of 75° to 80° F (24° to 27° C) during days and 70° to 74° F (21° to 23° C) during nights for most species.
- Keep the substrate sufficiently moist so that water is easily squeezed out of it, but not so much that the cutting base is saturated. The base of the cutting (fig. 1.14) needs air for proper rooting.
- Use warm water, 85° to 90° F (29° to 32° C), in the mist lines since cold water will lower the soil temperature during the day.
- Maintain high relative humidity in the air surrounding the cutting, 75 to 90%, to minimize transpiration, thereby slowing water loss.
- Prevent leaf wilting by applying overhead mist or fog

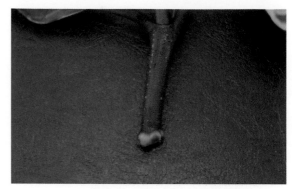

Figure 1.14. Stage 2 Sanchezia cutting showing callus formation.

or by using propagation tents.
- Increase and decrease mist frequency as the light and ambient temperatures change during the course of the day.
- Mist frequently during the night for the first three to five days, if required.
- Note that each wilting episode during Stage 2 adds at least one day to the rooting program.
- Maintain a light intensity of 500 to 1,000 f.c. (5 to 11 klux) for most species. A higher light intensity will increase plant stress due to excessive warming.
- Use retractable shade so that the light intensity can be increased as the cuttings mature.
- Begin foliar feeding with 50 to 75 ppm nitrogen from calcium nitrate or 20-10-20 if there is any loss in foliage color. Fertilizer may not be needed.
- Maintain a substrate pH of 5.5 to 6.2 and electrical conductivity (EC) below 0.78 to 0.80 mS/cm (2:1 water:media method). Maintain substrate leachate pH at 6.0 to 6.2.
- Avoid using growth regulators during Stage 2 if they were used during stock plant growth.
- Start applying appropriate growth regulators as soon as the cuttings are turgid, but only if growth regulators were not used during stock plant growth.
- Transfer cuttings to Stage 3 once 50% of the cuttings begin differentiating root initials.

Stage 3: Root development

In addition to roots forming (fig. 1.15), new top growth may be evident, and the cuttings remain turgid more easily.
- Maintain the substrate temperature at 66° to 70° F (19° to 21° C).
- Maintain air temperatures of 75° to 80° F (24° to 27° C) during days and 60° to 68° F (16° to 20° C) during nights.

Figure 1.15. Stage 3 Sanchezia cutting showing root formation.

- Begin drying out the substrate once roots are visible.
- Avoid drying out the air since this will increase evapotranspiration, which will reduce root zone temperature and increase water loss from cuttings.
- Reduce soil moisture by reducing or eliminating mist application during the dark period; reducing the duration and frequency of the mist; and/or reducing the amount of water applied per day by delaying the start of the mist period until 9:30 to 11:00 A.M. and ending the mist period earlier than 4:00 to 5:00 P.M.
- Begin increasing light intensity to 1,000 to 2,000 f.c. (11 to 22 klux) as the cuttings start to develop a rootball.
- Apply growth regulators, if needed, after misting is stopped.
- Apply fungicides to protect against botrytis, if needed, after misting is stopped.
- Begin feeding with 100 to 150 ppm nitrogen from nitrate-based fertilizers (15-0-15 or 14-0-14), then increase rapidly to 200 ppm. Increase the frequency and rate at each application to prevent high EC problems, or alternate fertilization with clear water to maintain substrate EC.
- Maintain the substrate pH at 5.5 to 6.2 and EC at 0.8 to 1.1 mS/cm.
- Monitor the pH and EC of the leachate on a daily basis. The pH should be 6.0, and the EC should stay at 0.5 to 1.0 mS/cm.

Stage 4:
Toning the rooted cutting

The cuttings should be toned for shipping or planting by reducing substrate moisture (figs. 1.16 and 1.17). Toned cuttings will be no longer be soft and wilt easily, allowing the cuttings to withstand the rigors of shipping, if necessary, and planting. While slight wilting is acceptable, severe wilting should not occur. Cuttings

TABLE 1.1

Planting priority for each species. Level 1 is the most urgent and should be planted first within one to two hours after arrival or harvest; levels 2 to 4 are increasing less urgent but should be planted within twenty-four hours.

SPECIES	PRIORITY LEVEL
Bacopa (*Jamesbrittania*)	
(see also Bacopa below)	1
Dahlia	1
Lantana	1
Geranium, ivy	
(*Pelargonium peltatum*)	1
Geranium, zonal	
(*Pelargonium x hortorum*)	1
Heliotropium	1
Lobelia	1
Thunbergia	1
Calibrachoa	2
Coleus	2
Diascia	2
Evolvulus	2
Impatiens, double	2
Impatiens, mini	2
Nemesia	2
Osteospermum	2
Petunia	2
Salvia	2
Snapdragon (*Antirrhinum*)	2
Verbena	2
Angelonia	3
Argyranthemum	3
Bacopa (*Sutera*)	3
Bidens	3
Bracteantha	3
Cuphea	3
Helichrysum	3
Impatiens, New Guinea	3
Impatiens, trailing	3
Gaura	3
Lamium	3
Monopsis	3
Portulaca	3
Sanvitalia	3
Scaevola	3
Strobilanthes	3
Lysimachia	4
Kalanchoe	4
Plectranthus	4

Figure 1.16. Stage 4 rooted marguerite daisy (*Argyranthemum*) cutting toned and ready to plant.

Figure 1.17. Strips of Stage 4 poinsettia cuttings toned and ready for shipping.

are at the "pullable plug" stage, meaning that the root-ball will hold together if pulled out of the flat.

- Maintain the substrate temperature at 64° to 66° F (18° to 19° C).
- Maintain air temperatures of 75° to 80° F (24° to 27° C) during days and 60° to 65° F (16° to 18 C) during nights. A lower constant day and night air temperature of 58° to 62° F (14° to 17° C) may be used, if practical, to reduce stem elongation and to thicken the leaves.
- Move the liners from the mist area into an area of lower relative humidity, lower temperature, and higher light intensity.

- Use a zero day and night temperature difference (DIF) if possible, (see chapter 5 for more information).
- Use growth regulators if DIF is positive.
- Increase the light intensity to 2,000 to 4,000 f.c. (22 to 43 klux). High light will maximize branch development, decrease internode elongation, and increase leaf and cuticle thickness. The increased thickness will allow cuttings to better survive the transition to the greenhouse production environment.
- Provide shade during the middle of the day to reduce temperature stress.
- Maintain the substrate pH at 5.5 to 6.2 and EC at 0.9 to 1.2 mS/cm.
- Fertilize once a week with 150 to 200 ppm nitrogen from 15-0-15 alternating with 20-10-20.

Buying Cuttings and Plugs versus Propagating In-House

Today many businesses purchase liners, plugs, and rooted or unrooted cuttings from specialists who efficiently propagate species on a large scale. Ultimately the decision to propagate crops internally or to purchase cuttings or rooted plants must be based on economics, quality, and dependable delivery. Consideration should also be given to materials, labor, and greenhouse space.

For every argument growers can muster in favor of growing their own stock plants, there are arguments against it. Many growers are lulled into a false sense of security by growing their own stock plants. After all, by managing the stock, they control the quality of the cuttings and the timing of their arrival. Both are sometimes issues of contention with purchased cuttings. However, growing stock plants is vastly different from producing finished plants: you may have plants for six to eight months. Over that period several production issues can occur, such as insect, disease, and nutritional problems. The yield of harvestable cuttings is directly impacted by how well the plants are produced. That's why purchasing from quality cutting suppliers, both domestically based and offshore, can be advantageous. Producing cuttings is the business of these suppliers: they live, breath, eat and sleep stock culture and stock maintenance. They should have a list of procedures to ensure consistent quality time and time again. If their delivery track record concerns you, ask to see their production protocol and request grower references.

Another advantage of purchased cuttings or plugs is that less space is required, which may allow more crops to be produced. For many growers, there's no reason to tie up greenhouse space, spend additional money on heat, containers, media, fertilizers, overhead, and so forth, or tie up labor for stock plants when cuttings are easily brought. In addition, purchasing plugs may also allow producers of bedding plants and field-grown cut flowers to forgo a propagation greenhouse or to start transplant production later in the winter or the spring.

Growers who produce hard-to-find varieties or species may need to maintain their own stock plants. However, these plants are often poorly maintained and not indexed for viruses or other latent diseases. If rare, hard-to-find species are your business, it is possible to work with labs to clean up your stock and maintain a clean source of supply for mother plants each year. In addition, plug suppliers may be able to custom-propagate most species as long as you purchase a minimum number of cuttings.

Many growers grow a small range of stock plants for some crops, but purchase cuttings for the rest. This decision will be based on a number of factors such as cost, cutting availability and timing, internal production issues, and specific market requirements for the finished plant. The trend is that growers are purchasing more cuttings and relying less on stock plants. For example, fifteen years ago nearly 75% of all vegetatively propagated geranium plants were grown from cuttings harvested from stock plants on-site. Today it is less than 50%. Poinsettias also mirror the trend toward buying cuttings, according to the Ecke Ranch. About fifteen years ago approximately 25% of finished flowering poinsettias were started using purchased rooted cuttings or unrooted cuttings, and 75% of finished plant producers grew their own stock plants. Today, however, about 60% of finished flowering poinsettias are started using purchased rooted or unrooted cuttings, and only 40% of growers grow their own stock.

Young Plant Industry

The young plant industry has been rapidly growing as more producers purchase cuttings and plugs rather than maintain stock. While figures for vegetative propagation alone are not available, estimates for the entire young plant industry are available for 2000 to 2004 from the U.S. Department of Agriculture (USDA). In 2000 the USDA estimated sales of $243 million, which increased to $332 million in 2002 and to $354 million in 2004. Not surprisingly, production is centered in areas with large concentrations of floriculture crops, including Florida, California, and Michigan. Pennsylvania also has a relatively high amount of production, primarily of perennial plants for outdoor use.

Well over half of the young plants are produced for the bedding plant segment of the industry, but cuttings and plugs are also grown for cut flower, potted plant, and foliage plant production. Imported unrooted cuttings, cane sections, and other propagation materials have been tracked for a longer period of time by the USDA and have increased from $12.7 million in 1993 to $55.3 million in 2004. This increase reflects a mounting number of cuttings being produced abroad in areas with favorable climates and lower production costs, such as Central America and Africa. The heavy reliance on hand labor can make cutting production expensive in developed countries. In addition, stock plant production of many species requires warm temperatures and high light, both major production costs when stock plants are maintained in northern climates.

Cultivar Protection, Licensing, and Leasing

As stated earlier, the goal of plant propagation is to reproduce a plant with a desirable set of characteristics. Although these characteristics may occur through spontaneous mutations (sports), new cultivars are typically produced through long-term breeding programs. Because of the substantial amount of time and money required to produce a new cultivar, a number of processes are available in the United States for plant breeders to protect their intellectual property and profit from it. These processes, which can be complicated, typically require the services of a federally registered patent agent or attorney.

Plant patents

Plant patents are the primary method of protecting asexually propagated plants in the United States. They can be obtained for asexually propagated plants that are new and unique. A patent is effective for seventeen to twenty years, after which time it expires and cannot be renewed; the plant can then be freely propagated and marketed. Plant patents are issued in the United States by the U.S. Patent and Trademark Office (USPTO). Many companies use the acronym

Figure 1.18. Plant label showing ®, ™, and PPAF (plant patent applied for).

PPAF, which means "Plant Patent Applied For" (fig. 1.18). This designation indicates that the patent has been filed but not yet granted. Plant patents are independent of trademarks.

The process of obtaining a plant patent in the United States begins with an application by the inventor or inventors who have bred or discovered the plant to be patented. Inventors may hold the patents in their names or may transfer a portion or the entire rights of the patent to another individual, entity, or company. The latter parties are known as assignees; they can also transfer rights to additional parties with the permission of the inventor.

Plant patents are granted if the plant is new and distinguishable from other plants by at least one characteristic, such as flower color, size, or degree of doubleness; foliage color or shape; or plant height or form. The inventor must declare that these distinguishing characteristics are stable and that the plant has been asexually propagated. The inventor must also certify that he or she bred or discovered the plant. If the plant was discovered, the inventor must indicate that it was found in a cultivated area such as a nursery or greenhouse. Forms of wild plants discovered in nature cannot be patented. The patent application may be rejected if the new cultivar was offered for sale for more than one year prior to the filing of the application.

The length of the patent depends on the date it was filed or granted. Prior to June 8, 1995, patents already granted will be in effect for seventeen years, and those that were filed and subsequently granted will be in effect for twenty years after the filing date. Patents filed on or after June 8, 1995, and subsequently granted will be in effect for twenty years after the filing date. Most of the time, the application is made for a cultivar's denomination, which is generally not the trade name of the variety. For example, 'Freedom Red' poinsettia was patented in U.S. Plant Patent 7825 as Eckespoint (490). In this particular case, the cultivar name Freedom has been protected with a trademark as well. Plant patents that have been granted are listed on the U.S. PTO website at *www.uspto.gov*.

The acronym PPAF is often used after the patent has been filed but before it has been granted. It is illegal to use PPAF without intending to patent the plant. Firms propagating a plant marked PPAF will be liable to the patent owner once the patent is granted.

Plant patenting allows the inventor and/or assignee to control asexual reproduction of the plant by excluding others from propagating and from using, offering for sale, and/or selling the plant in the United States. Through licensing agreements, the inventor can allow others to propagate, use, offer for sale, and/or sell the plant. These agreements are legally binding contracts that usually reimburse the inventor by means of an up-front lump sum payment or royalties based on the number of cuttings made or plants propagated. For the inventor, determining which type of payment to choose can be difficult; however, when plants have true market potential, royalties are often more lucrative than up-front payments.

Patent infringement

Patent infringement occurs when the plant is propagated without permission from the patent owner. Infringement is defined as follows (Plant Variety Protection Act of 1970):

- Asexual propagation of the new cultivar.
- Selling, offering for sale, exposing to sale, delivering, shipping, consigning, exchanging, soliciting an offer to buy, or any other transfer of title or possession of plants of the new cultivar.
- Importation or exportation of the new cultivar into or from the United States.
- Dispensing the new cultivar to another, in a form that can be asexually reproduced, without notice as to being a protected cultivar.
- Performing, instigating, or actively inducing performance of any of the aforementioned acts.

Trademarks

Trademarks can be words, symbols, or designs. A trademark "identifies the goods or services of one party as distinct from those of others and indicates the origin of the goods or services," according to Hutton (1991). For example, the name of a specific plant or series of plants (such as Sunblaze roses) can be trademarked. Trademarks are often combined with patents; however, trademarks do not expire. While a plant can be propagated and marketed after the patent expires, the plant's trademarked name cannot be used unless permission is obtained from the company holding the trademark. Note that the trademarked name of a plant is different from its cultivar name; the latter cannot be trademarked and can be freely used. For example, in the name Supertunia Lavender Morn, the trademarked word "Supertunia" cannot be used by anyone without permission by the trademark holder, but "Lavender Morn" can be readily used. Unregistered trademarks are noted with the symbol ™ and registered trademarks are noted by ®.

Other protections

Plant variety protection provides protection for inbred plant varieties produced from seed. Varieties need to be unique, uniform, and stable. Plant utility patents are often used by biotechnology companies to protect unique production processes, genes, plant parts, and physical traits associated with their products. In recent years, some hybrid flower seed cultivars have been protected with utility patents.

Proprietary rights can be used to control the propagation and marketing of a unique plant without patents, variety protection, or trademarks. Distribution of the plant material is controlled by contractual agreements, making propagation and marketing of a plant by anyone other than those specified in the contract illegal. Such agreements may specify the stage at which a plant or harvested cut flower may be sold, how it is packaged, in which outlets it may be sold, and what kinds of tags or other marketing support materials are to be used with the product.

Many countries other than the United States also have legislation to protect the work of firms and individuals developing new cultivars. The Union for the Protection of New Varieties of Plants (UPOV) is an international agreement among member countries to protect plant developers' work. However, some developing countries have not joined UPOV and do not recognize plant cultivar protection. In several cases, countries joined UPOV, but they signed old versions of the agreement. Those older versions do not include the most recent protections for intellectual property, and the laws passed in the signing country may represent protection on a reduced level. For example, while China joined UPOV in 1999, it signed UPOV 1961, which does not offer marketers of proprietary genetics in the floriculture industry much protection through Chinese law. In general, all developed nations in which floriculture is a vital segment of agricultural production have signed the most recent UPOV agreements and have a well-established body of law to protect the intellectual property of plant breeders.

Licensing and leasing

Once a cultivar has been legally protected, propagation by anyone other than the developer requires a license or a sublicense. In effect, propagators may not own the plant material, but rather lease or rent it from the plant developer. Generally, for each propagule (cutting or tissue-cultured plantlet) the grower pays a royalty to the plant developer. When a grower buys protected plant materials, the royalty has already been included in the price. Growers cannot legally propagate patented plants without a license from the developer and must appropriately label each plant. Unauthorized propagation of a plant constitutes infringement and is illegal. Failure to pay royalties for the propagation of protected plants is also illegal. Most plant breeders work with commercial firms that administer their royalty programs. These firms routinely visit the greenhouses of plant propagators and of growers who purchase patented and otherwise protected plants to audit for illegal propagation. Although it occurs infrequently, a number of growers have been prosecuted for illegally propagating varieties.

Trademarks can also be licensed. Propagators need to know which cultivars are protected with a trademark and obtain permission prior to propagation. Many species or cultivars are not protected and can be propagated freely. However, even if the plant patent has expired on a variety, as long as the name has been trademarked it is illegal to sell propagated plants using the same name without permission or payment of a royalty to the trademark owner. The propagator is responsible for determining the legal status of each cultivar.

References

Avent, T. 2003. *So You Want to Start a Nursery.* Timber Press, Portland, Oregon.

Craig, R. 1993. Intellectual property protection, pp. 389–404. In: *Geraniums IV*, 4th ed., J.W. White, ed. Ball Publishing, Batavia, Illinois.

Darke, R. 1991. A curator's viewpoint. *HortScience* 26:3 62–363.

Fowler, C. 1994. *Unnatural Selection.* Gordon and Breach, Yverdon, Switzerland.

Griffith, L. P. Jr. 1998. *Draceana fragrans*, pp. 122-123. In: *Tropical Foliage Plants: A Grower's Guide.* Ball Publishing, Batavia, Illinois.

Hartmann, H. T., D. E. Kester, F. T. Davies Jr., and R. L. Geneve. 2002. *Hartmann and Kester's Plant Propagation: Principles and Practice*, 7th ed. Prentice Hall, Upper Saddle River, New Jersey.

Hutton, R. J. 1991. New funds for plant breeding. *HortScience* 26:361–362.

Klopmeyer, M., M. Wilson, and C. Anne Whealy. 2003. Propagating vegetative crops, pp. 165–180. In: *Ball RedBook*, 17th ed., vol. 2, D. Hamrick, ed. Ball Publishing, Batavia, Illinois.

Joiner, J. N., R. T. Poole, and C. A. Conover. 1981. Propagation, pp. 284–306. In: *Foliage Plant Production*, J. N. Joiner, ed. Prentice Hall, Englewood Cliffs, New Jersey.

Lagerstedt, H. B. 1967. Propagation of begonias from leaf disks. *HortScience* 2(1):20–22.

Le Nard, M. and A. A. De Hertogh. 1993. General chapter on spring flowering bulbs, pp. 705–739. In: *The Physiology of Flower Bulbs*, A. De Hertogh and M. Le Nard, eds. Elsevier, Amsterdam.

Praktijkonderzoek Plant & Omgeving. 2001. Young plant material, pp. 105–106. In: *Handbook for Modern Greenhouse Rose Cultivation*, Wageningen, The Netherlands.

Rogers, O. M. 1991. Germplasm and how to protect it. *HortScience* 26:360–361.

UPOV. 1999. UPOV Notification No. 70: International Convention for the Protection of New Varieties of Plants of December 2, 1961, as revised at Geneva on November 10, 1972, and on October 23, 1978. Accession by the People's Republic of China in Geneva, Switzerland, March 23, 1999.

Williams, J. 2004. Ecke Ranch, Encinitas, California, personal communication, June 7, 2004.

2

Propagation Industry

Kimberly A. Williams

An increasingly complex network of businesses is linked together in the process of bringing cutting-propagated floral crops to consumers. The businesses range from large national and international breeding or propagation companies to local retail garden centers. Poinsettias, chrysanthemums, and geraniums (*Pelargonium*) were used to pioneer vegetative propagation in the modern floral industry. These were followed by New Guinea impatiens and an assortment of crops targeted for spring sales. Today the explosion of species and varieties available as vegetatively propagated bedding plants has renewed the product palette of the spring season. This chapter presents five business profiles summarizing the roles that a breeding company, rooting station, direct unrooted grower (root-and-sell propagator), wholesale greenhouse business, and retail garden center play in bringing cutting-propagated floral crops to consumers (fig. 2.1).

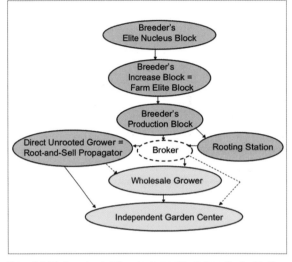

Figure 2.1. Diagram showing the many types of businesses involved in the development and production of vegetatively propagated plant materials.

Breeding Firm: Fischer USA (Boulder, Colorado)

Fischer USA is one of several breeding companies with an international reach that develop and distribute patented vegetatively propagated plant materials to the North American market. Other companies with similar roles in the breeding and marketing of new vegetative plant materials for the greenhouse industry include Ball FloraPlant, Dümmen USA, Fides, Oglevee Ltd., Paul Ecke Ranch, Selecta Klemm GmbH & Co., and Yoder Brothers. Some companies focus on a select group of plant species, while others have a broad and diverse patented product line. Breeding companies typically produce large quantities of cuttings for the North American market offshore, or in locations other than the United States. The primary reasons for this trend include the optimal climates of offshore farms and the lower labor costs.

Fischer's breeding program has generated the company's 103 varieties of zonal and ivy geraniums, 40 varieties of New Guinea impatiens, and 40 poinsettia cultivars. The profile of Fischer USA illustrates the multistep process of how cuttings are derived and shipped to greenhouses in North America.

In 1959 Fischer was founded in Germany by Gerhard Fischer. It was the first company in Europe to offer geraniums free of xanthomonas, and in 1983 Fischer introduced its first varieties, the 'Pelfi' geranium series. The main facility is located in Hillscheid, Germany (fig. 2.2), which is about 60 miles northwest of Frankfurt. The company's CEO is Josef Fischer, one of Gerhard's sons. The four companies that constitute Fischer's worldwide system are Fischer Germany in Hillscheid; Fischer France in Châtellerault, France; Fischer Asia in Shanghai, China; and Fischer USA in Boulder, Colorado. Fischer Germany and Fischer France serve all of Europe. Fischer USA, which was founded in the early

Figure 2.2. Fischer's plant breeding facility and site of elite nucleus blocks in Hillscheid, Germany. (Fischer Germany)

1980s, serves the North American market. Fischer Asia has recently begun to distribute and sell its products to the Chinese and Japanese markets. Today, worldwide the company sells more than 100 million cuttings per year.

The process of bringing a new cultivar to market begins with plant breeding and variety selection. All of Fischer USA's geraniums and New Guinea impatiens are bred in Germany, Portugal, and the Canary Islands; poinsettia breeding is done at its German facility. Plant breeders focus on improving current varieties as well as creating new genetic lines. Breeders make planned crosses to try to generate desirable characteristics in the resulting plants, such as earlier flowering, improved branching, and heat and drought tolerance (fig. 2.3). Thousands of geranium and New Guinea impatiens seedlings are evaluated at annual summer field trials in Hillscheid and Châtellerault; most are discarded. The most promising seedlings are sent to a tissue culture lab for cloning and disease indexing, which is an extensive process that maintains plant material free of all known systemic bacteria, fungi, and viruses (see chapter 9). In particular, through this process the bacterial diseases *Xanthomonas* and *Ralstonia* have been eliminated from geraniums and several viruses from New Guinea impatiens. Cuttings are propagated from poinsettia seedlings (figs. 2.4, 2.5, and 2.6) showing potential and are grafted onto current varieties to transfer a phytoplasma, a viruslike organism

responsible for improved branching in poinsettias (fig. 2.7). Many new poinsettia cultivars are developed from either natural or forced mutations that occur on currently marketed varieties. Most pink, purple, white, multicolor, and variegated poinsettias arise from mutations or sports, whereas most red and some white poinsettias are developed from seedlings. From the time that a new variety is observed by a plant breeder, generally three to five years is required before it can be released in the commercial market.

The millions of unrooted cuttings shipped to growers worldwide originate from small numbers of disease-free stock plants known as "elite nucleus

Figure 2.3. Planned crosses are carefully made on geranium plants to breed improved cultivars. (H. Lang)

Figure 2.4. To breed most red and some white poinsettia cultivars, crosses are made. (H. Lang)

blocks." Fischer maintains these highly scrutinized stock plants in special greenhouses in Germany under strict sanitation protocols (fig. 2.8). Greenhouses are outfitted with insect screening and positive-pressure double doorways, and each elite stock plant is grown and irrigated separately in a soilless substrate. In addition, each elite plant has its own disinfected knife and disposable gloves.

Figure 2.5. Poinsettia seeds are collected at the proper stage of maturation to ensure viability. (H. Lang)

Figure 2.7. Usable poinsettia seedlings are grafted onto rootstocks of current cultivars to transfer the viruslike phytoplasma, which is responsible for improved branching. (J. Dole)

Cuttings from the elite nucleus blocks are shipped to Fischer's overseas farms in Portugal, Kenya, Israel, Mexico, or the Canary Islands to become stock plants for cutting production; these plants are called

Figure 2.6. Poinsettia seedlings are evaluated for their commercial potential; most are discarded. (H. Lang)

"increase blocks" or "farm elite blocks." Strict sanitation procedures are also followed in the overseas greenhouses. Geraniums and New Guinea impatiens are tested regularly for vascular diseases, while poinsettias are monitored primarily for poor branching, whiteflies, and powdery mildew.

Cuttings taken from the increase block are rooted in an isolated, clean greenhouse and then shipped to Fischer's production greenhouses in Mexico, Kenya, or China, where they are grown as the stock plants for cuttings to be shipped to rooting stations and growers around the world. Most Fischer cuttings for the North American market are produced at the Vivero International S.A. de C.V. farm in Cuernavaca, Mexico, about ninety miles southeast of Mexico City. Even at this large production farm, sanitation is prac-

ticed carefully (fig. 2.9). Greenhouse workers must wear protective clothing, boots, and gloves that are disinfected before entering the stock plant area. Knives are sterilized before cuttings are taken from each stock plant. With the recent certification guidelines for geranium production passed down by the U.S. Department of Agriculture (USDA), these sanitation guidelines must be followed exactly. Much time is also put into disease and insect scouting, as well as employee training. Managers try to maintain stock plants in a non-flowering state and at a growth stage that is neither too woody nor lush for the production of high-quality cuttings by pruning selective-

Figure 2.8. Elite nucleus blocks of plantlets that have been disease indexed are maintained under strict sanitation protocols in Fischer's facility in Germany. (H. Lang)

ly and using chemical growth regulators. Anticipating the exact number of cuttings per square foot (meter) each week is challenging, since climate conditions are variable.

Fischer USA has four rooting stations and several independent root-and-sell operations that complete

Figure 2.9. Geranium stock plants at a cutting production farm in Mexico are grown in bags set on concrete blocks. (H. Lang)

Figure 2.10. Cuttings are taken according to strict sanitation practices; they are enclosed in plastic bags of 125 and labeled. (H. Lang)

the propagation phase by rooting cuttings and shipping them to other growers or retail garden centers to finish all over North America. Under ideal conditions, it takes about two days from the time cuttings are harvested in Mexico until they reach a rooting station or grower. For example, if cuttings are harvested in Mexico on Sunday (fig. 2.10), they are packed in insulated boxes, cooled with ice, and picked up by FedEx at the farm early on Monday morning. The shipment departs via FedEx planes from Mexico City and arrives in Miami on Monday afternoon; cuttings are put in coolers until USDA inspectors can clear the shipment (fig. 2.11). Cuttings are loaded back onto FedEx planes Monday evening and sent to the FedEx distribution center in Memphis, Tennessee. Growers receive the cuttings on Tuesday morning.

All stock plants are destroyed at the end of the cutting season and no old stock plants are reused. The entire process of establishing stock plants repeats itself each season. This annual stock renewal with disease-indexed plants, as well as routine testing throughout the cutting production process, provides as much of a guarantee of disease-free cuttings as possible for growers. Important challenges of breeding companies include selecting the best varieties from their breeders' trials, predicting consumer preferences, forecasting growers' cutting needs for each season, maintaining pest-free stock, and obtaining USDA approval and clearance of cuttings shipped into the United States.

Royalties of several cents per plant are paid on each patented cutting to the breeding company. This is necessary to support the work of breeding new cultivars, maintaining disease-free stock, and enhancing consumer sales of the cultivars with marketing programs. Breeders feel that patented plant materials usually outperform unpatented varieties, as documented by the extensive trialing conducted not only

by Fischer but also by university trial sites representing the extreme range of climates across North America. Royalty payments also support the development of information about cultural practices for growers and marketing programs to help increase sales to retailers and consumers.

Figure 2.11. Shipments of cuttings arrive in Miami and are picked up by an import broker; they are then delivered to the USDA–APHIS station near the airport for inspection. After being cleared, they are taken to FedEx for shipping to customers. (H. Lang)

Corporate leaders predict that the number of breeding companies will increase in the future because consumer demand for new and different plants that perform well in the garden and the home is far from satiated. Like other breeding companies, Fischer seeks out new plant materials and listens to its brokers and growers to determine what is in demand and what is missing from its product mix. For example, Fischer is currently adding a landscape type of hiemalis begonia to its product line. Ultimately, Josef Fischer believes that a combination of quality, branding, and innovation will capture the attention of growers and consumers.

More marketing partnerships will probably form in the future to help promote the plant materials that breeding companies offer. More branded plant materials are likely to appear on the market despite the difficulty of ensuring that quality is maintained through the end of the market channel, a necessary process in building consumer support for a particular brand. And the use of the Internet will undoubtedly become increasingly important in sales and marketing as well as in providing easy access to educational materials for products.

Most recently, Fischer took over the production and marketing of the vegetative varieties of Goldsmith Seeds to create the Goldfisch line, which includes angelonia, snapdragon, calibrachoa, impatiens, geranium (*Pelargonium*), petunia, and verbena. This strategic business alliance makes yesterday's competitors today's business partners.

Breeding companies fill a vital role in bringing improved and unique cultivars to the gardening public. They ensure that disease-free plants are available for production, introduce new products with proven garden performance, provide educational materials for growers, and support their products with marketing programs.

Rooting Station: EuroAmerican Propagators LLC (Bonsall, California)

Rooting stations produce rooted cuttings or liners that are sold to wholesale and retail production operations to finish for sale to gardeners. EuroAmerican Propagators is a rooting station cofounded by John Rader and Jerry Church in 1992, when they purchased the young plant production business of Weidner's Gardens in Encinitas, California. At the same time, Rader and Garry Grueber of Kientzler KG founded Proven Winners LLC, an international marketing cooperative that has created a successful national marketing strategy based on plant branding. In its first year EuroAmerican Propagators offered just four products: 'Golden Beauty' strawflower (*Bracteantha*), 'Toucan Tango' brachyscome, 'Trailing Tyrolean' carnation, and 'Blue Wonder' scaevola. Today EuroAmerican Propagators offers more than 400 varieties of plants and serves nearly 6,000 customers. In 2003 the Proven Winners group in North America sold approximately 120 million vegetative liners.

The Proven Winners brand is owned in equal shares by three production companies: EuroAmerican Propagators; Pleasant View Gardens in Loudon, New Hampshire; and Four Star Greenhouses in Carleton, Michigan. Josh Schneider, director of product development and education for EuroAmerican Propagators, defines Proven Winners in a nutshell as "three production companies that own a brand together and work together to market and produce great plants for the grower and gardener." Today, Proven Winners has divisions in Canada, Europe, Japan, Australia, and South Africa in addition to the United States. The Proven Winners marketing concept is to provide "new and unique, but always unusual, great garden performers for premium garden markets." The garden performance of potential new plant introductions under the Proven Winners label are tested over a two-year period at the California, New Hampshire, and Michigan sites of the three parent companies as well as at the University of Florida; these locations represent a wide range of U.S. climates. When all sites agree that plant performance is outstanding, production protocols for that variety are established. However, fewer than 5% of the plants trialed will be introduced to the marketplace. Josh Schneider explains that some great garden performers never make it to market. For example, false indigo (*Baptisia australis*) blooms for only a month and does not look good in a pot, which limits its market potential for high-volume sales. On the other hand, caricature plant (*Graptophyllum*) markets well, but production costs are high because these plants do not readily produce breaks after a pinch; few cuttings are harvested per stock plant, making the cost per cutting higher.

The search for outstanding and unique plants is never-ending, and Josh Schneider spends a lot of time locating new plants for the Proven Winners line. He works with breeders to encourage development of plant characteristics that improve garden appeal and performance, and he believes that his own inexperience in breeding is his greatest contribution to the process. He is not, he says, constrained by what is impossible, because he does not know any better. A case in point is his and Garry Grueber's discovery of a weed that appeared to be a relative of nemesia in the crack of a sidewalk in Capetown, South Africa; they discussed the possibility that it be crossed with cultivated forms of nemesia. While several successful plant breeders said that the cross would be impossible and the plants were likely to be genetically incompatible, Innovaplant, the company that Grueber works for, decided to accept the challenge of crossing them. The results are the 'Sunsatia' series released by Proven Winners in 2003; these plants are more tolerant of heat and cold than earlier hybrids and are available in colors never before seen in cultivated nemesia.

In looking back on advancements that fueled the growth of the vegetative propagation industry, Josh Schneider cites the innovations of FedEx and overnight delivery that allow for rapid transport of perishable cuttings all over the world. EuroAmerican Propagators' CEO John Rader believes that improvements in micropropagation techniques that provide the ability to produce clean stock through thermally treated tissue cultures is primarily responsible for the existence of the vegetative industry. For Proven Winners, the story began in about 1991 when Kientzler/Innovaplant, a European company, wanted to introduce its newly developed New Guinea impatiens to the U.S. market but found that much of the North American stock for this crop was infected with tomato spotted wilt virus (TSWV). After a few years of work, Innovaplant had a functioning clean stock program for New Guinea impatiens, which today includes maintenance of all cultivars in tissue culture, routine virus indexing for various viral diseases both *in vitro* and *in vivo*, and maintenance of elite mother stock in thrips-proof greenhouse facilities. As more species were introduced into the Proven Winners line, they became a part of the clean-stock program. Today Proven Winners maintains more than 2,400 different cultivars, species, and hybrids of plant materials in its laboratories.

EuroAmerican Propagators maintains at least 30% of the stock for any single variety that it offers on its site in Bonsall, with most of the remainder maintained at Innovaplant's facilities in Costa Rica. This strategy of splitting its stock plant supply provides security in case a pathogen outbreak decimates stock at one site. All of EuroAmerican Propagators' rooted cutting sales are handled through broker companies, and a royalty payment of about 10% of the cost of the liner is passed to the breeders of the individual varieties.

EuroAmerican Propagator's nearly eighty-acre location in northern San Diego County (fig. 2.12) provides an optimal climate for "putting roots on cuttings." Unlike its market partners Pleasant View Gardens and Four Star Greenhouses, which sell finished plants in addition to rooted cuttings, EuroAmerican Propagators is only a rooting station business growing and selling rooted liners. Because of its location in the western region and ideal production climate, sales of liners begin in early January (its week of greatest volume shipped is Week 5 in late January/early February) and continues well into the summer. This production focus allows the company to control the quality of product that it ships, starting with optimal stock plant maintenance. For example, if

Figure 2.12. EuroAmerican's rooting station facility in Bonsall, California. (EuroAmerican Propagators)

strawflower (*Bracteantha*) stock is allowed to wilt, cuttings are prone to develop downy mildew during the rooting process. When scaevola cuttings are harvested from poorly maintained stock plants, they can require up to twelve weeks to root, whereas rooting time is only three weeks when cuttings are harvested from healthy stock. The vast majority of liners produced by EuroAmerican Propagators, which can be considered a midwife of the Proven Winners Brand, are patented varieties. The company also roots roses for Jackson and Perkins, but no longer produces liners of geraniums (*Pelargonium*) or poinsettias.

The facilities for rooting cuttings in Bonsall consist of mesh benches with heating pipes underneath in passively cooled greenhouses. Boom irrigation and overhead watering provide water to cuttings, which are stuck in 82-cell trays containing peat-based media. Before shipping, cuttings are hardened in the field or in retractable-roof greenhouses. These relatively low-energy-input production facilities are possible because of the optimum production environment.

As an early innovator in the use of branding to market garden plants, EuroAmerican Propagators and Proven Winners have raised the bar for the entire industry; competing suppliers have reacted to the success of these companies by establishing their own lines of trademarked flowers.

Direct Unrooted Grower: H.M. Buckley and Sons Inc. (Springfield, Illinois)

H.M. Buckley and Sons has been involved in the propagation phase of the greenhouse industry since its very beginning. In the 1930s, the business was shipping rooted cuttings to customers on refrigerated rail cars.

Today fifth-generation Lad and Doug Buckley now run the company that was started in 1884 by their great-great-grandfather. The relationship that Paul Ecke Sr. established with the Buckley operation as one of Ecke's original poinsettia propagators in the 1940s continues today. In addition to poinsettias, Buckley and Sons root the Flower Fields line of spring plants along with other patented and unpatented plants.

Buckley operates from two locations with a production area totaling 1.2 million sq. ft. (11 hectares): the original greenhouse range in Springfield, Illinois, and a second location in Naples, Florida. Both sites produce unrooted cuttings and spring liners from September to April, finished spring bedding plants from March to June, and Ecke and Fischer poinsettia liners from July through September. Spring liner production accounts for over 80% of Buckley's propagation market, while poinsettia liner production is only about 20% and decreasing each year. With a primary customer base of garden centers that produce their own material and small wholesale growers, Buckley is subject to trends that impact this segment of the industry. For example, sales of fuchsia have been decreasing steadily because the plants do not hold up well for the end consumer, resulting in returns to garden centers. To respond to these market shifts, Buckley is continually trying new crops and anticipating the next trend. For example, it is moving into herb liner production, a growth area for the company (fig. 2.13).

Buckley was quick to notice the major swing in the greenhouse industry toward greater production of patented cutting propagated materials, and switched its product offerings in tandem. About half of its propagation is of unpatented species and varieties such as vinca vine (*Vinca major*), with patented plant materials accounting for the remainder. Though its product line is extensive, Buckley is especially well known for lantana. About 60% of the lantana that it roots and ships are from the patented 'Patriot' series, while the rest are unpatented varieties. As a licensed propagator for the Flower Fields, Buckley roots cuttings produced in Guatemala (figs. 2.14 and 2.15). The Flower Fields includes about twenty plant species, such as coleus, New Guinea impatiens cultivars, petunias, and portulaca. Buckley also roots the Athens Select series, a diverse group of plants ranging from cuphea and heliotrope to plectranthus and verbena that are also produced from cuttings produced offshore. However, Buckley still grows its own stock of many species, including lantana and poinsettia.

Figure 2.13 Herb propagation is a growth area for Buckley. (K. Williams)

Propagators are middlemen in the process of royalty collection for breeding companies. Buckley pays a royalty on each patented cutting that it roots. For example, royalties for the Flower Fields and Athens Select programs are $0.06 and $0.085 respectively per rooted liner, which includes a color tag for each plant. Royalties payments are generally accepted as part of doing business when they allow companies to bring new and unique plants to the market and to back them up with a marketing program, both of which are significant benefits for small growers and retailers. A downside of the current structure of royalty payments is that root-and-sell operations like Buckley pay the royalty for each plant that it roots, even if the company does not sell it. This results in tightening orders to avoid overproduction. Propagators would prefer that royalties be paid only on plants sold to the finisher.

When it comes to the production side of the propagation business, H.M. Buckley and Sons has seen it all. Prior to twenty years ago, the company rooted cuttings of crops such as ageratum and Cyclone impatiens (a predecessor of New Guinea impatiens) in beds of sand. Today, head grower Bill Boehm explains that Buckley likes to match its propagation medium to the needs of each individual crop. A favorite material is Preforma, a peat-blend substrate held together with a binding agent, which provides enough aeration for crops like osteospermum, fuchsia, and strawflower to thrive. Oasis wedges are the substrate of choice for poinsettias and New Guinea impatiens, and many other crops are rooted in a peat and perlite germination mix. Buckley uses 105-cell trays for nearly everything. Cuttings are rooted under automatic, intermittent mist and over bottom heat (fig. 2.16). Buckley's crop scheduling generally provides for an extra week of time past Stage 3 and into

Figure 2.14. Shipments of unrooted cuttings arrive via FedEx in the morning. (K. Williams)

Figure 2.15 Unrooted cuttings are stuck at H.M. Buckley and Sons. (K. Williams)

Stage 4, which results in shipping only well-rooted cuttings and provides a buffer for pulling orders. Orders of rooted cuttings are shipped overnight via major shipping companies; though Buckley used airlines in the past, doing so is no longer feasible since the September 11 terrorist attacks. Buckley's future plans for updating production focus on ever-increasing opportunities to automate propagation practices.

Buckley is known for its friendly, service-oriented style that is ideal for small growers and garden centers. It holds a plant trial each summer and invites customers to visit its Illinois operation and observe the field performance of the newest industry introductions. One advantage of having a customer base composed primarily of small production businesses is that it is a relatively stable market niche; swings in volume of production from gaining or losing a single account are not great

from year to year. The downside is that the number of small growers in the United States is slowly decreasing, and Buckley must look to new products and markets to maintain its customer base. Another challenge is that in the past, spring liner production was a niche market with only a handful of operations focusing on this specialty. Today, however, there are more than 250 rooting stations for spring liners, so competition has increased steadily over the years.

Figure 2.16. Lad Buckley and head grower Bill Boehm inspect a cutting at Buckley's Springfield, Illinois, facility. (K. Williams)

Since starting production more than a century ago as one of the very first rooting operations in the United States, the Buckley family has seen much change in the industry and knows that change is the only constant that a greenhouse business can count on. A fire in the summer of 2003 at Buckley's Illinois operation offered the opportunity to update and increase automation of its propagation space, which the company sees as essential in remaining competitive in the future. H.M. Buckley and Sons has thrived over the years by staying in tune with industry trends, always offering the newest plant introductions, and striving to do so with excellent service and a competitive pricing structure.

Wholesale Greenhouse Producer: Kaw Valley Greenhouses, Inc. (Manhattan, Kansas)

Kaw Valley Greenhouses has been the most rapidly expanding greenhouse business in Kansas in recent years, and an ever-increasing demand for the company's products by its market niche has fueled this growth. Kaw Valley Greenhouses produces crops almost solely for the spring market, and it has carved out a marketing strategy built on its service program. As a wholesale greenhouse operation that sells primarily to high-end grocery store chains in central and eastern Kansas, Kaw Valley Greenhouses delivers, restocks, and maintains the store displays of its spring plants. And if a plant fails to sell, it buys it back from the retail outlet at full price. Therefore, the company focuses on producing well-toned, high-quality bedding plants, hanging baskets, and mixed containers. Its retail prices are a little higher than those of local box stores, but so is its quality.

Kaw Valley Greenhouses was started in 1967 by Patricia and Leon Edmunds. As parents of nine children, they said they started the greenhouse business "to keep the kids occupied and out of trouble." In the days before it was a common practice for grocery stores to sell spring bedding plants, Pat and Leon convinced a local grocery store manager to offer their products if they stocked and maintained the displays themselves— and if they were paid only for products that sold. This market strategy of outsourcing has grown into the extensive service program that has become the backbone of their business and driven their growth.

Today, a second generation of Edmundses, daughter Chris and sons Joe, Knute, and Pete (fig. 2.17), run this business, which sells more than $3 million of bedding plants per year to more than one hundred grocery stores across Kansas. The Dillon's Supermarket chain, a regional subsidiary of Kroger, accounts for about 60% of its business. Kaw Valley Greenhouses is now a midsize wholesale greenhouse producer with about 200 employees during the busy season and about 30 employees year-round. Staff at peak season includes about 100 to 120 people working in production and distribution, and about 80 employees off-site to organize, stock, water, and maintain the store displays in cities that they serve. Sales volumes at individual grocery stores range from a low of $6,000 to over $140,000; an average store yields about $38,000 in sales.

To accomplish the improved shelf life and garden performance that is so crucial to its market niche, the company's production strategy includes using its own soil-based substrate of about 12% field soil with peat and perlite, which dries slowly. In addition to incorporating slow-release fertilizer into its root medium, it produces crops under cool temperatures, subjects them to Kansas winds, and tones them with fertilizer and water restrictions. This production regime helps the

Figure 2.17. Joe, Pete, Chris, and Knute (from left to right) comprise the current generation of Edmunds that owns and operates Kaw Valley Greenhouses. (Kaw Valley Greenhouses)

plants hold up between visits from Kaw Valley Greenhouses employees. And when customers get the plants home, they stand up to the harsh Kansas spring and summer weather with its strong, dry winds better than soft, lush plants would.

Kaw Valley Greenhouses propagates plants from both cuttings and seed. Its most popular products are spring bedding standards: petunias, geraniums (*Pelargonium*), pansies, vinca (*Catharanthus roseus*), marigolds, and impatiens. Species propagated from cuttings include New Guinea and double impatiens, some petunias and verbena, vinca vine (*Vinca major*), and perennials such as artemisia. Though in past years the company bought more rooted cuttings, it now finds it more cost effective to either produce its own stock or to buy unrooted cuttings. In particular, the high cost of shipping drives Kaw Valley Greenhouses to root as many species as it can. Production manager Knute Edmunds explains that when the company roots a new species, it starts with small numbers and then builds on its successes in the following years. Another factor influencing whether to buy rooted or unrooted cuttings is timing and space availability during the season. Kaw Valley Greenhouses does not hesitate to root on-site before February and March; in March, rooted cuttings start to arrive. Its propagation space empties out by April 1, when the first shipments of finished plants are made to Wichita and every square inch of space is used to finish crops.

Kaw Valley Greenhouses' cutting propagation area is outfitted with Netafin mist nozzles and Biotherm bottom heat on expanded metal benches (fig. 2.18). These benches are located in one of the passively cooled Nexus Zephyr structures with sidewalls and roof vents that the production staff manually opens

Figure 2.18 Rooting geraniums under overhead mist at Kaw Valley Greenhouses. (K. Williams)

mass merchandisers, and while Kaw Valley Greenhouses continues to produce the bread-and-butter basic spring crops, it does not hesitate to expand its product mix by trying a collection of new species each year. As the company keeps pace with industry and consumer trends, it finds itself producing more mixed containers filled with vegetatively propagated plants.

As a wholesale producer, Kaw Valley Greenhouses generates its spring products through both seed and cutting propagation. It utilizes all avenues to procure cuttings of plant materials, including buying rooted

and closes so that they can maintain the relative humidity at a level about 25% higher than what the environmental control system would allow. This space is readily converted to finished crop production when the propagation season wanes.

Though Kaw Valley Greenhouses is always looking for "cool new stuff" and offers an ever-changing product mix, it is well known for its geraniums. The company has been producing geranium stock plants and rooting its own geranium cuttings since the business started. The production cycle begins in late September, when it buys disease-indexed cuttings. Planting this early forces the company to hold the first crops but allows it to match propagation needs with labor availability. In late November and early December, it harvests the first batch of cuttings. This is followed by a moderate defoliation of the stock plants; workers leave eight to ten of the youngest fully expanded leaves and remove all the buds (fig. 2.19). Sanitation protocols, such as disinfecting the work space and knives between cultivars, to prevent disease spread are practiced. In January to early February, the second flush of cuttings is harvested. These stock plant geraniums are finished for a midspring sale; they are generally shipped about two weeks prior to Mother's Day. Kaw Valley Greenhouses has experimented with using ethephon (Florel) sprays to promote branching and control flower bud development on its stock geraniums, but it currently applies the spray prior to finishing ivy geraniums only.

Chris Edmunds, who plans the product mix of the operation and follows consumer and market trends closely, predicts continuing growth in the market segment that Kaw Valley Greenhouses serves. She finds that uncommon plants are increasingly available at

Figure 2.19. Stripping geranium stock plants after taking cuttings in February at Kaw Valley Greenhouses. These stock plants will be finished for Mother's Day sales. (K. Williams)

and unrooted cuttings as well as producing stock plants of geraniums from which it harvests two flushes of cuttings and then finishes as large plants for Mother's Day sales. As one of the first greenhouse businesses to develop an extensive service program, it has led the industry in adopting a marketing strategy of outsourcing or consignment sales, and this market niche drives its selection of propagation and production practices.

Garden Center: Randolph's Greenhouses (Jackson, Tennessee)

For "plantaholic" Rita Randolph, creating a successful mixed planter is both an art and a science. The colorful creations that Rita cooks up are well known throughout the Jackson, Tennessee, area, where Randolph's Greenhouses is located. With upward of 85% of its annual profits from spring season sales, this plant-oriented retail garden center specializes in unusual and difficult-to-find plant collections (fig. 2.20). To provide such a selection, Randolph's Greenhouses has found that both propagating in-house and purchasing rooted cuttings are necessary to meet its market needs.

Rita's father's pre-World War II hobby of hybridizing azaleas, hollies, and magnolias quickly became an actively growing greenhouse business on the site of a former cotton field. Rita grew up in the midst of this family-run wholesale and retail nursery operation, which she eventually purchased from her mother, Ruth Randolph, in 1989. Since then, she and her husband, Hamp McCall, have maintained a thriving company that now has ten greenhouses on 17 acres (6.9 hectares) and is growing. Rita recalls an instance that became a turning point for the business: she vividly remembers her family turning away a retail customer who offered to pay twice the price for plants that were being saved for a wholesale customer.

Randolph's Greenhouses is now solely a retail operation. Its greenhouse division produces about 90% of the annuals, perennials, ornamental grasses, tropicals, and aquatic plants that are sold in the company's 7,500 sq. ft. (700 m²) retail area. In the very early 1980s, well ahead of the curve of the mixed container craze, Randolph's Greenhouses began offering mixed planters of spring bedding plants, following the strategy that something in each of the combination planters would survive the customer's care and handling. The business now specializes in unique combination planters designed around color schemes. Rita does not bother putting price tags on the plants offered for sale in her retail space; this passionate plantswoman has found that the cost does not matter to the consumer when the end product is a unique and colorful planter overflowing with appealing and interesting plants.

Rita and Hamp have created a market niche for their nursery by minimizing hard-good sales and focusing on an extremely wide and varied selection of plant materials, from the latest trendy items to rare finds that cannot be located elsewhere. The business is closed, except by appointment, from early July through mid-September, and again from mid-December through mid-January. More than 85% of Randolph Greenhouses' profit accrues during April, May, and June, when it is open seven days a week. There is little need for advertising because Randolph's primary customers are dedicated repeat clients who bring in their containers each year to be planted by the company. Rita's regular column in the local newspaper and her frequent speaking engagements also generate an expanding customer base.

Figure 2.20. The front of Randolph's Greenhouses. (K. Williams)

In the 1970s and 1980s, Randolph's Greenhouses was a licensed propagator of poinsettias, chrysanthemums, and geraniums from stock that it produced. In fact, Rita recalls finishing ten greenhouses of poinsettias from outdoor-grown stock that the company itself produced. For the past decade, however, the firm has opted to purchase rooted cuttings of all patented varieties of spring bedding plants, primarily through its regional Ball representative, though it makes purchases through Michell's and Bodger Botanicals as well. Shipments of rooted cuttings arrive from January through March. While Randolph's Greenhouses still produces more geraniums and impatiens for spring sales than any other crops, it propagates an extraordinary mix of unpatented plant materials that range from abutilon, alternanthera, and cuphea to old but great selections of zonal geraniums. Rita and Hamp maintain one greenhouse of stock plants year-round; these stock plants, in combination with purchases of unpatented plants from buying trips to Florida and other states, are the basis for the half of their spring production that they propagate on-site.

Randolph's Greenhouses has found an appropriate balance between buying rooted cuttings and doing its own propagation of unpatented plants. Rita cites two reasons for on-site propagation: higher profit per plant (the plant material is less expensive, and no royalties are paid) and a more diverse product line that allows the company to offer not only the latest and greatest of the patented selections but also the tried-and-true plants that thrive locally. With its success in propagating unpatented plant materials, Randolph's

Figure 2.21. The propagation area of Randolph's Greenhouses. A newspaper cover helps recently stuck cuttings acclimate under hand misting. (R. Randolph)

might well choose to buy unrooted cuttings of patented varieties and root them on-site too. However, it comes down to limited time and space. Considering the amount of attention required to successfully propagate and grow the extremely wide

Figure 2.22. Rita Randolph looks up from a retail display in Randolph's Greenhouses that emphasizes variegated foliage and lots of color. (K. Williams)

range of unpatented plants that the company produces, Rita and Hamp just do not have the time or the space to root patented materials.

Randolph's propagation system looks a little different from that of most other growers. Hot water pipes under the benches provide the necessary bottom heat. Cuttings are stuck in a thoroughly moistened high

perlite mix and misted by hand, not automatically. The company manages the diversity of species and challenges of matching water requirement with the stage of cutting development by placing wet newspaper over recently stuck cuttings to manage moisture (fig. 2.21). The newspaper is removed each night, and as the cuttings callus it is no longer used. The 95% success rates that the company accomplishes with this unorthodox propagation strategy are hard to beat.

Over the years, Rita and Hamp have adapted their business to changing consumer trends while finding ways to keep it interesting for themselves. Rita's talent for predicting future trends had Randolph's Greenhouses carving out a market niche for container gardening long before it was an industry movement. She continues to create new container combinations that includes the integration of tropical plants and colorful foliage into mixed planters, so that their displays are still interesting after the blooms fade (fig. 2.22). As for the future, Rita and Hamp are working on a mail-order Web site that will focus on selling combinations of plants and rare specimens, such as topiary trees ready to grow on patios. Rita sees no decline in container gardening; instead, she predicts that hanging basket gardening, in particular, will continue to grow in popularity.

Final Thoughts

The business opportunities associated with cutting propagation are dynamic and ever-changing. A recent trend has resulted in stock plant production generally moving offshore for optimal production climate and less expensive labor costs; however, its future may be influenced by bioterrorism concerns and homeland security issues in the United States that restrict imports of live plant materials. During the spring seasons of 2003 and 2004, small outbreaks of Southern bacterial wilt, caused by the pathogenic bacterium *Ralstonia solanacearum* race 3 biovar 2, caused substantial losses for hundreds of operations in all five of the propagation business categories described in this chapter. Ultimately, more than four hundred facilities in forty-one states received shipments of three suspect geranium cultivars in 2004, and destruction of all plants of these cultivars was required by USDA-APHIS (Animal and Plant Health Inspection Service). Extreme measures were taken to eradicate this *Ralstonia* because it can also infect seed potatoes; if established, the bacterium would jeopardize the American potato production industry.

If offshore production continues to face problems with importation of diseases, the niche for U.S.-based propagation businesses could expand in the future. If more U.S. growers had to produce their own stock plants to meet spring cutting needs, this could have an interesting impact on the production of other floral crops. For example, filling more production space in the fall and winter seasons with geranium stock plants might reduce the number of poinsettias produced, which in turn could help raise prices of this commodity crop. However, the current reality is that more than 80% of all cutting-propagated geraniums are supplied by offshore farms, and eliminating labor-intensive stock plant maintenance allows U.S. growers to use valuable greenhouse space for finishing plants rather than propagating them. The bottom line is that U.S. growers would have to pay more for domestic cuttings, and most industry leaders believe that the advantage of lower cost will outweigh concerns about the quality of cuttings coming from offshore farms.

Another perennial challenge of the propagation industry is to ensure that the quality of a product is maintained through the end of the market channel, which is necessary to keep consumers coming back year after year. Proven Winners' John Gaydos, Director of Product Development and Promotion, has noted that the large colorful care tags with a plant photo often accompany plants to consumers' landscapes and these can serve as a tombstone marker just as readily as an effective marketing tool.

Along these lines, it is increasingly important for breeding companies to release only outstanding new cultivars because small producers and garden centers find royalties difficult to swallow when they are attached to ordinary plants. In fact, some companies are making an impact in the expanding market of vegetative propagation by providing cuttings of varieties that are not patented. For example, Florexpo in Costa Rica, whose unrooted cuttings are brokered through McHutchison Horticultural Distributors and McGregor Plant Sales in the United States, serves about a thousand medium to large production operations. About 80% of the 90 million cuttings it produced in 2004 were of unpatented plant selections. Future customers are expected to be growers who currently maintain their own stock of plant selections that are not patented.

Despite challenges, the cutting-propagation niche of the greenhouse production industry is poised to continue expanding. As long as the gardening public has an insatiable appetite for unique plants with outstanding landscape performance, cutting-propagated plants offer opportunity.

References

Funk, J. 2004. Unbridled enthusiasm. *Greenhouse Grower* 22(6):16–17.

James, L. 2002. Strength in variety. *FloraCulture International* 12(3):32–35.

Lang, H. 2002. A cutting's long journey. *GrowerTalks* 66(5):56–62.

Onofrey, D. 2004. Ahead of the game. *Greenhouse Grower* 22(1):172–176.

Schneider, J. 2003. From bench to basket. *Greenhouse Grower* 21(11):14–20.

Sheldon, B. 2000. Kansas consignment. *GrowerTalks* 64(4):132–133.

3

Stock Plant Management

James L. Gibson

Traditionally, stock plants were grown domestically to produce the amount of cuttings required for each growing season. While poinsettias and geraniums (*Pelargonium*) were the two most commonly grown stock plant crops, a number of crop species were produced using stock plants. On-site stock plant production has generally become a practice of the past for many producers because not only does domestic production of stock plants require large portions of greenhouse space, but the greenhouse industry experienced a cutting-propagated bedding plant revolution in the 1990s. The diversity of plant material exploded during this time period, offering growers opportunities to produce plants during nontraditional periods of the year. Propagation firms also developed offshore cutting production facilities to take advantage of inexpensive labor costs and better environmental conditions.

Other reasons for the reduction in domestic stock plant production were the rapid introduction of patent-protected cultivars and the commitment to clean stock programs. Illegal propagation of patent-protected varieties is a major issue in greenhouse production today. Before growing stock plants, growers should make sure that the species they want to grow are legal to propagate (see chapter 1). It should also be noted that the production of unpatented or patented cuttings should be for one's own operation; a special license is required to propagate plants for other firms. Please refer to M. Klopmeyer, M. Wilson, and C. Anne Whealy's 2003 chapter in the *Ball RedBook,* vol. 2 (17th edition), for information on U.S. patents and legal issues.

Growing stock plants requires time and attention to ensure healthy plant material for production. Before growing the plants, conduct a stock plant production and management checklist (table 3.1). Poor stock plant management leads to insufficient production and unhealthy cuttings, whereas proper management results in an abundant number of healthy cuttings.

TABLE 3.1

Stock plant production and management checklist.

- Are there separate greenhouses devoted solely to stock plant production?
- Are the right personnel on board to grow and manage stock plants?
- Are there financial resources for supplemental lighting and plumbing?
- Are protocols in place for year-round stock plant maintenance?
- Will greenhouse space be used efficiently?
- Have production costs been calculated to achieve optimal profitability?
- Will there be other crop conflicts?

Producers who have the time and resources to grow stock plants on-site should consider unpatented cultivars that are easy to produce and maintain. Examples include Mexican heather (*Cuphea hyssopifola*), licorice plant (*Helichrysum petiolare*), 'Blackie' sweet potato vine (*Ipomoea batatas*), vinca vine (*Vinca major*), and 'Homestead Purple' verbena (*Verbena canadensis*). These filler plants are just a few of the species that complement the numerous patented cultivars available today (fig. 3.1).

Young plant material for stock plants should be purchased from a reputable supplier. Healthy and disease-free plants are crucial to a successful stock plant program. Young plant material should be inspected immediately because these mother plants will be the source of finished greenhouse crops. Several young-plant suppliers guarantee that their plant material is pathogen free by culture-virus indexing (CVI). Plant viruses cannot keep up with the rapid growth of shoot

Figure 3.1. Licorice plant (*Helichrysum petiolare*) is an unpatented tender perennial often grown as an annual that serves as a great filler plant in containers. (J. Gibson)

tips. During culture indexing, new plants are propagated from these shoot tips on sterile media and disease tested over several months to ensure that the stock plant material is clean. This technique is also used to prevent bacteria or fungi from harboring in young plants. Virus indexing is a combination of laboratory tests including heat treatment, meristem culture, and a series of analyses that detect the presence of viruses (see chapter 9.)

With several species cuttings are harvested from plants in production to propagate subsequent crops. For example, potted roses are cut back one to several times to create fuller plants and control timing of flowering. The harvested shoots are used to make one-node cuttings. Periodically, new cuttings may need to be purchased from outside sources to supplement production or to reinvigorate the plant material.

For many non-patented bedding plant species the primary shoot can be harvested from cuttings after they have rooted and shoot growth has resumed. This acts as a pinch to increase branching. Growers should be aware, however, that harvesting these shoots from too low on the stem may reduce branching, and quality, of the original crop. In addition, extra crop time may be required to allow the primary shoot to grow long enough to harvest for a cutting as compared to simply pinching the tip of the shoot to increase branching.

Most stock plant producers regenerate their own stock year after year. While all stock plants should be healthy and vigorous, cuttings should only be selected from the best-looking stock plants for next year's plants. Be sure that the cuttings have the same characteristics as the cultivar, which is known as being "true-to-type." Healthy cuttings should be propagated in the same manner as other cuttings; however, cuttings designated for stock plant production should be transplanted into larger-celled containers after rooting is complete. This ensures that the plants do not become stunted and stressed before they are planted into the final stock plant container. If possible, new cuttings should be purchased annually from a reliable outside source.

The Growing Environment

Stock plants should be grown in areas away from general production and retail settings. They are grown mainly on benches or in hanging baskets to allow easy harvest by laborers. If benches are not available, stock plants can be placed on large inverted containers to avoid the potential spread of waterborne diseases (fig. 3.2). If plants possess a trailing habit, greenhouse purlins, or other supports, can be used to hang stock plants grown in hanging baskets.

Figure 3.2. Stock plants can be grown on the greenhouse floor, but they should be raised to make it easier to harvest cuttings. (B. Whipker)

Pest Exclusion and Sanitation

Insects can be a severe threat to a clean stock program (see chapter 10). In particular, western flower thrips can serve as a vector for impatiens necrotic spot virus (INSV) and tomato spotted wilt virus (TSWV). Symptoms include yellow or necrotic spots (rings) on leaves and stems as well as mottling. Routine inspections of the foliage for eggs and immature stages of the insect should be conducted. An excellent control measure for insects is screening (fig. 3.3). These fine-mesh screens prevent

Figure 3.3. Insect screening is required for the prevention of western flower thrips and other insect pests that can infest stock plants. (J. Gibson)

Figure 3.4. Drip emitters should be placed in the interior of the container to ensure uniform saturation of the root substrate. (J. Gibson)

insects such as whiteflies and thrips from entering a greenhouse through open vents. Before greenhouses are filled with stock plants, growers should make sure that pest populations are significantly reduced or eliminated. Propagators often allow two weeks between crops to eliminate pests from greenhouses. This is also an ideal time to remove weeds and plant debris and to sanitize benches, floors, roofs, and sidewalls. Surfaces can be cleaned with quaternary ammonium compounds such as ammonium chloride (Green Shield, Physan 20, Triathlon), or hydrogen dioxide (Zerotol).

Irrigation and Water Quality

An efficient irrigation system is required for optimum cutting production. The best way to avoid water stress is to have an automatic watering system in place. Single, double, or ring drip emitters are excellent water delivery systems for stock plants (fig. 3.4). While effective, overhead watering from sprinklers or by hand should be avoided because it creates the perfect environment for foliar diseases, and it can spread root diseases. Water testing should be conducted twice a year to monitor electrical conductivity (EC), pH, and alkalinity values. A high substrate EC or pH due to poor water quality can disrupt water relations, movement of water from the medium to the plant, and lead to nutrient disorders of the stock plants.

Containers

Popular container sizes for stock plants range from 6.5 to 7.5 in. (17 to 19 cm) azalea pots to hanging baskets. Large containers are preferred because they require

less frequent watering (fig. 3.5). However, if stock plants are grown for a short period of time (less than four months), smaller containers may be more appropriate. One advantage of growing in smaller containers is that the stock plants can be retailed after the cutting production season. Transplanting stock plants into larger containers such as planters or hanging baskets is routinely done with poinsettias, geraniums, and New Guinea impatiens; however, growers should note that these plants have been

Figure 3.5. Poinsettia stock plants are often grown in large containers. (J. Gibson)

repeatedly pinched, hedged, or trimmed, and it may take a while for them to develop into an attractive salable item. Stock plants for foliage plants are sometimes also grown in ground beds, primarily in Central and South American countries.

Root Substrate

Stock plant growers require a substrate that retains moisture but provides adequate oxygen and will support a plant for several months. The traditional components of horticultural substrates: perlite, vermiculite, peat, foam, coir (coconut fiber), bark, and sand are used, but since stock plants will be grown for several months, mixes should be selected that will not break down quickly.

While the likelihood of root rots is greater in substrates that are continually saturated, diseases can occur at any time. Preventative fungicide substrate drenches with chemicals, such as fosetyl-Al (Aliette), etridiazole plus thiophanate methyl (Banrot), or mefenoxam (Subdue Maxx), may be applied to stock plants.

Regular monitoring of the substrate pH allows producers to make a decision to lower or raise the pH during cutting production or to add more limestone to the substrate for future stock plant crops. Because stock plants are grown longer than finished crops, the substrate limestone charge, or content, should be carefully monitored. Dolomitic limestone, a source of calcium and magnesium, will eventually dissolve out of the substrate; therefore, producers may have to apply liquid limestone or finely ground limestone to the stock plant crop during the cutting production season.

Spacing

Spacing stock plants is different from spacing greenhouse crops. Stock plants are spaced as tightly as possible to produce a maximum number of cuttings per square foot. A general rule is to provide 0.5 to 1.5 sq. ft. per 6.5 to 7.5 in. pot (0.05 to 0.14 m² per 17 to 19 cm pot) on a bench. For example, poinsettia and New Guinea impatiens stock plants in 7 to 8 in. (18 to 20 cm) containers should be spaced every square foot (11 pots/m²). Once stock plants begin to be pinched, trimmed, and harvested, there will be some space between them. Some propagators grow stock plants "pot tight" to produce an expansive and dense canopy of cuttings for continual harvesting. If cuttings are not removed on a regular basis with this approach, the internodes will become stretched due to the greater degree of far-red light penetrating the stock plant's lower canopy. The red to far-red light ratio changes as light passes through foliage, increasing the percentage of far-red light. Far-red light encourages stem elongation.

Temperature

In general, stock plants should be grown in temperatures of 70° to 75° F (21° to 24° C) during days and 65° to 68° F (18° to 20° C) during nights. Cutting quantity and quality (caliper, internode length, and stem weight) are affected by greenhouse temperature (see chapter 5). Warmer temperatures speed up the development of cuttings, but excessive temperatures can delay growth. Just as with greenhouse crops, stock plants should be kept under shade during warmer periods of the year to reduce stress.

Light

Light is essential for creating chemical energy (sugars) in plants. These sugars or carbohydrates in cuttings contribute to root and shoot growth during propagation. The three components of light (duration, quantity, and quality) should be considered when growing stock plants. Duration of light, or photoperiod, is important to stock plant production because of its effects on the flowering of photoperiodic species. Flowering is not desired on cutting material and can inhibit leaf development and rooting. For example, fuchsias need to remain under twelve-hour photoperiods, while chrysanthemums require day lengths greater than fourteen hours of light to remain vegetative. Night-interruption lighting can assist stock plant managers in extending the day length.

The light intensity or quantity should be held above 3,000 f.c. (32 klux) and below 7,000 f.c. (75 klux) for most greenhouse species. Supplemental lighting has been shown to improve the quantity and quality of cuttings of several floriculture crops such as chrysanthemum, petunia, poinsettia, scaevola, and verbena. However, if light levels are below 300 f.c. (3 klux), undesired internode elongation may occur. Low light may also cause a decline in shoot growth, which can negatively impact cutting quality and the carbohydrate content of the tissue.

Planting

Stock plants are typically established for six to twelve weeks to enable them to develop a large canopy so that a greater number of cuttings can be produced during peak cutting demand times. Producers normally plant two to three cuttings per 6.5 to 7.5 in. (17 to 19 cm) container. For better establishment, spacing cuttings 3 to 5 in. (8 to 13 cm) apart within the container to allow light to penetrate the interior of the plants.

Pinching and Trimming

Soft or hard pinches are conducted before harvesting to keep stock plants in a vegetative state and to increase the number of lateral branches. These branches combine to form a dense "scaffold" of plant material so that a large number of cuttings are produced. Work at Clemson University, South Carolina, showed that for maximum cutting numbers of diascia, snapdragon, and verbena, the initial pinch on the stock plants should occur after six nodes can be left on the plant, and the resulting side shoots should also be pinched when six nodes can be left on the shoots. By contrast, pinching low and allowing only two nodes to remain with both pinches reduced the number of cuttings harvested. In addition, for marguerite daisy (*Argyranthemum*), nemesia, and verbena increasing the number of pinches from one to three on the stock plants before the cutting harvest commenced delayed the initial harvest but increased the total number of cuttings harvested.

Trimming is also conducted before harvesting so that the secondary shoots formed after pinching produce adequate amounts of cuttings. Trimming involves shaping the plant by removing weak or broken shoots and other branches outside the canopy. Trimming is a routine activity to allow more stock plants to be grown on benches and to improve airflow between plants. Trimming stock plants during low demand times for cuttings is also important in controlling excessive vegetation. Excessive trimming should be avoided, however, as this interrupts the fine balance of root to shoot growth and can subsequently affect stock plant vigor as well as cutting yield and quality. Watering excessively sheared plants the same

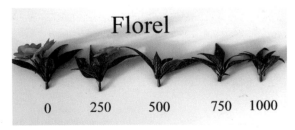

Figure 3.6. Effect of ethephon on flowering and leaf area of New Guinea impatiens. Cuttings were harvested two weeks after treatment with concentrations of 0 to 1,000 ppm. (B. Whipker)

as large canopied stock plants may introduce root and foliar diseases, nutrient deficiencies, and poor development of lateral shoots.

Plant Growth Regulators

Because flowers or flower buds are not desirable on cuttings, stock plant producers often apply ethephon (Florel) to control reproductive growth and, for some species, enhance branching (fig. 3.6). According to Peter Konjoian, ethephon has also been shown to decrease leaf area on stock plants of fuchsia, geranium (*Pelargonium*), and lantana. A general concentration range is 250 to 500 ppm; higher or improper application rates can delay flowering of the finished crop. Even at recommended rates, a slight reduction in leaf area may occur. It has also been reported that ethephon at 500 ppm resulted in a smaller stem length and stem diameter of geranium cuttings. Ethephon remains effective on stock plants for about four to six weeks. Ethephon sprays on stock plants are commonly applied two weeks prior to harvesting cuttings. Applying it at pinch or two weeks before pinching has been shown to increase the number of geranium cuttings.

Growth retardants may be also be applied to stock plants to provide compact cuttings or to prevent stem elongation during propagation. Since ethephon applications may also reduce stem elongation, be careful of applying other growth retardants in addition to ethephon.

Stock Plant Age

Stock plant producers should produce herbaceous cuttings that have actively growing shoots (meristems). Tissues that are too young or too old root more slowly than cuttings taken at the proper stage of maturity. Fully developed flowers on cuttings are a sure sign that tissue may be too old to root optimally. Cuttings that are too old do not branch as extensively as younger, softer tissue. A proper pinching and trimming program and/or regular harvests will eliminate most problems associated with cutting age.

Fertilization and Nutritional Monitoring

Nutrient-stressed stock plants produce nutrient-stressed cuttings. Stock plants that are fertilized appropriately produce cuttings with enough nutrient reserves to carry them through the early stages of propagation. Adequate nitrogen (N) content is crucial in cuttings because it is needed for nucleic acid and protein synthesis in plant tissue. However, if tissue nitrogen concentration is too high, rooting will be inhibited. Stock plants should be fertilized with both ammoniacal nitrogen (NH_4-N) and nitrate nitrogen (NO_3-N) to improve the quantity and quality of cuttings produced. Stock plants fertilized with high rates of NH_4-N will produce soft, lush cuttings that will not ship well. A general nitrogen concentration range for stock plants is 150 to 250 ppm. Because calcium and boron are essential for the development of new cell walls, it is critical that stock plants are not deficient in these nutrients. The use of a slow-release fertilizer is not recommended for stock plants because nutrients can be released rapidly during warm periods. Soluble fertilizer offers a steady rate of nutrients to the stock plant.

Growers should monitor stock plant nutrition with the PourThru method because it is a nondestructive way of measuring the pH and EC of the root substrate. For detailed information about this method visit www.pourthruinfo.com. An ideal pH range for most stock plants is between 5.8 and 6.2, and EC levels during cutting production should be maintained between 2.5 and 4.0 mS/cm for the PourThru extraction method. The 1:2 media:water dilution or saturated paste (saturated media extract) methods can be used if containers are too large for the PourThru method or if ground beds are used.

Harvesting

Healthy stock plants can tolerate frequent harvests. There are two types of harvest strategies: selective harvesting and hedging (grazing). If growers desire only the largest, highest-quality cuttings, then a selective harvest should be conducted. Selective harvesting works well when a specified number of cuttings are required each week. If growers need to meet the demands of a specific cutting window, then stock plants should be hedged. In hedging, all cuttings on the stock plant that fit the minimum quality standards of the propagator are harvested. With hedging, each harvest should be scheduled relative to trimming or the previous harvest.

Early morning is the best time to harvest, since plants are more turgid earlier than later in the day. Stock plants should be fully hydrated before harvesting to ensure that the cuttings can withstand the stress of severance from the stock plant. Employees should be instructed to take cuttings of similar size, quality, and stage of development. It is very important that propagators educate the employees about

Figure 3.7. A 10% bleach solution is used to sanitize cutting tools. (J. Gibson)

TABLE 3.2

A suggested stock plant production schedule for common vegetative annuals.

TIMING	CULTURAL PRACTICES
Week 0	Plant pest-free, healthy rooted cuttings. Fertilize with 100 to 150 ppm nitrogen. Apply preventative substrate drench
Weeks 2 to 4	Hard-pinch plants to five to six nodes above the substrate
Weeks 4 to 6	Soft-pinch plants to develop canopy. Fertilize with 200 to 250 ppm nitrogen
Weeks 6 to 8	Continue to pinch plants to develop canopy. Remove old leaves and shoots
Weeks 6 to 18	Apply ethephon (Florel) sprays at 150 to 300 ppm to minimize flowering and enhance branching
Weeks 8 to 20	Harvest cuttings. Conduct routine maintenance of stock plants

cutting quality before harvesting. Retraining may be required periodically, especially if new employees are hired. Each cutting should be between 1.5 to 3.5 in. (4 to 9 cm) in length and have at least three to five leaves on it, depending on the species. A cutting that is stretched with long internodes, has a thin stem caliper, and/or has a reduced leaf area will not root optimally. In addition, stock plant contamination can be reduced by providing a shallow basin for employees to wash their hands and forearms in a mild bleach and dish detergent solution of 2 fl. oz. bleach plus 1 tbsp. detergent per 5 gal. water (60 ml bleach plus 15 ml detergent per 19 L water) to use before harvesting.

Cutting Tools

Scissors, clippers, knives, and razor blades can be used to remove cuttings from stock plants. Sharp cutting tools are essential because they avoid the possibility of destroying the cutting base. Dull tools can crush the basal tissue and prevent or delay rooting. Cutting tools should be dipped in a 10% bleach solution or other disinfectant repeatedly during harvesting (fig. 3.7).

Conclusion

Producing and managing stock plants is a time-consuming responsibility that requires constant attention. The ultimate goal is to maximize production without reducing quality. Use the information outlined in this chapter as general guidelines for stock plant production and management. Table 3.2 provides a general stock plant production schedule for common vegetative annuals. Refer to individual species in parts 2 and 3 of the text for specific scheduling guidelines.

References

Baker, J. and E. A. Shearin. 2002. Insect screening for greenhouses. North Carolina State University, *Department of Entomology Insect Note*, www.ces.ncsu.edu/depts/ent/notes/O&T/production/note104.html.

Blazich, F. A. 1988. Mineral nutrition and adventitious rooting, pp. 61–69. In: *Adventitious Root Formation in Cuttings*, T.D Davis, B.E. Haissig, and N. Sankhla, eds. Dioscorides Press, Portland, Oregon.

Cavins, T. J., W. C. Fonteno, J. L. Gibson, and B. E. Whipker. 2000. Establishing a PourThru sampling program: Part 2. *Ohio Florists' Association Bulletin* 847:11–14.

Faust, J. E. and L. W. Grimes. 2004. Cutting production is affected by pinch number during scaffold development of stock plants. *HortScience* 39:1691–1694.

Faust, J. E. and L. W. Grimes. 2005. Pinch height of stock plants during scaffold development affects cutting production. *HortScience* 40:650–653.

Gibson, J. and L. Greer. 2002. Retail reflections: Profiting by propagating? *North Carolina State University, Commercial Floriculture*. www.ces.ncsu.edu/depts/hort/floriculture/RR/Propagation/prop_veg_annuals.htm.

Hamrick, D., ed. 2003. *Ball RedBook*, 17th ed., vol. 2. Ball Publishing, Batavia, Illinois.

Hartmann, H. T., D. E. Kester, F. T. Davies Jr., and R. L. Geneve. 2002. *Hartmann and Kester's Plant Propagation: Principles and Practices*, 7th ed. Prentice Hall, Upper Saddle River, New Jersey.

Healy, W. 1994. Vegetative plug production: Stock plant management and liners. *Professional Plant Growers' Association Newsletter* 25:2–5.

Konjoian, P. 2001. On-site propagators: Have you tried buying unrooted cuttings. *Ohio Florists' Association Bulletin*. 854:6–7.

Klopmeyer, M. 2003. Indexing for disease, pp. 181–184. In: *Ball RedBook*, 17th ed., vol. 2. D. Hamrick, ed. Ball Publishing, Batavia, Illinois.

Klopmeyer, M, M. Wilson, and C. A. Whealy. 2003. Propagating vegetative crops, pp. 165–180. In: *Ball RedBook*, 17th ed., vol. 2, D. Hamrick, ed. Ball Publishing, Batavia, Illinois.

North Carolina State University Extension. 2002. PourThru sampling. *North Carolina State University Commercial Floriculture*. www.ces.ncsu.edu/depts/hort/floriculture/crop/crop_PTS.htm.

Oglevee. 2005. Ensuring Oglevee quality: Producing clean stock. www.oglevee.com/Programs%20Products%20and%20Specials/cvi_variety.htm.

Pasian, C. Poinsettia stock plants. 2002. *The Ohio State University Horticulture*. floriculture.osu.edu/archive/may99/po-stock.html.

Paul Ecke Ranch. 2002. Fast crop stock plants. *Paul Ecke Ranch.* www.ecke.com/html/tibs/tib_fastcrop.html.

Sawaya, M. 1994. Vegetative plug production: Propagation principles and procedures. *Professional Plant Growers' Association Newsletter* 25:2-4.

University of New Hampshire Cooperative Extension. 2002. Cost of producing cuttings. *University of New Hampshire Horticulture.* http://www.ceinfo.unh.edu/Agric/AGGHFL/cutcolor.pdf

Williams, J. 2001. Vegetative cuttings (unrooted and rooted) for spring and summer success. *Ohio Florists' Association Bulletin* 854:7–8.

Williams, J. E. and P. Ruis. 1995. Stock plant production, pp.65–79. In: *New Guinea Impatiens,* W. Banner and M. Klopmeyer, eds. Ball Publishing, Batavia, Illinois.

Wulster, G. 2002. Poinsettia stock plant management: Fundamentals pay off. *Rutgers Floriculture.* www.aesop.rutgers.edu/~Floriculture/publications/POINTSTK.HTM.

Media

William C. Fonteno and John M. Dole

Stock plant production and cutting propagation are on opposite ends of the spectrum of production situations for selecting the best medium, or substrate. Stock plants are often grown for many months in large containers. Cuttings are usually rooted and grown for a few weeks in small cells with very limited volumes. Even though the properties of both substrates should be similar, the criteria for choosing substrates for these tasks are different. Where appropriate, we will discuss the different strategies for stock plant and cutting production.

Stock plants are typically grown in containers over 4 in. (10 cm) high. This allows for greater gravitational pull, more drainage, and better aeration. Unfortunately, lightweight organic mixes will decompose over time, causing the mix to shrink and reducing drainage and aeration. If the stock plants are growing vigorously, the large root system will help resist shrinkage, and aeration loss can be avoided. If the plant has a poorly developed root system, shrinkage and aeration loss will be more pronounced. It generally takes three to four months for the substrate to begin to shrink. Peat and coconut fiber–based media are more susceptible to degradation and shrinkage; barks (particularly pine bark) seem more resistant.

Herbaceous cuttings typically root in as little as three weeks, while woody cuttings can take longer. There is a wide range of substrates available for propagation; the biggest decision is whether to use a loose substrate or a preformed product. In both cases, the depth of these substrates is much shallower than those used for growing stock plants. Consequently, propagation substrates will drain much less and are more prone to overwatering. These products are also very lightweight, since most rooted cuttings are shipped by air transport.

Properties

Moisture retention and aeration

A stock plant substrate must be able to provide plant roots with both water and air. Pores, or spaces, of various sizes allow a substrate to accomplish both func-

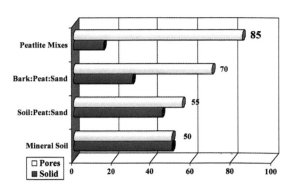

Figure 4.1. Total pore space and solid fractions (as percent volume) for mineral soil and horticultural substrates.

tions at once. Total porosity refers to all of the pore spaces within the substrate (fig. 4.1). While a plant is being watered from the surface, almost all the pores are filled with water. After irrigation is completed, the water filling the large pores, called *macro* or *noncapillary pores*, drains out the bottom of the pot by gravitational pull, and the pores refill with air. The smaller pores, known as *micro* or *capillary pores*, retain water. A suitable growing substrate contains a balance of capillary and noncapillary pores that allows optimal root growth.

The more shallow the pot, the shorter the substrate column. The shorter the substrate column, the less the gravitational pull and drainage (fig. 4.2, table 4.1). Very short containers, such as propagation flats, may not drain adequately to allow sufficient air to enter the substrate for good plant growth.

TABLE 4.1

Percentages of container volume occupied by water and air at container capacity for four substrates in pots, flats and plugs.

	6 in. (15 cm) standard pot	4 in. (10 cm) standard pot	48-cell bedding flat	512-cell plug flat
1 peat moss: 1 vermiculite				
Water (%)	67.9	75.2	79.5	84.8
Air (%)	19.0	11.7	7.4	2.1
3 pine bark: 1 sand: 1 peat moss				
Water (%)	51.5	57.6	61.4	66.9
Air (%)	18.9	12.9	9.1	3.6
1 soil: 1 peat moss: 1 sand				
Water (%)	47.2	51.2	52.9	54.3
Air (%)	7.4	3.4	1.7	0.3

Propagation substrates used in containers less than 2 in. (5 cm) tall should have more aeration.

Because horticultural mixes have a very high total porosity (> 70%), they do not tolerate rough handling. To maintain aeration after the substrates are mixed, do not pack substrate into the containers or

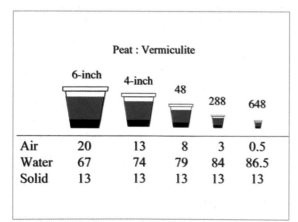

Figure 4.2. Effect of container size on percent water retention and aeration of three substrates. Note decrease in percent air and increase in percent water as the container becomes shorter from 6 in. (15 cm) pots, to 4 in. (10 cm) pots, 48-cell bedding plant flats, 288-cell plug flats or 648-cell plug flats.

Peat : Vermiculite BP Cell (48)

		Air Space	Unavailable Water	Available Water
Light		9	21	58
Medium		4	26	56
Heavy		2	30	52

Figure 4.3. The effects of compaction on a peat: vermiculite mix in a bedding plant cell (48 cells per tray).

Figure 4.4. Plug propagation trays that are nested directly on top of one another (right) causing substrate compaction. On the left are the same number of trays not nested together.

stack filled containers on top of each other, because the air space will decrease and the percentage of unavailable water will increase (figs.4. 3 and 4.4). Compaction result in overwatering and reduced plant growth (Fig. 4.5) Overhead irrigation frequently compresses the substrate over time, resulting in similar aeration problems. It is very important to match the substrate to the grower. Growers who grow stock

Figure 4.5. The plug on the left was compressed by tray stacking; the one on the right was not compressed, resulting in better aeration and therefore, better root/plant growth.

plants "on the dry side" can use a substrate with greater moisture retention, whereas growers who frequently irrigate will require a substrate with better drainage.

The amount of water held in a container by the substrate after it has been irrigated and drained is known as the *container capacity*. The water that is held in the substrate after irrigation is divided into two types: available and unavailable (fig. 4.3). The *available water* is loosely held between the substrate particles and can be absorbed by the plant's roots. The *unavailable water* is so tightly bound to the surface of the substrate particles that the roots are not able to absorb the water. When a plant has absorbed all of the available water, the plant has reached the *permanent wilting point.*

The rate of water uptake by a dry substrate can be increased with the incorporation of a *wetting agent.* Wetting agents decrease water surface tension, allowing the water to adhere to the surface instead of becoming a round bead. They are especially useful during the first irrigation in increasing the amount and rate of water uptake by substrate components that can be difficult to wet, such as dry peat moss or bark. Applications of a wetting agent before marketing a liner crop can also increase water retention in rooted cutting holding areas, where substrates can become quite dry between irrigations. Once a substrate is moist, however, wetting agents do not increase total water retention, only the amount retained immediately after a dry substrate is irrigated. Wetting agents are typically incorporated into premixed substrates and can be purchased if a firm is mixing its own substrates. Follow label recommendations and test wetting agents first, as phytotoxicity can occur.

Stability

The properties of a substrate continually change from the time the stock plant is potted until the last cutting is harvested and rooted. Thus a substrate may have the ideal properties at the time of potting, but less than ideal properties later in production. Stability is especially important for the production of stock plants that will remain in the same substrate for a long time. Stability can also be important with rooting cuttings to maintain consistent root mass and predictable rooting times.

One main cause of instability is biological degradation, the natural decomposition of organic matter. Although all organic matter eventually begins to decompose, not all organic matter decomposes at the same rate. One reason fresh sawdust is not used in substrates is because its rapid rate of decomposition alters the structure of the substrate. Peat moss and bark, however, decompose more slowly, allowing the substrate to retain its original properties much longer.

Vermiculite is also somewhat unstable due to physical compression over time. The natural compression from watering and plant root growth can cause the platelike structure of vermiculite to collapse. As a result, vermiculite particles lose a portion of their excellent moisture retention and aeration capabilities over time. Mixing and handling should be kept to a minimum in the preparation of any substrate containing vermiculite.

Another cause of instability is the variation in the quality of components used in substrates. Many times the quality of a component will differ in one or more of the properties discussed in this chapter, such as pH, air space, bulk density and so forth, resulting in variation in the properties of the final substrate and subsequent plant production. Variations in quality can be due to differences among manufacturers or due to decomposition if the components have been stored a long time. Most quality problems can be overcome at the time of formulation, but close attention must be made to the original components to ensure a stable uniform substrate.

Carbon: Nitrogen Ratio

Most substrates are composed primarily of organic matter, such as peat or bark. Organic matter is made up principally of carbon (C). In the process of decomposition, microorganisms feed on this carbon with the aid of available nitrogen (N). If a large amount of organic matter is broken down in a short time, nitrogen in the substrate can be quickly depleted by the microbes and not available for plant use. Lack of nitrogen can lead to nutritional deficiencies in plants growing in these substrates. Fortunately, most organic substrate components, such as peat moss, do not break down rapidly and so nitrogen depletion is minimal. The optimum ratio of carbon to nitrogen (C:N) for stable organic matter is 30 C to 1 N. Sawdust has a C:N ratio of 1,000:1 and therefore decays rapidly, resulting in significant nitrogen depletion. Barks also have high C:N ratios, 300:1 before composting, but are slow to decompose and are routinely composted prior to use. The composting process rapidly breaks down the small particles of organic matter in the bark, leaving larger pieces that do not break down rapidly. Thus nitrogen depletion occurs during the composting process, and properly processed bark will not deplete nitrogen in a substrate during stock plant production.

Bulk density

Bulk density refers to the dry weight of the substrate component relative to the volume. For example, sand has a high bulk density and perlite a low bulk density. Some components, such as peat moss, are very light when dry but have the ability to absorb a large amount of water and become heavy. For most stock plants, a substrate with a low to medium substrate bulk density of 6 to 20 lb./cu. ft. (100 to 320 g/L) is generally used to reduce the strain on workers. In some cases, a substrate with a greater bulk density may be necessary to prevent tall stock plants from falling over during production. Plug flat substrates should have a low bulk density to reduce worker strain and shipping costs.

Cation exchange capacity

Root substrate components such as peat moss, vermiculite, and bark have a negative electrical charge, which attracts positively charged ions (cations) in the substrate water solution. The cation exchange capacity (CEC) indicates the strength of the electrical charge in the substrate as well as the capacity of the substrate to hold positively charged nutrient ions. The greater the CEC, the more nutrient ions the substrate can hold. The CEC is based on volume (me/100 cc) for soilless substrates, and it should be high enough to allow the substrate to retain nutrients for the plants. Most of the plant nutrient ions are cations: ammonium (NH_4^+), potassium (K^+), calcium (Ca^{++}), magnesium (Mg^{++}), zinc (Zn^{++}), copper (Cu^{++}), manganese (Mn^{++}), and iron (Fe^{++}). Anions, or negatively charged ions, include phosphate ($H_2PO_4^-$), nitrate (NO_3^-), sulphate (SO_4^-), and cloride (Cl^-) Components with a high CEC include mineral soil, peat moss, and vermiculite; those with practically no CEC include perlite, Styrofoam, and sand.

pH

pH, which strongly influences the availability of nutrients to plant roots, is a measure of the concentration of hydrogen ions in the substrate's water solution. On a scale of 1.0 to 14.0, pH 7.0 is neutral, above 7.0 is basic (alkaline), and below 7.0 is acidic. The recommended substrate's pH will vary with the species being grown, but general recommendations have been developed.

For stock plant production, pH for substrates with no mineral soil should be 5.4 to 6.0. Substrates containing 25% or more mineral soil should have a pH between 6.2 and 6.8. Rooting substrates typically have no mineral soil and should have a pH of 5.6 to 6.2. Individual plant species will vary in their pH requirements.

Stock plant substrate pH often changes over time in response to fertilizers, water alkalinity, and pH. If the water alkalinity is high, the grower may want to begin the stock plants with a substrate pH at the low end of the recommended range and allow it to slowly drift upward without causing problems before the plant matures. On the other hand, the grower may want to start the crop at the upper end of the acceptable pH range if the water alkalinity and pH are low, if highly acidic fertilizers are being used, or if the water is acidified.

Soluble salts

Soluble salts are mineral salts found in substrates. They are the basis of nutrition in substrates. They typically come from fertilizers, but can also be found in water sources, organic matter such as composts, and other substrate components. For stock plant substrates, an initial fertilizer "starter" charge is usually incorporated into the mix. For rooting substrates, soluble salts should be much lower to prevent damage to sensitive young roots as they form. Many times fertilizers are not incorporated; liquid feeding at low concentrations of nitrogen may be applied after roots are formed.

Monitoring

Careful attention to pH and EC will prevent nutritional problems in stock plants. The best procedure for monitoring pH and EC in containerized stock plants is the PourThru technique. The 1:2 dilution or saturated media extract (SME) may be used with stock plants in beds or large containers (see chapter 7).

Substrate Components

While many materials can be used to grow plants, the most common materials used for stock plant production and loose-filled rooting substrates are listed here.

Peat moss

Peat is a natural accumulation of organic matter from four sources: sphagnum peat moss, hypnum peat moss, reed-sedge peat, and peat humus. The most important type of peat moss for horticultural use is sphagnum peat moss; the other types are used mainly outdoors as soil amendments or fuels. Fresh or dried sphagnum moss is also available but should not be confused with sphagnum peat moss. Sphagnum moss is used to line hanging baskets or cover the substrate in container gardens for aesthetic reasons, but it is not used as a substrate component. Sphagnum peat moss is the partially decomposed remains of various sphagnum moss species. It has a pH range of 3.0 to 4.0 and a fiber content of at least 66%; it is the major peat used commercially. Sphagnum peat moss is considered free of weeds, insects, and pathogens, and it can suppress fungal growth.

When purchasing peat moss, check the type, the degree of decomposition, the pH, the particle size, and—if buying it by weight—the percent of moisture. Peat moss is generally consistent within sources, but it can vary with the age and location of the bog and the harvest method.

Moisture retention and aeration: Excellent water retention and moderate aeration. Sphagnum peat moss can absorb up to 60% of its total volume in water. Peat moss can be difficult to wet if initially dry; the use of a wetting agent and/or warm water can facilitate wetting of dry peat moss. **CEC:** Moderate to high, 7 to 13 me/100 cc. **pH:** 3.0 to 4.0. **Stability:** Very stable. **C:N ratio**: 50:1, decomposition is slow. **Bulk density:** Low, 22 lb./cu. ft. (352 g/L). **Cost:** Moderate.

Bark

The type of bark available varies by area. The two general categories are softwood, which has a pH of 5.0 to 6.0, and hardwood, which has a higher pH of around 7.0. For both stock plant production and rooting substrates, pine bark is recommended. When purchasing pine bark, check the particle size, species, and degree of decomposition. Pine bark is more variable than peat moss, especially among sources. Bark can have disease-suppressive properties.

Moisture retention and aeration: Moderate water retention and excellent aeration after composting. Bark can be difficult to wet if allowed to dry below 34%. The use of a wetting agent and/or warm water can facilitate wetting of bark. **CEC:** High after composting, 12+ me/100 cc. **pH:** Softwood, 5.0 to 6.0. **Stability:** Very stable after composting. Despite having a high **C:N ratio** (300:1), the composting or aging is necessary to reduce the much less stable white wood and cambium left in the bark pile. Bark can be composted rapidly in four to six weeks by adding nitrogen, usually ammonium nitrate, at the rate of 3 lb. nitrogen/cu. yd. (1.8 kg/m³) and turning the pile once. Aging involves piling the bark for three to twelve months, usually without added nitrogen, and turning it occasionally when too hot (greater than 170° F [77° C]) or too dry (less than 34% moisture). **Bulk density:** Low to moderate, 32.7 lb./cu. ft. (523 g/L). **Cost:** Moderate, assuming the bark is not shipped from a great distance. Beware of exceptionally low-priced bark as it may be of poor quality.

Coir

Coir is similar in appearance to peat moss and is a by-product of the industry processing coconut husk fiber. Fibers and dust are removed during processing, composted, graded, dried, and pressed into bricks or bales, which are re-hydrated prior to use. It absorbs water more easily than dry peat moss. Coir is a relatively recent addition to the list of possible amendments, and quality varies with the source. In particular, total soluble salt, sodium, chloride, and potassium levels can be injuriously high. Coir dust does not contain weed seeds or pathogens.

Moisture retention and aeration: Excellent. **CEC:** Low to moderate, 3.9 to 8.4 me/100 cc. **pH:** 4.5 to 6.9. **Stability:** Excellent. Despite having a moderate **C:N ratio** (80:1), it decomposes slowly. **Bulk density:** Low, 22.3 lb./cu. ft. (357 g/L). **Cost:** High, due to shipping and expansion expenses.

Vermiculite

Vermiculite is manufactured from ground aluminum-iron-magnesium silicate that is heated to 1,400° F (760° C). Water trapped between the fine plate-like layers within the ore turns to steam and expands the ore fifteen to twenty times its original volume. The particles have a structure similar to tiny stacks of corrugated cardboard, resulting in excellent water retention. There are two sources of vermiculite: African and American. Vermiculite is also a minor source of calcium, magnesium, and potassium. Vermiculite can be purchased in different particle sizes, ranging from fine to coarse grades. The finer grades are used for propagation and the courser grades for potted plants.

Moisture retention and aeration: Excellent; do not use it with mineral soil, which will plug the pores of vermiculite particles. **CEC:** High, 10 to 16 me/100 cc. **pH:** African, 9.3 to 9.7; American, 6.3 to 7.8; however, pH generally has little effect on substrate pH. **Stability:** Chemically stable and sterile (**C:N ratio:** 0), but the particles compress easily, especially when wet, and should be avoided for long-term crops. Avoid over-handling, which will break down the structure. Vermiculite contains no organic matter to decompose. **Bulk density:** Low, 31.1 lb./cu. ft. (497 g/L). **Cost:** High.

Perlite

Alumino-silicate rock is ground and heated to 1,800° F (982° C), resulting in white popcornlike pieces. It has many characteristics similar to sand and is commonly used as a low-weight replacement for sand. Dust masks are recommended for handlers because mixing perlite can generate a considerable amount of irritating dust. Perlite has been erroneously reported to contain fluoride. It is actually safe to use with fluoride-sensitive species.

Moisture retention and aeration: Low water retention but excellent aeration. **CEC:** Very low, 0.15 me/100 cc. **pH:** Approximately 7.5, but it has little influence on substrates. **Stability:** Very stable and already sterile; contains no organic matter to decompose. **Bulk density:** Low, 20.8 lb./cu. ft. (333 g/L); may float to the top of the substrate in the container after watering. **Cost:** High.

Mineral soil

Mineral soil is seldom used in containers, but it is a component in ground beds. Soil generally contains little organic matter (1.5%), and it can vary in pesticide and herbicide content, mineral content, and the ratio of clay, silt, and sand. It is important either to know the source of the soil or to deal with a reputable supplier. The use of soil has decreased because of its heavy weight, its low aeration, and variable supplies; however, soil's high moisture retention, micronutrient

content, and CEC may still be useful in reducing water and nutrient runoff.

Moisture retention and aeration: Excellent water retention, but often poor aeration. **CEC:** Usually very high, up to 40 me/100 cc. **pH:** Variable; depends on the source of the soil. Test each new source. **Stability:** Very stable. The low organic content of most soils means that there is little to decay. Soil does not break down during pasteurization. **Bulk density:** High, 85.3 lb./cu. ft. (1,364 g/L). **Cost:** Generally low if you have your own source, but it can be expensive to purchase and ship.

Other components

The following are not as commonly used in production in the United States. However, some are popular materials in other countries. The choice of materials depends on local availability.

Rice hulls

Fresh rice hulls contain weed seeds and plant pathogens. Aged or composted hulls have fewer weeds and pathogens and retain their shape for several years in container media. Rice hulls are sometimes burned instead of composted. The ideal volume depends on the blending ratio with other materials; however, rice hulls have been successfully used at 20 to 50% on a volume basis. While not used extensively in the United States, rice hulls are a common component in tropical countries. They can be used effectively in both stock plant and rooting substrates.

Organic soils

Many tropical countries have highly organic soils that can be used in containers. These materials have a consistency of extremely degraded peat and should generally be used in small volumes (10 to 35%) for stock plant production. They are typically not used for rooting cuttings.

Calcined clay

Clay particles baked at 1,300° F (704° C) can vary with the type of clay used, but they are generally very porous. Calcined clays are also used as kitty litter, industrial spill absorbers, and other functions unrelated to floriculture. Calcined clay is quite heavy, 30 to 40 lb./cu. ft. (480 to 640 g/L), which limits its use. However, it has excellent moisture retention and aeration.

Sand

Sand is not commonly used in herbaceous stock plant production, but it is a common component in woody plant production. It is also used in propagation substrates for loose-filled beds. Coarse, concrete-grade sand (0.5 to 2.0 mm) should be used. Fine grade or beach sand as well as road or driveway sand, which could contain salt, should not be used. For best results, wash the sand to remove any clay particles, and pasteurize it before use. Sand was once one of the most commonly used components in substrates, but its use has declined as low-weight components with characteristics similar to those of sand, such as perlite and Styrofoam, were developed. If developing a new substrate with sand, be certain to test it first; sand can actually reduce aeration when combined with other components, particularly with fine-grade sand, which will fill the pores in the substrate.

Novel components

A variety of other materials can be incorporated in substrates. When deciding whether or not to use them, be sure to test them. In addition, make sure the component will be available over the long term. You do not want to waste the time it takes to test a new substrate and then have to abandon it because a key component is no longer available.

Substrate Preparation and Handling

For testing a new substrate or for potting only a few plants, small quantities of substrate can be mixed by hand. The proper amount of each component is spread out on a sterilized floor or bench and mixed together with a clean shovel. Be sure to thoroughly mix the components; fertilizers and other amendments should be spread out on the pile as evenly as possible before mixing to ensure uniform distribution of the amendments in the final substrate. Many growers and schools use a small cement mixer with a capacity of 1 to 6 cu. ft. (28 to 170 L), which generally produces a more uniform substrate than mixing by hand.

Larger volumes of substrate are mixed together using a large cement mixer or, more commonly, a commercially manufactured substrate mixing system. Such systems typically include a number of hoppers linked to a conveyor belt. The hoppers may include grinders to break up large bales of peat moss and to facilitate dropping the substrate components at the proper rate onto a conveyor belt that mixes or drops the substrate into a storage area or container. Mixing

systems are commonly integrated into a pot or flat filling machine for greater efficiency. The pot filler can also be linked to a conveyer belt for planting, labeling, and the first irrigation. The conveyer can continue into the greenhouse for transportation of containers to the growing benches.

During the mixing process, various amendments can be added to the substrates. Calcitic or dolomitic limestone can be added to raise the pH of peat-based substrates. Superphosphate (containing phosphorus and sulfur), controlled-release fertilizers (nitrogen, phosphorus, and/or potassium), gypsum (calcium and sulfur) and miconutrient mixes can also be incorporated. Most, if not all, commercial premixed substrates include wetting agents to allow rapid wetting after planting.

Regardless of the mixing method, it is important to produce a uniform, consistent mixture, especially for propagation flats with small volumes of substrate in each cell. Inconsistent mixing will lead to a variable crop that is difficult to water, fertilize properly, or use in machinery such as automatic transplanters. On the other hand, excessive mixing, such as occurs in rotating mixers, can break down the components and reduce aeration. The use of front-end loaders also leads to excessive substrate breakdown from compaction by the wheels.

Substrate components may need to be moistened prior to or during mixing to reduce dust from perlite and other components. Peat moss should be moistened prior to incorporation to facilitate wetting of the mixed substrate. If the mix is too dry, excessive shrinkage will occur after planting and subsequent irrigation. In such situations, water should be incorporated before the substrate is placed in the container rather than packing additional substrate into the container. In addition, dry substrates are difficult to rewet and require more than one irrigation to saturate the substrates. For pots, mix 1:1 water:dry substrate to obtain 50% moisture before planting. A higher moisture level is preferred for plug cells, mix 1:2 water:dry substrate to obtain 67% moisture. Substrates can also be moistened during the filling of containers and planting to reduce dust and add water to the substrate.

Experience and personal preference are required in determining the optimum amount of substrate to fill containers. Too much substrate leaves little room for water at the top of the substrate when the containers are watered by overhead irrigation, requiring frequent or lengthy irrigation to properly wet the substrate. In addition, there may not be enough room for pesticide or plant growth regulator drenches, producing incomplete coverage of the substrate. However, if insufficient substrate is used, stock plants will dry out rapidly, and pots may be too lightweight and fall over. To maintain proper aeration, never pack substrate into a container or stack containers directly on top of each other because that will also pack the substrate. Stagger flats and put pots into carry trays before stacking them.

Stock Plant Substrates

For stock plants, any high-quality commercial mix can be used (fig. 4.6). If you are employing a particular mix in your greenhouse operation with good results, try it for stock plant production. A common

Figure 4.6. Large bags of pre-mixed substrate.

lightweight mix-your-own-formula consists of 60% peat moss, 20% vermiculite, and 20% perlite. If the stock plants will be grown longer than six months, a mix with more pine bark is appropriate. For example, a heavier, longer-lasting formula would contain 60% bark, 20% peat, and 20% sand.

Rooting Substrates

Unrooted cuttings today are stuck in a variety of substrates, including peat-lite mixes, Ellepots, Jiffy pellets, Preforma, Oasis or Agri-foam, and Rubber Dirt. Some propagators prefer a coarser substrate such as a 50% peat and 50% perlite mixture, while others use a fine-grade plug mix. Molded substrates such as Rubber Dirt, Preforma, and foams may allow for earlier transplant than when loose mixes are used for rooting, because the root-ball remains intact even if the cutting is not very well rooted.

Loose-fill substrates

Substrates for rooting should be lightweight. A common formulation is 50% peat, 50% vermiculite. For more aeration use 50% peat, 50% perlite. For species that require long propagation periods, a mix containing fully composted ground pine bark may be best. For water-sensitive plants 100% perlite may be used, although prompt liquid fertilization may be necessary after two weeks. Several of the commercial mixes designed for seedling plug production can also be successfully used for rooting cuttings.

Jiffy pellets

Jiffy pellets are compressed peat blocks containing a specially formulated fertilizer (fig. 4.7). When placed in water they swell to five times their original size and are then ready to use. They are commonly used in producing geraniums and other herbaceous cuttings.

Figure 4.7. Jiffy pellets for propagation (www.jiffypot.com).

A newer product is the Jiffy-7 C, which is made of coir (coconut fiber) instead of peat and is wrapped in a nonwoven material for more aeration.

Rock wool

Rock wool is mineral rock melted and spun into various products (www.agrodynamics.com). It is most widely used in the home and industrial insulation industries. Rock wool is also made into slabs, blocks strips, and cubes for the horticultural industry. The slabs and blocks are used for growing many greenhouse cut flowers as well greenhouse vegetables, such as tomatoes, cucumbers and peppers. The strips, blocks and cubes are used for propagation of many edible and ornamental species. These materials are sterile and devoid of nutrients. They provide good aeration and water retention.

Rootcubes, horticubes, and wedges

These products made from rigid foam similar to florist foam are inert, very uniform, and sterile (fig. 4.8). Available in trays, strips, and holders of variety of sizes, they are used extensively for propagating poinsettias, geraniums, azaleas, and chrysanthemums, as well as other plants.

A

B

Figure 4.8. Various types of Oasis foam propagation substrates (www.smithersoasis.com/us/grower).

Fertiss

Fertiss is a European propagating plug containing a traditional peat, perlite, and vermiculite substrate

Figure 4.9. Fertiss propagation plugs (www.fertil.us/aboutfertil.htm).

bound by a non-woven membrane that can be penetrated by roots (fig. 4.9). Its pH is between 5.0 and 6.5. Shipped in a honeycombed tray, Fertiss is especially adapted to the propagation of cuttings.

Preforma plugs

These are loose-filled materials with a special binder that transforms them into a solid plug (fig. 4.10). It can be used in almost any tray configuration and with almost any substrate component formulation. As with other solid substrates, mechanical transplanting is less traumatic to the rooted cutting.

Figure 4.10. Preforma plugs (www.jiffypot.com)

Pathogen Control

Propagation of floriculture crops requires that substrates be free of plant pathogens, insects, and weeds. Many substrate components such as perlite, vermiculite, rock wool, and calcined clay are sterile as part of the high-temperature manufacturing process. Other components such as peat moss are not sterile but are judged to have few if any pests. The acidic nature of peat moss and the remote harvesting locations generally exclude plant pathogens, insects, and weeds from growing, and thus peat moss is considered ready to use without any further treatments for pathogens. Barks are usually considered ready to use because of the aging or composting process. The processing regime for coir makes it ready to use without pest problems.

Sphagnum peat, bark, and coir also appear to have varying degrees of natural disease-suppression properties. Light-colored sphagnum peat moss, which is harvested from the bog surface, suppresses pathogens for about six to twelve weeks. Composted softwood barks last five to six months, and composted hardwood barks up to two years. These components may host beneficial organisms that complete with or parasitize the pathogenic organisms. Barks also release phenolics that may suppress pathogens. The disease-suppressive properties are influenced by many physical, chemical, and biological factors that can produce variable results. Of course, even properly handled disease-suppressive substrate components may not be completely effective under high disease pressure.

Soil and sand, which usually contain plant pathogens, weed seeds, and insects, must be pasteurized. If only one or two components require treatment, they should be treated prior to mixing. Also ground beds for stock plants that are being replanted with a new crop need to be treated to eliminate any pathogens from the previous crop. Many times, treatment of the substrate is easier and more cost effective than removing, disposing, and replacing the old substrate.

Pasteurization

The most common way to control pathogens in greenhouse substrates for containers or ground beds is to heat substrates to 140° to 150° F (60° to 66° C) for thirty minutes. This pasteurization treatment is highly effective in eliminating most pathogens, insects, and nematodes, but unfortunately many nonpathogenic beneficial organisms are also killed. If weed seeds are a problem, heat substrates to 158° to 176° F (70° to 80° C). Substrates can be heated either by electricity or steam. Electrical pasteurization boxes are available to treat small quantities of soil or sand. Large amounts of soil or sand or ground beds are more economically treated with steam, applied either directly or with aeration. Although direct steam application is rapid, it often results in portions of the substrate being overheated at 212° F (100° C) to ensure that all of it reaches 160° F (71° C) for thirty minutes. Aerated steam can also be used, a process in which the steam is blended with air to 140° to 160° F (60° to 71° C). Aerated steam usually results in a more consistent pasteurization with no overheating, and it is more energy efficient.

With either steam method, substrates should be moist (approximately 25 to 40% water by volume) but not wet. Substrates with excess water will take

Figure 4.11. Steam pasteurization of substrate in a cart.

longer to pasteurize and may lead to incomplete pasteurization in that the substrate solution must also reach 160° F (71° C). However, substrates should not be dry because water facilitates the movement of the heat throughout the substrate. In addition, pathogens

Figure 4.12. Steam pasteurization of ground beds.

and dormant weed seeds are more resistant to heat in a dry state. Moisten the substrates, and store them for at least four hours and up to two weeks prior to pasteurization to allow weed seeds to begin germination and resting stages of pathogens and nematodes to become active. The moistening and storing process is especially helpful in controlling weeds. Steam pasteurization is also thought to improve the structure of substrates by slightly breaking down some of the organic matter, which then leads to increased bonding between substrate particles, resulting in greater porosity.

Specially designed carts have a perforated bottom to allow the steam to rise up through the substrate

Figure 4.13. Steam pasteurization of open soil in a greenhouse.

(fig. 4.11). The carts are covered with a tarp, which is then tied over the cart to hold in the steam. One side of the cart can usually be lowered horizontally to create a potting bench if needed.

The substrates in ground beds should be moist, loose, and slightly mounded to allow for adequate steam penetration (figs. 4.12 and 4.13). A perforated pipe extends down the length of the bed to carry the steam. The beds are then covered with a tarp, which is anchored to trap the steam.

One obvious disadvantage of steam pasteurization is the cost, which includes the expense of not only energy but also labor. Other potential problems are manganese and ammonium toxicity. Manganese toxicity can occur if the soil that is used contains large amounts of manganese in an unavailable form; the steam converts a portion of it into an available form. Pasteurization at too high a temperature or for too long can result in high manganese levels that are toxic to plants. Ammonium toxicity can occur because the pasteurization process at 160° F (71° C) kills the microorganisms responsible for the conversion of ammonium (NH_4^+) to nitrite (NO_2^-) to nitrate (NO_3^{-2}), causing the ammonium in the substrate to increase to a toxic level. If a substrate contains high levels of ammonium from compost, urea fertilizer, or highly decomposed peat, the ammonium can increase rapidly after pasteurization. The best solution is to avoid components with high ammonium levels and to incorporate ammonium-based fertilizers after the substrate has been pasteurized. If the problem occurs, the substrate can be stored for three to six weeks to allow the proper microorganisms to reestablish.

Solarization

Solarization is slow but inexpensive and free of chemicals. Greenhouse or field ground beds or pots of substrates are watered, drained, and covered tightly with clear (not black) 1.5 to 2 mil plastic. The plastic traps heat and increases the temperature of the substrates. This method is most effective during the summer or in areas with abundant sunshine, warm temperatures, and minimal wind. Leave the plastic on the substrates for four to six weeks. As with heat pasteurization, the substrates must be moist but not wet prior to treatment and free of clods or lumps. Be sure the plastic doesn't contain any holes and is tightly sealed; otherwise, some of the heat may escape, reducing its effectiveness.

For field or greenhouse ground beds the process works best if the plastic is laid close to the soil or substrate surface, which should be smooth without any protruding vegetation, rocks, or trash. Cultivate about 4 in. (10 cm) deep prior to applying the plastic. After solarization, avoid cultivating deeper than 3 in. (8 cm); deeper cultivation may bring up weed seeds that have not been killed.

Containers with substrates can be solarized by covering them with a tent of clear plastic. The containers or loose substrates to a depth of 12 in. (31 cm) can also be sandwiched between a layer of plastic on the ground, which is then folded over the substrates and sealed. Two layers of plastic, at least 0.5 in. (1.3 cm) apart, is more effective than single layers, resulting in temperatures up to 50° F (28° C) higher than single layers. Monitor the substrate temperature. All portions of a substrate should be 160° F (71° C) for thirty minutes. Especially effective solarization systems may reach the indicated temperatures in as little as a week.

Solarization is quite effective against insects, and it controls most fungi and weeds as well as some nematodes. Solarization is most effective against winter annual and perennial weed seeds and seedlings and is least effective against summer annuals. In fields the heat cannot penetrate deep into the soil, limiting solarization's effectiveness against established perennials weeds and other pests deep in the soil.

Fungicides

In an emergency, unpasteurized substrates can be drenched with fungicides to prevent possible pathogen problems. However, fungicides are expensive and may not be 100% effective in controlling substrate-borne pathogens. Using a pasteurized substrate or pathogen-free components is more practical and cost effective in the long run.

Chemical sterilants

Chemical sterilants are commonly used outdoors to eliminate weeds, insects, and diseases prior to planting. One of the most commonly used chemicals is the gas methyl bromide. Use of methyl bromide in the greenhouse has been limited because the gas is highly toxic to humans and the substrate needs to be aerated for seven to ten days prior to planting. In addition, some plant species such as carnations are particularly sensitive to methyl bromide. Environmental and toxicological concerns have limited the use of methyl bromide, which is scheduled to be removed from the market worldwide. Chloropicrin is available and can be used alone as a replacement for methyl bromide or in combination with methyl bromide. Together the two compounds are quite effective against fungi, insects, and nematodes and somewhat effective against weeds. Other chemicals and processes are being researched for outdoor soil sterilization and may have an application for greenhouse use as well.

References

Adams, R. and W. Fonteno. 2003. Substrates, pp. 19–27. In: *Ball RedBook*, 17th ed., vol. 2., D. Hamrick. Ball Publishing, Batavia, Illinois.

Barrett, J. 1997. Wetting agents: do they provide benefits after the first irrigation? *Greenhouse Product News* 7(10):26–28.

Dreistadt, S. H. 2001. *Integrated Pest Management for Floriculture and Nurseries.* University of California Division of Agriculture and Natural Resources Publication 3402.

Evans, M. R., S. Konduru, and R. H. Stamps. 1996. Source variation in physical and chemical properties of coconut coir dust. *HortScience* 31:965–967.

Fonteno, W. C. 1996. Growing substrates: types and physical/chemical properties, pp. 93–122. In: *Water, Substrates, and Nutrition for Greenhouse Crops*, D. W. Reed, ed. Ball Publishing, Batavia, Illinois.

Handreck, K. and N. Black. 2002. *Growing Substrates for Ornamental Plants and Turf*, 3rd ed. University of New South Wales Press, Sydney, Australia.

Konduru, S., M. Evans, and R.H. Stamps. 1999. Coconut husk and processing effects on chemical and physical properties of coconut coir dust. *HortScience* 34:88–90.

Meerow, A. W. 1997. Coir dust, a viable alternative to peat moss. *Greenhouse Product News* 7(1):17–21.

Nelson, P. V. 2003. Root substrate, pp. 197–236. In: *Greenhouse Operation and Management*, 6th ed. Prentice Hall, Upper Saddle River, New Jersey.

Sonneveld, C. 1991. Rockwool as a substrate for greenhouse crops, pp. 285–312. In: *High-Tech and Micropropagation I*, Y.P.S. Bajaj, ed. Biotechnology in Agriculture and Forestry, vol. 17. Springer-Verlag, Berlin.

5

Temperature and Light

Matthew G. Blanchard, Joaquin A. Chong, James E. Faust, and Erik S. Runkle

Temperature and light are the two environmental factors that drive plant growth and development. Temperature primarily controls the rate of plant development (for example, the time to flower or the production of roots), and light influences the accumulation of plant biomass (for example, leaf and stem thickness). Although temperature and light have distinct effects on plant growth and development, they interact in many ways.

For greenhouse growers to correctly manage temperature and light during propagation, they must first understand the fundamentals of how these two factors influence plant growth and development. When temperature, light, and humidity are optimized, propagation time is minimized, thus reducing the potential to encounter nutritional or pest problems. This chapter focuses on how temperature and light control plant growth and development, with an emphasis on how these parameters influence the propagation of floriculture crops.

Temperature

Temperature influences many physiological processes that occur during propagation, including photosynthesis, respiration, transpiration, and root and shoot development.

Average daily temperature (ADT)

The *average daily temperature* is the mathematical average temperature during a twenty-four-hour period. The formula for calculating ADT is: ADT = [(day temperature x hours) + (night temperature x hours)] ÷ 24

For example, a grower using a fourteen-hour day temperature of 68° F (20° C) and a ten-hour night temperature of 62° F (17° C) would calculate ADT as follows:

$$[(68 \times 14) + (62 \times 10)] \div 24$$
$$= [952 + 620] \div 24$$
$$= 65.5° \text{ F}$$

$$[(20 \times 14) + (17 \times 10)] \div 24$$
$$= [280 + 170] \div 24$$
$$= 18.8° \text{ C}$$

The ADT is important to calculate, since it influences the rate of growth and the development of a plant. The relationship between ADT and growth and development is linear between the base and optimum temperature. The *base temperature* is the temperature at or below which no growth occurs. At the *optimum temperature* plant development is most rapid. As the temperature increases beyond the optimum value, growth slows because plants experience heat stress. The base and optimum temperatures vary from species to species, and they can be considerably different. For example, the base temperature of cool-season plants such as petunia is approximately 35° F (2° C), while the base temperature for warm-season plants such as New Guinea impatiens is closer to 50° F (10° C).

Floriculture crops have an optimum temperature range for growth and development. Some cold-tolerant crops such as osteospermum perform best at 50° to 60° F (10° to 16° C), while cold-sensitive crops such as New Guinea impatiens perform best at 70° to 75° F (21° to 24° C). An important consideration when growing floriculture crops is that the optimum temperature often decreases as plants advance through different stages of development. In particular, the optimum temperature for the rooting of cuttings is usually higher than the optimum temperature for finishing crops. For example, a recommended temperature for snapdragons during cutting propagation is 68° to 72° F (20° to 22° C), while a recommended temperature after transplant is 57° to 65° F (14° to 18° C).

Many floriculture crops produce a set number of leaves before flower initiation. The rate of progress toward flower initiation can be quantified by tracking the number of leaves that appear (unfold) each day. The rate of leaf unfolding per day is primarily a function of

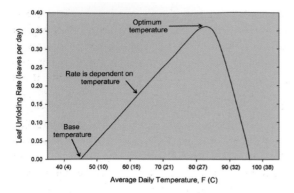

Figure 5.1. An example of plant leaf unfolding rate as a function of average daily temperature.

the average daily temperature. As the average daily temperature increases, the leaf unfolding rate increases until the temperature reaches its optimum level. A further increase in temperature will cause a decrease in the rate of leaf unfolding (fig. 5.1).

The *actual plant temperature* must be considered, not just the surrounding air temperature. The actual plant temperature may be several degrees cooler or warmer than the air temperature due to factors such as conduction, convection, transpiration, and radiation. For example, vinca (*Catharanthus roseus*) exposed to supplemental

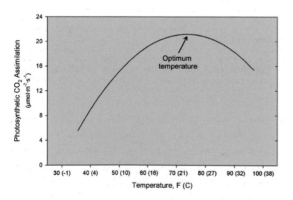

Figure 5.2. Generic response of photosynthetic rate to increasing plant temperature.

light from high-pressure sodium lamps at 380, 570, and 760 f.c. (4, 6, and 8 klux; 50, 75, 100 $\mu mol \cdot m^{-2} \cdot s^{-1}$) were, respectively, 2.2°, 2.7°, and 3.1° F (1.2°, 1.5°, and 1.7° C) warmer than plants in darkness. Knowledge of these variables and how actual plant temperature can change during the day and night allows growers to make adjustments in crop production schedules. During propagation, the temperature of the propagation medium must also be monitored because subop-

timal temperatures will slow rooting and increase disease susceptibility.

The rate of photosynthesis is positively correlated with temperature: the photosynthetic rate increases as temperature increases to an optimum. After the optimal temperature is reached, any further rise in temperature causes a decrease in the rate of photosynthesis and a decline in crop production (fig. 5.2).

Day and night temperature difference (DIF)

The relationship between day and night temperature can affect internode elongation and thus cutting length and plant height in a wide array of plant species. DIF is calculated as:

DIF = day temperature − night temperature

For example, a grower with a day temperature of 72° F (22° C) and a night temperature of 65° F (18° C) will have a +7° F (+4° C) DIF, while another grower with a day temperature of 62° F (17° C) and a night temperature of 68° F (20° C) will have a −6° F (−3° C) DIF.

Stem elongation is promoted when the day temperature is warmer than the night temperature ("positive DIF" or +DIF). When day temperature is cooler than the night temperature ("negative DIF" or −DIF), stem elongation is inhibited. The magnitude of the inhibition (−DIF) or promotion (+DIF) of stem extension increases as the day and night temperature difference increases. For example, internode length generally increases as the +DIF value increases.

Poinsettia producers commonly use cooler temperatures during the day than during the night (−DIF) to produce shorter plants. The use of DIF as a tool for managing plant height provides growers with an alternative to the use of plant growth retardants.

Plants grown under the same DIF will have a similar final height at flowering, regardless of different average daily temperatures. For example, poinsettias grown at 63° F (17° C) during the day and 68° F (20° C) during the night will have the same final height as plants grown at 68° F (20° C) during the day, and 73° F (23° C) during the night if all other conditions are similar. However, plant development will be hastened by growing the crop at a warmer average daily temperature compared with a cooler average daily temperature.

It is important to distinguish how ADT and DIF influence plant growth and development. DIF primarily influences the length of internodes and not the rate of plant development (fig. 5.3). In contrast, ADT controls the rate of plant development. Both of these concepts

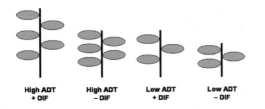

Figure 5.3. A schematic diagram of the effects of average daily temperature (ADT) and day and night temperature difference (DIF) on plant development and internode elongation.

can be used simultaneously to control the rate of plant growth as well as the characteristics of plant growth. For example, if rapid growth and short internodes are desirable, a grower could use a high ADT in which the day is cooler than the night temperature (–DIF).

Light

Light intensity

The light intensity is defined as the amount (or brightness) of light received by a plant at a specific period of time. The standard instantaneous unit of measurement often used by greenhouse growers in North America is the *foot-candle* (*f.c.*), while growers in Europe generally use the *lux* (or *klux*, which is 1,000 lux). The foot-candle unit refers to the brightness of a standard candle as it appears to the human eye 1 ft. away. The problem with using foot-candles as a unit of measurement for light intensity is that it is based on the amount of light perceived by the human eye and does not take into account light's capacity to drive plant photosynthesis.

A measurement system that is more appropriate for measuring light intensity for plant growth is the quantum system. Light energy travels in packets called quanta, or photons. The number of photons falling on a specific area (1 m^2) per unit of time (1 second) is expressed in the unit micro mole (µmol). (One µmol equals 6.022 x 10^{17}.) Light intensity measurements from quantum light meters are written as $\mu mol \cdot m^{-2} \cdot s^{-1}$. Affordable quantum light meters, which are available to greenhouse growers, provide an accurate measure of light intensity within the greenhouse.

It is important for growers to routinely measure and record the light intensity in all locations of the greenhouse throughout the year to determine the need for supplemental lighting. How much does the light intensity change during the year? During a clear summer day at noon, the maximum light intensity outdoors may approach 10,000 f.c. (108 klux, 2,000 $\mu mol \cdot m^{-2} \cdot s^{-1}$); during the winter months, the light intensity may reach

only 5,000 f.c. (54 klux, 1,000 $\mu mol \cdot m^{-2} \cdot s^{-1}$). Many crops have a target light intensity range at which plant growth is maximized and crop quality can be maintained. This information can be found in many crop production manuals. Plants from different parts of the world have adapted to different light intensities over time by changing characteristics such as the leaf area or leaf thickness, or developing a new plant growth habit.

The light intensity that is delivered to a crop has a direct influence on the rate of photosynthesis. As light intensity increases, the photosynthetic rate continues to rise until the photosynthetic system becomes saturated.

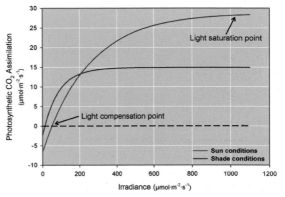

Figure 5.4. The response of photosynthesis to increases in light intensity for plants previously acclimatized to sun or shade conditions. Photosynthesis is saturated at a much higher light intensity (770 $\mu mol \cdot m^{-2} \cdot s^{-1}$, approximately 3,850 f.c. or 41 klux) for sun-acclimatized plants grown under sunny conditions compared with shade (400 $\mu mol \cdot m^{-2} \cdot s^{-1}$, approximately 2,000 f.c. or 22 klux). At light intensities below 200 $\mu mol \cdot m^{-2} \cdot s^{-1}$ (approximately 1,000 f.c. or 11 klux) shade-acclimatized plants are more efficient at using light energy than sun-acclimatized plants. The light compensation point (production of sugars is equal to the utilization of sugars) is reached at a lower light intensity for shade-acclimatized plants compared with sun-acclimatized plants.

The saturation level for photosynthesis differs among plant species, but it is usually higher for plants that naturally grow in sunny conditions compared with those that naturally grow in shade (fig. 5.4). When the photosynthetic rate is maximized for a plant, crop production is efficient and quality is usually high. If the light intensity for a crop is too high, meaning the light intensity is above the saturation level, damage to the plant can occur. Excessive light levels can result in the destruction of chloroplasts, which manifest as chlorotic or bleached leaves, "cupped" leaves, and leaf necrosis.

During propagation, light levels need to be controlled because young plant material is more susceptible to damage from higher light intensities due to the lack of roots and the development of specialized cells and protective pigments. As a result, shading during propagation is usually required to reduce light levels and prevent plant injury.

On the other extreme, if the light intensity is too low for a prolonged time period, the photosynthetic rate decreases, rooting is slow, and plant quality declines. At low light intensities, carbohydrate levels decrease in plant tissues, and many physiological processes are delayed. During propagation, suboptimal light intensities can result in undesirable internode stretching, weak stems, and most importantly, a slower rate of root development. This situation can occur even in high light climates when excessive shading is used to control temperature under propagation tents. The combination of low light and high temperature can stress cuttings, resulting in slow and erratic rooting and high disease incidence. In some situations, propagation tents may not be feasible (see chapter 11).

Daily light integral (DLI)

Daily light integral is a term used to describe the total amount of light received in a given area during a twenty-four-hour period. The daily light integral is expressed in *moles per square meter per day* ($mol \cdot m^{-2} \cdot d^{-1}$). Many growers are familiar with light measurements that are reported as an instantaneous measure of light intensity delivered at a specific time of day. These instantaneous measurements are often expressed in units of foot-candles, klux, or $\mu mol \cdot m^{-2} \cdot s^{-1}$ and do not take into account the length of the day. For example, an instantaneous light measurement taken at noon on a sunny day in January may be the same as a measurement taken on a cloudy day in June, but the DLIs would be different. Why? The day length is longer in June than in January, allowing greenhouse crops more time to harvest the sun's energy. Greenhouse growers who are familiar with the DLIs in their locales during a given time of year will be more efficient at growing crops and maintaining plant quality.

The DLI measured outdoors can range from 5 to 50 $mol \cdot m^{-2} \cdot d^{-1}$ during the year, while the measurements inside a greenhouse can range from low values (2 $mol \cdot m^{-2} \cdot d^{-1}$) to high values (25 $mol \cdot m^{-2} \cdot d^{-1}$) during the year; the range in values is due to factors such as the seasonal angle of the sun, cloud cover, and day length (fig. 5.5). For example, the DLI inside a greenhouse can range from 15 to 40 $mol \cdot m^{-2} \cdot d^{-1}$ in Phoenix, Arizona, (33° north latitude) while in East Lansing, Michigan, (43° north latitude) the DLI can vary from 6 to 29 $mol \cdot m^{-2} \cdot d^{-1}$ (fig. 5.6). However, values above 25 $mol \cdot m^{-2} \cdot d^{-1}$ are generally not observed in a greenhouse, since greenhouse shading is often necessary to help prevent excessive heat loads during the summer.

A useful tool for greenhouse growers in the United States has been the development of daily integral maps,

Figure 5.5. The average daily light integrals for the contiguous United States for each month of the year.

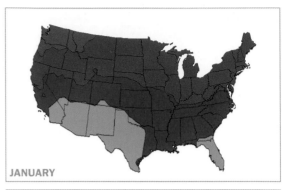

JANUARY

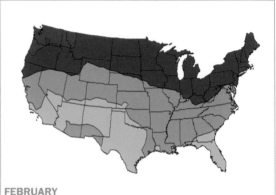

FEBRUARY

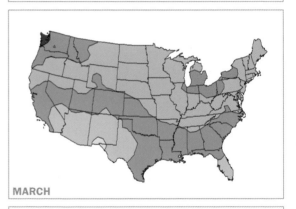

MARCH

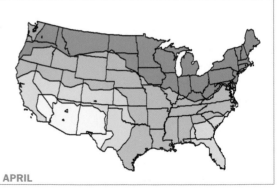

APRIL

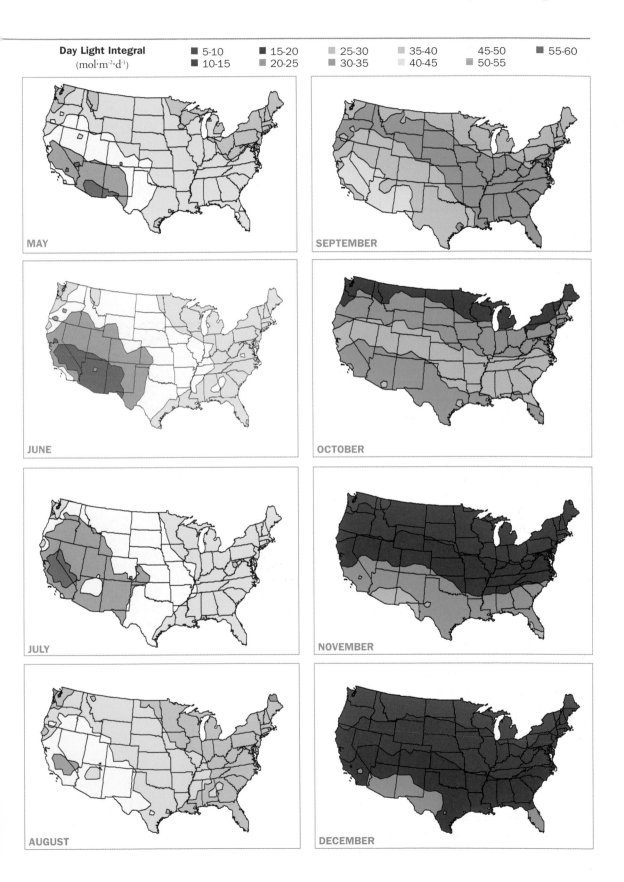

Day Light Integral (mol·m⁻²·d⁻¹)
- 5-10
- 10-15
- 15-20
- 20-25
- 25-30
- 30-35
- 35-40
- 40-45
- 45-50
- 50-55
- 55-60

MAY

SEPTEMBER

JUNE

OCTOBER

JULY

NOVEMBER

AUGUST

DECEMBER

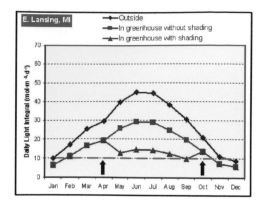

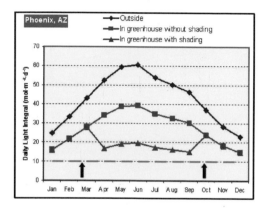

Figure 5.6. The average daily light integrals during the year in East Lansing, Michigan, (43° north latitude) and Phoenix, Arizona, (33° north latitude) outdoors and inside a typical greenhouse (65% light transmission) with and without shading. Arrows indicate when whitewash (reducing light transmission by 50%) would normally be applied or removed by the grower during the year. The dashed line indicates the minimum desirable daily light integral, 10 mol·m^{-2}·d^{-1}, to produce high quality floriculture crops.

Photoperiod

Photoperiod is the duration of light during a specific time span (twenty-four hours). For example, a fourteen-hour photoperiod refers to fourteen hours of light and ten hours of darkness. *Photoperiodism* is a term used to describe the response of an organism to changes in the length of day and night. Research has shown that the length of the dark period (night) controls photoperiodic responses in plants. Examples of photoperiodic responses in plants include the formation of storage organs (for example, bulbs and corms), cold acclimation, dormancy induction, seed germination, leaf development, stem elongation, and flower initiation and development. The critical photoperiod is the photoperiod that separates the occurrence of a plant photoperiodic response and the absence of the response. For example, 'Blue Clips' Carpathian harebell (*Campanula carpatica*) has a critical

Figure 5.7. The critical photoperiod for 'Blue Clips' Carpathian harebell (*Campanula carpatica*), an obligate long-day plant, is approximately sixteen hours. In other words, flowering occurs when the night length is shorter than eight hours. Plants were forced at 68° F (20° C) and did not receive any cold treatment at 41° F (5° C). NI = night interruption lighting from 10:00 P.M. to 2:00 A.M. (E. Runkle)

which provide estimations of the amount of light delivered to different areas of the country for each month of the year. It is important to remember that the DLI outside the greenhouse is higher than inside the greenhouse due to the loss of light transmission through the greenhouse glazing and overhead structures. Growers can estimate the amount of light that actually reaches the greenhouse crop by taking a measurement of the light intensity outside the greenhouse on a clear day and then measuring the light intensity inside the greenhouse. From these measurements a light transmission percentage can be calculated, and growers can get a general idea of the amount of light that is actually reaching the greenhouse crop. A recommend benchmark for most greenhouse crops is a minimum DLI of 10 to 20 mol·m^{-2}·d^{-1} for stock plants and finished crops, and approximately 3 to 5 mol·m^{-2}·d^{-1} for rooting of cuttings.

photoperiod of sixteen hours. This means that plants uniformly initiate flowers when night lengths are shorter than eight hours, and plants remain vegetative when night lengths are longer than eight hours (fig. 5.7).

Most floriculture crops can be divided into three main categories based on how photoperiod influences flower initiation and development: long-day plants, short-day plants, and day-neutral plants. *Long-day plants* initiate flowers when the night length is less than some critical duration (in other words, the day length is longer than the critical photoperiod). *Short-day plants* initiate flowers when the night length is longer than some duration (in other words, the day length is less than a critical photoperiod). *Day-neutral plants* initiate flowers under a wide range of photoperiods, and photoperiod has no effect on time to flower. A small percentage of plants have a dual photoperiod requirement for flower initiation, for example, a short photoperiod followed by a long photoperiod.

Plant responses to photoperiod can be further classified into two groups: *obligate* (qualitative) and *facultative* (quantitative). Greenhouse crops that have an obligate response require a certain photoperiod for the initiation of flowers. Plants that are characterized as having a facultative response will flower more rapidly and uniformly under certain photoperiods, but will eventually flower under all photoperiods. For example, a facultative long-day plant flowers under all natural day lengths, but will flower faster when the day length is long.

When the natural day length is short, it can be extended with light from lamps to create an artificial long day. Alternatively, night interruption lighting can be provided during the middle of the dark period (for example, from 10:00 P.M. to 2:00 A.M.). All major lamp types used in greenhouses can be used for photoperiodic lighting. The light intensity for photoperiodic lighting should be a minimum of 10 f.c. (108 lux, 2 $\mu mol \cdot m^{-2} \cdot d^{-1}$), although many plant species perceive lower light intensities.

Effects of Temperature and Light on Stock Plants, Cuttings, and Propagation

Temperature and light are key factors that affect cutting yield, size, quality, and rooting. The specific ways that environmental parameters influence these parameters are discussed here.

Cutting yield

Stock plant productivity, or cutting yield, depends primarily on the greenhouse temperature and light environment as well as cultural procedures such as pinching and cutting removal techniques. Cutting yield will be addressed by differentiating two phases of stock plant production: the build-up and the mature phases.

Build-up phase

The build-up phase refers to the initial stage of cutting production that occurs while the rate of cuttings harvested increases weekly. The build-up phase is *node limited*, meaning that productivity during this phase is limited by the number of nodes on the stock plants. At this time, each shoot is near the top of the stock plant canopy, so light is not limiting unless the ambient light levels are low (less than 10 mol·m⁻²·d⁻¹). Temperature is particular-

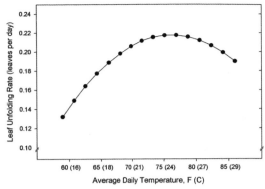

Figure 5.8. Temperature response curve for poinsettia leaf development. (Adapted from Berghage et. al., 1990.)

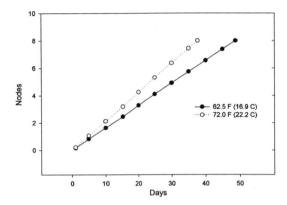

Figure 5.9. Days to produce an eight-node poinsettia cutting at 62.5° and 72° F (17° and 22° C). At 62.5° F (17° C), one node is produced approximately every 6.25 days and a cutting requires forty-eight days. At the higher temperature 72° F (22° C), one node is produced approximately every five days and a cutting requires forty days.

ly important during the build-up phase, since it is the primary factor that determines the rate at which nodes are produced on the developing shoots.

For many species, the optimal rate of leaf development (or leaf unfolding) occurs near 70° to 75° F (21° to 24° C). The effect of temperature on leaf production can be demonstrated with a relatively simple model using poinsettia (fig. 5.8). At 72° F (22° C), the leaf unfolding rate is estimated to be 0.20 leaves per day; thus a new node is produced every 5 days. At 62.5° F (17° C), the leaf unfolding rate is 0.16 leaves per day; thus a new node is produced every 6.25 days (Fig. 5.9). For poinsettia, a typical cutting contains eight unfolded leaves, while two nodes are left below the removed cutting. Using this poinsettia model, 50 days are required to produce a ten-node shoot (yielding an eight-node cutting) at 72° F (22° C), while 62.5 days are required to produce a simular cutting at 62.5° F (17° C).

As the stock plant size increases during the build-up phase, light interception by stock plants increases as does cutting production. The duration of the build-up phase is determined by plant spacing: the closer the spacing between stock plants, the shorter the build-up phase. Once the leaves of neighboring stock plants grow close together, cutting production per square foot is maximized, and plants reach the mature phase.

Mature phase

The mature phase refers to the second stage of stock plant production and is characterized by a steady rate of cutting production. The mature phase starts once neighboring stock plants begin to overlap and form a canopy. At this point, individual plants cannot be differentiated.

During the mature phase, cutting production is primarily *light limited*. In the mature canopy, only the uppermost shoots intercept sufficient light to produce cuttings. The amount of light delivered to the canopy determines how many shoots are actively maturing into cuttings. The canopy contains more nodes than can be supported by the light intercepted by the stock plants, so shoot growth and cutting production are not *node limited* as is the case during the build-up phase.

Regular cutting removal is required during the mature phase to create a steady supply of cuttings. Even if cuttings are not needed, it is important to remove shoots that have reached a mature cutting stage, since those that are not removed become too mature and reduce the productivity of the underlying shoots.

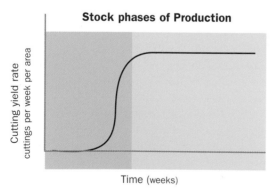

Stock phases of Production

Figure 5.10. Cutting yield rate (cuttings per week) increases rapidly during the build-up phase of stock production, then levels off and produces regular weekly harvests throughout the mature phase.

Finally, cutting yield greatly depends on the size of the cutting harvested. Cutting yield increases as the cutting specifications (for example, node number, stem caliper, and leaf size) are reduced. In other words, if small cuttings with fewer leaves are acceptable, more cuttings can be harvested from the stock plant during each week of the mature phase (fig. 5.10).

Cutting size

Choosing the proper cutting size to harvest depends on the grower's needs. Larger cuttings (longer stems, larger leaves, thicker stems, and more nodes) require longer stock production time and more propagation bench space, but often less bench time following transplant. Smaller cuttings are more quickly produced by the stock

Figure 5.11. Poinsettia cuttings from stock plants harvested at a rate of (from left to right) six, four, and two cuttings per square foot per week (sixty-five, forty-three, and twenty-two cuttings per square meter per week). The fewer cuttings harvested per week, the larger the cutting. (J. Chong)

plants and require less propagation space, but usually require more bench time following transplant.

Cutting size has a great impact on stock plant productivity. Ideally, stock plants produce a continuous cycle of cuttings throughout the peak harvest season. When a cutting is harvested, a new cycle of growth starts from the nodes left below the harvested cutting. If small cuttings are harvested, the cycle is faster and more shoots are actively developing in the stock canopy. If large cuttings are harvested, the cycle is slower and fewer shoots are actively developing in the stock canopy.

The rate of cutting removal from stock plants is termed the *harvest intensity*, which can be expressed as the number of cuttings harvested per square foot (square meter) per week. Harvest intensity affects cutting quality, described in terms of cutting length, stem caliper, and leaf area per cutting (fig. 5.11).

Cutting quality

Cutting quality is usually a subjective observation based on characteristics such as leaf thickness, stem flexibility, stem caliper, and leaf area. However, cutting quality can be quantified to some extent. Cutting quality is closely correlated to the temperature and light environment. The ratio of light to temperature (*photothermal ratio*) is a concept that describes the interactive effects of temperature and light on plant growth and development.

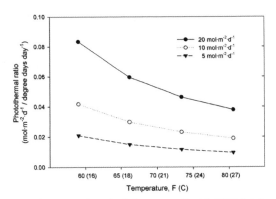

Figure 5.12. The photothermal ratio increases as the daily light integral (DLI) increases or temperature decreases. Plant quality also increases as the photothermal ratio increases.

Temperature determines how fast plants develop, such as the number of days to develop a new node. Light determines plant growth, such as the amount of photosynthesis per leaf or the amount of carbon fixed per leaf (measured in terms of dry weight). The combination of temperature and light influences the amount of dry weight formed per leaf or flower. Thus temperature influences the time over which a particular plant organ (for example, a leaf) develops, while the amount of light intercepted during that time period influences the amount of dry weight accumulated in that leaf.

For example, a plant grown at a cool average daily temperature, less than 65° F (18° C), develops relatively slowly. During this time, a considerable amount of light can be intercepted if the light levels are relatively high. Thus the highest-quality plants are often grown under cool temperatures and high light levels (greater than 10 mol·m⁻²·d⁻¹). These plants have relatively thick stems, small but thick leaves, a large number of branches, excellent root growth, large flowers, and high flower counts. In contrast, the lowest-quality plants are grown at warm average daily temperatures, greater than 75° F (24° C), and low light levels (less than 10 mol·m⁻²·d⁻¹). These conditions result in rapid development and very little light intercepted during shoot development. As a result, plant quality is poor; the plants have thin stems, thin leaf tissue, few branches, small flowers, and low flower counts.

Increasing the photothermal ratio is one method of improving quality. This is done by increasing the light level and/or decreasing the temperature (fig. 5.12). However, one must be careful to recognize that cooler temperatures also result in slower cutting production, while higher light can result in more flower development. The latter situation can be a problem with highly reproductive species. If a stock plant develops flowers too

rapidly, then cutting production can be reduced. In such cases, additional shade is required. The shade will reduce cutting quality, but may be necessary to produce large quantities of vegetative cuttings.

Finally, cutting quality can be improved by removing large leaves near the top of the stock plant canopy. This allows more light to penetrate the stock canopy, which enables higher light interception by the developing shoots (future cuttings). Leaf removal is effective in improving cutting quality on many species, such as geraniums (*Pelargonium*) and New Guinea impatiens, as the stock canopy matures and excessive foliage blocks light penetration.

Cutting propagation
The goal of propagation is to maintain turgid cuttings and minimize stress while promoting rapid root formation. However, the warm, moist propagation environment is conducive to pathogen development, and misting promotes leaching of nutrients; thus cuttings should be rooted as quickly as possible, using the least amount of water possible, to minimize disease and nutritional problems. Most cuttings can be successfully propagated in two to four weeks if proper environmental conditions are maintained during propagation.

Temperature
Air and growing media temperatures must be controlled during propagation. The combination of a warm growing medium and a cooler air temperature promotes rapid root growth without excessive shoot growth. For most plants, bottom heat should be utilized to maintain the medium between 73° and 77° F (23° and 25° C). It is important to directly measure the temperature of the rooting medium with a temperature probe, since evaporation from the wet medium may cause the growing medium to be cooler than the surrounding air temperature. For most species, air temperature should be maintained between 70° and 73° F (21° and 23° C). Once root initiation occurs, the soil temperature can be decreased to 66° to 70° F (19° and 21° C), and the air temperature reduced to 65° to 70° F (18° to 21° C). This temperature reduction may reduce unwanted stem stretch and also acclimate the cuttings prior to transplant. Plant growth regulators may be required in propagation if warm air temperatures cannot be avoided. Higher propagation and finishing temperatures may be necessary for warm-season species such as ornamental sweet potato (*Ipomoea batatas*), and lower temperatures for cool-season species such as osteospermum.

Light levels

Although the appropriate light levels during propagation can vary with species, some generalizations can be made. Vegetative cuttings require a minimum quantity of light for proper root development. Light quantities below this minimum result in little or no root development (fig. 5.13). Too much light can reduce root formation because of excessive stress. During the early stages of propagation (from stick to callus formation), light levels should be maintained between 600 and 1,000 f.c. (7 and 11 klux; 120 and 200 $\mu mol \cdot m^{-2} \cdot s^{-1}$), resulting in approximately 3 to 5 $mol \cdot m^{-2} \cdot d^{-1}$. In addition, light should ideally be indirect, or diffuse, to improve the uniformity of light in the propagation house.

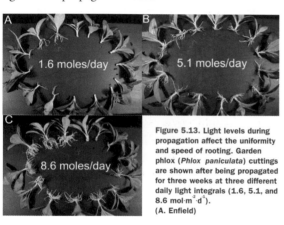

Figure 5.13. Light levels during propagation affect the uniformity and speed of rooting. Garden phlox (*Phlox paniculata*) cuttings are shown after being propagated for three weeks at three different daily light integrals (1.6, 5.1, and 8.6 $mol \cdot m^{-2} \cdot d^{-1}$). (A. Enfield)

After root initiation (generally five to twelve days after stick), light levels should be increased to 1,000 to 2,000 f.c. (11 to 22 klux; 200 to 400 $\mu mol \cdot m^{-2} \cdot s^{-1}$) resulting in 5 to 10 $mol \cdot m^{-2} \cdot d^{-1}$. Shade can be provided during the hottest part of the day if needed to prevent excessive drying of the cuttings and propagation medium. An ideal propagation house would have a retractable shade curtain, so that light levels can be optimized throughout the day. With a retractable shading system, the curtain can remain open on cloudy days and in the morning and late afternoon on sunny days. The curtain can be closed during the brightest hours of the day to prevent excessive light levels.

Once the cuttings are well-rooted (generally two to three weeks after stick), light levels should be increased to near production levels, generally 2,000 to 4,000 f.c. (22 to 43 klux; 400 to 800 $\mu mol \cdot m^{-2} \cdot s^{-1}$) or 10 to 15 $mol \cdot m^{-2} \cdot d^{-1}$. Higher light levels promote branching, prevent excessive stem elongation, and help to acclimate the cuttings to the postpropagation environment.

Photoperiod

If photoperiod affects flowering in a particular plant species, then photoperiod should be managed to prevent or reduce premature flower induction. Generally, the length of time required for rooting is sufficiently short to prevent flowering in propagation. However, this is only true if the stock plants have been properly maintained. If cuttings are harvested from reproductive stock plants, flower development during propagation can delay or inhibit root formation. Senescing flowers will also increase botrytis problems. Finally, flower development on cuttings may reduce the growth potential for those plants following transplant.

References

Berghage, R. D., R. D. Heins, and J. E. Erwin. 1990. Quantifying leaf unfolding in the poinsettia. *Acta Horticulturae* 272:243–247.

Enfield, A., E. Runkle, R. Heins, and A. Cameron. 2003. Herbaceous perennials: *Phlox paniculata*. *Greenhouse Grower* 21(6):66–74.

Erwin, J. E. and R. D. Heins. 1995. Thermomorphogenic responses in stem and leaf development. *HortScience* 30:940–949.

Faust, J. E. and R. D. Heins. 1998. Modeling shoot-tip temperature in the greenhouse environment. *Journal of the American Society for Horticultural Science* 123:208–214.

Fisher, P. and E. Runkle. 2004. *Lighting Up Profits: Understanding Greenhouse Lighting.* Meister Media Worldwide, Willoughby, Ohio.

Joeright, D., D. Tschirhart, R. Heins, A. Cameron, and W. Carlson. 2001. Herbaceous perennials: propagation. *Greenhouse Grower* 19(4):38–45.

Korczynski, P. C., J. Logan, and J. E. Faust. 2002. Mapping monthly distribution of daily light integrals across the contiguous United States. *HortTechnology* 12:12–15.

Liu, B. and R. D. Heins. 2002. Photothermal ratio affects plant quality in 'Freedom' poinsettia. *Journal of the American Society for Horticultural Science* 127:20–26.

Williams, J. E. and P. Ruis. 1995. Stock plant production, pp. 65–79. In: *New Guinea Impatiens*, W. Banner and M. Klopmeyer, eds. Ball Publishing, Batavia, Illinois.

6

Water

Kimberly A. Williams

All metabolic processes performed by plant cells depend on water. Water maintains protoplasm, which is the site of all enzyme-mediated physiological processes. Photosynthesis is one such process that creates the energy (carbohydrates) necessary to develop new roots. Water is critical for the cell division and elongation that occurs during rooting. Water is the hydraulic agent that maintains plant cells, without the aid of lignified cells that are found in woody plant tissues, in a fully expanded (turgid) condition and keeps plants standing upright. Water is the solvent in which nutrients are transported into and throughout the plant. And water cools the plant via transpiration, which is the evaporation of water from its leaves.

Figure 6.1. These New Guinea impatiens cuttings have just been stuck. A water deficit is obvious because of their lack of turgidity. (K. Williams)

The problem during propagation is that the water supply from the roots to the leaves has been severed, and the foliage is still losing water through transpiration. The goals are to minimize transpiration until roots form and to replace water to the rooting cutting that is lost via transpiration. A lack of water—called a *water deficit*—occurs whenever more water is lost than absorbed (fig. 6.1). If the water content of the cuttings is too low, rooting will be delayed, or worse yet, death will occur before root formation is accomplished.

Providing proper moisture management during vegetative transplant production seems straightforward; however, there are many pitfalls that can result in substantial losses, as well as many opportunities to use water management to influence the quality of the final product. Optimizing moisture management is made more difficult by the wide diversity of crops and the turns (different stages of the same crop) that are often rooted in the same propagation space. Delivering the right amount of water at the right time during vegetative propagation is the challenge.

Humidity and Vapor Pressure Deficit

The water status in plants is determined principally by the balance between water absorption from the rooting medium and water loss to the atmosphere. Humidity is the most important factor affecting water loss. Although humidity has only two direct effects on plants—transpiration of water through plants and the opening or closing of the tiny pores (stomata) through which leaves absorb carbon dioxide for photosynthesis—these effects may be quite significant. The rate of transpiration depends primarily on the "steepness" of the humidity gradient, or the difference between humidity on the inside and outside of the plant leaf. Secondarily, transpiration depends on the degree of stomatal opening. Since the atmosphere inside the leaf is always essentially saturated, the humidity gradient and thus the rate of water loss is determined mainly by the humidity of the atmosphere outside of the leaf. As atmospheric humidity decreases, transpiration increases; this is not desired during the early stages of propagation before roots form. Therefore, a primary goal of optimizing the rooting environment is humidity management.

Humidity can be difficult to control in a greenhouse environment. We commonly think of humidity in terms of *relative humidity*, which is the fraction or percentage of water vapor in the air compared to the amount that the air could actually hold at a particular temperature. However, this is a relative measure, and an absolute measure would be more useful. *Vapor pressure deficit (VPD)*, which quantifies the difference (deficit) between the amount of moisture in the air and how much moisture the air can hold when it is saturated, provides an absolute measure of humidity.

Vapor pressure is a measure of how much water vapor, or water in the form of gas, is in the air. More water vapor in the air translates to a greater water vapor pressure. When air reaches its maximum water vapor content, this is called saturation vapor pressure, which varies with the air temperature. The amount of water vapor that the air can hold approximately doubles with every 20° F (11° C) increase in temperature. Therefore, the difference between the saturation vapor pressure and the actual vapor pressure is the mathematical definition of VPD. In other words, VPD quantifies how close the greenhouse air is to saturation at any given temperature. A higher VPD, under low humidity, for example, means that the air has a higher capacity to hold more water, which stimulates transpiration. Lower VPD means that the air is near saturation, so transpiration will be minimized under these high humidity conditions. Environmental humidity-control equipment has been designed to function based on VPD.

Managing Water Applications

Stock plant water management

Stock plants should be completely turgid when cuttings are harvested, since the stomates will close and the cutting will be maintained only by internal water content through the initial stages of rooting. Experimental evidence from as far back as the early 1950s supports the importance of harvesting cuttings from turgid stock because rooting was reduced in cuttings that were harvested from stock plants with a water deficit. Because stock plant turgidity at the time of cutting harvest is critical, it is often desirable to take cuttings early in the morning before stock plant transpiration is increased by warm temperatures and higher light intensities.

Cutting water management

Research by Wilkerson and colleagues (2005) with poinsettia cuttings helped define the relationship between rooting stage and how a grower should manage humidity and root medium moisture content. After a cutting is severed from the stock plant, the cutting stomates close and transpiration and gas exchange are halted. The responsiveness of stomates and the ability of cuttings to transpire increased only after visible roots formed on the poinsettia cuttings. In addition, transpiration increased in response to light only following root emergence. Cuttings had to be well rooted to absorb enough water from the rooting medium to avoid moderate VPD stress at this stage. This research indicates that the propagator should alter humidity and root medium moisture content over the course of the rooting process.

Stage 1:
Cutting arrival or harvest and sticking

If unrooted cuttings are purchased, the goal is to reduce stress on the cuttings during transport and help them become turgid as quickly as possible after arrival. One option is to open the shipping boxes and place the cuttings under the mist system while still in their opened bags. This is the best option for growers who do not have adequate cooler space. Unstuck cuttings of many species can be left under mist for up to twenty-four hours without damage as long as the cuttings stay moist and are misted frequently.

The second option is to open the boxes and store them in a cooler overnight, which often allows them to become turgid again. Geraniums (*Pelargonium*) can tolerate temperatures down to 33° F (0.5° C), while New Guinea impatiens are best stored between 45° and 50° F (7° and 10° C). Poinsettias should not be stored for any length of time at lower than 45° F (7° C). Do not cold store cuttings for more than twenty-four hours, if possible. Some cuttings that are susceptible to ethylene, such as geraniums, can develop excessive leaf yellowing under propagation when they have been stored in boxes for more than twenty-four hours. Do not store cuttings in closed boxes; always open the boxes to allow for good air exchange, as long as the cuttings are placed in a cool or high humidity environment

The rooting medium should be on the propagation bench and thoroughly moistened in preparation for sticking the cuttings. Begin misting once the cuttings are stuck to reduce water stress and reestablish cutting turgor. If many cuttings are to be propagated, misting may need to commence before all are stuck. The frequency of mist application will vary widely depending on the crop, local weather conditions, and greenhouse environment, and though a propagator should not limit mist during this stage, excessive water application can contribute to future disease problems. A typical mist routine consists of misting for three to eight seconds every five to ten minutes over a twenty-four-hour period, reduced to every ten minutes after three to four days (fig. 6.2).

Typically, cuttings should be stuck 0.5 to 0.75 in. (1.3 to 2 cm) deep into a rooting medium. Cuttings

Figure 6.2. These trays of ivy geranium cuttings were stuck earlier in the day at Neosho Gardens in Council Grove, Kansas. Mist application is frequent during the first couple days after sticking to help cuttings regain turgidity and acclimate to the propagation environment. (K. Williams)

that are stuck too shallow are prone to falling over, and cuttings stuck too deep may have root initiation and development hampered by a lack of oxygen. Most rooting containers have a perched water table that remains one-quarter to one-half the depth of the cell, so the base of a cutting should be stuck just above this water level.

Water uptake in cuttings usually declines after the cuttings are initially inserted into the rooting medium. The decline may be caused by blocked xylem vessels, the cells that conduct water up the shoot; this problem is also observed in cut flowers. It is important to maximize the contact area between the cut surface and the rooting medium.

In northern climates, propagators should mist with tempered water heated to greater than 70° F (21° C) during the winter months, to reduce the significant cooling effect that cold water can have on the rooting medium. Fluctuations in soil temperature can

easily add days or weeks to rooting times. Water for the mist system may ideally be heated to 75° to 85° F (24° to 29° C).

Stage 2: Callusing

Callusing actually begins immediately after cutting harvest as a layer of dead cells forms over the wound to reduce water loss and help protect against pathogen entry. Callus cell development continues through Stage 2, and moisture management should be the main focus during this phase of development. The goal is to maintain nearly 100% relative humidity as well as a constantly moist root medium without having the medium waterlogged, which would limit root gas exchange. A typical misting routine is to mist for three to five seconds every ten to twenty minutes, and to extend the frequency of mist to every twenty to fifty minutes as the cuttings end Stage 2. It should be possible to squeeze water from the rooting medium during this stage. These conditions, coupled with warm soil temperatures, are ideal for rapid, uniform callus development and root initiation.

Stage 3: Root development

With the onset of root development, stomates are now regaining normal function for gas exchange. Wilting becomes less frequent because the cuttings can absorb water from the root medium with their newly forming root systems; the water they absorb replaces water lost from transpiration. Aggressively manage all aspects of the propagation environment, including water relations as described in the next paragraph, during this stage to maximize root development and minimize excessive shoot growth.

A few days after roots are visible, a propagator can begin to apply less water by allowing the root medium to dry down, which will promote root growth. In fact, mist may be discontinued and water applied by syringing by hand as needed. Because the cutting can now absorb water through a root system, much less frequent mist is required. The only time that excess water should be present in the rooting medium is immediately after watering; at all other times, the medium should be substantially drier than during Stage 2, and only a small amount of water should be able to be squeezed from the rooting medium between water applications.

Stage 4: Toning the rooted cutting

The propagator's goal is now to prepare the cuttings for transplanting and finishing. Root growth should continue simultaneously so that the well-developed root ball will transplant easily and sustain the plant immediately afterward.

Water management is still critical for growth control and the best tool for toning the cutting, allowing the cutting to withstand the rigors of shipping, if necessary, and planting. The root medium can dry down even more between waterings, inducing a slight water stress that will toughen the plant and push the developing root system. Misting can definitely be discontinued during this stage. However, the root medium should not dry enough to induce a severe wilt. Rather, allow the root medium to dry to the point of being a lighter color than when it is wet, with no free water present. But do not allow it to become much lighter than its wet color or shrink away from the walls of the cell. If water content is managed correctly, a soilless medium will crumble apart when squeezed.

Very little, if any, mist is applied during this stage. The lack of mist will result in a relative humidity that fluctuates dramatically during the day and mimics that of the production environment. This will further tone the cuttings and prepare them for transplanting.

Other water management comments

While cuttings that are in the process of rooting must never be allowed to dry down completely, a saturated rooting medium can restrict oxygen and contribute to the development of disease. The smaller the rooting cell, the easier it is to create waterlogged conditions in the root zone. Soft new growth on shoots with thin, large leaves and a poorly developing root system are visual indicators that the rooting environment is too wet.

Do not presume that regular mist applications result in a moist rooting medium. Foliage of the cutting or neighboring cuttings often deflects mist droplets from reaching the rooting medium. And while high relative humidity maintains plant turgidity, the rooting process can be slowed if the rooting medium—where new root cells are forming—is too dry. This problem is most noticeable with foam-type rooting media. Propagators must check the moisture content of the media frequently, and watering with a hose and wand is often required to supplement the mist. This is especially critical during the early stages of rooting.

High humidity, and thus lower vapor pressure deficit, is the goal during most of the propagation process. However, humidity in propagation areas is characterized by large fluctuations caused by the vents, doors, and windows being opened; irrigation; temperature changes; and changes in the weather. Take note of where air currents from HAF (horizontal airflow) fans or convection tubes blow down the mist table, and increase misting or syringing as needed.

Cuttings of some species, such as poinsettias, chrysanthemums, and geraniums, can be direct-stuck into their final production containers if adequate mist space or boom irrigation is available to maintain a highly humid environment (fig. 6.3). Some easy-to-root genera, such as peperomia, do not even require mist space (fig. 6.4). Principles of managing water for direct-stuck cuttings are the same as stated in this chapter, but maintaining high humidity to reduce water loss may be more difficult because of greater environmental fluctuations in production areas compared with propagation areas.

Figure 6.3. Chrysanthemum cuttings have been stuck directly into the final container and rooted under mist at Stutzman's Greenhouses in Hutchinson, Kansas. (K. Williams)

Figure 6.4. Leaf cuttings of peperomia are stuck directly into their final pot and rooted under overhead irrigation at Costa Nursery Farms in Homestead, Florida. (K. Williams)

Equipment for Water Application and Management

Key facilities for propagators include bottom heat on the propagation bench or floor, a good shade system with one or two shading options (to reduce water loss and transpiration because the light intensity and temperature are lower), and a fine mist system that provides uniform coverage across the propagation area (fig. 6.5). It is essential to filter water for mist or fog systems to prevent plugging of the small nozzle openings; filter selection is discussed later in this chapter. This section will focus on facility options to provide mist and/or a high-humidity rooting environment.

Figure 6.5. Geranium cuttings rooted under overhead mist (Netafin nozzles) and over Biotherm bottom heat at Kaw Valley Greenhouses in Manhattan, Kansas. (K. Williams)

Fog cooling systems

Two types of evaporative cooling systems are available to actively cool greenhouse operations: fan-and-pad systems and fog cooling. The lesser-used of these is fog cooling, which has been available since about 1980. Filtered water is pumped to a high-pressure pumping apparatus that generates a fog of water droplets less than 10 microns (one-tenth the thickness of a human hair). These droplets are suspended in the air, and as they evaporate, the air is cooled. Droplets are so small that people and plants stay relatively dry; however, the humidity is extremely high, as the air is nearly saturated with water vapor. A space outfitted with this type of cooling system can be used as a propagation area because of the ideal rooting environment that it provides. Cuttings would typically be removed from this environment midway through Stage 3.

Mist systems

Intermittent mist systems, in which the mist is "on" for a specific period of time and "off" for a specified period, give propagators excellent control over the rooting environment; they are the standard equipment for rooting cuttings in the greenhouse industry (figs. 6.6, 6.7, and 6.8). Solenoid valves control the flow of water through the system; the "normally open" type should always be selected for use because if the power becomes disconnected, the valve will

Figure 6.6. Mist nozzles attached to riser pipes at Frisby Greenhouses in Vinita, Oklahoma. (K. Williams)

Figure 6.7. Overhead sprinklers with Netafin fittings for cutting propagation at H.M. Buckley and Sons in Springfield, Illinois. (K. Williams)

remain open and allow water to pass through, which will keep the mist operating in the event of a power failure.

Misting of cuttings started in the early 1940s. Very fine droplets of water emitted by the system maintain a high-humidity environment and reduce air and leaf temperature, all of which reduces transpiration. In experiments where the leaf temperatures

Figure 6.8. Overhead mist provided by Netafin nozzles at Neosho Gardens in Council Grove, Kansas. (K. Williams)

Figure 6.10. Geranium cuttings rooted under overhead mist provided by a moving boom and over a heated flood floor at Neosho Gardens in Council Grove, Kansas. (K. Williams)

were recorded with thermocouples, leaves under mist were 10° to 15° F (6° to 8° C) cooler than leaves not under mist. In general, it is only necessary to apply mist during daylight hours, except during the early periods of Stage 1.

A number of different nozzle types are available, and the most satisfactory ones break water droplets into very fine particles so that they fill the atmosphere around the cuttings, wetting both sides of the leaves (fig. 6.9). The smaller the water particles, the faster

Figure 6.11. Aster propagation under mist provided by a moving boom at Metrolina Greenhouses near Charlotte, North Carolina. (K. Williams)

Figure 6.9. Mist nozzles attached to a pipe running parallel to a production bed at H.M. Buckley and Sons in Springfield, Illinois. (K. Williams)

they evaporate and the higher the humidity, both of which are appropriate for propagation applications. A droplet size smaller than 100 microns (μm) (0.004 inch, 0.1 mm) is preferred.

Boom irrigation systems

Booms fitted with nozzles move up and down a greenhouse bench distributing water droplets evenly on closely spaced trays (figs. 6.10 and 6.11). This

type of system is commonly used when establishing cuttings that have been direct-stuck in their final container or when establishing large plots of rooting cuttings. An advantage of a boom is the uniformity of water application.

Tent systems

There are many variations of tenting. The simplest is to lay a thin (0.03 mil) layer of polyethylene film or spun-bonded polyester over a well-watered bed of cuttings with the plastic directly touching the leaves and then tucking it in around the edges. Another technique involves building a framework to support the poly in a bow shape (fig. 6.12). Boxlike designs may result in condensation forming on the ceiling of the tent, causing the poly to sag and moisture to drip on the cuttings underneath. It is common to use clear polyethylene in the winter and white polyethylene during the summer to help manage heat buildup under the closed tent.

Figure 6.12. Hibiscus cuttings being propagated under tents. (H. Wilkins)

An advantage of this type of system is flexibility. A grower can place cuttings taken on different days in the same tent, and newly stuck cuttings do not have to be placed on a "first-day" mist schedule. Because tents are usually closed, it is critical to prevent excessively high temperatures that may make shading and ventilation necessary. Another potential drawback is that some plants, such as geraniums, are susceptible to ethylene buildup in closed tents.

Figure 6.13. Mist timer for a propagation space at Frisby Greenhouses in Vinita, Oklahoma. (K. Williams)

Hand misting
Hand misting is typically done only to mist dry areas or to syringe as needed. Special mist nozzles are required, such as Fogg-It nozzles, which put out a fine mist particle of between 50 to 100 microns. Some growers have combined multiple Fogg-It nozzles with a mini handheld boom made of PVC pipe to cover large areas faster. Larger droplet sizes can be provided with soaker nozzles; typically, they are necessary to penetrate foliage when the goal is to thoroughly wet the propagation medium.

Controlling Mist Frequency
Time clocks and computers
Electrically powered timer mechanisms, or time clocks, are available to operate the mist at desired intervals, often with several mist zones (fig. 6.13). Two timers could be placed to act together in a series: the first turns the entire system on in the morning and off in the evening, and the second serves as an interval timer to produce an intermittent mist during daylight hours. The biggest disadvantage of timers is that they do not respond to daily fluctuations in light intensity, relative humidity, and temperature.

Timed irrigation patterns are called constant-cycle and variable-cycle. The former is a preset system where each valve is cycled between on and off at a constant rate during the daytime when mist is applied. A time clock or controller typically allows a time period to be set when the mist system turns on and off; the cycle length (total duration of each mist cycle) and pulse width (amount of time that irrigation valves will be on during each cycle) is preset by the grower for each zone.

Preset systems may or may not respond to environmental conditions. If the system has an environmental override, such as a photocell that allows a predetermined amount of light accumulation to override the preset time clock and trigger a mist application, the system is a hybrid between constant-and variable-cycle irrigation.

Variable-cycle irrigation is more powerful than constant-cycle irrigation, because the cycle length and pulse width are varied from a user-selected minimum/maximum as a function of temperature, light level, or humidity. For example, when humidity is the control parameter, higher humidity results in a shorter pulse width and a longer cycle. As humidity increases due to mist application, the cycle length decreases proportionally from its maximum duration.

On-demand variable cycle irrigation is usually complex enough to require computer control and is typically based on one or a combination of up to three factors: accumulated light (see page 68); vapor pressure deficit (a computer accumulates the total VPD hours until the desired VPD is met, triggering a mist application; a percentage daily increase or decrease in water is often a feature); and evapotranspiration (ET). Light, temperature, relative humidity, and other factors are combined in an ET model to calculate plant's ET; when a given amount of water has been lost, water is applied to increase the water content of the rooting medium to container capacity.

Computerized mist-control systems can be designed that provide a propagator with the choice of using several of these timing methods in an integrated fashion.

Accumulated light system

Photoelectric cells control mist based on the relationship between light intensity and cutting transpiration rate. The photoelectric cell conducts electrical current in proportion to light intensity. This activates a magnetic counter, or charges a condenser, so that after a certain light threshold is met, a solenoid valve opens and mist comes on. The light threshold can be automatically increased or decreased based on the stage of plant growth. Because light is typically the most important environmental factor that contributes to evapotranspiration of cuttings, this type of controller efficiently controls mist in many different production situations.

Electronic leaf

An electronic leaf system maintains a uniform level of humidity at the leaf surface. It consists of two carbon electrodes set in a small circular ebonite block and placed under the mist with the cuttings. The alternate wetting and drying of the terminals connects and breaks the low-voltage circuit, which is connected to a solenoid valve. An advantage of this system is that it is responsive to environmental changes. However, salt deposits, which conduct electricity, build up between the terminals, causing erroneous operation.

Gravimetric scales

This system utilizes a screen balance that is based on the weight of water. A small screen made of stainless steel attaches to a lever that actuates a switch. When the mist is on, water collects on the screen until its weight trips the switch, turning off the solenoid valve. Screen balances are subject to salt deposits, algal growth, and air currents that distort balance accuracy.

Water Quality and Sources

Water quality is defined by the type and concentration of chemical elements or compounds found in water that determines its suitability for plant production. Essentially, water-quality reports indicate what contaminants are in the water, and how much of each is present. These chemicals may be toxic or may alter pH sufficiently to restrict plant growth. At the very least, any nutrients present in the water should be considered as fertilizer and taken into account in a fertilizer program. In addition, the water supply can be a source of inoculum for some plant pathogens.

Using water with minimal problems is critical during the propagation phase of production. Because propagation media are contained in small low-volume cells, a toxicity or pH problem can occur quickly. In addition, many propagation media contain unbuffered inert materials; therefore, they rapidly conform to the pH of the water. If the water quality is poor, cuttings in the process of rooting are likely to be exposed to its ill effects. Finally, plants are very susceptible to disease during propagation. The important point is that water appropriate for routine crop production may be unusable for propagation. For example, a potted-crop grower may have no trouble using water with 130 ppm sodium, but this same water may be unusable for a propagator.

Water-quality guidelines

Water-quality guidelines are well established for greenhouse production (table 6.1), and a number of excellent resources detail the characteristics of each water-quality parameter. When adapting these guidelines for water used in propagation, remember that plants are most sensitive during this phase, and one should err on the side of least contaminants.

Water sources

In most greenhouse operations, the water is from one of five possible sources, each with its own advantages and disadvantages: groundwater from wells, surface water, drainage ponds, rainwater, and municipal water.

Well water

Groundwater supplied by wells is water that has drained through the soil profile to a depth where all pore spaces are filled with water; the geological formation is called an aquifer. In general, there are two types of aquifers: confined and unconfined. Confined aquifers are water-saturated rock with an impermeable layer of rock or clay above and below it, keeping the water level relatively constant year-round. An unconfined aquifer, on the other hand, does not have an upper impermeable boundary, so the saturated zone, or water table, may rise and fall dramatically over the course of a year.

The quality of well water depends primarily on the parent material of the saturated zone. Because the parent material is limestone in many parts of the

TABLE 6.1

Desirable characteristics of high-quality irrigation water for floriculture crop production. Plants can often tolerate much higher levels of some individual ions.

CHARACTERISTIC	DESIRED LEVEL	UPPER LIMIT
Soluble salts (EC)	0.2 to 0.5 mS/cm	0.75 mS/cm for plugs
		1.5 mS/cm for general production
Soluble salts (total dissolved salts)	128 to 320 ppm	480 ppm for plugs
		960 ppm for general production
pH	5.5 to 6.8	7.0
Alkalinity (CaCO$_3$ equivalent)	40 to 65 ppm (0.8 to 1.3 meq/L)	150 ppm (3 meq/L)
Bicarbonates	40 to 65 ppm (0.7 to 1.1 meq/L)	122 ppm (2 meq/L)
Hardness (CaCO$_3$ equivalent)	< 100 ppm (2 meq/L)	150 ppm (3 meq/L)
Sodium (Na)	< 50 ppm (2 meq/L)	69 ppm (3 meq/L)
Chloride (Cl)	< 71 ppm (2 meq/L)	108 ppm (3 meq/L)
SAR[a]	< 4	8
Nitrogen (N)	< 5 ppm (0.36 meq/L)	10 ppm (0.72 meq/L)
Nitrate (NO$_3$)	< 5 ppm (0.08 meq/L)	10 ppm (0.16 meq/L)
Ammonium (NH$_4$)	< 5 ppm (0.28 meq/L)	10 ppm (0.56 meq/L)
Phosphorus (P)	< 1 ppm (0.3 meq/L)	5 ppm (1.5 meq/L)
Phosphate (H$_2$PO$_4$)	< 1 ppm (0.01 meq/L)	5 ppm (0.05 meq/L)
Potassium (K)	< 10 ppm (0.26 meq/L)	20 ppm (0.52 meq/L)
Calcium (Ca)	< 60 ppm (3 meq/L)	120 ppm (6 meq/L)
Sulfates (SO$_4$)	< 30 ppm (0.63 meq/L)	45 ppm (0.94 meq/L)
Magnesium (Mg)	< 5 ppm (0.42 meq/L)	24 ppm (2 meq/L)
Manganese (Mn)	< 1 ppm	2 ppm
Iron (Fe)	< 1 ppm	5 ppm
Boron (B)	< 0.3 ppm	0.5 ppm
Copper (Cu)	< 0.1 ppm	0.2 ppm
Zinc (Zn)	< 0.2 ppm	0.5 ppm
Aluminum (Al)	< 2 ppm	5 ppm
Fluoride (F)	< 1 ppm	1 ppm

[a]Sodium Adsorption Ratio relates sodium to calcium and magnesium levels.

Table adapted from Dole and Wilkins (2005).

country, ground water is often high in carbonates, which increases media pH during the rooting process. If well water has a high iron content, iron-fixing bacteria may develop, producing a bluish bronze sheen on plant surfaces, plugging submersible pumps, or clogging mist nozzles with a slimy yellowish mass. The depth of the well, the season of the year, and the amount of pumping all influence water quality from wells; therefore, at a minimum, well water should be tested at the end of the driest month, during the wettest month, and in the middle of both summer and winter. The advantages of well water are that it is typically inexpensive and pathogen-free due to natural filtration.

Surface water

Surface water is pumped from creeks, streams, rivers, and lakes. As with well water, the composition of rock and soil directly in contact with the water affects its quality. Most surface water is fairly low in salts, except in the western United States, where sodium and boron are problems. Concerns about surface water include contamination from substances added upstream, such as phytotoxic industrial chemicals or herbicides from farming operations. In addition, surface water is a common inoculum source for plant pathogens. Therefore, growers should not pump surface water directly to the crop, but filter and treat it before use.

Drainage ponds

Water in drainage ponds is generally a combination of rainwater and drain-tile runoff or water captured for recycling from the production operation. These ponds are typically smaller than 4 acres (1.6 hectares) and less than 20 ft. (6 m) deep, and it therefore may freeze in the winter in cold climates. Pond water often contains fertilizer and other agricultural chemicals, and it is commonly a source of plant pathogens. Thus, unless it has been treated, pond water is not usually an acceptable source of water for propagation.

Rainwater

Rainwater is collected precipitation from greenhouse roofs that is held in a cement or vinyl-lined cistern. Contamination is minimal, making this an excellent source of water for propagation. In some regions, the pH of rainwater may be low due to acid rain; however, this is typically not a problem for propagation because rain water is unbuffered. The challenges of using rainwater as a water source are generally related

to collection and storage, which depend not only on the volume of water used by the greenhouse but also on the amount and frequency of precipitation.

Municipal water

Municipal or city water is water supplied by a municipality. Therefore, it has been treated to remove suspended solids, pathogenic bacteria, and herbicides; it often contains fluoride, sodium, and/or chloride, sometimes at levels that are detrimental to plant growth. For example, 250 ppm chloride is typically the upper regulatory limit, but plant growth, especially for propagation, is affected at levels as low as 10 ppm. In fact, the growth of geraniums (*Pelargonium*) and begonias are affected at 2 ppm chlorine, and pepper and tomato growth declines at levels between 3

Figure 6.14. Reverse osmosis system at Kaw Valley Greenhouses in Manhattan, Kansas. (K. Williams)

and 8 ppm. The cost of municipal water varies, but it is usually prohibitive as a primary water source for a production operation. Municipal water is commonly used as a back-up source for propagation when the main water supply for a production operation is unacceptable, due to pathogens (for example, pond water) or high soluble salt level, and is not being treated prior to application.

Reverse osmosis water

Reverse osmosis (RO) water is produced by forcing water through a semipermeable membrane that allows water but not salts to pass through (fig. 6.14). Between 90 and 99% of salts in the original water source are left behind. RO water may be appropriate

TABLE 6.2

Water-quality characteristics that lead to a clogging hazard.

CLOGGING FACTOR	CLOGGING HAZARD		
	MINOR	MODERATE	SEVERE
Physical			
Suspended solids (ppm)	< 50	50–100	> 100
Chemical			
pH	< 7.0	7.0–8.0	> 8.0
Dissolved solids (ppm)	< 500	500–2,000	> 2,000
Manganese (ppm)	< 0.1	0.1–1.5	> 1.5
Total iron (ppm)	< 0.2	0.2–1.5	> 1.5
Hydrogen sulfide (ppm)	< 0.2	0.2–2.0	> 2.0
Biological			
Bacterial population (count per liter)	< 10,000	10,000–50,00	> 50,000

Table adapted from Rolfe et al. (2000).

to use to back-mix with another water source to reduce salt content for propagation. RO purification is not particularly effective at removing boron from water supplies. It is expensive, but it is the gold standard for propagation facilities, because it ensures water that is free of pathogens and has excellent quality attributes. Deionization, distillation, and electrodialysis methods are available for treating water with high ion content, but these methods are more expensive than reverse osmosis and typically cannot produce the volume of water needed.

System clogging problems

There are three main causes of blockages in irrigation systems: solid particles, biological growth, and chemical sediment. Table 6.2 indicates water-quality properties that result in potential clogging hazards. Solid particles include suspended inorganic particles such as sand, silt, clay, and plastic, and organic materials such as pieces of plants. Biological blockages typically result from algae and bacterial growth forming a gelatinous, sticky tissue in the pipes and the water. Bacterial slimes occur based on water pH, temperature, and sources of organic carbon. Aerobic sulfur slime may occur when water contains hydrogen sulfide and more than 0.1 ppm of total sulfides. Iron slime can develop when water contains more than 0.1

TABLE 6.3

Minimum filter opening sizes necessary to remove suspended solids.

MATERIAL	MESH[a]	INCHES	MM
Leaves, twigs	30	0.023	0.58
Gravel	10	0.075	1.91
Coarse sand	70	0.008	0.20
Fine sand	600	0.001	0.025
Algae	2,000	0.0002	0.005
Silt	3,000	0.0001	0.003

[a]Human hair is about 150 mesh = 0.004 inch = 0.1 mm.
Table adapted from Bartok (2000).

ppm of iron. Iron-fixing bacteria can cause a bluish sheen on leaf surfaces or a yellowish mass that clogs irrigation nozzles. Often a basin aeration pump that simply keeps the water moving helps precipitate the iron, removing it as a food source for the bacteria.

Finally, chemical sediment may settle in various components of the greenhouse plumbing. For example, in hard water whose pH is greater than 7.5 and alkalinity is greater than 300 ppm, calcium and magnesium carbonates may settle. Iron and manganese sulfides or metal hydroxides may form a scale on pipe walls.

Filtering water

Physical sanitation methods such as filtering are essential for propagation facilities. Two types of filtering may be necessary: first, filtering for particulate matter, and second, using an activated carbon filter to remove herbicides and other chemicals. Because suspended solids such as organic matter and chemical precipitates can clog fine nozzles in propagation areas, it is essential to protect your irrigation system with a good filtering system. Municipal water and rainwater are the two sources least likely to contribute to clogging.

Key considerations for filter selection include the type and quantity of solids present in the water source, the flow rate needed to supply your irrigation system, and the level of filtration needed (table 6.3). The pressure loss created by the filter should be minimal.

Several types of filters are available. *Screen filters* can be purchased in all sizes and shapes. Intake screens may be placed on the suction end of the pipe supplying water from a pond or stream to remove large debris and algae. Small-aperature in-line screen filters, which have one or two cylindrical screen elements, can be used as a final filtration if the water is fairly clean. These filters are inexpensive and available across a wide range of flow rates. The most common models must be manually disassembled for cleaning, though models with automated hydraulic flushing of the screen are available.

Disk filters consist of many flat, grooved rings that are stacked tightly together; the degree of filtration is determined by the size and number of the grooves. Intake water surrounds the filter element and is forced through the grooves, which traps the suspended debris. Cleaning is accomplished by reversing the water flow, which expands the disk stack; then pressurized air and water spray spin the disks, throwing off any debris. This type of filter is best for water with a low concentration of suspended solids.

Media filters are ideal for removing algae, slime, and small suspended inorganic silt and clay particles. The filter is a plastic or steel tank containing quartz or another inert material that provides filtration; the particle size of the inert material determines the level of filtration. Intake water flows through the bed,

depositing solids. When the pressure loss decreases, back-flushing begins and clean water is forced up from the bottom, which causes an expansion of the media filter material. This loosens the trapped solids, which then flow through a separate drain valve.

Finally, *centrifugal separators* are best for removing sand or other heavy particulate matter. Inlet water is introduced in a spinning motion inside a steel cone. Heavier particles as small as 200 mesh are forced by centrifugal action to the outside; they slide down to a collection chamber at the bottom. This type of filter is low cost, creates little pressure loss, and is very efficient. Separators can be arranged in tandem to increase capacity.

Water Treatment for Pathogen Control

Pathogen control is a major issue, because disease organisms including *Ralstonia*, *Phytophthora*, *Pythium*, and *Colletotrichum* are carried in recirculating water. Options to treat water before reapplication to plants include the following.

Chemical treatment

Oxidizing agents such as ozone and chlorine are effective in eradicating plant pathogens in water. The effectiveness of chemical treatment is related to chemical concentration, exposure time, and water quality. Chemical treatments are low cost and effective against a wide range of pathogens; however, they may damage plant tissue, which is especially critical during propagation.

Ozonation

Ozonation involves injection of ozone gas (O_3) into a reaction tank. The gas is commonly prepared by passing dry air through an electrical discharge. All pathogens are effectively destroyed by the oxidation process, provided that a high enough concentration and long enough exposure time are used.

Air is passed through a corona discharge generator; the ozone produced is then bubbled into the water so it can dissolve and disperse. Ozone is a toxic gas that needs to be applied in completely airtight tanks. Large holding tanks are required for the treated water to pass through before moving out into the irrigation system to achieve needed exposure times. However, the time required to hold water with ozone is shorter than with chlorine: 1.5 ppm ozone, held for twenty minutes (compared with thirty minutes for chlorine), is required. Like chlorine, ozone reacts with organic residues and iron chelates.

Chlorination

Chlorination is the common means to disinfect drinking and pool water. Gaseous chlorine (Cl_2) reacts with water to form hypochlorous acid (HClO, also known as "free available chlorine") and hypochlorite (ClO^-). The HClO is the most dominant form of chlorine between pH 5.0 and 6.5 and the most effective at killing pathogens. To disinfect water, chlorine is supplied as sodium or calcium hypochlorite, so that HClO is present at concentrations of at least 2 to 10 ppm.

The effectiveness of chlorine treatment depends on six factors: the chlorine concentration, the pathogen type, the initial cleanliness and pH of the water, the water temperature, and the duration of the pathogen's exposure to chlorine. The higher the concentration of chlorine, the more quickly it disinfects. Dirty water binds chlorine, reducing its effectiveness; thus the dirtier the water, the higher the chlorine rate needed to clean it. A neutral pH is best, because chlorine is most stable at that pH. A water temperature greater than 68° F (20° C) or less than 50° F (10° C) may decrease the effectiveness of chlorine. The effective length of time for a pathogen to be exposed to chlorine ranges from one minute to twenty-four hours. Adequate exposure requires that a holding-tank system be in place. The proper dose must be put into the water and held there for thirty minutes of oxidation time.

There are three methods for incorporating chlorine into irrigation water: sodium hypochlorite (commercial bleach), which has 100,000 to 140,000 ppm chlorine per liter and can be an explosion hazard if stored improperly; calcium hypochlorite, which has 350,000 ppm chlorine; and chlorine gas, which is the least expensive of the three materials but is dangerous to handle.

A chlorination system can be expensive to install, as well as dangerous and difficult to maintain. However, the operation costs associated with chlorine injection are low because it requires limited energy. Chlorine compounds react with inorganic compounds and organic residues in the water, reducing the efficacy of this system against microbes. In addition, toxic residues called trihalomethanes, which are suspected to be carcinogenic and are toxic to human health, may be formed. For this reason, some European countries have recently banned the use of chlorination. Perhaps the greatest concern about chlorinating water that will be used for propagation is the potential for phytotoxicity to plants; the damage is most severe when the crop is grown in an inert growing medium, such as many of the propagation media used today.

Chlorine dioxide (ClO_2) is being studied as a low-cost technique to treat large volumes of water, especially to control *Fusarium*. This compound is a water-soluble gas that is itself biocidal. It is formed by mixing sodium chlorite and hydrochloric acid as they are simultaneously injected into the water stream. It kills a wide range of pathogens at concentrations as low as 0.5 to 3 ppm. Like chlorination, its activity is reduced through reactions with organic solutes, and it may also react with nitrate, iron, and manganese. No holding time is required.

Bromination

Bromine is a member of the same chemical family as chlorine and acts similarly in disinfecting water. When sodium bromide is added to sodium hypochlorite, hypobromous acid is formed. Hypobromous acid is a very effective disinfectant across a wider pH range than hypochlorous acid: at pH 8.5, 60% of bromine is still present in this form, which is not true of chlorine. Interestingly, research in Australia has shown that bromination may be more advantageous and economical than chlorination over a wider range of water qualities. Currently, however, it is not frequently used in the United States.

Peroxides

Peracetic acid or hydrogen peroxide (H_2O_2) at a rate of 200 ppm has been recommended as an effective and safe rate to use. Peroxide is not stable in air, so old product loses efficacy. No holding time is needed, which is an advantage. However, peroxides provide no residual activity.

Copper ionization

Copper ions in solution are generated by passing an electrical charge between copper electrodes. Concentrations of 0.5 to 1 ppm copper are desired. This method is not effective if the water pH is greater than neutral, because the copper ions will precipitate at a higher pH.

Ultraviolet light

UV light, or wavelengths of radiation between 200 and 400 nm, can be used to kill fungal spores and microbes. The effective irradiation dose is the product of UV intensity and exposure time as measured in joules per square meter. Most bacteria succumb to UV treatment at lethal doses below 300 J/m^2. Plant pathogenic fungi, however, have variable sensitivity to UV treatment. Pseudomonads, *Erwinia*, and zoospores of water molds are easy to kill with UV light, but xanthomonads, *Fusarium*, and *Thielaviopsis* are more difficult to kill. To eliminate all relevant pathogens, including viruses and nematodes, 1,000 to 2,500 J/m^2 is recommended. High-pressure systems typically have one very strong UV bulb, and low-pressure systems have numerous lower-power bulbs.

Low-pressure mercury vapor lamps are relatively efficient sources of UV radiation; they emit 40% of the electrical energy input in the form of UVc, which is 200 to 280 nm. A set of stainless steel tubes, each with a UV lamp in a quartz glass tube, comprises the system. The water layer should be less than 10 mm for the greatest efficiency. Radiators have a working life of about 7,000 hours. Costs for this type of system are intermediate compared with other techniques. Because dissolved organic matter and other particles can reduce the system's efficacy by blocking UV light, prefiltration is essential. A potential drawback is that UV radiation can interact with iron chelates in fertilizer solution to reduce iron availability and may even cause plant deficiency, though this is not probably an issue during cutting propagation.

Biofiltration

Although membrane filtration has not proved to be a useful means of removing pathogens from water, biofiltration shows promise because of its simplicity and effectiveness. Raw water percolates very slowly through a bed of fine sand or rock wool granulate that works as a filter. The rate should be about 4 to 12 in. (10 to 30 cm) per hour. A skin forms on the surface of the filter bed that consists of various active microorganisms and organic and inorganic material. Cleaning the filter bed is necessary after a few weeks to a few months, depending on the quality of the raw water, to prevent clogging. A couple of inches of the top layer are scraped off with each cleaning, so the starting thickness of the bed should be 32 to 48 in. (80 to 120 cm). This process is effective against fungi, such as *Pythium* and *Phytophthora*, and bacteria, though viruses and nematodes are not satisfactorily eliminated with this technique.

Slow filtration of water through fine sand (0.15 to 0.35 mm) traps pathogens, and beneficial microbes develop on the sand surface for biocontrol of pathogens. This method is usually limited to small-scale operations with adequate space. The drawbacks of this system are that large areas are needed to process high volumes of water, and clogging may be a problem depending on initial water quality.

Heat treatment or pasteurization

The ability of heat to destroy plant pathogens depends on both temperature and exposure time. A suitable combination of these two factors is 203° to 207° F (95° to 97° C) for thirty seconds, which has proved to be effective at controlling plant pathogens including viruses and nematodes. Although the treatment is very effective, the cost of equipment and the energy to operate it can be prohibitive.

The principal components include two heat exchangers, a heater, and a pipe system. The filtered recycled water is often acidified to a pH less than 5.0 before heat treatment to avoid precipitation of carbonates in the heat exchangers. The water is heated to 176° to 194° F (80° to 90° C) in the first heat exchanger; in the second exchanger, the temperature is increased to 203° to 207° F (95° to 97° C) and maintained for at least thirty seconds. The treated water is then cooled down to 77° to 86° F (25° to 30° C). Recent research indicated that exposure to lower temperatures for a longer time, for example, 185° F (85° C) for three minutes, provides the same efficacy but reduces energy costs.

Summary

Water management is arguably the most critical aspect of the environment to manage during the rooting of cuttings. In addition, water-quality factors related to chemical properties and pathogen control are closely tied to most of the common problems that propagators face during the rooting of cuttings. Therefore, successful cutting propagation requires a pathogen-free water source with limited mineral contaminants and aggressive management of humidity and water application in the propagation environment.

References

Bailey, D., T. Bilderback, and D. Bir. 1999. Water considerations for container production of plants. *Horticulture Information Leaflet* 557, Department of Horticultural Science, North Carolina State University. www.ces.ncsu.edu/depts/hort/floriculture/hils/HIL557.pdf

Bartok, J. W. 2000. Protect your water system with a good filter. *GMPro* 20(2):61–62.

Dole, J. M. and H. F. Wilkins. 2005. Water, pp. 79–93. In: *Floriculture Principles and Species*, 2nd ed. Prentice Hall, Upper Saddle River, New Jersey.

Loach, K. 1988. Water relations and adventitious rooting, pp. 104–116. In: *Adventitious Root Formation in Cuttings.* T. D. Davis, B. E. Haissig, and N. Sankhla, eds. Dioscorides Press, Portland, Oregon.

Prenger, J. J. and P. P. Ling. 2001. *Greenhouse Condensation Control: Understanding and Using Vapor Pressure Deficit (VPD).* Ohio State University Extension Fact Sheet AEX-804.

Rolfe, C., W. Yiasoumi, and E. Keskula. 2000. *Managing Water in Plant Nurseries: A Guide to Irrigation, Drainage, and Water Recycling in Containerized Plant Nurseries,* 2nd ed. NSW Agriculture, Orange, New South Whales.

Wilkerson, E. G., R. S. Gates, S. Zolnier, S. T. Kester, and R. L. Geneve. 2005. Transpiration capacity in poinsettia cuttings at different rooting stages and the development of a cutting coefficient for scheduling mist. *Journal of the American Society for Horticultural Science* 130:295–301.

Wilson, M. 2002. Beating stage fright. *GrowerTalks* 66(5):40–49.

7

Stock Plant
and Cutting Nutrition

James L. Gibson

Many production factors can affect cutting propagation of floral crops: irrigation, light (photoperiod, intensity, and quality), temperature, plant growth regulators, and mineral nutrition. Mineral nutrition has been investigated by propagators and researchers to improve cutting quality and yield as well as root regeneration of cuttings. Research has shown that adventitious root formation is affected by both initial nitrogen levels and carbohydrate status. For example, in tomato a high carbon-nitrogen ratio (C:N) increased rooting of stem cuttings. This chapter will focus on the effects of mineral nutrition on cutting size (for example, stem diameter, stem length, and leaf area), yield, and rooting response. In addition, it will provide the tools to manage a nutritional program.

NPK Fertilization

Recommendations for stock plant nutrition are usually limited to growing plants at the optimum level for the species. However, nutrition not only affects cutting yield but also the rooting of cuttings. For example, at the University of Maryland geranium (*Pelargonium*) stock plants were fertilized with deficient, optimal, or excessive nutrient levels of nitrogen (N), phosphorus (P), and potassium (K). The N level resulted in a more pronounced variation in the rooting of cuttings than either P or K. Deficient and optimal levels of N resulted in a significantly higher percentage of rooted cuttings (67%) than the excessive level (56%). Although the rooting percentages were lower with the highest level of N, the number and length of roots were greater.

Fertility studies on the rooting of chrysanthemum, poinsettia, coleus, and carnation cuttings under mist by researchers at Cornell University demonstrated the

importance of proper nutrition to stock plants. The total mineral nutrient content per cutting was the same before and after rooting; therefore, little or no leaching from these herbaceous species occurred. Leaching in herbaceous cuttings is typically minimal due to quick metabolization of nutrients within cells and cell walls. For herbaceous cuttings to increase in dry weight, macronutrients are redistributed from mature parts of the cuttings to the new growth. Roots and leaves of chrysanthemum cuttings, propagated under distilled water mist, developed and grew due to the redistribution of N, P, and K. This research demonstrates the importance of adequately fertilizing stock plants. After roots have formed, providing a low-concentration fertilizer solution with low ammoniacal-N and P is recommended for floral crops (fig. 7.1).

Figure 7.1. Cuttings of vegetative strawflower (A) thirty-six, (B) thirty-three, (C) thirty, (D) twenty-seven, (E) twenty-four, and (F) twenty-one days after sticking in a nutrient-free environment. Notice the lower leaf chlorosis (nitrogen deficiency) after twenty-one days in propagation.

Effects of N and K concentration on cutting yield, quality, and adventitious rooting were measured at North Carolina State University to establish research-based stock plant fertility programs. Stock plants of 'Grenada' New Guinea impatiens, which has a low fertilizer requirement, and 'Purple Fan' scaevola, which has a moderate to heavy fertilizer requirement, were fertigated (water-soluble fertilizer was applied through an irrigation system) with all combinations of 100, 200, or 300 ppm N and K. The greatest yield of high-quality cuttings and optimum rooting occurred with 300 ppm N. Fertilizing with K at 200 to 300 ppm generally did not improve New Guinea impatiens or scaevola cutting yield and rooting, with the one exception of greater shoot dry weight in scaevola with K at 300 ppm. However, an increase in shoot dry weight without a concomitant increase in root weight would be undesirable. A high root to shoot ratio is recommended for newly rooted cuttings, because it avoids factors that reduce plug quality: stretched internodes (fig. 7.2), excessively soft foliage, and a poorly developed root system. For this reason, K at 100 ppm appears optimal. Based on the research, the standard fertilization ratio of 1N:1K is

Figure 7.2. A high root to shoot ratio is recommended for newly rooted cuttings, because it avoids the stretched internodes and excessively soft foliage shown here.

not applicable to cutting production. Successful propagation of New Guinea impatiens and scaevola occurred at a ratio of 300 ppm N:100 ppm K.

Nutrient Stresses on Stock Plant Yield and Subsequent Rooting of Stem Cuttings

Little has been published on the effects of nutrient stresses on the rooting of stem cuttings. When a nutrient stress occurs, a greater part of the residual nutrient is used by the root system for growth. Optimal rooting typically occurs when nitrogen is marginally low and carbohydrates are high in cuttings; high nitrogen tends to inhibit rooting. Stock plants fertilized with high rates of ammoniacal nitrogen will produce soft, lush cuttings that will not ship well. Because calcium and boron are essential for the development of new cell walls, it is critical that stock plants are not deficient in these nutrients. Zinc is required by the plant for the formation of auxin, which stimulates adventitious root formation in cuttings.

Nutrient stress research on young plants improved the visual appearance of bedding plant plugs at North Carolina State University. Low applications of phosophorus (restricting it to 15 to 20% of the nitrogen level) reduced plant height, improved tone, and increased rooting. Propagators who reduce phosphorus may achieve shorter cuttings; however, too little phosphorus in the cutting may cause undesirable purple pigmentation and perhaps necrosis

Figure 7.3. Undesirable pigmentation and necrosis has occurred on petunia cuttings that have been phosphorus restricted.

(fig. 7.3). When crops such as impatiens (*Impatiens walleriana*) were subjected to phosophorus deficiencies, plants were more compact and deeper green than fertilized plants, but were delayed by five days.

Research at North Carolina State University determined the impact of a light (incipient) and a moderate deficiency of each of eleven essential mineral nutrients on the rooting of stem cuttings of strawflower (*Bracteantha bracteata*). Stem cuttings were harvested when initial foliar symptoms were first expressed and later under moderate deficiency symptoms. Nutrients at a light or moderate stage of

Figure 7.4. Phosphorus-deficient cuttings expressed darker, more slender leaves than control cuttings.

Figure 7.5. Zinc-deficient cuttings had less root growth than control cuttings.

deficiency that reduced rooting were phosphorus (fig. 7.4), calcium, and zinc (fig. 7.5). Interestingly, stem cuttings from potassium-deficient stock plants were shorter and had more roots than cuttings receiving all essential nutrients.

Specific Nutrient Effects on Stock Plant Yield and Rooting Response

Nitrogen

Nitrogen is important for nucleic acid and protein synthesis in plant tissue. Levels of nitrogen in cuttings have a direct influence on rooting performance. When chrysanthemum stock plants in Germany were fertilized at a low, moderate, or high concentration of nitrogen, the high nitrogen rate resulted in fewer harvested cuttings. In addition, as the nitrogen concentration increased, root initiation and development decreased.

However, another study in Germany showed no decrease in the rooting of chrysanthemum cuttings when nitrogen concentrations were high. Stock plants were fertilized once a week with 60, 150, or 400 ppm nitrogen. As the nitrogen rate increased, the nitrogen concentration in prerooting tissue in the cuttings and the number and length of adventitious roots increased.

Nitrogen form: NO_3-N/NH_4-N ratio effects

Not only has the concentration of nitrogen been investigated, but the effect of the nutrient's form as either ammoniacal nitrogen (NH_4-N) or nitrate nitrogen (NO_3-N) on cutting quantity has also been studied.

Researchers in Israel evaluated the effect of 200 ppm nitrogen supplied at ratios of 40:60, 60:40, and 70:30 NH_4-N:NO_3-N on the quality of geranium (*Pelargonium*) stock plants and cutting yield. The NH_4-N:NO_3-N ratio did not affect the number of stem cuttings produced per plant under natural light conditions, approximately 95% of sunlight transmittance, or 7,000 to 8,000 f.c. (75 to 86 klux). However, under low light levels, approximately 70% of sunlight transmittance, or 5,000 to 6,000 f.c. (54 to 65 klux), fertilizing with a NH_4-N:NO_3-N ratio of 70:30 reduced cutting yield per plant. In addition, as the NH_4-N:NO_3-N ratio decreased from 70:30 to 40:60, rooting percentage increased from 83 to 89% under natural light levels, but decreased from 94 to 88% under low light levels. Cutting quality was also greater when the cuttings were harvested from stock plants grown under low light levels with 60:40 or 70:30 NH_4-N:NO_3-N ratios.

A second study by the Israeli researchers investigated the effect of 50, 100, 200, or 400 ppm nitrogen and 30:70, 40:60, and 60:40 NH_4-N:NO_3-N ratio on

geranium stock plant growth and cutting yield. Cutting number was not affected by fertilizer rates or ratios, except for stock plants fertilized with nitrogen at 50 ppm, which produced lower numbers of vegetative cuttings. The nitrogen form did not affect the production of cuttings or the fresh weight of cuttings. Root fresh weight and the root to shoot ratio of the stock plants decreased with increasing nitrogen concentration and increasing NO_3-N percentage.

In summary, cutting production was maximized at a high light level, but rooting percentage was maximized at a low light level. Greenhouse propagators of geraniums need to adjust their NH_4-N:NO_3-N balance in accordance with the light levels during the stock plant production season. While root growth of the stock plant decreased when the nitrogen concentration increased, cutting yield was not affected. Based on this research, geranium stock plants should be fertilized with nitrogen at 100 to 200 ppm with an NH_4-N:NO_3-N ratio of 60:40.

Poinsettia stock plants researched at the University of Minnesota were fertilized with nitrogen at 250 ppm with three NH_4-N:NO_3-N ratios of 0:1, 1:2, and 2:1 to investigate the influence of the nitrogen form on the poinsettia disorder leaf edge burn (LEB) and cutting production. When plants were fertilized with NH_4-N:NO_3-N ratios of 1:2 or 2:1, the number of LEB leaves increased nearly 100%, but the number of cuttings per plant increased nearly 40%. Thus, nitrate-only fertilizers limited LEB, but maximum cutting production required a combination of both ammoniacal and nitrate nitrogen.

An increase in cutting number from poinsettia stock plants fertilized with higher NH_4-N:NO_3-N ratios was also demonstrated by researchers at Pennsylvania State University. Stock plants were fertilized with nitrogen at 200 ppm with ratios of 0:1, 1:2, and 2:1. Shoot and root dry weight, number of cuttings, and shoot lengths were greater from stock plants fertilized with solutions containing ammoniacal nitrogen. Stock plant height was slightly less when fertilized at an NH_4-N:NO_3-N ratio of 0:1.

Cutting Nutrition: Growth Control

Researchers at the University of Georgia recommend the preplant or postplant fertilization program be reduced or eliminated to achieve shorter plugs and cuttings. They recommend reducing phosphorus and potassium concentrations for impatiens, petunia, and salvia (*Salvia splendens*) plug production because of the ineffectiveness of those nutrients on shoot growth and there is no need to overfertilize. However, researchers at North Carolina State University found that eliminating the preplant or reducing the postplant nitrogen, phosphorus, and potassium reduced plant tone, but did not delay production of the finished crop.

Fertilizer Selection and Delivery for Cuttings

Fertilizing through overhead mist emitters is normally not recommended for floral crops unless the cuttings are on the propagation bench for an extended period of time, typically more than four weeks.

Figure 7.6. Undesirable stretch due to excessive applications of 20-10-20 at 200 ppm nitrogen.

Figure 7.7. Poinsettia cuttings on the left were fertigated with 15-0-15, while plants on the right were treated with a phosphorus-containing fertilizer, 20-10-20.

Fertilizers may clog mist emitters if salts precipitate in the water line. Therefore, cuttings of floral crops should be fertigated through a hose. In general, the first application of a soluble fertilizer can occur at signs of a visible callus, using 50 to 75 ppm nitrogen. Normally, this occurs around five to ten days after sticking cuttings. Once the root initials protrude from the cutting base, cuttings can be lightly fertilized with 100 ppm nitrogen from a complete fertilizer. Cuttings should never be fertilized when the rooting substrate is dry.

A fertilizer low in phosphorus and ammoniacal nitrogen should be used during propagation. High levels of phosphorus have been shown to increase stem elongation (fig. 7.6) and promote flowering; they are also toxic to some native Australian species such as scaevola and marguerite daisy (*Argyranthemum*). Ammoniacal nitrogen, on the other hand, causes lush cutting growth. Propagators should use fertilizers such as 13-2-13 and 15-5-15 in the propagation area weekly at concentra-

tions of 50 to 100 ppm nitrogen. Propagators who desire short poinsettia cuttings often fertigate with dark weather feed, which has a low ammoniacal nitrogen concentration (fig. 7.7). Acidic fertilizers like 20-10-20 should be used if growers have moderate levels of alkalinity in their irrigation water. To moderate the high phosphorus and ammoniacal nitrogen of the commonly used 20-10-20, a low rate can be applied to provide micronutrients, and growers can rotate the feedings with a dark weather formula or calcium nitrate [$Ca(NO_3)_2$].

Fertilizer Selection and Delivery for Stock Plants

Fertilizers can be supplied through preplant incorporation into the substrate or by fertilization through the irrigation system. Preplant incorporation can be accomplished by small amounts of soluble fertilizers intended to serve only as a short-duration starter fertilizer or by various controlled-release fertilizers intended to last for the entire crop cycle. In the first case, the nutrients last only about two weeks under normal irrigation frequencies and must be followed by a routine fertilization program. Be sure to check premixed media, since many brands contain starter charges. While controlled-release fertilizers have the advantage of potentially reducing both labor costs and the waste of nutrients through leaching, the lengthy period that stock plants are typically cultivated makes the use of controlled-release fertilizers as the sole source of nutrition more difficult. However, controlled-release fertilizers can be readily combined with constant liquid fertilization, or fertigation.

Fertigation

Fertigation is the application of water-soluble fertilizers through the irrigation water. Typically, nutrients are applied at every irrigation (constant liquid fertilization, or CLF) when the plants are actively growing. At times, fertilizer drenches with high fertilizer rates can be used to raise media electrical conductivity (EC), or individual nutrients can be applied to correct potential deficiencies.

The CLF concentration depends on a number of variables, the most important of which are the species being grown, the irrigation frequency, and the leaching fraction (the percentage of water that runs out the bottom of the container). Species vary greatly in their fertilizer requirements, but they can be placed into three general categories: high, medium, and low nutritional requirements. For example, poinsettias require higher levels of nutrients than double impatiens. Many growers are forced to grow a number of crop species using the same fertilizer rate from one injector. In such cases, the nutritional level can be individually tailored to each crop's needs by setting the fertilizer rate for the species requiring the highest fertilizer rate and then combining fertigation with clear water irrigation for the other species. The lower the nutritional requirements of the species, the more frequent the clear water irrigation. The other approach is to set the fertigation rate low and incorporate a controlled-release fertilizer into the substrate or top-dress the substrate with a controlled-release fertilizer for those species that require high nutrition.

Irrigation frequency and leaching fraction are interrelated in that both influence the rate at which nutrients are lost from the substrate and must be replaced. Growers who irrigate frequently and have a high leaching fraction will leach more nutrients from the substrate and will require higher fertigation rates.

Other variables that influence a plant's nutrient requirements include the season (a higher rate in summer than winter), the substrate (the higher the cation exchange capacity, the lower the fertilizer rate), and the stage of plant growth (a higher rate at the middle of the production cycle when plants are growing fast and a reduced rate or no fertilizer at the end of the production cycle).

If controlled-release micronutrients have not been incorporated into the substrate prior to planting, water-soluble micronutrient mixes must be applied as a water-soluble fertilizer. Micronutrients are also frequently fertigated.

Mixing water-soluble fertilizers

While small quantities of fertilizers can be dissolved and applied by handheld watering cans, injectors or proportioners are used to inject specific amounts of concentrated fertilizer (stock) solution into the irrigation water. Backflow preventors are required to stop the siphoning of stock solution back into the general water system, unless a space exists between the water supply line and the stock tank. The space must be equal to twice the diameter of the supply line. Individual states may have different requirements.

The ratio of fertilizer concentration to water varies from 1:16 to 1:1,950, depending on the injector. Greenhouses generally use a ratio between 1:16 and 1:200. Some injector models allow the ratio to be adjusted lower for difficult-to-dissolve fertilizers that must be dissolved in a less-concentrated solution. Injectors also vary in flow rate and pipe sizes. High flow rates are needed for greenhouses in which multiple areas are being fertigated. The stock tank should be large enough to prevent the need for constant mixing of the fertilizer concentrate. The electrical conductivity (EC) of fertilized water should be monitored periodically to ensure that the proper ratio is being maintained. An EC meter can be installed in the water line for constant monitoring or for regulation of the fertilizer level in the irrigation water. EC meters can be equipped with an automated alarm system if the EC becomes too high or too low. Improper functioning of the injectors can lead to serious problems from high soluble salts or deficiencies from inadequate nutrition.

Depending on the concentration of the injector solution, the fertilizers may be difficult to dissolve in the stock tank solution. In such cases, hot water is required to dissolve them. Constant agitation of stock solution may also be required to ensure application of a uniform nutrient solution. Not all fertilizers are compatible with each other in the stock tank, and may either exhibit reduced solubility or produce insoluble precipitates. In each case, the nutrients are not reaching the plant materials, and the injector may be damaged or plugged. For example, sulfuric acid cannot be directly mixed with calcium nitrate. In such cases, injectors with two or more injector heads are used to allow the fertilizers to be diluted in the irrigation water prior to be being mixed together.

When fertigating, growers have the option of using a premixed fertilizer or mixing their own. As is the case with media, premixed fertilizers are usually more expensive than buying individual components, but much of the dollar savings of self-mixed fertilizers can be lost in the labor needed to mix them. The production of specialized species may dictate that growers mix their own fertilizers or add additional nutrients to premixed fertilizers. For larger producers, mixing their own fertilizers is often economically justified, although, as with media, the price of premixed fertilizers usually drops with increasing volumes purchased.

Small producers generally have many tasks to perform, and the higher cost of premixed fertilizers is offset by the convenience. In addition, mixing one's own fertilizer increases the chance of error. With fertilizers, a simple mistake can rapidly damage a crop, especially when micronutrients are being applied.

Developing a Nutritional Program

The first step in developing a nutritional program is to determine which nutrients are contributed by the substrate and the water. Premixed media usually contain a small amount of fertilizer intended for the first couple of weeks of production, but the amount is usually not enough to affect the nutritional program. Firms mixing their own media may include fertilizers intended to last for the entire crop cycle, indicating that the amount applied through fertigation should be reduced. While high-quality water should have relatively low EC, the water may contain high levels of various nutrients.

The second step is to decide how to supply micronutrients. Because of the long crop time typical of stock plant production, micronutrients present in the substrate will be depleted long before the stock plants are replaced. Large firms frequently apply the micronutrients through fertigation. Micronutrients can also be incorporated into the substrate. Some firms incorporate one-half of the required amount of micronutrients into the substrate and supply the other half through fertigation. Remember that premixed fertilizers often contain micronutrients, but they may not provide enough for long-term crops.

Determining which water-soluble fertilizer to use depends mainly on the desired media pH, which is influenced by alkalinity of the water (see chapter 6). Ammonium and urea-based fertilizers tend to be acidic, reducing media pH; nitrate-based fertilizers tend to be basic, increasing the pH. The fertilizer bag should list the potential acidity, which is expressed as the amount of calcium carbonate required to neutralize the acidity in 1 ton (907 kg) of the fertilizer. The higher the number, the more acidic the fertilizer. Similarly, potential basicity is expressed as the amount of calcium carbonate that would equal the basicity in 1 ton of the fertilizer. Although many premixed fertilizers have relatively high ammonium levels and are acidic, basic nitrate-based fertilizers are available. In addition, growers can combine potassium nitrate and calcium nitrate to make their own basic fertilizer. Unfortunately, high-ammonium fertilizers are not feasible in some situations, thus limiting the ability of growers to control media pH through fertilizer choice. Producers can rotate between acidic and basic fertilizers as needed to help manage media pH.

pH Management

In an aqueous solution a certain number of water molecules (H_2O) are split into the ions H^+ and OH^-. pH is a measure of the concentration of H^+ ions in a solution, usually the substrate water solution, and is measured on a scale from 0 to 14. At pH 7.0 the solution is neutral, and the H^+ concentration is equal to the OH^- concentration. A pH of less than 7.0 is acidic, and a pH of greater than 7.0 is basic or alkaline. pH has a major effect on the availability of nutrients in the substrate. The recommended pH for soilless media is 5.4 to 6.0; for soil-based media containing at least 25% soil, the recommended pH is 6.2 to 6.8. Specific crop species may have other pH requirements; see the sections on individual species in parts 2 and 3. A number of factors affect the pH of a substrate, including the components, the water, the fertilizers, and the plant itself. For example, peat moss is acidic, water pH can vary greatly depending on the source, ammonium-based fertilizers are acidic, and some plants respond to high pH-induced iron deficiency by releasing hydrogen ions, thus lowering the pH immediately around the roots and increasing iron availability and uptake.

Increasing substrate pH

Calcitic or dolomitic limestone is most commonly used to increase substrate pH prior to planting. It is more difficult, however, to raise substrate pH after the crop has been planted. One method is to use basic fertilizers, such as calcium and potassium nitrate, and reduce the use of acidic fertilizers, such as ammonium nitrate. Generally, this technique can only moderately alter substrate pH. Manipulating substrate pH through fertilizer choice is best done before the substrate pH is too low. For faster and greater action, flowable lime, which is a suspension of lime, can be applied. If faster action is required, hydrated lime ($CaOH$) can be applied to the substrate; it should be applied carefully since it can burn foliage. Recommendations call for mixing 1 lb. (0.45 kg) of hydrated lime in 5 gal. (19 L) water and applying only the liquid portion, since not all the hydrated lime will dissolve. Do not use hydrated lime with controlled-release fertilizers containing ammonium or when liquid feed is over 25% ammonium because ammonia gas may be produced. In cases of chronically low pH, potassium bicarbonate can be injected into the irrigation water to increase alkalinity and substrate pH.

Decreasing substrate pH

Before planting, there are several options for lowering substrate pH. Elemental sulfur can be incorporated into the substrate; at 5 lb./sq. yd. (3 kg/m³) it will reduce substrate pH about 0.5. Iron sulfate can also be used, for quicker action. Of course, adding sphagnum peat moss or increasing the amount of peat moss used can create a substrate with a lower pH.

After planting, iron sulfate can be used to lower substrate pH but may produce inconsistent results. At 3 lb./100 gal. (0.36 kg/100 L) the pH may be reduced by up to 1.0 point. Apply iron sulfate only to the substrate since it is toxic to foliage, and be sure to monitor the EC because the iron sulfate can increase soluble salts in the substrate. Using acid fertilizers such as ammonium nitrate can also decrease media pH.

Acid injection to reduce the water's pH is a routine practice in many greenhouses. Continual acid injection is best used to maintain substrate pH at the desired level. If the substrate pH already is high (for example, close to 7.0), acid injection will only slowly decrease it and may lower it just 0.5 to 1.0 point. Phosphoric, nitric, and sulfuric acid are most commonly used, especially in areas with highly alkaline water or by large producers.

Soluble Salts Management

The term "soluble salts" refers to the total dissolved ions in media water solutions. Soluble salts are measured by electrical conductivity (EC): the greater the concentration of soluble salts in a substrate, the more easily an electrical current will pass through a water solution of the substrate. Common symptoms of high soluble salts include slow growth, necrotic leaf margins (especially on the lower leaves), reduced or erratic rooting of cuttings, and increased susceptibility to root and crown diseases. In general, optimum root growth is obtained with low media EC. Since cuttings have limited root systems, they are most susceptible to high soluble salts. Plant species vary greatly in their sensitivity to high soluble salts; some species, such as New Guinea impatiens, are particularly susceptible while others, such as poinsettia, are tolerant.

High soluble salt levels can occur either from the overapplication of fertilizers or through inadequate leaching. Many ions, such as NO_3^- or Mg^{++}, are absorbed by the plant. Other ions, such as Cl^- or Na^+, are not absorbed in high quantities and tend to accumulate in the substrate. The problem is best prevented by reducing fertilizer rates or by irrigating with unfertilized water as often as required. For example, many growers routinely use constant liquid fertilization during the week, and they use unfertilized water every weekend, once every two weeks, or once every sixth irrigation, depending on the desired substate EC. Growers can also control the problem by regularly overirrigating by 10 to 20%; however, this practice is less desirable due to pollution and the wasted water and fertilizer. Growers with high soluble salts in the irrigation water before fertilizers are added will have greater difficulty controlling soluble salts. Once the substrate has high soluble salts, the only control is through leaching, which is most effective if plants are irrigated with two applications of unfertilized water within two to four hours of each other.

Monitoring Nutrition

Growers always need to vigilantly monitor the nutritional status of their crops. The natural variations in weather, irrigation frequency, leaching, water quality, media nutrient content, and plant growth will combine to make each crop unique.

Visual

The simplest monitoring method is to visually assess the crop; this is best done by an experienced grower. Visually monitoring is not effective by itself in the long term, and it may not be adequate to produce the highest plant quality. By the time symptoms are noted, damage has already occurred to the crop, reducing cutting quality and quantity in the case of stock plants. For most crops, plant growth slows as the nutrient level drops, but actual deficiency symptoms may not be visible yet. Thus plant quality may decrease before the grower is aware of any nutritional problems.

In-house pH and EC testing

A more effective monitoring method is to routinely track media pH and EC levels with pH and EC meters. The best results are obtained when the same person conducts the tests each time. Preferably that person should not be the owner, manager, or grower, since these individuals are often unable to regularly perform the tests due to time constraints.

A variety of pH and EC measuring devices are available from greenhouse supply firms. Meters can range from approximately $50 to several hundred dollars. Meters should be calibrated regularly with solutions of a known pH and EC. Such solutions can also be purchased. Four methods are currently available for testing media pH and EC in-house: PourThru, dilution, press, and saturated media extract. (See table 7.1.)

PourThru

The PourThru method is quicker than either the dilution or the saturated medium extract method, because no media samples are collected. The PourThru method involves applying sufficient distilled water to the substrate surface of a plant to collect enough runoff to test, usually ¼ to ½ cup or 50 to 100 ml. The pot, cell pack, or basket is placed over a water collection tray or saucer. A saucer with upward projections or a raised ridge will allow the pot to drain and collect enough runoff for another test to be started. Plants should be irrigated one hour before testing to provide a uniform substrate moisture level. Varying amounts of water in the substrate prior to testing will either increase or decrease the ion concentration and result in fluctuations in the EC reading. If using constant liquid fertilization, irrigate with the usual fertilizer solution.

Each reading using the PourThru method is from only one container. Readings from several containers, at least five, within each crop should be taken and averaged to provide accurate results representative of the entire crop. The samples should be taken from plants that have been similarly produced. Different production conditions such as pot size, nutritional regime, temperature, or even cultivar may result in variable test results. Generally, 3.0 to 5.2 mS/cm is suitable for established plants.

Dilution

With the dilution method the substrate is mixed with distilled water in a 1:2 or 1:5 ratio, stirred well, allowed to stand thirty to sixty minutes, and pH and EC are then recorded. Filtering to remove substrate particles will improve the accuracy of the readings but is not necessary. For consistency, the substrate should be air-dried first and a standard amount of water added to the sample, but few growers do this. When using a moist substrate be sure that it has not been recently watered and is not wet. A greater amount of water in the substrate will dilute the ions and reduce the EC reading, compared with air-dried samples. This problem is not as great using a 1:5 dilution.

Usually ¼ to ½ cup or 50 to 100 ml of substrate is sufficient. A core of the substrate, from the top to the bottom of the pot should be taken, and the upper 0.5 in. (1.3 cm) discarded. Soluble salts are usually high in the upper layer of the substrate, and roots do not normally grow there. For plugs and bedding plant flats with small cells, it is easiest to harvest the entire root-ball, because taking a core is impractical. Extra plug flats may need to be grown to provide flats for sampling. In addition, the nutrient content of plug media changes rapidly due to leaching or plant nutrient uptake. Plug media samples should be collected one to two hours after fertilization to provide the most reliable and accurate assessment of nutrient content.

Small subsamples should be taken randomly from at least five pots, flats, baskets, or locations in the ground beds and combined. The greater the number of subsamples, the more reliable the results and the more likely the results will accurately reflect the status of the entire crop. Taking subsamples from only a few plants on the edge of the bench may lead to inaccurate results and poor decisions. The samples should be taken from plants that have been similarly produced. Different production conditions such as pot size, nutritional regime, temperature, or even cultivar may result in variable test results.

Press

The press method was developed as an easy way to sample plug media. The surface of the plug is pressed, forcing the substrate water solution out in a cup. Each plug will produce two to three drops of solution; one row of plugs should provide sufficient solution to measure the pH and EC. Collect separate samples from at least five flats to gauge the status of the crop. For the best results, the samples should be collected one to two hours after fertigation.

Saturated media extract

The saturated media extract (SME) is the most complex test to administer and requires an experienced person to conduct it. The SME is, however, considered to be the most reliable test, because the moisture content and the amount of media have no effect on the results. The SME method is most commonly used by commercial laboratories. Distilled water is added to 1 pt. (470 ml) of substrate until the substrate is just saturated. There should be little or no water standing on the surface of the substrate, even though the substrate is saturated. Determination of when the material is saturated requires experience, especially with a soilless substrate. The substrate is allowed to stand for

TABLE 7.1

Interpretation of substrate soluble salt concentrations (EC) using various extraction methods. Values are in mS/cm. 1 mS/cm (EC meters commonly use this unit) = 1 dS/m = 1 mmho/cm = 100 mmho 10^{-5}/cm = 1,000 µmhos/com = 640 to 700 ppm. Recommendations for individual species may vary.

POURTHRU/ PRESS	1:5 SUBSTRATE: WATER SUSPENSION	1:2 SUBSTRATE: WATER SUSPENSION	SATURATED PASTE EXTRACT	INTERPRETATION/ACTION
0 to 1.0	0 to 0.11	0 to 0.25	0 to 0.75	Low; increase nutrient levels for optimum growth
1.0 to 2.5	0.12 to 0.35	0.26 to 0.75	0.76 to 2.0	Low to satisfactory; suitable for cuttings, many bedding plants, and salt-sensitive plants
2.6 to 4.6	0.36 to 0.65	0.76 to 1.25	2.1 to 3.5	Satisfactory; maintain this range for most established plants; upper limit for species sensitive to soluble salts
4.7 to 6.5	0.66 to 0.89	1.26 to 1.75	3.5 to 5.0	High; may be okay for most established plants, but may be damaging to sensitive plants; reduce fertilization rate and/or leach lightly once
6.6 to 7.8	0.9 to 1.1	1.76 to 2.25	5.0 to 6.0	Very high; potential damage to most plants; leach heavily at least twice
7.8+	1.1+	2.25+	6.0+	Extreme; most crops will be damaged; leach heavily at least twice

thirty minutes, and the water is drained using a vacuum filter. Media samples are collected as directed previously under the dilution method.

Substrate tests

At times growers need to know the individual nutrient levels in the substrate, in addition to the pH and EC. Media testing by professional laboratory is relatively inexpensive and will provide levels of macronutrients as well as pH and EC. Some laboratories may also be able to determine certain micronutrient levels. It is important to use the same laboratory for all media testing because results may vary slightly among labs due to different handling and analysis procedures. Also choose a laboratory

that is prompt in returning results. Media tests are only a "snapshot in time," and the nutrient status of a crop is dynamic. Therefore, the usefulness of a test will diminish if the results are not returned and used promptly to make changes in the nutrient regimes. If an apparent nutritional problem is occurring, be sure to send in samples from the plants with the problem as well as from a healthy symptomless plant to serve as a comparison.

Although most laboratories require at least 1 pt. (470 ml) of substrate, some request more. Samples are taken in the same manner as described for in-house pH and EC testing.

Interpretation of media test results requires guidelines with which to compare the results. The analysis provided by the commercial laboratories will be useful initially, but these are general guidelines, and the optimum nutrient levels for a particular crop or production environment may be different. If nutritional problems are suspected, media from healthy plants and from problem plants should be tested to allow comparison. Over time, the results from the healthy plants will allow a firm to develop specific nutrient level guidelines for its own operation.

When studying the results of a substrate test, the first datum to check is the pH. The pH strongly affects the availability of nutrients, and some nutrient problems may be due to excessively high or low pH. Nutrients may be present in the substrate but not available to the plant because of high or low pH. Altering the pH may correct the initial problem. The second datum to check is the EC level (table 7.1). Again, correcting a high EC problem by leaching fertilizers or correcting a low EC problem by applying additional fertilizers may be all that is needed. Finally, the last data to check are the individual nutrient levels, which should be within acceptable nutrient ranges and in balance with each other. For example, calcium levels may be adequate in the substrate, but the presence of high magnesium levels may result in calcium deficiency in the plant.

Tissue tests

Tissue tests have the advantage of being more accurate than substrate tests. The results indicate nutrient levels actually in the plant versus nutrient levels in the substrate. Tissue tests also include most micronutrients and sodium, which can be of concern in regions with high amounts of sodium in the water. On the other hand, tissue tests do not include substrate pH and EC levels; thus a substrate sample should be sent with the tissue sample. Together the two tests will provide a complete description of the nutritional situation.

Harvest approximately 1 oz. (28 g) of leaf tissue, without petioles; up to sixty or seventy leaves may be needed if the leaves are small. With small plugs or cuttings, the entire plant may be harvested. Samples should be randomly harvested from as many plants as possible. If the leaves have substrate, fertilizer, or pesticide residue, gently wash or dip the foliage in distilled water, then blot and air-dry it. Do not vigorously wash the leaves, since nutrients may be leached out. In some cases, a mild detergent may be added to the water to aid in the removal of substances not easily washed off. The commercial lab will have more information about when washing or soaking is appro-

priate and how to do it. The leaves should not be sent wet, because they may rot or deteriorate by the time the lab can handle them.

As with media tests, tissue harvesting and handling should be consistent from one sampling date to the next. Most tissue test standards are based on the "most recently mature leaf," or the youngest leaf that is fully expanded. The recommended tissue to harvest may be different for some crops. It is important to properly select the appropriate leaf tissue because nutrient levels can vary greatly depending on which part of the plant the leaves are harvested from. The laboratory can provide information on properly harvesting tissue. If a specific problem is being addressed, harvest tissue from the same location on both symptomatic and healthy plants.

Correcting Nutritional Problems

Deficiencies

Nitrogen, phosphorus, and potassium deficiencies can be readily corrected by increasing the rate of constant liquid fertilization or by applying a drench of fertilizer high in the specific nutrient needed. If a calcium or magnesium deficiency is indicated, apply a drench of calcium nitrate or magnesium sulfate, respectively. If the calcium deficiency is related to environmental conditions, increase transpiration by increasing air movement or decreasing humidity. Routine foliar sprays of calcium chloride can be used as a preventative with some crops such as poinsettias. Although sulfur deficiency is rare, the deficiency can be readily corrected by drenching with any sulfate-containing compound, such as magnesium or potassium sulfate.

With micronutrients, examine the pH first and adjust it if needed (see the pH section earlier in the chapter). Excessively high or low pH frequently causes micronutrient deficiencies. If the pH is acceptable, water-soluble micronutrient treatments can be applied. Often if only one element is deficient, a complete micronutrient mix can be applied, since other micronutrients may also be low. However, do not apply a complete mix at the full rate if one has been used within two to four months. Consequently, the specific nutrient may need to be applied to correct the deficiency. Remember that micronutrients are usually difficult to leach, and the cure could lead to toxicities that are hard to correct.

Toxicities

Toxicity problems related to macronutrients, although rare, often appear first as soluble salt damage. The solution, of course, is to leach the substrate with unfertilized water (see the soluble salts section earlier in this chapter). Toxicity problems are most likely to occur with micronutrients, which can also produce symptoms similar to high soluble salts. Unfortunately, micronutrients are difficult to leach out of the substrate, so options are limited. Routine monitoring of the media EC will help eliminate the possibility of a high soluble salts problem.

Conclusion

Propagators should adopt a nutrient program that produces the maximum number of high quantity cuttings. Nutrition is one of the factors that affects stock plant development and the production of cuttings. Propagators should consider other external factors such as humidity, light, and temperature before establishing a fertilization program. Asexual propagation has become a means of producing plants that have historically been grown from seed, such as coleus, impatiens, strawflower, and verbena. Our knowledge about how to propagate these floral crops has been gleaned from what we know about plants traditionally propagated from cuttings, such as chrysanthemum, geranium (*Pelargonium*), poinsettia, and New Guinea impatiens. Unfortunately, mineral nutrition of stock plants and cuttings requires practical knowledge specific to the species and information from other species will only be of limited usefulness. What is required to maximize the productivity of stock plants may differ greatly from common growing strategies for the finished product.

References

Blazich, F. A. 1988. Mineral nutrition and adventitious rooting, pp.61–69. In: *Adventitious Root Formation in Cuttings*. T. D. Davis, B. E. Haissig, and N. Sankhla, eds. Dioscorides Press, Portland, Oregon.

Druege, U., S. Zerche, and R. Kadner. 1998. Relationship between nitrogen and soluble carbohydrate concentrations and subsequent rooting of *Chrysanthemum* cuttings. *Advances in Horticultural Science* 12:78–84.

Druege, U., S. Zerche, R. Kadner, and M. Erns. 2000. Relationship between nitrogen status, carbohydrate distribution, and subsequent rooting of chrysanthemum cuttings as affected by pre-harvest nitrogen supply and cold storage. *Annals of Botany* 85:687–701.

Ganmore-Neuman, R., and A. Hagiladi. 1990. Effect of the NO_3^-/NH_4^+ ratio in nutrient solution on *Pelargonium* stock plants: Yield and quality of cuttings. *Journal of Plant Nutrition* 13:1241–1256.

Ganmore-Neuman, R., and A. Hagiladi. 1992. Plant growth and cutting production of container-grown *Pelargonium* stock plants as affected by N concentration and N form. *Journal of the American Society for Horticultural Science* 117: 234–238.

Good, G. L., and H. B. Tukey. 1966. Leaching of metabolites from cuttings propagated under intermittent mist. *Proceedings of the American Society for Horticultural Science* 89:727–733.

Good, G. L., and H. B. Tukey. 1967. Redistribution of mineral nutrients in *Chrysanthemum morifolium* during propagation. *Proceedings of the American Society for Horticultural Science* 89:384–388.

Hartmann, H. T., D. E. Kester, F. T. Davies Jr., and R. L. Geneve. 2002. *Hartmann and Kester's Plant Propagation: Principles and Practices*, 7th ed.. Prentice Hall, Upper Saddle River, New Jersey.

Haun, J. R. and P. W. Cornell. 1951. Rooting response of geranium cuttings as influenced by nitrogen, phosphorus, and potassium nutrition of the stock plant. *Proceedings of the American Society for Horticultural Science* 58:317–323.

Krause, J. 1981. Effect of stock plant nutrition on the yield of chrysanthemum cuttings. *Acta Horticulturae* 125:47–50.

Krause, E. J. and H. R. Kraybill. 1918. *Vegetation and reproduction with special reference to tomato*. Oregon Agricultural Experiment Station Bulletin 149.

McAvoy, R. 1995. Basic principles of vegetative plant propagation. *Connecticut Greenhouse Newsletter* pp. 1–6.

Mills, H. A. and J. B. Jones. 1996. *Plant Analysis Handbook II*. MicroMacro Publishing, Athens, Georgia.

Nelson, P. V. 2002. Nutrition and water, pp. 23–27. In: *Tips on Regulating Growth of Floriculture Crops*. M. Gaston, L. A. Kunkle, P. S. Konjoian, and M. F. Wilt, eds. Ohio Florists' Association, Columbus.

Nelson, P. V., J. S. Huang, W. C. Fonteno, and D. A. Bailey. 1996. Fertilizing for perfect plugs, pp. 86–90. In: *GrowerTalks on Plugs II*, D. Hamrick, ed. Ball Publishing, Batavia, Illinois.

Bierman, P., J. Dole, C. Rosen, and H. Wilkins. 1989. Calcium deficiency on poinsettia stock plants. *Minnesota State Florists Bulletin* 38(2):1–3.

Read, P. E., C. D. Fellman, A. S. Economou, and Y. Quiguang. 1985. Programming stock plants for propagation success. *Combined Proceedings of the International Plant Propagators' Society* 35:84–91.

Rose, M. A. 1992. Growth of poinsettia stock plants with high ammonium fertilizer. *Pennsylvania Flower Growers Bulletin* 411:3–4.

Smith, F. W. and J. F. Loneragan. 1997. Interpretation of plant analysis: Concepts and principles, pp. 3–33. In: *Plant Analysis: An Interpretation Manual*, 2nd ed., D. J. Reuter and J. B. Robinson, eds. CSIRO Publications, Australia.

Styer, R. and D. S. Koranski. 1997. *Plug and Transplant Production: A Grower's Guide*. Ball Publishing, Batavia, Illinois.

Van-Iersel, M. W., P. A. Thomas, R. B. Beverly, J. G. Latimer, and H. A. Mills. 1998. Fertilizer effects on the growth of impatiens, petunia, salvia, and vinca plug seedlings. *HortScience* 33: 678–682.

Van-Iersel, M. W., P. A. Thomas, R. B. Beverly, J. G. Latimer, and H. A. Mills. 1998. Nutrition affects pre- and posttransplant growth of impatiens and petunia plugs. *HortScience* 33:1014–1018.

Veirskov, B. 1988. Relations between carbohydrate and adventitious rooting, pp.70–78. In: *Adventitious Root Formation in Cuttings*. T. D Davis, B. E. Haissig, and N. Sankhla, eds. Dioscorides Press, Portland, Oregon.

Wilson, J. B. 1988. A review of evidence on the control of shoot:root ratio, in relation to models. *Annals of Botany* 61:433–449.

Zakkour, C., J. Dole, and H. Wilkins. 1986. The influence of ammonium vs. nitrate forms of nitrogen on calcium levels and leaf edge burn in poinsettia (*Euphorbia pulcherrima* Willd. Ex. Klotsch). *HortScience* 21:240.

8

Rooting Hormones and Plant Growth Regulators

Brian E. Whipker, James L. Gibson, and Christopher B. Cerveny

Rooting hormones and plant growth regulators are used extensively during plant propagation. These chemicals aid in rooting and preventing excessive plant stretch. Both types of chemicals are excellent additions to a grower's toolbox. Factors related to their use are discussed in this chapter.

Rooting Hormones

The need for rooting compounds depends on the species being propagated. Rooting hormones are essential for economical rooting of some species, but they are not effective or needed with others. For many species, rooting compounds are not required for rooting but will accelerate root initiation, increase root uniformity, and increase the number and quality of roots produced. Rooting compounds are most economical on species that are difficult to root or when uniformity is required (figs. 8.1 and 8.2). Refer to table 8.1 for a list of species that may benefit from a rooting hormone application.

In general, the application of rooting hormones is not required for most herbaceous species. The added labor cost of application is not necessary with easy-to-root cuttings; however, with moderate and difficult-to-root species rooting hormones may enhance rooting percentages. Exogenously (externally) applied hormones also facilitate rooting where cultural practices or environmental conditions are not ideal. Examples of less-than-ideal situations include uneven misting, suboptimal propagation temperatures, and in some cases, reduced light levels during winter.

Perhaps the situation in which rooting hormones are best utilized is in propagation of the "new and unusual." In today's marketplace, customers often demand new products faster than they can be devel-

Figure 8.1.
Crops such as marguerite daisy (*Argyranthemum*) may benefit from an application of rooting hormone. (J. Gibson)

Figure 8.2. Difficult-to-root species such as mandevilla benefit from a rooting hormone application. (J. Gibson)

oped; the green industry is no stranger to this phenomenon. Rooting hormones can improve the commercial viability of temperate and tropical annual and perennial species by increasing propagation success. Common or prized woody ornamental groups such as vines, groundcovers, and flowering shrubs add a multitude of new possibilities to a grower's plant inventory with the use of rooting hormones.

Auxins

Rapid, uniform root development on cuttings can be hastened by the application of auxins. The naturally occurring indole-3-acetic acid (IAA) can be used, but it is unstable and easily degrades. Fortunately, synthetic auxins, such as indole-3-butyric acid (IBA) and

Figure 8.3. The influence of rooting hormones on the propagation of pentas (top row) and mandevilla (bottom row): (1) untreated, (2) K-IBA at 1,000 ppm, (3) K-IBA at 5,000 ppm, (4) K-IBA at 10,000 ppm, (5) Dip 'n' Grow, semihardwood concentration, (6) Dip 'n' Grow, softwood concentration, (7) Hormodin #1, (8) Hormodin #2, and (9) Hormodin #3. (J. Gibson)

Figure 8.4. Cutting bases can be sprayed with rooting hormones; efficiency is increased when they are treated in bundles. (J. Gibson)

Figure 8.5. Propagation of perennial plants with semihardwood tissue using rooting hormones. (J. Gibson)

naphthalene acetic acid (NAA), are longer lasting and more reliable than IAA. Since the development of synthetic IBA, that auxin has also been found to occur naturally.

A number of rooting powders and liquids are available containing a range of auxin concentrations (table 8.2). For example, Hormex Rooting Powder #1 contains 0.1% (1,000 ppm) IBA in talc, which is used for most greenhouse crops; #2 contains 0.3% (3,000 ppm) IBA; and #3 contains 0.8% (8,000 ppm) IBA. Products with higher IBA rates are available and are generally used on woody plants. Other products, such as Hormodin, also include IBA. Some rooting compounds contain more than one type of auxin and/or cytokinins, fungicides, and other chemicals. For example, Rootone contains benzyladenine (BA), NAA, fungicide, and other unspecified chemicals. Rooting compounds are most effective on species that root naturally but development is slow, and are least effective on species that root rapidly (fig. 8.3).

Cultural practices

Plant response to rooting hormones varies with each species, but before rooting hormones are introduced, growers should implement a few simple cultural practices to reduce the number of propagation challenges. Cuttings, whether are grown from on-site or offshore stock plants, should be thoroughly inspected before planting (fig. 8.4). Softwood cuttings that have an actively growing shoot tip should be selected (fig. 8.5). Tissues that are too young or too old will root more slowly than cuttings that are at the proper stage of maturity. Cuttings that are too old also tend not to branch as well as younger, softer tissue. Therefore, it

is important to visually inspect the lower portion of the cutting to check for woody tissue that is brown or grayish brown in color. Cuttings that exhibit this hardwood tissue may need to be trimmed closer to the shoot tip. Fully developed flowers on cuttings are sometimes another sign that tissue may be too old to root optimally. Mist and light levels should be regulated appropriately; a propagation medium that is too saturated (low oxygen) or light levels that are too intense will inhibit rooting.

Hormone concentrations

Generally speaking, auxin-based rooting products are applied at concentrations of 500 to 1,500 ppm for herbaceous and softwood cuttings. Rates between 1,000 to 3,000 ppm may be used for woodier tissue, but the maximum recommended concentrations are not more than 5,000 ppm for semihardwood cuttings and 10,000 ppm for hardwood cuttings.

Care should be taken with rooting hormones

TABLE 8.1
Rooting hormone requirement for selected floriculture crops.

NONE	OPTIONAL	ESSENTIAL
Angelonia	Argyranthemum	Bougainvillea
Bacopa (Sutera)	Calibrachoa	Brachyscome
Coleus (Solenostemon)	Diascia	Dahlia
Cuphea	Fuchsia	Heliotrope
Impatiens, Bedding	Nemesia	Hibiscus, tropical
Impatiens, New Guinea	Salvia (certain species)	Lobelia
Petunia	Scaevola	Mandevilla
Perilla	Snapdragon (Antirrhinum)	Mimulus
Plectranthus	Strobilanthes	Osteospermum
Portulaca	Verbena	Thunbergia

TABLE 8.2
Partial list of commercially available rooting hormones for herbaceous plant propagation.

TRADE NAME	SOURCE	FORMULATION	INGREDIENT
Chryzopon	ACF Chemiefarma Maarssen, The Netherlands	Powder (talc)	0.1 to 8% IBA
C-mone C-mone K C-mone K+	Coor Farm Supply Service, Inc. Smithfield, North Carolina	Liquid (isopropyl alcohol)	1 and 2% IBA 1% KIBA 1% KIBA + 0.5% NAA
Dip' N Grow	Dip' N Grow, Inc. Clackamas, Oregon	Liquid (ethyl alcohol)	1% IBA + 0.5% NAA + boron
Hormex	Brooker Chemical Corp. Chatsworth, California	Powder (talc) Liquid	Rooting Powder: 0.1 to 4% IBA Hormex Concentrate: 0.013% IBA + 0.24% NAA + vitamin B1
Hormodin	E.C. Geiger, Inc. Harleysville, Pennsylvania	Powder (talc)	0.1, 0.3, and 0.8% IBA
Hormo-Root	Rockland Chemical Co. Newfoundland, New Jersey	Powder (talc)	0.1 to 4.5% IBA
IBA Water Soluble Salts	Hortus USA Corp. Inc. New York, New York	Liquid (water)	20% IBA
Rhizopon	Hortus USA Corp. Inc. New York, New York	Powder and water-soluble tablet form	0.1, 0.3, and 0.8% IBA
Woods Rooting Compound	Earth Science Products Corp. Wilsonville, Oregon	Liquid (ethanol)	1.03% IBA + 0.56% NAA

because overapplication of some formulations can cause damage to the cutting base. Formulations dissolved in alcohol are more prone to burn or dehydrate plant tissue. Auxin in excessive concentrations may inhibit bud development and cause leaf yellowing or abscission, stem blackening, and even cutting death. It has also been reported that misapplication to leaves may result in curling or otherwise distorted plant growth. When optimal treatments are applied, cuttings should exhibit the following characteristics: the basal portion of the cuttings shows some swelling, callus tissue forms, and root initials emerge just above the cutting base.

Methods of application

There are several accepted methods of application for growers wishing to use rooting hormones. When dipping the cutting bases into a rooting hormone, it is more efficient to dip several cuttings at once rather than to dip them individually. It is also better to use a small portion of the hormone mixture in a separate container, away from the stock batch, and to change it frequently. This will minimize the potential for disease spread and cross contamination.

Powders

Auxin-based rooting hormones may be mixed with talc and applied to the base of cuttings. The cuttings are dipped in the powder, then lightly tapped to remove excess chemical. To increase adhesion of the powder to the cutting bases, stem tissue can be recut or dipped in water or alcohol before application. However, this will lead to a more rapid deterioration of the rooting hormone batch and may increase the potential for disease spread.

Powdered forms of rooting hormones are generally less effective than liquid formulations applied at the same concentration. Auxin uptake by the cutting base is often inhibited by a rough textured stem and by talc being removed when the cutting is inserted into the propagation medium. However, talc-based products have the advantage of being less toxic and more sanitary than liquid formulations. These factors may ultimately make powders more cost effective.

Quick-dip solutions

Quick-dip solutions follow the same general principle of application as powders in that they are auxin-based products mixed with a carrier (usually alcohol or water) and are applied to the base of the cutting (fig. 8.6). Auxin can also be dissolved in 50% ethanol or

Figure 8.6. The quick dip is a popular technique used to apply rooting hormones. (C. Cerveny)

isopropyl alcohol and 50% water. Cuttings are dipped for one to five seconds at a depth of 0.25 to 0.75 inches (0.6 to 2 cm). Dipping the cuttings deeper in the solution can be used to compensate for lower auxin concentrations.

Quick-dip solutions have the advantage of being highly uniform, consistent, and easy to use. However, the risk of disease contamination is higher with liquid formulations than with powders. These formulations also tend to increase in auxin concentration as the solution evaporates. It is important to change the solution periodically throughout the day, especially in hot, dry environments, and to keep containers tightly sealed when not in use to prevent evaporation of the alcohol. It is also a good idea to throw out any unused solution at the end of the planting period rather than put it back into the stock container.

Figure 8.7. K-IBA is a water-soluble rooting hormone that has enormous potential with floriculture crops. (J. Gibson)

Water-soluble compounds

Water-soluble formulations of rooting hormones such as K+ or potassium salt formulations of IBA and NAA, which have traditionally been used by propagators of woody ornamentals, show promise for herbaceous plant propagation (fig. 8.7). Because these compounds are readily dissolved in water rather than alcohol, it tends to make their use by growers safer and easier.

Stem base sprays

As an alternative to dipping cuttings in talc or a liquid, rooting hormones can be applied to cutting bases or the foliage as a spray. A preplant foliar spray directed toward the stem base can be applied with a spray bottle; the spray is most practical when applied to bundles of cuttings before planting. This form of application eliminates the need for a common dipping container, reducing the incidence of disease spread.

Postplant foliar sprays

With postplanting applications of rooting hormones, much lower concentrations (50 to 100 ppm) of auxin are required than with conventional application methods. The material is sprayed to the point of runoff. The advantages of this treatment are that fewer workers handle the chemicals, and applications can be made up to twenty-four hours after planting. One challenge to this alternative method of application is that limited information on rates and concentrations for specific crops is available.

Plant Growth Regulators

Undesirable stretching due to high temperatures, lush growth, or low light can be a problem during propagation. Therefore, plant growth regulation is an integral part of the production program of many vegetatively propagated plants. Growers must be prepared to prevent excessive stem elongation. A number of nonchemical and chemical control options are available to manipulate plant growth so that well-proportioned, compact plants can be produced.

The two primary control options for controlling plant growth are physical and chemical. For most greenhouse operations, a combination of factors within each of these options can be used to manipulate plant growth.

Physical control

Knowing how the growing environment and cultural practices can affect plant growth will help in managing a crop's growth.

Nutrition

The type of nitrogen supplied can impact plant growth. Relying on nitrate nitrogen instead of ammoniacal nitrogen or urea nitrogen, both of which encourage lush growth, will help prevent excessive growth. Phosphorus also promotes plant growth. Plug producers commonly use low-phosphorus fertilizers such as 13-2-13 Cal-Mag or 15-0-15, which contain little or no phosphorus, to help limit stem elongation. In-depth fertilizer recommendations are covered in chapter 7.

Light

High light levels limit plant elongation, resulting in shorter plants. Low light conditions, typical of propagation environments, can lead to leggy plants if cuttings are allowed to remain in the propagation area. Additional details about light quality are discussed in chapter 5.

Temperature

Temperature manipulation can be very effective in controlling plant growth. Higher day temperatures than night temperatures (positive DIF) promote stem elongation, while lower day temperatures than night temperatures (negative DIF) limit elongation. Zero or negative DIF is very effective in controlling plant growth of many plant species, including poinsettias, chrysanthemums, and snapdragons.

Interestingly, a large percentage of the daily stem elongation occurs early in the day just prior to and after sunrise, thus cool temperatures (negative DIF) for at least two hours starting just before first light in the morning will reduce stem elongation. This cool, early morning pulse is known as the temperature DROP and should extend up to four hours after first light to be more effective. However, very warm temperatures during the rest of the day (positive DIF) may negate much of the effects of the temperature DROP. More detailed information on temperature control is covered in chapter 5.

Container size

Vegetative cuttings can be relatively large in comparison with seed-produced crops. Competition between plants can occur during rooting when the leaves begin to overlap. The use of plug trays with larger cells allows more room for the plants to grow before they begin to stretch. Economically, however, it may not be feasible to use larger cell plug trays, because of the lower number of cuttings generated per unit of propagation area and the added cost of shipping.

Timing

One of the most effective methods of controlling excessive plant growth is crop timing. The simple method of staggering the finish time of a set of cuttings is very effective in the propagation of many vegetative annuals. Staggered finish times avoid the need to hold a crop and ensure that a new supply of cuttings will always be available.

Chemical control

To control excessive plant growth, many crops require the use of chemical plant growth regulators (PGRs). Most of the commercially available PGRs are antigibberellins, which work by inhibiting gibberellin (GA) synthesis within the plant. GAs promote cellular elongation; without them, cells do not elongate as much, and plants do not grow as tall.

PGR types

A number of PGRs are available for height control

Figures 8.8a and b. Chlormequat can cause leaf phytotoxicity on (a) geranium and (b) poinsettia when applied at rates greater than 1,500 ppm or when the plant is stressed. (B. Whipker)

TABLE 8.3

Plant growth regulator concentration ranges for beginning foliar spray trials. Conduct trials initially on a small number of plants to determine the short-term and long-term efficacy.

CHEMICAL	FOLIAR SPRAY CONCENTRATION(ppm)
Ancymidol (A-Rest)	3 to 10
Chlormequat (Cycocel)	300 to 1,000
Daminozide (B-Nine, Dazide)	1,500 to 3,000
Daminozide + chlormequat (B-Nine + Cycocel) tank-mix	Daminozide: 800 to 2,500 + Chlormequat: 800 to 1,500
Ethephon (Florel)	200 to 500
Paclobutrazol (Bonzi, Paczol, or Piccolo)	1 to 30
Uniconazole (Sumagic)	0.5 to 5

(table 8.3). Ancymidol (A-Rest) has been available for a number of years. Its activity, or effectiveness at a given concentration, is greater than daminozide (B-Nine, Dazide) or chlormequat (Cycocel), but less than uniconazole (Sumagic), flurprimidol (Topflor), or paclobutrazol (Bonzi, Piccolo, Downsize, Paczol). Ancymidol is actively transported within the plant and can be applied as either a spray or a drench. It can be used on a number of crops, and growers use it on plugs and many bedding plants. Because of its low residual activity, it is ideal for applying to cuttings.

Daminozide is the most widely used PGR in the U.S. market. It is actively transported within the plant and used only as a foliar spray. It has a low degree of residual activity, so it is also ideal for use on cuttings.

Chlormequat also is actively transported within the plant. It can be applied as a foliar spray or a drench. It is used extensively on finished geraniums (*Pelargonium*) and poinsettias; multiple spray applications are usually applied. Phytotoxicity can occur

tion applied per area. To prevent overdosing and phytotoxicity, multiple applications at lower concentrations can be used to provide the same results as higher rates.

Foliar sprays require uniform applications to obtain consistent results. To accomplish this, a dose is based on measuring a known amount of chemical, adding it to a known volume of water, and applying a spray to a known bench area. Most foliar sprays are applied at the rate of 1 gal. per 200 sq. ft. (1 L/4.9 m^2) of bench area.

When mixing PGRs, great care must be given to accurately measuring and applying the chemical. As always, the label contains the legal mixing information. The North Carolina State University Web site www.pgrinfo.com contains a free downloadable Excel spreadsheet that will enable you to calculate PGR rates. A CD version can also be purchased from the North Carolina Commercial Flower Growers' Association (919-334-0093).

PGR rates

Recommended rates for the commonly grown floricultural crops are listed on the chemical label. These should be used as guidelines, and adjustments should be made for your particular location. Suggested rates for beginning your own trials are listed in table 8.3. Keeping complete records on how well a PGR application worked will assist you in customizing future PGR rates to your own operation. The records should include stage of development, fertilization program, and weather conditions. Table 8.4 provides suggested rates for some crops; it was compiled from recommendations by Klopmeyer and colleagues (2003) and actual grower rates.

Conclusion

From a practical standpoint, most of the plant species used by the greenhouse industry root relatively easy. The propagation process can often be hastened by treating cuttings with commercially available rooting hormones. Improved cutting performance and greater finished plant quality can be achieved with these tools; however, growers have to consider the added expense of hormone application and debate the cost versus increased product diversity and the potential for increased revenue.

Excessive stretching due to high temperatures, lush growth, or low light can be a problem during propagation. The two primary control options for controlling plant growth are physical, though manipulating nutritional program, light levels, temperatures, container size, and crop timing, and chemical plant growth regulators. For most greenhouse operations, a combination of factors within each of these options can be used to manipulate plant growth.

References

Blazich, F. A. 1988. Chemical formulations used to promote adventitious rooting, pp. 132–149. In: *Adventitious Root Formation in Cuttings.* T.D. Davis, B.E. Haissig, and N. Sankhla, eds. Dioscorides Press, Portland, Oregon.

Davidson, H., R. Mecklenburg, and C. Peterson. 2000. *Nursery Management: Administration and Culture.* Prentice Hall, Upper Saddle River, New Jersey.

Davis, T. D., B. E. Haissig, and N. Sankhla, eds. 1988. *Adventitious Root Formation In Cuttings.* Dioscorides Press, Portland, Oregon.

Dole, J. M. and H. F. Wilkins. 2005. *Floriculture: Principles and Species*, 2nd ed. Prentice Hall, Upper Saddle River, New Jersey.

Hartmann, H. T., D. E. Kester, F. T. Davies, Jr., and R. L. Geneve. 2002. *Hartmann and Kester's Plant Propagation: Principles and Practices.* 7th ed. Prentice Hall, Upper Saddle River, New Jersey.

Klopmeyer, M., M. Wilson, and C. A. Whealy. 2003. Propagating vegetative crops, pp. 165–184. In: *Ball RedBook*, 17th ed, vol. 2., D. Hamrick, ed. Ball Publishing, Batavia, Illinois.

9

Disease Management

Gary W. Moorman

The concept is simple and logical. Healthy stock plants yield healthy cuttings, and diseased stock plants yield diseased cuttings. This concept has probably been recognized since humans began propagating plants vegetatively, even before the causes of plant disease were fully understood. In the highly integrated plant industry in which one grower maintains stock plants and sells thousands or hundreds of thousands of cuttings to other growers, recognizing the importance of this concept and acting on it are crucial to the well-being of the entire industry. If the primary propagator, the person who roots the plants, or the grower who finishes the plants allows a pathogen into the system, not only are reputations and profits lost but consumers lose confidence that they can buy healthy plants. For these reasons, it is important to know which pathogens pose the greatest threat to the production of healthy vegetatively propagated plants and to understand the following about those pathogens: where they enter the production system, how they are spread and maintained in the crop, and how they can be eliminated.

Although any plant pathogen infecting a stock plant can be carried along in the production system, only certain ones pose a great threat to the industry. Pathogens like *Botrytis*, which causes gray mold (fig. 9.1), and *Rhizoctonia* and *Pythium*, which cause root and stem rots, are ubiquitous. These pathogens attack hundreds of different kinds of plants, and not just vegetatively propagated ones; they are not the pathogens of major concern. Such pathogens pose a chronic threat that must be managed by everyone throughout the process, from stock plant production to finishing the plant for sale. Growers at every level of the industry recognize the constant presence of such pathogens in their greenhouses as well as on plants immediately outside their greenhouses. Knowing this, they take steps to minimize the impact of these pathogens on plant health. Sanitation in the production facility, removal of plants other than crop plants from the growing area, and suppression of weeds outside the greenhouse vents and doors all help to minimize the introduction of these common pathogens.

The greatest threat to vegetatively propagated crops is from the host-specific pathogens and obligate parasites (those that survive and reproduce only on live plant

Figure 9.1. Gray mold of geranium caused by *Botrytis*.

material) that stay associated primarily with the propagated species, and it continues from the time of initial infection until the crop is killed, severely damaged, or shipped elsewhere as a symptomless carrier. The viruses, fungi, nematodes, and bacteria that systemically infect almost all parts of the plant pose the greatest industry-wide threat to successful plant production (table 9.1).

Pathogens that Pose the Greatest Threat (Target Pathogens)

Viruses

Viruses are composed of a small piece of genetic material surrounded by a protein coat; RNA is the genetic material in most plant-infecting viruses, and

TABLE 9.1

Diseases and associated pathogens of importance in vegetative propagation of herbaceous ornamental crops.

COMMON NAME	SCIENTIFIC NAME
Viruses	
Arabis mosaic virus	
Flower breaking of geranium	
Impatiens necrotic spot virus	
Tobacco mosaic virus	
Tomato ringspot virus	
Tobacco ringspot virus	
Bacteria	
Bacterial blight of geranium	*Xanthomonas campestris* pv. *pelargonii*
Bacterial canker of poinsettia	*Curtobacterium poinsettia*
Bacterial leaf spot of poinsettia	*Xanthomonas campestris* pv. *poinsettiicola*
Bacterial wilt	*Ralstonia solanacearum*
Bacterial wilt of carnation	*Pseudomonas caryophylli*
Fungi	
Carnation rust	*Uromyces caryophyllinus*
Geranium rust	*Puccinia pelargonii-zonalis*
Fuchsia rust	*Pucciniastrum epilobii* and *P. pustulatum*
Fusarium wilt of cyclamen	*Fusarium oxysporum* f. sp. *cyclaminis*
Scab of poinsettia	*Sphaceloma poinsettiae*
Verticillium wilt	*Verticillium albo-atrum* and *V. dahliae*
White rust of chrysanthemum	*Puccinia horiana*
Nematodes	
Foliar nematode	*Aphelenchoides fragariae* and *A. ritzemabosi*

DNA in only a few. Viruses direct the chemical functions of the host plant to produce more viral genetic material and protein coat. Most viruses survive only in live plant cells; they lose infectivity when the plant tissue dies or when virus-containing sap dries on a surface outside the plant cell.

Some viruses are spread among plants through the transfer of sap (mechanical transmission) if moved rapidly on workers' hands or tools. Most viruses are spread during the feeding or probing activity of thrips, aphids, or other insects or nematodes. An important exception to this generality is tobacco mosaic virus (TMV), which retains infectivity in dead, dry plant material and in sap dried on hands, clothing, pots, tools, and equipment. TMV is usually spread mechanically and seldom by insects.

Regardless of the virus's identity, virus particles must be introduced into live cells, where they direct the plant to produce more virus components. The virus components assemble and move from cell to cell infecting, in most cases, all but a few young cells at the root and shoot growing tips (meristems). Any part of the plant composed of more than those few young cells of the meristem harbor virus particles. Thus infected stock plants are the source of viruses in the production system. If insects are eliminated from the production area and steps are taken to ensure that the virus is not spread mechanically, the only way that the virus remains a threat is through cuttings taken from infected stock plants.

One significant problem with viruses is that several important ones, including TMV and impatiens necrotic spot virus (INSV), have enormous host ranges. The host range of a pathogen is the list of different plants that the pathogen can infect. Because of this, many different species of plants can be sources of viruses with large host ranges whether these plants are inside a greenhouse, under the benches, immediately outside the greenhouse, in the business office, or in workers' homes and handled by workers before they handle the crop. Insects, especially aphids and thrips that have fed on infected plants and then are allowed access to the crop, can also introduce viruses into the production system. And in the case of TMV, cigars, cigarettes, and smokeless tobacco products can be sources of the virus.

Bacteria

Bacteria are single-celled organisms that have a rigid cell wall. Their genetic material (DNA) is in the form of a circular strand. Most bacteria also harbor plasmids, small DNA-containing units, that also impart some characteristics to bacteria (including antibiotic resistance in some cases). From just a few cells, bacteria can multiply very rapidly under favorable conditions. Plant pathogenic bacteria generally survive in infected plants, debris from infected plants, and in a very few cases infested soil. Most require a wound or natural opening to gain entry to the plant, and they need warm, moist conditions to cause obvious disease symptoms. Bacteria grow between plant cells on the nutrients that leak into that space or within the vascular tissue of the plant. They release enzymes that degrade cell walls, toxins that damage cell membranes, growth regulators that disrupt normal plant growth, or complex sugars that plug water-conducting vessels; the damage depends on the species of bacteria involved and the tissue infected.

Systemically infecting plant pathogenic bacteria that reside in the vascular tissue (fig. 9.2) of the plant (for example, *Xanthomonas campestris* pv. *pelargonii*, *Xanthomonas campestris* pv. *begoniae*, and *Ralstonia solanacearum*) can be found discontinuously throughout most of the plant's xylem from the roots to the shoots and branches (fig. 9.3). Because the vascular tissue arises from cells at the base of the meristematic tissue, the cells at the tip of the meristem, away from the differentiated xylem, are free of bacteria. Vascular wilt bacteria are usually maintained in a crop by propagating from infected stock plants. It should be noted that *Ralstonia solanacearum* (formerly *Pseudomonas*), unlike most systemically infecting bacteria, survives very well in soil and that all bacteria can inhabit the surface of the plant for some time without inducing symptoms.

Some bacteria, such as *Curtobacterium poinsettia* (the cause of bacterial canker in poinsettia) and *Xanthomonas campestris* pv. *poinsettiicola* (the cause of bacterial leaf spot in poinsettia), do not infect systemically; they are associated primarily with one species of host plant in the production system and do not infect other species in production. Similarly, *Pseudomonas caryophylli* attacks carnations and few other plants. Such pathogens tend to stay associated with the host plant, and they are carried from generation to generation in infected stock plants and in or on the surface of cuttings from infected stock. In addition to being spread from plant to plant in sap on tools, equipment, and workers' hands, bacteria can be readily spread in splashing droplets of water during irrigation or in condensation dripping from inside the greenhouse structure onto plants.

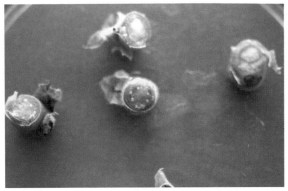

Figure 9.2. Bacteria oozing from the vascular tissue of a heavily infected geranium.

Figure 9.3. Vascular wilt.

Rhodococcus fascians (formerly *Corynebacterium*) causes abnormal branching and stem development near the base of infected plants. This bacterium can attack many different species of host plant but tends to stay associated with infected live plants. It is maintained in the production system when cuttings are taken from infected plants. The bacterium does not survive long outside the plant, but it can be spread via cutting knives and other tools.

Erwinia carotovora (the cause of bacterial soft rot) does not infect systemically but survives well in soil, rooting media, and plant debris; it is also known to survive in irrigation systems. It is readily spread from these sources and poses a significant threat to most crops that are vegetatively propagated, especially during the rooting phase of production.

Fungi

Fungi are a very large, diverse group of multicelled organisms. Their cells are generally threadlike strands (hyphae) that have rigid cell walls. Most fungi reproduce asexually by forming spores or by the fragmentation of the hyphal threads. Some fungi also reproduce sexually by forming spores resulting from mating. The vascular wilt fungus *Verticillium* resides in soil and in many different susceptible plants. *Verticillium* has, to a large extent, been eliminated as a threat to vegetatively propagated crops, since most growers no longer use soil in the production system. Those who do use soil treat it to eliminate pathogens before planting (see chapter 4). Like xylem-infecting bacteria, *Verticillium* is found discontinuously throughout the xylem of an infected plant but is not found among the meristematic cells. Cuttings taken from infected stock plants are the main source of *Verticillium* in vegetatively propagated crops today.

Figure 9.4. Geranium rust.

Other fungi that pose a threat to vegetatively propagated crops are those that are host specific or have a very small host range. These fungi stay associated with and survive on infected host plants. Rust fungi—such as geranium rust, *Puccinia pelargonii-zonalis* (fig. 9.4); carnation rust, *Uromyces caryophyllinus*; and fuchsia rust, *Pucciniastrum epilobii* or *P. pustulatum*—and powdery mildew of poinsettia are

obligate parasites that survive only on live host plants and spread among plants within that crop. Because these pathogens attack very few or no other species, plants other than the crop in production are not a source of them. However, once a pathogen is in a production facility, its spores are carried by wind currents throughout the greenhouse. The spores can also be deposited on skin and clothing and subsequently brushed off onto other plants of the same species.

Nematodes

Nematodes are non-segmented roundworms. Plant parasitic species are distinguished by the mouthpart, called a stylet; it is a hollow spearlike structure used by the nematode to probe plant cells, inject digestive enzymes, and withdraw digested plant components. Most plant parasitic nematodes reside in the soil. They can be eliminated from production by pasteurizing the soil before planting, not using soil as a potting component, or removing cuttings from the plant well above the soil to regenerate new plants in nematode-free potting media.

Important exceptions are species of foliar nematode (*Aphelenchoides* spp.) that live on or inside the aboveground portions of host plants. Although foliar nematodes can be easily detected by tearing a portion of infected plant tissue apart in a clear drop of water and examining the drop with magnification, many host plants do not exhibit obvious symptoms, even when thousands of nematodes are present within the tissue. In such cases, it is not unusual for these symptomless carriers to be the source of foliar nematodes for other plants. *Aphelenchoides fragariae* and *A. ritzemabosi* attack many different species of plants including herbaceous ornamentals.

Management of Pathogens That Threaten Vegetative Propagation: Primary Propagation

Recalling the concept stated at the beginning of this chapter that healthy stock plants yield healthy cuttings, it is obvious that the way to eliminate the pathogens that pose the greatest threat to production is to establish healthy stock plants, keep them free of pathogens, and then remove propagules, plant parts used for production, only from those healthy plants. For several decades, the use of "pathogen-free" stock plants has been recommended. What is really meant is that stock plants must be free of those target pathogens that pose the greatest threat to production. Other pathogens such as *Botrytis* may be present on "pathogen-free" plants.

To obtain an economically valuable, pathogen-free plant, the first task of the primary propagator is to find an apparently healthy plant that has all the desired horticultural characteristics. The next step is to verify that plants derived from this plant are indeed free of the target pathogens. Obligate parasitic fungi and foliar nematodes can be detected by the naked eye or through microscopic observation or will manifest themselves in a relatively short period of time if the growing conditions are conducive to their development. Infected plants can be identified and discarded with relative ease. Then those fungi and bacteria not readily observed can be sought for elimination from desired plants.

Some argue that it is impossible to free a plant totally of pathogens and all that is achieved is to a reduction of target pathogens to levels so low that they are difficult to detect. However with skill, attention to detail, and repetitive processing of plant material, it should be technically possible and statistically probable for a primary propagator to completely free a few plants of target pathogens. And once the plants are free of target pathogens, it should be possible to maintain them in that condition by isolating them from all other plants, imposing strict sanitation conditions, and educating those who work with the plants to take steps to prevent the introduction of pathogens.

Culture indexing

The plant or some part of the plant must be verified free of the pathogen in question. Most of the bacteria and some of the fungi targeted for elimination will grow in artificial culture, separate from plant tissues. In a process called culture indexing, plants are tested for the presence of bacteria and fungi; a separate indexing protocol must be followed to test for viruses.

Culture indexing is a system whereby a portion of the cutting is removed and placed in a medium, usually a broth that fosters the growth of target organisms. The initial plant yielding those cuttings is discarded. Cuttings are labeled and records kept, noting which cuttings originated from a particular plant. If bacteria or fungi grow from one or more cuttings from a given plant, all the cuttings from that plant are discarded. When all cuttings from a particular plant

yield no microbial growth, those cuttings are retained and used as stock plants for the next generation of cuttings. Because an organism present in very low numbers may not always be detected, testing is repeated, usually two more times.

Culture indexing is not applied to viral pathogens because viruses do not grow in culture. Virus particles are submicroscopic, and virus symptom development can be suppressed by environmental conditions. For example, geraniums (*Pelargonium*) infected by one of several geranium viruses can be totally free of obvious symptoms when conditions are good for plant growth. However, when cool, dark conditions prevail, severe symptoms may be expressed (fig. 9.5). Then when good conditions return, new tissues will be free of symptoms even though the virus is still present.

One method of detecting the presence of viruses is to inoculate indicator plants with sap from the candidate plant. Certain plants, including *Chenopodium quinoa*, exhibit distinct dead spots (called "local

Figure 9.5. Leaf crinkle cause by a virus in geranium. Symptoms often abate when growing conditions for the plant are good, even though the virus is still present in the tissue.

lesions") even when inoculated with a low concentration of any one of a wide variety of viruses. Although the identity of the virus causing such a nonspecific symptom cannot be determined, the presence of a virus is indicated. Cuttings are taken from an apparently healthy plant, and small portions are excised, ground in a buffer, and rubbed onto the indicator plant. If a symptom develops in the indicator plant, all the cuttings from that particular plant are discarded. When no symptoms develop in the indicator plant inoculated with sap from a group of cuttings from a particular plant, those cuttings are retained. As in culture indexing, plants are tested repeatedly over time to verify that viruses are not present. This method has been proved very reliable.

Immunochemical and nucleic acid-based tests have been used in place of indicator plants for viruses and some bacteria. A separate test is required for each targeted pathogen, but many different tests can be run simultaneously and rapidly. Some of these tests not only determine the identity of the pathogen, but they also give an indication of the numbers of bacterial cells or virus particles present.

For indexing large numbers of plants, immunochemical tests such as the Enzyme-Linked Immunosorbant Assay (ELISA) are used for some pathogens. It is not adequate if the pathogen is present in very low numbers, as is the case with tobacco ringspot and tomato ringspot viruses. For the bacterium *Xanthomonas campestris* pv. *pelargonii*, it is generally recognized that 1,000 to 10,000 cells/ml must be present to successfully detect its presence with ELISA.

In the immunofluorescence technique, bacterial cells are exposed on microscope slides to antibodies tagged with a fluorescent dye. Either the bacteria must be extracted from the plant tissue or the plant tissue must be sliced thinly enough for the dye to come in contact with the bacteria. Although this is a sensitive serological test, detection limits are still above 1,000 cells.

Detection and identification methods based on DNA sequences or probes designed to hybridize with specific pathogen DNA sequences have been developed. Employing the polymerase chain reaction (PCR), single-stranded DNA and RNA probes can detect as few as 100 or even 10 bacterial cells per sample. A PCR test has been developed for the simultaneous detection of *Ralstonia* and *Xanthomonas* in geraniums.

Meristem tip culture

To increase the likelihood of obtaining a plant free of target pathogens, often meristem tip culturing is performed rather than using relatively large pieces of plant tissue as propagation material. The few cells at the growing point, or meristem, are still dividing to give rise to new plant parts but are a few cells away from vascular tissue; those cells are most likely to be free of internal infections by most viruses, bacteria, and fungi. Pathogens on the outer surface of these cells can be washed away or neutralized with mild disinfectants.

In general, it is faster and technically easier to regenerate a plant from 100 to 200 cells that include the meristem and some differentiated cells than from 10 to 20 meristematic cells alone. If it is suspected

that a pathogen may be present in a plant, pathogen reproduction can sometimes be suppressed while the rest of the plant continues to grow. The result is a larger volume of tissue free of the pathogen. For example, geraniums grown at very high temperatures continue to grow slowly, while many viruses do not replicate at those temperatures. This process increases the volume of virus-free tissue, making it more likely that the tissue removed for meristem propagation will be free of viruses.

Combining culture indexing and meristem tip culture

There are at least two ideas about the order in which culture indexing and meristem tip culture should be conducted. Both require that the plants have all the desired horticultural characteristics and that they are apparently healthy. One philosophy holds that culture indexing should be performed first. Once the plants are free of fungi and bacteria, then plant manipulation, meristem tip culturing, and virus indexing should done to establish virus-free plants. The second philosophy holds that manipulation of the plants (such as growing them at high temperatures), meristem culturing, and virus indexing should be done first to establish virus-free plants. During this process, it is very likely that fungi and bacteria will simultaneously be eliminated.

Regardless of the approach taken, the procedures need to be repeated on subsequent generations of plants and all target pathogens tested until it is certain that the resulting plants are "pathogen-free" —that is, free of all the target pathogens. When very sensitive tests are combined with repeated testing, it is likely that target pathogens can be detected if they are present.

Elite nucleus stock

When it appears that a plant no longer has any of the target pathogens, that plant becomes the parent of subsequent generations of cuttings. At the end of this repetitive procedure, the final cuttings are retained and are sometimes called the elite nucleus stock plants. These pathogen-free plants must be isolated from all other plants in a facility that excludes insects, mites, and people other than those educated and trained to maintain the health and isolation of these plants. The elite nucleus stock plants must be handled individually and steps taken to sanitize hands and tools before approaching the next plant. Some primary propagators ensure isolation by placing individual stock plants in screened, latched cages within the greenhouse. The time, effort, and resources expended in indexing for viruses and culturable organisms make the elite nucleus plants extremely valuable. Every effort must be made to keep them pathogen free. Only workers well educated in the reasons why these plants are particularly important should have access to them. Outside visitors, regardless of status or importance, should not be allowed access to these plants.

Of crucial importance is the unidirectional flow of plants through the system from this point onward. Cuttings taken from the elite nucleus stock must be rooted in a different facility and never returned to the elite stock house. Any plants that are identified as candidates for becoming elite nucleus stock must be put through the culture indexing and meristem tip culture process outlined here and assumed to be contaminated until proven pathogen free. To do otherwise is to risk the health of all the plants in the elite nucleus stock house.

Increase block

Once the elite nucleus stock is established, cuttings are taken to increase the number of stock plants that can provide healthy cuttings. An area with the capacity to

Figure 9.6. Powdery mildew on poinsettia.

house significantly more plants than the elite stock house is required. However, these secondary stock plants must also be isolated from all other plants; protected from the common pathogens such as *Botrytis*, powdery mildew (fig. 9.6), *Pythium*, and *Rhizoctonia*; and handled by as few well-trained employees as possible. These secondary stock plants constitute the increase block. Cuttings taken from the increase block are used to establish, in a different greenhouse, the production block that yields cuttings for sale.

Several companies have adopted this type of system to obtain healthy stock plants, increase blocks, and production blocks. Through company-enforced rules and regulations governing the processing, testing, and handling of plants, these elite primary propagators work to supply the rest of the industry with plants of known good health. In Pennsylvania, for example, the Pennsylvania Department of Agriculture (empowered by a legislative rule passed by the state government) tests and certifies that geraniums produced in such a system are free of viral pathogens.

Management of Pathogens That Threaten Vegetative Propagation: Secondary Propagation

Once plants leave the elite nucleus and increase blocks, they are grown in numbers that require larger facilities and contact with more workers. Great care must be taken to use sanitation practices and insect, mite, and disease control measures to maintain the health of these plants. When cuttings from the primary propagator are sold to other firms for increase and sale, the opportunity for reintroduction of target pathogens from that point in the production system significantly increases because of the large number of plants involved, the space needed, the number of workers required, and exposure to the wider variety of other plant species grown by most secondary propagators. Although it is not possible to maintain the strict isolation afforded elite and increase block plants, nevertheless sanitation as well as insect, mite and disease control measures must be in place to maintain the health of the plants.

Secondary propagators often purchase different cultivars of a given species from several different elite propagators who hold patent or propagation rights to certain cultivars. When plants arrive from a source, those plants should be kept together as a block and not mixed with plants from other sources. Through this procedure, the source of plants found to harbor one or more of the target pathogens can be readily identified. If plants from several sources are mixed together, it is very difficult to determine the origin of pathogens found later. Some pathogens such as *Ralstonia solanacearum* and *Erwinia carotovora* can be spread via irrigation water; thus until the new plants have been observed for a length of time sufficient to verify that they are healthy, new plants should not be placed in an ebb-and-flow system or other system where water is shared or recycled among many plants.

In Pennsylvania, for example, it is possible for secondary propagators of impatiens to receive government certification of plant health. However, most secondary propagators must develop and institute rules and regulations governing the procedures they use to propagate, test, and maintain the health of plants on their own without the benefit of an outside, unbiased agency.

Controlling Pathogens in Stock Plants: Primary or Secondary Propagation

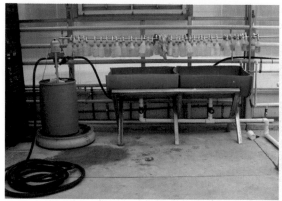

Figure 9.7. Hand-washing station. Note the bottles of disinfectant above the sink ready to be filled and carried by workers for use in the production area.

An extremely important way that pathogens can become widespread among vegetatively propagated crops is through pathogen movement from plant to plant on workers' hands and tools. Viruses and bacteria are readily vectored these ways. To combat this movement, hand-washing stations (fig. 9.7) should be readily available, and bottles of soapy water or disinfectant should be carried and used frequently by workers who handle plants. In the elite stock plant houses, it is mandatory that hands be washed thoroughly after working with one stock plant and before moving to the next stock plant. An even more effective strategy would be to use disposable gloves and to change gloves between plants.

In increase stock plant houses it is not reasonable to do so between each stock plant; however, washing and disinfecting hands or changing disposable gloves should be done as frequently as feasible, and tools should be changed between stock plants. A used tool should be placed in disinfectant for eight to ten minutes while using another tool. The number of tools available to a given worker is determined by the number of times a clean tool must be obtained over the ten-minute period. In relation to the crop losses that could occur through the spread of pathogens on tools, the cost of multiple reusable cutting knives per worker is insignificant. Alternatively, branches removed for cuttings can be broken off rather than severed with a knife, and the worker can change and discard disposable gloves.

As noted previously, several pathogens pose a chronic threat to all plants in greenhouses. However, certain species and cultivars are particularly susceptible to specific pathogens, and records should be kept over the years to document which pathogens create

problems and when those problems occur. For example, of all the vegetatively propagated crops, geranium is arguably the most susceptible to gray mold attack. *Botrytis* is favored by the dark, cool, humid conditions within the crop canopy that prevail in late autumn and early winter in many production locations. Begonias frequently are infected with one of the powdery mildews, a fungus that produces massive numbers of spores during cool, humid nights and releases them during warm, dry days. Conditions conducive to powdery mildew often occur in the spring and again in the autumn but tend to lessen during the summer. *Botrytis* and the powdery mildews are spread by air currents from plants either inside or outside the facility, and it is impossible to totally exclude their presence; thus it is important to maintain environmental conditions within the crop canopy that are unfavorable to them. Also growers should be prepared to apply chemical or biological control agents to protect plants from attack. Neither chemicals nor biocontrols are very effective in curing a plant that is already infected; they are most effective when used preventively.

Botrytis poses a threat to almost all species and is often difficult to control among stock plants. One reason is that most stock plants are large with a dense canopy that is difficult to penetrate thoroughly with fungicides or biological control agents. It is crucial to suppress spore production within stock plant houses to protect the stock and, more importantly, to minimize the number of spores on cuttings. If not controlled adequately, spores will be released whenever there is activity in the greenhouse, creating "spore showers." The result is that cuttings will have *Botrytis* spores on them even though no symptoms are obvious. These spores will germinate and infect cuttings during rooting or shipping (fig. 9.8).

Figure 9.8. A geranium cutting infected with *Botrytis*.

Low relative humidity among the plants is inhibitory to *Botrytis*, which needs moisture on leaf surfaces in order to invade. Thus *Botrytis* activity can be slowed by spacing plants well, using horizontal airflow systems, encouraging warm air to rise up through the canopy, or employing other strategies to sweep humid air out of the canopy. *Botrytis* is most aggressive when it has a base of nutrients and is invading new plant tissue. If stock plants flower and the flowers are allowed to senesce and fall, this tissue is excellent for the production of huge numbers of spores by *Botrytis*. If an infected petal falls on a healthy leaf, *Botrytis* readily grows from that petal and into the leaf (fig. 9.9). Plants such as geraniums and impatiens are prone to this problem and should never be hung above other stock plants or have other plants hung above them. If the irrigation system for hanging plants results in drip onto the plants below, the problem is magnified.

Great care should be taken in the selection of fungicides, the timing of their use on stock plants, and the protective equipment provided to those who must then work with the crop. It is well known that some chemicals, including chlorothalonil, can cause a rashlike dermatitis. Strict adherence to the reentry period legally required by the product label and the use of protective sleeves, overalls, and gloves even after the reentry period has expired can minimize worker exposure. If rashes develop, it should not be immediately assumed that pesticide exposure is the cause. The sap of some plants, geranium for one, is very irritating to some people's skin. Also, some people develop sensitivity to the latex in the gloves they wear for protection; they must then wear gloves made from other materials such as nitrile.

Stock plants are usually grown for several months within a facility, increasing the opportunity for various other pathogens to be inadvertently brought into contact with them. *Pythium*, *Rhizoctonia*, *Fusarium*, *Thielaviopsis*, and other soilborne pathogens can be

Figure 9.9. *Botrytis* growing from an infected flower petal into a leaf on which it has fallen.

brought into the greenhouse on workers' shoes and on dirty tools. Sanitation practices such as scraping soil off shoes and tools and then swabbing them with disinfectant can help to minimize this movement. Disinfectants do not penetrate soil or organic matter well. Therefore, before treatment clean the surface to be disinfected fairly well. Longer disinfectant times (five to ten minutes) are more effective than short times (seconds to one to two minutes).

Some supply houses and businesses catering to the pesticide-applicator industry sell preentry floor mats that can be charged with disinfectants. These mats are placed in strategic locations (fig. 9.10) so that workers can walk through them and thereby treat their footwear. To be effective at all, the disinfectant must be changed or recharged frequently: at the beginning of the workday, at morning break, after lunch, and in midafternoon if traffic flow is high. The very short treatment time that results and the likelihood that large bits of soil will not be penetrated well by the disinfectant make it doubtful that these mats are truly effective; however, they serve as a constant reminder to the workers of the need to prevent the movement of pathogens into the production area.

In addition to chemical fungicides such as etridiazole (Terrazole and Truban), mefenoxam (Subdue Maxx and Quell), PCNB (Terraclor), fosetyl-Al (Aliette), triflumizole (Terraguard), and fludioxonil (Medallion) (table 9.2), several biological control agents are now available for managing soilborne plant pathogens (table 9.3). None of them will cure a plant once it is infected. And none are effective indefinitely after application. For these reasons, biological control agents should be applied as soon as roots are available on the plant material for them to colonize, and they should be applied again at an interval recommended on the product label. As with chemicals, if growing conditions are very favorable to the root-infecting fungi, biological agents will not completely control the pathogen. As roots grow, mature, degenerate naturally, and are replaced by new roots, the amount of organic matter that an opportunistic pathogen such as *Pythium* can use increases. This makes it very important that *Pythium* is excluded from the production area through sanitation procedures. With care, fungicides and biological control

Figure 9.10. A floor mat charged with disinfectant.

agents can be used on the same plants. As a general rule, ten days should elapse between the application of a chemical and the application of a biological control agent or vice versa. When in doubt about their combined use, a company representative for the bio-control agent should be consulted.

Disease Threats During Rooting

The major threats to new cuttings during rooting are *Botrytis* already on the cuttings, *Botrytis* spread from other plant material already in the cutting bed, bacteria (primarily *Erwinia* species that cause soft rots) on cuttings taken from infected stock plants, bacteria infesting the rooting medium, and *Pythium* or *Rhizoctonia* in the rooting medium.

As noted already, good control of *Botrytis* on stock plants will minimize the number of spores brought into the rooting area on cuttings. If stock plants have been treated with a fungicide or a combination of fungicides that tend to have long residual activity (a long period after application during which they remain effective), protection may carry through the rooting period. Although systemic chemicals can have long residual activity, they are at the greatest risk for

the selection of fungicide-resistant *Botrytis* (see the information concerning the threat of resistance). Combinations of nonsystemic chemicals can have long residual activity. In general, *Botrytis* and other fungi have not developed resistance to nonsystemic protectants.

To further manage *Botrytis* during rooting, plants should be monitored frequently to determine the earliest time when misting can be curtailed and humidity reduced. It seems likely that fungal and bacterial biological agents available for *Botrytis* control would perform adequately under the high-humidity conditions during rooting if applied early in the process. Finally, some disinfectants continuously injected into the mist water line to manage the buildup of algae in the propagation area may also suppress *Botrytis*. Care must be taken to first determine that this use of disinfectant is legal in your locale and that the concentration of disinfectant is not toxic to the cuttings.

Unrooted cuttings are vulnerable to other foliar

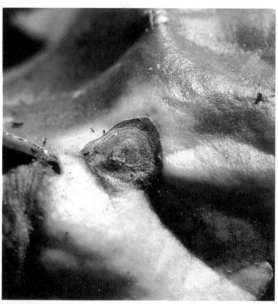

Figure 9.11. Alternaria leaf spot on geranium.

pathogens in the high-humidity conditions found during rooting. Fungi that normally cause little or no damage, including *Alternaria* (fig. 9.11) and *Myrothecium*, can cause significant damage. In general, if a good *Botrytis* control strategy is in place, these other fungi will be managed as well. If an organism other than *Botrytis* appears to be a problem, obtain an accurate diagnosis as soon as possible to determine what action should be taken. This is particularly important in light of the fact that no single fungicide

TABLE 9.2

Common names and trade names of some fungicides and disinfectants. Those grouped together have similar modes of action and should not be alternated or mixed together in an attempt to avoid fungicide resistance.

COMMON NAME	TRADE NAME
Disinfectants	
Ammonium chloride	Green Shield, Triathlon
Chlorine disinfectant	Clorox
Hydrogen dioxide	OxiDate, TerraCyte, ZeroTol
Fungicides	
†Azoxystrobin	Heritage, Quadris
Carbonic acid salt or potassium bicarbonate	Armbicarb, First Step, Kaligreen, Milstop, Remedy
Chlorothalonil	Bravado, Bravo, Chlorostar, Concorde, Countdown, Daconil, Echo, Fung-Onil, PathGard
Copper salts	Camelot, Tenn-Cop 5E
Copper sulfate	Cuprofix Disperse
Copper sulfate pentahydrate	Phyton 27
Cupric hydroxide	Champion, Kocide 101, Nu-Cop
Copper oxychloride	Microsperse COC
Tribasic copper sulfate	Tennessee Tri-Basic
Cupric sulfate + mancozeb	Cuprofix MZ
Copper hydroxide + mancozeb	Junction, Mankocide
Etridiazole	Terrazole, Truban
Etridiazole + thiophanate methyl	Banrot
†Fenarimol	Rubigan
*†Fenhexamid	Decree
Fludioxanil	Medallion
†Fosetyl-Al	Aliette
*†Iprodione	Chipco 26019, Sextant
†Kresoxim methyl	Cygnus
Mancozeb	4 Flowable, Dithane, FORE, Junction, Pentalthlon, Protect T/O
Mancozeb + dimethomorph	Stature
Mancozeb + thiophanate methyl	Duosan, Zyban
Maneb	Maneb
*†Mefenoxam	Mefenoxam 2, Quell, Subdue Maxx
*†Metalaxyl	Subdue
†Myclobutanil	Eagle, Nova, Systhane
Paraffinic oil	SunSpray Ultra-fine
PCNB	Terraclor
Phosphites, sodium, potassium, and ammonium salts	Biophos, Phostrol
Piperalin	Pipron
Potassium salts of fatty acids	M-Pede
Potassium salts of phosphorus acid	Quest, Resyst
†Propiconazole	Alamo, Banner, Propiconazole Pro

(Continued on page 112)

(Continued from page 111)

COMMON NAME	TRADE NAME
Sodium carbonate peroxyhydrate	TerraCyte
Sodium methyl dithiocarbamate	Vapam
Streptomycin sulfate	Bac-Master, Streptrol
Sulfur	Enduro Sulfur, Kumulus, Lime Sulfur, Micro Flo, Microsperse Wettable Sulfur, Orthorix, Thiolux
†Thiophanate methyl	Bonomyl, Cavalier, 3336F, Domain FL, Topsin. OPH 6672
†Thiophanate methyl + chlorothalonil	ConSyst, Spectro 90
†Thiophanate methyl + flutolanil	SysStar
†Thiophanate methyl + mancozeb	Duosan, Zyban
†Triadimefon	Bayleton, Strike
†Trifloxystrobin	Compass
†Triflumizole	Terraguard
†Triforine	Funginex, Triforine
Ziram	Ziram

* currently recognized to be at risk for the development of resistance in one or more pathogens
† systemic or locally systemic in some plants

TABLE 9.3

Scientific names and trade names of biological control organisms.

SCIENTIFIC NAME	TRADE NAME
Agrobacterium radiobacter	Galltrol A, Norbac
Ampelomyces quisqualis	AQ10
Bacillus subtilis	Companion, Epic, Kodiak, Serenade
Burkholderia cepacia	Deny
Candida oleophila	Aspire
Gliocladium catenulatum	Primastop
Streptomyces lydicus	Actionvate
Streptomyces griseoviridis	Mycostop
Trichoderma harzianum	PlantShield, Trichodex
Trichoderma virens	SoilGard

effectively controls all fungi.

If it is determined that bacterial pathogens are causing crop losses during rooting, the health of the stock plants must be assessed. If the bacteria are traced to a stock plant, the stock plant must be destroyed immediately. Sanitation measures being used during cutting harvest should be evaluated also to ensure that workers are not spreading bacteria on their hands or tools. The rooting medium in which bacteria-infected cuttings were struck must be discarded and the sur-rounding area thoroughly washed down and disinfected. Finally, the possibility that the irrigation water is contaminated should be considered.

If rooting hormones are applied to cuttings, the hormone should be dusted or sprayed on the cuttings. If the cuttings are dipped into a common container of hormone and the container contents become contaminated with a pathogen, each batch of cuttings subsequently treated will be exposed to that pathogen.

Disease Threat During the Shipment of Cuttings

Botrytis and soft rot bacteria pose the greatest threat to cutting health during shipping. The health of cuttings is directly related to their health at the time of packing, the length of time they are in shipment, the temperatures and relative humidity during shipment, the length of time the customer leaves the plants in the boxes after arrival, and the environmental conditions during the time the customer continues to hold the plants in the boxes. To determine "what went wrong," each of these possibilities must be examined. Attempts made to enclose fungicide-releasing products in shipping boxes have, to date, been unsuccessful. Cooling the plants during shipment and scheduling the shortest possible transit time continue to be the best approaches in ensuring that the plants are as healthy upon arrival as they were when initially packed.

For the Good of the Entire Industry

All propagators, whether primary or secondary, should determine which pathogens, insects, and mites pose a particular threat to the crop being propagated and develop a strategy for protecting the crop. Great care should be taken to select the most appropriate control methods that have long-term benefits to the entire industry. One issue that should not be overlooked is the fact that because plant propagators sell plants throughout the industry, any pathogen allowed to infect or take up residence on plants could be distributed far and wide.

In addition to the elimination of target pathogens and the production of "pathogen-free" plants, the manner in which *Botrytis*, powdery mildews, *Pythium*, insects, and mites are managed must be of concern. If a propagator uses a pesticide in a way that fosters resistance, those resistant organisms will be spread in the industry on the plants. The result is that growers will find that pesticide ineffective, even if they never used it, because the pathogen or pest they are dealing with and that was inadvertently shipped to them developed resistance elsewhere. All plant propagators should stay up-to-date on the recommended strategies for preventing the development of pesticide resistance. They should avoid the repeated and prolonged use of chemicals known to be at high risk for the development of resistance (table 9.2). And it should become a standard industry-wide practice to maintain and make available a list of pesticides that have been used on each batch of cuttings so that those purchasing the plants can select pesticides accordingly.

References

Baker, R. R., P. E. Nelson, and R. H. Lawson. 1985. Carnation, pp. 507–563. In: *Diseases of Floral Crops*, vol. 1, D. L. Strider, ed. Praeger Scientific, New York.

Barker, K. R. 1998. Introduction and synopsis of advancements in nematology, pp. 1–20. In: *Plant and Nematode Interactions*, K. R. Barker, G. A. Pederson, and G. L. Windham, eds. American Society of Agronomy, Crop Science Society of America, and Soil Science Society of America, Madison, Wisconsin.

De Boer, S. H., D. A. Cuppels, and R. D. Gitaitis. 1996. Detecting latent bacterial infections, pp. 27–57. In: *Pathogen Indexing Technologies*, S. H. De Boer, J. H. Andrews, and I. C. Tommerup, eds. Academic Press, New York.

Glick, D. L., C. M. Coffey, and M. A. Sulzinski. 2002. Simultaneous PCR detection of the two major bacterial pathogens of geranium. *Journal of Phytopathology* 150:54–59.

Hausbeck, M. K., and G. W. Moorman. 1996. Managing *Botrytis* in greenhouse-grown flower crops. *Plant Disease* 80:1212–1219.

Hausbeck, M. K., and S. P. Pennypacker. 1991. Influence of grower activity and disease incidence on concentrations of airborne conidia of *Botrytis cinerea* among geranium stock plants. *Plant Disease* 75:798–803.

Hausbeck, M. K., S. P. Pennypacker, and R. E. Stevenson. 1996. The use of forced heated air to manage *Botrytis* stem blight of geranium stock plants in a commercial greenhouse. *Plant Disease* 80:940–943.

Haygood, R. A., and D. L. Strider. 1985. Bacterial diseases, pp. 229–252. In: *Diseases of Floral Crops*, vol. 1, D. L. Strider, ed. Praeger Scientific, New York.

Lawson, R. H. 1985. Viruses and virus diseases, pp. 253–294. In: *Diseases of Floral Crops*, vol. 1, D. L. Strider, ed. Praeger Scientific, New York.

Moorman, G. W., and R. J. Lease. 1992. Residual efficacy of fungicides used in the management of *Botrytis cinerea* on greenhouse-grown geraniums.

Plant Disease 76:374–376.

Munnecke, D. E. 1956. Development and production of pathogen-free geranium propagative material. *Plant Disease Reporter Supplement* 238:93–95.

Oglevee-O'Donovan, W. 1993. Clean stock production, pp. 277–286. In: *Geraniums IV*, J. W. White, ed. Ball Publishing, Geneva, Illinois.

Riedel, R. M. 1985. Nematode problems, pp. 295–312. In: *Diseases of Floral Crops*, vol. 1, D. L. Strider, ed. Praeger Scientific, New York.

Strider, D. L., and R. K. Jones. 1985. Poinsettias, pp. 351–404. In: *Diseases of Floral Crops*, vol. 1, D. L. Strider, ed. Praeger Scientific, New York.

10

Insect, Mite, and Slug Management

Raymond A. Cloyd and Christine A. Casey

Propagation poses special pest management challenges for the grower. Clean cuttings must be produced, but the unique conditions under which both stock plants and cuttings are grown can make this difficult. Stock plants that are held for too long may become a permanent source of infestation, while the high moisture level surrounding cuttings under mist can encourage fungus gnats and shore flies. Young plants are especially sensitive to pesticides and the wide mixture of plant species often grown together in the greenhouse increases the potential for many different insects or mites to be present simultaneously. Pesticides, or pest control materials, include insecticides, miticides, and molluscicides.

Insect, mite, and slug pests of cutting propagation can be divided into two categories: those that are a problem on stock plants and those that are a problem during propagation. The major arthropod pests of stock plants include whiteflies, thrips, aphids, mealybugs, and twospotted spider mites. The major pests that occur during propagation are fungus gnats, shore flies, and slugs. Dealing with pests in each of these situations requires different management strategies.

Greenhouse producers must implement a regular scouting program to effectively manage the major insect and mite pests. Detecting pest populations early and avoiding overlapping generations will increase the effectiveness of any control strategy. Yellow sticky cards can be used to detect the presence of pests such as whiteflies, thrips, winged aphids, and fungus gnat and shore fly adults. Routine visual inspection of stock plants, particularly leaf undersides, will be useful in detecting pest populations early. In addition, routinely checking yellow sticky cards and/or visually inspecting plants will also help to time spray applications of insecticides and miticides at the most vulnerable (susceptible) life stage.

The management of insect and mite pests on stock plants, and unrooted or rooted cuttings typically involves the use of pesticides. However, biological control has also been included in this chapter and should be considered along with the use of pesticides. To obtain control with pesticides, greenhouse producers must implement strategies that initially reduce pest populations, such as removing heavily infested leaves, older leaves, heavily infested plants, plant and substrate debris, and weeds.

Pesticides

Pesticides are one of the main control methods used against insects and mites. Pesticides can be divided into two groups based on their method of control: contact and systemic. Contact pesticides are those that actually contact the pest's body or are ingested by the pest. Systemic insecticides are absorbed by the plant, usually the roots, and move throughout the plant. A pest is controlled when it ingests plant material, such as leaf tissue or plant sap, containing the active ingredient. Although systemic insecticides may be able to control insects that are difficult to reach, most systemics do not accumulate in flowers, woody stems, and old leaves. Thus systemic insecticides may be most useful when young stock plants are first established and have a limited effect on older stock plants.

Timing

Pesticides are generally applied as soon as an infestation is apparent. They are often reapplied, depending on the residual life of the material, the pest life

115

cycle, and the method of control (systemic or contact). Be sure to consult the label for information on reapplication intervals.

Formulations

Pesticides are available in a variety of formulations, including wettable powders, emulsifiable concentrates, aerosols, fogs, smokes, soluble concentrates, water-soluble packets, and granules; some products or materials are available in more than one formulation. When considering which formulation to use, the ease of application includes the labor required to apply the product and the amount of time required to clean the equipment. For example, aerosols are easy to apply and require little labor, but they may not effectively control insects or mites located deep within the dense foliage of stock plants.

Pest resistance

Many insects and mites have developed resistance to one or more pesticides. As insects reproduce, genetic modifications can occur that are passed on to the offspring. In some cases, these gene changes make the insect more likely to survive an application of a particular insecticide. At first the gene may be rare in an insect population. If a product kills 95% of the insects it reaches, the remaining 5% may continue reproducing and pass the gene for resistance to their offspring. If insecticides with the same mode of action are used in successive applications, the gene becomes much more prevalent. Since the gene confers a survival advantage, insects without the resistance gene will be killed. This process continues until the insecticide eventually becomes ineffective. This process can also occur with mites and miticides.

Choosing and correctly applying the right insecticides and miticides as well as integrating pesticides with other tactics can lower the likelihood of resistance. In the past, growers were taught to rotate chemical classes to delay resistance. However, as more information became available on pesticide activity, it was discovered that different classes may have similar modes of action. Now the accepted way to reduce the probability of resistance is to rotate among pesticides with different modes of action after each generation, because insects and mites resistant to one mode of action may not be resistant to another. The Insecticide Resistance Action Committee (IRAC) has proposed a new rotation system based on pesticide mode of action (table 10.1), which will be printed on new pesticide labels.

Finally, remember that there are many reasons why an insecticide or miticide application may not provide control. The product may have been stored, mixed, or applied incorrectly, or the wrong product or rate may have been used. If a pesticide application appears ineffective, be sure to eliminate other causes of poor insect and mite control before deciding that resistance is the problem.

Phytotoxicity

Phytotoxicity can occur with the use of any insecticide or miticide. Before applying any pest control material to a crop, check the label to determine if the product is labeled for use on that plant species. Symptoms of phytotoxicity include one or more of the following: marginal necrosis, chlorotic or necrotic spots, and blighted or malformed flowers, buds, and young leaves.

A number of factors will increase the likelihood of phytotoxicity. Petals, bracts, and young leaves are more sensitive and likely to be damaged than mature tissue. Water stress or any other plant stress will also increase susceptibility to damage. The likelihood of phytotoxicity is higher at temperatures above 80° F (27° C); 65° to 80° F (18° to 27° C) is generally a safe temperature range. During warm periods of the year, apply insecticides and miticides late in the evening or early in the morning (before 9:00 A.M.). Phytotoxicity is also likely when the foliage is wet for an extended period (greater than six hours), and the pest control materials are applied by means of fogs, smokes, or aerosols.

Do not apply tank mixtures of two or more pest control materials unless thoroughly tested beforehand. Do not exceed recommended label rates, and use wetting agents only when warranted or specified on the label. Finally, be sure the application equipment has never been used to apply herbicides, and apply pest control materials uniformly to the crop. Generally, young plants damaged by chemical applications may grow new foliage that covers up the damaged tissue, but injury sites may encourage the development of botrytis.

Pesticide compatibility

Tank-mixing two or more pest control materials can increase effectiveness, but may also increase the potential for phytotoxicity. Do not mix pesticides unless you are certain that they are compatible. Consult the supplier or manufacturer to determine which pesticides can be applied together. Mixing

TABLE 10.1
Mode of action of greenhouse pest control materials

1. ACETYLCHOLINE ESTERASE INHIBITORS
Inhibit the enzyme cholinesterase (ChE) from clearing the acetylcholine (ACh) transmitter. This prevents termination of nerve impulse transmission and results in an accumulation of acetylcholine leading to hyperactivity, respiratory failure, exhaustion of metabolic energy, and death. Pest control materials:
- Acephate (Orthene or Precise)
- Chlorpyrifos (DuraGuard)
- Methiocarb (Mesurol)

2. GABA-GATED CHLORIDE CHANNEL BLOCKERS
Act on the gamma-aminobutyric acid (GABA) receptor by binding to the chloride channels thus preventing chloride ions from entering neurons. This disrupts GABA activity, which leads to hyperexcitation, paralysis, and death. Pest control material:
- Endosulfan (Thiodan)

3. SODIUM CHANNEL BLOCKERS
Destabilize nerve cell membranes by working on the sodium channels in the peripheral and central nervous system; slowing down or preventing closure. This results in stimulating nerve cells to produce repetitive discharges, eventually leading to paralysis and death. Pest control materials:
- Bifenthrin (Talstar, Attain)
- Cyfluthrin (Decathlon)
- Fenpropathrin (Tame)
- Fluvalinate (Mavrik)
- Lambda-cyhalothrin (Scimitar)
- Permethrin (Astro)
- Resmethrin

4. NICOTINIC ACETYLCHOLINE RECEPTOR DISRUPTORS
Act on the central nervous system, causing irreversible blockage of the post-synaptic nicotinergic acetylcholine receptors leading to disruption of nerve transmission and uncontrolled firing of nerves. This results in rapid pulses from a steady influx of sodium, leading to hyperexitation, convulsions, paralysis, and death. Pest control materials:
- Acetamiprid (TriStar)
- Clothianidin (Celero)
- Dinotefuran (Safari)
- Imidacloprid (Marathon)
- Thiamethoxam (Flagship)

5. NICOTINIC ACETYLCHOLINE RECEPTOR AGONIST
Disrupt binding of acetylcholine at nicotinic acetylcholine receptors located at the post-synaptic cell junctures, and negatively affect the gamma-amino butyric acid (GABA) gated ion channels. Pest control material:
- Spinosad (Conserve)

6. GABA CHLORIDE CHANNEL ACTIVATORS
Affect gamma-amino butyric acid (GABA) dependent chloride ion channels by increasing membrane permeability to chloride ions leading to inhibition of nerve transmission, paralysis, and death. Pest control material:
- Abamectin (Avid)

7. JUVENILE HORMONE MIMICS
Arrest development by causing insects to remain in a young or immature stage primarily by inhibiting metamorphosis (change in form). As a result, insects are unable to complete their life cycle. Pest control materials:
- Fenoxycarb (Preclude)
- Kinoprene (Enstar II)
- Pyriproxyfen (Distance)

8. CHITIN SYNTHESIS INHIBITORS
Prevent the formation of chitin, which is an essential component of an insect's exoskeleton causing the insect's cuticle to become thin and brittle. As a result, insects (and mites in the case of etoxazole) die while attempting to molt from one stage to the next. Pest control materials:
- Buprofezin (Talus)
- Cyromazine (Citation)
- Diflubenzuron (Adept)
- Etoxazole (TetraSan)
- Novaluron (Pedestal)

(Continued on page 118)

(Continued from page 117)

9. GROWTH AND EMBRYOGENESIS INHIBITORS

Disrupt the formation of the embryo during development or inhibit larval maturation. However, the specific mode of action and target site of activity are still not known. Pest control materials:

- Clofentezine (Ovation)
- Hexythiazox (Hexygon)

10. SELECTIVE FEEDING BLOCKERS

Inhibit feeding behavior of insects by interfering with neural regulation of fluid intake in the mouthparts. Pest control materials:

- Flonicamid (Aria)
- Pymetrozine (Endeavor)

11. DISRUPTORS OF INSECT MIDGUT MEMBRANES

Bind to specific receptor sites on the gut epithelium resulting in degradation of the gut lining and eventual starvation of the insect. Crystals release protein toxins (endotoxins) that bind to the mid-gut membrane receptor sites creating pores or channels. This paralyzes the digestive system and ruptures the midgut cell walls allowing ions to flow through the pores disrupting potassium and pH balances. As a result, the alkaline contents of the gut spill into the blood resulting in gut paralysis and death. Pest control materials:

- *Bacillus thuringiensis* var. *israelensis* (Gnatrol)
- *Bacillus thuringiensis* var. *kurstaki* (Dipel)

12. OXIDATIVE PHOSPHORYLATION UNCOUPLER

Uncouple oxidative phosphorylation, which is a major energy-producing step in cells, by disrupting the H+ gradient, which prevents the formation of adenosine tri-phosphate (ATP). Pest control material:

- Chlorfenapyr (Pylon)

13. OXIDATIVE PHOSPHORYLATION INHIBITOR

Inhibit oxidative phosphorylation at the site of dinitrophenol uncoupling, which disrupts the formation or synthesis of adenosine triphosphate (ATP). Pest control material:

- Fenbutatin-oxide (Vendex)

14. ECDYSONE ANTAGONIST

Disrupt the molting process by inhibiting biosynthesis or metabolism of the molting hormone—ecdysone. Pest control materials:

- Tebufenozide (Confirm)
- Azadirachtin (Azatin/Ornazin)[a]

15. MITOCHONDRIA ELECTRON TRANSPORT INHIBITORS

Inhibit Complex (site) I electron transport or act on the NADH-CoQ reductase site, or bind to the Qo center of Complex III in the mitochondria reducing energy production by preventing the synthesis of adenosine triphosphate (ATP). Pest control materials:

- Acequinocyl (Shuttle)
- Fenpyroximate (Akari)
- Pyridaben (Sanmite)

16. DESICCATION OR MEMBRANE DISRUPTORS

Damage the waxy layer of the exoskeleton of soft-bodied insects and mites by altering the chitin so that it cannot hold fluids resulting in desiccation (drying up) or smother insects by covering the breathing pores (spiracles). Pest control materials:

- Neem oil (Triact)
- Paraffinic oil (SunSpray UltraFine Oil)
- Potassium salts of fatty acids (Insecticidal Soap)

17. GABA-GATED ANTAGONIST

Blocks or closes gamma-amino butyric acid (GABA) activated chloride channels in the peripheral nervous system. Pest control material:

- Bifenazate (Floramite)

18. LIPID BIOSYNTHESIS INHIBITOR

Blocks the production of lipids, which are a group of compounds made up of carbon and hydrogen including fatty acids, oils, and waxes. Disrupts cell membrane structures and reduces sources of energy. Pest control materials:

- Spiromesifen (Judo)

[a]In addition to acting as an insect growth regulator, azadirachtin acts a feeding deterrent/inhibitor, oviposition inhibitor, repellent, egg-laying deterrent, sterilant, and/or direct toxin.

pesticides that are incompatible may result in phytotoxicity, decreased effectiveness of one or both products, and lead to the formation of insoluble precipitates. To test for compatibility, collect a sample of the spray solution in a clear jar after the pesticides have been mixed in water, and check the sample after fifteen to twenty-five minutes. If the materials are compatible, the solution should appear homogenous. If the materials are incompatible, they will separate and a noticeable layer will be present.

Pesticide safety

It is important to handle and apply pesticides properly. Many countries have regulations designed to protect the safety of workers when pesticides are being used. In the United States, the federal Worker Protection Standard (WPS) is one of the most important regulations. Most states and some local governments have additional safety and licensing requirements for individuals who apply pesticides. Anyone who works with pesticides or supervises personnel who work with pesticides may need to obtain a license or be certified. Extension service personnel or the Department of Agriculture in each state should be able to provide further information.

Biological Control

Biological control is an option that may be used in integrated pest management (IPM) programs. Use of biological control can help avoid pesticide phytotoxicity to mixed crops as well as alleviate concerns regarding reentry intervals and worker safety. However, the challenges of using biological control in propagation are the short production time (which may be too short for effective control) and the need for cuttings to be free of insects (although natural enemies might remain on the cuttings). Despite these challenges biological control can be part of a successful IPM program during propagation. This chapter will review the biology and use of common natural enemies and provide examples of IPM programs. In all cases, information presented about release rates and timing is intended only to serve as a guideline, since specific conditions in individual greenhouses may differ. Consult your supplier of natural enemies or Extension advisor for more information.

Getting started
with biological control

You must be fully committed to undertaking a bio-

logical control program, because natural enemies are living organisms that function differently from other pest control tactics. Natural enemies do not act as quickly as pesticides, and they may be shipped in a stage that does not attack pests, so they generally are not used as rescue treatments. The best use of natural enemies in propagation is through prophylactic releases, typically when pests are first observed, but occasionally before pests are discovered, if they are expected and have been problems in the past. The use of natural enemies must be carefully evaluated, so biological control should not be implemented unless a scouting program is already in place. Start by using biological control for one pest problem on a specific crop in a limited area of the greenhouse. Practice by ordering a small quantity of natural enemies before you make your first release, so you are familiar with the process of receiving the shipment and assessing its viability. Expand to larger areas and more crops as you gain experience and confidence.

Issues that must be considered before any biological control program is initiated are cost, availability and efficacy of natural enemies, compatibility with pesticides, and appropriate environmental conditions. In addition, you should find a reputable supplier and order your natural enemies early enough so the supplier can provide you with quality product. Consult your Extension advisor or biological control supplier regarding release rates and timing of releases. Biological control programs are typically designed to maintain a balance between pest and natural enemy populations so there is always a viable food source for the natural enemies and the population does not disappear. In short-term greenhouse crops, however, it is often recommended to release higher numbers (inundative releases) to increase pest mortality.

Cost

Biological control will often cost more initially than the use of pesticides. However, in the long term, the cost of using biological control may be comparable to the use of pesticides. Additionally, the cost of natural enemies might be offset by their advantages, such as no reentry intervals and reduced worker, environmental, and phytotoxicity risks.

Compatibility with pesticides

In most cases, insecticides and miticides do not distinguish between natural enemies and harmful insects and mites. However, many natural enemies and pesticides can be used together, especially when using reduced-risk pesticides, which may be less harmful to natural enemies than conventional or older pesticides. If biological control is going to be used successfully, the entire pest management program must include methods compatible with natural enemies. Consult a biological control supplier to obtain information on the pest control materials that are compatible with natural enemies. Most biological control suppliers maintain web sites with compatibility information.

Compatibility is not an all-or-nothing situation. Insecticides and miticides may be harmful when they contact a natural enemy directly but are safe when dry. Thus delaying a release until after a pesticide application may be sufficient, depending on the pesticide. Also, a pesticide may be more harmful at a higher rate than a lower rate. In situations where the pest control material causes some mortality of the natural enemies, a higher release rate may be warranted.

In general, insecticidal soap and horticultural oil are not harmful to natural enemies once the applications have dried. However, natural enemies may be killed by direct sprays of both materials. Fungicides and insect growth regulators are generally compatible with most natural enemies, whereas organophosphate, carbamate, and pyrethroid-based pest control materials are not compatible with natural enemies. Many of the newer pesticides are more specific in their activity than older broad-spectrum materials and thus are more likely to be compatible. Pesticide formulation may also influence compatibility.

Insecticide and miticide residues may impact natural enemies, so allow a one- to three-week interval before making any releases. However, this depends on the type of pest control material. Pesticide residues remaining in sprayers may pose a risk to natural enemies and microbials that are applied with a sprayer, such as insect pathogens and entomopathogenic nematodes, which are microscopic worm-shaped organisms that causes disease in insects. It is best to dedicate sprayers for applying pesticides separate from those used for applying natural enemies.

Viability of natural enemies

Biological control suppliers try to ensure that the natural enemies they sell are healthy and packaged properly. Despite this, problems may develop during production or shipping. You should examine natural enemies when they arrive at the greenhouse to be sure they are alive. Natural enemies should be scheduled to arrive at the greenhouse within one to two days, and someone should be available to receive the shipment. Be sure to protect packages from extreme heat, sun, or cold, and refrigerate them, if specified by the supplier. Make releases immediately upon arrival, and avoid using any yellow sticky cards for at least one week after releasing natural enemies, especially parasitoids, which may be attracted to the yellow sticky cards.

Efficacy of Natural Enemies

In general, natural enemies do not kill pests as quickly as pesticides, and some insects and mites will continue to feed while they are being killed; biological control must therefore be initiated when pest populations are low. Natural enemies are often most effective at maintaining low pest populations, rather than reducing a high pest population. Some natural enemies will starve if they eliminate their prey, so additional releases may be required if pests return. Several natural enemies can switch to alternative food sources until the preferred prey returns.

Using biological control on stock plants

Propagating from clean stock plants is the first step to producing pest-free cuttings. Biological control is often not considered on these plants, because some insects or mites (either harmful or beneficial) may remain on the stock plants. Growers who use biological control during production, however, might consider the presence of natural enemies a benefit.

In some cases, using natural enemies on stock plants may be preferable to using pest control materials. For example, mealybugs, which have an extended development time, can be unnoticed on stock plants and are difficult to control with insecticides. Natural enemies may be able to control small pest populations more effectively than insecticides. In addition, the dense canopies of stock plants often reduce the effectiveness of pesticide applications, whereas natural enemies can more easily penetrate the foliar canopy.

Using biological control on poinsettias

Biological control is often not considered for controlling whiteflies on poinsettias because of the efficacy of systemic insecticides. However, biological control of whiteflies during poinsettia propagation may complement an insecticide program. For example, poinsettia cuttings that initially contain immature stages of whiteflies may be dipped into a solution of the insect pathogen *Beauveria bassiana* according to label directions. Additionally, using biological control during propagation may enable growers to start finished plant production with clean cuttings free of potentially harmful insecticide residues.

Also, if a systemic insecticide is used during production, it may not be used during propagation. Be sure to read the label before making more than one application to a crop. Unfortunately, most systemic insecticides remain effective for only eight to eleven weeks, which is three to four weeks less than the production time. The concern over damaging poinsettia bracts, which are especially sensitive to pesticide applications, means that it may be more appropriate to use another insecticide initially and delay the application of a systemic insecticide until the third or fourth week of production. The use of natural enemies may be an option early in production to allow the grower to delay the application of a systemic insecticide.

Pests of Stock Plants

Whiteflies
Biology and damage
The primary whitefly species encountered on stock plant material include the silverleaf whitefly, *Bemisia argentifolii*, and the greenhouse whitefly, *Trialeurodes vaporariorum* (fig. 10.1). In addition, the bandedwing whitefly, *Trialeurodes abutiloneus*, may be present in the greenhouse from late summer through early fall. However, the bandedwing whitefly is less problematic than the other two whitefly species.

The whitefly life cycle consists of egg, three nymphal stages, pupa, and adult. Most whitefly life stages are generally located on leaf undersides. The insects use their piercing-sucking mouthparts to feed within the vascular tissues of plants.

Adult whiteflies are typically white, narrow, and approximately 0.08 to 0.1 in. (2 to 3 mm) in length. Adult females deposit eggs on the underside of mature leaves. Greenhouse whitefly females tend to lay their eggs in a crescent-shaped pattern, whereas silverleaf whitefly females lay their eggs scattered over the leaf surface. The spindle-shaped eggs are

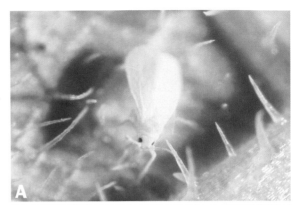
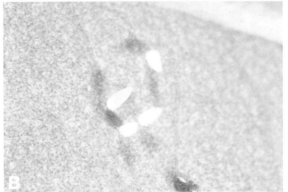

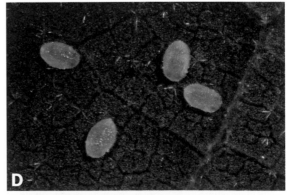

Figure 10.1. Whiteflies shown in various life stages: (A) adult silverleaf whitefly, *Bemisia argentifolia*; (B) whitefly eggs on the underside of a leaf; (C) whitefly nymphs feeding on a leaf underside; and (D) whitefly pupae stage, which is tolerant of most insecticides. (R. Cloyd)

white when first laid, but eventually turn amber brown (silverleaf whitefly) or dark gray (greenhouse whitefly).

The eggs hatch in approximately ten to twelve days at temperatures between 65° to 75° F (18° to 24° C). The first nymphal stage, or crawler, hatches from the egg, migrates a short distance of 0.25 to 0.33 in. (6 to 8 mm) and eventually settles down to feed. At this stage, the nymphs do not move from the spot until they undergo a pupal stage, and then emerge as adults. Approximately four to five days before adult emergence, the nymph enters a pupal stage. At this time, the red eyespots of the developing adult are visible through the insect skin or pupal case.

Silverleaf whiteflies take approximately thirty-two days and greenhouse whiteflies approximately thirty-nine days to develop from egg to adult at temperatures between 65° to 75° F (18° to 24° C). The life cycle takes less time as temperatures increase, especially during late spring and summer. It is important to realize that sixteen to twenty days of the developmental time are spent in life stages (egg and pupa) that are tolerant of many foliar and systemic insecticides. A single female adult whitefly can lay eggs one to three days after emerging as an adult, and she can lay up to 200 eggs and live about twenty-five to thirty days, depending on environmental conditions. Silverleaf and greenhouse whitefly identification can be confirmed using the pupal and adult stages. Silverleaf whitefly pupae appear rounded, dome shaped, and do not have parallel sides; the pupae have no hairs around the edges. Adult silverleaf whiteflies have a light yellowish body with white wings, and the wings are held rooflike over the body at a 45° angle. Greenhouse whitefly pupae have parallel sides that are perpendicular to the leaf surface, giving a disk- or cake-shaped appearance; the pupae have fringed hairs (setae) around the edges. Greenhouse whitefly adults have a white body and white wings, with the wings held almost horizontally over the body.

The nymphal or immature stages of whiteflies cause direct plant damage by feeding on plant fluids with their piercing-sucking mouthparts, which may result in leaf yellowing, leaf distortion, plant stunting, plant wilting, and possibly plant death, depending on the level of infestation. Additionally, during the feeding process the nymphal stages produce a clear, sticky liquid material called honeydew, which serves as a growing medium for black sooty mold fungi. The sooty mold fungi can reduce the ability of stock plants to photosynthesize or manufacture food. Heavily infested plants, if disturbed, produce a cloud of flying whitefly adults. These adults may also be very obvious when at rest on leaf undersides. In addition to causing direct plant injury, whiteflies have the ability to cause indirect injury by transmitting various diseases, including bacteria and viruses.

Chemical management

Insecticides with whitefly activity include a number of systemic, contact, and insect growth regulators. Systemic insecticides are generally less effective on older stock plants due to the woodiness of the plant material. In addition, it will take longer to obtain adequate control, and the time it takes to achieve sufficient control may not prevent overlapping generations from occurring. When using short-residual contact insecticides or insect growth regulators, it is important to obtain thorough coverage, particularly on the underside of leaves, where a majority of the whitefly life stages reside.

A number of insecticides have translaminar activity, which means that the material resides within the leaf tissue, providing a reservoir of active ingredient. Be sure to read the label to determine which insecticides have translaminar activity. When using these materials, coverage is not as important because whiteflies will take up the active ingredient when feeding within the leaf tissues. High-volume applications are generally needed to obtain sufficient coverage on the underside of leaves. Aerosols are less effective when stock plants have a dense canopy of foliage; as a result, it is difficult to obtain sufficient coverage to provide control. Rotate insecticides with different modes of action to avoid the development of resistant whitefly populations.

Biological control

Biological control methods for greenhouse whiteflies and silverleaf whiteflies have been extensively researched, resulting in the commercialization of several predators, parasitoids, and pathogens. All whitefly parasitoids attack the nymphs, while predators and pathogens affect all life stages. Parasitoids, often referred to as parasitic wasps, kill by parasitism and host feeding, which occurs when a female wasp punctures the body of a whitefly nymph and feeds on the body fluids that exude out. Higher kill rates may occur from host feeding than from parasitism. The female wasp may also lay an egg in the same nymph. Regular releases of parasitoids are often required on short-term crops. *Encarsia fomosa* is a parasitic wasp that is most effective on greenhouse whitefly, with only limited success on silverleaf whitefly. This wasp parasitizes immature whiteflies, primarily the third and fourth instars, and will host feed on smaller instars. All whitefly life stages are often present on a crop at the same time, so regular releases are generally needed until all whiteflies have progressed through the susceptible stages. *Encarsia* is shipped as parasitized whitefly pupae glued to cards that are placed in the greenhouse, usually once a week. Place the cards face down, as close as possible to the bottom of the plant. Because whitefly nymphs are located on leaf undersides, inverting the cards mimics the orientation from which the wasps normally emerge. In addition, the wasps fly in an upward spiral as they emerge, so placing cards near the bottom ensures they will encounter nymphs as they fly upward. Consult a biological control supplier to determine release rates. *Encarsia* is most effective at 80° F (27° C) and 50 to 80% relative humidity. It is susceptible to wet sprays of many pest control materials, but is compatible with insecticidal soap, horticultural oil, most insect growth regulators, and certain fungicides when residues have dried.

Eretmocerus eremicus is a parasitic wasp used for controlling silverleaf whitefly, although it will also attack greenhouse whitefly. This wasp parasitizes immature whiteflies, preferring the second and third instars. In addition, host feeding may kill all immature stages. Because all whitefly life stages are typically present in a crop, regular releases are generally required until all whiteflies have progressed through the susceptible stages.

Eretmocerus is shipped as parasitized whitefly pupae glued to cards that are placed in the greenhouse, usually once a week. As with *Encarsia*, cards are placed face down, as close as possible to the bottom of the plant, to increase the likelihood that the wasps will encounter nymphs as they fly upward. The suggested release rate is three to five wasps per plant per week, but consult a biological control supplier to determine release rates for your greenhouse operation. These wasps are attracted to yellow sticky cards, which should be removed before making any releases. *Eretmocerus* develops faster than the silverleaf whitefly at temperatures between 77° and 84° F (25° and 29° C). Products containing a mixture of *Encarsia formosa* and *Eretmocerus eremicus* are available for use in greenhouses with both whitefly species.

Delphastus catalinae is a predatory lady beetle that feeds on all stages of whitefly. Both the larval and adult stages are predaceous. It is most successful against high whitefly populations and is typically released in whitefly hot spots, in conjunction with other whitefly natural enemies. The beetles will reproduce in the greenhouse if they are able to consume large numbers of whitefly eggs. Yellow sticky cards should be removed before releasing any beetles.

Beauveria bassiana is an insect pathogen that may be used to control whiteflies. The fungal spores germinate and develop into hyphae (threadlike strands), which penetrate the whitefly cuticle and initiate infections. Infected whiteflies turn orange-brown. Uninfected whiteflies may pick up spores as they walk across a leaf containing spores or an infected host. Unlike most insect pathogens, *Beauveria* can infect whiteflies at a relative humidity as low as 45%, although it is more effective at humidity levels greater than 75%. The fungus should be used when the whitefly population is low. Delay fungicide applications for forty-eight hours after applying *Beauveria* to avoid killing any spores.

Thrips
Biology and damage
The western flower thrips, *Frankliniella occidentalis*, is the primary thrips species that is a problem on stock plants and the only species covered in this section (fig. 10.2). Its life cycle consists of egg, nymph, pupa, and adult. The western flower thrips is less than 0.08 in. (2 mm) in length and possesses piercing-sucking mouthparts. Adult thrips females lay eggs in leaf tissue. The female may live for up to forty-five days and can lay between 150 to 250 eggs during her lifetime. Eggs hatch into nymphs, which feed on leaves and flowers. Thrips may pupate in leaf debris or substrates. Later, adults emerge; they normally feed on the new growth and flowers of stock plants.

The life cycle is temperature dependent, generally requiring two to three weeks from egg to adult. During cooler temperatures, the life cycle from egg to adult takes longer. However, as temperatures increase, the thrips life cycle is shortened, causing populations to rise dramatically. For example, the life cycle can take seven to ten days to complete at 85° F (29° C). As a result, thrips populations may fluctuate over the course of the growing season.

Western flower thrips directly damage stock plants by feeding in terminal buds before they open, causing premature bud abortion, distortion, or deformation of new growth. Thrips feeding on leaf buds before they open can result in leaf scarring. Western flower thrips also cause indirect damage by vectoring impatiens necrotic spot virus (INSV) and tomato spotted wilt virus (TSWV). Since there are no pest control materials that control viruses, all infected stock plants and neighboring plants must be removed promptly.

Chemical management

There are a number of effective insecticides that can be used to control western flower thrips on stock plant material; however, relying solely on insecticides to manage thrips will most likely lead to the development of resistant thrips populations. Contact insecticides are primarily used to control thrips, and applications must be made before thrips enter the terminal growth of stock plants. Once thrips enter the buds, they are very difficult to control. As a result, high-volume applications are generally needed to increase the likelihood of contacting thrips inside the buds. Because of the small size of the spray particles, aerosols are not very effective in penetrating the unopened terminal growth. When using insect growth regulators to manage thrips, it is important to make applications before thrips populations build up, because these insecticides are active only on the immature or larval stages. It is extremely important to rotate insecticides with different modes of activity to avoid the development of resistant thrips populations.

Biological control

Neoseiulus cucumeris (also known as *Amblyseiulus cucumeris*) is a predatory mite that feeds on first instar thrips larvae. The mite is distributed in the greenhouse in sachets placed every 25 to 30 sq. ft. (2.3 to 2.8 m²) on the bench so that the sachets touch the plant canopy. Each sachet contains bran and bran mites that serve as a food source for the approximately 200 predatory mites, which reproduce in the sachet and emerge over a six-week period. This predator can also be purchased in a bulk formulation that is distributed by hand. The mite is most effective when the temperature is 70° F (21° C) or higher, and the relative humidity is greater than 70%.

Neoseiulus should be released before thrips populations begin increasing or are well-established. This predator will disperse more readily if pots or foliage of adjacent plants are touching. Individual sachets

Figure 10.2. Western flower thrips, *Frankliniella occidentalis*, (A) adult, (B) adult on leaf, and (C) nymph. (D) Feeding injury to chrysanthemum leaf; note the silvered appearance. (R. Cloyd)

can be placed on hanging baskets as well. Replace one-fourth to one-third of the sachets every three weeks to maintain a constant supply of predators. Avoid getting the sachets wet since moisture can cause the bran to rot. If present, slugs and mice occasionally feed on the sachets. *Neoseiulus* will feed on pollen as an alternative food source if thrips populations are low.

Beauveria bassiana is an insect pathogen that may be used to control thrips. The fungal spores germinate and develop into hyphae, which penetrate the thrips cuticle and initiate infections. Uninfected thrips may pick up spores as they walk across a leaf containing spores or an infected host. In contrast to most insect pathogens, *Beauveria* can infect thrips at a relative humidity as low as 45%, although it is more effective at humidity levels greater than 75%. The fungus should be used when the thrips population is low. Delay any fungicide applications for forty-eight hours after applying *Beauveria* to avoid killing spores.

Aphids
Biology and damage
Aphids can be one of the most difficult insect pests to control on stock plants (fig. 10.3). A number of different aphid species attack stock plants; they include the green peach aphid, *Myzus persicae*; rose aphid, *Macrosiphum rosae*; chrysanthemum aphid, *Macrosiphoniella sanborni*; melon or cotton aphid, *Aphis gossypii*; foxglove aphid, *Aulacorthum solani*; and potato aphid, *Macrosiphum euphorbiae*. Aphid color will vary depending on the particular host plant fed upon; color therefore should not be used to identify aphid species.

Aphids are small, soft-bodied insects approximately 0.04 to 0.10 in. (1 to 3 mm) long that possess tubes, called *cornicles*, on the end of the abdomen. Male aphids are typically absent from the greenhouse. Females do not need to mate to reproduce; this process is called *parthenogenesis*. Females give birth to live female offspring that can start producing their own young, or nymphs, in seven to ten days. Each of these females can then give birth to sixty to one hundred live young per day for twenty to thirty days.

The ability of aphids to reproduce rapidly can create large population explosions within a short period of time, particularly during late spring and summer. Aphid reproduction depends on plant quality and the nutritional content of plant tissues. Aphids in

Figure 10.3. Aphids are shown on a leaf (A); notice the tubes (cornicles) emerging from their backs. They use their piercing-sucking mouthparts to remove fluids from vascular tissue; here they are shown feeding on (B) plant tissues, (C) terminal growth, and (D) a leaf underside. (R. Cloyd)

greenhouses are normally wingless; however, winged forms will develop when the host plant gets crowded or when plant quality declines, thus expediting aphid movement throughout a greenhouse.

Aphids typically feed on new terminal growth and on the underside of stock plant leaves. However, distribution on plants will vary depending on the aphid species. For example, green peach aphid populations are commonly located on the upper leaves and stems, whereas melon or cotton aphid populations are distributed throughout the plant canopy.

Aphids damage foliage by removing plant fluids with their piercing-sucking mouthparts. Feeding on new growth results in young leaves appearing crinkled, curled, or distorted. Aphids may also cause plant stunting. Additionally, aphids produce a clear sticky liquid material called honeydew, which serves as a growing medium for black sooty mold fungi. The sooty mold fungi can reduce the ability of stock plants to photosynthesize or manufacture food. Aphids are also capable of transmitting many destructive viruses.

Chemical management

A number of insecticides are active on aphids. With contact insecticides thorough coverage of all plant parts is essential. Rotate insecticides with different modes of action to avoid the development of resistant aphid populations. High-volume applications are generally needed to obtain sufficient coverage on the underside of leaves. Aerosols are less effective when stock plants have a dense plant canopy; as a result, it is difficult to obtain adequate plant coverage with sprays to control the aphids.

Systemic insecticides, which are insecticides that are translocated throughout the plant, are generally less effective on older stock plants due to the woodiness of the plant material. In addition, it takes longer to obtain adequate control, and the time it does take to achieve sufficient control may not prevent overlapping generations from occurring. When using short-residual contact insecticides or insect growth regulators it is important to get thorough coverage, particularly on plant parts where aphids tend to reside.

Biological control

There are several natural enemies commercially available for both the green peach aphid and the melon or cotton aphid. These natural enemies must be used when aphid populations are low, since aphids can multiply rapidly and will develop faster

than they are killed. The convergent lady beetle, *Hippodamia convergens*, is a predator that may be released for aphid control. Both adults and larvae prey on aphids, but may switch to other insects, honeydew, or nectar when aphids are low in number or not present. If beetle eggs or larvae are not observed, then additional releases may be necessary. Adults may be compatible with certain pest control materials.

The green lacewing species *Chrysoperla rufilabris* tolerates humid conditions more than *Chrysoperla carnea*, so it is the one typically used in greenhouses. Adults feed on nectar, pollen, and honeydew. The larvae feed on aphids as well as other greenhouse pests, including mites and whiteflies. The larvae are cannibalistic and must be released in a manner that minimizes encounters with other lacewing larvae. All lacewing life stages can be purchased from commercial biological control suppliers; however, eggs or larvae are preferred because adults may disperse to search for food before laying eggs. Green lacewings are compatible with certain pest control materials.

The aphid midge, *Aphidoletes aphidimyza*, is another predator used to control various aphid species. The midge larvae bite aphids on their legs, inject a toxin, and extract body fluids. The adults feed on honeydew and are rarely seen because they are short lived and active at night. They are effective summer predators but will enter diapause, which is a period of slow growth and development, that occurs under short days unless supplemental lighting is provided. *Aphidoletes* are shipped as pupae, so they must pass through the adult and egg stages before they begin foraging for aphids.

Aphidius colemani is a parasitic wasp that attacks green peach and melon or cotton aphids. The wasp lays an egg in an immature aphid or adult, and the developing larva feeds within the aphid, causing it to turn brown and papery. These are called aphid mummies, and an adult wasp emerges from them. Mummies are visible among a population of aphids, so parasitism can be determined.

Aphidius matricariae is a parasitic wasp similar to *A. colemani*, but it is specific to the green peach aphid. It kills aphids in the same manner as *A. colemani*, and percent parasitism can be determined in the same manner. Adults of this species feed on nectar or honeydew.

The insect pathogen *Beauveria bassiana* may be used against aphids. It is most effective against adults because the rapidly developing immature aphids shed their skins before the fungus can penetrate, resulting in the need for additional applications for adequate control.

Twospotted spider mite
Biology and damage

The primary mite species of stock plants is the twospotted spider mite, *Tetranychus urticae*, particularly in late spring and summer (fig. 10.4). It is a problem on stock plants for a number of reasons including small size, which makes it difficult to detect; rapid life cycle; wide host range; feeding location primarily on leaf undersides, making it hard to see; and resistance to miticides.

Twospotted spider mites prefer warm, dry conditions with low relative humidity. It is typically oval shaped and yellow-orange, green, or red. Adults have two dark spots on both sides of the abdomen. Females are larger than males. Adult females live approximately thirty days and lay small spherical transparent eggs on leaf undersides. A single adult female can lay between 50 and 200 eggs. The eggs hatch into six-legged larvae that undergo two eight-legged nymphal stages before reaching adulthood. The life cycle from egg to adult generally takes one to two weeks, depending on temperature. For example, the life cycle from egg to adult takes fourteen days at 70° F (21° C) and seven days at 85° F (29° C).

Twospotted spider mite populations are normally located on the underside of older leaves of stock plants, where they feed within plant cells, removing chlorophyll (green pigment) with their styletlike mouthparts. The mites feed primarily near the midrib and veins of plant leaves. Damaged leaves appear stippled and bronzed with small silvery gray to yellowish speckles, and eventually fall off the plant. If high populations are present, then webbing will be noticeable.

Chemical management

Various miticides are effective in controlling twospotted spider mites on stock plants. Most have contact activity, so thorough coverage of all plant parts, especially leaf undersides, is critical. A number of miticides have translaminar activity, which means that the material resides within the leaf tissue, providing a reservoir of active ingredient. Be sure to read the label to determine which miticides have translaminar activity. With these materials coverage is not as important, because mites will take up the

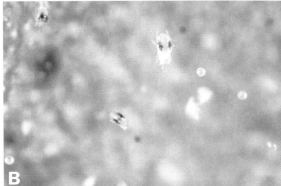

Figure 10.4. Two-spotted spider mite, *Tetranychus urticae*, (A) adult, and (B) adult with eggs, the spherical objects, on the underside of a leaf. Plant injury caused by the two-spotted spider mite is shown on young foliage (C) and (D) New Guinea impatiens; notice the stippling and, in the case of the New Guinea impatiens, the bronzing of the leaves. (R. Cloyd)

active ingredient when feeding within the leaf tissues. Some miticides have ovicidal (egg-killing) activity. These miticides must be used on stock plants before the spider mites become abundant, or they may be tank-mixed with a miticide that is active on larvae, nymphs, and/or adults. Be sure to read the label before tank-mixing any miticides.

During late spring and summer the interval between spray applications should be no more than seven days for short-residual contact miticides to prevent the development of excessively high mite populations. High-volume applications are generally needed to obtain sufficient coverage to contact mites on the underside of leaves. Aerosols are generally less effective when stock plants have a dense canopy of foliage; as a result, it is difficult to obtain adequate coverage to provide control. Rotate miticides with different modes of activity to avoid the development of resistant twospotted spider mite populations.

Biological control

The predatory mite *Phytoseiulus persimilis* may be used to control the twospotted spider mite. *Phytoseiulus* works best at temperatures between 70° and 85° F (21° and 29° C) and high relative humidity (70 to 90%). Plants that are touching will facilitate predator movement among plants and will promote high relative humidity within the canopy. It is important to release the predator when twospotted spider mite levels are low. The onset of cool, short days in late fall and winter may can cause twospotted spider mites to turn orange. They should not be confused with the rapidly moving predatory mite, which is slightly larger, bright orange, and pear-shaped. The spider mite predator *Neoseiulus* (formerly known as *Amblyseius*) *californicus* should be used under cool temperatures and short-day conditions, or when spider mite populations are low.

Mealybugs
Biology and damage

The primary mealybug species that is a problem on stock plants is the citrus mealybug, *Planococcus citri* (fig. 10.5). Mealybugs cause direct plant injury by feeding on plant fluids in the vascular tissues (in the phloem) with their piercing-sucking mouthparts. This causes leaf yellowing, plant wilting, and stunting. In addition, mealybugs excrete honeydew, a clear sticky liquid that serves as an excellent growing medium for black sooty mold fungi. The sooty mold

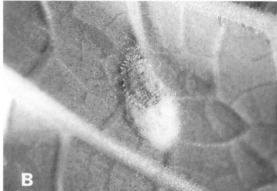

Figure 10.5. Citrus mealybug, *Planococcus citri*, (A) adult; (B) female laying eggs within the cottony mass; (C) immature stage after molting (note the white object on the right is the cast-skin); and (D) various life stages including adults and immatures. (R. Cloyd)

fungi can reduce the ability of stock plants to photosynthesize or manufacture food. Mealybugs prefer to congregate in large numbers at leaf junctures (where the petiole meets the stem), on the underside of leaves, and on stem tips.

The general mealybug life cycle consists of egg, several immature (crawler) stages, and adult. Before females die, they lay eggs underneath their bodies. The eggs hatch into mobile crawlers that move around seeking a place to settle and feed. Once settled, mealybugs go through several growth stages, or instars, before becoming adults. Male mealybugs eventually become winged individuals that mate with females and then die, whereas females continue developing and then die after laying eggs. The eggs remain protected under the body of the dead female until they hatch. A single mealybug female is capable of laying up to 600 eggs.

Mealybugs have a longer developmental period from egg to adult than most other greenhouse pests including aphids, whiteflies, thrips, and spider mites. The life cycle from egg to adult generally takes around sixty days, depending on temperature. Since mealybugs (except for adult males) do not fly, they will not be caught on yellow sticky cards, which means that visual inspections will be required to detect early mealybug infestations.

Chemical management

Adult mealybugs are difficult to control because they form a waxy protective covering that is impervious to most insecticides. In addition, because most insecticides have no activity on eggs, at least two to three applications may be needed to achieve satisfactory control, especially when dealing with overlapping generations. The crawler stage, which does not possess a waxy covering, is the most susceptible to insecticides including insect growth regulators, insecticidal soap, and horticultural oils.

Thorough coverage is essential when using contact insecticides because mealybugs are located in inaccessible areas, such as the base of leaf petioles and the underside of leaves. Adding a surfactant such as a spreader-sticker to the spray solution may help in improving coverage and penetration. Systemic insecticides have activity on the feeding stages of mealybugs; however, they need to be applied before mealybug populations become excessive and while the plants are actively growing, so the active ingredient can move to the locations where mealybugs feed.

Biological control

Two natural enemies of mealybugs can be purchased commercially. The mealybug's waxy coating and inaccessible feeding locations can hinder insecticidal control; therefore, biological control can be an important part of a mealybug management program. The mealybug destroyer, *Cryptolaemus montrouzieri*, is a beetle that consumes all stages of the citrus mealybug. The predator is released as an adult and is most effective at 80° F (27° C). Under favorable conditions, when temperatures are above 68° F (20° C) and an ample food supply is available, the mealybug destroyer will reproduce in the greenhouse. It will feed on scale crawlers or immature whiteflies if mealybugs are not present. This predator is most effective when mealybugs are abundant but usually will not eliminate a population.

Using the mealybug destroyer in combination with *Leptomastix dactylopii* will ensure better control of citrus mealybug. *Leptomastix dactylopii* is a parasitic wasp that attacks only citrus mealybugs. It prefers to lay its eggs in larger mealybug stages, such as the third and early fourth instars and female adults. The wasp is very effective at locating citrus mealybugs when the populations are low. *Cryptolaemus* will feed on newly parasitized mealybugs, but will avoid them as the wasp reaches maturity. Both of these natural enemies are compatible with certain pest control materials.

Pests During Propagation

Fungus gnats
Biology and damage

Fungus gnats, *Bradysia* species, are among the few greenhouse pests in which the damaging larval stage is located in the growing substrate (fig. 10.6). Fungus gnats have a life cycle consisting of egg, four larval stages, pupa, and adult. A generation can be completed in twenty to twenty-eight days, depending on temperature. Fungus gnat adults are winged, 0.125 in. (3 mm) long, with elongated legs and antennae. The adults, which live for approximately seven to ten days, tend to fly around the surface of the substrate.

Females deposit 100 to 200 eggs into the cracks and crevices of growing media. They are highly attracted to microbially active substrates containing peat moss and pine bark. Eggs, which are yellowish white to opaque, hatch into white transparent or slightly translucent legless larvae that are approximately 0.25 in. (6 mm) long. A characteristic diagnostic feature of fungus gnat larvae is the presence of a black head capsule, which is absent in shore fly larvae (described below). Larvae are generally located within the top 1 to 2 in. (2.5 to 5 cm) of the substrate. However, they may be found throughout the substrate profile. The larvae are highly attracted to cuttings before callus formation.

Fungus gnat larvae are a problem during propagation because they tunnel into cuttings and stems, causing the collapse and eventual death of cuttings. In addition, wounds created during feeding may allow secondary pathogens, such as *Pythium*, to enter. Both the adult and larva are capable of disseminating and transmitting diseases.

Chemical management

Insecticides can be used to control fungus gnats and shore flies; however, they must be used in conjunction with algae control. It is important not to rely solely on insecticides to control these pests. Many of the insecticides registered for fungus gnats and shore flies are insect growth regulators (IGRs). Insect growth regulators are primarily effective on the larval stage, having no adult activity. A number of conventional insecticides and a bacterial insecticide can be used to control fungus gnat larvae. In propagation systems these insecticides are applied as a drench or a "sprench," which is a high-volume spray application to the substrate. Be sure to use the lowest label rate of an insecticide to avoid damaging any cutting roots. Both adult fungus gnats and shore flies may be controlled with conventional insecticide sprays or aerosols.

Biological control

Several options are available for fungus gnat control and are all directed against the larvae. *Hypoaspis miles* is a soil-dwelling predatory mite that feeds on fungus gnat larvae. The mite is packaged in vermiculite, which is distributed over the soil surface or incorporated into the substrate before planting. Mites are released at approximately 10 mites per sq. ft. (108/m²). *Hypoaspis* will reproduce in the greenhouse, so one or two applications are often sufficient. The mites are active when soil temperatures are above 50° F (10° C), and they are most effective in pot-to-pot spacing or flats as both situations facilitate mite dispersal. They will feed on alternative prey (such as thrips pupae) in the absence of fungus

Figure 10.6. Fungus gnat, *Bradysia* species. (A) adult on yellow sticky card—note the Y-shaped vein in the forewings; (B) larvae—note the black head capsule; and (C) eggs. (D) Larval damage to dahlia; the plant on the left had at least seventy fungus gnat larvae in the pot, whereas the plant on the right contained fewer than ten larvae in the pot. (C image from E. Zaborski, Illinois Natural History Survey; the remainder from R. Cloyd)

gnat larvae. Certain pest control materials applied as drenches are compatible with *Hypoaspis*.

Bacillus thuringiensis var. *israelensis* is the subspecies of a soilborne bacterium used for the control of fungus gnat larvae. This bacterium specifically attacks certain larvae in the order Diptera, the flies. However, the material has no activity on shore fly larvae. It must be ingested by the fungus gnat larva, after which a lethal protein crystal is released into the insect's gut. Although feeding stops within a few hours, death can take several days.

Bacillus is most effective on young fungus gnat larvae that are actively feeding; older larvae must feed longer to ingest a lethal dose. One to three applications may be needed, depending on fungus gnat populations. This material should not be tank-mixed with fertilizer concentrates (but dilute fertilizer solutions may be applied at the same time) or with any compound containing more than 100 ppm copper or chlorine. *Bacillus* has a shelf life of two years when stored properly.

Steinernema feltiae is an entomopathogenic nematode that may be used to control fungus gnat larvae. The nematodes are mixed with water and applied through an injector or a sprayer under low pressure with the filters removed. Nematodes move through the substrate in the moisture film and enter fungus gnat larvae through natural body openings. The nematodes release a bacterium that kills the larvae in one to two days. The nematodes reproduce within the larvae and eventually leave to infect other fungus gnat larvae. Adequate soil moisture is required for the nematodes to migrate through the substrate and locate fungus gnat hosts. One application is sometimes sufficient, especially if used in conjunction with the bacterium *Bacillus*.

Shore flies
Biology and damage
Shore flies, *Scatella* species (fig. 10.7), are less of a pest problem during propagation than fungus gnats are. Shore flies have a life cycle consisting of egg, three larval stages, pupa, and adult. A generation can be completed in sixteen to twenty days, depending on temperature. Adult shore flies resemble houseflies; they are 0.125 in. (3 mm) long with deep black bodies. Each wing usually contains at least five light-colored spots. The antennae and legs are short, and the head is small. The larvae are opaque yellowish brown, with no head capsule, and 0.25 in. (6 mm) long.

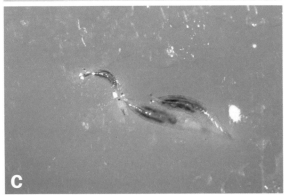

Figure 10.7. Shore flies, *Scatella* species, (A) adult with a fungus gnat adult on a yellow sticky card, (B) adult on a yellow sticky card—note the white spots on the wings, (C) larvae—note there is no black head capsule, and (D) adult on a plant leaf. (A and B images from R. Cloyd; C and D images from R. Lindquist, Olympic Horticultural Products)

Shore fly adults are stronger fliers than fungus gnats. They are less likely to cause direct plant injury than fungus gnats; however, shore fly adults are more easily seen flying around plants and are readily captured on sticky cards. Although adult shore flies are generally considered a nuisance pest, they may leave black fecal deposits on the leaves of cuttings, which may affect the ability of cuttings to root. In addition, the fecal deposits may contain a water-mold pathogen, such as *Pythium aphanidermatum*. Larvae typically do not feed on cuttings or the newly established roots, since they are primarily algae feeders.

Chemical management
See the chemical management section under fungus gnats for information on shore flies.

Biological control
Limited options for biological control of shore flies exist. Naturally occurring parasitoids, such as *Aphaerata debilitata*, may sometimes enter the greenhouse if pesticide use is minimal. The rove beetle, *Atheta coriaria*, is a predator that feeds on fungus gnat and shore fly larvae. Both immature and adult stages are predaceous, and the adults can fly, which enhances dispersal within the greenhouse. Approximately 1 beetle is released for every 4 to 5 sq. ft. (0.37 to 0.46 m²) of greenhouse space. Rove beetles may consume *Hypoaspis miles*, the soil-dwelling predatory mite that also feeds on fungus gnat larvae, so the two species should not be used together. The first release of either species is made as soon as the cuttings come into the greenhouse; a second release may be made approximately ten days later.

Slugs
Biology and Damage
Slugs are destructive pests that may be a problem during propagation. They can completely devour young seedlings or cuttings overnight. A slug is classified as a mollusk, related to clams and oysters; it is often referred to as a "naked snail" because it lacks a shell, which snails possess. Slugs can live from one to six years. They lay clusters of translucent, pearl-shaped eggs under debris or buried beneath the soil or the surface of the substrate. Each slug can lay between twenty and one hundred eggs several times per year. Slugs are *hermaphroditic*, which means they have both male and female sex organs. As a result, a slug can mate with itself if another slug isn't present.

Figure 10.8. Slugs and slug damage on gerbera foliage. (R. Cloyd)

Slugs vary in length from 0.5 to 1.5 in. (1.3 to 4 cm) and in colors from white to yellow, lavender, purple, or black, depending on the species. Some have brown specks or mottled areas on their bodies.

Slugs are able to move due to a large structure called the *foot*, which runs the length of the slug. The underside of the foot is called the *sole*. Near the front of the sole under the head is a gland that produces two types of slime, or mucus. One form of mucus is free flowing, whereas the other is more viscous. The combination of these two substances forms the slime trails for which slugs are famous. These slime trials remain in the morning and will glisten.

Slugs have chewing mouthparts and cause plant damage by creating large irregular holes with tattered edges in leaves (fig. 10.8). They feed using a structure called a *radula*, which is in the mouth and is covered with small teeth. This allows slugs to scrape away the surface of plant tissue.

The activity of slugs is highly dependent on soil moisture, which facilitates their movement; the moist environment in a propagation area may allow them to become a major problem. Slugs are primarily active at night (nocturnal) when humidity is high. They hide during the day under plant and other debris, weeds, and benches.

Management
Managing slugs involves a combination of strategies such as hand picking, habitat modification, traps, and commercial molluscicides. Monitoring is important to determine the effectiveness of slug management strategies. This involves going out in the evening with a flashlight and looking for the presence of slugs. During this time, hand picking

can be performed to reduce slug populations; it is especially effective during moist weather conditions. Placing slugs in a container with soapy water will kill them.

Habitat modification is one of the most effective strategies in reducing slug populations. This involves eliminating hiding places such as weeds and debris. For stock plants, proper watering practices can also minimize slug populations. Avoid watering plants late in the day, because moist conditions are conducive for slug activity. It is best to water early in the morning.

Copper barriers can be placed around the base of benches or on bench legs. Slugs receive a slight electric shock when their moist bodies contact the copper, which repels them. Be sure to avoid leaving sharp edges on the barriers, which may be hazardous to workers or customers.

Diatomaceous earth, shredded bark, eggshells, and wood ash have been used as barriers to prevent slugs from feeding on plants. These materials work best during dry periods, when slugs are less active. However, the effectiveness of these materials is reduced by irrigation, which limits their use in mist or propagation greenhouses. These materials lose their effectiveness after becoming wet, which means they have to be reapplied regularly. Overall, these types of materials are not feasible for use in greenhouses.

Traps such as wood boards, rolled-up newspapers, or old tuna cans may be placed where slugs are feeding. Check traps early in the morning and at least twice a week.

Commercial molluscicides can be applied to areas such as underneath greenhouse benches or around plants. The commercially available molluscicides kill slugs either by ingestion, contact, or acting as nerve poisons that interfere with nerve-impulse transmission. One type of molluscicide works by paralyzing slugs and causing them to secrete excessive amounts of mucous. Death generally occurs from water loss and/or exposure to direct sunlight. However, under cool, moist conditions slugs may recover. Most molluscicides are less effective in dry areas of the greenhouse. Irrigating before applying these materials is recommended to promote slug activity. Localized spot applications should be made, as opposed to broad-scale applications.

References

Web sites
Biobest compatibility information, www.biobest.be
Koppert compatibility information, www.koppert.com
Syngenta Bioline compatibility information, www.syngenta-bioline.co.uk

11

Structures and Equipment

John M. Dole and Ted E. Bilderback

Propagation Facilities

Depending on the size of the production facility, the propagation area can be either a separate greenhouse or a section within a larger greenhouse used for stock plants or finished plant production. Most facilities prefer segregating the propagation area in a separate house because the warm temperatures, low light levels, and high humidity required are incompatible with finished plant production of most floriculture crops.

Provided that light levels and temperatures are not too high, however, high-humidity enclosures can often be placed in greenhouses used in finished plant production. These facilities are especially useful for propagating directly in the final container. Mist and fog systems can be constructed within production houses if the propagation area is separated by a wall of plastic sheeting either from floor to ceiling or to at least to a couple of feet or a meter above the top of the cuttings. Mist systems can be placed on individual benches that are surrounded by plastic sheeting to keep air movement within the greenhouse from lowering the humidity too much around the cuttings. Such systems are most effective if temperatures and light levels on the individual benches can be controlled.

sand beds. In such cases, the sand needs to be periodically pasteurized, usually with steam, to eliminate weed seeds, insects, and diseases. Other propagators use a similar propagation method but insert the cuttings into flats of sand or lightweight perlite for ease of handling. While regular bedding plant flats can be used, they are lightweight and do not hold up well to the rigors of repeated use and cleaning; furthermore, they may not be deep enough for some species. Deep flats made of heavy plastic are durable, long lasting, and easier to sterilize for repeated use.

Figure 11.1. A mist propagation area with nozzles on risers. Note the header pipe, solenoid, and mist lines. (T. Bilderback)

Benches and Beds

Almost any type of weight-bearing structure can be used for benches, at least temporarily. Bench tops are often made of expanded metal sheets, with the sharp edges wrapped in metal edging for safety. Bench tops can also be made of welded wire, treated wood, snow fence, or plastic panels, all of which are prone to warping or bowing and decompose rather quickly in the hot and humid propagation environment. Supports can be made of concrete blocks, metal posts, or treated wood.

In the past, cuttings were propagated in beds of sand and removed after roots were well developed. Some propagators, primarily of woody ornamentals, still use

When determining the amount of bench or bed space required for propagation, be sure to provide as much room as possible in the propagation area for adequate air circulation. Leaves from one cutting should not shade the shoot tip of an adjacent cutting, since this may delay rooting of the shaded cutting.

Propagation Environment

Cutting propagation of most species requires an area with high humidity and moisture to prevent cuttings from desiccating before they form roots. Humidity and media moisture levels can be maintained through mist,

Figure 11.2. A mist propagation area with hanging nozzles. (T. Bilderback)

fog, or high-humidity enclosures (see chapter 6). Mist applies water directly to cuttings to reduce transpiration and maintain cutting turgidity, thus allowing root development (figs. 11.1 and 11.2).

However, fogging and high-humidity enclosures are often preferred because prolonged misting can promote diseases (due to excessive foliar wetness) and leach nutrients from the substrate and foliage. Fog systems produce much smaller water particles than mist systems,

Figure 11.3. High-humidity tent propagation. (H. Wilkins)

which reduces the amount of water applied and the resulting nutrient leaching from leaves. The amount of fog provided can be adjusted to either wet the foliage or evaporate enough so that 100% humidity is maintained without water droplets falling on the cutting foliage. The latter situation is typically preferred. Tents of various types maintain high humidity, reducing transpiration without the constant application of water (fig. 11.3).

Mist systems

The purpose of propagation irrigation is to apply a thin

film of small water droplets uniformly over the young fragile plants. Therefore, low-volume, high-pressure sprinkler nozzles (emitters) that produce a fine mist are

recommended. If a large volume of water is applied, it will saturate the propagation substrate, reducing rooting percentages due to poor soil aeration, and increased algae growth and disease pathogens. Many new mist nozzles have been introduced in recent years. Depending on the size and type of nozzle, discharge rates

Figure 11.4. An in-line disk filter. (T. Bilderback)

vary from 0.6 to 14 gph (2.3 to 53.0 L/h) when operated at 40 psi (276 kPa) water pressure.

A typical propagation irrigation system consists of a

Figure 11.5. A 24-volt solenoid valve. (T. Bilderback)

supply manifold, a line filter or strainer, and one or more lateral lines on which the nozzles are located. Mist nozzles may be equipped with strainers, but an in-line filter is recommended. The in-line filter is installed between the water source and the solenoid (figs. 11.4 and 11.5). This filter removes sediment algae and particulates from the water, and it reduces the possibility of clogging in the nozzles and in the diaphragm of the solenoid valve.

Nozzles

Nozzles may be mounted directly on lateral lines, mounted on risers higher than plants in the propagation unit, or suspended from drop lines mounted above propagation areas (see figs 11.1 and 11.2). A variety of inserts and couplers are available for installation of the nozzles. Many propagation nozzles are fitted with antidrip devices to avoid creating wet areas in propagation trays or in beds below the nozzles. The nozzles are normally spaced 3 to 4 ft. (90 to 120 cm) apart running down the middle of the bench. In the case of wide benches or beds, more than one line of nozzles may be

Figure 11.6. Boom irrigation. (J. Dole)

needed. Even distribution of water over the propagation area is important to ensure that all cuttings are uniformly moistened and free from moisture stress.

Traveling boom mist systems outfitted with appropriate nozzles can be used for propagation (fig. 11.6). These systems travel the length of the greenhouse over propagation benches, flats, or beds. The height above the benches, the speed of travel, and the nozzle arrangement can be adjusted to apply the correct amount of water. Conical and flat-fan spray nozzles can be used. The system can be adjusted to spray in the forward and reverse travel mode, or in only one direction. Right- and left-side booms can be controlled separately so that only one side of the boom can be operated if needed.

Valves

Solenoid valves that operate in the "normally closed" mode are most commonly used for irrigation purposes. "Normally open" solenoids are available for propagation which is an advantage in case of a power failure to prevent cuttings from drying out. Regardless, propagators should check mist propagation areas frequently to prevent over- and underwatering. Also low-voltage (24 VAC) solenoids should be used, since they present less danger to people working around them in case of an electrical malfunction. Plastic pipe—typically black, soft polyethylene (PE) or typically white, hard polyvinyl chloride (PVC)— is most frequently used for manifold and lateral lines. Schedule 80 PVC pipe, which is typically gray, is more rigid and reduces light penetration and algal growth. Schedule 40 PVC is better than more flexible Class 160 or Class 200 PVC pipe, both of

which are thinner walled. Schedule refers to the thickness of the pipe wall with lower numbers thicker.

Operating the system

An electronic controller, a mechanical clock, or an artificial leaf are used to operate a propagation mist system. An electronic controller with multiple stations can operate multiple solenoid valves. Electronic controllers

Figure 11.7. A solid-state irrigation controller. (T. Bilderback)

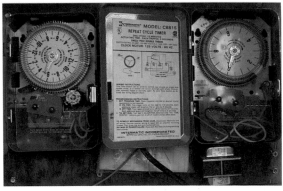

Figure 11.8. A twenty-four-hour and interval timer with a 110 to 24 volt transformer attached. (T. Bilderback)

allow great flexibility in choosing the time between mist cycles and the length of time each solenoid is open for mist application (fig. 11.7). Some propagation misting systems still use mechanical time clocks, consisting of a twenty-four-hour master clock, a "slave" or interval timer, and a 110 to 24 volt transformer (fig. 11.8). The master twenty-four-hour timer activates the system in the morning and cuts if off in the evening. During the time period when the master clock is on, the interval timer controls the frequency and duration of each misting cycle. Some automated mist systems are equipped with a light sensor that overrides mist intervals on cloudy days.

Figure 11.9. An artificial leaf screen mist controller. (T. Bilderback)

The frequency and duration of the mist or fog can also be controlled by devices that measure solar radiation, evaporation, or vapor pressure deficit. Such control systems allow mist or fog application to be tied more directly to the environmental conditions, thus reducing the chance of over- or undermisting the cuttings. Some propagators prefer using artificial leaf controllers (fig. 11.9).

The artificial leaf controller consists of a threaded pivot arm about 12 in. (30 cm) long and a piece of 2 by 3 in. (5.0 by 7.6 cm) window screen soldered to one end, an adjustable counter balance nut attached to the other end, and a mercury switch fastened to the pivot arm near the counter balance nut. The mercury switch is wired electrically to the solenoid valve. Everything except the wire mesh is enclosed in a light-gauge metal housing, and the entire controller is set on the propagation bench. When the mesh screen is dry, the mist is activated. As water from the mist nozzles collects on the mesh screen, the screen gets heavier and pivots downward. The mercury switch breaks contact, and the solenoid valve is closed, shutting off the mist. As water evaporates from the mesh screen, it gets lighter and pivots upward. The mercury switch activates the solenoid valve, and the mist is started. An advantage of this system is that misting depends on the rate of evaporation. If the system is properly set, the seedlings never become too wet. However, wind or moderate air movement will disrupt the proper operation of the artificial leaf.

Increasingly, the propagation environment is computer controlled with mist application govern by accumulated light, vapor pressure deficit (VPD), or evapotranspiration (ET). The latter is calculated from light levels, temperature, relative humidity and other factors. The computer controller can employ one or more methods to determine when to start or shut off misting for the day, how long each misting episode will last, and the time between misting episodes. Computer controllers are explained in greater detail in chapter 6.

Protecting plants from overmisting

Misting or fogging at nighttime may be required if the air is warm and dry, but it can generally be discontinued after a few days. Misting is commonly controlled by time clocks, but time intervals set for sunny conditions will result in overmisting during overcast weather, which can delay rooting and increase the incidence of pathogens. Overmisting can also result in foliar nutrient leaching and yellowing. To prevent either from occurring, low levels of nitrogen and potassium can be applied to cuttings. A mixture of 2 oz. (57 g) of potassium nitrate (KNO_3) and 3 oz. (85 g) of calcium nitrate [$Ca(NO_3)_2$] per 100 gal. (379 L) provides approximately 55 ppm nitrogen and potassium. Fertilizer can be applied through the mist system, but precipitation of salts will clog the nozzles. Because of this maintenance issue, periodic applications of nutrients should be made through a hose with a mist nozzle (see chapter 7). Regardless of the control system, reduce misting frequency as cuttings begin to form roots or during low light conditions. The mist may be turned off completely if day temperatures can be controlled or if the ambient humidity is high.

Fog

A fog of minute water particles is injected into the greenhouse from nozzles located on the ceiling, sidewalls, or pipes that drop down from the ceiling. The droplets produced should be small enough, typically 15 μm in diameter, to evaporate before settling on the foliage; larger droplets will increase the potential for diseases. For fog to be most effective, use high-quality water with low electrical conductivity (EC). With poor-quality water, soluble salts precipitate, plug the nozzles, and cause frequent maintenance problems.

Since a relatively low amount of water is required, it can be treated to remove salts and particulates prior to use. In-line filtration is especially important for fog systems because of the small aperatures on the nozzles (See chapter 6). In areas with low humidity, fog can also cool the air substantially—a factor that should be taken into account. Fog does not cool the substrate as much as misting; thus less media heating may be required. However, fog systems are typically more expensive to install and maintain than mist systems. Fog systems are especially useful for slow-to-root species, which must remain in high-humidity environments for a long time.

High-humidity enclosures
Tents
High-humidity tents are generally preferred over misting systems because tenting eliminates overwatering, algae growth on floors, and concerns with system malfunctions while ensuring a uniform propagation environment. Compared with misting, high-humidity tents reduce nutrient leaching from the leaves, lessen the amount of free moisture on the foliage, and decrease the incidence of disease. Tenting also eliminates the need for a mist or fog system, which can make it more feasible to propagate directly in the final container. Major drawbacks of tent propagation are the additional labor required to set up, remove, and dispose of the plastic.

Figure 11.10. A high-humidity propagation tent. Note the additional layer of black plastic used to provide artificial short days. (H. Wilkins)

Tenting may not be feasible in areas with high light intensity or high temperatures due to heat buildup under the tent, even with extra shade to reduce the light intensity. Generally, clear plastic is used in the winter under low light conditions and white plastic in summer, when light levels are greater. In warm or high-light climates, white plastic should be used year-round. To provide short-day photoperiods (see chapter 5) during propagation for plants such as potted campanula, the tents can be covered at night with an additional layer of black plastic (fig. 11.10).

To construct a tent, cover a bench with perforated plastic sheeting so that at least 12 in. (30 cm) hangs over the side of the bench. A capillary mat and perforated black plastic covering can be placed over the bench top. Place containers on the plastic sheeting or, if used, on capillary mats that have been watered. Hand mist the cuttings once. Cover the bench area with white or clear plastic held above the plants by hoops; the humidity is held in the tent by a water seal between the two plastic sheets. The tent should be totally closed for the first twenty-four hours, after which time it can be opened daily for increasing amounts of time to allow fresh air to enter and to harden the cuttings after they have begun to root. Ultimately, the plastic is removed.

If bench heating is available, then thermostats should be placed in the tent. Thermostats sense the temperature; if it falls below the set point, the thermostat will turn on the bench heating.

Direct-contact enclosures
Many species are able to tolerate materials being laid directly on the cuttings. Such materials can include nonperforated polyethylene plastic sheeting, typically white, perforated polyethylene sheeting, such as Vispore, or spun-bonded polyester cloths, such as Remay. The cuttings are stuck in the substrate and watered in. This simple system is especially useful for propagating rapidly rooting species in the final container. In some cases, plastic sheeting should be placed on the bench under the pots to prevent excessive drying. If spun-bonded cloth or perforated polyethylene sheeting is used, it can be misted occasionally to maintain high humidity around the cuttings. As the cuttings root, misting can be decreased, lowering the humidity level and hardening the cuttings. Plastic covers may need to be opened periodically to reduce the humidity and harden the cuttings if plastic sheeting has been placed on the bench under the containers. When the roots are sufficiently developed, the plastic or cloths can be completely removed.

Types of Containers
Several considerations must be made when containers are used for stock plant production and cutting propagation. For stock plants grown in pots and hanging baskets, the containers should be strong enough to last the length of the crop cycle, which may be many months to several years. In addition, use of large containers is recommended because they do not dry out as rapidly as smaller containers, especially when the stock plants become large. The various types of containers that can be used for propagation are discussed here. Propagation strips are discussed in chapter 4.

Plug flats
Plug flats are temporary intermediate containers used for the propagation of seeds and cuttings. After the cut-

Figure 11.11. Rooted poinsettia plug showing ribs in the root-ball that prevent root circling. (J. Dole)

tings root, they are transplanted out of the plug flat and into other containers such as pots, hanging baskets, or other flats. Plug flats vary in the number of cells per flat (18 to 800) and in the shape (round, square, or hexagonal), diameter, and depth of the cells. Plug flats used for cuttings typically have larger cells with 72 to 105 per flat. Ribbed, square, or hexagonal cells are thought to reduce root spiraling around the cell that can lead to poor establishment of a plant after transplanting (fig. 11.11). Most plug flats are made of plastic, but some are also made of Styrofoam.

Flats and inserts

Bedding plant flats and inserts are typically used for marketing the final product. However, they can also be used for propagation, especially for species with large stems or leaves requiring more room in the flat. Flats are identified by the overall dimensions. Currently, the standard 1020 flat, which has an actual dimension of 10.5 by 21 in. (27 by 53 cm), is quite common. Dimensions for the 1020 flat will vary with the manufacturer. Other types of flats are narrower than the standard 1020 flat and are used to increase the number of flats produced per bench. Other factors that vary include the depth, the style of the bottom (webbed or solid), and the number and configuration of ribs within the flat. Ribs are raised ridges or walls within the flat to make the flat more rigid. Depending on the configuration of the ribs, they may prevent some cell packs from being used in certain flats. Most flats are black or dark green.

The inserts match the dimensions of the flats and are identified by the number of separable cell packs within each flat and the number of cells within each pack. Inserts are designated by a three- or four-digit number indicating the number of cells in each pack (the last two digits) and the number of packs in a flat (the first one or two digits). For example, an 1801 insert has 18 containers, each of which contains one cell, and a 1206 insert has twelve cell packs, each of which contains six cells.

Recycling Containers

Containers can be reused by washing and soaking them in a disinfectant. Generally, new sterile containers should be used during propagation because of the possibility of disease, even after chemical disinfection. A typical greenhouse, however, will accumulate many damaged or unusable odd-sized containers, especially flats. In Europe and some areas of the United States and Canada, facilities are available for recycling leftover plastic containers. Contact your local supplier about a recycling program in your area. Flats and inserts are the most commonly recycled containers.

Temperature

Proper temperatures are critical to rapid, successful cutting propagation (see chapter 5 for more information). Media heating is especially important for rooting the cuttings of many species. Generally, the substrate should be at least 70° F (21° C), with 73° to 77° F (23° to 25° C) optimum for most species. If misting is used during propagation, evaporation of the mist may reduce the temperature of the substrate, and additional heat may be required. Cold water can delay rooting substantially, especially during cool weather; heat the water to 85° to 90° F (29° to 32° C). The air temperature should be 70° to 73° F (21° to 23° C), since maintaining a lower temperature in the air than in the substrate will encourage rooting without excessive shoot growth. Specific species may have a higher or lower optimum substrate temperature for propagation.

To provide warm substrate temperatures, heating cables can be placed on the bench for small-scale propagation systems. In larger propagation facilities one of several heating systems may be used at or under the bench; they include microclimate tubing, fan-jet tubes, and hot-water or steam pipes. A microclimate tubing system consists of a network of small, flexible, black rubber tubes laid on the bench top or attached underneath it. Hot water is circulated from water heaters through the tubes, allowing the heat to rise and warm the substrate above it. Large polyethylene fan-jet tubes can also be used to direct the heat from forced-air heaters under the bench; however, care must be taken to prevent excessive drying of the cuttings by using plastic to cover the bench top underneath the propagation containers. In greenhouses with hot water or steam heating, the pipes can be placed under each bench and individually controlled so that each bench is maintained at the correct temperature. With all of the heating systems, temperature sensors should be placed in the substrate to maintain the proper temperature.

Figure 11.12. An external shade system. (J. Dole)

Light

Propagation areas require lower light levels than production areas to reduce transpiration and desiccation of the cuttings until roots form (see chapter 5 for more information). Optimum propagation is achieved when the light level can be altered according to the stage of propagation. For most species, the initial light levels should be 500 to 1,000 f.c. (5 to 11 klux) and 1,000 to 2,000 f.c. (11 to 22 klux) after root initiation. When the cuttings are well rooted, the light levels should be increased to ranges close to the optimum for production; the exact range will vary with the species. In general, light levels need to be reduced from ambient for propagation.

Figure 11.13. An internal automatic shade system. (J. Dole).

Reducing light levels

Two common ways to reduce the light intensity in a greenhouse are with shade cloth and shading compounds. Shade cloth is available in a variety of types that reduce light by 25 to 98%. One common type regulates the amount of shade produced by varying the number of threads per inch used to weave the fabric. It can be used to cover specific benches, or more commonly, the entire house. Placing the shade cloth over the greenhouse also reduces photodegradation of the glazing, such as occurs with polyethylene film or polycarbonate, and provides extra protection against wind and hail damage.

Figure 11.14. Lightweight spun-fiber cloth provides a temporary high-humidity enclosure over cuttings. (J. Dole)

External shading is more effective than internal shading because in the latter case the light has already entered the greenhouse and is absorbed by the screen, raising the internal greenhouse temperature (fig. 11.12). However, internal shading allows growers to regulate light levels by opening the shade cloth during cloudy days and closing it during sunny days (fig. 11.13). This process is often mechanized by using pho-tosensors to automatically open and close the shade cloth. The cloths are subject to photodegradation and should be stored out of sunlight when not in use.

Another type of shade cloth is made of lightweight white spun-bonded fiber, such as Remay. Spun-bonded cloths are not strong enough to be used externally, and they are often used to cover individual benches or beds (fig. 11.14). The cloth is so lightweight that it can be laid directly on the plants for a temporary light screen, for example, immediately after transplanting cuttings; if kept wet, this type of cloth can also be used for a high-humidity enclosure.

Shading compounds can be used to reduce light intensity but are now rarely used. The white compounds can be applied directly to the outside of the glazing in one heavy layer or in two to three diluted layers. Shading compounds specific for greenhouses can be purchased and diluted at one part compound to six parts water for heavy shade or one part compound to fifteen to twenty parts water for light shade. Generally, most of the shading compound wears off gradually during the summer, but the remainder may need to be scrubbed off at the end of the season; scrubbing is generally not a pleasant job, but it must be done if any residue remains. Commercial shading compounds designed for greenhouses are easier to remove than diluted latex paint.

Increasing light levels

In some situations, light levels are low and supplemental high intensity discharge (HID) lighting is advised. For example, light levels during the winter, especially in northern or cloudy climates, can be too low for optimum propagation. Another common problem is that in warm climates heavy shade is used to reduce greenhouse or tent temperatures, sometimes below the amount of light needed for propagation. In such cases supplemental HID lighting can be used below the shade to restore optimum light levels.

While supplemental lighting is often cost-effective in propagation because large numbers of plants are typically packed into a relatively small area, a cost-benefit analysis must be completed to determine if the expenses of energy, light fixtures, installation, and maintenance will be offset by increased growth, quality, and reduced crop production times. Minimum supplemental light requirements vary with each species, but 300 to 600 f.c. (3 to 6 klux) is a general recommendation for supplementary lighting. Greater use can be obtained from light fixtures in some situations by installing them on a track system and moving the lights from one section to another. The process is automatically controlled and can be used to light two crops with the same light fixtures. HID lighting in greenhouses can be used to supplement sunlight during the day or to extend the day. Supplemental lighting can be applied during the night to take advantage of low, off-peak electricity rates.

Automation

Floriculture has traditionally been a labor-intensive industry, and cutting harvest and propagation is one of the highest labor-requiring segments of the industry. Automation can allow current employees to increase output or allow them to accomplish more important tasks. Automation can have a variety of other benefits as well, including reducing employees' muscle strain, improving plant quality, and increasing benching efficiency. The counting feature of many machines can even eliminate the annoying distraction of keeping track of the number of cuttings harvested or flats stuck (fig. 11.15).

Figure 11.15. A homemade cutting counter. As cuttings are harvested, they are dropped through the opening and automatically counted when they break a beam of light. (J. Dole)

Virtually every commercial greenhouse already uses some type of automation, such as environmental controllers to heat and cool greenhouses and to switch air circulation equipment on and off. However, greenhouse controllers are only the start of automation. Every business should analyze its operation. The first step is to see what can be done to improve the efficiency of the operation by simplifying the layout and decreasing employee movements. For example, are the media and related supplies stored close to the potting area? Harvesting can be notoriously inefficient: do the employees pack and ship an entire bench or a section of a bench at once, or do they walk the benches selecting specific flats for harvest? After analyzing its operation, each firm should make appropriate changes to improve efficiency. The next step is to determine those areas suitable for mechanization.

Irrigation

Automated irrigation has become a requirement for large-scale production of any crop. Even small operations can benefit from automated irrigation systems and should install them wherever possible. For plug production, choose a low-volume sprinkler, boom, and/or flood system.

Each irrigation system has specific advantages and disadvantages, but all systems are cost-effective in the long run. Some systems, such as low-volume sprinklers, will pay for themselves within a year. More expensive systems may have longer payback periods. In addition to labor savings, automated systems may reduce water and fertilizer use and runoff as well as their associated expenses. Some systems, such as flood system, can reduce foliar and crown diseases and fungicide use because there is no wetting of the foliage compared with hand watering or overhead watering systems. Automated irrigation systems generally increase crop uniformity, which reduces production problems and eases shipping and handling. Automated systems work best when the crop is uniform in size, stage of development, and species at planting, and they help to maintain uniformity from potting to shipping.

Media mixing and planting

Media mixers and flat fillers are now used in many greenhouses. Plug extractors remove plugs from plug flats, and automatic transplanters insert them into the substrate.

Figure 11.16. Automatic irrigation of newly transplanted material. (J. Dole)

Water is sprayed onto the media during mixing and before or after planting (fig. 11.16). Taggers insert labels into flats after they are filled with media. While these types of machines usually require one or two people to check and correct skips, they can greatly increase employee output.

Figure 11.17. An automatic sorting system for potted flowering plants. (J. Dole)

The next stage of automation may be to integrate video cameras into the transplanting and production process. Video can be used to grade plug quality prior to planting and to check for skips. Video can also be incorporated during production to grade plants and sort them by size (fig. 11.17). Thus the flats of smaller plants can be held back, if needed, for additional time to grow, and the larger plants moved to the next production stage.

Plant movement

A wide variety of equipment and processes can reduce the number of motions required to produce a crop. Carts, conveyers, and monorails can be used to transport flats within the greenhouse, greatly reducing strain on employees and saving time (fig. 11.18). Carts operate most easily on concrete walkways, but models with large or wide wheels can be used on gravel aisles. Consider carts that can be connected together and pulled with an electric vehicle. Conveyors can work well for short distances, such as from the potting area to the

Figure 11.18. A conveyor for moving flats around the greenhouse. (J. Dole)

cooler. They can be portable and moved around as needed or used as benches for short-term crops when placed on supports. Overhead monorails generally work best with an open greenhouse, but they can also be a great way to move plants between numerous small greenhouses (fig. 11.19). Some systems allow carts to be attached to the monorail, increasing flexibility of both the monorail and the carts.

A step up in automation is to use mobile benches (also called bench trays or Dutch trays), which consist of bench tops filled with plants. They allow numerous plants to be handled as one unit rather that individual flats having to be handled separately. The bench trays can be carried by forklift and placed on the bench supports, carried by automatic mechanized trolleys, or moved manually on rollers. The most sophisticated systems link each component of the propagation and production systems together via conveyors or mechanized trolleys. In some systems, the trolleys are programmed by computer to deliver trays from the potting area to an assigned location in the production area. After moving through production, the trays are emptied for shipping and marketing. The trays are then returned to the headhouse for cleaning, storage (if needed), and replanting to complete the cycle. The trays can be loaded or emptied by hand or with automatic flat grippers that grab, move, and set flats at the proper spacing on the bench tray.

Mobile benches are most efficient when used in a first-in–first-out production system. They can also allow high benching efficiency of more than 90%, but such systems often prevent easy access to plants in the center of the greenhouse. Cranes can be used to access the center trays.

Spray applications
The spraying of pesticides, growth regulators, and other chemicals is often a hot and uncomfortable job for the applicators. Mechanized spraying equipment is available, in which robots are programmed to spray specific areas. Robots can be programmed during regular working hours or during times when employees are not around.

Cutting harvesting
The process of counting and keeping track of the number of cuttings harvested can slow harvesters down. Cutting counters can be constructed to record via electronic eye the number of harvested cuttings employees drop through openings in collection containers. Carts can also be designed to make cutting harvesting more efficient by providing easy access to supplies such as knives, disinfectant solution, gloves, and containers.

Harvest and postharvest handling
Video grading systems are available to scan finished flats with cameras, rate them by foliage percentage and height, and assign them specific grades.

Economics
The advantages of automation are obvious, but are they worth the cost? Every operation should compare expenses and potential savings. The less tangible benefits of some machinery, such as reduced muscle strain or less boredom for employees, must also be considered. Remember, with any new equipment, it takes time to incorporate the machinery into an operation; up to two years may be required before the full savings are realized.

Implementation
A couple of problems tend to occur when implementing a new handling process or installing a new piece of equipment. The first problem is resistance by the employees involved, and the second is lack of use or abandonment after a period of time. Try to prevent these problems in the following ways.

- Make sure that the change solves an actual problem or results in a genuine improvement. If employees don't see the need for a change, they are less likely to implement it.
- Be sure the new equipment or process flows well with the rest of the system. For example, installing media-mixing machinery may not save money if too many different mixes are used. Even a change as simple as buying carts can be ineffective if the carts do not handle well or do not move down the aisles easy.
- Reassure employees that they are not going to be replaced, if that is the case. Many types of labor-saving machinery require a number of people to operate them smoothly. Often the same number of employees is required; the employees simply get more work done. If positions are going to be eliminated, it may be best to implement the changes when the operation expands; that will reduce the need to hire additional workers and not eliminate current employees.

References
Aldrich, R. A., and J. W. Bartok Jr. 1989. *Greenhouse Engineering*, 2nd ed. Northeast Regional Agricultural Engineering Service, Cornell University, Ithaca, New York.

Beytes, C. 2003. *Ball RedBook*, 17th ed., vol. 1. C. Beytes, ed., Ball Publishing, Batavia, Illinois.

Hanan, J. J. 1998. *Greenhouses: Advanced Technology for Protected Horticulture*. CRC Press, Boca Raton, Florida.

Hartmann, H. T., D. E. Kester, F. T. Davies Jr., and R. L. Geneve. 1997. *Hartmann and Kester's Plant Propagation: Principles and Practice*, 7th ed. Prentice Hall, Upper Saddle River, New Jersey.

Nelson, P. V. 2003. *Greenhouse Operation and Management*, 6th ed. Prentice Hall, Upper Saddle River, New Jersey.

12

Postharvest

James E. Faust, Amy L. Enfield, Sylvia M. Blankenship, and John M. Dole

Prior to 1990, the majority of vegetative cuttings were produced and propagated in-house. The most commonly produced stock plants included zonal geraniums and poinsettias. In recent years, the floriculture industry has become increasingly segregated, so now growers are often specialized as stock plant growers, propagators, or finishers. The high labor requirements to maintain stock plants and har-

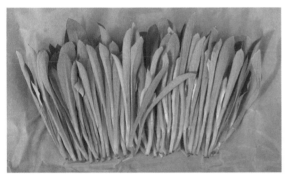

Figure 12.1. Unrooted yellow buttons (*Chrysocephalum*) cuttings. (J. Faust)

vest cuttings have resulted in an increased number of companies producing and supplying cuttings from offshore production facilities. Consequently, more unrooted cuttings (URC) as well as rooted cuttings (RC) are being shipped on trucks and airplanes than ever before. This has increased the need for understanding the postharvest requirements of vegetative cuttings and for developing methods of packaging and shipping cuttings.

Figure 12.2. Callused poinsettia cuttings are most commonly used in direct-stick production. (A. Enfield)

Figure 12.3. Rooted coleus cuttings are most often shipped in plug flats. (J. Dole)

Vegetative cuttings are shipped in three forms: unrooted (fig. 12.1), callused (fig. 12.2), and rooted cuttings (fig. 12.3). Unrooted cuttings have a relatively short lifespan and are particularly sensitive to the postharvest environment. Callused cuttings typically perform better in the postharvest environment than unrooted cuttings; they are most often used in direct-stick propagation. For rooted cuttings, physical damage is a common shipping issue; most efforts have focused on designing shipping packages and rooting media that minimize the physical damage.

Fundamentals

Proper postharvest handling of cuttings centers on managing four key issues: temperature, water, ethylene, and pathogens. All of these issues are related because warm temperatures during shipping will dehydrate cuttings, increase ethylene production, and result in disease problems. It is important, however, to understand each issue and how it relates to postharvest handling of cuttings.

145

Respiration

Respiration is the metabolic process in plants and animals whereby carbohydrates (sugars and starches) are broken down to produce energy that is used to build and maintain cells. During respiration, carbon dioxide is produced while oxygen is consumed. Cuttings continue to respire even after they are harvested from the mother plant. When plant material is placed in enclosed environments, such as plastic bags, carbon dioxide can accumulate to toxic levels and/or oxygen can be depleted, resulting in anaerobic conditions. Respiration continues until the plant material has substantially deteriorated. Therefore, all cuttings need to be treated as living things, since they are respiring and carrying on the basic metabolism of life.

The rate of respiration varies tremendously among plants and plant parts. Generally, a higher respiration rate leads to a shorter storage life. A dormant woody cutting has a much lower respiration rate than a leafy cutting from young tissue; in fact, woody dormant tissue can be stored much longer than herbaceous young cuttings. The rate of respiration can be a limiting factor influencing longevity when storing or shipping plant material. As carbohydrates are depleted from the cuttings due to respiration, the cuttings will experience slower and less uniform rooting, and even death may occur.

Temperature has the dominant effect on the rate of respiration. A general rule in chemistry says that for every 19° F (10° C) rise in temperature, the rate of a chemical reaction will double. This is referred to as the Q_{10}. In plants this is true only for a specific temperature range, and at times it can even more than double. Cold temperatures can slow metabolism and respiration. This is the basis for using refrigeration to make plant products, such as cuttings, last longer. The rate of respiration needs to be kept as low as possible to extend the storage life of a cutting. The lowest desirable temperature is termed the *base temperature*. For chilling-sensitive species, such as New Guinea impatiens and poinsettia, the base temperature is 50° to 55°F (10° to 13° C), while cold-tolerant species are best held at 35° to 50° F (2° to 10° C).

Temperature

For each species there is an optimum temperature for the maximum storage life of a cutting. This optimum temperature should be low enough to slow metabolism and respiration, but not so low that it causes chilling or freezing injury. The origin of the plant is often a key to storage temperature. For cold-tolerant temperate species a common storage temperature is 35° to 50° F (2° to 10° C). However, many species can be stored as low as 32° to 34° F (0° to 1° C). Plants of tropical origin cannot with-stand cold temperatures, usually below 50° F (10° C), and should be stored at 50° to 60° F (10° to 16° C). Symptoms of chilling injury include blackened or water-soaked tissue, wilted foliage and stems, and desiccated tissue from water loss caused by cellular damage. Decay will frequently accompany chilling injury; however, the decay may not appear until the plants are removed from the cooler and rewarmed.

High storage temperatures will rapidly shorten the storage life and survival of the cuttings. Anyone handling cuttings should periodically check the coolers to ensure the cuttings are as cold as desired. During periods of heavy use, coolers may stay excessively warm due to open doors and the placement of large amounts of warm material in the cooler.

Depending on the packaging, cuttings may lose water rapidly. If water is present, high temperatures will promote pathogenic infection. A common problem is the condensation that forms when plant material packaged in plastic undergoes temperatures changes during handling and shipping. This condensation results in free water on the plant surfaces that leads to cutting deterioration and pathogen growth.

Water

Cuttings should be turgid prior to shipping and storage, but tissue surfaces should be dry. The presence of water on the foliage or stems may allow diseases to develop. However, dehydration during shipping and storage may cause leaf abscission, necrotic tissue, and reduced rooting in propagation. The longer and greater the dehydration event, the more likely that problems will develop during subsequent propagation.

Pathogens

Botrytis and bacterial soft rot (primarily *Erwinia* species) are the primary diseases that cause problems during shipping and storage. Botrytis is a common fungus within production greenhouses, and spores can be readily found on cuttings. The botrytis spores require moisture (free water) to germinate and high humidity to grow. Transpiration from plant material packed in sealed boxes provides high humidity. Spores will germinate if there is water on the cuttings prior to packing or from condensation during shipping and storage. If the cuttings are exposed to warm temperatures at any time, botrytis will develop rapidly and destroy the cuttings. The optimum temperature for botrytis development is approximately 68° F (20° C). Even if the cuttings are kept relatively cool, botrytis can develop and limit the length of time the cuttings can be stored.

While bacterial diseases are not as prevalent in production greenhouses, if they are present they can also rapidly destroy cuttings during storage and shipping. Occasionally, cuttings will appear healthy when unpacked, but both bacterial soft rot and botrytis will become apparent within hours of being placed under the mist because of the infection that occurred during improper shipping and storage. Chronic disease problems during shipping and storage may require preventative pesticide applications. However, the best control is to produce clean cuttings and to keep storage and shipping temperatures and times as cold and short as possible. See chapter 9 for information on diseases that occur in stock plant and propagation areas.

Ethylene

Ethylene is a hydrocarbon gas of low molecular weight that is produced by plants and other more industrial sources. It functions as a plant hormone on leaves, stems, roots, flowers, and fruit. Ethylene effects include yellowing of green tissues; dropping of leaves, petals, and flowers; death of buds; poor growth; and stunting of growth. Ethylene has very little odor, and we have no way of knowing it is present other than by testing the air or observing ethylene-sensitive plants.

Sources of ethylene

Ethylene can be produced by several sources. Plant material—particularly fruit such as apples, tomatoes, pears, and bananas—produces ethylene. Decaying, diseased, or wounded plant material can produce ethylene. In storage and production situations, equipment with internal combustion engines, burning propane, or other fuels is a common source of ethylene. This includes forklifts, cleaning equipment, and heaters. Welding will generate ethylene as a consequence of using acetylene. Natural gas contains ethylene; leaks in natural gas lines have been known to defoliate plants. Smoke from fires and exhaust from trucks, automobiles, and aircraft all contain ethylene. Air pollution in urban and industrial areas can account for ethylene in "normal" air.

Time, concentration, temperature, and plant interaction

The question is often asked, "How much ethylene will damage my plants?" Unfortunately, it is difficult to say how much ethylene will damage a particular plant because of the interactions that occur between exposure time, ethylene concentration, temperature, and the age and type of plant material.

Damaging concentrations could be as low as parts per billion in some plants. Anything over 1 ppm is almost certainly a problem. However, it is not uncommon to see amounts less than 1 ppm causing damage, particularly if plants are exposed for a long period of time. The higher the concentration of ethylene, the less time needed to induce damage. Low concentrations may induce damage over more extended periods of time. The longer the exposure to ethylene, the greater the damage. Most ethylene damage occurs when exposure is at least several hours. It could take several days to induce damage if the concentration and temperature are low. Minutes of exposure are not long enough to induce damage. For example, if you walked with a package of cuttings through an apple storage room containing several parts per million ethylene, it would not hurt the cuttings. However, if you stored the cuttings in the apple storage room for several days, you might see damage.

In most situations, the higher the temperature, the more likely you are to see damage. For example, cuttings exposed to ethylene at 70° F (21° C) might get damaged, whereas cuttings at 40° F (4° C) will not. The type of plant material also influences how much ethylene will cause damage. Older plant material is more easily damaged than young tissue; you might see the older foliage drop off a cutting, but the tip remains alive. Some plant species are much more sensitive than others to ethylene. In some species the leaves are sensitive to ethylene while the flowers are not, and in other species the flowers are sensitive while the foliage is not.

Symptoms of ethylene damage

Ethylene exposure can cause a variety of symptoms, many of which look like stress or senescence. Loss of chlorophyll, or yellowing, is common. Dropping of leaves, petals, or flowers is also common. Lantana cuttings typically defoliate when exposed to ethylene (fig. 12.4). While older leaves tend to drop first, flower buds can be particularly susceptible in some plants. Premature aging and shattering of flowers is symptomatic of ethylene exposure. Often the meristematic regions appear to be undamaged while the rest of the plant shows symptoms. Ethylene exposure typically does not cause spots or necrotic areas on leaves.

Epinasty is an ethylene condition in which the petioles turn downward, giving a wilted appearance, but on close inspection the petioles are turgid. Poinsettia leaves typically show epinasty when exposed to ethylene. Plants can recover from epinasty if placed in an ethylene-free environment. Slight epinasty can be difficult to notice unless an ethylene-free plant is available for comparison.

Figure 12.4. Defoliation of lantana cuttings due to exposure to 1 ppm ethylene is shown on the left. On the right are untreated cuttings that retained foliage. (J. Dole)

Ethylene damage can be difficult to diagnose if the concentrations of ethylene are low and exposure occurs over a long period of time. In one case, the plants of a poinsettia grower were not growing and developing on schedule, but there was no sign of any stress on the plants. After looking at a multitude of possible causes for the lack of growth, the air in the greenhouses was tested and found to be contaminated with ethylene from the heaters. Once the heaters were repaired, the ethylene was eliminated, and the plants started growing again. There was no leaf drop, as you might expect with a higher concentration of ethylene.

Larger doses of ethylene have more dramatic effects. For example, in an outdoor setting a grower was faced with damaging cold temperatures, so large propane heaters were rented and the plants were enclosed in plastic. The result was that the plants were not cold damaged, but the leaves turned bright yellow and dropped due to ethylene exposure from the heaters.

Controlling ethylene

By far, the best solution to a problem of ethylene damage is to remove the source of the ethylene. This may mean limiting equipment use, repairing equipment, or using electric equipment. It may be possible to increase ventilation and reduce the concentration of ethylene to an unharmful level. In some situations, lowering the temperature may help reduce ethylene damage. Ethylene-producing products should not be stored in the same area as sensitive products.

Ethylene absorbents, including potassium permanganate and activated charcoal, are commercially available. However, both are dependent on the air coming into contact with the absorbent; if the air does not pass over the absorbent at a high enough rate, ethylene may not be reduced enough to prevent damage. Absorbents

come in small packages, which can be included in a packed box or can be used as air filters in cold storage or other facilities. While these products often do reduce ethylene, they do not always reduce it enough to prevent damage.

A reduction in oxygen and an increase in carbon dioxide can mitigate an ethylene response, which is the basis for controlled atmosphere storage or modified atmosphere packaging. Controlling ethylene effects by altered atmospheres can be beneficial in some products. However, most successful modified atmospheres are the result of considerable engineering efforts to match the packaging material to the plant, temperature, and humidity requirements. Simply putting cuttings in a plastic bag does not protect them from ethylene because ethylene will diffuse through most plastics.

Two ethylene inhibitors are available. Silver thiosulfate (STS) has long been used by the cut flower industry to protect cut stems against ethylene. STS prevents damage from internal ethylene produced by the plant itself as well as external ethylene from outside sources. STS is available as a floral preservative into which the cut stems are placed. The effects are long lasting for most species. However, STS is not labeled for use on stock plants or cuttings, and disposal of the solution has caused some environmental concerns. In addition, phytotoxicity may be an issue; in a research study 2 mM STS injured pothos cuttings sufficiently to reduce rooting percentage, number of roots, total root length, and dry weight compared with untreated cuttings.

1-methylcyclopropene, 1-MCP (EthylBloc) also prevents ethylene action from internal and external ethylene, and it appears to be more suitable for application to cuttings. It is available either as a powder that must be measured or as a premeasured packet; when mixed with water or a buffer solution, it releases a gas, 1-MCP, that penetrates the plant. Plant material is treated in an enclosed space such as a cooler, room, greenhouse, truck trailer, or shipping container. The treatment area must be tightly sealed; leaks can be sealed with plastic sheeting, tape, caulking or other sealants. Plastic sheeting can be used to enclose an area, but metal or glass structures are best, since 1-MCP penetrates plastic sheeting and will dissipate relatively quickly from the enclosure. An internal air circulation system will ensure uniform gas distribution. The volume of treatment area must be calculated (length x width x height) to determine the amount of EthylBloc to use. Pour the water or buffer solution into a plastic container, and add the water-soluble EthylBloc powder or packets. The water or buffer can be poured out after treatment is complete.

The recommended treatment time is four to eight hours at 50° to 75° F (10° to 24° C). Lower EthylBloc rates can be used if treatment times are longer (at least ten hours). However, higher rates or longer treatment times are required if temperatures are from 35° (2° C) to less than 50° F (10° C). If necessary, plant material can be treated more than once without any problems, since phytotoxicity has never been recorded.

The effectiveness of 1-MCP is dependent on the plant material, and side effects have been noted. For example, 1-MCP reduced leaf drop and yellowing of unrooted 'Isabel' geranium (*Pelargonium*), hibiscus (*Hibiscus rosa-sinensis*), croton, and pothos cuttings compared with untreated control cuttings. Unfortunately, 1-MCP may reduce rooting of geranium, hibiscus, and chrysanthemum cuttings; 1-MCP had no effect on leaf yellowing of 'Coral Charm' chrysanthemum unrooted cuttings.

Figure 12.5. A worker counts and bags poinsettia cuttings in the greenhouse. (J. Faust)

Figure 12.6. Boxes of poinsettia cuttings are stored in a cooler prior to shipment. (J. Faust)

Handling and Shipping

Cuttings are harvested from stock plants during the morning and early afternoon (fig. 12.5). The cuttings are usually counted and bagged in the greenhouse or field and then placed in a cooler, where the orders are sorted and boxed (fig. 12.6). Cuttings of cold-tolerant species should be held at 35° to 50° F (2° to 10° C) and those of chilling-sensitive species at 50° to 60° F (10° to 16° C). Vacuum cooling (fig. 12.7) or forced-air cooling is often performed to remove the greenhouse heat from the packages of cuttings. Frozen gel packs or ice may be included in the packed boxes to maintain cool temperatures during transit.

Then the cuttings are taken to the airport in the afternoon or evening and transported by plane to a port of entry, such as Los Angeles or Miami. In some situations, the boxes are re-iced at the port of entry—that is, the melted ice or gel packs are replaced with frozen ice or gel packs. USDA-APHIS (U.S. Department of Agriculture's Animal and Plant Health Inspection Service) inspects the cuttings; if acceptable, the boxes are transported to the customer via an express mail carrier or a temperature-controlled truck. Express mail shipments are usually delivered to the customer within forty-eight hours from the time the cuttings are harvested. Truck delivery may require an additional day; however, temperature control can be maintained throughout the additional time.

Growers must check the cuttings immediately upon arrival for any noticeable signs of damage, disease, or death. The condition of the cuttings affects

Figure 12.7. A vacuum cooler is used to remove the greenhouse heat from boxes of cuttings prior to shipment. (J. Faust)

Figure 12.8. A typical unrooted cutting shipping container made of cardboard box lined with polystyrene sheets. (J. Faust)

Figure 12.11. Cuttings are often wrapped in moistened paper to help keep them hydrated during shipment. (J. Faust)

Figure 12.12. The use of ice or gel packs adds further temperature control during shipment. (J. Faust)

Figure 12.9. (A) Cuttings are placed in individual plastic bags, with (B) one cultivar per bag. (J. Faust)

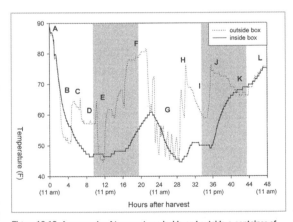

Figure 12.13. An example of temperatures inside and outside a container of unrooted cuttings shipped internationally during August: Shaded areas of the graph represent nighttime (nine p.m. to six a.m.). The temperature inside the box is effectively maintained between 50° and 60° F (10° and 16° C), despite outside temperatures ranging from 45° to 80° F (7° to 27° C). The temperature inside the box warms up to ambient (outside temperatures) during the last few hours of shipping, underscoring the importance of proper handling when the boxes arrive at the greenhouse.

Letters on graph refer to shipping stages: A = cuttings harvested in the greenhouse (August 1, 11:00 A.M.), B = vacuum cooling, boxing, and placing in cooler, C = delivery of boxes (via truck) to airport, D = boxes held at the airport prior to flight, E = flight to U.S. Port of Entry, F = boxes held in customs—USDA-APHIS inspection, G = boxes held in cooler, H = flight to regional distribution center, I = boxes held at regional distribution center, J = flight to local distribution center, K = on local delivery truck, L = delivery to greenhouse (August 3, 11:00 A.M.)

Figure 12.10. Some cuttings, such as poinsettias, are placed in wax-coated cardboard trays. (J. Faust)

their storage longevity as well as their performance in propagation. Ideally, the cuttings should be stuck immediately upon arrival. However, if the cuttings cannot be stuck right away and if they are sufficiently hydrated, they can be stored in a cooler with high relative humidity (80 to 95%) for up to twenty-four hours. The temperature should be 35° to 50° F (2° to 10° C) for cold-tolerant species (which includes most species), and 50° to 60° F (10° to 16° C) for chilling-sensitive species. Some growers will schedule the cuttings to be placed in the cooler prior to stick, since cooled cuttings maintain turgidity better when stuck. If no cooler is available, the cuttings can be placed on the propagation bench under mist and shade cloth until they can be stuck. The mist should keep the cuttings well hydrated; however, if the cuttings are laid horizontally, the stems will bend, making them more difficult to stick. The cuttings will decline rapidly after arrival if the boxes are placed in a location warmer than 70° F (21° C). Botrytis often limits the storage longevity of unrooted cuttings, even when cuttings are held at optimal temperatures.

Shipping containers
Unrooted and calloused cuttings
Shipping containers for unrooted and calloused cuttings are usually made of corrugated cardboard and lined with polystyrene sheets to provide temperature insulation (fig. 12.8). The outside of the box may be white to reflect sunlight and thus limit the heat buildup inside the box. Cuttings are placed in plastic bags by cultivar (one cultivar per bag) (Fig. 12.9) or arranged in wax-coated cardboard trays (fig. 12.10). Depending on cutting size, there are normally 100 to 200 cuttings per bag or tray. Holes may be poked into the bags to increase ventilation within the package; they will reduce ethylene and carbon dioxide accumulation and decrease oxygen depletion inside. Additionally, the cuttings may be wrapped in moistened paper to reduce cutting desiccation during shipping (fig. 12.11). Only USDA-approved packing materials, such as paper, plastic, or vermiculite, can be used for importation of cuttings into the United States. Other importing countries may have similar requirements. Calloused cuttings are usually packed at a lower density (number of cuttings per box) than unrooted cuttings.

Ice or gel packs are often added to the shipping containers for further temperature management (fig. 12.12). The cuttings must be shielded from direct contact with the ice in order to prevent cold damage. Temperature management is the primary limiting factor

Figure 12.14. Rooted cuttings can be removed from the propagation trays prior to shipping in order to decrease freight costs. For example, chrysanthemums are placed in plastic bags in groups of fifty rooted cuttings. (J. Dole)

Figure 12.15. Plug trays are sometimes protected with bubble wrap during shipment. (J. Faust).

Figure 12.16. Plug trays are placed inside cardboard inserts and then layered in the shipping box. (J. Faust)

for successful shipment of cuttings, since precise temperature control cannot be done with current airfreight shipping methods. Containers of cuttings leave the off-shore production facilities at "cool" temperatures of 50° to 60° F (10° to 16° C) and are usually maintained at that level during shipment for the first twenty-four hours (fig. 12.13). Temperatures inside the boxes may vary widely during the second day of shipping, depending on the external environment. As shipping temperatures inside the box increase, so do respiration rates, ethylene production, dehydration, and cutting degradation; thus it is important for growers to quickly place boxes of cuttings into a temperature-controlled area or to unpackage the cuttings. Each additional hour in a warm package will negatively impact cutting performance and survival.

Rooted cuttings

Physical damage, temperature management, dehydration, botrytis blight, and ethylene are primary factors that affect rooted cuttings during shipping. Considerable effort has gone into designing the liners and packages to minimize physical damage. Containers for shipping rooted cuttings are usually constructed from corrugated cardboard; during the winter months, they are lined with polystyrene sheets. Rooted cuttings are often grown in a foam product such as Oasis or a special substrate containing a bonding agent or polymer additive, such as Preforma. The substrate helps maintain the integrity of the root-ball during shipping and prevents the plugs from becoming bare-rooted.

Rooted cuttings can be shipped with or without plug trays. For example, rooted cuttings of chrysanthemums are removed from the plug tray, then packaged and shipped in plastic bags (fig. 12.14). Rooted cuttings shipped in plug flats are placed on racks when they are shipped by truck or boxed for shipping by express mail carrier. The boxed flats are usually wrapped with nylon netting, bubble wrap (fig. 12.15), or spun-bonded fabrics to help protect the plants and prevent dislodging.

The wrapped trays are then placed inside corrugated cardboard inserts, which are fitted in layers inside the box (fig. 12.16).

References

Abeles, F. B., P. W. Morgan, and M. E. Saltveit Jr. 1992. *Ethylene in Plant Biology.* Academic Press, San Diego, California.

Gibson, J. L., B. E. Whipker, S. Blankenship, M. Boyette, T. Creswell, J. Miles, and M. Peet. 1999. Ethylene pollution can kill your plants. *GM Pro* 19(11):55–63.

Hardenburg, R. E., A. E. Watada, and C. Y. Wang. 1986. *The Commercial Storage of Fruits, Vegetables, and Florist and Nursery Stocks.* U.S. Department of Agriculture. Agricultural Handbook 66. Superintendent of Documents, Washington, D.C.

Muller, R., M. Serek, E. C. Sisler, and A. S. Andersen. 1997. Poststorage quality and rooting ability of *Epipremnum pinnatum* cuttings after treatment with ethylene action inhibitors. *Journal of Horticultural Science* 72:445–452.

Muller, R., M. Serek, E. C. Sisler, and A. S. Anderson. 1998. Ethylene involvement in leaf abscission, chlorosis, and rooting of *Codiaeum variegatum* var. *pictum* (Lodd.) Muell. 'Aucubaefolia'. *Gartenbauwissenschaft* 63:66–71.

Nowak, J. and R. M. Rudnicki. 1990. *Postharvest Handling and Storage of Cut Flowers, Florist Greens, and Potted Plants.* Timber Press, Portland, Oregon.

Serek, M., A. Prabucki, E. C. Sisler, and A. S. Andersen. 1998. Inhibitors of ethylene action affect final quality and rooting of cuttings before and after storage. *HortScience* 33:153–155.

Wills, R., B. McGlasson, D. Graham, and D. Joyce. 1998. *Postharvest: An Introduction to the Physiology and Handling of Fruit, Vegetables and Ornamentals,* 4th ed. CAB International, New York.

Part 2

13

Cutting Propagation of Specialty Bedding Plants

John M. Dole and James L. Gibson

Introduction

What is a bedding plant? It is any plant that provides temporary color or texture to the landscape. Years ago the answer used to be much more specific: an herbaceous annual or tender perennial sold in a bedding plant flat and used for temporary color in the landscape. Today, however, the lines are increasingly blurred between bedding plants and other groups of plants, such as indoor foliage plants, perennials, and woody trees, shrubs, and vines. Increasingly, landscapers and the general public use specific plants as bedding plants because of their color, size, and price, and they do not care if the plant was "supposed" to be something else.

Many indoor foliage plants make excellent outdoor bedding plants; they include rex and angel wing begonias, bromeliads, spider plant (*Chlorophytum comosum*), *Pilea*, plectranthus, nephthytis (*Syngonium podophyllum*), and wandering Jew (*Tradescantia*). Perennials and woody ornamentals with colorful foliage, such as coral bells (*Heuchera*) and hosta, can be also used for one season and replaced along with traditional bedding plants. Mixed containers often contain a range of plant types from "tropical foliage" to "hardy perennials" (figs. 13.1 and 13.2). The right plant for the right garden location at the right price has become the guiding principle.

Today the category "bedding plants" includes flat-grown plants (packs), which are primarily annual and tender perennial ornamentals and vegetables (fig.

Figure 13.1. A mixed container with hosta, streptocarpella, *Spilanthes*, impatiens, and fuchsia.

13.3); pot-grown plants, which encompass annual, tender perennial, and perennial ornamentals and vegetables (fig. 13.4); and hanging baskets, which are generally limited to annual and tender perennial ornamentals (fig. 13.5). A wide variety of plants are grown as specimens in large containers as patio plants; among the most popular is the tropical hibiscus, a tender woody shrub. Mixed plantings of several species in

Figure 13.2. A mixed container with 'Sundance' *Cordyline*, coleus, centradenia, and other species.

Figure 13.3. Flat of 'Tricolor' salvia.

Figure 13.5. Hanging baskets of 'Fiesta ole Frost' impatiens.

Figure 13.4. Pots of 'Designer Whitefire' geranium.

Figure 13.6. Mixed container with calibrachoa, coleus, and other plants.

Figure 13.7. Mixed container with fuchsia, impatiens, coleus, and abutilon.

large pots and hanging baskets, which are also known as combo pots and baskets, have become especially popular (figs. 13.6 and 13.7).

Many commonly used vegetatively propagated bedding plant species have already been covered in this text in separate chapters. The remainder of this chapter lists a variety of additional cutting-propagated bedding plant species.

Abutilon x hybridum and A. megapotamicum

COMMON NAME: Flowering maple, Chinese lantern, abutilon.
FAMILY: Malvaceae.

Description and uses

A. x *hybridum* is a charming tender perennial grown for bell-shaped flowers available in a wide array of mostly pastel colors including white, pink, rose, peach, red, and various shades in between. It grows to 18 in. (45 cm) tall in temperate climates, but to 8 ft. (2.4 m) tall in warm climates. The foliage resembles maple leaves—hence the common name, flowering maple. It can be either seed- or cutting-propagated, is not frost tolerant, and is grown in the spring in pots or hanging baskets. The related species, *A. megapotamicum*, is a spreading version of flowering maple and makes a great hanging basket. It has either solid green or variegated green and yellow foliage and bright red and yellow flowers that hang down from the stems.

Propagation and production

Tip cuttings are taken and rooted at 70° to 75° F (21° to 24° C) using bottom heat. Use rooting hormone (750 ppm KIBA) on some cultivars. Cuttings are ready in four to five weeks. One rooted cutting is used per 4 in. (10 cm) pot, two or three per 6 in. (15 cm) pot, and four to six per 8 to 10 in. (20 to 25 cm) hanging basket. After they are established, plants may be pinched to encourage branching. Ethephon (Florel) sprays at 500 ppm can also be used in conjunction with the pinch to encourage branching. Plants in 4 or 6 in. (10 or 15 cm) pots are ready to sell in eight to ten weeks, and those in 10 in. (25 cm) baskets in ten to twelve weeks. In the summer plants are ready two weeks earlier.

Temperature
Grow plants at 60° to 70° F (16° to 21° C) night temperature. Temperatures below 60° F (16° C) will slow growth greatly, and above 85° F (29° C) may cause flower bud abortion.

Height control
Paclobutrazol (Bonzi) sprays at 5 ppm or chlormequat (Cycocel) at 750 ppm can be used.

Comments
Fertilize with nitrogen at 100 to 150 ppm to prevent excessive canopy growth which would reduce visibility of flowers. Plants grow best in partial shade in the home garden, and can be kept as houseplants during the winter.

Figure 13.8. 'Cloud Nine Blue' ageratum.

Figure 13.9. 'Cloud Nine White' ageratum.

Ageratum houstonianum
COMMON NAME: Ageratum, floss flower.
FAMILY: Compositae.

Description and uses
This annual ornamental is grown in pots. The clusters of small fuzzy-appearing flowers are available in blue, purple, white, and pink (figs. 13.8 and 13.9). Bedding cultivars grow 5 to 8 in. (13 to 20 cm) tall. Tall cultivars can be used as for cut flowers. Both seed- and cutting-propagated cultivars are available.

Propagation and production
Propagate terminal cuttings at 70° to 75° F (21° to 24° C) using bottom heat. Insert one cutting per cell if using plug flats. Rooting hormone is not required for this easy-to-root species. Provide mist for the first five to eight days, and decrease misting as soon as possible to reduce stem elongation during propagation. Rooting should be completed in three to four weeks.

Use one plug per 4 in. (10 cm) pot, and one to three per 6 in. (15 cm) pot. Long days speed flowering. Plants may be pinched after cuttings are established to encourage branching. Plants in 4 in. (10 cm) pots are ready to sell in seven to nine weeks, and those in 6 in. (15 cm) pots in nine to eleven weeks.

Temperature
Ageratum is generally grown at 55° to 62° F (13° to 17° C) night temperature, but may be grown at cooler temperatures, down to 45° F (7° C).

Height control
Sprays of daminozide (B-Nine) at 2,500 to 5,000 ppm or uniconazole (Sumagic) at 5 to 10 ppm are effective. Grow ageratum on the dry side, and use minimal fertilizer to obtain compact, rapid-flowering plants.

Comments
Ageratum flowers, especially those of white cultivars, may turn brown in the summer. Do not allow the plant to dry out, which can lead to substantial leaf yellowing and a papery burn that becomes distinct within the canopy.

Bidens ferulifolia

COMMON NAME: Bidens, tickseed.
FAMILY: Compositae.

Description and uses

This heat- and drought-tolerant plant is native to Mexico and the southwestern United States. It is grown for its multitude of small yellow daisylike flowers (fig. 13.10). The mounding tender perennial grows 5 to 15 in. (13 to 38 cm) tall and equally wide. Although the plant can be seed propagated, it is primarily cutting propagated. Bidens is not frost tolerant and is grown in the spring in pots or hanging baskets as more of a companion plant than a monoculture crop. Flowering tends to diminish in the heat of summer in warm climates.

Figure 13.10. 'Solaire Yellow' bidens.

Propagation and production

Propagate terminal cuttings at 70° to 75° F (21° to 24° C) using bottom heat. Insert one to two rooted cuttings per cell if using plug flats. Rooting hormone, 2,500 ppm IBA or IBA plus NAA, should be used. Reduce misting as soon as possible to prevent a delay in rooting. Rooting should be completed in three to four weeks.

One plug is used per 4 or 6 in. (10 or 15 cm) pot, and two to four per 8 in. (20 cm) pot. Avoid high soluble salts. Generally, 4 in. (10 cm) pots are ready to sell in four to six weeks, 6 in. (15 cm) pots in six to eight weeks, and 8 in. (20 cm) pots in eight to ten weeks.

Temperature

Grow plants at 55° to 60° F (13° to 16° C) night temperature, but cooler temperatures down to 45° F (7° C) can be used to hold the plants.

Height control

During propagation sprays of daminozide (B-Nine) at 2,500 to 3,000 ppm or a tank-mix spray of ancymidol (A-Rest) at 6 to 12 ppm and daminozide at 1,250 to 2,500 ppm can be used fourteen to twenty-four days after sticking an unrooted cutting.

Comments

Along with coreopsis, this is another plant with an unattractive common name, tickseed. The name bidens is better but not by much.

Brachyscome species

COMMON NAME: Swan river daisy, brachyscome.
FAMILY: Compositae.

Description and uses

The white, yellow, violet, or blue daisylike flowers have yellow or black centers and are 1 in. (2.5 cm) wide (figs. 13.11 and 13.12). Plants grow to 10 in. (25 cm) tall. *B. iberidifolia* is an annual that is primarily seed propagated; *B. angustifolia*, *B. multifida*, and *B. segmentosa* are annuals or tender perennials that are primarily cutting propagated (fig. 13.13). Numerous hybrids exist. None of the species are frost tolerant, and all are grown in packs, pots, or hanging baskets.

Propagation and production

Propagate terminal cuttings at 70° to 75° F (21° to 24° C) using bottom heat. Rooting hormone, 2,500 ppm IBA or IBA plus NAA, should be used. With plug flats, one or two cuttings are usually inserted per cell. Rooting should be completed in three to four weeks.

One plug and no pinch are used with 4 and 5 in. (10 and 13 cm) pots, one to two plugs and one to two pinches with 6 in. (15 cm) pots, and three to four plugs and one to two pinches with 8 to 10 in. (20 to 25 cm) pots. Plants in 4 to 6 in. (10 to 15 cm) pots are ready to sell in four to six weeks, and those in 8 to 10 in. (20 to 25 cm) pots in ten to twelve weeks. The crop finishes two to four weeks earlier in the spring.

Temperature

Grow these plants at 63° to 68° F (17° to 20° C) night temperature. Finish at cooler temperatures, down to 45° to 50° F (7° to 10° C), for the best quality.

Figure 13.11. 'New Amethyst' brachyscome.

Figure 13.12. 'Mini Yellow' brachyscome flats ready for market.

Figure 13.13. Brachyscome rooted cuttings ready to transplant.

Height control
Usually no growth regulators are required, but daminozide (B-Nine) at 2,500 to 5,000 ppm can be used. Ancymidol (A-Rest) or paclobutrazol (Bonzi) are also effective.

Comments
These plants are day-neutral.

Felicia amelloides
COMMON NAME: Felicia, blue marguerite.
FAMILY: Compositae.

Description and uses
This spreading plant is grown for its blue to white daisies. The plant grows to 20 in. (50 cm) tall and is hardy to Zone 9. Felicia is not frost tolerant and is grown in the spring in pots or mixed containers. It performs best in areas with cool nights and low humidity. Felicia can be grown in the spring in warm climates.

Propagation and production
Propagate terminal cuttings at 70° to 75° F (21° to 24° C) using bottom heat. Insert one cutting per cell if using plug flats. Rooting hormone should be used on this species. Provide mist for the first five to ten days. Rooting should be completed in four to five weeks.

One plug is used per 4 in. (10 cm) pot, two or three per 6 in. (15 cm) pot, and four or five per 8 to 10 in. (20 to 25 cm) pot. Plants should be pinched as soon as rooted liners are established, and they may need to be pinched again during production. Generally, 4 in. (10 cm) pots are ready to sell in eight to ten weeks, 6 in. (15 cm) pots in nine to eleven weeks, and 10 in. (25 cm) pots in ten to twelve weeks.

Temperature
Grow plants at 50° to 55° F (10° to 13° C) night temperatures.

Height control
A tank-mix spray of daminozide (B-Nine) at 2,500 to 4,000 ppm and chlormequat (Cycocel) at 1,000 to 1,500 ppm can be used.

Comments
Unfortunately, this charming plant is not able to be widely grown due to its specific temperature requirements outdoors.

Iresine herbstii

COMMON NAME: Bloodleaf, chicken gizzard, beefsteak plant, iresine.
FAMILY: Amaranthaceae.

Description and uses

While originally used as an indoor foliage plant passed from family to family, this species has been reborn as a colorful outdoor bedding plant. It is grown for its purple or green foliage variegated with white, pink, red, or yellow (figs. 13.14 and 13.15). The flowers are insignificant. Spreading forms grow 6 to 8 in. (15 to 20 cm) tall and 3 to 4 ft. (90 to 120 cm) wide. Upright forms grow up to 24 in. (60 cm) tall. Iresine can be either seed or cutting propagated. This tender perennial is not frost tolerant and is grown in the spring in pots or hanging baskets. Iresine can be grown in sun to partial shade in the home garden.

Propagation and production

Propagate terminal cuttings at 70° to 75° F (21° to 24° C) using bottom heat. Insert one cutting per cell if using plug flats. Rooting hormone is optional for this species. Provide mist for the first four to seven days. Rooting should be completed in three to four weeks.

One plug is used per 4 in. (10 cm) pot, one or two per 6 in. (15 cm) pot, and four or five per 8 to 10 in. (20 to 25 cm) pot. Plants should be pinched as soon as rooted liners are established, and they may need to be pinched frequently during production. Plants in 4 in. (10 cm) pots are ready to sell in six to eight weeks, those in 6 in. (15 cm) pots in seven to ten weeks, and those in 10 in. (25 cm) pots in ten to thirteen weeks.

Temperature

Grow iresine at 62° to 65° F (17° to 18° C) night temperatures.

Height control

None is generally required. Restrict water and fertilizer or provide a soft pinch to hold plants back if they appear to be growing too tall.

Comments

Ethylene at 0.1 to 1 ppm did not influence leaf abscission or cutting rooting.

Figure 13.14. 'Blazin Rose' iresine.

Figure 13,15. Iresine plug flat.

Lotus berthelotii

COMMON NAME: Parrot's beak, coral gem.
FAMILY: Leguminosae.

Description and uses

The unusual orange-red to scarlet or purple pealike flowers have a long slender beak and occur in loose terminal clusters on low-growing vines (fig. 13.16). The foliage is silvery gray. This tender cutting-propagated perennial is not frost tolerant, and it is sold in the spring in pots and hanging baskets.

Propagation and production

Propagate terminal cuttings at 70° to 75° F (21° to 24° C) using bottom heat. Insert one cutting per cell if using plug flats.

One plug is used per 4 in. (10 cm) pot, one or two per 6 in. (15 cm) pot, and three or four per 8 to 10 in. (20 to 25 cm) pot. Plants grown in 6 in. (15 cm) or larger containers should be pinched; the first pinch

Figure 13.16. 'Amazon Sunset' parrot's beak.

should occur when six to eight leaves have formed, and additional pinches can be made when two leaf pairs can remain. In the spring, 4 in. (10 cm) pots are marketable in five to six weeks, 6 in. (15 cm) pots in six to seven weeks, 8 in. (20 cm) hanging baskets in eight to ten weeks and 10 in. (25 cm) hanging baskets in ten to twelve weeks. Crop time is one to two weeks shorter during the summer.

Temperature
Grow plants at 50° to 60° F (10° to 16° C) night temperature. Plants require a four- to eight-week-long cold treatment at 40° to 45° F (4° to 7° C) for flower initiation. Once initiated, flowering will continue as long as the night temperature remains below 60° F (16° C). Plants may stop flowering during the summer but may flower again in the fall.

Height control
None is usually required.

Comments
Even, consistent irrigation is important.

Mentha species
COMMON NAME: Mint, peppermint, spearmint.
FAMILY: Labiatae.

Description and uses
This well-known herb was the original source of one of the most ubiquitous flavorings in candy, desserts, and a variety of other products. Many species of mint with attractive foliage, flowers, and fragrance also make wonderful garden perennials. Be aware, howev-

er, that they can be invasive in the home garden because of the numerous stolons, underground stems, that they produce. Unless the right contained location is found in the landscape, mints can be more easily grown in pots. Dozens of species and cultivars are available in a range of leaf colors, plant habits, and fragrances including citrus, apple, pineapple, chocolate, and ginger. Two of the more common and popular species are spearmint, *M. spicata*, which grows 30 in. (75 cm) tall and peppermint, *M.* x *piperita*, which grows to 36 in. (90 cm) tall. Mints are both seed and cutting propagated, but those with the best fragrance are cutting propagated.

Propagation and production
Plants can be propagated from either 3 to 4 in. (8 to 10 cm) terminal cuttings or stolon segments. Most species of mints produce stolons, which can be harvested and cut into pieces for propagation. Stolon development typically starts anytime from when flower buds are first visible until just after flowering. Peak stolon production occurs at the end of flowering. Propagate cuttings at 72° to 77° F (22° to 25° C). If using terminal cuttings, rooting hormone (500 ppm KIBA) may be helpful with some cultivars. Plants can be readily propagated in the final container. Cuttings should be rooted within seven days. After roots are present, begin fertilizing with 50 to 75 ppm nitrogen from 14-0-14 with every other irrigation, and reduce misting. Once cuttings are well rooted, lower the substrate temperature to 65° to 72° F (18° to 22° C), increase light levels, and reduce humidity.

One plug is used per 4 in. (10 cm) pot, and one to three per 6 in. (15 cm) pot. Plants should be pinched as soon as rooted liners are established. Older plants can be pinched as needed. Plants in 4 in. (10 cm) pots are ready to sell in three to four weeks. Add one to two weeks for plants in 6 in. (15 cm) pots.

Temperature
Grow plants at 58° to 64° F (14° to 18° C) night temperature. Avoid day temperatures above 86° F (30° C).

Height control
None is usually required.

Comments
Be aware of insects such as whitefly and thrips, and use appropriate control measures.

Mimulus x hybridus

COMMON NAME: Mimulus, monkey flower.
FAMILY: Scrophulariaceae.

Description and uses

The tubular white, yellow, orange, or red flowers are produced on 8 to 12 in. (20 to 30 cm) tall plants. The plants are not frost tolerant and are sold in the spring in packs, pots, and hanging baskets. Both seed- and cutting-propagated cultivars are available, but those propagated from cuttings are most commonly grown.

Propagation and production

Propagate terminal cuttings at 70° to 75° F (21° to 24° C) using bottom heat. Insert one cutting per cell if using plug flats. Pinch cuttings in propagation three weeks after sticking.

Use one plug per 4 in. (10 cm) pot, one or two per 6 in. (15 cm) pot, and three to four per 10 in. (25 cm) basket. Pinching is useful. Fertilize at 150 to 200 ppm nitrogen, and maintain substrate pH at 5.5 to 6.2. Provide high light of at least 5,000 to 6,000 f.c. (54 to 65 klux). Plants do not tolerate water stress, which causes lower leaves to turn yellow and drop. Plants are ready to sell in twelve to fourteen weeks, regardless of container size.

Temperature

Grow mimulus initially at 60° to 65° F (16° to 18° C) night temperature, then lower to 50° to 55° F (10° to 13° C) for production. Reduce the temperature to 40° to 45° F (4° to 7° C) to hold plants.

Height control

Daminozide (B-Nine) at 1,500 to 2,500 ppm or chlormequat (Cycocel) at 1,500 ppm can be used for height control.

Comments

Mimulus is a long-day plant requiring day lengths of thirteen hours or longer.

Nolana humifusa

COMMON NAME: Nolana.
FAMILY: Nolanaceae.

Description and uses

This low-spreading plant grows to 6 in. (15 cm) tall and has small blue flowers. Plants are not frost toler- ant and are grown in the spring in hanging baskets and mixed containers.

Propagation and production

Propagate terminal cuttings at 70° to 75° F (21° to 24° C) using bottom heat. Insert one cutting per cell if using plug flats. Three to five plugs are used in a 10 to 12 in. (25 to 30 cm) hanging basket, which finish in ten weeks. Use a well-drained substrate with a pH of 6.0 to 6.5. Keep plant evenly moist, and avoid high soluble salts in the substrate, especially during short days. Plants are ready to sell in ten weeks.

Temperature

Grow plants at 60° to 65° F (16° to 18° C) night temperature.

Height control

Ethephon (Florel) sprays can be used at 500 to 1,000 ppm, but they will delay flowering.

Comments

While not well known, this species is becoming more common.

Otacanthus caeruleus

COMMON NAME: Brazilian snapdragon.
FAMILY: Scrophulariaceae.

Description and uses

Intense blue flowers are this tender perennial's main attraction. Flowering is minimal in the heat of summer in warm climates but occurs heavily in the fall. The plant grows 36 in. (90 cm) tall and is used in pots and mixed containers.

Propagation and production

Propagate terminal cuttings at 70° to 75° F (21° to 24° C) using bottom heat. Insert one cutting per cell if using plug flats. Use one plug per 4 or 6 in. (10 or 15 cm) pot, three per 8 in. (20 cm) pot, and four per 10 in. (25 cm) pot. Pinch plants above the second node after plugs are established. A second pinch may be needed on larger containers. Use a well-drained substrate with a pH of 5.6 to 6.2; higher pH may cause interveinal chlorosis on young leaves. Keep plants evenly moist, and avoid high soluble salts in the substrate, especially during short days. Plants in 4 in. (10 cm) pots are ready to sell in nine weeks, those in 6 in. (15 cm) pots in twelve weeks, and those in 8 in. (20 cm) pots in nine weeks.

Temperature
Grow plants at 60° to 65° F (16° to 18° C) night temperature.

Height control
Daminozide (B-Nine) sprays at 2,500 ppm can be used.

Comments
Brazilian snapdragon is considered a tropical perennial. In northern locations it should be produced later in spring when the day length is longer and the ambient air temperatures are warmer. Beginning production too early results in stalled growth and wasted production resources.

Perilla frutescens
COMMON NAMES: Perilla.
FAMILY: Labiatae.

Description and uses
This coleus-like plant is grown for its green, bronze, or purple foliage. Newer cultivars with bright pink and white variegated foliage have renewed interest in the formerly little-used plant (fig. 13.17). The flowers are small and not particularly attractive. A heat-tolerant annual that grows 24 to 36 in. (60 to 90 cm) tall and 18 to 24 in. (45 to 60 cm) wide, perilla is primarily cutting propagated. It is not frost tolerant and is grown in the spring in pots or large baskets. Variegated cultivars lose some of their color when grown in the shade in the home garden.

Propagation and production
Propagate terminal cuttings at 70° to 75° F (21° to 24° C) using bottom heat. Insert one cutting per cell if using plug flats. Rooting hormone is not required for this easy-to-root species. Provide mist for the first four to seven days, and decrease misting as soon as possible to reduce stem elongation during propagation. Rooting should be completed in two to three weeks.

One plug is used per 4 in. (10 cm) pot, one or two per 6 in. (15 cm) pot, and three or four per 8 to 10 in. (20 to 25 cm) pots. Pinch plants as needed to shape them and to reduce their height. Plants in 4 in.

Figure 13.17. 'Magilla' perilla.

(10 cm) pots are ready to sell in five to seven weeks, those in 6 in. (15 cm) pots in six to eight weeks, those in and 10 in. (25 cm) pots in eight to eleven weeks.

Temperature
Grow plants at 60° to 70° F (16° to 21° C) night temperature.

Height control
Daminozide (B-Nine) at 2,500 to 4,000 ppm can be used. Multiple sprays may be necessary.

Comments
Ethylene at 0.1 to 1 ppm did not influence leaf abscission or cutting rooting.

Phlox drummondii
Common name: Annual phlox.
Family: Polemoniaceae.

Description and uses
This annual version of the stately perennial garden phlox also has clusters of white, pink, apricot, rose, red, or lavender flowers (fig. 13.18). Plants are only 8 to 10 in. (20 to 25 cm) tall and flower all season. The species can be propagated either by seed or cuttings; however, cuttings tend to be more vigorous and floriferous. In mild climates, Zones 9 to 11, some cultivars have excellent heat and cold tolerance and may flower year-round. In cool climates plants are grown during the summer.

Propagation and production

Propagate terminal cuttings at 72° to 75° F (22° to 24° C) using bottom heat. Insert one cutting per cell if using plug flats. Rooting hormone is not required but may be beneficial; if so, 1000 ppm KIBA can be

Figure 13.18. 'Intensia Lavender Glow' annual phlox.

used. Provide mist for the first six to ten days. Rooting should be completed in four to five weeks, but additional time may be required to produce a plant ready for transplanting.

Use one plug per 4 to 6 in. (10 to 15 cm) pots, and three for larger pots and hanging baskets. Pinching can be used but is usually not required. Plants are day-neutral. Overwatering promotes root rot. Use 200 ppm nitrogen from low to moderate ammonium fertilizers. Plants in 4 to 6 in. (10 to 15 cm) pots finish in five to seven weeks, and those in larger pots and hanging baskets in six to eight weeks.

Temperature

Grow plants at 63° to 68° F (17° to 20° C) night temperature, although plants can be grown much cooler, down to 45° F (7° C).

Height control

Daminozide (B-Nine) sprays at 2,500 to 5,000 ppm are effective.

Comments

The heat tolerance of newer cultivars has made them exceptional garden plants.

Phygelius aequalis and *P. capensis*

COMMON NAMES: Phygelius, cape fuchsia.
FAMILY: Scrophulariaceae.

Description and uses

This charming plant produces loose open spikes of drooping trumpet-shaped flowers on plants to 4 ft. (1.2 m) tall. The flowers range in color from white, pink, and salmon to orange, and the foliage can be bright green or bronze (fig. 13.19). While plant habit is typically upright, phygelius can be grown in both pots and hanging baskets. Plants can be propagated by cuttings or seed. Plants are cold hardy to Zone 7 and remain evergreen down to 20° F (–7° C).

Propagation and production

Propagation requires two to three weeks, and finished plants in 6 in. (15 cm) pots are ready to sell in six to eight

Figure 13.19. 'Croftway' phygelius.

weeks. Rooting hormone (750 ppm KIBA) may be helpful. Use one plant per 6 in. (15 cm) pot. Use high light, above 5,000 f.c. (54 klux), and 150 ppm nitrogen from moderate to low ammonium fertilizers. The pH of the substrate should be 5.5 to 5.8. Plants should be pinched after cuttings are established to encourage branching. Plants can also be sheared if overgrown and allowed to rebloom in three to five weeks. Plants tend to flower in flushes, and they can be sheared between the flushes.

Temperature

Plants are generally grown at 60° to 65° F (16° to 18° C) night temperature.

Height control

Paclobutrazol (Bonzi) drenches at 0.25 to 0.5 ppm can be used. Do not overwater, which will cause excessive stem elongation.

Comments

These new and uncommon plants can make a charming addition to the landscape.

Rosmarinus officinalis

COMMON NAMES: Rosemary.
FAMILY: Labiatae.

Description and uses

This small to medium-size shrub with its gray-green, needlelike aromatic foliage is one of the most popular herbs (fig.13. 20). Plants grow to 4 ft. (1.2 m) tall and are sold in the spring in various pot sizes. Several cultivars are available; they vary in height, plant shape (upright or reclining), cold hardiness (to Zone 6), and flower color (pink to purple).

Propagation and production

Propagate 4 to 6 in. (10 to 15 cm) terminal cuttings at 70° to 75° F (21° to 24° C) using bottom heat. Insert one cutting per cell if using plug flats. Rooting hormone, 2,500 ppm IBA or IBA plus NAA, should be used. Provide mist for the first six to ten days. Reduce misting as soon as possible to prevent rotting. Rooting should be completed in three to four weeks.

Figure 13.20. Rosemary plant.

Use one plug per 4 in. (10 cm) pot, two to three per 6 in. (15 cm) pot, and three to five per 8 to 10 in. (20 to 25 cm) pots. Plants may be pinched after cuttings are established to encourage branching. Plants may also be trimmed at any time. Use a well-drained substrate with a pH of 6.5 to 6.8. Even, consistent irrigation is important; however, the substrate should be allowed to dry between irrigations. Avoid overirrigation, especially after transplanting plugs. Plants in 4 in. (10 cm) pots are ready to sell in six to eight weeks, those in 6 in. (15 cm) pots in seven to nine weeks, and those in 8 to 10 in. (20 to 25 cm) pots in eight to ten weeks.

Temperature

Grow plants at 62° to 68° F (17° to 20° C) night temperature.

Height control

None is usually required.

Comments

Potted rosemary can be sheared into topiary shapes or standards to make a high-dollar specialty item.

Santolina chamaecyparissus

COMMON NAME: Lavender cotton, santolina.
FAMILY: Compositae.

Description and uses

This mounding, compact plant makes a great perennial hedge or edging. The fine-textured foliage is green to grayish and fragrant. Small yellow flowers are produced but are not the main attraction. Cultivars vary in height from 6 to 18 in. (15 to 45 cm). Plants are hardy to Zone 7 but struggle in areas of high humidity and rainfall. They are sold in small pots in the spring.

Propagation and production

Propagate terminal cuttings at 70° F (21° C) using bottom heat. Cuttings should be made from the soft green growth; avoid using woody cuttings since they take longer to root, resulting in higher losses. Use two to three cuttings per plug flat cell. Do not overmist this species.

Use one plug per 4 in. (10 cm) pot, and one to three per 6 in. (15 cm) pot. Grow the plants on the dry side since they are easily overwatered, which will result in root and crown rot and soft growth. If using large or mixed containers, transplant plugs to an intermediate-size container first to prevent overwatering. The fertilizer rate should also be relatively low, at 100 to 125 ppm nitrogen. Give plants a pinch one to two weeks after transplanting, and trim older plants as needed. Plants in 4 in. (10 cm) pots will be ready to sell in six to seven weeks, and those in 6 in. (15 cm) pots in eight to ten weeks.

Temperature

Plants are grown at 60° to 65° F (16° to 18° C) night temperature and finished at 45° to 50° F (7° to 10° C).

Height control

None is usually required.

Comments

The similar *S. rosmarinifolia* is grown occasionally; it has narrower leaves that are green.

Strobilanthes dyerianus
COMMON NAME: Persian shield.
FAMILY: Acanathaceae.

Description and uses
This tender perennial shrub is grown for its large striking purple, silver, and green leaves (figs. 13.21 and 13.22). Spikes of small flowers occur but are not desirable (fig. 13.23). The species reaches 4 ft. (1.2 m) tall. Plants are typically grown in containers.

Propagation and production
Propagate terminal cuttings at 70° to 75° F (21° to 24° C) using bottom heat. The jury is still out on this plant regarding its photoperiod requirements. Juvenility of the tissue and day length may influence flowering. In general, plants produce flowers during short days and become less vigorous in habit. Growers can keep plants vegetative by extending the day length to fourteen hours. Insert one cutting per cell if using plug flats. Rooting hormone is not required for this species but can be used. Provide mist for the first seven to twelve days. Pinch cuttings eighteen to twenty-one days after sticking to improve branching. Rooting should be completed in four to five weeks.

Use one or two plugs per 6 in. (15 cm) pot, and three to five per 10 in. (25 cm) pot. One or more pinch may be required. The brightest color is obtained with moderate light of 3,000 to 6,000 f.c. (32 to 65 klux). Pinch as needed to encourage branching and to shape the plants. Plants in 6 in. (15 cm) pots are ready to sell in eight to ten weeks, and those in 10 in. (15 cm) pots in ten to thirteen weeks. Fertilize with 200 to 250 ppm nitrogen, rotating between 20-10-20 and 15-0-15 to keep the pH at 5.6 to 6.0.

Temperature
Grow plants at 60° to 65° F (16° to 18° C) night temperature.

Height control
None is generally required. Daminozide (B-Nine) at 2,500 to 5,000 is used for maintaining compact growth in smaller containers.

Comments
Ethylene at 0.1 to 1 ppm did not influence leaf abscission or cutting rooting.

Figure 13.21. Persian shield plants in the landscape.

Figure 13.22. Persian shield foliage.

Figure 13.23. Persian shield flowers on stock plants.

Thunbergia alata

COMMON NAME: Black-eyed Susan vine.
FAMILY: Acanthaceae.

Description and uses

This tender perennial vine has tubular flowers with white, pale lavender, yellow, or orange petals and a throat color ranging from light to dark brown (fig. 13.24). Plants are not frost tolerant and are sold in the spring in pots and hanging baskets (fig. 13.25). Both seed- and cutting-propagated cultivars are available.

Propagation and production

Stick cuttings within one or two hours after harvest or arrival. Propagate cuttings using 3,000 ppm IBA and 70° to 75° F (21° to 24° C) bottom heat. Either terminal or stem cuttings can be used; with the latter be sure at least one node touches the surface of the substrate. Insert one cutting per cell if using plug flats. Provide mist for the first seven to twelve days. Use night mist for the first seven to eight days, and do not ever let the cuttings dry out. Pinch cuttings eighteen to twenty-one days after sticking to improve branching. Rooting should be completed in four to five weeks, and plugs ready to transplant in five to six weeks. It is important to implement a fungicide program during Stage 3 of propagation because of the incidence of devastating foliar diseases, such as rhizoctonia.

Use one plug per 4 in. (10 cm) pot, two to three per 6 in. (15 cm) pot, and three to five per 10 in. (25 cm) basket. Pinching can be useful to increase branching; use one pinch for 4 in. (10 cm) pots, two for 6 in. (15 cm) pots, and two to three pinches for large containers. Use high light, between 5,000 and 8,000 f.c. (54 to 86 klux) and 200 to 250 ppm nitrogen. Maintain a pH of 5.8 to 6.2. Excessive growth can occur if phosphorus or ammonium levels are too high. Foliar chlorosis can be treated either with iron chelate sprays or drenches or with iron sulfate drenches. If using iron sulfate, be sure not to get any on the foliage. Plants in 4 in. (10 cm) pots are ready to sell in six to ten weeks, those in 6 in. (15 cm) pots in seven to eleven weeks, and those in 10 in. (25 cm) baskets in ten to fourteen weeks.

Temperature

Grow plants at 60° to 65° F (16° to 18° C) night temperature. Growth will be greatly slowed if the plants are grown at cooler temperatures than indicated.

Figure 13.24. Black-eyed Susan vine flower.

Figure 13.25. Black-eyed Susan vine pots ready for market (B. Whipker).

Figure 13.26. Flat of black-eyed Susan vine cuttings with disease.

Height control

None is usually required.

Comments

Black-eyed Susan vine is a day-neutral plant. Cuttings are susceptible to various rots (fig. 13.26).

Thymus species

COMMON NAME: Garden thyme, lemon thyme, common thyme.
FAMILY: Labiatae.

Description and uses

These short, prostrate shrubs are grown for their fragrant foliage and profuse clusters of tiny flowers (fig. 13.27). Plants grow from 4 to 15 in. (10 to 38 cm) tall, depending on the species. A number of species can be grown, including lemon thyme, *T.* x *citriodorus*, and common thyme, *T. vulgaris*. Many of the species have cultivars available, including some with variegated foliage. Most species are hardy to Zone 7, but some, such as *T. serpyllum*, are hardy to Zone 5. The spreading growth habit of the various thymes makes them suitable for the edges of urns, window boxes, or hanging baskets in addition to use in the herb garden.

Propagation and production

Most thyme cultivars are propagated by 3 to 6 in. (8 to 15 cm) long cuttings at 70° F (21° C) bottom heat. Cuttings should be made from the soft green growth; use two to three cuttings per plug flat cell or four to six cuttings per 3 in. (8 cm) pot. Avoid using woody cuttings since they take longer to root, resulting in higher losses. Rooting hormone is generally not needed. Do not overmist thyme.

Use one plug per 4 in. (10 cm) pot, and one to three per 6 in. (15 cm) pot. Grow plants on the dry side since they are easily overwatered, which will result in root and crown rot and soft growth. If using large or mixed containers, transplant plugs to an intermediate-size container first to prevent overwatering. The fertilizer rate should also be relatively low, at 100 to 125 ppm nitrogen. Plants in 4 in. (10 cm) pots are ready to sell in five to seven weeks.

Temperature

Plants are grown at 60° to 65° F (16° to 18° C) night temperature and finished at 50° to 60° F (10° to 16° C).

Height control

None is normally required on these low-growing plants. In addition, chemical plant growth regulators cannot be used on plants that might be consumed.

Comments

These multiuse plants should be used more in mixed containers for their great texture and fragrance.

Figure 13.27. 'Orange Balsam' common thyme (*Thymus vulgaris*).

Other Specialty Bedding Plants

The difficulty with any discussion of specialty bedding plants is deciding what to include. The following species have much to offer but, unfortunately, relatively little nonproprietary information is available about them. Several are represented by unpatented cultivars and are readily obtainable.

Acalypha hispida (chenille plant) and *A. pendula* (dwarf creeping chenille)

This charming plant produces long pendulous spikes of small bright red flowers. In tropical areas (cold hardiness Zone 11 and 12) it can grow to 6 ft. (1.8 m) tall, but in temperate areas it is grown primarily as a striking plant for hanging baskets and mixed containers. Dwarf creeping chenille (*A. pendula*) is a durable tropical perennial hardy to Zones 8 to 11; it can be used as a containerized ornamanetal or groundcover (fig. 13.28). Dwarf creeping chenille, which has very few pest problems, performs best in dry acidic to slightly alkaline soils and full sun conditions. Fertilizer recommendations for chenille plant suggest using 200 to 250 ppm nitrogen to increase the length of flowers.

Acalypha wilkesiana (copper leaf)

This old-time tender shrub is grown for its large multicolor leaves ranging in shape from long and narrow to large and wide. Several cultivars are available in a range of colors including copper (of course), red, cream, pink, and yellow. In Zone 10 or warmer areas, the plant grows 10 ft. (3 m) tall; however, in most temperate landscapes it grows only 2 to 4 ft. (60 to 120 cm) in a summer.

Figure 13.28. Chenille plant (*Acalypha hispida*) (N. McCue).

Figure 13.29. 'Wildcat Blue' pimpernel (*Anagallis*).

Allamanda species (allamanda)

Large bright yellow flowers and thick shiny green leaves are produced on a woody vine that grows several feet in temperate climates to over 12 ft. (4 m) in tropical areas. Allamanda is grown as a container plant and is hardy only to Zone 11. It is reported to be propagated easily by using semihardwood cuttings in summer and fall, with up to 2,000 ppm IBA applied. Allamanda should be grown using 65° F (18° C) night temperature.

Aloysia triphylla (lemon verbena)

Although rather unassuming, this tender shrub (hardy to Zone 8) is one of the best lemon-scented plants available. Besides great fragrance, the plant offers shiny green leaves and fast growth. The flowers, however, are small, and the plant can appear lanky and unkempt late in the season. In a single growing season, it will reach 4 to 5 ft. (1.2 to 1.5 m) tall. Softwood cuttings root easily in the spring; more mature cuttings are taken in the summer and the fall.

Anagallis hybrids (pimpernel)

This low-growing plant produces scores of beautiful small blue or orange flowers (figs. 13.29 and 13.30). It is best suited to cool climates and is hardy to Zone 7. Seed-propagated cultivars have been available for years, but recent hybrids have greatly improved the plant. Look for more cultivars to become available.

Centradenia hybrid (centradenia)

This hybrid is grown for its bright purple flowers and green foliage that is bronzy when young (fig. 13.31). The stems are also bronze colored. The plant grows 10 to 14 in. (25 to 35 cm) tall, and its long arching stems spread 24 in. (60 cm) wide. It is hardy to Zone 9 and is grown in hanging baskets, pots and mixed containers.

Figure 13.30. 'Wildcat Orange' pimpernel (*Anagallis*).

Duranta erecta (golden dewdrop)

Known formerly as *D. repens*, this tropical woody shrub can grow 10 to 12 ft. (3 to 4 m) tall, though it usually reaches only 1 to 4 ft. (30 to 120 cm) tall in temperate climates. Cultivars with bright yellow or variegated green and yellow foliage are quite pop-

Figure 13.31. 'Purple Showers' centradenia.

ular. The flowers are mostly purple, but also can be white, and are carried in clusters. Yellow or variegated cultivars are less floriferous. Golden dewdrop is hardy only to Zone 10. Other *Duranta* species and hybrids are available.

Graptophyllum pictum (caricature plant)

This drought- and heat-tolerant species has large leathery bronze or green leaves generously marked in cream, pink or yellow. Plants can grow to 6 ft. (2 m) tall in the tropics but typically reach only 3 to 4 ft. (90 to 120 cm) in temperate climates. The species is hardy to Zone 10. Flowers are rarely produced.

Helichrysum apiculatum (yellow buttons)

Formerly known at *Chrysocephalum apiculatum,* this low-growing native of Australia is hardy to Zone 8. Its small bright yellow flower clusters are the buttons to which the common name refers (fig. 13.32). Plants should be pinched to encourage canopy development.

Hemigraphis alternata and *H. repanda* (waffle plant)

Figure 13.32. Yellow buttons (*Helichrysum apiculatum*).

These low-growing plants are favored for their purplish green leaves. *H. repanda* has narrow leaves, and *H. alternata* wide ones. Both species are slow growing, reach only 6 in. (15 cm) tall, and are hardy to Zone 10. Terminal cuttings will root in two to three weeks at 70° to 75° F (21° to 24° C).

Mandevilla species and hybrids (mandevilla)

Mandevilla is a member of the same family as *Allamanda,* Apocynaceae. It is an evergreen climbing vine characterized by large five-lobed rose, pink, or white flowers, sometimes with a yellow throat, appearing in mid- to late summer. The twining woody tissue that grows several feet in temperate climates to over 12 ft. (4 m) in tropical areas (fig. 13.33) should be supported on a trellis or other structure. The large leath-

Figure 13.33. Mandevilla flower.

ery leaves are shiny dark green and quite attractive. Mandevilla, which is hardy to Zone 10, is grown as a container plant. Single-node hardwood cuttings with half of each of the leaves removed are generally used. Use a rooting hormone (2,500 ppm IBA) and propagate at 70° to 75° F (21° to 24° C) bottom heat. Rooting should be completed in four to five weeks.

Origanum species (oregano, marjoram)

Several species of plants are known as oregano or marjoram, including *O. majorana* and *O. vulgare,* which are hardy to Zones 7 and 5, respectively. Oregano is well-known as a cooking herb. It is a low-growing or weakly upright plant with numerous small hairy leaves. Other species are also grown for their white, pink, or rose-colored flowers. Use terminal cuttings and some cultivars root best with rooting hormone (500 to 750 ppm KIBA).

Pachystachys lutea (golden shrimp plant, golden candles)

This is another old-time plant experiencing a revival, in this case because of its striking yellow upright inflorescences (figs. 13.34 and 13.35). Most of the color is provided by the numerous bracts, but the white tubular flowers are also attractive. Plants can grow to 6 ft. (2 m) tall, but generally they average 24 to 36 in. (60 to 90 cm) in the temperate garden. Plants are tropical and hardy to Zone 10.

Sanchezia speciosa (sanchezia)

This striking and durable tender shrub has large shiny green leaves with the veins boldly marked in yellow and red. The thick reddish stems add even more color. A heat- and drought-tolerant plant, sanchezia

Figure 13.34. Golden shrimp plant (*Pachystachys lutea*) flower.

Figure 13.35. Golden shrimp plant (*Pachystachys lutea*) plant.

makes an excellent addition to mixed containers. The large leaves and thick stems make it difficult to handle in propagation, and limited cutting production has reduced its availability. Plants grow 3 to 4 ft. (90 to 120 cm) tall in a season and are hardy to Zone 10. Plants rarely produce flowers in temperate climates, but the main attraction is the foliage.

Streptocarpella saxorum (streptocarpella)

Ugly name for an attractive plant. This species has beautiful delicate blue flowers produced on wiry stems arching above the plant canopy. As with many gesneriads, the foliage is sensitive to cold water, which produces cream-colored spots and patches on the velvety light green leaves. The plant is perfect for hanging baskets and small pots, growing about 8 in. (20 cm) tall and 12 to 20 in. (30 to 50 cm) wide. It requires some shade outdoors.

References

Faust, J. E. and L. W. Grimes. 2005. Pinch height of stock plants during scaffold development affects cutting production. *HortScience* 40:650–653.

Gaston, M. L., L. A. Kunkle, P. S. Konjoian, and M. F. Wilt, eds. 2001. *Tips on Regulating Growth of Floriculture Crops*, Ohio Florists' Association Services, Columbus, Ohio.

Hamrick, D., ed. 2003. *Ball Redbook*, 17th ed., vol. 2. Ball Publishing, Batavia, Illinois.

Mattson, N. S. and J. E. Erwin. 2005. The impact of photoperiod and irradiance on flowering of several herbaceous ornamentals. *Scientia Horticulturae* 104:275–292.

Moyer, M. and R. Schoellhorn. 2004. Phygelius possibilities. *GPN* 14(8):22–24.

Nemeth, E. and T. V. Pham. 1995. Vegetative propagation of four menthe species. *Gartenbauwissenschaft* 60:34–37.

Starman, T. W., M. C. Robinson, and K. L. Eixmann. 2004. Efficacy of ethephon on vegetative annuals. *HortTechnology* 14:83–87.

Whipker, B. E. 2003. Growth regulators for floricultural crops, pp. 439–448. In: *2003 North Carolina Agricultural Chemicals Manual*. College of Agriculture and Life Science, North Carolina State University, Raleigh, North Carolina.

Williams, J. 2005. Smoothie thunbergia. *GPN* 15(2):90.

Yoder Green Leaf Perennials. 2004. *Handling unrooted perennials.* www.green-leaf-ent.com/URC_Handling_2004.pdf.

14

Cutting Propagation of Herbaceous Perennials

Holly L. Scoggins

We lump a tremendous variety of plants under the heading "perennials." This medley of physiology and morphology—dicots, monocots, creeping, climbing, grasslike, and so on—all affects how the plants are propagated. Ken Druse, author of *Making More Plants* (2000), points out that most perennials suitable for cutting propagation tend to be shrubby, branched dicots. Most have soft, green stems, but some are semiwoody. Some species of herbaceous perennials have yet to experience "cultivarization" to the degree that annuals have, so what is in the trade is the straight, or original, species. Many of these can be successfully and economically propagated by seed. Others, including common monocots like hosta and daylily (*Hemerocallis*), lack the stems to cut, and are best propagated by division. With such a diverse group of plants there are many exceptions to every generality.

In regard to cutting propagation, other chapters cover the general techniques, but this chapter briefly reviews what works specifically for perennials. It also discusses how environmental factors such as photoperiod and vernalization can play a much greater role in the physiology, and in turn, the propagation of hardy perennials than they do with annuals.

Types of Cuttings Used

Stem cuttings

The various types of stem cuttings are the most common. Terminal or tip cuttings include the apical tissue and are usually 2 to 3 in. (5 to 8 cm) in length. Sections taken farther down the stem are known as subterminal or butt cuttings. Several members of the Lamiaceae, or mint family, such as spotted dead net-

tle (*Lamium maculatum*) and anise hyssop (*Agastache*), will root equally well at each and every node. A few species root whether or not a node is present below the media surface. But some species require two nodes, one of which will be stuck into the rooting medium, with the other in the air. For example, false indigo (*Baptisia*) is notoriously hard to root unless you know this little trick. Leaf bud cuttings include a small chunk of stem along with the leaf. Several species and hybrids of sedum root readily this way.

Basal cuttings

A basal cutting differs in that it comes from the crown of the plant, which is that part of the plant where new stems are produced each growing season (fig. 14.1). It may include some stem or just foliage and a piece of

Figure 14.1 A basal cutting of 'Moonshine' yarrow (*Achillea*) ready to stick at Riverbend Nursery, Riner, Virginia.

the crown tissue. These cuttings are most prolific and usable in the early spring, just as new growth is emerging. Be sure to get a bit of the juvenile crown tissue. A greater number of cuttings of "stemless" perennials, such as *Geranium* and yarrow (*Achillea)* species and hybrids, will root. And on all aerial cuttings, keep one or two leaves for the best rooting. If the leaves are large, cut them back to half their surface area to prevent the "umbrella effect" (water applied overhead is blocked from reaching the root zone).

Rhizome and root cuttings

These other types of cutting propagation are used successfully with fleshy-rooted and rhizomed perennials, such as bear's breeches (*Acanthus*), *Bergenia,* Siberian bugloss (*Brunnera macrophylla*), and bleeding heart (*Dicentra spectabilis*). Sections of roots 2 to 3 in. (5 to 8 cm) long should sprout both shoots and roots. But orientation can matter: the end closest to the stem (the proximal end) should point up and be even with the surface of the medium, and the end farthest from the stem (the distal end) should point down. An old trick of the trade is to make a blunt cut at the end destined to become a shoot and a slanted cut at the rooting or distal end. Or if there's enough space, plant them horizontally.

Unfortunately, rhizome and root cuttings rarely yield uniform results and are a lot of work, but they are the best method of propagation for a few species. One of my favorite native perennials, *Astilbe biternata,* is notoriously tough to propagate. However, Dr. Allan Armitage reported serendipitous results in plant multiplication when a dormant plant in the University of Georgia trial garden was accidentally broken apart during cultivation. Which brings us to the topic of the actually taking of the cuttings. I like the advice of Dr. Leonard Perry, from the University of Vermont, on the best tools for perennial cuttings: "Any that work and are appropriate for plant and method; pruners, knives, single-edge razor blade, reciprocating saw. . . ."

Cultural and Environmental Specifics

Cell size

Perennials can be rooted in a wide range of cell sizes, but the 76 to 54 cells per tray size is commonly used (fig. 14.2). As with most crops, the larger the starter plant, the shorter the finish time in the final container. The mass of the cutting often dictates a larger cell; for example, a leaf and stem cutting of 'Autumn Joy' sedum is much bigger than a 2 in. (5 cm) piece of bacopa (*Sutera*) stem. Rooting cuttings in trays that hold 30 to 36 cells yields fewer plants per square foot (square meter) of propagation space, but the shorter amount of time required to finish may result in substantial savings.

Media

Any well-drained soilless medium will work for root-

Figure 14.2. 72-cell tray of 'Hidcote' English lavender (*Lavandula angustifolia*) cuttings, five weeks after sticking.

ing cuttings. Experienced propagators suggest a lighter, better-draining medium for cool-season propagation; adding perlite may be enough. In hot weather, however, excessive transpiration and evaporation may cause plugs to dry out quickly. A medium with a high peat content can help conserve moisture.

Moisture

One of the most common reasons for poor rooting and survival is too much moisture, both on the foliage and in the medium. Just as is the case with some annuals, not all perennial species tolerate constant misting. Reduce the mist cycle for *Artemisia, Gaura*, and Mediterranean herbs such as rosemary and lavender. The survival rate of cuttings improves for most perennial species if they are removed from mist as soon as roots appear.

Leo Blanchette of Blanchette Gardens, Carlisle, Massachusetts, recommends that small-scale propagators consider the use of humidifiers in lieu of a mist system. This method maintains high relative humidity without constantly wet foliage. Propagation with fog may also be an option for large-scale perennial propagators. Experienced in growing sedum and other succulents, John Valleau of Valleybrook Gardens in Niagara-on-the-Lake, Ontario, Canada, notes that sedum tip cuttings root well on a dry bench, with no mist necessary. So many of the propagation houses I have been in seem to grow great crops of algae and other unwanted organisms. Cutting back on mist, providing plenty of light, and keeping a clean, well-ventilated area will greatly enhance success.

Rooting hormones

As with annuals, externally applied hormones can speed root development. Some of the woodier species, such as *Caryopteris* and *Buddleia*, benefit from a dip or a spray, especially if the cuttings are taken in the semihardwood stage in summer. Most perennials root equally well with rooting hormones in talc or solution. A great idea when working with several concentrations or combinations is to color-code the solution with a drop of food coloring. Note that some species may be sensitive to the alcohol used as a solvent for pure (reagent grade) compounds. The potassium salts of indolebutyric acid and napthalenacetic acid (KIBA and KNAA, respectively) do not require alcohol; water can be used as the solvent. An alternative method of auxin application is the poststick spray. Within twenty-four hours of sticking, apply a uniform spray, just until runoff, to dry the foliage.

Research at Auburn University, Alabama, on *Ajania pacifica* found that spray applications of 50 ppm IBA plus 25 ppm NAA gave similar rooting results as a dip of 1,000 ppm IBA plus 500 ppm NAA. Yoder Green Leaf's tip sheet on handling unrooted perennials gives all hormone treatment recommendations as a spray application. One of the main benefits of this method of application is that fewer workers handle chemicals compared with the traditional dip-and-stick routine.

The Roles of Photoperiod and Vernalization

No discussion of propagating perennials can take place without a review of what makes them flower. Whether cuttings are rooted for personal use or to sell to a finishing grower, the way they are handled as plugs can impact when they will flower. Color sells, whether in the form of annuals or perennials; it is more difficult to market green plants. Though this chapter is concerned with propagation, proper environmental management of the cutting once it is rooted is necessary for many species to ensure uniform flowering of the finished product. Conversely, manipulation of the environment may be necessary to maintain a vegetative stock plant.

Perennials may have specific requirements for flowering; photoperiod (day length) and temperature affect many species. However, armed with night-interruption lights, night-extending black cloths, and coolers, we can force plants into flowering long before they would in the landscape. University of Georgia and, more recently, Michigan State University

Figure 14.3. *Coreopsis grandiflora* 'Sunray' lights up the garden in June. (Hahn Horticulture Garden, Virginia Tech)

researchers have invested much time and energy into unlocking the required combinations of cool temperatures and photoperiod for numerous species. They have developed cookbook-style recommendations for species where flowering is desirable, grouping species with similar requirements to streamline production—a tremendous boon to propagators and growers.

But with so many species and cultivars now being produced commercially on a large scale, researchers cannot keep up. To further complicate the situation, flowering responses may vary among different species of the same genus or even cultivars of the same species. For example, the MSU researchers found that certain cultivars of the perennial tickseed *Coreopsis grandiflora* have different needs: 'Early Sunrise' does not require a cold treatment, while 'Baby Sun' and 'Sunray' require ten to fifteen weeks of cold to force flowers (fig. 14.3).

Photoperiod

Many species require long days, and flowering in the landscape will be delayed until that critical photoperiod occurs. These are known as *obligate* long-day plants. Other species would flower eventually in short days, but providing long days speeds the process; these are known as *facultative* long-day plants. Light quality is important. Though incandescent bulbs are sufficient for photoperiodic lighting, research has shown that high intensity discharge (HID) lights such as high-pressure sodium lamps can greatly increase plant quality, which is usually defined as plant mass (see chapter 5). To achieve long-day conditions, the grower can either extend the daylight hours (sixteen hours is effective for most long-day species) or provide night-interruption lighting (usually for four hours from 10:00 P.M. to 2:00 A.M.).

Vernalization

The issue of vernalization separates perennial from annual production. Many species require a period of cold temperatures before flowering will occur in the coming growing season. Growers who propagate their own perennials will often plant the rooted liners in late summer and early fall, then hold them over the winter in a white opaque polyethylene-covered cold frame or outdoors, ensuring that the plant gets the chilling it needs. Another method of ensuring a proper cold period is to place trays of rooted liners in a lighted cooler and gradually decrease the temperature to just above freezing. For most species, eight or ten weeks at 40° to 45° F (5° to 7° C) is sufficient to provide the required vernalization period.

Care must be taken not to overwater dormant plants, nor to allow them to dry out. A fungicide drench prior to chilling can help protect against crown and root rots. When growing plants in a cold frame, watch for increasing temperatures as spring progresses. Some method of ventilation will be necessary on sunny days. Ease the plants into "natural" conditions by midspring, first by ventilating them by opening doors and frame ends, then by perforating the plastic at the top of the house.

Many perennial growers purchase liners that are already vernalized for late winter or early spring potting. They are, essentially, gambling that someone else has applied the proper temperatures and duration. If vernalization is not complete, they can be stuck with green plants in the spring sales window, not an enticing prospect when they invested $1.00 or so in each liner.

Effect of photoperiod and temperature on stock plant management

The flowering response to temperature and photoperiod also complicates the maintenance of stock plants. But you can take the information on forcing perennials into

flower and work backward, doing whatever it takes to prevent floral initiation and maintaining a vegetative state. For example, pot or cut chrysanthemums are held under short days to increase the size of the plant before forcing flowering with long days. The same technique works for some perennial species, creating robust stock plants with no flower buds.

When to Take Cuttings

The ideal perennial (in a propagator's eyes) would yield large numbers of fast-rooting, uniform cuttings year-round. Unfortunately, that is not the case for most genera. Whether the limiting factor is flowering, lack of branching, or mature plants that refuse to root, a propa-

Figure 14.4. Recently transplanted *Gaura lindheimeri* in March, when lack of supplemental lighting in the greenhouse resulted in compact growth.

gator has to control or work around these physiological problems to ensure uniform, rootable cuttings. Like most other categories of ornamental plants, herbaceous perennials tend to be more difficult to root if they are flowering.

Figure 14.5. Cuttings of *Euphorbia amygdaloides* var. *robbiae* are flowering when they're not supposed to!

For some species, it is necessary to take cuttings in the summer or to provide artificial long days. *Gaura lindheimeri* tends to stay too compact and unbranched, almost rosettelike, under short days (fig. 14.4). Long days (sixteen hours) result in elongated and well-branched stems that yield many quality cuttings.

Some plants, such as wood spurge (*Euphorbia amygdaloides* var. *robbiae*) are best propagated in the spring because floral initiation occurs in the late summer and fall. Cuttings taken in the fall will put their energy into forming flowers instead of a vegetative mass (fig. 14.5).

Woody plant propagator Richard Bir of North Carolina State University turns his attention occasionally to herbaceous plants—in particular, studying how propagation influences overwinter survival. Bir and Joseph Conner, North Carolina State University, working on the notoriously hard-to-root hybrid 'Purple Smoke' baptisia, found a much greater overwintering survival rate if the cuttings were taken in late spring (early May) rather than summer and if they had a vegetative bud below the medium surface. A well-established root system enhanced chances for survival. Time of sticking also impacted flowering the following year, with more than 50% of the cuttings propagated earlier in the year producing flowers. Other perennials reported to overwinter best with early establishment include *Solidaster, Aster, Astrantia, Coreopsis* 'Moonbeam', *Geranium, Monarda* 'Petite Delight', *Vernonia*, and *Solidago*, according to Ohio grower John Murray of Millcreek Gardens, Ostrander, Ohio.

Early summer is the best time to obtain leafy softwood cuttings of woody species grouped with perennials, such as *Caryopteris* and *Buddleia*. But in the *Reference Manual of Woody Plant Propagation*, Michael Dirr notes of *Buddleia davidii*, "If all plants rooted as easily as this species and the cultivars, plant propagation would not be a challenge." Rooting of semihardwood cuttings taken later in the year can be hastened with rooting hormone.

Potential Problems with Stock Plants

John Friel of Yoder Green Leaf Perennials summed up problems with stock plants as follows: "Stock plant management is an expensive practice, fraught with perils: variety mix-ups, weeds, pests and pathogens,

Figure 14.6. *Physostegia virginica* 'Vivid' in the Hahn Horticulture Garden, Virginia Tech.

Figure 14.7. Mass planting of *Solidago rugosa* 'Fireworks' at the Chicago Botanic Garden.

Figure 14.8. Toad lilies, such as *Tricyrtis hirta* 'Miyazaki', are increasing in popularity for shade gardens.

TABLE 14.1

Cutting propagation of herbaceous perennials. Little information on flowering and stock plant management is available for the hundreds of species, hybrids, and cultivars on the market. Photoperiod or vernalization requirements for flowering are given if documented. Some information may be specific only to that particular species or cultivar. For many of these perennials, the straight species can also be propagated from seed. Consult the resources, where listed, for more detailed information on production. LD = long day; SD = short day; NI = night interruption.

PERENNIAL COMMON NAME	TYPE OF CUTTING[A]	HORMONE RECOMMENDATIONS IF KNOWN[B]	SPECIAL PROPAGATION SUGGESTIONS	PHOTOPERIOD AND/OR COLD PERIOD (32° TO 45° F [0° TO 7° C]) REQUIREMENT TO FLOWER IF KNOWN	RESOURCE[C]
Achillea filipendulina, A. millefolium Yarrow	Basal	None except for 'Coronation Gold' 1,000 ppm IBA		LD	
Aegopodium podagraria 'Variegatum' Bishop's weed	Stem and basal	None			BPM
Ajania pacifica (Chrysanthemum pacificum) Gold and silver chrysanthemum	Stem	1,000 ppm IBA + 500 ppm NAA dip or 50 IBA + 25 NAA foliar spray after sticking			Blythe et al., 2002
Ajuga reptans Bugleweed	Stem and basal	1,000 ppm IBA	Stem cuttings taken in midsummer root easiest; basal cuttings including a small piece of root very fast.		BPM
Amsonia hubrichtii, A. tabernaemontana Blue star flower	Tip	1,500 ppm IBA	Take before flowering in early spring; up to six weeks to root		
Armeria maritima Sea thrift	Basal	1,000 ppm IBA	Take anytime except during flowering		BPM
Artemisia silver-leaved species and hybrids Wormwood	Stem	None	A. schmidtiana 'Siver Mound' is especially susceptible to overly wet rooting conditions		BPM
Artemisia dracunculus Tarragon	Stem	500 ppm KIBA			Yoder
Aster species and hybrids (late summer and fall blooming)	Stem		Shear after flowering to encourage new growth; take 1 to 2 in. (2.5 to 5 cm) of new growth	LD	BPM

PERENNIAL COMMON NAME	TYPE OF CUTTING[A]	HORMONE RECOMMENDATIONS IF KNOWN[B]	SPECIAL PROPAGATION SUGGESTIONS	PHOTOPERIOD AND/OR COLD PERIOD (32° TO 45° F [0° TO 7° C]) REQUIREMENT TO FLOWER IF KNOWN	RESOURCE[C]
Baptisia alba, B. australis, B. 'Purple Smoke' False indigo	Stem	1,250 ppm IBA (Yoder recommends 3,500 ppm)	Take two-node cuttings mid- to late spring, before flowering; stick at least one node into medium		Conner and Bir, 2001
Bergenia cordifolia and hybrids Heartleaf bergenia	Basal		Take basal shoots in spring and early summer		BPM
Boltonia asteroides Boltonia	Stem		Take stem sections in spring or early summer; four weeks to root	LD	BPM
Buddleia davidii and hybrids Butterfly bush	Stem (greenwood or softwood)	1,000 to 3,000 ppm IBA talc or solution	Take cuttings in summer; wounding the stem speeds rooting		
Campanula 'Birch Hybrid' Bellflower	Stem	1,000 ppm IBA	Highest quantity and quality cuttings from stock under SD	Facultative LD; fastest with high light intensity, cold for six to nine weeks	FUP
Campanula carpatica, C. persicifolia Bellflower	Stem or basal		Take basal cuttings in spring		FUP
Caryopteris divaricata Bluebeard	Stem (greenwood or softwood)	1,000 to 1,500 ppm IBA	Take cuttings in spring and early summer; stick one node into medium		Dirr
Ceratostigma plumbaginoides Leadwort	Stem	1,500 ppm KIBA	Take cuttings in spring and summer (shoots are late to emerge in landscape); non-flowering stems root faster and better		Yoder, BPM
Chelone lyonii Turtle's head	Tip		Best success in late spring or early summer, before flower initiation		BPM
Clematis species and hybrids Clematis	Stem (softwood from young shoots)	None or 2,000 to 3,000 ppm IBA (species dependent)	Stem section should include leaf nodes; stick in medium up to point where leaf meets stem; wound if slightly woody; slow to root		BPM

(Continued on page 180)

(Continued from page 179)

PERENNIAL COMMON NAME	TYPE OF CUTTING[A]	HORMONE RECOMMENDATIONS IF KNOWN[B]	SPECIAL PROPAGATION SUGGESTIONS	PHOTOPERIOD AND/OR COLD PERIOD (32° TO 45° F [0° TO 7° C]) REQUIREMENT TO FLOWER IF KNOWN	RESOURCE[C]
Chrysogonum virginianum Green and gold	Tip, stem with part of creeping rootstock	500 to 750 ppm IBA			Yoder, BPM
Coreopsis rosea, C. verticillata and hybrids Tickseed	Stem	None, except for *C.* 'Creme Brulee', *C.* 'Limerock Ruby', and *C. rosea* 'Sweet Dreams'; Yoder recommends 1,000 ppm KIBA	For *C. verticillata*, stock management is tricky: LD results in many cuttings but flowering is induced and rooting percentage lower; SD (less than fourteen hour) yields fewer but faster-rooting cuttings	Obligate LD (less than fourteen hours); cold is not required but may increase bud count and speed flowering	FUP Yoder
Delosperma species and hybrids Ice plant	Stem	1,000 ppm KIBA			Yoder
Echinacea purpurea cultivars ('Magnus', 'Ruby Star')	Basal	1,000 ppm IBA		No requirements, but fastest flowering with fourteen-hour day length or NI; ten weeks of cold will hasten flowering; beware of over-wintering problems	FUP
Erigeron species Fleabane	Stem	500 to 100 ppm KIBA			Yoder
Eupatorium species and hybrids	Stem (softwood)	500 ppm IBA			
Euphorbia species and hybrids		1,000 ppm IBA			
Gaillardia cultivars	Stem or basal	500 ppm IBA			
Gaura lindheimeri	Stem	None or 1,000 ppm IBA; do not leave too long under mist	Best lateral branch production in summer (or grow stock under LD)	Facultative LD (more than fourteen hours)	FUP, Yoder

PERENNIAL COMMON NAME	TYPE OF CUTTING[A]	HORMONE RECOMMENDATIONS IF KNOWN[B]	SPECIAL PROPAGATION SUGGESTIONS	PHOTOPERIOD AND/OR COLD PERIOD (32° TO 45° F [0° TO 7° C]) REQUIREMENT TO FLOWER IF KNOWN	RESOURCE[C]
Geranium species and hybrids, except *G. dalmaticum* Hardy geranium	Basal	1,000 ppm KIBA			Yoder
Geranium dalmaticum Dalmatian geranium	Stem	1,000 ppm IBA	Best-quality cuttings from stock under SD	Facultative LD; six weeks or more of cold	FUP
Hedera helix English ivy	Stem	1,000 to 3,000 ppm IBA for more profuse roots	Summer or fall is ideal, but roots at any time of year		WPP
Helianthemum nummularium Rock rose	Stem (softwood after flowering)	2,000 ppm IBA		Take cuttings in late summer or fall after flowering	BPM
Helianthus species and hybrids Perennial sunflower	Stem	1,000 ppm KIBA			Yoder
Heliopsis helianthoides False sunflower	Stem	1,000 ppm IBA	Take cuttings in early spring, before flower buds develop		BPM
Heuchera sanguinea Coral bells	Basal				
Hypericum species and hybrids St. John's wort	Tip	1,000 ppm IBA talc or solution (no alcohol)	Root easily mid-summer through fall		WPP
Iberis sempervirens Candytuft	Stem	1,000 to 3,000 ppm IBA talc.	Take cuttings in summer		WPP
Lamium galeobdolon (Lamiastrum galeobdolon) Yellow archangel	Stem	None			Yoder
Lamium maculatum Spotted dead nettle	Stem	None			Yoder

(Continued on page 182)

(Continued from page 181)

PERENNIAL COMMON NAME	TYPE OF CUTTING[A]	HORMONE RECOMMENDATIONS IF KNOWN[B]	SPECIAL PROPAGATION SUGGESTIONS	PHOTOPERIOD AND/OR COLD PERIOD (32° TO 45° F [0° TO 7° C]) REQUIREMENT TO FLOWER IF KNOWN	RESOURCE[C]
Lavandula species and hybrids Lavender	Tip	1,000 ppm IBA		For *L. angustifolia* LD until visible bud; cold for fifteen weeks; plugs should have twenty or more nodes before cold treatment for most uniform flowering	FUP
Leucanthemum x *superbum* Shasta daisy	Tip			With prior cooling, facultative LD (more than sixteen hours or NI) provides fastest flowering; obligate LD without cooling; faster, more uniform flowering with six weeks cold	FUP
Mentha x *piperita* Peppermint	Stem	500 ppm IBA			
Monarda didyma Beebalm	Stem	None	Stick a second node into medium if cutting is taken in late summer		
Nepeta species and hybrids Catmint	Stem	500 ppm KIBA			Yoder
Oenothera fruticosa Sundrops	Tip, basal offsets after flowering	None	Obtain greatest number of vegetative cuttings under SD	Facultative LD; best with at least three weeks of cold	FUP
Penstemon species and hybrids Beard-tongue	Stem	500 ppm IBA		For *P. digitalis* 'Husker Red', no photoperiod requirement; cold for nine to fifteen weeks speeds flowering	FUP
Perovskia atriplicifolia Russian sage	Stem	None			Yoder
Phlox divaricata, P. stolonifera Woodland phlox	Stem		Late spring		
Phlox paniculata Garden phlox	Stem	1,000 to 1,250 ppm IBA	Best results in spring	Be sure at least one node is in the medium	Bir and Conner, 1996
Phlox subulata Moss phlox	Tip	1,000 ppm KIBA			Yoder

PERENNIAL COMMON NAME	TYPE OF CUTTING[A]	HORMONE RECOMMENDATIONS IF KNOWN[B]	SPECIAL PROPAGATION SUGGESTIONS	PHOTOPERIOD AND/OR COLD PERIOD (32° TO 45° F [0° TO 7° C]) REQUIREMENT TO FLOWER IF KNOWN	RESOURCE[C]
Physostegia virginiana Obedient plant (fig. 14.6)	Stem	None	Keep under SD; vegetative cuttings root faster	Facultative LD (more than sixteen hours or NI); cold for ten weeks	FUP
Potentilla fruticosa Bush cinquefoil	Stem (softwood)	1,000 ppm IBA	Remove from mist once roots appear; sensitive to excess moisture		WPP
Rosmarinus officinalis Rosemary	Stem (greenwoodor softwood)	500 to 1,000 ppm IBA talc or KIBA solution	Easy on the mist; too much moisture reduces rooting		WPP
Ruellia brittoniana Hardy petunia	Stem	1,000 ppm KIBA			Yoder
Salvia species and hybrids Sage	Stem	500 to 1,000 ppm IBA			
Saxifraga species and hybrids Saxifrage	Stem	750 ppm IBA	Watch overwatering; very susceptible to rhizoctonia root and crown rots.	For *S.* x *arendsii* 'Triumph', facultative LD (more than sixteen hours); cold for nine to twelve weeks	FUP
Sedum x 'Autumn Joy' (*Hylotelephium* x 'Autumn Joy') Stonecrop	Stem	None	After late spring terminal cuttings have flower buds but stem cuttings do not; vegetative cuttings root faster; ten- to thirteen-hour day length helps keep stock plants vegetative	LD	FUP
Sedum kamtschaticum, S. spurium, and similar species Stonecrop	Stem	None			BPM, Yoder
Solidago species and hybrids Goldenrod (fig. 14.7)	Tip or basal	None	Take cuttings in spring and summer, before flowering		BPM
Teucrium chamaedrys Germander	Stem	1,000 ppm KIBA			Yoder

(Continued on page 184)

(Continued from page 183)

PERENNIAL COMMON NAME	TYPE OF CUTTING[a]	HORMONE RECOMMENDATIONS IF KNOWN[b]	SPECIAL PROPAGATION SUGGESTIONS	PHOTOPERIOD AND/OR COLD PERIOD (32° TO 45° F [0° TO 7° C]) REQUIREMENT TO FLOWER IF KNOWN	RESOURCE[c]
Thymus species Thyme	Stem	None			Yoder
Tricyrtis species and hybrids Toad lily (fig. 14.8)	Stem	None			Yoder
Verbena canadensis Canadian verbena	Stem		Nonflowering shoots root faster; needs to be well established to overwinter		BMP
Veronica species Speedwell	Stem		Take cuttings with two or three nodes; keep stock plants warm to avoid flowering	For *V. longifolia* 'Sunny Border Blue', no photoperiod requirements; cold for ten weeks is optimal	FUP
Vinca minor Periwinkle	Stem	1,000 ppm IBA + 500 ppm NAA	Take cuttings with single nodes; best rooting from fall cuttings		Landon and Banko, 2002

[a]*Type of cutting.* "Stem" also includes the terminal or tip cuttings.

[b]*Hormones.* IBA: (recommendations from Yoder Greenleaf is for K salt of indole-3-butyric acid, also known as KIBA); NAA: naphthalene acetic acid

[c]*Resources.*

BPM = *Ball Perennial Manual,* Nau, J., 1996.

WPP = *The Reference Manual of Woody Plant Propagation: From Seed to Tissue Culture,* Dirr, M.A. and C.W. Heuser, Jr., 1987.

FUP = *Firing Up Perennials,* Michigan State University and Greenhouse Grower Magazine, 2000.

Yoder = *Handling Unrooted Perennials,* Yoder Green Leaf Perennials, 2004.

Other resources are found under "References."

winter kill, bench space that can't be turned. . . . Hence the rapidly growing popularity of offshore URCs [unrooted cuttings] like ours."

The age of the stock plant is important to propagative success. Cuttings from young plants are more likely to root than those from old stock. Plan to replace stock plants each year if possible. Maintaining stock of perennial plants in a greenhouse environment can be difficult due to the number of species and diseases. The alterna-

tive of keeping outdoor stock blocks limits cutting availability to the actual growing season.

Alternatives to stock plants
Unrooted cuttings

As previously mentioned, the option of buying unrooted cuttings, quite popular on the vegetative annual scene, has now crossed over to the perennial market. The lower costs compared with buying rooted liners in media have helped fuel this rapidly expanding sector of the young plants market. Shipping costs are minimal with no trays or media to add weight. Sellers of unrooted cuttings tout "ideal" conditions: most of the cuttings are produced in Central American countries such as Costa Rica, home of high light and moderate temperatures. The cuttings are usually carefully graded, yielding a level of uniformity seldom seen in self-propagated material. After unpacking unrooted cuttings, handle them the same as if you had just taken them yourself. If they cannot be stuck immediately, store them in a cooler around 40° F (4° C) to slow deterioration.

Keep those plug trays rolling

Don't overlook your rooted (or rooting) cuttings as a source for more material. Shelton Singletary, journeyman perennial propagator, recommends *rolling* a flat, propagating cuttings off of the young plants to obtain a second or even third batch of cuttings, depending on the vigor of the species. *Tipping*, or removing a one- or two-node shoot, also encourages branching of the original plant as with pinching. And in an extreme example of rolling, he has also experimented with "macro micropropagation": using a benzyladenine (BA) spray on Stage 3 tissue-cultured plants such as hosta. A naturally occurring cytokinin, BA encourages proliferation of plantlets, turning one young plant into several in a matter of weeks. Work like this is expanding the frontier of perennial propagation. Similar tricks of the trade are slowly making their way into the mainstream as the popularity of and demand for perennials continue to rise.

References

Armitage, A. M. 1997. *Herbaceous Perennial Plants,* 2nd ed. Stipes Publishing, Champaign, Illinois.

Bir, R. E., and J. L. Conner. 1996. How and when herbaceous cuttings are stuck influences winter survival, pp. 312–314. In: *Proceedings of the Southern Nursery Association Research Conference,* Atlanta, Georgia. Proceedings since 1992 available online at http://www.sna.org/research/researchproceedings.

Blanchette, L. 1998. New ideas in asexual perennial propagation, pp. 141–143. In: *Proceedings of the 1998 Perennial Plant Symposium,* Boston, Massachusetts.

Blythe, E. K., J. L. Sibley, K. M. Tilt, and J. M. Ruter. 2002. Evaluation of an alternative method of auxin application in cutting propagation, pp. 348–351. In: *Proceedings of the Southern Nursery Association Research Conference,* Atlanta, Georgia.

Conner, J. L. and R. E. Bir. 2001. Propagating Baptisia 'Purple Smoke' and keeping it alive, pp. 411–412. In: *Proceedings of the Southern Nursery Association Research Conference,* Atlanta, Georgia.

Dirr, M. A. and C. W. Heuser Jr. 1987. *The Reference Manual of Woody Plant Propagation: From Seed to Tissue Culture.* Varsity Press, Inc., Athens, Georgia.

Druse, K. 2000. *Making More Plants.* Clarkson N. Potter, New York.

Michigan State University, 2000. *Firing Up Perennials.* Michigan State University and *Greenhouse Grower* Magazine. Meister Media, Willoughby, Ohio.

Landon, A. and T. Banko. 2002. Factors affecting rooting of *Vinca minor* single-node cuttings, pp. 328–331. In: *Proceedings of the Southern Nursery Association Research Conference,* Atlanta, Georgia.

Murray, J. K. 2000. Overwintering perennials at Millcreek Gardens LLC, pp. 60–62. In: *Proceedings of the 2000 Perennial Plant Symposium, Toronto, Ontario.*

Nau, J. 1996. *Ball Perennial Manual.* Ball Publishing, Batavia, Illinois.

Yoder Green Leaf Perennials. 2004. Handling Unrooted Perennials. www.green-leaf-ent.com/URC_Handling_2004.pdf.

15

Cutting Propagation of Specialty Cut Flowers

Lane Greer

In the early 1990s, specialty cut flowers became an important crop for several reasons.

- Farmers began to diversify into high-value specialty crops.
- Retail florists began asking for new and unusual flowers, many of which could not be grown in South America or shipped well.
- Consumers had more disposable income and were willing to spend some of it on flowers.
- More farmers markets were established throughout the country, and flowers became an integral part of those markets.
- Martha Stewart, HGTV, and similar phenomena in the media brought home and garden decoration into the forefront of American minds.

As a result of these changes, growers began asking for more information on cut flower production, and there are now numerous resources available on this topic. Resources for propagating new cut flower material are still rare, however. This is due to several factors: many cut flower growers are small scale, less than 10 acres (4 hectares), and have no propagation facilities; some growers are inexperienced; and many new varieties are easy to grow from seed. Perhaps more important is the amount of time that must be expended on propagation. The life of a cut flower grower is demanding. At any time up to thirty species may be flowering; they have to be harvested, treated, bunched, and shipped, often in the same day. The need for constant harvesting and replanting is time consuming, to say the least. The time and skill necessary for propagation may not be available to many small and medium-sized growers. Furthermore, the market for selling vegetative material to cut flower producers is small.

So why consider vegetative propagation of cut flowers? Most often, growers who propagate do so because they cannot find an adequate supply of a species from other sources. A Texas grower may have found a native plant, for instance, with good postharvest life but little seed production. Finding a supplier of the plant in Wisconsin may not help the Texas grower, since ecotypes can vary so much that many Wisconsin plants are not likely to perform well in Texas. Instead, the Texas grower uses vegetative propagation techniques to get an exact copy of the parent plant.

Economics play a role in this choice, as well. Many cut flowers are not patented and can be propagated vegetatively, but the market for selling vegetative material is small. Woody cut flower growers use vegetative cuttings more often than herbaceous plant growers because they want quicker production from trees and shrubs.

Growers who propagate have the necessary facilities, such as a propagation house or mist system. They also have the knowledge necessary to begin producing their own material. Additionally, they have time— or workers who have time—to spend on this venture.

Small-Scale Propagation Equipment

The key to successful vegetative propagation of leafy cuttings is to keep them from wilting and drying out until roots are produced. High humidity (between 95 and 100%) and temperatures ranging from 70° to 80° F (21° to 27° C) give cuttings a much better chance of survival. The best way to keep most plants turgid is to provide high humidity through a mist system (fig. 15.1). Intermittent mist is usually used to keep cuttings cool and to provide water without leaching nutrients and waterlogging the medium. Overhead mist systems consisting of PVC pipes, mist nozzles, and a timing system are relatively inexpensive and easy to install and maintain (see chapter 11). However, they do require some space and may be more permanent than some operations prefer.

Figure 15.1. A mist system for propagation.

Small-scale propagation units can be as simple as a large aquarium or terrarium, either filled with individual pots or with cuttings stuck directly into the medium (fig. 15.2). In this case, 2 to 4 in. (5 to 10 cm) of media can be placed in the bottom of the container. Waxed cardboard boxes can also be used. A glass or clear plastic cover should be used to keep humidity high. Other small-scale operations might use individual pots covered with plastic from 2-liter soda bottles or with large clear plastic bags. With these simple structures, placement is crucial. Indirect light, north-facing windows, or fluorescent lights are recommended. Direct sun will quickly cause desiccation and death.

Temperatures should not rise above 80° F (27° C) or fall below 65° F (18° C). Even with good placement, these structures will

Figure 15.2. A Wardian case can be used for small-scale propagation. Be sure to monitor temperatures to prevent overheating.

Figure 15.3. An on-bench heating system (notice white pipes) for propagating cuttings into plugs.

still require careful monitoring for moisture loss. Add water if the medium appears dry or if no water condenses on the inside of the structure overnight.

Just as heating the medium speeds seed germination, increasing soil temperatures leads to faster rooting of cuttings (fig. 15.3). Blowing warm air under benches, using heating mats, and circulating warm water through PVC pipes are relatively easy ways to increase the temperature of the medium to 73° to 77° F (23° to 25° C) Cuttings taken in summer rarely need supplemental heat.

Growers who are propagating large numbers of cuttings should consider investing in a small propagation house. In a separate house, proper temperatures can be more easily maintained, intermittent mist systems can be permanently installed, and propagation equipment can be held in one location. Heated ground beds can also be used. Additionally, sanitation is imperative in propagation houses, which is often easier to achieve in a small separate house. See chapter 11 for more information on large-scale propagation facilities.

Propagating Herbaceous Plants

Cuttings from herbaceous plants should be selected from specimens showing the best characteristics in the field. Mark the best plants when they are in flower for later propagation. Several cutting types can be harvested, depending on the species and time of year. Many plants are most successfully propagated in the spring.

Terminal or *tip cuttings* include the stem apex, young leaves, and one or more mature leaves, and they generally produce a finished crop the quickest. *Subterminal* or *butt cuttings* also have several nodes but are harvested farther down the stem and do not include the stem apex. *Basal cuttings* are a type of terminal cutting harvested from the crown, which is that part of the plant where new stems are produced each growing season of perennials; they typically include a piece of the crown tissue for rapid rooting. *Leaf bud cuttings* are a type of subterminal cutting with only one node. *Rhizome cuttings* are simply stems growing underground; they are cut into pieces, each containing at least one node. In addition, some species can be propagated from roots or leaves without any stem tissue. See chapter 1 for more information.

Propagating Woody Plants

Timing of propagation is crucial for many woody species. Cuttings of forsythia (*Forsythia* x *intermedia*), for example, can be successfully rooted at any time during the year, but lilac (*Syringa vulgaris*) cuttings must be taken in spring if they are to be successful. There are three kinds of woody cuttings: *softwood*, *hardwood*, and *semihardwood*.

Softwood cuttings are taken in spring when the wood is still soft and easily bent, hardwood cuttings are taken in late winter, and semihardwood cuttings are taken sometime in between, before the stem tissue has become woody. Softwood cuttings contain almost no carbohydrate reserves; they can be difficult to root unless they are placed in a mist system or otherwise kept near 100% relative humidity. Hardwood cuttings are easier to maintain but require more time to form roots. Softwood cuttings of crape myrtle (*Lagerstroemia indica*), for example, will form roots in three weeks, while hardwood cuttings from the same plant require two to four months for root formation. A semihardwood cutting of crape myrtle, taken during the summer, will root in one to two months. While a mist system or indoor facility is usually required for softwood and semihardwood cuttings, hardwood cuttings can be stuck in a medium in fall and then placed outdoors to continue rooting during the winter months. For outdoor propagation, protection such as row covers, mulching, or low tunnels will improve rooting.

For most woody species, cuttings should be 3 to 6 in. (8 to 15 cm) long, with four to eight leaves. Larger cuttings will dry out more quickly. For best results, take cuttings from the current season's growth from vigorous plants showing the characteristics desired. Take cuttings in the early morning, and keep them from drying out. Remove any flowers or flower buds. While not necessary for most herbaceous plants, wounding will improve the chance of success in rooting woody species. To wound a cutting, remove the bark from the bottom 1 to 2 in. (2.5 to 5 cm) of the cutting. Then 1 in. (2.5 cm) up the stem, make a shallow cut that is deep enough to enter the xylem (heartwood) of the cutting. One or two such cuts are adequate. Rooting hormones may also increase the likelihood of rooting for numerous woody species. A medium consisting of equal parts of sphagnum peat and perlite is adequate for rooting most woody species, unless otherwise noted in table 15.1. Pine bark is not recommended for sticking cuttings, since it is too coarse to hold water and nutrients well.

Transplanting to the Field

After cuttings have established roots and have begun to show new shoot growth, they can be transplanted

TABLE 15.1
Cut flower species suitable for vegetative propagation.

SPECIES NAME	COMMON NAME	OTHER PROPAGATION METHODS	RECOMMENDATIONS
Achillea 'Coronation Gold'	Coronation Gold yarrow	Division	Take subterminal stem cuttings in summer after flowering. Keep well watered. Divide three-year-old plants after flowering. Larger crowns will produce flowers the first year after division.

(Continued on page 190)

(Continued from page 189)

	SPECIES NAME	COMMON NAME	OTHER PROPAGATION METHODS	RECOMMENDATIONS
 Figure 15.4. 'Gold Plate' yarrow (*Achillea filipendulina*).  Figure 15.5. Established yarrow plants in the field.	*Achillea filipendulina*	Fernleaf yarrow	Division	Take basal cuttings as soon as shoots emerge in spring. Divide after flowering, preferably in early spring or early fall.
 Figure 15.6. Common yarrow (*Achillea millefolium*).	*Achillea millefolium*	Common yarrow	Division	Take basal cuttings as soon as shoots emerge in spring. Root cuttings or root pieces also produce new plants. Divide in early summer after flowering. Divide every three to four years.
	Achillea ptarmica	Sneezewort	Division	Take subterminal stem cuttings in summer after flowering. Take basal cuttings as soon as shoots emerge in spring. Divide every three to four years. Vegetatively propagated plants have larger flowers and are more fully double.
	Adenophora liliifolia	Ladybells	Division	Take basal cuttings immediately after shoots emerge. Division can be difficult, and roots tend to rot.

	SPECIES NAME	COMMON NAME	OTHER PROPAGATION METHODS	RECOMMENDATIONS
\n\nFigure 15.7.\nButterfly weed.	*Asclepias tuberosa*	Butterfly weed		Take terminal stem cuttings 3 to 4 in. (8 to 10 cm) long in spring, prior to flowering. Do not use rooting hormone, but place in a high-humidity area (mist system is best). Rooting occurs in four to six weeks. For root cuttings, take 2 to 3 in. (5 to 8 cm) pieces from roots closest to the mother plant, and place them vertically in a well-drained, sterilized medium. Keep warm and moist. See Part 3 for additional information.
	Aster hybrids	Aster	Tissue culture, division	For basal cuttings, remove new shoots that appear at the base of the mother plants. Terminal shoot cuttings result in shorter plants and should not be used for cut flower production. Take basal cuttings after flowering in late fall, winter, or spring. Place unrooted cuttings in a well-drained medium at 70° to 75° F (21° to 24° C) and maintain high humidity (mist system). These cuttings root in seven to fourteen days. Rooting hormones increase propagation success. Plants held in long-day conditions will produce long stems the first year. Tissue culture ensures virus-free plants and is used for most new cultivars. See Part 3 for additional information.
\n\nFigure 15.8. Buddleia.	*Buddleia davidii*	Butterfly bush		Take softwood cuttings in late spring, and hardwood cuttings in late summer or fall. A quick dip of 1,000 to 3,000 ppm IBA will improve rooting. As soon as cuttings root, place them in lower humidity since cuttings rot rapidly.

(Continued on page 192)

(Continued from page 191)

	SPECIES NAME	COMMON NAME	OTHER PROPAGATION METHODS	RECOMMENDATIONS
 Figure 15.9. Boxwood.	*Buxus sempervirens*	Boxwood		Terminal cuttings root easily with 1,000 ppm IBA.
 Figure 15.10. American beautyberry.	*Callicarpa americana*	American beautyberry		Softwood cuttings root easily under mist. Rooting hormone is not necessary.
	Callistephus chinensis	China aster		Take terminal stem cuttings. Hold stock plants in short-day conditions.
	Caryopteris x *clandonensis* and *Caryopteris incana*	Blue mist spirea and blue spirea		Take 2 to 3 in. (5 to 8 cm) cuttings of vegetative shoot tips during summer. Use a rooting hormone (IBA, NAA, or 1,000 ppm IBA) and bottom heat to decrease rooting time to seven to ten days.
	Centranthus ruber	Red valerian		Take terminal stem or basal cuttings. Basal cuttings should be taken before any buds are visible.
	Chrysanthemum x *morifolium* (*Dendranthema* x *grandiflorum*)	Chrysanthe-mum		Terminal cuttings 2 to 3 in. (5 to 8 cm) long will root easily under mist, fog, or plastic tents. Stock plants must be kept under long-day conditions. See Part 3 for more information.
	Coreopsis grandiflora	Coreopsis	Division	Take subterminal cuttings. Divide every three years in spring or fall.

	SPECIES NAME	COMMON NAME	OTHER PROPAGATION METHODS	RECOMMENDATIONS
	Cornus sericea	Red twig dogwood		Take hardwood cuttings in early spring. Rooting hormone and bottom heat will improve rooting. Use a 1,000 ppm IBA dip on cuttings taken in June and July. Hardwood cuttings 8 to 10 in. (20 to 25 cm) long can be stuck directly into the field in late winter or early spring.
 Figure 15.11. Flowering dogwood.	*Cornus florida*	Flowering dogwood		Take softwood cuttings immediately after flowering, and treat them with 1,000 ppm IBA. For best results, place in a peat-perlite mix under intermittent mist and supplemental lighting. Do not disturb until shoot growth is observed.
 Figure 15.12. 'Marble Ball' dahlia.	*Dahlia* hybrids	Dahlia	Division	Take terminal cuttings from actively growing plants. Cuttings taken from greenhouse-forced tubers in winter provide best results. Place two- to three-node cuttings in a well-drained medium in high humidity and at 65° to 72° F (18° to 22° C). Roots appear in three to four weeks. Transplant rooted cuttings to 4 to 6 in. (10 to 15 cm) pots or 18-cell bedding plant flats and grow at 60° to 68° F (16° to 20° C) until transplanting to the field. To divide, cut tuberous roots into pieces, each with at least one terminal adventitious bud (eye). See Part 3 for more information.

(Continued on page 194)

(Continued from page 193)

SPECIES NAME	COMMON NAME	OTHER PROPAGATION METHODS	RECOMMENDATIONS
Delphinium	Delphinium hybrids	Tissue culture	Take 3 to 4 in. (8 to 10 cm) long terminal cuttings of new basal shoots. Make sure the base of the cutting is solid, not hollow. Place in a well-drained medium under mist for three to four weeks for optimal rooting. Most new hybrids are produced from tissue culture or seed and are sold as plugs.
Dianthus species	Dianthus		Place terminal or basal cuttings in a well-drained medium, and hold them at 64° to 68° F (18° to 20° C). It is particularly important to use disease-indexed stock, since *Dianthus* are prone to numerous diseases. See Part 3 for more information.
 *Echinacea purpurea*	Purple coneflower	Division	Take 1 to 3 in. (2.5 to 8 cm) root cuttings in early spring, and place them upright in a 60:40 sand-peat mix or similar medium. Root cuttings can also be placed flat and lightly covered with medium. Use rooting hormone for best results. Take basal cuttings in spring. Divide every three years in spring or fall.
Echinops bannaticus	Globe thistle	Division	Take basal cuttings from new juvenile ground shoots. For root cuttings, take 1 to 2 in. (2.5 to 5 cm) long pieces in spring, and place them vertically in a well-drained medium in a warm, humid location. Shoots appear in two to three weeks. Divide in spring after flowering.

Figure 15.13. Purple coneflower.

	SPECIES NAME	COMMON NAME	OTHER PROPAGATION METHODS	RECOMMENDATIONS
 **Figure 15.14.** **Sea holly.**	*Eryngium planum*	Sea holly	Division	Take basal cuttings from new juvenile ground shoots. Take 2 to 4 in. (5 to 10 cm) root cuttings from mature roots in late winter while the plant is dormant. Plant upright in a well-drained medium in high humidity at 68° to 75° F (20° to 24° C). Division can be done, but it is difficult.
	Eustoma grandiflorum	Lisianthus		Take terminal cuttings from stock plants held under long-day conditions. Rooting occurs in two weeks when cuttings are held under mist at 75° F (24° C). Cutting-propagated plants may be of lower quality than seed-propagated plants.
	Forsythia x intermedia	Forsythia		Softwood cuttings root easily in three to four weeks. Use 1,000 to 3,000 ppm KIBA quick dip. Hardwood cuttings can also be used.
	Goniolimon tataricum	German statice	Division	Root cuttings made in spring provide the best new plants, but they can also be made in fall. Cut the roots into 1 to 3 in. (2.5 to 8 cm) pieces. Place thick roots upright in the medium; place thinner pieces horizontally and cover them lightly. Division must be done carefully; spring is preferable for plants that are to be immediately replanted. If dividing in fall, grow the new plants in the greenhouse for three to four weeks before overwintering them in an unheated but protected area.

(Continued on page 196)

(Continued from page 195)

	SPECIES NAME	COMMON NAME	OTHER PROPAGATION METHODS	RECOMMENDATIONS
	Gypsophila paniculata	Baby's breath	Tissue culture	Take terminal cuttings in summer and place them under mist in a well-drained medium at 68° to 75° F (20° to 24° C). See Part 3 for more information.
 Figure 15.15. Sneezeweed.	*Helenium autumnale*	Sneezeweed	Division	Take terminal or basal cuttings in spring and early summer. Divide in spring.
	Heliopsis helianthoides	Sunflower heliopsis	Division	Take terminal or basal cuttings in early spring prior to bud set. Divide in spring or fall.
	Hydrangea macrophylla	Hydrangea		Take two- to three-node softwood tip cuttings in late spring to early summer (April through early July). For best results, remove half the leaf. Dip the entire cutting in a mild systemic fungicide, and use a rooting hormone. Place the cuttings in a waxed cardboard box with a lid, and leave in 55° to 75° F (13° to 24° C) for ten to fifteen days. Then plant the rooted cuttings in 4 in. (10 cm) pots or 18-cell bedding flats in a well-drained medium. A more traditional technique is to use 1,500 ppm IBA or 1,000 ppm KIBA, and place the cuttings in 1:3 peat-perlite medium under mist or fog at 70° to 74° F (21° to 23° C). The medium should be sterile with a pH around 6.0. Place cuttings in shade, in 2,500 to 3,000 f.c. (27 to 32 klux). Rooting should occur in two to five weeks. See Part 3 for more information.

	SPECIES NAME	COMMON NAME	OTHER PROPAGATION METHODS	RECOMMENDATIONS
	Hypericum species	Hypericum	Division	Use softwood cuttings for best results. Divide in spring.
 Figure 15.16. Deciduous holly fruit.	*Ilex* species	Deciduous holly		Softwood cuttings root in six to eight weeks. Cuttings collected in June and July should be treated with IBA at 1,000 to 3,000 ppm.
	Leucanthemum x superbum	Shasta daisy	Division	Double forms and some single forms must be propagated by terminal cuttings or division. Use rooting hormone for best results. Take cuttings from field-grown plants during summer. Cuttings from greenhouse-grown plants can be taken any time of year, but photoperiod must be increased to fourteen hours to keep plants vegetative. Keep cuttings in mist for two weeks. Divide every three years in spring or fall.
	Liatris spicata	Gayfeather	Division	Take terminal cuttings from newly emerged stems. Vegetatively produced corms are more productive than seed-grown corms. Divide plants in spring or fall.
	Limonium latifolium	Statice or sea lavender	Division	Take root cuttings. Divide in spring.
	Lobelia species	Lobelia	Division	Take terminal or subterminal cuttings. Divide in spring or fall.
 Figure 15.17. Gooseneck loosestrife.	*Lysimachia clethroides*	Gooseneck loosestrife	Division	Take terminal cuttings. Divide rhizomes after flowering.

(Continued on page 198)

(Continued from page 197)

	SPECIES NAME	COMMON NAME	OTHER PROPAGATION METHODS	RECOMMENDATIONS
 **Figure 15.18.** **Wax myrtle.**	*Myrica cerifera*	Wax myrtle		Take softwood cuttings in early summer, and treat them with 10,000 ppm IBA. Root cuttings can also be made in early winter. Use 2 to 3 in. (5 to 8 cm) long pieces, and place them in coarse sand rather than a peat mix.
 **Figure 15.19.** **Summer phlox.**	*Phlox paniculata*	Summer phlox	Division	Terminal stem cuttings root in two to three weeks. Most growers place them in plug trays in a well-drained medium. Root cuttings can also be taken.
	Physalis alkekengi	Chinese lantern	Division	In spring or fall, dig and divide underground stems (rhizomes), then pot them up.
	Physostegia virginiana	Obedient plant	Division	Subterminal stem and root cuttings are most successful when bottom heat is used. Spray 10 ppm benzyladenine (BA) three times weekly for five weeks to increase branching. Divide mature one-year-old plants in early spring.
	Rudbeckia fulgida	Rudbeckia	Division	Take basal cuttings in spring. Vegetatively produced plants have larger, brighter flowers. Divide every three years in spring or fall.
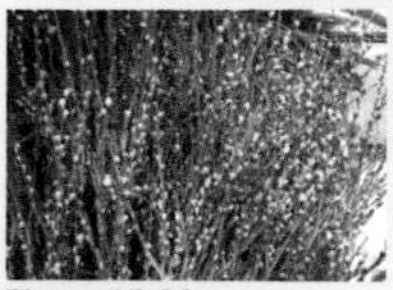 **Figure 15.20.** **Forced cut pussy willow** **(*Salix*).**	*Salix* species	Willow		Softwood and hardwood cuttings taken at any time of the year root easily. Neither rooting hormone nor bottom heat is needed.

	SPECIES NAME	COMMON NAME	OTHER PROPAGATION METHODS	RECOMMENDATIONS
\n\nFigure 15.21.\nMexican sage.	Salvia leucantha	Mexican sage		Take 2 to 3 in. (5 to 8 cm) long terminal cuttings before flower buds form. Place in a 1:2 peat-perlite mix or similar medium at 70° to 75° F (21° to 24° C) in high humidity (preferable to intermittent mist). Field plants can be dug and over-wintered in a unheated greenhouse. Take cuttings from these stock plants in late winter and spring, but keep mother plants under long-day conditions. See Part 3 for more information.
	Scabiosa caucasica	Pincushion flower	Division	Take basal cuttings. Divide every two to three years if plants are large enough to warrant it.
	Solidago hybrids	Goldenrod	Division	Terminal or basal cuttings root easily. Divide every two to three years. See Part 3 ` for more information.
\n\nFigure 15.22.\nStokes aster.	Stokesia laevis	Stokes aster	Division	Take root cuttings while plants are dormant. Divide in spring or autumn.
	Verbena bonariensis	Tall verbena		Take terminal cuttings 2 to 3 in. (5 to 8 cm) long of new growth; they root in three to five weeks. Root cuttings can also be taken in spring.
\n\nFigure 15.23.\nSpeedwell.	Veronica spicata	Speedwell	Division	Take terminal cuttings in late spring or early summer. Divide every two to three years in spring or fall.

(Continued on page 200)

(Continued from page 199)

SPECIES NAME	COMMON NAME	OTHER PROPAGATION METHODS	RECOMMENDATIONS
Veronicastrum virginicum	Culver's root	Division	Take 2 to 3 in. (5 to 8 cm) long terminal or subterminal stem cuttings in spring or early summer before flowering. Rooting occurs in two to three weeks. Divide every two to three years in spring or late summer.

to the field. Before transplanting, however, the cuttings should be hardened off by growing them in a sunny but sheltered location outdoors for one to two weeks, just as with seedlings. This will reduce the incidence of transplant shock, which usually manifests itself as severe wilting or rapid loss of foliage. During hardening off, the greatest risk to plants is water stress. A fully formed root system is contained within a very small, usually black pot. Soil temperatures can quickly rise to 100° F (38° C), which kills new roots.

The best time to transplant is in early morning, when temperatures are cool and the soil is evenly moist but not wet. Planting late in the evening can also be successful. The worst-case scenario is planting in a dry field on a sunny afternoon. No matter when the plants are set out, the key to success is to water them immediately. As soon as a row is planted, the plants should be irrigated from an overhead source. Once the soil around each new plant has been thoroughly soaked, soil replaces air around the plant roots and decreases the chances of transplant shock. The plants should be checked every day after transplanting until the next good rain and during any dry spells.

For cuttings transplanted in very early spring or late fall, row covers may be necessary. Translucent row covers diffuse sunlight and create more indirect light while simultaneously holding in heat and increasing air temperature 2° to 6° F (1° to 3° C), depending on the row cover material. Unless you plan to monitor them constantly, your row covers should have some method for heat release. Slitted clear plastic covers obviate the need for constant monitoring. Row covers without slits may be pulled over the plants at night and pulled off every morning. For most cut flowers, row covers will have to be supported by wire hoops or stakes. Otherwise, a heavy dew can pull down the row cover, toppling the plant stems.

Division

Many of the plants listed in table 15.1 are herbaceous perennials and benefit from division every two to four years. The plant is divided into two or more pieces, each containing roots and shoots. Division is more labor-intensive than cutting propagation; however, division will produce a plant with harvestable flowers more quickly than cutting propagation. Since the "stock" plants for cut flower growers are actually the cut flower production beds, there is little to no cost in maintaining "stock" plants. Thus, division is an economical method for producing the large numbers of plants required for a cut flower operation. In addition, many species require division periodically as older plantings become less productive, bearing small flowers on shorter stems.

Generally, spring-blooming plants should be divided in fall, fall-blooming plants should be divided in spring, and summer-blooming plants can be divided in fall or spring. However, there are numerous exceptions to this rule of thumb. The best time to divide plants is during dormancy. As a practical matter, however, cold or wet field conditions may prevent heavy equipment from entering the field. Furthermore, division is labor-intensive and therefore expensive, and a grower's labor force may be at its smallest during this time.

To divide plants, use a shovel or garden fork to dig up the entire plant. For large operations, modified potato diggers can be used to uproot plants. Shaking off loose soil decreases the weight of the root-ball but increases time and labor. Use a shovel, machete, or saw to separate the roots. Pulling roots apart is generally not feasible on a commercial scale. The amount of vegetative material that should accompany the new roots will depend on the species, but most plants require some shoot growth for rapid reestablishment. Newly divided plants should be replanted as quickly as possible.

References

Armitage, A. M. and J. M. Laushman. 2003. *Specialty Cut Flowers*. Timber Press, Portland, Oregon.

Ball, V., ed. 1998. *Ball RedBook*, 16th ed. Ball Publishing, Batavia, Illinois.

Bir, R. E. 1992. *Growing and Propagating Showy Native Woody Plants*. University of North Carolina Press, Chapel Hill, North Carolina.

Dirr, M. A. 1998. *Manual of Woody Landscape Plants*. Stipes Publishing, Champaign, Illinois.

Dole, J. M. and H. F. Wilkins. 2005. *Floriculture: Principles and Species*, 2nd ed. Prentice Hall, Upper Saddle River, New Jersey.

Nau, J. 1996. *Ball Perennial Manual*. Ball Publishing, Batavia, Illinois.

16

Cutting Propagation of Foliage Plants

Jianjun Chen and Robert H. Stamps

Foliage Plants: Their Origins and Uses

Defined literally, foliage plants would include all plants grown for their beautiful leaves rather than for flowers or fruits. In general horticultural terms, however, foliage plants are those with attractive foliage and/or flowers that are produced in shaded greenhouses or shade houses and are used as living specimens for interior decoration or whose foliages are harvested and used in floral arrangements. Foliage plants grown in containers are commonly referred to as houseplants. Foliages used in decorative arrangements are called florists' greens or cut foliages. In the subtropics and tropics, these plants may also be grown under shade as landscape plants.

Plants from at least 130 genera and probably more than 1,000 species have been produced as foliage plants. Most foliage plants are indigenous to tropical and subtropical regions. Foliage plants native to the understory of tropical rainforests are generally tolerant of low light, sensitive to chilling temperatures, and day-neutral to photoperiod; whereas foliage plants originating from the subtropics tolerate limited degrees of heat, drought, and chilling temperatures and may also show dormancy in winter. Only a few foliage plants are indigenous to temperate zones. The most common temperate foliage plant species are *Fatsia japonica*, a tree, and *Hedera helix* (English ivy), a vine. Some plants used indoors are native to climatically extreme conditions such as deserts. These plants, predominantly succulents and cacti, can adapt to heat and drought stresses.

The value of foliage plants lies in their aesthetic appearance, ability to survive under indoor low light, potential to reduce pollutants while growing indoors, and durability when used as cut foliage. The beauty of foliage plants—reflected by their wide variety of overall forms and sizes; varied leaf shapes, textures, and variegation; and colorful flowers—has fascinated people for a long time. The grand drawing rooms of Victorian houses were filled with palms and ferns. Because of their tolerance to low light levels, foliage plants have been widely used for decorating building interiors to bring beauty and comfort to our surroundings and remind us of nature. Interiorscapes with foliage plants fulfill a psychological need, enhance our indoor environment, and are also a satisfying hobby. In addition, plants inside buildings reduce dust, act as natural humidifiers, and purify indoor air. A NASA-funded project concluded that foliage plants can remove nearly 87% of air pollutants from sealed chambers within twenty-four hours. For example, each *Spathiphyllum* 'Mauna Loa' (peace lily) plant removed 16 mg formaldehyde, 27 mg trichloroethylene, and 41 mg benzene from sealed chambers after a twenty-four-hour exposure to each chemical.

The aesthetic and psychological enhancement of interior environments and the purification of indoor air have become catalysts in promoting the production of foliage plants and increasing their use indoors. The national wholesale value of foliage plants increased from $13 million in 1949 to $639 million in 2004, a forty-nine-fold increase in fifty-three years. The wholesale value of cut foliage added another $92 million in 2004. The steady increase in wholesale value may also be attributed to increased introduction of new plants and cultivars, as well as to technological advances in propagation and production. This chapter is intended to cover the current status of foliage plant propagation, with a major emphasis on cutting propagation.

203

TABLE 16.1

Methods of foliage plant propagation.

FAMILY	GENUS	COMMON NAME(S)
Acanthaceae	*Aphelandra*	Zebra plant
	Fittonia	Mosaic plant, net leaf
	Hemigraphis	Waffle plant
	Hypoestes	Polka dot plant
	Ruellia	Monkey plant
	Sanchezia	Sanchezia
Agavaceae	*Agrave*	Century plant
	Cordyline	Ti plant
	Dracaena	Corn plant, dracaena
	Nolina	Bottle palm, pony tail
	Sansevieria	Snake plant
	Yucca	Spanish bayonet, yucca
Amaryllidaceae	*Eucharis*	Amazon lily
Araceae	*Aglaonema*	Chinese evergreen
	Alocasia	Elephant's-ear plant
	Anthurium	Flamingo flower
	Dieffenbachia	Dumb cane
	Epipremnum	Pothos, devil's ivy
	Homalomena	Homalomena
	Monstera	Swiss-cheese plant
	Philodendron	Philodendron (vining)
	Philodendron	Philodendron (upright)
	Spathiphyllum	Peace lily
	Syngonium	Arrowhead vine, nephthytis
	Zamioculcas	ZZ plant
Araliaceae	*Dizygotheca*	False aralia
	Fatsia	Fatsi, Japanese fatsia
	Hedera	English and other ivies
	Polyscias	Ming and other aralias
	Schefflera	Schefflera, umbrella tree
Araucariaceae	*Araucaria*	Norfolk Island pine
Asclepiadaceae	*Ceropegia*	Rosary vine
	Dischidia	Ant plant
	Hoya	Wax plant
Aspleniaceae	*Asplenium*	Bird's-nest fern
Begoniaceae	*Begonia*	Rex begonia
Bignoniaceae	*Radermachera*	China doll
Blechnaceae	*Blechnum*	Hard ferns
Bromeliaceae	*Aechmea*	Silver vase bromeliad
	Ananas	Ornamental pineapple
	Billbergia	Queen's tears
	Cryptanthus	Earth star

	CUTTING			DIVISION	GRAFTING	LAYERING[b]	TISSUE CULTURE	SEEDS/ SPORES
CANE[a]	EYE	LEAF	TIP					
	2[c]		1				1	
	2		1			3		
	2		1					
			2					1
	2		1					
	2		1	3				
				1				2
2			1				1	3
2			1					3
				2				1
		2		1				
1				2				
				1				
3			1	2			1	
				1			1	2
				2			1	3
3			2	4			1	
	1		2					
3			2				1	
		3	1			2		1
	1							
				2			1	3
				2			1	3
	2						1	3
		1		2				3
			2					1
	2		1					1
	1		2					
			1				1	1
	4		3				1	2
			3			2		1
	1			2				3
	1			2				
	1		2					3
				2			1	1
2		1						
			2					1
				1				2
				2			1	1
		2		1			1	
				1				2
				1				

(Continued on page 205)

(Continued from page 205)

FAMILY	GENUS	COMMON NAME(S)
	Dyckia	Dyckia bromeliad
	Guzmania	Guzmania
	Neoregelia	Blushing bromeliad
	Nidularium	Bird's nest bromeliad
	Tillandsia	Air plant
	Vriesea	Painted feather bromeliad
Cactaceae	*Cereus*	Column cactus
	Echinocactus	Barrel cactus
	Opuntia	Opuntia, prickly pear
	Pereskiopsis	Pereskiopsis
	Rhipsalis	Mistletoe cactus
	Schlumbergera	Christmas cactus
	Selenicereus	Queen of the night
Commelinaceae	*Callisia*	Inch plant, striped inch plant
	Cyanotis	Teddy-bear vine, pussy ears
	Geogenanthus	Seersucker plant
	Siderasis	Brown spiderwort
	Tradescantia	Wandering Jew, inch plant, spiderwort, spider-li
Compositae (Asteraceae)	*Gynura*	Velvet plant, purple passion
	Mikania	Plush vine
	Senecio	String-of-beads, wax plant
Cornaceae	*Aucuba*	Spotted laurel
Crassulaceae	*Crassula*	Jade plant
	Kalanchoe	Kalanchoe
	Sedum	Sedum, burro's tail
Davilliaceae	*Davallia*	Footed fern
Dicksoniaceae	*Cibotium*	Mexican tree fern
	Dicksonia	Tasmanian tree fern
Dryopteridaceae	*Cyrtomium*	Asian netvein, holly fern
	Polystichum	Christmas fern, shield fern, holly fern
	Rumohra	Leatherleaf fern
Euphorbiaceae	*Codiaeum*	Croton
Gesneriaceae	*Aeschynanthus*	Lipstick plant, black pagoda
	Columnea	Goldfish plant
	Episcia	Flame violet
	Saintpaulia	African violet
Heliconiaceae	*Heliconia*	Lobster claw, heliconia
Labiatae (Lamiaceae)	*Plectranthus*	Swedish ivy
Leeaceae	*Leea*	West Indian holly, leea
Liliaceae	*Aloe*	Aloe
	Asparagus	Fern asparagus, sprengeri asparagus
	Aspidistra	Cast-iron plant
	Chlorophytum	Spider plant
	Haworthia	Zebra haworthia, pearl haworthia
	Ruscus	Ruscus
Loganiaceae	*Buddleia*	Indoor oak
Marantaceae	*Calathea*	Peacock plant, calathea

CUTTING				DIVISION	GRAFTING	LAYERING[b]	TISSUE CULTURE	SEEDS/ SPORES
CANE[a]	EYE	LEAF	TIP					
				1				2
				1			1	2
				1			1	2
				1				2
				1				2
				1			1	2
1				2	3			1
					1			1
1				2	3			
					1			
					1			
1				2	3			
					1			
	2		1					
			1	2				3
	1		2					
	1		2	3				
	1		2	3				
	1		2	3				
	1		2					
	1		2					
1			2					3
	2	3	1					
	2	3	1					
	1	1	2					
				1			1	2
				1				
							1	1
							1	1
								1
				1			1	2
			1			2		
			1					2
	2		1					
	2	3	1					
		1						
				1				
		2	1					
			2					1
				2				1
				2				1
				1				
				1			2	1
				1				2
				1			1	
1								
				2			1	

(Continued on page 208)

(Continued from page 207)

FAMILY	GENUS	COMMON NAME(S)
	Ctenanthe	Never-never plant
	Maranta	Prayer plant
	Stromanthe	Stromanthe
Melastomataceae	Bertolonia	Jewel plant
	Sonerila	Frosted sonerila
Meliaceae	Trichilia	Natal mahogany
Moraceae	Ficus	Fig (vine)
	Ficus	Fig (upright)
Musaceae	Musa	Banana plant
Myrsinaceae	Ardisia	Coralberry
Oleandraceae	Nephrolepis	Boston fern
Orchidaceae	Ludisia (Haemaria)	Jewel orchid, gold-lace orchid
Palmae (Arecaceae)	Chamaedorea	Parlor palm, neanthe bella
	Chrysalidocarpus	Areca palm
	Howea	Sentry palm, kentia palm
	Phoenix	Date palm
	Ravenea	Majesty palm
	Rhapis	Lady palm
Pandanaceae	Pandanus	Screw pine
Piperaceae	Peperomia	Peperomia
Pittosporaceae	Pittosporum	Pittosporum
Podocarpaceae	Podocarpus	Podocarpus
Polygonaceae	Coccoloba	Sea grape
Polypodiaceae	Aglaomorpha	Bear's paw fern
	Platycerium	Elkhorn fern, staghorn ferns
	Polypodium	Hare's foot, polypodium
Pteridaceae	Adiantum	Maidenhair fern
	Pellaea	Button fern
	Pteris	Brake, table fern
Rubiaceae	Coffea	Coffee
Saxifragaceae	Saxifraga	Mother of thousands
	Tolmiea	Piggyback plant
Strelitziaceae	Strelitzia	Bird of paradise
Taccaceae	Tacca	Devil flower, bat flower
Urticaceae	Pellionia	Pellionia
	Pilea	Aluminum plant
	Soleirolia	Baby's tears
Vitaceae (Vitidaceae)	Cissus	Grape ivy
Zingiberaceae	Alpinia	Shell ginger
	Curcuma	Curcuma ginger
	Globba	Globba ginger
	Hedychium	Ginger lily, butterfly ginger
	Kaempferia	Peacock ginger
	Zingiber	Common ginger, pinecone ginger

a Cane includes upright and horizontal (rhizome) stem cuttings.
b Layering includes both air and root layering.
c Numbers indicate preference with 1 = first choice(s), 2 = second choice(s), etc. Preferences may change depending on plant species or cultivars, costs, uses, markets, product size, therefore, multiple propagation methods for a plant may have the same rating based on these factors.

	CUTTING			DIVISION	GRAFTING	LAYERING[b]	TISSUE CULTURE	SEEDS/ SPORES
CANE[a]	EYE	LEAF	TIP					
				1				
			1	2			1	
				1				
		2						1
			1					
	2							1
	1			1				
	2	2	1			1	1	2
				2			1	3
			2					1
				1			1	
				1				
				2				1
				2				1
				2				1
				2				1
				2				1
				2				1
				1				2
	2	3	1					
			1					2
		2	1					1
			1			2		1
				2				1
				1			1	2
				1			1	2
				1			1	1
				3			2	1
				1			1	2
			2					1
				1				
		2		1				
				2				1
			2					1
	2		1					
	2		1					
	3	2	1	1				
	2		1			3		
				1			1	2
				1			1	
				1			1	2
				1			1	2
				1				
				1			1	

Methods of Foliage Plant Propagation

Foliage plants are propagated mainly through vegetative means, although some plants are propagated by seeds or spores. Methods of vegetative propagation include cuttings, division, grafting, layering, and tissue culture. Table 16.1 lists methods for propagation of 131 foliage plant genera. Since many genera can be propagated by more than one method, the preference of the methods for each genus is ranked in the table. The rank, however, may require modifications when propagation methods for a particular species of a genus differ from the rest, such as with certain species of *Chlorphytum*. Seed germination is the first choice for propagation of *Chlotophytum amaniense*, whereas division is the preferred method of propagation of *C. comosum*. In addition, the preferred propagation method may change in response to the availability of stock plants, the cost of cutting production, and the market demand for a genus, a species, or a cultivar.

Cuttings

Portions of stems, roots, or leaves are cut from stock plants and chemically induced or wounded under an appropriate microenvironment to form roots in a culture medium and then to produce shoots. The new independent plants are true (genetically identical) to the parent in most cases, providing sizable starting materials for marketable or finished plant production. This method is useful to propagators because it is a convenient and inexpensive way to increase the number of plants. Foliage plant cuttings are traditionally categorized as cane, eye or leaf-bud, leaf, and tip cuttings. Details for each of the cutting methods are discussed in later sections in this chapter.

Division

The separation or splitting of plants through the root system is known as division. The term also applies to the separation of bulbs, rhizomes, offsets, runners, stolons, and suckers. A number of foliage plant genera have vegetative structures, such as bulbs (*Eucharis grandiflora*) and rhizomes (*Alocasia, Aspidistra, Colocasia, Strelitzia reginae, Zamioculcas zamiifolia*, some orchids, ornamental ferns and ginger, and tuberous begonia), which can be used for division. Propagation is carried out by separating the bulbs or cutting the rhizomes into sections containing at least one lateral bud per piece and then planting the bulbs or pieces of rhizome in a growing medium. *Rumohra*, the predominant florists' green, is mostly propagated from rhizome pieces (predominantly rhizome tip cuttings) without the use of any growth regulators.

An offset is a characteristic type of lateral shoot or branch that develops from the base of the main stem. Foliage plants that produce offsets include *Anthurium, Dieffenbachia, Spathiphyllum*, and many bromeliads. Offsets in some cacti, such as *Schlumbergera truncata* (Christmas cactus) and *Hatiora gaertneri* (Easter cactus), are known as phylloclades or pups. Offsets and pups are removed by cutting close to the main stem with a sharp knife and then transplanted into a growing medium, usually after letting the wounded surfaces heal.

Runners are specialized stems that arise from leaf axils. They grow horizontally above and along the ground and produce plantlets at their nodes or apices. *Nephrolepis* (Boston fern) produces runnerlike branches (stolons), and plantlets form along them. *Saxifraga stolonifera* (mother of thousands) produces long slender red runners that also bear miniature plants at their ends. *Chlorophytum comosum* (spider plant) produces its plantlets from the apex of stolons. The plantlets are important commercial propagules, which are plant parts used for production.

A sucker is a shoot that arises on a plant from belowground. The most precise use of this term is to designate a shoot that arises from an adventitious bud on a root. Suckers are produced by several foliage plants including *Aglaonema, Calathea, Maranta*, and *Sansevieria*. Suckers are cut from stock plants and transplanted into containerized media for finished plant production.

Grafting

Two or more separate plants are united so that they function as one, creating a strong healthy plant that has the best characteristics of its two parents. The term "scion" is used to designate the portion of the one plant that is attached to the other, which is called the stock. The stock is usually rooted so that it may gather nourishment from the soil or rooting medium and furnish it to the scion. Among the foliage plants, cacti can be propagated by grafting. A grafted cactus will grow faster, flower sooner, and usually produce more seeds than its ungrafted counterparts.

Layering

The induction of adventitious roots on stems that are still attached to stock plants is called layering. Some plants—such as juvenile *Hedera helix, Epipremnum aureum,* and *Philodendron scandens*—have a natural propensity to regenerate by self-layering, forming adventitious roots from the stems that stay in contact with the growing medium. Stems of other plants can only produce roots at the site of a wound while they are still attached to the parent plants. Once rooted, the stems or layers are severed from the parent plant and grown individually. Layering is commonly used when other propagation methods are not effective for a particular species.

Air layering is a method of producing a rooted stem by wrapping a moistened medium, such as sphagnum peat, around a wounded area on a stem and covering it with plastic or some other type of moisture-retentive wrap. Pinning of stems to the ground or growing medium to allow adventitious root formation from stems covered by the soil or medium is known as simple layering. Leggy stems of dieffenbachia can be layered by curving them and placing them into medium-filled containers.

Tissue culture

The production of multiple new plants from very small pieces of plants, such as embryos, seeds, stems, shoot tips, root tips, calluses, single cells, and pollen grains on artificial media under aseptic conditions, is termed micropropagation by Hartmann et al. (1997). At least 50% of foliage plant genera have been reported to be tissue culturable. Some major foliage plant genera or groups that are commercially micropropagated include *Alocasia, Anthurium, Calathea, Colocasia, Dieffenbachia, Ficus, Musa, Philodendron, Spathiphyllum, Syngonium,* ferns, and bromeliads. Commercial tissue culture laboratories are able to produce millions of plantlets that are transplanted into medium-filled plug trays. The plants are commonly known as liners and are uniform, well rooted, and generally pathogen free. Since plantlets are continually transferred from laboratories to greenhouses, liners provide a year-round source of plant propagules. Use of liners has also given producers the option of converting space formerly used to maintain stock plants into production areas for finished plants.

Seeds

Some foliage plant species, such as *Araucaria heterophylla, Asparagus setaceus, Chamaedorea elegans, Chrysalidocarpus lutescens, Coffea arabica, Ficus altissima, Howea forsteriana, Hypoestes phyllostachya, Phoenix roebelinii, Ravenea rivularis, Schefflera actinophylla,* and some cacti, are exclusively grown from seeds. *Aglaonema, Anthurium, Dieffenbachia, Philodendron, Spathiphyllum,* and some bromeliads are seed propagated primarily for evaluating progeny from breeding programs.

Spores

Spores are used to propagate many ferns. Germinating spores produce a *prothallium,* on which *archegonia* (female reproductive organs producing eggs) and *antheridia* (male reproductive organs producing sperms) are formed. An antheridium produces mobile *antherozoids,* which swim to an archegonium and fertilize the eggs when the prothallium is covered with a film of water. In the past, spores were germinated on a peat-based medium in a shaded greenhouse, but they are now predominantly germinated in nutrient agar under aseptic conditions. Spores are typically decontaminated prior to sowing. Spore germination is favored by using a nutrient-free medium, but growth of the prothallus is improved by the addition of inorganic salts and sucrose. Germination occurs in two to three weeks, and the developing ferns can be transplanted into appropriate media in two to three months.

Cutting Production, Shipping, and Storage

Propagation by cuttings is still the dominant method of producing starting materials for finished foliage plant production, even though tissue culture has become increasingly popular over the last twenty years. Among the 131 genera in table 16.1, about 70% list cuttings as either the first or second choice of propagation. Cuttings formerly were produced in-house for self-sufficient individual nurseries, but now cutting production is an important separate business in the foliage plant industry, both nationally and internationally.

According to the USDA Agricultural Statistics Service (2005), the wholesale value of unfinished propagules of foliage plants in the United States in 2004 was $48 million, of which unrooted cuttings accounted for a great portion. In addition, the USDA Foreign Agricultural Service (2004) reported that the value of unrooted foliage plant cuttings imported from Central and South America in 2002 was $34 million. In general, the cost of unrooted cuttings is 10% of the national foliage plant wholesale value. Since the wholesale value in 2004 in the United States was $639 million, the estimated cost of unrooted cuttings in 2004 could be $64 million. This value did not include millions of *Dracaena sanderiana* (lucky bamboo) cane cuttings imported from Asia.

Stock plants

All cuttings are harvested from stock plants or from plants already in production. Some foliage plants, particularly vines, such as *Epipremnum* (pothos) and *Cissus* (grape ivy), are periodically trimmed to shape the plants and increase branching. The resulting shoots are sometimes propagated for the next generation of finished plants.

The genetic makeup of a stock plant and its physiological status have profound effects on the rooting ability of cuttings. For example, either tip or leaf-bud cuttings of any *Ficus benjamina* cultivar readily root in media, whereas cuttings of *F. binnendykii* 'Amstel King' are difficult to root. This difference in rooting is determined by the genetic makeup of plants. However, the percentage of successfully rooted *F. benjamina* cuttings may vary depending on the physiological status of the cuttings. Tip cuttings and leaf-bud cuttings that are closer to the apex root more quickly than cuttings made from the stem base. In some other species, such as *Schefflera arboricola*, however, cuttings taken from a more basal portion of the stem tend to root better than tip cuttings. This is likely because tip cuttings are too young, without a well-established xylem vessel, causing the cuttings to easily dehydrate during rooting.

Some species, such as *Epipremnum aureum*, *Ficus pumila*, *Hedera helix*, *Monstera deliciosa*, and *Philodendron scandens*, have both juvenile and mature forms, a characteristic called dimorphism. The rooting ability of cuttings derived from the juvenile stage differs significantly from that of cuttings derived from the mature stage. Cuttings from mature *Ficus pumila* required 3,000 ppm exogenous auxin to obtain maximum rooting percentage and root number, whereas cuttings from juvenile plants only needed 1,000 ppm auxin. A study of *Hedera helix* showed 100% rooting success for cuttings from juvenile forms, but only 16% rooting success for cuttings from mature forms with or without auxin treatment. In the foliage plant industry, only the juvenile forms of dimorphic plants have been widely used as stock for producing cuttings.

Aging is another aspect of the physiological status of stock plants that influences adventitious root formation. Many species have no dimorphic characteristics, but the rooting ability of cuttings declines with the increasing age of stock plants. For example, *Aphelandra squarrosa* stock plants must be replaced periodically because repeated use of the same stock plants results in cuttings with poor rooting ability. The same phenomenon occurs in *Aeschynanthus*, *Cissus*, *Codiaeum*, *Fittonia*, *Maranta*, and *Peperomia*. The reasons for the reduced rooting potential with aging are still poorly understood. One explanation is that aged plants may have low levels of phenols, which are postulated to be auxin cofactors or synergists in root initiation. Pathogen infection, particularly viruses, and pest infestation, as well as inappropriate environmental conditions and cultural practices may also be implicated in the decreased rooting potential of cuttings from aged plants.

Stock plants should be maintained in optimal environmental conditions with appropriate cultural management. Plants used as stock should be vigorous, free of diseases and insects, and without nutritional deficiencies. To meet these requirements, stock plants must be genetically sound. They should be 1) selected from seed-germinated or tissue-culture-generated plants that are free of pathogens, 2) isolated from a large cutting population that is full of vitality, and/or 3) derived from new hybrids exhibiting hybrid vigor. Generally, these selected stocks need to be replaced using the same selection process every three to five years to avoid aging and pathogens. However, some dracaena species produce the highest yields of cuttings when stock plants are ten to fifteen years old.

There are two methods of stock plant production: containerized production and field production. In the first, stock plants are produced in containers in a shaded greenhouse or a shade house, either raised off the ground (on benches or in hanging baskets) or directly on the ground. Off-the-ground production of stock plants is strongly recommended, since root rot diseases, soilborne nematodes, and other problems, such as snails, are more common to plants cultivated on or in the ground. Containerized production is used by self-sufficient nurseries or nurseries specialized in producing commercial cuttings of certain foliage plant genera. In the second method, stock plants are produced in the field in the tropics and subtropics. Field production is done by professionals specialized in cutting production for export.

Regardless of production type, stock plants should be grown in appropriate light, temperature, and relative humidity and maintained with adequate irrigation, fertilization, and pest-control practices to ensure that the best physiological status is attained. Joiner

(1981) and Griffith (1998) are references for appropriate environmental control and cultural practices for foliage plant production. However, stock plant production may differ slightly from finished plant production because the plants are used for different purposes.

In general, light levels for stock plant production should be higher than those for finished plant production. For example, the maximum recommended light level for stock production of *Epipremnum aureum* 'Golden Pothos' is 5,000 f.c. (54 klux) compared to 1,500 to 3,000 f.c. (16 to 32 klux) for acclimatized finished plants. Foliage plants grown under higher light intensities may not be attractive, but they accumulate more carbohydrates that can be used in the rooting process; they also yield a higher number of cuttings than plants grown under low light conditions. Cutting yield of *Peperomia obtusifolia* increased 77% at 5,000 f.c. (54 klux) compared with 2,500 f.c. (27 klux).

With increased labor costs and further production specialization in the United States, more cuttings are now imported from tropical America. Major stock-producing countries include Colombia, Costa Rica, Dominican Republic, Guatemala, Honduras, Jamaica, and Mexico. Cuttings imported are mainly *Aglaonema*, *Aphelandra*, *Araucaria*, *Codiaeum*, *Cordyline*, *Dracaena*, *Epipremnum*, *Peperomia*, and *Philodendron*. In addition, Hawaii supplies unrooted and rooted cuttings of *Dracaena*, *Cordyline*, and *Codiaeum* to the mainland. Most cuttings (except cactus) will root better if fresh cuttings are stuck into a growing medium. In commercial production, however, cuttings are frequently purchased from stock plant suppliers and may have been shipped a long distance and even stored for days after shipping. As a result, packing, shipping, and storage are additional factors influencing the quality of foliage plant cuttings.

Packing, shipping, and storage

Cuttings should be taken from healthy stock in the morning when plants are turgid. When necessary, cuttings may be washed and sprayed with USDA-approved fungicide and/or insecticide. *Aglaonema*, *Calathea*, *Cordyline*, *Dracaena sanderiana*, and *Strelitzia* cuttings range in length from 4 to 20 in. (10 to 50 cm) long with ten per bunch. Bunches are usually packed in USDA-approved packing materials, including exfoliated vermiculite, paper, perlite, polymer-stabilized cellulose, and sphagnum moss. In addition to any of these packing materials, cuttings should be wrapped in newspaper to provide insulation and moisture retention, then placed in a strong one-piece or full-telescoping (overlapping box segments that slide out to form a larger box) waxed fiberboard box lined with polyethylene film. When shipping to areas with extremely hot or cold weather, the box should be lined with polystyrene foam. The box should be sized to fit on a standard 40 by 48 in. (102 by 122 cm) pallet.

Temperatures of 60° to 65° F (16° to 18° C) and a relative humidity of 90 to 100% should be maintained during transportation and storage of most cuttings. The moderately low temperature along with the high humidity reduces water loss from transpiration and preserves the cuttings' carbohydrates for rooting. Foliage plant cuttings in general are sensitive to chilling; *Aglaonema* 'Silver Queen' is among the most sensitive plants; it can be injured at 55° F (13° C). Cuttings are usually transported by air cargo when they are exported. Importers should check with USDA-APHIS (United States Department of Agriculture-Animal and Plant Health Inspection Service) for current information and restrictions that may apply to their products. Almost all plant materials require a permit to enter the U.S. Most other countries also require permits and certificates.

It may take four to fifteen days from the time of harvest until the cuttings arrive in nurseries where rooting will take place. If cuttings are imported by brokers, which is common in the industry, the delay can be even longer. Therefore, cuttings should be unpacked and inspected for physical damage and pest problems; acceptable cuttings should be stuck immediately upon arrival. Moisture and light are important factors. If cuttings cannot be stuck or potted immediately, the boxes should be left open to reduce water condensation and to allow the cuttings to receive artificial light while being maintained near 65° F (18° C). A test of storage temperature and duration influencing propagation of *Dracaena fragrans* 'Massangeana' showed that root growth and shoot sprout of 12 in. (30 cm) canes after six weeks of storage at 60° F (16° C) or 70° F (21° C) were comparable to the controls that were rooted without being stored. *Codiaeum* cuttings had excellent quality when stored for five to ten days at 60° to 86° F (16° to 30° C) or fifteen days at 60° to 68° F (16° to 20° C).

Cultural Practices and Environmental Conditions Required for Rooting

Achieving high-quality rooted cuttings requires not only the availability of healthy and turgid cuttings, but also appropriate cultural practices and environmental conditions during rooting. Cultural practices include container and medium selection, water and nutrient management, growth regulator application, and disease and pest controls. Environmental conditions refer mainly to light intensities, relative humidity, and temperatures.

Cultural practices

Container selection

Plastic plug trays, pots, and hanging baskets have been used for rooting foliage plant cuttings. The North American standard plug tray for ornamentals is 11 by 22.5 in. (28 by 57 cm), but varies in the number of cells, ranging from 18 to 800, depending on the size of each cell. Plug trays are temporary containers that are used mainly for root establishment. The most commonly used tray has 72 cells; small eye or tip cuttings are singly stuck in each cell filled with growing medium. Rooted cuttings as plugs are then transplanted into larger containers.

Hanging baskets and pots are identified by diameters; typical sizes include 4, 6, 8, and 10 in. (10, 15, 20, and 25 cm). Cuttings can also be stuck directly in pots or hanging baskets; the number of cuttings per pot varies depending on plant species and pot size. For example, four cuttings of *Philodendron scandens* may be rooted in a 4 in. pot, six in a 6 in. pot, eight in an 8 in. pot, and ten in a 10 in. pot. Hanging baskets usually have saucers or other devices to collect drainage; however, saucers are generally not used during rooting and production but are attached just prior to marketing the plant.

Rooting media selection

Cuttings are almost exclusively rooted in soilless media. A vital component of a rooting medium is organic matter, such as pine bark, peat, coir dust (a coconut by-product), or compost. Other components including perlite, vermiculite, sand, and polystyrene beads are used in various combinations with the organic materials to formulate growing media (see chapter 4). Additional ingredients may include dolomite, fertilizer, and a wetting agent. Media companies usually prepare and sell different formulations, and they may also mix specific combinations to fulfill a grower's request. For example, Vergo Container Mix A (Verlite Co., Tampa, Florida), a widely used pre-mixed packaged medium for foliage plant propagation and production, consists of 60% Canadian peat, 20% vermiculite, and 20% perlite based on volume

and is supplemented with 8 lb./cu. yd. (4.7 kg/m^3) of dolomite. Large nurseries usually have their own formulas and may prepare their container media from component ingredients on-site. Commonly used media for foliage plant propagation and production are listed in table 16.2.

Rooting media should hold and provide water and nutrients, permit gas exchange with roots, and physically support the cuttings and subsequent new plants. Various physical and chemical parameters have been taken into account to determine the quality of container media. In general, media with the following physical properties are considered to be suitable for propagation of foliage plant cuttings: bulk density ranging from 0.09 to 0.46 oz./in.^{3} (0.16 to 0.8 g/cm^3) based on dry weight, total porosity of 50 to 75%, container capacity between 20 and 60% by volume, moisture content of 50 to 75%, and air space of 10 to 20% (5 to 10% for cell plugs). Desirable chemical properties of container media include a carbon to nitrogen ratio of less than 25; concentrations of sodium less than 80 ppm, boron less than 4 ppm, and fluorine less than 1 ppm; pH 5.5 to 7; soluble salts (electrical conductivity) of root-zone solution 1.0 to 2.0 mS/cm extracted using the PourThru method; and cation exchange capacity of 5 to 50 meq/100 g.

Some foliage plant genera, such as *Chlorophytum*, *Cordyline*, and *Dracaena*, are sensitive to fluoride. Tipburn followed by leaf necrosis are typical symptoms. Superphosphate, which used to be a common container substrate amendment, was shown to be a fluoride carrier and is no longer routinely added to growing media. Additionally, media should be free of pathogens and nematodes, and disinfection and/or pasteurization may be needed if pathogenic fungi, bacteria, or nematodes are present. Potting machines have been widely used for filling containers with media; depending on the type of machines used, 900 to 3,500 containers can be filled in one hour.

Water management

Mature shoots of foliage plants by weight are largely water: *Aglaonema* (80%), *Anthurium* (84%), *Dracaena fragrans* (86%), *Syngonium* (91%), *Dieffenbachia* (92%), *Schefflera* (96%), and *Spathiphyllum* (98%). Success in rooting is directly related to the water status of the cuttings and the available water in the medium. Water loss from transpiration and water gain from uptake must be in balance to maintain turgor. The cutting base that touches the rooting medium is the main entry point for

TABLE 16.2
Components of common growing mixes used for foliage plant propagation and production.

GROWING MIX	COMPONENTS
Cornell Foliage Plant Mix[a]	50% sphagnum peat, 25% vermiculite, and 25% perlite, supplemented with ground limestone, superphosphate, potassium nitrate, fritted trace elements, and granular fertilizer (10-10-10) at 8.3, 2.0, 1.0, 0.12, and 2.7 lb./cu. yd. (4.9, 1.2, 0.6, 0.07, and 1.6 kg/m³), respectively.
Cornell Epiphytic Mix	33% sphagnum peat, 33% perlite, and 33% Douglas fir bark, supplemented with ground limestone, superphosphate, potassium nitrate, fritted trace elements, iron sulfate, and granular fertilizer (10-10-10) at 7.1, 4.0, 1.0, 0,12, 0.5, and 2.7 lb./cu. yd. (4.2, 2.4, 0.6, 0.07, 0.3, and 1.6 kg/m³), respectively.
Coir Dust Mix 1[b]	50% coconut coir dust, 25% vermiculite, 25% perlite, supplemented with dolomite at 7.1 lb./cu. yd. (4.2 kg/m³).
Coir Dust Mix 2	40% coconut coir dust, 30% vermiculite, 30% pine bark, supplemented with dolomite at 7.1 lb./cu. yd. (4.2 kg/m³).
Fafard Mix 2-B[c]	50% Sphagnum peat, 30% pine bark, 10% perlite, and 10% vermiculite, supplemented with dolomite and gypsum at 6 and 1.2 kg/m³, respectively, and liquid wetting agent at 4.2 fl. oz./cu. yd. (160 mL/m³).
Scotts Redi-Earth with coir[d]	50% coconut coir pith, 50% medium-grade vermiculite, starter nutrient charge, and other ingredients.
Uinversity of Florida Foliage Plants Mix 1[e]	50% sphagnum peat, 25% pine bark, and 25% shavings; dolomite and fertilizers may be supplemented.
University of Florida Foliage Plants Mix 2	50% sphagnum peat and 50% pine bark; dolomite and fertilizers may be supplemented.
University of Florida Foliage Plants Mix 3	75% sphagnum peat and 25% sand; dolomite and fertilizer may be supplemented.
Vergo Container Mix A[f]	60% Canadian peat, 20% vermiculite, and 20% perlite, supplemented with dolomite at 6.7 lb./cu. yd. (4 kg/m³).

[a] Boodley and Scheldrake, 1977. [c] Fafard Inc., Apopka, Florida. [e] Poole et al., 1981.
[b] Stamps and Evans, 1997. [d] The Scotts Co., Marysville, Ohio. [f] Verlite Co., Tampa, Florida

water. It is essential that cuttings establish a firm contact with the medium by a thorough watering of the medium right after potting.

The availability of water to cuttings depends primarily on the quantity of water stored in the container medium and its relationship to the water potential (the ability of a substance to draw water to itself) of the medium. In general, media should contain about 20 to 30% by volume of easily available water for optimal rooting. At the same time, the rooting environment should be manipulated to minimize the water vapor pressure difference between the cuttings and the surrounding air. These requirements are attained in foliage plant propagation by rooting cuttings in shaded greenhouses or shade houses under enclosed tents, intermittent mist, or fogging systems.

Mist systems have been shown to increase rooting percentage; thus it is the preferred irrigation method in the propagation of foliage plant cuttings. Until roots become established, mist is normally turned on at nine a.m. and turned off at sunset using timers. A common mist cycle used in foliage plant propagation in humid climates is fifteen seconds of mist per thirty minutes, although twelve seconds on for every six minutes has been shown to be best for *Schefflera arboricola*. Systems should be adjusted according to the plant species and types of cuttings, the temperature, the humidity, the light intensity, and the rooting medium's water-holding capacity. Cane cuttings may require a lower frequency of misting than tip cuttings. If tip cuttings have several leaves that possess a high transpiration rate, mist frequency and duration should increase. It may be appropriate to select a rooting medium designed to drain excess water so that the cuttings do not rot. Products such as Oasis (cubes or wedges made from open-celled, water-absorbing foam) are designed for such a purpose.

Groundwater is the primary source of water for irrigating foliage plants in many operations. A water source with the following chemical properties is reported to be acceptable for foliage plant propagation and production: alkalinity less than or equal to 100 ppm; soluble salts (electrical conductivity) less than 0.5 mS/cm; pH 5 to 7; turbidity less than 1.5 ntu; NH_4-N, NO_3-N, P, and SO_4 each less than 5 ppm; Cl less than 140 ppm; Ca less than 120 ppm; Mg less than 24 ppm; Na less than 50 ppm; and fluoride (F) less than 0.5 ppm. Be aware that hard water (containing calcium greater than 80 ppm) applied through mist may result in residue deposits on leaves and may affect market value if rooted cuttings are sold. Additionally, since groundwater is the primary source of water for irrigation, appropriate filters should be used to prevent plugging of mist or fog nozzles and subsequent disruption of irrigation cycles during propagation.

Nutrient management in rooting

The potential leaching of nutrients from the rooting medium during misting has been a concern. Studies of different rates of controlled-release fertilizers or water-soluble fertilizers affecting the rooting of *Aglaonema, Aphelandra, Codiaeum, Dieffenbachia, Epipremnum, Maranta, Philodendron,* and *Schefflera* showed that additional fertilizers had no effects on root numbers, and high fertilizer rates even reduced root grades. These results can be explained by the fact that the process of root formation at the base of a cutting can be divided into three stages: initiation, elongation, and root growth and development. Mineral nutrients within cuttings can generally support the root initiation process; thus the application of fertilizers during the period of root initiation has no effect on root numbers. On the other hand, high fertilizer rates may create a root environment with high soluble salts, which inhibits root elongation. Therefore, as long as the rooting medium has an initial soluble salts level of 1 to 2 mS/cm, measured by the PourThru extraction method, no fertilization is needed during the root initiation process (generally seven to fourteen days, depending on species). Subsequent fertilization for root growth and development is needed if rooting media soluble salts levels drop below 1 mS/cm.

A common practice in monitoring nutrient status and pH of rooting media is to extract root-zone solutions from the media and analyze nutrient concentrations, pH, and soluble salts of the solutions. Four procedures have been used for root-zone solution extraction of containerized plants: the 1:2 dilution, the 1:5 dilution, the PourThru, and the saturated-paste methods (see chapter 7). Two methods were developed for extracting root-zone solution of plug trays: press extraction and multicavity collection method. Medium pH has been found to be independent of extraction methods. However, soluble salts and mineral element concentrations vary with the method used for solution extraction. Thus interpretations of medium testing should specify which method was used for the root-zone solution extraction.

Growth regulator application

Foliage plant cuttings are generally easily rooted, but the addition of auxin can improve rooting of some species. When comparing the use of the natural auxin indoleacetic acid (IAA) and synthetic ones, such as indolebutyric acid (IBA) and naphthalene acetic acid (NAA), IBA has been used more frequently than the rest. Table 16.3 lists rooting indexes of twenty-eight foliage plant species after their cuttings were dipped in a dry powder containing 0.1, 0.3, or 0.8% IBA. Species that showed significant root index differences compared with the control (without IBA treatment) were *Aglaonema costatum, A. crispum, Begonia* Rex Cultorum hybrids, *Cissus antarctica, Codiaeum variegatum, Ficus benjamina, Fittonia verschaffeltii, Gynura aurantiaca, Hedera helix, Peperomia obtusifolia, Pilea cadierei, Polyscias fruticosa, Sansevieria trifasciata, Senecio rowleyanus,* and *Syngonium podophyllum*.

TABLE 16.3

Rooting index[a] of foliage plant cuttings treated with three indolebutyric acid[b] (IBA) concentrations (adapted from Miller and Poole, 1982)[c]. IBA was beneficial for the highlighted species at the shaded rates.

PLANT	TYPE OF CUTTING	DAYS IN MIST	UNTREATED CONTROL	IBA		
				0.1%	0.3%	0.8%
Aeschynanthus pulcher	Tip	40	4.7 a[d]	4.5 a	4.4 a	3.5 b
Aeschynanthus pulcher	Eye	40	4.4 ab	4.2 b	4.7 a	4.7 a
Aglaonema costatum	Tip	21	2.8 c	3.2 b	3.8 a	1.8 d
Aglaonema crispum	Tip	21	2.5 c	3.3 b	4.3 a	3.5 b
Ardisia crenata	Tip	38	4.9 a	5.0 a	4.7 a	4.1 b
Begonia Rex Cultorum hybrids	Leaf	45	4.1 b	3.7 c	4.1 b	4.7 a
Cissus antarctica	Eye	37	2.7 b	3.1 a	3.2 a	2.7 b
Cissus rhombifolia	Eye	37	1.5 a	1.7 a	1.5 a	1.2 b
Codiaeum variegatum	Tip	35	3.3 b	2.7 c	3.1 c	4.1 a
Dieffenbachia amoena	Tip	19	3.7 a	3.6 a	3.3 a	3.3 a
Dracaena deremensis	Tip	32	4.6 ab	4.7 a	4.4 b	4.8 a
Dracaena marginata	Tip	32	3.9 a	4.6 a	2.5 c	2.6 c
Dracaena surculosa	Eye	20	4.1 a	4.0 a	3.4 b	3.1 b
Episcia cupreata	Tip	18	3.1 a	3.4 a	3.8 a	3.4 a
Epipremnum aureum	Eye	47	4.6 a	3.6 b	3.9 b	4.3 a
Ficus benjamina	Tip	35	4.1 b	3.7 bc	3.2 c	4.7 a
Fittonia verschaffeltii	Tip	34	2.9 c	3.9 b	4.7 a	4.0 b
Gynura aurantiaca	Eye	34	3.7 b	3.7 bc	4.1 ab	4.5 a
Hedera helix	Eye	45	3.6 c	4.0 bc	4.2 b	4.9 a
Hoya carnosa	Eye	41	4.8 a	4.5 a	4.7 a	4.7 a
Peperomia obtusifolia	Tip	26	3.2 c	4.5 a	4.5 a	4.0 b
Philodendron scandens	Eye	47	4.6 a	4.1 b	4.4 a	4.3 ab
Pilea cadierei	Tip	18	3.4 b	3.8 a	3.7 ab	3.7 ab
Plectranthus australis	Tip	15	4.2 a	4.0 a	4.2 a	4.0 a
Podocarpus macrophyllus	Tip	48	4.0 a	2.4 b	2.9 b	2.7 b
Polyscias fruticosa	Tip	23	3.0 b	4.0 a	1.8 c	3.0 b
Sansevieria trifasciata	Leaf	48	3.4 c	4.9 a	3.9 b	4.0 b
Senecio rowleyanus	Eye	49	3.2 c	3.7 ab	3.9 a	3.4 bc
Syngonium podophyllum	Eye	54	1.7 b	2.2 b	1.7 b	3.1 a

[a]Rooting index with a scale of 1 = no roots, 2 = very little rooting, 3 = fair rooting,
4 = good rooting, and 5 = heavy rooting.
[b]IBA in a powder form, with active IBA concentrations of 0.1, 0.3, and 0.8%.
[c]Rooting took place in a shaded greenhouse with a maximum light level of 1,200 (13 klux)
and air temperatures of 64° to 86° F (18° to 30° C). Rooting medium was maintained at 75° F
(24° C) by bottom heating and misted for five seconds every six minutes from ten a.m. to four p.m.
[d]Means in a given row followed by the same letter are not significantly different according to
Duncan's new multiple range test ($P \leq 0.05$).

Disease control

Commonly occurring bacterial, fungal, and viral diseases in foliage plants have been well documented. See *Foliage Plant Diseases: Diagnosis and Control* by A.R. Chase (1997) for detailed information. Among the pathogens listed, three fungi (*Rhizoctonia*, *Phytophthora*, and *Pythium*) and one bacterium (*Xanthomonas*) cause the most common diseases in foliage plants.

Rhizoctonia, *Phytophthora*, and *Pythium* can cause root rot diseases in a wide range of foliage plants. To control these pathogens, the first measure is to use disease-free cuttings and surface-sterilize clippers used for taking cuttings between plants. The second is to exercise sanitary cultural practices in the rooting process, including scrubbing reused pots and trays to remove sclerotia and sterilizing containers with a labeled quaternary ammonium compound or other effective disinfectant. To help prevent colonization by fungi growing medium components and mixed media should not be stored on the ground. Native soil incorporated into media mixes must be pasteurized. See chapter 9, for more information on disease management. Also see *Integrated Pest Management for Floriculture and Nurseries* by S. H. Dreistadt (2001) for integrated management of pathogens and insects.

The bacterium *Xanthomonas* infects all of the major tropical foliage plants, such as *Aglaonema*, *Anthurium*, *Dieffenbachia*, *Epipremnum*, *Philodendron*, *Spathiphyllum*, and *Syngonium*. The infection is through entrance at hydathodes (epidermal structures specialized for secretion, or exudation, of water) on the leaf margins or by entering wounds. Symptoms occur on the plants as chlorotic water-soaked spots on leaf margins, which grow rapidly to form characteristic necrotic V-shaped lesions. Most plants exhibit symptoms within two to three weeks after infection. Eventually, infected plants wilt and die. In other plants, such as ivy, ficus, and schefflera, the bacteria enter via the leaf stomata and become only locally systemic. In this case, removal of infected leaves will lower inoculum levels. The primary mechanism of movement of *Xanthomonas* within the nursery is splashing water; limiting the amount of water on leaf surfaces is advantageous to disease control, but it is difficult to accomplish since intermittent mist is often used during rooting. The most important step for controlling this pathogen is the use of clean cuttings and rooting media.

Another aspect of disease control is to avoid importing exotic plant pathogens. The importation of large numbers of cuttings from the tropics increases the risk of introducing new pathogens even through samples are inspected. For example, the bacterial pathogen *Ralstonia solanacearum* is known to infect hundreds of plant species. A new race of this pathogen, race 1, which is more virulent than the others, was isolated from *Epipremnum aureum* cuttings imported from a tropical region.

Insect and mite control

The major insect pests of foliage plants are aphids, mealybugs, scales, and thrips. They feed by sucking plant sap, which results in distorted new growth, leaf yellowing, and leaf drop. Mites are arachnids and belong to the same animal class as spiders and ticks. Mites puncture plant cells with their mouthparts and suck the exuding fluid, which causes plant tissue to discolor or distort. Fortunately, insect and mite infestations generally do not occur during propagation if cuttings are initially free of pests.

Fungus gnats, however, commonly occur on organic materials when conditions are damp. They are not only a nuisance during propagation but also damage newly formed roots, young stems, and germinated seedlings. In addition, fungus gnats can contaminate media with fungi including *Botrytis*, *Fusarium*, and *Pythium*. Besides cultural control, such as sanitation and exclusion, the most effective method for controlling fungus gnats is soil drenches with insect growth regulators, since more than half of a fungus gnat's life span is spent in larval and pupal stages confined to the growing medium. See chapter 10 for more information.

Parasitic nematode control

Parasitic nematodes include root knot nematodes (*Meloidogyne javanica*, *M. incognita*, and *M. arenaria*), cactus cyst nematode (*Heterodera cacti*), root lesion nematodes (*Pratylenchus penetrans*, *P. brachyurus*, *P. coffeae*, and *P. zeae*), and burrowing nematode (*Radopholus similes*). Cuttings infested with nematodes lose vigor and/or eventually fall over.

Foliage plants susceptible to infection by root knot nematodes include *Aglaonema*, *Ardisia*, *Asparagus*, *Aspidistra*, *Schefflera*, *Calathea*, *Chamaedorea*, *Dieffenbachia*, *Maranta*, and *Sansevieria*. Species in the cactus family (Cactaceae) are susceptible to cactus cyst nematodes. *Aglaonema*, *Ananas comosus*, *Begonia*, and *Chamaedorea* are often damaged by root lesion nematodes. Although root lesion nematodes, especially *Pratylenchus penetrans*, are regularly isolated from *Rumohra adiantiformis*, negative effects on yield have not been confirmed experimentally under current production conditions. The burrowing nematode can infect *Anthurium, Calathea, Chamaedorea, Dieffenbachia, Monstera,* and *Philodendron.* Nematode infection is a major problem in *Aglaonema*; it has been reported that plants have been widely infested by lesion and root knot nematodes in tropical stock farms.

Stock plant growers generally treat their fields two to three times a year with nematicides. However, the use of nematicides is not favored because most of the chemicals are rather toxic.

Environmental conditions and control

Cuttings are rooted under fog, mist, or in tents in shaded greenhouses and shade houses where light levels range from 1,000 to 1,500 f.c. (11 to 16 klux), air temperature ranges from 70° to 86° F (21° to 30° C), and relative humidity is 80 to 100%. If rooting takes place in winter and early spring, the rooting medium temperature is probably more critical to the rooting process than the air temperature. Cuttings are stuck in a soilless medium confined by different sizes of containers, and medium temperatures fluctuate more in smaller containers than in larger containers.

For example, the air temperature in a shaded greenhouse without heat in central Florida in February dropped from 57° F (14° C) at 5:00 P.M. to 45° F (7° C) at 6:00 A.M., while the medium temperature of 4 in. (10 cm) pots decreased from 69° F (21° C) to 54° F (12° C) during those hours. On the other hand, changes in the air temperature in a shaded greenhouse and medium temperature of 8 in. (20 cm) pots were almost identical, decreasing from 77° F (25° C) at 4:00 P.M. to 64° F (18° C) at 4:00 A.M. in February in central Florida. In the same experiment, *Aglaonema* 'Silver Queen' growing in root-zone-heated pots maintained in a temperature range from 72° to 81° F (22° to 27° C) produced five times more lateral shoots and 50% more dry weight than plants grown in unheated containers.

Root-zone heating, or bottom heating, is often accomplished by using steam or hot water pipes beneath the growing benches and skirting the benches to retain heat. In addition, hot air may be forced through convection tubes under the benches or commercial heating systems may be utilized. A study of the interactions between light and root-zone heating on the rooting of *Codiaeum variegatum* 'Gold Dust' and *Ficus benjamina* found that the number of roots in *C. variegatum* was unaffected by either light or medium heating, but both factors enhanced root elongation.

However, rooting of *F. benjamina* was improved in a heated medium and was unaffected by light.

Systems used for controlling the rooting environment include thermostats and timers, analog step controllers, dedicated microprocessor controls, and integrated computer controls. Thermostats and timers are low-cost systems that provide limited control. Thermostats are simple temperature-sensing devices in propagation tents that turn a switch on at one temperature and off at another. Timers are used for other functions such as turning mist on and off. Analog step controllers divide a propagation greenhouse's heating and cooling equipment into steps, or stages, called a sequence of operation. They are generally most appropriate for simple greenhouse zones limited to six to eight total stages of heating and cooling or for smaller operations with no anticipation of expansion. Step controllers have a low initial cost and provide better control of the greenhouse environment than either single- or multiple-stage thermostats.

Dedicated microprocessors are devices that bring the benefits of computerization to the step-controller concept. They have more output connections than the step controller, allowing more devices to be integrated in the system, and a full range of optional sensors for controlling irrigation, lighting, and temperature. Using the built-in keypad and the menu-driven on-screen interface, growers can customize the system based on their needs. Some systems also allow for remote programming and monitoring using personal computers. With proper programming, microprocessor controls provide improved accuracy and better equipment coordination.

Integrated computer controls (ICC) are an advance from microprocessor controls; they combine the capability of step or microprocessor and other individual control devices into an integrated computer system. Integrated computer controls can coordinate virtually all greenhouse environment functions, including ventilation, heating, cooling, air circulation, irrigation, fertilization, boiler control, lighting, and carbon dioxide dosing, based on multiple settings entered by the grower. The benefits of the ICC include more stable and accurate environmental control, energy conservation, improved rooting, and lower labor costs. The installation of a control system in foliage plant propagation largely depends on labor availability and costs, propagation materials and needs, current infrastructure, energy consumption, and other considerations.

Rooting of Cuttings

Propagation from cuttings exploits the ability of a piece of plant tissue from a stem, a leaf, or a root to regenerate into a fully developed plant with roots and shoots. Rooting can be conducted at any time of the year, but certain times may be better than others for specific crops. Good times are early spring (before new growth starts and when plants are responding to increasing temperature) and fall (after good summer growth). In theory, each living cell is capable of regenerating a complete plant, and each differentiated plant cell is able to *dedifferentiate* into a meristematic cell. Propagation by cane, eye, and tip cuttings exploits the ability of cells to form adventitious roots, but leaf cuttings require initiating both adventitious roots and shoots.

There are two types of adventitious roots: *preformed* and *wound roots*. Preformed roots develop naturally on stems, such as juvenile *Epipremnum aureum*, *Hedera helix*, and *Ficus pumila*, while they are still attached to the parent plant and may emerge prior to severing the stem piece. Wound roots develop only after living cells at the cut surfaces are injured and exposed. Wound healing results in certain cells in the vicinity of the vascular cambium and phloem beginning to divide; specific cells then dedifferentiate and form root initials. Subsequently, the root initials develop into organized root *primordia* and the growth and emergence of the primordia outward results in root tips. Therefore, the initial rooting process is visually considered as initiation and elongation. In the rooting of juvenile cuttings of *Ficus pumila*, four days are required to allow the dedifferentiation to occur in phloem ray parenchyma cells, two more days are needed for the growth and emergence of primordia, and then on day seven roots protrude from stems as root tips.

Another phenomenon associated with root initiation is *callus*, which develops at the basal end of cuttings under a favorable rooting environment. Callus is an irregular mass of parenchyma cells generally originating from the vascular cambium. Callus and root formation often occur simultaneously, and roots appear through callus but they are independent of each other. In some difficult-to-root species, however, callus appears to be a precursor of adventitious root formation. For example, adventitious roots of *Sedum* and mature *Hedera helix* originate in the callus tissue formed at the base of cuttings.

The following discussion will focus on the rooting of cane, eye, tip, and leaf cuttings, since they are the most common cutting types in the foliage plant industry. Important plant genera that are propagated by preferred cutting methods will be mentioned. Procedures for rooting each type of cutting will be outlined using selected genera or species as examples.

Cane cuttings

Cane and rhizome cuttings are basically stem cuttings. Because some foliage plant genera have canelike stems, cane cuttings became a popular term. *Aglaonema*, *Cordyline*, *Dieffenbachia*, *Dracaena*, *Homalomena*, *Yucca*, and some cacti can be propagated by cane cuttings. Among these, *Dracaena fragrans* 'Massangeana' and *D. deremensis* 'Warneckii' and 'Hawaiian Lisa Cane' have been, and will continue to be, propagated primarily by canes because the crown of leaves that sprouts from the top of the cane gives an instant palm effect.

Canes are harvested either in Central and South America or Hawaii and cut into lengths ranging from 1 to 5 ft. (0.3 to 1.5 m). The bottom inch of the cane is sometimes dipped into an alcohol solution containing 10,000 ppm IBA for approximately two seconds. Cane tips are then dipped into a mixture of portland cement and sealing wax to prevent drying and splitting during shipping. The treated canes are placed in an upright position on pallets in crates with a plastic and moss-lined bottom to maintain high humidity during shipping. Canes are shipped at 60° to 65° F (16° to 18° C) for five to fourteen days, and they can be stored at 60° to 70° F (16° to 21° C) for an additional two weeks without influencing rooting or sprouting.

Rooting dracaena canes vertically

Have containers with 8 in. (20 cm) diameters or larger and a good-quality rooting medium ready. Inspect canes immediately upon arrival and discard any that are dehydrated or infected with pathogens. Pot the canes in containers with a growing medium. After potting, water the rooting medium thoroughly, and place the containers in a mist system that applies approximately twelve seconds of mist every thirty minutes. Rooting should take place under 2,000 to 3,000 f.c. (22 to 32 klux) maximum light, 68° to 86° F (20° to 30° C) temperatures, and 80 to 100% relative humidity.

Research has shown that initial bud-break in *D. fragrans* 'Massangeana' was hastened by soaking the base in a solution containing 50 ppm IBA for eighteen hours. Another report indicated that immersion of *D. fragrans* 'Massangeana' and *D. deremensis* 'Warneckii' and 'Janet Craig' cuttings in 120° F (49° C) hot water for ten minutes for insect control, followed by 0.8% IBA basal treatment increased rooting and root number. Usually three different lengths of canes are potted in an equilateral triangle in a pot. Each potted cane should stand straight and be stable. In general, cuttings spout in four to five weeks and roots appear in five to six weeks.

Rooting dieffenbachia canes horizontally

Inspect canes and prepare propagation medium and containers as described immediately above. Cut the canes into pieces with one or two nodes, and allow the two ends of each piece to suberize (harden off) for about two days. Place the cuttings horizontally, buds uppermost, in the medium; cover them until their surfaces are barely visible. Rooting should take place under mist at fifteen seconds every thirty minutes in a shaded greenhouse with 2,000 to 3,000 f.c. (22 to 32 klux) maximum light, 68° to 86° F (20° to 30° C) temperatures, and 80 to 100% relative humidity. A study has shown that single-node cuttings from the uppermost part of the *Dieffenbachia amoena* cane, just below the leaves, produced larger plants than cuttings from basal nodes. The height of plants after four months of growth was directly related to the diameter and length of the cutting. In addition, cuttings planted 3 in. (8 cm) deep produced smaller plants than those just barely covered by the medium.

Rooting cacti cuttings

Cut straight across the stem of vigorous stock plants, such as column cactus, *Cereus peruvianus*, using a clean, thin-bladed knife. The rootstock left in the pot should be about 3 in. (8 cm) tall. Cut the stem into 9 in. (23 cm) sections, and allow them to form callus for one to fourteen days in a warm and dry place. It is important to remember which ends of each piece are the top and bottom. Use a small pot in which the cuttings will stand upright. Fill the bottom 1 in. (2.5 cm) with a rooting medium, then add a 0.5 in. (1.3 cm) layer of fine gravel. Water the medium immediately after sticking (bottom end down, of course), and keep it moist but not wet thereafter. Cactus cuttings are usually rooted under light levels of 3,000 to 5,000 f.c. (32 to 54 klux) maximum and temperatures of 70° to 85° F (21° to 29° C). Propagating cacti through cuttings provides larger plants much more quickly than propagating from seed, but far fewer plants can be obtained. The main concern with cac-

Figure 16.1. Propagation of *Dracaena fragrans* 'Massangeana' canes. (A) Canes of different lengths ready for rooting were imported from Costa Rica (note that the top end of each cane was sealed with wax); (B) four canes of different lengths were stuck in each 12 in. (30 cm) pot; (C) canes sprouted first and then roots appeared (inset); and (D) rooted canes in commercial production. (Stewarts Nursery, Winter Garden, Florida)

tus cutting propagation is not water loss, but fungal infection, mainly *Drechslern cactivora*, which causes a dry basal rot, as well as *Pythium debaryanum* and *Phytophthora cactorum*, both of which result in a wet basal rot.

Eye or leaf-bud cuttings

Eye cuttings or leaf-bud cuttings consist of a leaf blade, petiole, and a short piece of the stem with the attached axillary bud. In the foliage plant industry, the term "eye cutting" is often used to refer to cuttings derived from plants with vinelike stems, which includes *Aeschynanthus, Cissus, Columnea, Epipremnum, Episcia, Gynura, Hedera helix, Hoya, Mikania, Philodendron scandens, Senecio,* and *Syngonium.* Leaf-bud cuttings are commonly made from plants with upright growth habits, such as *Aphelandra, Fatsia, Ficus, Geogenanthus, Ruellia, Sanchezia,* and *Schefflera.* Eye or leaf-bud cuttings require adventitious root formation since shoots can be initiated from the axillary bud of the attached leaf. This type of cutting is particularly useful when propagating material is limited because it will produce at least twice as many new plants from the same amount of stock material.

Rooting *Epipremnum*
(pothos) eye cuttings

Select healthy vines with fourteen or fifteen leaves and desirable patterns of foliar variegation (if any), and cut at the fourth or fifth leaf from the base (fig. 16.2). Eye cuttings are taken just above the node, resulting in single-eye, or single-node, cuttings. The cuttings should be up to 2 in. (5 cm) long with the stem cut 1.2 in. (3 cm) below the node. Sometimes double-eye, or double-node, cuttings are taken as well. As mentioned earlier, *Epipremnum,* along with *Hedera helix* and *Ficus pumila,* generate preformed roots. These adventitious roots should be preserved during cutting harvest.

Stick the cuttings singly per cell in plug trays or use multiple cuttings in individual containers. Cuttings are more commonly stuck in containers: four per 4 in. (10 cm) pot, six per 6 in. (15 cm) pot, or eight per 8 in. (20 cm) pot. Rooting hormones are not necessary since pothos cuttings root easily. Water the cuttings well initially, and apply mist for five seconds every five minutes for about three weeks. Cuttings root in three to four weeks under a light level of 3,000 f.c. (32 klux) and temperatures ranging from 75° to 90° F (24° to 32° C). Research has shown

Figure 16.2. Propagation of *Epipremnum aureum* 'Golden Pothos' eye cuttings. **(A)** On a healthy plant with fourteen leaves a cut is made above the fourth leaf from the base; **(B)** single-eye cuttings are made from the cut vine, leaving any adventitious roots intact; **(C)** four cuttings are stuck in each 5 in. (13 cm) pot; and **(D)** a rooted eye cutting.

that an extra three to five weeks of mist increased vine lengths but did not increase fresh weight. Vine length increase without a corresponding fresh weight or dry weight increase is undesirable in pothos production. If rooting takes place in winter, bottom heat with a medium temperature at 82° F (28° C) can increase root length, vine length, root numbers, and root and shoot dry weights.

Rooting ficus leaf-bud cuttings

Select healthy stems produced from the current season; they should be soft at the tip but firm at the base (fig. 16.3). Cut the stems just above each node to obtain single-node leaf-bud cuttings. Fill either containers or cells of plug trays with a rooting medium, and stick each cutting just deep enough for it to be able to stand upright. Firm the medium around the cuttings, and water thoroughly. The cuttings should be misted for five seconds every five minutes under 2,000 to 3,000 f.c. (22 to 32 klux) light levels and 75° to 90° F (24° to 32° C) temperature. Bottom heat at 82° F (28° C) may be helpful for rooting in winter and early spring.

Since more cuttings are produced per plant than either air layering or tip cutting, the leaf-bud cutting has been an important method of quickly propagating *F. benjamina, F. binnendykii, F. elastica, F. lyrata, F. retusa,* and *F. salicifolia.* A propagation study in central Florida with *F. elastica* 'Decora' showed that 90% of single leaf-bud cuttings rooted, and shoots produced from them reached a height of 12 in. (30 cm) in six months. However, leaf-bud cuttings of *F. elastica* and *F. lyrata* can occupy extra space on propagation benches because of their large leaves. In a study conducted to increase space utilization efficiency, leaves were either rolled longitudinally and held in place with a rubber band or partially cut off. Results showed that the leaf should not be rolled during propagation; however, removal of 50% of the leaf permitted adequate rooting while taking up less space.

Tip cuttings

As the name implies, tip cuttings are taken only from the tips of stems. Usually 4 to 10 in. (10 to 25 cm) long with two to five leaves, they are a popular way of propagating *Aglaonema, Aphelandra, Cordyline, Dieffenbachia, Dracaena, Fastina, Ficus, Fittonia, Maranta, Peperomia, Pittosporum, Polyscias,* and *Rumohra.* This propagation method results in desirable plants in a short period of time, but it yields fewer cuttings per plant compared with eye or leaf-bud cuttings. Small tip cuttings often root faster and

Figure 16.3. Propagation of *Ficus benjamina* 'Midnight' leaf-bud cuttings. (A) Removing a healthy branch from a stock plant; (B) three-leaf cuttings; (C) cuttings stuck singly in 4 in. (10 cm) pots; and (D) rooted cuttings.

require less space. The depth to which cuttings are stuck is important since root initiation and growth require a large amount of oxygen. Cuttings should be stuck just deep enough to stabilize and support the cuttings.

Dieffenbachia and dracaena cuttings should be allowed to suberize (harden off), and ficus cuttings should have milky sap dried at the end of the cutting surface before being stuck into the rooting medium. *Dracaena marginata* cuttings allowed to suberize in an open greenhouse in Hawaii for four days had a 100% survival rate without infection compared with only 30% of those cuttings that were not hardened. Cuttings will root better if they are appropriately spaced, as opposed to being potted in a clump. Additionally, tip cuttings may require an increased frequency of mist, since they have more leaves that may increase water loss through transpiration compared with those from eye or leaf-bud cuttings.

Rooting *Aglaonema* tip cuttings

Select cuttings, either imported or harvested in-house, that are healthy, free from pathogens and nematodes, and have about five leaves (fig. 16.4). A cutting that is too large (more than seven leaves) may fall over in the pot and will have a stretched appearance later on. If the cutting is too small (fewer than four leaves), the tender stem is more susceptible to pathogens. Dip the cutting base in rooting hormone powder containing 0.3% IBA, tap the stem gently to remove any excess powder, and stick the cutting in the container medium. *Aglaonema* is usually produced in pots with a diameter of 8 in. (20 cm) or larger, and three or more cuttings are rooted per pot. Water the medium thoroughly after potting, and keep it moist but not wet. Cuttings root in three to four weeks under light levels from 1,500 to 2,000 f.c. (16 to 22 klux) and air temperature of 75° to 90° F (24° to 32° C). The medium temperature should be maintained at 79° to 86° F (26° to 30° C). *Aglaonema* is still primarily propagated by tip cutting because tissue culture methods for this genus have not been established.

Propagating *Rumohra* tip cuttings

Use stout, anthracnose-free terminal rhizome (stem) pieces 4 to 6 in. (10 to 15 cm) long with several fronds (leaves) attached. These cuttings are broken off, not cut off, the parent rhizomes (fig. 16.5). The fronds should be healthy and not so large that they make the cuttings fall over and pull out of the ground

Figure 16.4. Propagation of *Aglaonema* 'Silver Queen' tip cuttings.
(A) Potted stock plants; (B) cuttings with five or six leaves;
(C) single cuttings stuck in 4. in (10 cm) pots; and (D) rooted tip cuttings.

Figure 16.5. Propagation of *Rumohra adiantiformis* by rhizome tip cuttings. (A) Creation of furrows in ground beds to accept terminal stem pieces; (B) rhizome mat prior to the selection of rhizome tips for planting; (C) terminal rhizome section suitable for planting; (D) rhizome tips laid in furrows; (E) newly planted ground bed; and (F) established field planting.

or potting medium. Rhizome tips should be whitish tan at the apex with no sign of physical damage or decay. Larger-diameter tip cuttings typically become established more quickly and produce larger fronds than thinner cuttings. Plant the cuttings horizontally in loosened soil or a well-drained potting medium as soon as possible after the cuttings are made. The top of the rhizomes should be about 1 to 1.5 in. (2.5 to 4 cm) below the medium surface. Planting cuttings too deep can be detrimental. No rooting hormone or mist is necessary.

Water the medium thoroughly after planting, and keep it moderately moist thereafter. Planted rhizome tips should be held under maximum light levels from 2,000 to 3,000 f.c. (22 to 32 klux) and air temperatures of 68° to 86° F (20° to 30° C). Rhizomes should become established and produce new fronds in eight to twelve weeks. Two to three rhizome pieces are typically planted per 6 in. (15 cm) diameter pot. For ground beds, one and a half to two tips are usually planted per linear foot (30 cm) of furrow. Although plants derived from tissue culture are available, most

Rumohra plants are still propagated commercially using tip cuttings.

Leaf cuttings

Leaf cuttings require the formation of new roots and shoots, which develop from either primary or secondary meristems. Small plantlets derived from leaf cuttings of *Kalanchoe pinnata* originate from primary meristem, or *foliar embryos*. The foliar embryos are formed in the early stages of leaf development from small groups of cells at the edges of the leaf. A leaf cutting of ZZ plant, *Zamioculcas zamiifolia*, produces a tube from the wounded main vein, and a petiole bearing leaflets grows up from the tube. However, leaf cuttings from other foliage plants, such as *Begonia* Rex Cultorum hybrids, *Crassula*, *Peperomia*, *Saintpaulia*, *Sansevieria*, and *Sedum*, form adventitious roots and shoots from the secondary meristem. In other words, a group of cells that have differentiated and functioned in leaf tissue dedifferentiate into new meristematic zones, resulting in the regeneration of new plant organs.

Rooting *Saintpaulia* (African violet) leaf cuttings

Select fully expanded and healthy leaves with a petiole length of 1 to 2 in. (2.5 to 5 cm) from stock plants (fig. 16.6). Separate the leaf from the petiole base by either using a sharp knife or simply pulling it off, and insert the petiole into medium-filled cell plugs or containers. Water the medium thoroughly after sticking, and keep it moist thereafter. Rooting should take place under 1,000 to 1,500 f.c. (11 to 16 klux) light levels. Plantlets will appear from the base in ten to fourteen weeks. A study has reported that plantlets can be harvested in eight to twelve weeks if a rooting medium temperature is maintained at 75° F (24° C) and the air temperature is 64° F (18° C). Pot harvested plantlets in cell plugs or transplant them into 4 in. (10 cm) or larger pots for finished plant production.

Rooting *Zamioculcas* (ZZ plant) leaf cuttings

Cut the leaflets from the petioles and insert them singly in medium-filled plug trays or 4 in. (10 cm) pots (fig. 16.7). The leaflets may also be cut into several pieces and propagated by placing the wounded side into the medium. Place the plug trays on benches in a shaded greenhouse, and keep the medium moist during rooting. Maintain the greenhouse temperature from 75° to 90° F (24° to 32° C), relative

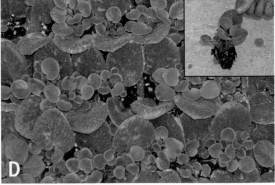

Figure 16.6. Propagation of *Saintpaulia* leaf cuttings; an assortment of cultivars were used. (A) Leaves with petioles cut from or pulled off a stock plant; (B) petioles, cut to about 1 in. (2.5 cm), inserted into medium-filled cell plugs; (C) leaf cuttings in 72-cell trays; (D) plantlets growing from leaf cuttings and (inset) a well-rooted healthy plug. (Green Masters, Inc., Apopka, Florida)

humidity between 60 and 100%, and light intensities from 550 to 1,000 f.c. (6 to 11 klux). Callus will form around the main vein in two to three weeks after sticking. A small rhizome (tuber) will become visible in another two weeks. One week later, roots will appear in the rhizome. One month after the rhizome is visible, a petiole bearing alternate pinnate leaflets will emerge from the rooting medium.

Rooting cuttings in water or solution

In addition to rooting cuttings in soilless media, eye or tip cuttings of *Begonia*, *Cissus*, *Cordyline*, *Epipremnum*, *Ficus pumila*, *Hedera helix*, *Philodendron scandens*, and *Syngonium*, leaf cuttings of *Saintpaulia*, and cane cuttings of *Dracaena sanderiana* can be rooted in aerated tap water or a diluted fertilizer solution (such as a 50 ppm nitrogen solution made from a 24-8-16 water-soluble fertilizer containing micronutrients). Containers should be opaque or shielded from light to avoid algal growth. Rooting will take place under 500 to 1,000 f.c. (5 to 11 klux) light and 75° to 82° F (24° to 28° C) temperatures. After roots form, transplant the plants to a container medium for finished plant production. The most common water-rooted cuttings are *Dracaena sanderiana* canes, called lucky bamboo, which are produced in straight, braided, curled, wavy, and various other configurations. After buds break, the canes or tips are placed in decorative vases containing either water or diluted solution and used directly for interior decoration.

Summary

Commercial foliage plant production has become truly global as rooted and unrooted cuttings, seedlings, and tissue-culture liners from the Caribbean, Central America, China, India, Korea, Thailand, the Netherlands, the United States, and elsewhere are grown in the United States and sold nationally and internationally, primarily in Canada and Europe. The future of the industry is bright as interiorscaping with foliage plants and cut foliage has become an integral part of contemporary life. With increasing worldwide urbanization, interior decoration with foliage plants will continue to grow, and the foliage plant industry will face increased demand for diverse and high-quality plants. This increased demand will require more propagules for production.

Even though micropropagation will move forward and expand, the other methods of foliage plant propagation will continue to be important, particularly

Figure 16.7. Propagation of *Zamioculcas zamiifolia* leaf cuttings. (A) Leaflets cut from a petiole; (B) individual leaflets stuck in medium-filled cell plugs; (C) leaflet without rhizome (left) and rhizomes with roots (center and right); and (D) rhizome without leaf (left), rhizome with one leaf (center) and rhizome with two leaves (right).

cutting propagation. Cutting propagation is not only a simple and convenient way of quickly producing sizable cloned propagules, but it is also the preferred choice for propagation of new plants and cultivars when other methods may not be immediately available or may not effectively increase the number of plants. Future research in cutting propagation should focus on underutilized species and develop procedures for their propagation; pursue innovative ways to effectively reproduce difficult-to-propagate plants; optimize environmental conditions and cultural practices for producing healthy, vigorous, and uniformly rooted cuttings in a short period of time; and deliver these techniques to nurserymen for improving cutting and foliage plant production.

Acknowledgments

The authors thank Kelly Everitt for collecting some data and reading the manuscript, Loretta Satterthwaite for reviewing the manuscript, and Russell D. Caldwell and Mitcheal Thompson for assisting in the preparation of figures. The authors appreciate Green Masters Inc., Apopka, Florida, and Stewarts Nursery, Winter Garden, Florida, for providing *Saintpaulia* and *Dracaena* propagation materials, respectively, for photographing. This study was supported by the Florida Agricultural Experiment Station and approved for publication as Journal Series No. R-10936.

References

Boodley, J. W., and R. S. Sheldrake. 1977. *Cornell Peat-Lite Mixes for Commercial Plant Growing.* Cornell Plant Science Information Bulletin 43.

Chase, A. R. 1997. *Foliage Plant Diseases: Diagnosis and Control.* APS Press, St. Paul, Minnesota.

Chen, J., D. B. McConnell, R. J. Henny, and D. J. Norman. 2005. The foliage plant industry. *Horticultural Reviews* 31:45–110.

Dole, J. M., and H. F. Wilkins. 1999. *Floriculture: Principles and Species.* Prentice Hall, Upper Saddle River, New Jersey.

Dreistadt, S. H. 2001. *Integrated Pest Management for Floriculture and Nurseries.* University of California Division of Agriculture and Natural Resources Publication 3402.

Griffith, L. P. 1998. *Tropical Foliage Plants: A Grower's Guide.* Ball Publishing, Batavia, Illinois.

Hartmann, H. T., D. E. Kester, F. T. Davies Jr., and R. L. Geneve. 1997. *Plant Propagation: Principles and Practices.* 6th ed. Prentice Hall, Upper Saddle River, New Jersey.

Henny, R. J., and J. Chen. 2003. Cultivar development of ornamental foliage plants. *Plant Breeding Reviews* 23:245-290.

Joiner, J. N. 1981. *Foliage Plant Production.* Prentice Hall, Englewood Cliffs, New Jersey.

Miller, V. J., and R. T. Poole. 1982. *IBA Effects on Foliage Plant Cuttings.* University of Florida, Agricultural Research Center, ARC-Apopka Research Report RH-82-11.

Nehrling, A., and I. Nehrling. 1962. *Propagating House Plants.* Hearthside Press, Great Neck, New York.

Nelson, P. V. 2003. *Greenhouse Operation & Management.* 6th ed. Prentice Hall, Upper Saddle River, New Jersey.

Poole, R. T., C. A. Conover, and J.N. Joiner. 1981. Soils and potting mixtures. pp. 179–202. In: *Foliage Plant Production.* J. N. Joiner, ed. Prentice Hall, Englewood Cliffs, New Jersey.

Stamps, R. H., and M. R. Evans. 1997. Growth of *Dieffenbachia maculata* 'Camille' in growing media containing sphagnum peat or coconut coir dust. *HortScience* 32:844–847.

U.S. Department of Agriculture. 2005. *Floriculture Crops 2003 Summary.* Washington, D.C.

U.S. Department of Agriculture, Foreign Agricultural Service. 2004. *BICO Import Commodity Aggregations.* Washington, D.C.

Part 3

Crop-by-Crop Cutting Propagation

Achimenes

Common name: Achimenes, hot water plant.
Scientific name: *Achimenes* hybrids.
Family: Gesneriaceae.
Other propagation methods: Rhizome scales, seed.

Description, Uses, and Status

The profuse flowers are single, five lobed, and 1 to 2.5 in. (2.5 to 6 cm) across. The plants are short stemmed and have three to four pubescent leaves per node. Achimenes is popular as a potted herbaceous flowering plant or hanging basket plant.

Flowering Control and Dormancy

Flowering will occur regardless of day length after the development of the third or fourth leaf whorl, and achimenes should be considered a day-neutral plant. However, at the end of the summer growing period and under short days, rhizomes form, plant growth slows, stems dry, and rhizomes become dormant. Depending on the cultivar, dormancy is broken either when freshly harvested rhizomes are placed in a moist substrate at 85° F (29° C) or when they are stored at 50° to 60° F (10° to 16° C) for forty days and then moved to 72° F (22° C). Pupation, which is the formation of a new and equally dormant rhizome on the top of the old rhizome at the site of the uppermost apical bud, occurs at 68° to 77° F (20° to 25° C). Dormancy lasts two to five months when older plants or stock plants are cut back and stored at 50° F (10° C). When such plants are recycled, two to four months are required for flowering, with production beginning in February to April. Dormancy can be induced by allowing the plants to dry.

Stock Plant Management

Achimenes develops from short 0.5 to 1.5 in. (1.3 to 4 cm) rhizomes formed at the base of the shoots. European production is based on cuttings produced from rhizomes. First, rhizomes for the future stock plants are laid 2 in. (5 cm) apart on a porous substrate, then covered with 0.5 in. (1.3 cm) of substrate and kept warm and moist until shoots appear. Rhizomes are placed end to end, and 250 to 300 can be planted in a 16 by 24 in. (40 by 60-cm) tray. Shoots are pinched when there are two mature leaves. Soaking rhizomes in 50 ppm gibberellic acid (GA₃) or 50 ppm benzyladenine (BA) for eight hours can improve sprouting after two to three weeks' storage at 77° F (25° C).

Cutting Harvest

Five to seven flushes, producing 500 to 1,000 cuttings/sq. yd. (600 to 1,200 cuttings/m²), are taken from February to June. Nonterminal leaf cuttings can also be used with two to three nodes per cutting. One to two pairs of leaves are always left on the mother plant when cuttings are removed. As spring advances, cutting quality decreases; therefore three to five cuttings are rooted in a 4 in. (10 cm) pot.

Propagation

Propagation can occur under tents or light mist. The rooting substrate should be heated from the bottom and held at 73° to 75° F (23° to 24° C) during propagation. Cuttings root rapidly in fourteen to eighteen days.

Plant Growth Regulators

Plant growth regulators can be used, results will vary with the cultivar. One or more spray applications of ancymidol (A-Rest) at 50 ppm, daminozide (B-Nine) at 5,000 to 7,000 ppm, paclobutrazol (Bonzi) at 100 ppm, or chlormequat (Cycocel) at 3,000 to 5,000 ppm are effective. Daminozide can delay flowering and reduce flower size; paclobutrazol delayed flowering and reduced flower number; and chlormequat can cause leaf chlorosis.

Production and Schedule

When rhizomes are planted in January, two to three weeks are required for new shoots to develop from the dormant rhizomes. Another two to three weeks are required for cutting production to begin in February at temperatures of 75° to 80° F (24° to 27° C) during days and 60°F (16°C) during nights. Cuttings root in fourteen to eighteen days. During early spring eight to nine additional weeks are required to produce a marketable plant by April; later only seven to eight weeks are needed. The ideal day temperature ranges from 70° to 90° F (21° to 32° C) and ideal night temperature from 65° to 70° F (18° to 21° C).

Diseases

Botrytis can be a problem when ventilation is not adequate. Tobacco mosaic virus has also been noted.

Postharvest

Achimenes is a tropical plant. Do not store rhizomes or cuttings at temperatures below 41° F (5° C).

References

Kuehny, J. 2001. Gloxinias and other gesneriads, pp. 93–95. In: *Tips on Regulating Growth of Floriculture Crops,* M. L. Gaston, L. A. Kunkle, P. S. Konjoian, and M. F. Wilt, eds. Ohio Florists' Association Services, Columbus, Ohio.

Nowak, J., and R. M. Rudnicki. 1990. *Postharvest Handling and Storage of Cut Flowers, Florist Greens, and Potted Plants,* Timber Press, Portland, Oregon.

Vlahos, J. C. 1989. Effects of GA₃, BA and NAA on dry matter partitioning and rhizome development in two cultivars of *Achimenes longiflora* DC. under three levels of irradiance. *Acta Horticulturae* 251:79–92.

Vlahos, J. C. 1990a. Daylength influences growth and development of *Achimenes* cultivars. *HortScience* 25:1595–1596.

Vlahos, J. C., and W. Brascamp. 1989. The influence of the growth retardants paclobutrazol, ancymidol and S-3307 on growth and development of *Achimenes longiflora* DC. 'Viola Michelssen' grown under two light regimes. *Acta Horticulturae* 251:75–77.

Vlahos, J. C., G. F. P. Martakis, and E. Heuvelink. 1992. Daylength, light quality, and temperature influence growth and development of *Achimenes*. *HortScience* 27:1269–1271.

Wikesjö, K. 1982. Growing hybrid *Achimenes* as a pot plant. *Florists' Review* 168(4357):34, 120, 122.

Wiles, L. S. 1988. Cultural notes—*Achimenes*. *GrowerTalks* 15(12):12.

Zimmer, K., and K. Junker. 1985. *Achimenes*, pp. 391–392. In: *Handbook of Flowering*, vol. I, A. H. Halevy, ed. CRC Press, Boca Raton, Florida.

Angelonia

Common name: Angelonia, summer snapdragon.
Scientific name: *Angelonia angustifolia.*
Family: Scrophulariaceae.
Other propagation methods: Seed.

Two angelonia cultivars: 'Angelmist Purple Stripe' (left) and 'Angelmist Purple Improved' (right).

Description, Uses, and Status
Angelonia is covered with loose upright spikes of striking white, pink, purple, or bicolor tubular flowers up to 1 in. (2.5 cm) across. This heat- and drought-tolerant tender perennial is a popular bedding plant for ground beds and containers. Cultivars vary from low and spreading to strongly upright with a height of up to 30 in. (75 cm). Plants are hardy only to Zone 9; they can withstand light frosts and are sold in the spring in pots. Spreading forms can be used in hanging baskets. Angelonia can also be used as a cut flower.

Flowering Control and Dormancy
Angelonia is day-neutral. High light encourages rapid flowering, improved branching, and compact growth.

Stock Plant Management
Keep stock plants regularly pruned to maintain shoot numbers and to prevent flowering.

Cutting Harvest
Terminal cuttings 1 to 2 in. (2.5 to 5 cm) long are har-vested. Avoid thin weak stems, and remove flowers to improve rooting efficiency.

Propagation

Stage 1:
Cutting arrival or harvest and sticking
- Stick cuttings immediately in a substrate with a high starter charge.
- Rooting hormones are not required. However, 2,500 ppm IBA can be used on cutting bases.
- Store cuttings at 50° to 60° F (10° to 16° C) for up to twenty-four hours if planting is going to be delayed.

Stage 2: Callusing

- Maintain substrate temperatures of 70° to 75° F (21° to 24° C).
- Maintain air temperatures of 75° to 80° F (24° to 27° C) during days and 68° to 70° F (20° to 21° C) during nights.
- Keep the rooting substrate sufficiently moist so that water is easily squeezed out of it, but not so much that the cutting base is waterlogged.
- Use tempered water, 85° to 90° F (29° to 32° C) in the mist lines.
- Increase and decrease mist frequency as the light and ambient temperature change during the course of the day. Do not overmist.
- Maintain a light intensity of 500 to 1,000 f.c. (5 to 11 klux).
- Begin foliar feeding with 50 to 75 ppm nitrogen from 15-0-15 if there is any loss in foliage color. Fertilizer may not be needed.
- Transfer the cuttings to Stage 3 in five to seven days, once 50% of the cuttings begin differentiating root initials.

Stage 3: Root development

- Maintain substrate temperatures of 68° to 72° F (20° to 22° C).
- Maintain air temperatures of 75° to 80° F (24° to 27° C) during days and 68° to 70° F (18° to 21° C) during nights.
- Begin drying out the substrate once roots are visible.
- Begin reducing the duration and frequency of mist.
- Increase light intensity to 1,000 to 2,000 f.c. (11 to 22 klux).
- Fertilize with 100 ppm nitrogen from 15-0-15 alternating with 20-10-20, then increase rapidly to 150 ppm.
- Roots should develop in seven to fourteen days.

Stage 4: Toning the rooted cutting

- Maintain air temperatures of 70° to 75° F (21° to 24° C) during days and 62° to 68° F (17° to 20° C) during nights.
- Move the liners from the mist area.
- Increase the light intensity to 2,000 to 3,000 f.c. (22 to 32 klux).
- Fertilize once with 150 to 200 ppm nitrogen from 15-0-15 or 20-10-20.
- Pinch three weeks after sticking.

Plant Growth Regulators

Daminozide (B-Nine) sprays at 1,500 to 3,000 ppm can be used. A tank mix of daminozide at 1,250 to 2,500 ppm) and chlormequat (Cycocel) at 750 to 1,000 ppm is effective as a spray. Another possible tank mix for spraying is ancymidol (A-Rest) at 4 to 10 ppm and B-Nine at 1,500 to 2,500 ppm. Sprays of paclobutrazol (Bonzi) at 5 to 80 ppm, uniconazole (Sumagic) at 10 to 20 ppm, or flurprimidol (Topflor) at 45 to 60 ppm are useful during production. Bonzi drenches at 4 to 8 ppm can be applied to plugs prior to transplanting, or 1 to 4 ppm drenches can also be used when plants are nearly finished size. Ethephon (Florel) has been used to increase branching, but it will cause foliar tip burn and may delay flowering.

Production and Schedule

Grow the cuttings at 75° to 90° F (24 to 32° C) during days and 65° to 70° F (18° to 21° C) during nights. High light levels of 6,000 to 10,000 f.c. (65 to 108 klux) will produce a short, well-branched, early-flowering plant. Since this crop prefers relatively warm temperatures and high light, do not start production too early, especially in the north, since plant growth will be minimal until later in the season.

Maintain substrate pH at 5.5 to 6.0 and EC at 2.0 to 2.5. Fertilize plants with 150 to 200 ppm nitrogen. Do not allow the substrate to become completely dry, because leaf tip burn may occur.

One rooted cutting is used per 4 in. (10 cm) pot, and one or two per 6 in. (15 cm) pot. Plants should be pinched ten to fourteen days after potting or when roots have reached the edge of the container. Generally, three to five nodes should remain after the pinch. A second pinch can be used with pots larger than 4 in. (10 cm). Typically, 4 in. (10 cm) pots are ready to sell in six to ten weeks, and 6 in. (15 cm) pots in seven to eleven weeks.

Diseases

Botrytis and root rots are common. Do not allow the rooting substrate to stay wet for long periods.

Disorders

Too much fertilizer, especially high ammonium levels, will cause excessive foliage, few flowers, and weak stems. Delayed flowering or an overabundance of foliage may also be due to low light levels and excessive or late ethephon applications. Iron deficiency may cause foliar chlorosis.

Postharvest

Cuttings can be stored at 50° to 60° F (10° to 16° C) for up to twenty-four hours. Exposing unrooted cuttings to 1 ppm ethylene for up to twenty hours had no effect on leaf abscission or cutting rooting.

References

Hamrick, D. 2003. *Angelonia,* pp. 224–226. In: *Ball Redbook,* 17th ed., vol. 2, D. Hamrick, ed. Ball Publishing, Batavia, Illinois.

Miller, A., and A. M. Armitage. Temperature, irradiance, photoperiod, and growth retardants influence greenhouse production of *Angelonia angustifolia* Benth. Angel Mist series. *HortScience* 37:319–321.

Schoellhorn, R. 2000. Control vegetative plug growth with PGRs. *GMPro* 20(12):53–55.

Schoellhorn, R. 2002. Angelonia—the warm season snapdragon. *GPN* 12(3):76, 78.

Antirrhinum

Common name: Snapdragon.
Scientific name: *Antirrhinum majus.*
Family: Scrophulariaceae.
Other propagation methods: Seed, tissue culture.

Description, Uses, and Status

Flowers are borne in spikes; each flower has five lobed petals fused into a tube at the base. The three lower lobes or lips are typically spreading, and the two upper lobes or lips are erect and form a "mouth"—hence the name snapdragon. Some cultivars have opened-faced flowers ("butterfly"). Flower colors include white, red, rose, pink, yellow, orange, and bicolors. Plant habit ranges from tall and upright to short and trailing. Snapdragons have many uses as cut flowers, garden plants, and bedding plants. Cutting-propagated types are primarily short or trailing and are used as bedding plants. Trailing types are more heat tolerant than most seed-grown cultivars, and many are fragrant.

'Luminaire Hot Pink' bedding snapdragon.

Flowering Control and Dormancy

The snapdragon is a facultative long-day plant in that flowering occurs faster under long photoperiods; however, flowering can occur under short days. A wide variation exists among cultivars in response to long days and temperature. Juvenile plants that have fewer than a specified leaf number will not respond to long days. While the juvenile period is not known for cutting propagated cultivars, for cut flower cultivars the juvenile period lasts until eighteen to twenty two leaves have formed.

Stock Plant Management

Work at Clemson University showed that for maximum cutting numbers, the initial pinch on the stock plants should occur after six nodes can be left on the plant, and the resulting side shoots should also be pinched when six nodes can be left on the shoots. In contrast, pinching low and allowing only two nodes to remain with both pinches reduces the number of cuttings harvested. For example, pinching to two nodes both times produced 60 cuttings per stock plant over the course of the experiment, while pinching to six nodes produced 140 cutting per stock plant, a 230% increase in cuttings. Thus building the stock plant scaffold is important to future cutting production.

Cutting Harvest

Terminal cuttings are harvested with one or two nodes ranging in size from 1.25 to 2 in. (3 to 5 cm). Thin weak stems or "butterfly" cuttings (having two opposite leaves and axillary buds) should be avoided because of poor rooting efficiency.

Propagation

Stage 1:
Cutting arrival or harvest and sticking

- Stick cuttings in a substrate with a pH of 5.6 to 5.8.
- Stick one cutting per cell if using plug flats.
- Use a rooting hormone, 2,500 ppm IBA, on cutting bases. Experimentally, NAA at 500 ppm is also effective.
- Store cuttings at 50° to 60° F (10° to 16° C) for up to twenty-four hours if planting is going to be delayed.

Stage 2: Callusing

- Maintain substrate temperatures of 68° to 72° F (20° to 22° C).
- Maintain air temperatures of 75° to 80° F (24 to 27 C) during days and 68° to 70° F (20° to 21° C) during nights.
- Maintain a light intensity of 500 to 1,000 f.c. (5 to 11 klux).
- Begin foliar feeding with 50 to 75 ppm nitrogen from 15-0-15.
- Transfer the cuttings to Stage 3 in five to seven days, once 50% of the cuttings begin differentiating root initials.

Stage 3: Root development

- Maintain substrate temperatures of 68° to 72° F (20° to 22° C).
- Maintain air temperatures of 75° to 80° F (24 to 27 C) during days and 68° to 70° F (20° to 21° C) during nights.
- Increase the light intensity to 1,000 to 2,000 f.c. (11 to 22 klux) as the cuttings begin to root.
- Fertilize with 100 to 150 ppm nitrogen once a week from 15-0-15 alternating with 20-10-20.
- Roots should develop in seven to fourteen days; rooting will be more efficient if the substrate is moist but not saturated.

Stage 4: Toning the rooted cutting

- Maintain air temperatures of 75° to 80° F (24° to 27° C) during days and 62° to 68° F (17° to 20° C) during nights.
- Fertilize twice a week with 150 to 200 ppm nitrogen from 15-0-15 alternating with 20-10-20. Pinch three weeks after sticking.

Plant Growth Regulators

While most bedding snapdragons are compact, various plant growth regulators can be used, including sprays of ancymidol (A-Rest) at 15 to 20 ppm, paclobutrazol (Bonzi or Piccolo) at 10 to 30 ppm, daminozide (B-Nine) at 1,500 to 2,500 ppm, chlormequat (Cycocel) at 800 to 1,500 ppm, and uniconazole (Sumagic) at 20 to 45 ppm. Tank-mixed sprays of daminozide at 800 to 1,000 ppm and chlormequat at 800 to 1,000 ppm or of ancymidol at 4 to 10 ppm and daminozide at 1,250 to 2,500 ppm can also be used. Day and night temperature difference (DIF) is effective on snapdragon; a 0 or negative DIF should be maintained for bedding and potted plants (see chapter 5 for more information). Ethephon (Florel) is not recommended for use on this crop.

Production and Schedule

Grow snapdragons at 72° to 75° F (22 to 24° C) during days and 62° to 65° F (17° to 18° C) during nights. Reduce the night temperature to 45° to 50° F (7° to 10° C) after the plants are established. Provide levels of 5,000 to 6,000 f.c. (54 to 65 klux).

Substrate pH should be 5.5 to 6.2. Fertilize with 150 to 200 ppm nitrogen; increase to 200 to 300 ppm after the plants are established. Low fertilizer levels will decrease branching. Monitor substrate pH and EC, and leach as needed to avoid high soluble salts. Excessive drying will cause foliar necrosis.

Use one rooted cutting per 4 in. (10 cm) pot, two per 6 in. (15 cm) pot, and four to five per 10 in. (25 cm) hanging basket. Plants should be pinched two to three weeks after potting or when roots have reached the edge of the container. A second pinch can be used with pots larger than 4 in. (10 cm). Pinch or shear as needed to maintain plant shape. Generally, 4 in. (10 cm) pots are ready to sell in six to twelve weeks, 6 in. (15 cm) pots in eight to fourteen weeks, and 10 in. (25 cm) hanging baskets in ten to fourteen weeks.

Diseases

Slow root degeneration and wilting are related to poor aeration, excessive watering, and *Pythium*. *Botrytis* and *Pythium* are two of the more common diseases observed. Tomato spotted wilt virus and impatiens necrotic spot virus can cause brown or black stem lesions, which often do not appear until just before flowering.

Disorders

Too much foliage growth can be due to high nitrogen levels, too much fertilizer under low light conditions, and overwatering. Iron deficiency can occur if the root substrate pH is high or is not allowed to dry between waterings.

Postharvest
Cuttings can be stored at 50° to 60° F (10° to 16° C) for up to twenty-four hours.

References
Barrett, J. E., and T. A. Nell. 1989. Comparison of paclobutrazol and uniconazole on floriculture crops. *Acta Horticulturae* 251:275–280.

Bell, M. 2001. Bedding plants and seed geraniums, pp. 54–62. In: *Tips on Regulating Growth of Floriculture Crops,* M. L. Gaston, L. A. Kunkle, P. S. Konjoian, and M. F. Wilt, eds. Ohio Florists' Association Services, Columbus, Ohio.

Cockshull, K. E. 1985. *Antirrhinum majus,* pp. 476–481. In: *Handbook of Flowering,* vol. I, A. H. Halevy, ed. CRC Press, Boca Raton, Florida.

Faust, J. E., and L. W. Grimes. 2005. Pinch height of stock plants during scaffold development affects cutting production. *HortScience* 40:650–653.

Hamrick, D. 2003. *Antirrhinum,* pp. 230–239. In: *Ball RedBook,* 17th ed., vol. 2, D. Hamrick, ed. Ball Publishing, Batavia, Illinois.

Hanan, J. J., and R. W. Langhans. 1963. Soil aeration and moisture controls snapdragon quality. *New York State Flower Growers Bulletin* 210:3–6.

Laughner, L., and B. Corr. 1996. Snapdragons: Formula for success. *GrowerTalks* 60(6):57, 62.

Maginnes, E. A., and R. W. Langhans. 1961. The effect of photoperiod and temperature on initiation and flowering of snapdragon (*Antirrhinum majus* var. Jack Pot). *Proceedings of the American Society for Horticultural Science* 77:600–607.

Neily, W. G., P. R. Hicklenton, and D. N. Kristie. 1997. Temperature and developmental stage influence diurnal rhythms of stem elongation in snapdragon and zinnia. *Journal of the American Society for Horticultural Science* 122:778–783.

Starman, T. W., M. C. Robinson, and K. L. Eixmann. 2004. Efficacy of ethephon on vegetative annuals. *HortTechnology* 14:83–87.

Argyranthemum

Common name: Marguerite daisy.
Scientific name: *Argeranthemum frutescens.*
Family: Compositae.
Other propagation methods: Seed.

'Madeira Santana' marguerite daisy.

Description, Uses, and Status
The white, pink, or yellow daisylike flowers may be single with a yellow center, or they may be double. This drought-tolerant tender perennial is used as a bedding plant for ground beds and containers. Plants are hardy only to Zone 9 but are frost tolerant and sold in the spring in large cell packs or pots. In warm climates marguerite daisy is sold as an early spring flower because flowering is sparse or nonexistent in the heat of the summer. In cooler climates it flowers profusely all during the growing season.

Flowering Control and Dormancy
Plants are day-neutral, but they flower faster under the longer days of spring.

Stock Plant Management
Building the stock plant scaffold is important to future cutting production. If there is sufficient time after establishment, stock plants should be pinched up to three times before cuttings are harvested. Increasing the number of pinches from one to three on stock plants before the cutting harvest commences delays the initial harvest but increases the total number of cuttings harvested. Pinching plants only once allowed cuttings to be harvested more quickly after establishment of the stock plants but reduced the total number of cutting produced. After establishment, stock plants should be trimmed regularly to avoid flowering and the excessive shoot elongation that occurs if cuttings are not harvested routinely.

Cutting Harvest

Terminal cuttings 1 to 2 in. (2.5 to 5 cm) long are harvested. Remove flowers from cuttings to improve rooting efficiency.

Propagation

Stage 1:
Cutting arrival or harvest and sticking

- Stick cuttings in a substrate with a low starter charge and a pH of 6.0 to 6.5.
- Apply a rooting hormone to the cutting bases, using a rate appropriate for herbaceous cuttings.
- Stick one cutting per cell if using plug flats.
- Store cuttings at 40° to 45° F (4° to 7° C) for up to twenty-four hours if planting is going to be delayed.

Stage 2: Callusing

- Maintain substrate temperatures of 68° to 75° F (20° to 24° C).
- Maintain air temperatures of 70° to 75° F (21° to 24° C) during days and 68° to 70° F (20° to 21° C) during nights.
- Maintain a light intensity of at least 500 to 1,000 f.c. (5 to 11 klux).
- Begin foliar feeding with 50 to 75 ppm nitrogen from 15-0-15 if there is any loss in foliage color.
- Callus formation can be extensive in propagation trays with little sign of rooting. Monitor for fungus gnat larvae regularly, since infestations can have devastating effects on root development.
- Transfer the cuttings to Stage 3 after five to seven days, once 50% of the cuttings begin differentiating root initials.

Stage 3: Root development

- Maintain a substrate temperature of 68° to 75° F (20° to 24° C).
- Maintain air temperatures of 70° to 75° F (21° to 24° C) during days and 68° to 70° F (20° to 21° C) during nights.
- Begin drying out the substrate once roots are visible.
- Begin increasing the light intensity to 1,000 to 2,000 f.c. (11 to 22 klux) as the cuttings start to root out.
- Fertilize once a week with 100 to 150 ppm nitrogen, alternating between 15-0-15 and 20-10-20.
- Roots should develop in seven to nine days.

Stage 4: Toning the rooted cutting

- Maintain air temperatures of 68° to 75° F (20° to 24° C) during days and 62° to 68° F (17° to 20° C) during nights.
- Allow the substrate to dry without wilting cuttings.
- Increase the light intensity to 2,000 to 4,000 f.c. (22 to 43 klux).
- Fertilize once a week with 150 to 200 ppm nitrogen from 15-0-15 alternating with 20-10-20.
- The cuttings should be toned for seven days.

Once cuttings are rooted they should be pinched to produce compact, well-branched specimens. A pinching protocol similar to that used for garden mums can be used, with one pinch prior to or soon after planting while still applying a PGR later.

Plant Growth Regulators

Chlormequat (Cycocel) sprays at 750 to 1,500 ppm are effective and may be reapplied every two weeks as required. Sprays of daminozide (B-Nine) at 1,500 to 2,500 ppm, uniconazole (Sumagic) at 15 to 20 ppm, or flurprimidol (Topflor) at 60 to 75 ppm can be used. Also effective is a tank-mixed spray of ancymidol (A-Rest) at 4 to 10 ppm and daminozide at 1,250 to 2,500 ppm. Ethephon (Florel) sprays at 500 ppm can be used to increase branching.

Production and Schedule

Grow finished plants at 65° to 75° F (18° to 24° C) during days and 45° to 55° F (7° to 13°C) during nights. The best plant quality is obtained with cool production temperatures, but plants can be grown warmer to decrease production time. High light levels of 5,000 f.c. (54 klux) or greater should be used.

Marguerite daisy plug ready for planting.

Space plants as needed to prevent stretching.

Plant in a substrate with a high starter charge and a pH of 6.0 to 6.5. Fertilize with nitrogen at 150 to 200 ppm constant liquid fertilization. A magnesium sulfate application at 0.5 to 1 lb./100 gal. (0.6 to 1.2 g/L) is recommended to improve tone. Keep plants moist without chronic overwatering, which can cause plant collapse. Foliar burn can occur with excessive drying, however.

One unrooted cutting is used per 4 or 5 in. (10 or 13-cm) pot, and one or two per 6 in. (15 cm) pot. Plants in 4 in. (10 cm) pots may be pinched four to five days after potting or when roots have reached the edge of the container. Larger containers may be pinched up to two weeks after potting. Allow five to six sets of leaves to remain. In the winter 4 in. (10 cm) pots will be ready to sell in eight to nine weeks, 5 in. (13 cm) pots in nine to ten weeks, and 6 in. (15 cm) pots in ten to eleven weeks. The crop finishes two to three weeks earlier in the summer.

Diseases

Botrytis and various root rots are problems.

Disorders

Excessive foliage can be due to high nitrogen levels, light that is too low, or overwatering. Iron deficiency can be an issue if the root substrate pH is too high or is constantly saturated.

Postharvest

Cuttings can be stored at 40° to 45° F (4° to 7° C) for up to twenty-four hours.

References

Faust, J. E., and L. W. Grimes. 2004. Cutting production is affected by pinch number during scaffold development of stock plants. *HortScience* 39:1691–1694.

Hamrick, D. 2003. *Argyranthemum,* pp. 242–244. In: *Ball RedBook,* 17th ed., vol. 2, D. Hamrick, ed. Ball Publishing, Batavia, Illinois.

Asclepias

Common name: Butterfly weed.
Scientific name: *Asclepias tuberosa.*
Family: Asclepiadaceae.
Other propagation methods: Seed, tissue culture.

Butterfly weed flowers

Description, Uses, and Status

Plants up to 40 in. (1 m) tall support umbels of small pale yellow to reddish orange flowers. Bright orange is the most common flower color. The sap is clear, unlike many other milk weeds. Butterfly weed is used as a cut flower and as a long-lived ornamental in the garden landscape. The plant is hardy in Zone 4 to 9.

Flowering Control and Dormancy

Young plants remain vegetative for one year. Both young and mature plants cease to form leaves and shoot elongation stops under short days. Photoperiods of thirteen hours or longer must be maintained for both floral induction and development, with fourteen- to sixteen-hour day lengths optimum. Basal branching, however, is inhibited under long days. A one-hour night break resulted in 100% flowering as part of research conducted in Israel. Flowering is perpetual if plants are kept under long days and protected from heat. Under short nine-hour photoperiods, flower bud abortion occurs and blind shoots develop (axillary shoots which fail to form flower buds). If crowns become dormant after flowering under natural autumn or short-day conditions, a cold treatment apparently becomes a requirement for further growth.

Stock Plant Management

Multiple pinches upon establishment will increase branching of this typically upright plant. Clean cutting tools are essential to avoid stem rots and transmission of vascular and foliar diseases. Gloves should be worn to avoid contact with skin and the latex sap that exudes from newly harvested cuttings.

Cutting Harvest

Stem cuttings 3 to 4 in. (8 to 10 cm) long should be taken prior to flowering. For root cuttings, the taproot is cut in sections 2 to 3 in. (5 to 8 cm) long and placed vertically in flats. Rooting hormones are not required.

Propagation

Cuttings will root in three to four weeks under mist at 70° F (21° C). Plugs should be transplanted as soon as possible to prevent damage to the taproot, which develops rapidly. A plant will decline if it becomes root bound; grow it in as large a container as practical.

Plant Growth Regulators

The height of potted plants can be controlled with three to four sprays of 5,000 ppm daminozide (B-Nine) or four sprays of 30 ppm paclubutrazol (Bonzi) applied at intervals of ten to fourteen days. Day and night temperature difference (DIF) is strongly effective; see chapter 5 for more information.

Production and Schedule

The appropriate forcing temperature is between 63° and 77° F (17° and 25° C). Plants will flower in eight to ten weeks after being vernalized. High light levels are required. Be careful not to overwater butterfly weed. Plants can be fertilized with nitrogen at 100 ppm constant liquid fertilization. Plants are spaced 18 by 24 in. (45 by 60 cm) apart for cut flower production. Butterfly weed is a long-lived perennial, and its clump size increases annually. One to three layers of support netting are required for both field and greenhouse production. Once plants are established, replanting or division is not needed for three to five years.

Diseases

Several diseases can occur outdoors. Root rot can be a problem.

Disorders

Flower abortion occurs under low light intensities or if plants are moved from long days to short days.

Postharvest

Fall-harvested crowns can be stored successfully for up to six months in polyethylene-lined crates at 28° to 36° F (−2° to 2° C).

References

Albrecht, M. L., and Lehmann, J. T. 1991. Day length, cold storage, and plant production method influence growth and flowering of *Asclepias tuberosa*. *HortScience* 26:120–121.

Armitage, A. M. 1996. Forcing perennials in the greenhouse. *GrowerTalks* 60(3):86, 88, 93, 94, 96, 97.

Armitage, A. M., and J. M. Laushman. 2003. *Asclepias tuberosa*, pp. 111–116. In: *Specialty Cut Flowers,* 2nd ed. Timber Press, Portland, Oregon.

Bhowmilk, P. C., and J. D. Bandeen. 1978. The biology of Canadian weeds, *Asclepias syriaca L. Canadian Journal of Plant Science* 56:579–589.

Latimer, J. G. Herbaceous perennials, pp. 98–110. In: *Tips on Regulating Growth of Floriculture Crops,* M. L. Gaston, L. A. Kunkle, P. S. Konjoian, and M. F. Wilt, eds. Ohio Florists' Association Services, Columbus, Ohio.

Lyons, R. E. 1986. *Asclepias tuberosa*, pp. 22–28. In: *Handbook of Flowering,* vol. V, A. H. Halevy, ed. CRC Press, Boca Raton, Florida.

Lyons, R. E., and Booze, J. N. 1983. Effect of photoperiod on first year growth of two *Asclepias* species. *HortScience* 18(4):575. (Abstract).

Maqbool, M., and A. C. Cameron. 1994. Regrowth performance of field-grown herbaceous perennials following bare-root storage between −10 and +5C. *HortScience* 29:1039–1041.

Nordwig, G. J. 1999. *Evaluation of Floral Induction Requirements and Commercial Potential of Asclepias Species.* M.S. thesis, University of Minnesota, St. Paul.

Shannon, T. R., and R. Wyatt. 1986. Reproductive biology of *Asclepias exaltata. American Journal of Botany* 73(1):11–20.

Warner, R. M., and J. E. Erwin. Temperature, pp. 10–17. In: *Tips on Regulating Growth of Floriculture Crops,* M. L. Gaston, L. A. Kunkle, P. S. Konjoian, and M. F. Wilt, eds. Ohio Florists' Association Services, Columbus, Ohio.

Aster

Common name: Perennial aster, novi-belgii aster, New York aster, Michaelmas daisy.
Scientific name: *Aster novi-belgii.*
Family: Compositae.
Other propagation methods: Division, tissue culture.

'Caitlyn' aster

Description, Uses, and Status
This 4 ft. (1.2 m) tall native of Eastern North America is known for its large clusters of small daisy-shaped flowers with blue-violet petals has been transformed into a myriad of cultivars with white, pink, red, or purple petals. Dwarf cultivars are also available. This aster species and its cultivars are used as potted flowering plants, cut flowers, and garden ornamentals.

Flowering Control and Dormancy
The natural sequence of events leading to the flowering of perennial asters is vernalization under winter conditions; stem elongation and branching under the long days of late spring and early summer; and flowering under the short days of late summer and fall. At the base of flowering stems rosette growths develop from axillary buds below the soil surface. The formation of these vegetative basal shoots occurs at the same time as autumn flowering. These basal shoots are vernalized by winter temperatures, and the growth cycle is repeated. Thus perennial aster should be considered a long-day–short-day plant for floral initiation and subsequent development.

Stock Plant Management
Perennial asters are similar to poinsettias and chrysanthemums in that apices go reproductive after a certain number of nodes are formed, regardless of the correct photoperiod for vegetative growth. Consequently, stock plants must constantly be renewed from tissue culture sources.

Stock plants also need to be managed carefully to ensure that vegetative cuttings are available for harvest. Typically, high light and temperatures above 68° F (20° C) are used to maintain vegetative plants. The following are three regimes used for cutting production.

Type 1: Cut flower crop grown with pinch. Stock plant is produced using *in vitro* propagation and kept under short days. Cuttings are continuously harvested, rooted, and planted in beds for cut flower production.

Type 2: Cut flower crop grown without pinch. Stock plant is produced using *in vitro* propagation and kept under long days. Cuttings are harvested, rooted, and planted in beds under long days for closely spaced cut flower production.

Type 3: Potted plants. The stock plant is kept under long days. Cuttings are harvested, rooted, and planted in pots for potted plant production.

When a plant has flowered and experienced cool winter temperatures and short days, numerous vegetative rosettes form. These juvenile rosettes root with ease at 70° F (21° C). The presence of a rhizome piece is critical for the preservation of juvenility in the rosette form. Rosette shoots form on outdoor plantings in late fall, winter, or early spring and can be used as cuttings. However, if cuttings are taken in the summer, rooted, and subsequently pinched, the shoots from these cuttings quickly form an inflorescence with little shoot elongation, regardless of photoperiod. Thus, these mature summer-grown axillary shoots are not reliable sources of cuttings, even though they root easily.

Cutting Harvest
Cuttings that have wide leaves and very short internodes are highly vegetative. Cuttings with narrow leaves, longer internodes, and thin stems are from inferior reproductive shoots and should be discarded. Remove lower leaves that would be below the substrate after sticking the cuttings. Sort cuttings by size and caliper before planting to create uniform blocks.

Propagation
Cuttings should be stuck in a substrate with a pH of 5.5 to 6.5 and a temperature of 65° to 68° F (18° to 20° C). Place rooted liners under long days (sixteen hours) to avoid morphological changes (narrow leaves, long

internodes, and thin stems). Cuttings should be under sixteen-hour days and 3,000 to 3,500 f.c. (32 to 38 klux). Roots will be initiated within seven to ten days, and rooting will be completed within ten to fourteen days. Apply 200 to 300 ppm nitrogen from 20-10-20 when roots are initiated.

Plant Growth Regulators

For potted flowering plants, daminozide (B-Nine) sprays at 1,500 to 5,000 ppm, paclobutrazol (Bonzi) sprays at 160 ppm, and uniconazole (Sumagic) sprays at 80 to 160 ppm can be used. A 5 to 15 ppm Bonzi drench may also be used.

Production and Schedule

In greenhouses, plants are forced at temperatures of 62° to 68° F (17° to 20° C) during days and 54° to 57° F (12° to 14° C) during nights. For optimal flower initiation, fourteen to sixteen hours of light are required, regardless of previous vernalization treatments. Three weeks of twelve to fourteen hours of light is the minimum, with thirteen hours optimal. In greenhouses, plants are forced in full light; shading occurs only when temperature control is needed. Supplemental high intensity discharge (HID) lighting is needed for winter production at most latitudes.

Nutrition levels of 150 to 200 ppm nitrogen from a balanced NPK fertilizer are adequate. High soluble salts should be avoided for potted plants. Any well-drained substrate is acceptable with a pH of 5.5 to 6.5.

Various schedules can be devised, depending on the type of propagation material, location, and season. A typical schedule for potted flowering plants is to propagate cuttings directly in the final pot for three weeks, then pinch and apply growth regulators one to two weeks later. At the time the plant growth regulators are applied, plants are spaced and provided with thirteen-hour short days. Plants will flower four to five weeks later.

For greenhouse cut flower production, plant rooted cuttings in beds and provide five to six weeks of long days. Apply short days thereafter, and flowering will occur seven to ten weeks later. Cut flower crops can be cut back after harvest, given four to five weeks of long days, and reflowered five to six weeks after the start of short days.

Diseases

Powdery mildew (*Erysiphe cichoracearum*), gray mold (*Botrytis cinerea*), stem rot (*Sclerotinia sclerotiorum*), and root and stem rot (*Rhizoctonia*) can be problems in the greenhouse. A variety of other diseases have been noted; they include fusarium wilt (*Fusarium*), verticillium wilt (*Verticillium dahliae*), root rot (*Pythium* and *Phytophthora*), rust (*Coleosporium asterum* and *Puccinia*), leaf spot (*Septoria*), tomato spotted wilt virus, and aster yellows.

Disorders

Flower buds fail to develop or abort if long days are not of sufficient duration prior to moving the plants into short days or if the number of short days are not sufficient.

References

Armitage, A. M., and J. M. Laushman. 2003. Aster, pp. 116–128. In: *Specialty Cut Flowers,* 2nd ed. Timber Press, Portland, Oregon.

Dreistadt, S. H. 2001. *Integrated Pest Management for Floriculture and Nurseries.* University of California Division of Agriculture and Natural Resources Publication 3402. Oakland, California.

Faber, W., and J. McGrew. 1998. Aster (Perennial), pp. 372–385. In: *Ball RedBook,* 16th ed., V. Ball, ed. Ball Publishing, Batavia, Illinois.

Farina, E., C. D. Guda, and E. Scordo. 1994. Flowering and morphogenic responses of new *Aster* hybrids to photoperiod. *Physiologia Plantarum* 91:312–316.

Horst, R. K. 1990. Aster (Perennial), p. 543. In: *Westcott's Plant Disease Handbook,* 5th ed. Van Nostrand Reinhold, New York.

Kristiansen, K., C. W. Hansen, and K. Brandt. 1997. Flower induction in seedlings of *Aster novi-belgii* and selection before and after vegetative propagation. *Euphytica* 93:361–367.

Oren-Shamir, M., L. Shaked-Sachray, A. Nissim-Levi, and D. Weiss. 2000. Effect of growth temperature on *Aster* flower development. *HortScience* 35:28–29.

Schwabe, W. W. 1986. *Aster novi-belgii,* pp. 29–41. In: *Handbook of Flowering,* vol. V, A. H. Halevy, ed. CRC Press, Boca Raton, Florida.

Wallerstein, I., A. Kadman-Zahavi, H. Yahel, A. Nissim, R. Stav, and S. Michal. 1992. Control of growth and flowering in two Aster cultivars as influenced by cutting type, temperature, and day length. *Scientia Horticulturae* 50:209–218.

Wallerstein, I., A. Kadman-Zahzvi [sic], A. Nissim, R. Stav, and S. Michal. 1992. Control by photoperiod and the rhizomatous zone over the production of basal buds and the preservation of the rosette form in *Aster* cultivars. *Scientia Horticulturae* 51:237–250.

Whipker, B. E., R. T. Eddy, F. Heraux, and P. A. Hammer. 1995. Chemical growth retardants for height control of pot asters. *HortScience* 30:1309.

Begonia, Hiemalis

Common name: Hiemalis begonia, elatior begonia, Rieger begonia.
Scientific name: *Begonia* x *hiemalis.*
Family: Begoniaceae.
Other propagation methods: Seed, tissue culture.

Hiemalis begonia flowers.

Description, Uses, and Status

Hiemalis begonias are known for their large clusters of white, yellow, red, or orange flowers. Plants in the genus are monoecious, with unisexual male (staminate) and female (pistillate) flowers appearing within the same inflorescence. Hiemalis begonias are used as upright potted flowering plants, marketed in various pot sizes and hanging baskets, and occasionally as bedding plants.

Flowering Control and Dormancy

Hiemalis begonia is an obligatory short-day plant at temperatures greater than 75° F (24° C); at lower temperatures, flower initiation can slowly occur under long days. At 75° F (24° C) the critical maximum photoperiod for floral initiation is twelve to thirteen hours for most cultivars. Regardless, new cultivars in the United States are selected to flower under long days at temperatures greater than 65° F (18° C). Furthermore, in winter plants must be given a fourteen-hour photoperiod at temperatures greater than 65° F (18° C), or the plants will tuberize and go dormant. However, some cultivars may not be responsive to photoperiod, and some cultivars may be responsive when young but not after four to six tiers of leaves have formed.

The decision to switch from long days to short days is made when the vegetative plant has formed sufficient foliage to cover the pot. The number of long days for vegetative growth and the number of short days for floral initiation depends on the time of year and the cultivar.

The critical number of continuous short days is only seven for flower induction, but plants will have low flower numbers. Commercially, two to three weeks of short days are given, followed by long days for normal plant development and abundant flower numbers. If short days continue for longer than three weeks, the plants may become dormant, and the number of future flowers will be reduced due to fewer leaf axils.

Stock Plant Management

For terminal cutting production, stock plants are kept vegetative by long days of sixteen hours, and they are grown at temperatures of 64° to 68° F (18° to 20° C). For leaf cuttings, stock plants should be under short days (twelve to thirteen hours of light) for four weeks, because shoot production is promoted when leaves are used from reproductive stock. Stock plants should be maintained at 60° to 68° F (16° to 20° C) for optimal leaf unfolding and leaf-cutting production numbers.

Cutting Harvest

Either terminal or leaf-bud stem cuttings can be used. Both should have one fully expanded leaf.

Propagation

A rooted terminal vegetative stem cutting with one fully expanded leaf is commonly used in Europe and North America. Cuttings are best rooted directly in the pot in which they are to be sold. Propagation can be under white plastic tents in the summer, clear plastic in the winter, or intermittent mist. Mist should be used only in areas where temperatures are too high for tents to be used.

Stage 1:
Cutting arrival or harvest and sticking
- After harvest cuttings can be held at 48° F (9° C) to reduce the tissue temperature.
- Do not crush or otherwise damage foliage and stems during propagation, since that may encourage disease problems.
- Stick cuttings in a substrate with a pH of 5.6 to 5.8.

- Store cuttings at 50° to 60° F (10° to 16° C) for up to twenty-four hours if planting is going to be delayed.

Stage 2: Callusing

- Maintain substrate temperatures of 68° to 72° F (20° to 22° C).
- Maintain air temperatures of 70° to 80° F (21° to 27° C) days and 68° to 70° F (20° to 21° C) during nights.
- Maintain a light intensity of 500 to 1,000 f.c. (5 to 11 klux).
- Begin foliar feeding with 50 to 75 ppm nitrogen from 20-10-20 if leaves begin to lose color.
- Transfer the cuttings to Stage 3 in fourteen to twenty-one days, once 50% of the cuttings begin differentiating root initials.

Stage 3: Root development

- Maintain substrate temperatures of 68° to 72° F (20° to 22° C).
- Maintain air temperatures of 70° to 80° F (21° to 27° C) during days and 68° to 70° F (20° to 21° C) during nights.
- Increase the light intensity to 1,000 to 2,000 f.c. (11 to 22 klux) as the cuttings begin to root out.
- Fertilize with 100 to 200 ppm nitrogen once a week from 15-0-15 alternating with 20-10-20.
- Roots should develop in seven to fourteen days.

Stage 4: Toning the rooted cutting

- Increase the light level to 2,000 to 3,000 f.c. (22 to 32 klux), reduce the humidity, and lower the air temperature.
- Fertilize cuttings twice a week with 150 to 200 ppm nitrogen from 15-0-15 alternating with 20-10-20.
- The cuttings can be toned for seven days.

Leaf cuttings are used in Europe and are frequently imported into North America. Better-quality plants are produced from leaf cuttings than terminal cuttings, since the plants will have more branches and adventitious shoots. However, terminal cuttings reduce the production time compared with leaf cuttings, because leaf cuttings must produce both new roots and new shoots. While short days hasten shoot formation from leaf cuttings, they also induce flowering and should not be used for longer than two weeks. A leaf cutting requires ten to thirteen weeks to form a plantlet with a good root system and three to five shoots.

Plant Growth Regulators

Chlormequat (Cycocel) is commonly used as a spray at 500 to 3,000 ppm; the concentration is cultivar related, but 500 to 1,000 ppm is commonly used to reduce internode length. Ancymidol (A-Rest), paclobutrazol (Bonzi), and uniconazole (Sumagic) are also effective. Hiemalis begonias do not respond to negative day and night temperature difference (DIF) during the vegetative phase, but they do respond to DIF during the flowering phase of growth. Plants also respond to a two-hour temperature drop (DROP) at the end of the night or at the beginning of the day (see chapter 8 for more information).

Production and Schedule

The optimum temperature is 65° F (18° C) for the long-day stage prior to and after the pinch, and 68° to 70° F (20° to 21° C) for the short-day stage. Plants should be forced at a night temperature of 64° F (18° C) for quality plants with short internodes, appropriate-sized leaves, large-diameter flowers, and bright colors. Reducing the temperature to 59° to 63° F (15° to 17° F) prior to marketing is recommended for optimal postharvest quality and life.

Leaf injury can occur under high light levels, and an interaction with temperature exists. At 64° F (18° C) and below, high light levels of 3,000 f.c. (32 klux) can be briefly tolerated; at 70° F (21° C) 2,000 f.c. (22 klux) can be tolerated; and at 81° F (27° C) 1,500 f.c. (16 klux). Excessively high light can cause slow, hardened growth; cupping of leaf margins; reddening or darkening of the leaf; and sunburned necrotic areas. Supplemental high-intensity discharge (HID) lighting can be used at 200 to 600 f.c. (2 to 6 klux) during the winter. Approximately twenty hours of light a day are used prior to short days to stimulate vegetative growth; during short days ten to twelve hours of light a day are used; and after floral initiation sixteen to twenty-four hours a day of light are used for rapid flower development.

Hiemalis begonias do not require high fertilizer levels. A constant liquid fertilizer of 100 to 125 ppm nitrogen is adequate. The growing substrate is typically high in organic matter and should be well drained with a pH of 5.5 to 6.5. The plants have a fibrous root system and can easily be injured if a peat-based substrate becomes excessively dry or overly moist for long periods.

The most vigorous shoots can be removed with a soft pinch to improve plant shape and to control plant height. Pinching can occur at the end of propagation in the summer or two weeks after propagation in the winter. With purchased transplants, pinching occurs from two to three weeks after potting. Plants can be heavy and floppy, requiring staking and possibly tying.

Once a plant is out of propagation, ten to twelve weeks are required for flowering from June to December, and thirteen to sixteen weeks from January to May.

Diseases

Bacterial soft rot (*Erwinia*) on stems or leaves, *Botrytis* on leaves and flowers, and powdery mildew (*Oidium*) on leaves and flowers are seen during production. Fungal root and stem rots (*Phytophthora, Pythium, Rhizoctonia solani, Sclerotinia sclerotiorum, Sclerotium rolfsii,* and *Thielaviopsis basicola*) can also be present. Armillaria root rot (*Armillaria mellea*), powdery mildew (*Erysiphe*), leafspot (*Phyllosticta*), bacterial blight (*Erwinia chrysanthemi*), soft rot (*Erwinia carotovora*), bacterial leaf spot (*Xanthomonas campestris* pv. *begoniae*), and various viruses have also been recorded.

Disorders

High night temperatures above 75° F (24° C) have been reported to delay flowering. On the other hand, premature flowering may also be triggered by moisture stress, low nutrition, sudden temperature changes, and growth retardants. Edema, a rupturing and corking of epidermal cells on the underside of the leaf, is thought to be caused by high substrate moisture content and extremely high day and low night temperature. Edema may also occur when the substrate stays warm at night and the air temperature is low, resulting in excessive leaf turgor pressure. Control edema by reducing moisture, maintaining constant temperatures, and reducing humidity.

Postharvest

While cuttings can be stored at 50° to 60° F (10° to 16° C) if necessary before sticking, storage is not recommended.

References

Dreistadt, S. H. 2001. *Integrated Pest Management for Floriculture and Nurseries.* University of California Division of Agriculture and Natural Resources Publication 3402. Oakland, California.

Gooder, M. 2,000. How we grow: hiemalis begonias. *GrowerTalks* 64(5):83, 88.

Grindal, G., and R. Moe. 1995. Growth rhythm and temperature DROP. *Acta Horticulturae* 378:47–52.

Hamrick, D. 2003. *Begonia,* pp. 253–256. In: *Ball RedBook,* 17th ed., vol. 2, D. Hamrick, ed. Ball Publishing, Batavia, Illinois.

Hilding, A. 1982. Production av *Begonia* x *elatior.* Trädgård 220. Swedish University of Agricultural Sciences Research Information Center, Alnarp, Sweden. (in Swedish)

Karlsson, M. G. 1992. Leaf unfolding rate in *Begonia* x *hiemalis.* HortScience 27:109–110.

Karlsson, M. G., and R. D. Heins. 1992. *Begonias,* pp. 409–427. In: *Introduction to Floriculture,* 2nd ed., R. A. Larson, ed. Academic Press, San Diego, California.

Mikkelsen, J. C. 1973. Production requirements for quality Rieger begonias. *GrowerTalks* 37(6):3–9.

Moe, R., K. Willumsen, I. H. Ihlebekk, A. I. Stupa, N. M. Glomsrud, and L. M. Mortensen. 1995. DIF and temperature drop responses in SDP and LDP, a comparison. *Acta Horticulturae* 378:27–33.

Myster, J., O. Junttila, B. Lindgård, and R. Moe. 1997. Temperature alternations and the influence of gibberellins and indoleacetic acid on elongation growth and flowering of *Begonia* x *hiemalis* Fotsch. *Plant Growth Regulation* 21:135–144.

Roodenburg, J. W. M. 1952. Environmental factors in greenhouse culture, pp. 117–126. In: *Report of the 13th International Horticultural Congress.*

von Hentig, W.-U. 1976. Zur Vermehrung von Elatiorbegonien 'Riegers Schwabenland' und 'Riegers Aphrodite.' *Gartenwelt* 76:95–100. (in German)

von Hentig, W.-U. 1978. Zur Vermehrung von Weitere Ergebnisse mit Rieger-Sorten. *Gärtnerbörse und Gartenwelt* 78(9):193–195. (in German)

Wikesjö, K., and H. Schüssler. 1982. Growing Rieger begonias year-round. *Florists' Review* 170 (4396):30, 72–74.

Begonia, Rex

Common name: Rex begonia.
Scientific name: *Begonia* Rex Cultorum hybrids.
Family: Begoniaceae.
Other propagation methods: Seed, division.

'Denver Lace' rex begonia.

Description, Uses, and Status

Hybrid rex begonias have short stems and fleshly rhizomes. Leaf size and leaf character (spiral or nonspiral) are the basis of group designations. Their leaves are large, 8 to 12 in. (20 to 30 cm) long and 6 to 8 in. (15 to 20 cm) wide, with wrinkled surfaces and frequently with wavy margins. Leaf colors include metallic green, silver gray, green, purple, or reddish brown in various patterns of spots or blotches. The monoecious flowers (with unisexual male (staminate) and female (pistillate) flowers appearing within the same inflorescence) are typically inconspicuous. Rex begonias are useful as specimens or focal points because of their unusual leaf colors and patterns. Large specimens are spectacular mass-planted in raised or ground beds; small plants are used in planters. They may be grown outdoors in areas of shade or under protection. The begonia family is quite large, with many beautiful species that can be grown for their foliage and flowers. Various other types of begonias, cane begonias in particular, have foliage as beautiful as rex begonias and are excellent for mixed containers, patio plantings, and landscape beds.

Flowering Control and Dormancy

Rex begonias are grown exclusively for their foliage, although plants do flower in the winter and spring in North America. Under short days and low temperatures, plants may go dormant.

Stock Plant Management

Because of the plants' large robust foliage and/or vigorous habit, propagators should trim the foliage during slower harvesting periods. Fertilizer applications should be light, 100 to 150 ppm nitrogen.

Cutting Harvest

Terminal cuttings with at least two or three leaves should be harvested from cane-type begonia stock plants, and petiole cuttings from clumping or rhizomatous-types. Leaf-petiole sections should be 2 to 4 in. (5 to 10 cm) in length with 0.75 to 1.25 in. (2 to 3 cm) of leaf blade on either side of the petiole.

Propagation

With leaf propagation, which is the most common method of propagation, mature leaves are cut into sections (called "chips") with a well-developed vein. The chips are placed in the rooting medium at a 45° angle. Whole leaves can also be used. Propagation can be in sand or in a peat-lite medium with 75° to 78° F (21° to 24° C) bottom heat. A clump of plantlets develops from each leaf-piece cutting; these are separated and used as transplants. Cuttings from rhizomes are possible. Stem cuttings can be used to propagate cultivars that have upright stems. Rooting hormones are recommended for all types of cuttings; powders are the most popular type of treatment.

Plant Growth Regulators

None are typically required.

Production and Schedule

An average daily temperature of 73° F (23° C) is recommended, with a slightly lower temperature of 62° F (17° C) at night and a slightly higher one of 85° F (29° C) during the day. Proper light intensity is critical for the most vivid coloration of leaves. Generally, 2,000 to 2,500 f.c. (22 to 27 klux) is adequate. Plants growing in excessively high light are more compact, and their color patterns and intensities are reduced. Commercially, plants can even be grown under the greenhouse bench where light intensity is low.

Although rex begonias require that their roots be kept continually moist, they do not tolerate overwatering. Humidity is the most important factor in growing quality plants; an average of 50% is recommended across all cultivars. More specifically, cultivars with heavy leaf textures require less (40 to 50%), and those with velvety textures require more humidity (50 to 60%). Low humidity turns leaf margins dry or brown; excessive humidity can cause rotting of leaves and rhizomes.

Nutritional requirements are minimal; feeding 100 ppm nitrogen every two weeks is advised. Avoid high soluble salts. The medium should be light and porous.

Rooted plugs are typically purchased from specialty propagators, and finished plants require nine to twelve weeks after planting.

Diseases
Bacterial leaf spot (*Xanthomonas campestris* pv. *begoniae*), botrytis blight (*Botrytis cinerea*), pythium root and stem rot (*Pythium*), fusarium stem rot (*Fusarium*), rhizoctonia root and stem rot (*Rhizoctonia solani*), and myrothecium leaf spot (*Myrothecium roridum*) are some of the diseases encountered. Also recorded are root and stem rot (*Phytophthora*), cottony rot (*Sclerotinia sclerotiorum*), black root rot (*Thielaviopsis basicola*), armillaria root rot (*Armillaria mellea*), powdery mildew (*Erysiphe* or *Oidium*), leafspot (*Phyllosticta*), bacterial blight (*Erwinia chrysanthemi*), soft rot (*Erwinia carotovora*), and various viruses.

Disorders
Dormancy is cultivar dependent and can occur during short days in winter. Chilling damage can occur if temperatures are low, 35° F (2° C), but above freezing. Sudden temperature shifts (cold or hot) should also be avoided, because dormancy may be induced or leaf injury may occur.

References

Dreistadt, S. H. 2001. *Integrated Pest Management for Floriculture and Nurseries.* University of California Division of Agriculture and Natural Resources Publication 3402. Oakland, California.

Henley, R. W., A. R. Chase, and L. S. Osborne. 1991. Begonia (foliage types). *Foliage Plant Research Note RH-91-18.* Central Florida Research and Education Center. Apopka, Florida.

Horst, R. K. 1990. Begonia, pp. 554–555. In: *Westcott's Plant Disease Handbook,* 5th ed. Van Nostrand Reinhold, New York.

Poole, R. T., and R. W. Henley. 1989. Production of foliage begonias for interiorscape market. *Proceedings of the Florida State Horticultural Society* 102:280–282.

Post, K. 1949. *Begonia,* pp. 248–342. In: *Florist Crop Production and Marketing.* Orange Judd Publishing. New York.

Thompson, M. L., and E. J. Thompson. 1981. Rex cultivars, pp. 172–177. In: *Begonias: Complete Review and Guide.* Times Books, New York.

von Hentig, W.-U., and G. Przyrembel. 1973. Einfluss der Ernährung von Rex-Begonien—Mutterpflanzen auf die Entwicklung von Jungflanzen aus Blattstucken. *Gartenwelt* 73(3):49–51. (in German)

White, E. A. 1923. *Begonia,* pp. 326–334. In: *The Principles of Floriculture.* Macmillan Publishing, New York.

Begonia, Wax

Common name: Wax begonia, bedding begonia, fibrous-rooted begonia.
Scientific name: *Begonia* Semperflorens-Cultorum hybrids.
Family: Begoniaceae.
Other propagation methods: Seed.

Description, Uses, and Status
The wax begonia has fibrous roots, and its stout stems are succulent and well branched. The glossy ovate leaves range from green to red, bronze-red, and mahogany red; they may even be variegated green and white. The

'Doublet Rose' begonia.

monoecious (with unisexual male [staminate] and female [pistillate] flowers appearing within the same inflorescence) flowers are single or double in colors including red, pink, pale orange, and white. Dragonwing begonias are produced similarly to wax begonias, but they are more vigorous and include some characteristics of angel-wing begonias, such as a more elongated leaf and a more unidirectional growth habit. Wax and dragonwing begonias are commonly used as bedding plants, adaptable to both shady and sunny areas.

Flower Control and Dormancy

Wax begonias are day-neutral and need no specific photoperiod or temperature. High light is required for rapid flowering. Branching is controlled mainly by the available photosynthates, whereas flowering is controlled by temperature.

Stock Plant Management

Some types are vigorous and should be pinched to maintain sufficient yield and avoid legginess of cuttings. Clean sterile cutting tools should always be used.

Cutting Harvest

Terminal cuttings 1.5 to 2 in. (4 to 5 cm) long with one fully expanded leaf are used.

Propagation

Cultivars with unusual green and white variegated foliage or double flowers are propagated by cuttings. Cuttings will root in three to four weeks under mist at 70° F (21° C). Avoid overmisting, since excessive moisture encourages diseases.

Plant Growth Regulators

Chlormequat (Cycocel) sprays at 500 to 1,000 ppm can be used. Ancymidol (A-Rest) sprays can be used at 6 to 12 ppm after transplanting plugs and at 10 to 12 ppm for finished plants. A tank mix of 1,000 to 1,250 chlormequat and 800 to 1,250 daminozide (B-Nine) can also be used.

Production and Schedule

For optimum growth, temperatures of 72°F (22° C) during days and 65° F (18° C) during nights is recommended for the first two weeks after planting, after which the temperature can be lowered to 67° F (19° C) during the day and 60° F (16°C) at night. High light of 4,000 to 5,000 f.c. (43 to 54 klux) is required for rapid flowering, and supplemental light is often beneficial.

Fertilize with 150 to 200 ppm nitrogen with every other irrigation. Using the PourThru method, maintain the substrate EC at 2.0 to 3.0 mS/cm during cool seasonal periods, but reduce by half in summer. Work at the University of Georgia, however, suggests that begonias are not sensitive to substrate EC, since they grew well with an EC ranging from 1.7 to 6.1 mS/cm. A crop of rooted cuttings typically requires the following amount of time to finish: five to seven weeks for 4 in. (10 cm) pots containing one cutting and 6 in. (15 cm) pots with three cuttings; eight to ten weeks for 8 in. (20 cm) pots with three cuttings; and nine to eleven weeks for 10 in. (25 cm) hanging baskets with three to four cuttings.

Diseases

Botrytis blight (*Botrytis cinerea*) and powdery mildew (*Oidium*) are common. Bacterial leaf spot (*Xanthomonas campestris* pv. *begoniae*), fusarium stem rot (*Fusarium*), and tomato spotted wilt virus can also be encountered. Cottony rot (*Sclerotinia sclerotiorum*), black root rot (*Thielaviopsis basicola*), armillaria root rot (*Armillaria mellea*), powdery mildew (*Erysiphe*), leafspot (*Phyllosticta*), bacterial blight (*Erwinia chrysanthemi*), soft rot (*Erwinia carotovora*), and various viruses have also been recorded.

Disorders

All green foliage may occur on variegated-leaf cultivars. Remove all green shoots from stock plants to help maintain variegation.

References

Bell, M. 2001. Bedding plants and seed geraniums, pp. 54–62. In: *Tips on Regulating Growth of Floriculture Crops*, M. L. Gaston, L. A. Kunkle, P. S. Konjoian, and M. F. Wilt, eds. Ohio Florists' Association Services, Columbus, Ohio.

Daughtrey, M., and A. R. Chase. 1992. Begonia, pp. 43–44. In: *Ball Field Guide to Diseases of Greenhouse Ornamentals*. Ball Publishing, Batavia, Illinois.

Dreistadt, S. H. 2001. *Integrated Pest Management for Floriculture and Nurseries*. University of California Division of Agriculture and Natural Resources Publication 3402. Oakland, California.

Ewart, L. C. 1980. A grower's guide to begonias. *American Vegetable Grower and Greenhouse Grower* 28(1):6.

James, E. C., and M. W. van Iersel. 2001. Fertilizer concentration affects growth and flowering of subirrigated petunias and begonias. *HortScience* 36:40–44.

Kessler, R., A. M. Armitage, and D. S. Koranski. 1991.

Acceleration of *Begonia* x *semperflorens cultorum* growth using supplemental irradiance. *HortScience* 26:258–260.

Kuehny, J. S., A. Painter, and P. C. Branch. 2001. Plug source and growth retardants affect finish size of bedding plants. *HortScience* 36:321–323.

Bougainvillea

Common name: Bougainvillea.
Scientific name: *Bougainvillea* x *buttiana, B. glabra,* and *B. spectabilis.*
Family: Nyctaginaceae.
Other propagation methods: Air layering.

Bougainvillea are ideal candidates for hanging basket production.

Description, Uses, and Status

Plants in this genus are noted for the vivid color of their bracts; the tubular flowers are inconspicuous within the bracts. The leaves are alternate and occasionally variegated, and the woody stems, which have thorns, form a vigorous vine with support. Bougainvillea is a prized ornamental shrub-vine in landscapes where heavy frosts or freezes are uncommon, and it is found in hot sunny areas as well as cool coastal regions around the world. This plant has also become an important plant for pots and hanging baskets in Europe and North America.

Flowering Control and Dormancy

Bougainville is a facultative short-day plant. Plants will eventually flower under long days, but fewer buds are formed. Factors other than photoperiod may induce flowering. High light levels result in the most rapid flowering. Cool night temperatures may also be a factor. Older plants flower sooner than newly rooted plants.

Stock Plant Management

Stock plants are typically grown in hanging baskets to allow for easy harvest of the long stems. Cuttings should be taken from wood that is mature to the point that it starts to become stiff. Care should be taken when harvesting cuttings because of the 1 to 1.5 in. (2 to 4 cm) sharp thorns that arise from the axils. When propagating by softwood cuttings, night temperatures should be above 55° F (13° C), whereas hardwood cuttings root more efficiently when night temperatures are below that level.

Cutting Harvest

The published literature offers varying information on length of stem cuttings and position. Succulent terminal cuttings 3 to 3.5 in. (8 to 9 cm) long were typically used. Other suggested cutting lengths include 4 to 5 in. (10 to 12 cm), 8 to 10 in. (20 to 25 cm), and 32 to 40 in. (80 to 100 cm) with

Bougainville cuttings with the succulent tips removed.

top portions removed back to 6 in. (15 cm) of total length. Stems up to 6 ft. (1.8 m) long and 1.2 in. (3 cm) in diameter can be harvested, leaves removed, staked, and propagated to produce the trunk of standard bougainvillea plants.

Another, perhaps more effective, means of determining cutting length in bougainvillea is by counting the number of nodes. The optimum number of nodes is less well defined, with recommendations including two nodes, three or four nodes, or five to nine nodes. Most sources agree that cuttings should be severed 0.5 in. (1.3 cm) below the bottom node.

Propagation

Bougainvillea cuttings often fail to produce roots, and the rooting percentage is low, even during spring and summer. The root system is also known to be extremely fine and fragile. Removing the lower leaves and using a rooting hormone are recommended. One report indicated that 0.2% NAA powder with Captan and Benomyl produced a higher percentage of rooted cuttings than 0.2 to 0.4 % IBA. Other researchers have used 4,000 to 16,000 ppm IBA, depending on the cultivar and time of year. Any well-drained substrate or rooting cube can be used; the substrate should be held at 75° to 81° F (24° to 27° C). Mist or fog can be used to maintain leaf turgidity. Rooting may be improved by using polyethylene plastic tents or laying the plastic directly on the cuttings. Cutting propagation requires two to four weeks.

Plant Growth Regulators

Several chemicals are effective on bougainvillea, but all chemicals should be tested carefully on a few plants of each cultivar because wide variations in response, due to cultivar, season, and geographical location, are typical. A drench of ancymidol (A-Rest) at 50 ppm or one of paclobutrazol (Bonzi) at 25 to 100 ppm can be applied. Dikegulac sodium (Atrimmec) sprays increased axillary branching and flowering in some cultivars but not in others. However, dikegulac sodium drenches at 1,600 ppm are generally recognized as the most effective way to reduce shoot elongation.

Production and Schedules

Day temperatures of 70° to 85° F (21° to 29° C) and night temperatures of 65° to 70° F (18° to 21° C) are recommended. High light levels and inductive eight-hour short days promoted flowering. Low light levels delayed flowering, even under inductive short-day cycles and optimal temperatures. High light of 4,000 to 5,000 f.c. (43 to 54 klux) encourages rapid compact growth and numerous well-colored flowers. While excessive water stress may result in abscission of flower bracts, plants are best grown on the dry side during greenhouse production.

Bougainvillea responds to constant fertilization of 150 to 200 ppm nitrogen. The plant is reported to have a high magnesium, iron, and manganese requirement. Excess salts can cause root damage. Avoid ammonium-nitrogen if plants are grown cool. Any well-drained substrate with a pH of 5.5 to 6.0 is acceptable. A substrate pH above 6.5 may lead to iron deficiency.

Plants can be soft pinched once growth starts (approximately ten days after propagation) or when new growth is 3 in. (8 cm) long. Plants can be pinched every four weeks if needed. Some production

schedules, however, do not include any pinching. An increase in branching can be obtained with two spray applications of benzyladenine (BA) at 50 to 100 ppm; the applications are made twenty-four hours after the first and second pinches.

After planting two rooted cuttings per 8 in. (20 cm) hanging basket, grow the plants for four weeks until they are pinched. Grow the plants for another two to three weeks, then start short days. Flowering will occur twelve to fifteen weeks later.

Diseases

Plants are relatively disease free, but a number of leaf spots (*Cercospora bougainvilleae, Cladosporium arthinioides,* and *Pseudomonas andropogonis*) and blights (*Phytophthora parasitica*) can be problems.

Disorders

Iron chlorosis is a common problem of plants grown in containers; it can result from root rot or from the substrate having a high pH, poor aeration, or high EC.

References

Aldrich, J. H., and J. G. Norcini. 1995. Copper hydroxide-treated pots improve the root system of bougainvillea cuttings. *Proceedings of the Florida State Horticultural Society* 107:215–217.

Allard, H. A. 1935. Response of the woody plants *Hibiscus syriacus, Malvavicus conzatti,* and *Bougainvillea glabra* to day length. *Journal of Agricultural Research* 51:27–34.

Atzmon, N., Z. Wiesman, and P. Fine. 1997. Biosolids improve rooting of bougainvillea (*Bougainvillea glabra*) cuttings. *Journal of Environmental Horticulture* 15:1–5.

Auld, R. E. 1987. The basics of propagating *Bougainvillea. Combined Proceedings of the International Plant Propagators' Society* 36:211–213.

Broschat, T. K. 1998. Nitrogen source affects growth and quality of *Bougainvillea. HortTechnology* 8:346–348.

Cameron, A. C., and M. S. Reid. 1983. Use of silver thiosulfate to prevent flower abscission from potted plants. *Scientia Horticulturae* 19:373–378.

Criley, R. A. 1977. Year round flowering of double bougainvillea: Effect of daylength and growth retardants. *Journal of the American Society for Horticultural Science* 102:775–778.

Criley, R. A. 1997. *Bougainvillea,* pp. 28–31. In: *Tips on Growing Specialty Potted Crops,* M. L. Gaston,

S. A. Carver, C. A. Irwin, and R. A. Larson, eds. Ohio Florists' Association, Columbus, Ohio.

Czekalski, M. L. 1989. The influence of auxins on the rooting of cuttings of *Bougainvillea glabra* Choisy. *Acta Horticulturae* 251:345–352.

Dierking, C. M., and K. C. Sanderson. 1985. Effect of various chemical spray treatments of *Bougainvillea spectabilis* Willd. *Proceedings of the Southern Nurserymen's Association of Research Conference* 30:220–222.

Hackett, W. P., and R. M. Sachs. 1966. Flowering in *Bougainvillea* 'San Diego Red'. *Proceedings of the American Society for Horticultural Science* 88:606–612.

Hackett, W. P., and R. M. Sachs. 1985. *Bougainvillea,* pp. 38–47. In: *Handbook of Flowering,* vol. II, A. H. Halevy, ed. CRC Press, Boca Raton, Florida

Higginbotham, R. 1992. *Bougainvillea* propagation. *Combined Proceedings of the International Plant Propagators' Society* 42:37–38.

Horst, R. K. 1990. Bougainvillea, p. 561. In: *Westcott's Plant Disease Handbook,* 5th cd. Van Nostrand Reinhold, New York.

Kamp-Glass, M., and M. A. H. Ogden. 1991. *Bougainvillea. GrowerTalks* 55(8):17.

Mudge, K. W., V. N. Mwaja, F. M. Itulya, and J. Ochieng. 1995. Comparison of 4 moisture management-systems for cutting propagation of bougainvillea, hibiscus, and kei apple. *Journal of the American Society for Horticultural Science* 120:366–373.

Norcini, J. G., J. H. Aldrich, and J. M. McDowell. 1994. Flowering response of *Bougainvillea* cultivars to dikegulac. *HortScience* 29:282–284.

Schoellhorn, R., and E. Alvarez. 2002. *Warm Climate Production Guidelines for Bougainvillea* Vol. ENH874, p. 5, Electronic Data Information Source, University of Florida.

Singh, B., P. K. Majumdar, and J. Prasad, 1976. Response of bougainvillea cuttings under bottom heat [Propagation], *Delhi Garden Magazine,* p. 13.

Bracteantha

Common name: Strawflower, golden everlasting, yellow paper daisy.
Scientific name: *Bracteantha bracteata.*
Family: Compositae.
Other propagation methods: Seed.

Description, Uses, and Status
This annual native of eastern Australia has 1 to 2 in. (2.5 to 5 cm) wide flowers with many rigid papery glossy bracts available in white, pink, rose, purple, yellow, and orange. Plants grow 18 to 30 in. (45 to 75 cm) tall, and they are typically grown in containers but occasionally in packs and hanging baskets. Vegetative strawflower is hardy in Zones 8 to 11, can withstand several light frosts, and performs best in well-drained situations.

Strawflower flower. (A. Williams)

Flowering Control and Dormancy
Strawflower is a day-neutral plant.

Stock Plant Management
Successive pinches are required to maintain a productive canopy of shoot tips. Allow two to three weeks of good root development before commencing to pinch. Use sterile cutting tools to avoid transmitting foliar pathogens and vascular diseases.

Cutting Harvest
Terminal stem cuttings are used. The long leaves can be cut in half before propagation.

Propagation
Treat cuttings with 2,500 ppm IBA and insert into a

substrate with a pH of 5.5 to 6.3. Stick one cutting per cell if using plug flats. Maintain the substrate at a temperature of 70° to 75° F (21° to 24° C). Because excessive misting will delay rooting, reduce misting as soon as possible. Begin fertilization the second week with 150 ppm nitrogen from 20-10-20. Rooting will occur in four to five weeks.

Plant Growth Regulators

None are generally required but paclobutrazol (Bonzi or Piccolo) sprays at 5 to 10 ppm or uniconazole (Sumagic) sprays at 10 to 20 ppm are effective. A tank-mixed spray of ancymidol (A-Rest) at 4 to 10 ppm and daminozide (B-Nine) at 1,250 to 2,500 ppm can be used. Ethephon (Florel) can be applied at 300 to 500 ppm to increase lateral branching.

Production and Schedule

Grow at temperatures of 65° to 75° F (18 to 24° C) during days and 55° to 60° F (13° to 16° C) during nights, and provide high light of 6,000 to 10,000 f.c. (65 to 108 klux). Pinching is often not required, especially for 4 to 5 in. (10 to 13 cm) pots, but may be needed for larger containers. Avoid wilting or overwatering since both lead to problems. Use a growing substrate with a pH of 5.5 to 6.3 and containing low amounts of phosphorus, because plants are sensitive to that element.

Use one rooted cutting per 4 in. (10 cm) pot, one or two per 6 in. (15 cm) pot, and three to five per 10 in. (25 cm) basket. Plants in the smaller pots are ready to sell in four to six weeks, those in the larger pots in seven to nine weeks, and those in the baskets in ten to twelve weeks.

Diseases

Root roots (especially from *Pythium, Rhizoctonia,* or *Phytophthora*) are common and can cause a rapid collapse if plants are overwatered. *Botrytis* can also be a problem, either as a flower blight or a stem canker.

Disorders

Yellowed foliage is fairly common. If older leaves are yellow, watch for low nutrition, especially nitrogen, high substrate EC, magnesium deficiency, or root rot. If younger leaves are yellow, check for low nutrition or iron deficiency, which may be due to high substrate pH. Delayed flower initiation can be due to low light levels, short days, or high night temperatures.

Postharvest

The cuttings should be removed from shipping boxes immediately and propagated as soon as possible. They are sensitive to cold damage if exposed to low temperatures.

References

Hamrick, D. 2003. *Bracteantha,* pp. 265–267. In: *Ball RedBook,* 17th ed., vol. 2, D. Hamrick, ed. Ball Publishing, Batavia, Illinois.

Calibrachoa

Common name: Calibrachoa, mini petunia.
Scientific name: *Calibrachoa* hybrids.
Family: Solanaceae.
Other propagation methods: Seed.

Description, Uses, and Status

This cutting-propagated perennial carries numerous small showy purple, pink, white, yellow, orange, or bicolor flowers. Calibrachoa is similar to the petunia, but has finer-textured foliage, a more pronounced trailing habit, and more flowers. Hybrids between calibrachoa and petunia are becoming available. The calibrachoa plant habit is trailing to weakly upright and

Overwintered 'Lirica Showers Rose' calibrachoa flowering in early spring in Zone 7.

mounding to 6 in. (15 cm) tall. It is cold tolerant and hardy to Zone 7 but is most reliable in Zone 8 or warmer areas. Plants can take temperatures down to 15° F (–9° C) in some situations. Plants that overwinter make a great color display quite early in the spring. Plants are sold in the spring in pots and hanging baskets.

Flowering Control and Dormancy

Calibrachoa is a facultative long-day plant; provide long days during propagation and production, if possible. Plants often stop flowering during the middle of the summer when temperatures are high.

Stock Plant Management

Maintain a well-trimmed stock plant to generate short terminal cuttings with thick stems. Ethephon (Florel) sprays at 500 to 1,000 ppm can reduce flowering and decrease internode elongation.

Cutting Harvest

Terminal cuttings are harvested with one or two mature leaves. Cuttings should be 2 to 3 in. (5 to 8 cm) long.

Propagation

Stage 1:
Cutting arrival or harvest and sticking
- Store the cuttings for at least two hours at 48° F (9° C) to reduce cutting temperature. Determine how many cuttings can be stuck in one to two hours, and store the remainder in a cool location or a cooler until they can be planted.
- Store cuttings at 40° to 45° F (4° to 7° C) for up to twenty-four hours if planting is going to be delayed.
- Rooting hormones are not required, but 2,500 ppm IBA on cutting bases may be beneficial.
- Stick one cutting per cell if using plug flats.

Stage 2: Callusing
- Maintain substrate temperatures of 70° to 75° F (21° to 24° C) for most cultivars.
- Maintain air temperatures of 70° to 75° F (21° to 24° C) during days and 68° to 70° F (20° to 21° C) during nights for most cultivars.
- Keep the substrate sufficiently moist so that water is easily squeezed out of it, but not so much that the cutting base is waterlogged. The base of the cutting needs air for proper rooting.
- Maintain a light intensity of 500 to 1,000 f.c. (5 to 11 klux). Supplemental lighting of 400 to 500 f.c.

(4 to 5 klux) may be beneficial in northern or cloudy climates.
- Begin foliar feeding with 50 to 75 ppm nitrogen from 15-0-15 as soon as the leaves begin to show any color loss.
- Maintain a substrate pH of 5.8 to 6.2.
- Transfer the cuttings to Stage 3 after five to seven days, once 50% of the cuttings begin differentiating root initials.

Stage 3: Root development
- Lower the substrate temperature to 68° to 74° F (20° to 23° C).
- Maintain air temperatures of 70° to 75° F (21° to 24° C) during days and 68° to 70° F (20° to 21° C) during nights.
- Begin drying out the substrate once roots are visible.
- Begin increasing light intensity to 1,000 to 2,000 f.c. (11 to 22 klux) as the cuttings begin to root out.
- Increase fertilization to once a week with 100 ppm nitrogen, alternating between 15-0-15 and 20-10-20, then increase to 200 ppm nitrogen.
- Roots should develop in nine to fourteen days.

Stage 4: Toning the rooted cutting
- Lower the air temperature to 70° to 75° F (21° to 24° C) during the day and 62° to 68° F (17° to 20° C) at night.
- Increase the light intensity to 2,000 to 4,000 f.c. (22 to 43 klux).
- Provide shade during the middle of the day to reduce temperature stress.
- Move the liners from the mist area into an area of lower relative humidity.
- Fertilize once a week with 150 to 200 ppm nitrogen from 15-0-15 alternating with 20-10-20.
- The cuttings can be toned for seven days.

Plant Growth Regulators

While calibrachoa is typically grown as a trailing plant, plant growth regulators are sometimes used to control growth and prevent the stems of plants in neighboring containers from intertwining. Daminozide (B-Nine) sprays at 2,500 to 3,000 ppm, paclobutrazol (Bonzi or Piccolo) sprays at 5 to 30 ppm, and uniconazole (Sumagic) sprays at 10 to 20 ppm can be used. A tank mix of ancymidol (A-Rest) at 4 to 10 ppm and daminozide at 1,250 to 2,500 ppm is also effective. Ethephon (Florel) sprays at 500 to 1,000 ppm can also be used but may delay flowering.

Production and Schedule

Grow calibrachoa at temperatures of 60° to 85° F (16° to 29° C) during days and 60° to 65° F (16° to 18° C) during nights. Cooler temperatures down to 55° F (13° C) can be used to improve plant quality, but growth will slow considerably. Warm production temperatures above 90° F (32° C) will decrease flower size. Maintain 5,000 to 9,000 ft. (54 to 97 klux) light levels.

The substrate pH should be maintained at 5.5 to 6.0. Plants are susceptible to iron chlorosis induced by high pH; it can be controlled by a lower pH or by the application of iron chelates. Calibrachoa requires high fertilizer rates of 200 to 300 ppm nitrogen. Maintain a substrate EC of 2.5 to 2.8 mS/cm. Allow plants to dry well between irrigations, since they are susceptible to overwatering.

Use one rooted cutting per 4 in. (10 cm) pot, one or two per 6 in. (15 cm) pot, and three to five per 10 in. (25 cm) basket. While typically not required, plants may be pinched at any time after establishment to increase branching and improve plant shape; however, pinching will delay marketing by two or more weeks. Plants in 4 in. (10 cm) pots are ready to sell in four to six weeks, those in 6 in. (15 cm) pots in seven to nine weeks, and those in 10 in. (25 cm) baskets in nine to eleven weeks.

Diseases

Botrytis, powdery mildew, and root rots can be problems.

Disorders

Maintain substrate pH at 5.5 to 6.0; iron deficiency may occur at pH levels above 6.0. Calibrachoa is quite tolerant of low substrate pH. Too much vegetative growth can occur if plants are subjected to high ammonium levels, low light conditions (especially with high fertilizer rates), or overwatering.

Postharvest

Cuttings can be stored at 40° to 45° F (4° to 7° C) for up to twenty-four hours.

References

Hamrick, D. 2003. *Calibrachoa,* pp. 278–280. In: *Ball RedBook,* 17th ed., vol. 2, D. Hamrick, ed. Ball Publishing, Batavia, Illinois.

Starman, T. W., M. C. Robinson, and K. L. Eixmann. 2004. Efficacy of ethephon on vegetative annuals. *HortTechnology* 14:83–87.

Campanula

Common name: Campanula, bellflower, harebell, bluebell.
Scientific name: *Campanula* species.
Family: Campanulaceae.
Other propagation methods: Seed, division.

Description, Uses, and Status

The leaves are alternate. The showy and bell-like flowers (hence one of its common names, bellflower) vary in size and form. The five-lobed corolla can be violet-blue, purple, pink, or white. Most campanula species form rosettes before stem elongation and flowering. Campanulas are commonly used as bedding plants, potted flowering plants, and cut flowers. They are important crops in northern Europe, especially in Scandinavia, where they are grown for spring sales in 4 in. (10 cm) pots or in hanging baskets.

Campanula glomerata 'Joan Elliot'.

Flowering Control and Dormancy

Reproductive growth occurs for *C. carpatica* and *C. isophylla* when the light period is longer than fourteen hours. While the critical day length decreases with increasing temperatures, it is fourteen hours at 59° to 70° F (15° to 21° C). Research at Michigan State University recommended sixteen-hour day lengths for *C. carpatica;* cold had no effect on flowering. These long-day treatments must be maintained even after the visible bud stage has been reached because shoots revert back to vegetative growth if returned to short days.

Stock Plant Management

Stock plants must be kept vegetative under short-day photoperiods of eight to twelve hours. Stock plants are grown at 60° to 65° F (16° to 18° C).

Cutting Harvest

Terminal cuttings 0.8 to 2 in. (2 to 5 cm) long with at least one fully expanded leaf are used.

Propagation

For the propagation of cuttings, keep the substrate temperature at 70° F (21° C) and the air temperature at 65° F (18° C). Rooting hormone, 500 to 1,000 KIBA, can be used depending on the species.

Plant Growth Regulators

If growth is excessive, daminozide (B-Nine) sprays at 2,500 to 5,000 ppm or flurprimidol (Topflor) sprays at 10 to 60 ppm can be used. Chlormequat (Cycocel), ancymidol (A-Rest), paclobutrazol (Bonzi), and uniconazole (Sumagic) are also effective. Both *C. carpatica* and *C. isophylla* respond to day and night temperature difference (DIF).

Production and Schedule

The best quality is obtained at 58° to 62° F (14° to 17° C), which produces floriferous, uniform plants. *C. carpatica* flowered more quickly but with fewer and smaller flowers as the temperature increased from 57° to 79° F (14° to 26° C).

The cultivated campanula species are long-day plants, which should be forced under high natural light. Supplemental high intensity discharge (HID) lighting is used in northern Europe. Reduce the light level at the end of the crop cycle to enhance flower color.

Most campanulas are sensitive to overwatering, which encourages disease, especially on open flowers. Nutrient levels should be at 200 ppm nitrogen from a complete fertilizer. Any well-drained substrate with a pH of 6.0 to 7.0 can be used.

With both *C. carpatica* and *C. isophylla,* eight to nine weeks are required from rooting cuttings to the time the plants are ready to sell. Long days begin six weeks after transplanting, and flowering occurs eight weeks later.

Diseases

Campanula has problems with *Botrytis.* Other problems include root and stem rot (*Fusarium, Rhizoctonia solanii,* and *Sclerotinia sclerotiorum*), aster yellows, and powdery mildew (*Erysiphe cichoracearum*).

References

Adams, R. 1991. "GrowerTalks" on Pot Culture: Campanula, pp. 50–51. *GrowerTalks,* Geo. J. Ball Publishing, Geneva, Illinois.

Horst, R. K. 1990. Campanula, p. 577. In: *Westcott's Plant Disease Handbook,* 5th ed. Van Nostrand Reinhold, New York.

Latimer, J. 2001. Herbaceous perennials, pp. 98–110. In: *Tips on Regulating Growth of Floriculture Crops,* M. L. Gaston, L. A. Kunkle, P. S. Konjoian, and M. F. Wilt, eds. Ohio Florists' Association Services, Columbus, Ohio.

Madson, P., and K. Madson. 1986. Campanula—A bright star in the future. *Bedding Plants International News* 16:7.

Moe, R., and O. M. Heide. 1985. *Campanula isophylla,* pp. 119–122. In: *Handbook of Flowering,* vol. II, A. H. Halevy, ed. CRC Press, Boca Raton, Florida.

Niu, G., R. D. Heins, A. Cameron, and W. Carlson. 2001. Temperature and daily light integral influence plant quality and flower development of *Campanula carpatica* 'Blue Clips', 'Deep Blue Clips', and *Campanula* 'Birch Hybrid'. *HortScience* 36:664–668.

Runkle, E. S., R. D. Heins, A. C. Cameron, and W. H. Carlson. 1998. Flowering of herbaceous perennials under various night interruption and cyclic lighting treatments. *HortScience* 33:672–677.

Serek, M., and E. C. Sisler. 2001. Efficacy of inhibitors of ethylene binding in improvement of the postharvest characteristics of potted flowering plants. *Postharvest Biology and Technology* 23:161–166.

Whitman, C., R. Heins, A. Cameron, and W. Carlson. 1995. Production guide for *Campanula carpatica* as a flowering plant. *Professional Plant Growers Association News* 26(4):2–3.

Whitman, C., R. D. Heins, A. C. Cameron, and W. H. Carlson. 1997. Cold treatment and forcing temperature influence flowering of *Campanula carpatica* 'Blue Clips'. *HortScience* 32:861–865.

Whitman, C., R. D. Heins, A. C. Cameron, and W. H. Carlson. 1998. Lamp type and irradiance level for daylength extensions influence flowering of *Campanula carpatica* 'Blue Clips', *Coreopsis* grandiflora 'Early Sunrise', and *Coreopsis verticillata* 'Moonbeam'. *Journal of the American Society for Horticultural Science* 123:802-807.

Yoder Green Leaf Perennials. 2004. *Handling Unrooted Perennials.* www.green-leaf-ent.com/URC_Handling_2004.pdf.

Chrysanthemum

'Sunny Gretchen' garden chrysanthemum.

Common name: Chrysanthemum, florist chrysanthemum.
Scientific name: *Chrysanthemum* x *morifolium* (formerly *Dendranthema* x *grandiflorum*).
Family: Compositae.
Other propagation methods: Seed, division.

Description, Uses, and Status
Chrysanthemum cultivars come in an astonishing variety of colors (white, green, yellow, red, bronze, and pink), color combinations, and petal styles (spoon, quill, and flat). The central disc florets may be numerous to nearly absent; the outer ray florets may also be numerous or have only one or two rows. This herbaceous perennial plant is one of the most popular floriculture species in the world, grown as a cut flower, potted flowering plant, and garden plant for fall color.

Flowering Control and Dormancy
Flowering is controlled by the naturally shortening day lengths of late summer and fall, with flowering occurring from early fall to winter. Long days are used to maintain vegetative growth of stock plants and cuttings prior to placing young plants under short days for flowering. The critical photoperiod is twelve hours or less for reproductive growth, and fourteen hours or more for vegetative growth. Floral induction can occur at or less than fourteen hours, but normal flower development does not continue. While most cultivars for cut flower and potted plant production are obligate short-day plants, many cultivars for garden use are facultative short-day plants. In addition, day-neutral breeding lines exist.

Cultivars are grouped into response groups, which are based on the required number of weeks from the start of short days to flowering. The time from the beginning of short days to flower initiation is relatively uniform; however, the time from initiation to development of the inflorescence varies among cultivars. Consequently, the total number of weeks from the beginning of short days to harvest or anthesis (visible pollen) varies. Cultivars that flower six to eight weeks after the start of short days are generally garden types; cultivars that flower eight to eleven weeks after short days are generally flowering potted plants; and cultivars that flower eight to fifteen weeks after short days are cut flowers.

Stock Plant Management
Stock plants must be grown under long days to keep them vegetative. However, if stock plants are continually kept under long days, they eventually form a terminally reproductive structure called a *crown bud,* which rarely reaches anthesis. For this reason, propagators must renew stock plants up to four times a year, depending on the cultivar grown. Old shoots with a large number of leaves are more likely to produce crown buds than are younger shoots. In addition, cutting quality declines as a stock plant ages.

Commercially, long days are generally created by using incandescent lamps as a night break. As the light intensity or the duration increases, the inhibition of reproductive growth is increased. Often cyclic lighting is used, for example, six minutes on and twenty-four minutes off, for a four-hour night break. Cool white fluorescent lamps are more efficient in electrical consumption and more effective at floral inhibition than incandescent lamps. Regardless, the incandescent lamp is more commonly used because of ease and low cost of installation.

For cyclic night-break lighting the intensity should be at least 10 f.c. (108 lux) at the shoot apex. High intensity discharge (HID) lighting can also be used to maintain vegetative growth under long days. If continuous lighting is used, the intensity required is 7 to 10 f.c. (76 to 108 lux).

Duration of the night break in the winter varies with the latitude. Five-hour night breaks are recommended for locations at 40° to 50° latitude, four hours at 24° to 40° latitude, and three hours at 25° latitude to the Equator from August 1 to May 30. Lighting for vegetative growth is necessary year-round from 15° latitude to the Equator. Commercial cutting propagators light year-round.

Stock plant handling affects the quality and rooting of the resulting cuttings. HID lighting and supplemental carbon dioxide of stock plants increased the number and quality of cuttings. Cuttings from plants grown under HID lights also produced more roots, which increased subsequent growth of the resulting plants. Stock plants must also have proper nutrition to provide for optimum nutrient levels in the cuttings. For example, cuttings low in nitrogen have fewer and shorter roots.

Cutting Harvest

Terminal cuttings 2.5 to 3 in. (6 to 8 cm) long are sold either unrooted or rooted. Because chrysanthemums are generally direct-stuck with multiple cuttings per pot, the grading and sorting of cuttings are especially important. Sort cuttings by stem caliper, length, and node number.

Propagation

Cuttings root with ease in one to two weeks under mist, fog, or plastic (white in the summer and clear in the winter) laid directly over the cuttings. A rooting hormone of 1,500 ppm IBA may be dusted on the base of the cuttings to speed rooting. Unrooted cuttings are often direct-stuck in the final container. With plug flats, one cutting is inserted per cell. Use a well-drained substrate with a pH of 5.8 to 6.2. Maintain a substrate temperature of 70° to 74° F (21° to 23° C) and air temperatures of 70° to 85° F (21° to 29° C). Avoid air temperatures less than 60 F (16° C) or greater than 95° F (35° C).

The frequency and duration of misting, if used, should decrease rapidly during propagation. For example, during Stage 2 apply mist every five to ten minutes for the first three days, and every twenty minutes for the next four days; during Stage 3 apply mist every thirty minutes. The actual mist program will vary with the time of year, the cultivar, etc. Overmisting will cause foliage yellowing; apply 100 ppm nitrogen if this occurs. Begin applying 200 to 300 ppm nitrogen once weekly upon visible root initials.

Cuttings should receive a high light level of 3,000 to 3,500 f.c. (32 to 38 klux), and HID lighting may be beneficial during propagation, especially in the winter or in cloudy climates. However, a lower light level or shading may be necessary for the first week or until the first roots are present.

To maintain vegetative growth, cuttings are kept under long days. The number of days that cuttings are kept under long days depends on the desired plant size and flowering date and the time of year. Lower light levels and temperatures in the winter delay development, requiring a greater number of long days to produce sufficiently large plants. In some cases, long days will extend past the propagation phase.

Plant Growth Regulators

With potted flowering plants, plant growth regulators are required to reduce internode elongation. One or more sprays of daminozide (B-Nine) at 1,000 to 5,000 ppm are commonly used. Paclobutrazol (Bonzi) is quite effective and can be applied as 31 to 125 ppm sprays or as 1 to 4 ppm drenches. Uniconazole (Sumagic) can also be applied as 2.5 to 10 ppm sprays or as 0.1 to 1 ppm drenches. Apply flurprimidol (Topflor) sprays at 7.5 to 15 ppm to sensitive cultivars, or 15 to 25 ppm to vigorous cultivars. Furthermore, temperature day and night temperature difference (DIF) and DROP techniques can be used to aid in height control (see chapter 8 for more information).

Production and Schedule

Rooted cuttings are directly planted in pots or beds and kept fogged or misted for several days until established. For potted plants, be sure to sort cuttings by root development in addition to stem caliper, length, and node number.

Chrysanthemums can be scheduled to flower any day of the year by lighting to keep plants vegetative or by placing plants under black cloth to induce flowering. Many garden mum cuttings are in the six- to seven-week response groups. Most potted flowering chrysanthemums are eight-week cultivars, and most cut flower cultivars are eleven-week cultivars. Regardless of the response group, for all cut flowers three or four weeks of long days are given after planting the rooted cutting to lengthen the stem, compared with two weeks for many of the pot mum cultivars.

Floral initiation and development are temperature dependent, and inappropriate temperatures during short days will delay floral initiation and development. Plants are typically grown at 72° to 82° F (22° to 28° C) day temperatures and 60° to 62° F (16° to 17° C) night temperatures. The delay of floral induction and early development is common if temperatures are above 85° F (29° C) during the early portion of the short-day period. This problem is known as heat delay; it can be prevented by pulling the black cloth late in the evening as temperatures drop and opening it in the middle of the night to release the heat under the cover. Regardless, the cloth must be left covering the plants for twelve or more hours. It is better to leave the cloth on longer in the cool of the morning versus pulling the cloth at 4:00 P.M. when workers go home. Automated controls allow the opening and closing of black cloths after workers have left.

Plants should be grown in high light, 4,500 to 7,000 f.c. (48 to 75 klux). In low light areas, HID lighting at 175 to 300 f.c. (2 to 3 klux) is commonly used to supplement natural winter days during the long-day vegetative period. The production of high-quality plants requires supplemental HID lighting in northern regions. Even though the time span from planting an unrooted cuttings to the start of short days is only two to six weeks, HID lighting increases quality. HID lighting is rarely used during short days, when it is of little benefit.

Nutrition rates depend not only depend on the stage of growth but also on whether the crop is being grown in beds (200 ppm nitrogen constant liquid fertilizer is frequently used) or in a soilless substrate in pots (250 to 400 ppm nitrogen is used). As soon as the cuttings are rooted, fertilization commences and continues until the flowers are in color; fertilization ceases prior to harvest for optimum postharvest life. During the last third of the production period, fertilizer levels can be reduced because vegetative growth is almost completed and only flower development is occurring. A wide range of media have been successfully used with pH ranging from 5.7 to 6.2.

For cut flowers and potted flowering plants, cuttings are usually pinched, and the time span from planting a rooted cutting to pinching varies from winter to summer.

Potted and cut chrysanthemum cultivars are frequently classified as having a disbud or spray inflorescence. If disbudded, all subtending axillary buds are removed as soon as they can be handled by the employees, leaving only the apical or terminal bud to develop into one large flower. If a spray inflorescence is desired, only the apical flower bud is removed, breaking apical dominance and allowing all the subtending axillary flowers to develop. This results in a full inflorescence with all flowers opening at the same time; if the older terminal bud is not removed, it will reach anthesis before the axillary flowers open. The terminal bud is removed when the buds develop some pigmentation.

Diseases

Cuttings from cultured-indexed stock plants and the use of pasteurized, well-drained media have eliminated most diseases. *Pythium, Rhizoctonia,* and *Sclerotinia* stem rots can occur. *Botrytis* on foliage and flowers can also occur if moisture and humidity are excessive and air movement is low. Fusarium wilt (*Fusarium oxysporum* f. sp. *chrysanthemi* and *F. oxysporum* f. sp. *tracheiphilum*), bacterial leaf spot and flower blight (*Pseudomonas cichorii*), white rust (*Puccinia horiana*), brown rust (*Puccinia tanaceti*), and tomato spotted wilt virus can be found on chrysanthemums. A number of other diseases have been reported, including verticillium wilt (*Verticillium dahliae*), ray blight (*Didymella ligulicola*), ray speck (*Stemphylium lycopersici*), sclerotinia rot (*Sclerotinia sclerotiorum*), powdery mildew (*Erysiphe cichoracearum*), septoria leaf spot (*Septoria chrysanthemi*), bacterial blight (*Erwinia chrysanthemi*), hollow stem (*Erwinia carotovora*), crown gall (*Agrobacterium tumefaciens*), and aster yellows.

Disorders

Crown buds form even under long days after a certain number of leaves develop on a shoot or a certain number of cuttings are removed from a stock plant. These crown buds differ from true flower buds and do not develop normally. Frequently, crown buds are removed and discarded at a pinch. However, if single-stem plants are grown, crown buds may appear. Crown buds may also form when flower initiation occurs under short days, but the correct conditions for further flower development are not present—that is, day length is too long or the temperature is too high. Regardless of the cause, vegetative shoots frequently develop below the crown buds. Low levels of ethylene have also been known to halt bud development and encourage vegetative bypass shoots.

Postharvest

Rooted cuttings of some cultivars can be stored at 32° to 37° F (0° to 3° C) for four to six weeks, whereas other cultivars can be stored for only one week. The variation among cultivars was related to carbohydrate status. Light intensity of 67 f.c. (721 lux) from cool white fluorescent lamps during cold storage improved cutting quality, regardless of the cultivar. Unrooted cuttings were stored successfully at close to 32° F (0° C) for up to three weeks if the cuttings came from stock plants that were fertilized with 100 to 200 ppm nitrogen. If stock plants received only low nitrogen levels (50 ppm), the number and length of roots on the cuttings were lower after three weeks' storage.

While some considered the chrysanthemum to be sensitive to ethylene, others noted that potted chrysanthemums were among the few species completely insensitive to ethylene. Treatment of cuttings with the antiethylene agent 1-MCP (EthylBloc) reduced rooting.

References

Accati-Garibaldi, E., A. M. Kofranek, and R. M. Sachs. 1977. Relative efficiency of fluorescent and incandescent lamps in inhibiting flower induction in *Chrysanthemum morifolium* 'Albatross.' *Acta Horticulturae* 68:51–58.

Anderson, N. O., and P. D. Ascher. 2001. Selection of day-neutral, heat-delay-insensitive *Dendranthema x grandiflora* genotypes. *Journal of the American Society for Horticultural Science* 126:710–721.

Barrett, J. E., M. E. Peacock, and T. A. Nell. 1986. Height control of exacum and chrysanthemum with paclobutrazol, XE-1019, flurprimidol and RSW-0411. *Proceedings of the Florida State Horticultural Society* 99:254–255.

Berghage, R. D., J. E. Erwin, and R. D. Heins. 1991. Photoperiod influences leaf chlorophyll content in chrysanthemum grown with negative DIF temperature regime. *HortScience* 26:708. (Abstract)

Borowski, E., P. Hagen, and R. Moe. 1981. Stock plant irradiation and rooting of chrysanthemum cuttings in light or dark. *Scientia Horticulturae* 15:245–253.

Cockshull, K. E. 1985. *Chrysanthemum morifolium*, pp. 238–257. In: *Handbook of Flowering*, vol. II, A. H. Halevy, ed. CRC Press, Boca Raton, Florida.

Cockshull, K. E., and A. M. Kofranek. 1985. Long-day flower initiation by chrysanthemum. *HortScience* 20:296–298.

Daughtrey, M., and A. R. Chase. 1992. Chrysanthemum, pp. 30–39. In: *Ball Field Guide to Diseases of Greenhouse Ornamentals*. Ball Publishing, Batavia, Illinois.

DeRuiter, H. A. 1993. Improving cutting quality in chrysanthemum by stock plant management. *Scientia Horticulturae* 56:43–50.

Dreistadt, S. H. 2001. *Integrated Pest Management for Floriculture and Nurseries*. University of California Division of Agriculture and Natural Resources Publication 3402. Oakland, California.

Druge, U., S. Zerche, R. Kadner, and M. Ernst. 2000. Relation between nitrogen status, carbohydrate distribution and subsequent rooting of chrysanthemum cuttings as affected by pre-harvest nitrogen supply and cold-storage. *Annals of Botany* 85:687–701.

Hicklenton, P. R. 1984. Response of pot chrysanthemum to supplemental irradiation during rooting, long day, and short day production stages. *Journal of the American Society for Horticultural Science* 109:468–472.

Hicklenton, P. R. 1985. Influence of different levels of timing of supplemental irradiation on pot chrysanthemum production. *HortScience* 20:374–376.

Higgins, E. 2001. Chrysanthemums, pp. 68–70. In: *Tips on Regulating Growth of Floriculture Crops*, M. L. Gaston, L. A. Kunkle, P. S. Konjoian, and M. F. Wilt, eds. Ohio Florists' Association Services, Columbus, Ohio.

Kadner, R., and S. Zerche. 1997. Influence of differential nitrogen supply from mother plants on capability for storage and rooting of chrysanthemum cuttings (*Dendranthema grandiflorum* hybrids). *Gartenbauwissenschaft* 62:184–189.

Karlsson, M. G., R. D. Heins, J. E. Erwin, R. D. Berghage, W. H. Carlson, and J. A. Biernbaum. 1989a. Temperature and photosynthetic photon flux influence chrysanthemum shoot development and flower initiation under short day conditions. *Journal of the American Society for Horticultural Science* 114:158–163.

Karlsson, M. G., R. D. Heins, J. E. Erwin, and R. D. Berghage. 1989b. Development rate during four phases of chrysanthemum growth as determined by preceding and prevailing temperatures. *Journal of the American Society for Horticultural Sciences* 114:234–240.

Mastalerz, J. W. 1977. Duration of irradiation, pp. 221–270. In: *The Greenhouse Environment*. John Wiley and Sons, New York.

Nell, T. A. 1993. *Dendranthema grandiflora*, pp. 35–38. In: *Flowering Potted Plants, Prolonging Shelf Performance*. Ball Publishing, Batavia, Illinois.

Rajapakse, N. C., W. B. Miller, and J. W. Kelly. 1996. Low temperature storage of rooted chrysanthemum cuttings: Relationship to carbohydrate status of cultivars. *Journal of the American Society for Horticultural Science* 121:740–745.

Rajapakse, N. C., D. W. Reed, and J. W. Kelly. 1989. Effects of pre-treatments on transpiration of *Chrysanthemum morifolium* in the dark. *HortScience* 24:998–1,000.

Sachs, R. M., and A. M. Kofranek. 1979. Radiant energy required for the night break inhibition of floral initiation as a function of day time light input in *Chrysanthemum x morifolium* Ramat. *HortScience* 25:609–610.

Serek, M., A. Prabucki, E. C. Sisler, and A. S. Anderson. Inhibitors of ethylene action affect final quality and rooting of cuttings before and after storage. *HortScience* 33:153–155.

Whealy, C. A., T. A. Nell, J. E. Barrett, and R. A. Larson. 1987. High temperature effects on growth and floral development of chrysanthemum. *Journal of the American Society for Horticultural Science* 112:464–468.

Wilfret, G. J. 1991. Effect of growth regulators on potted chrysanthemums. *Proceedings of the Florida State Horticultural Society.* 104:314–316.

Clerodendrum

Clerodendrum thomsoniae variegatum.

Common name: Clerodendrum, tropical bleeding heart, glory bower.
Scientific name: *Clerodendrum paniculatum, C.* x *speciosum, C. thomsoniae,* and *C. ugandense.*
Family: Verbenaceae.
Other propagation methods: Air layering, root cuttings.

Description, Uses, and Status

Of the clerodendrum species listed, *C. thomsoniae* has been cultivated for many years and is the most common. This vigorous twining evergreen shrub is a prized flowering specimen with large ovate shiny green leaves 5 in. (13 cm) long. The inflorescence consists of flowers with a pure white calyx, a crimson corolla, and long curved stamens. With age, the calyx turns from white to pink or purple. Forms with variegated foliage are available. In recent years *C. paniculatum* and *C.* x *speciosum* have been gaining in popularity. Both types have a red calyx and corolla, and the plants are less vigorous than *C. thomsoniae*. *C. paniculatum* has very large inflorescences. *C. ugandense* has also been used in floriculture because of its unusual flowers: the corolla has three pale blue lobes and one violet-blue lobe; the calyx is crimson, the filaments purple, and the anthers blue. Clerodendrums are spectacular potted or hanging basket plants when in flower, and they are especially popular in conservatories because of their beautiful floral displays.

Flowering Control and Dormancy

Both *C. thomsoniae* and *C.* x *speciosum* can be made to flower year-round with day-length control. In *C. thomsoniae* flower initiation may be independent of day length, but flower development is favored by short days. In *C.* x *speciosum* short days also promote flowering, and long days promote vegetative growth. For both species, once an inflorescence is initiated, the terminal growing point ceases growth and becomes dormant. Terminal growth commences again only when the flowers senesce. Renewed terminal growth is always vegetative, regardless of day length, light level, or temperature. Hence, flowering will subsequently occur on axillary shoots. Normally, five or six axillary flowering shoots form. *C. ugandense* is day-neutral, and temperature does not effect flower initiation. Flower induction occurs after six or seven leaf pairs have formed on a shoot. *C. paniculatum* is a long day plant with a critical night length of less than twelve hours.

Stock Plant Management

Large containers greater than 6 in. (15 cm) should be used. Internode growth should be managed by repeated pinching and routine trimming of shoots. Keep *C. paniculatum* stock plants under short days to prevent flowering.

Cutting Harvest

Commercial propagation of *C. thomsoniae* and *C.* x *speciosum* is by single-node cuttings; terminal cuttings can be used if the tissue is sufficiently hardened before propagation. Uniform propagation of *C. ugandense* is by terminal cuttings with two nodes; stem cuttings produced thin axillary shoots. *C. paniculatum* is also propagated by terminal cuttings.

Propagation

The recommended temperatures for propagation range from 70° to 75° F (21° to 24° C) for the substrate and 68° to 77° F (20° to 25° C) for the air. No rooting hormones are needed, and two to five cuttings are placed in a 2.75 to 4 in. (7 to 10 cm) pot. Rooting can occur within three to five weeks under propagation tents or mist. Plants should be slowly acclimated.

Plant Growth Regulators

Numerous attempts have been made to control internode elongation, since clerodendrons are vigorously growing vines. For *C. thomsoniae,* ancymidol (A-Rest) sprays at 100 to 750 ppm and drenches at 0.5 to 1.0 mg a.i. per pot are effective. Paclobutrazol (Bonzi) sprays at 100 to 200 ppm and drenches at 100 ppm or 0.5 to 1.0 mg a.i. per pot can also be used. Paclobutrazol must be used to control internode elongation in *C. ugandense,* with 5 to 15 mg a.i./pot required. Day and night temperature difference (DIF and DROP) are effective (see chapter 8 for more information). No information is available on vine control of *C. paniculatum.*

Production and Schedule

Rapid growth of *C. thomsoniae* and *C. ugandense* does not occur at temperatures below 64° F (18° C), and plants can shed their leaves and go dormant. Growing temperatures commonly used for *C. thomsoniae* range from 68° to 77° F (20° to 25° C) during days and 64° to 68° F (18° to 20° C) during nights.

All commercially important species require full light; the higher the light intensities the better. When light intensity decreases, the number of flowers decrease. High soluble salts can injure roots, and iron deficiencies can occur if a substrate pH of 5.5 to 6.5 is not maintained. Generally, 100 ppm nitrogen can be used.

Roughly nine to eleven nodes of *C. x speciosum* must develop before flowering occurs. For example, if a shoot is pruned to seven nodes, three additional nodes on the axillary shoot must develop before flowering; if it is pruned to five nodes, six to seven nodes on the axillary shoot must develop; and if it is pruned to two to three nodes, eight nodes on the axillary shoot must develop.

Propagation of *C. thomsoniae* and *C. ugandense* in northern Europe commences in January and continues into spring. Five months are required for production when these species are propagated in January. The main season for rapid growth and flowering is the spring for summer sales. *C. paniculatum* plants grown at 86° F (30° C) during days and 73° F (23° C) during nights flowered thirty days after the start of long days.

Diseases

Pythium root rot and mildew can be a problem in the winter, when temperatures are low, humidity is high, and routine fungicidal treatments are not used. Leaf spots (*Septoria phylctaenioides* and *Cercospora appii*) have also been noted.

Postharvest

Chilling injury can occur after forty-eight hours at 36° F (2° C).

References

Andersen, A. K., T. Wingreen, and L. Andersen. 1993. *Clerodendrum ugandense* Prain. propagation, retardation and post-production performance as an indoor potted plant. *Acta Horticulturae* 337:31–42.

Adriansen, E. 1980. The effect of day length and method of ancymidol application on growth and flowering of *Clerodendrum thomsoniae* Balif. *Tidsskrift for Planteavl* 84:399–413. (in Danish)

Anonymous. Undated. *Clerodendrum thomsoniae. Proceedings from Production of New Ornamental Plants.* Bavarian State Institute for Wine and Horticulture, Veitshochheim, Germany.

Alvensleben, R. V., and M. Steffens. 1989. *Clerodendrum thomsoniae. Gärtnerbörse und Gartenwelt* 50:2445–2447. (in German)

Beck, G. E. 1975. Preliminary suggestions for the culture and production of clerodendrum. *Ohio Florists' Association Bulletin* 547:6–7.

Delaune, A. 2005. *Aspects of production for Clerodendrum as potted flowering plants.* M.S. thesis, Louisiana State University, Baton Rouge, Louisiana.

Dipner, M. 1973. *Clerodendron thomsoniae. Gärtner Meistner* 81:97. (in German)

Hildrum, H. 1972. New pot plant. *New York State Flower Industry Bulletin* 29.

Horst, R. K. 1990. Clerodendrum, p. 605. In: *Westcott's Plant Disease Handbook,* 5th ed. Van Nostrand Reinhold, New York.

Sanderson, K. C., W. C. Martin Jr., and J. McGuire. 1990. New application methods for growth retardants to media for production of *Clerodendrum. HortScience* 25:125.

Shillo, R., and R. Engel. 1985. *Clerodendrum speciosum,* pp. 302–307. In: *Handbook of Flowering,* vol. II, A. H. Halevy, ed. CRC Press, Boca Raton, Florida.

Strömme, E., and H. Hildrum. 1985. *Clerodendrum thomsoniae,* pp. 299–301. In: *Handbook of*

Flowering, vol. II, A. H. Halevy, ed. CRC Press, Boca Raton, Florida.

Tandler, J., A. Borochov, and A. H. Halevy. 1989. Chilling effects on clerodendrum: interactions of water balance and ethylene. *Acta Horticulturae* 261:333–336.

von Hentig, W.-U. 1987. *Clerodendrum thomsoniae,* p. C3. In: *KulturKartei Zierpflanzenbau.* Verlay Parey, Berlin and Hamburg. (in German)

Crossandra

'Orange Marmalade' crossandra.

Common name: Firecracker flower, flame flower, crossandra.
Scientific name: *Crossandra infundibuliformis.*
Family: Acanthaceae.
Other propagation methods: Seed.

Description, Uses, and Status
Crossandra is grown not only for its orange, yellow, red, salmon, or pink flowers, but also for its smooth dark green foliage. The glossy gardenia-like leaves are opposite and 2 to 5 in. (5 to 13 cm) long. The flowers overlap each another to form a dense erect inflorescence. Each individual flower is a corolla composed of a slender tube that flares and forms a 1.5 in. (4 cm) wide lip with five rounded lobes. Plants can grow to 36 in. (90 cm) tall. Though a minor crop, it is an excellent plant for added variety during major spring holidays, and for large container gardens and baskets. Crossandra is used mainly as a 4 to 5 in. (10 to 13 cm) pot plant, but it can also be grown in larger pot sizes or as a bedding plant.

Flowering Control and Dormancy
Once the plant is rooted, high nutrition, warm temperatures, and the long days of summer are conducive to flowering. Plants will typically not flower if grown at light levels less than 1,800 f.c. (19 klux). Crossandra is not photoperiodic.

Stock Plant Management
Maintain actively growing stock plants at relatively low light levels to prevent flowering.

Cutting Harvest
Terminal cuttings 1 to 2 in. (2.5 to 5 cm) long with at least one mature leaf are used.

Propagation
Terminal cuttings root in four to five weeks with a rooting hormone, 3,000 ppm IBA, when propagated directly into 2.5 in. (7 cm) pots or cell packs. Use one cutting per cell. The substrate should have a pH of 5.8 to 6.2 and a temperature of 70° to 75° F (21° to 24° C). The air temperatures should be 75 to 85° F (24° to 29° C) during days and 68° to 70° F (20° to 21° C) during nights. Light intensity is reduced to 1,500 to 1,800 f.c. (16 to 19 klux). Remove any flower and buds during propagation. To prevent cuttings from stretching during propagation, daminozide (B-Nine) sprays at 3,000 ppm or chlormequat (Cycocel) sprays at 1,000 ppm can be applied. Apply 175 ppm nitrogen once per week starting with the second week of propagation. Propagation is easier and faster under white plastic tents in the summer or clear plastic in the winter.

Plant Growth Regulators
The most common plant growth retardant is

daminozide applied as a 1,500 to 3,000 ppm spray. Chlormequat at 1,000 ppm can also be used.

Production and Schedule

In Europe the optimum air temperatures have proved to be 66° F (19°C) during the day and 55° F (13° C) at night, and the optimum substrate temperature 72° F (22° C). A low forcing temperature was better when light intensities were low and high plant quality was desired. In the United States temperature recommendations are 78° to 82° F (26° to 28° C) during the day and 70° F (21° C) at night for six weeks after propagation, then switching to 75° F (24° C) during the day and 65° F (18° C) at night.

The recommended light intensity during production is 3,000 to 3,500 f.c. (32 to 38 klux). Growth is adequate between 2,600 and 3,000 f.c. (28 to 32 klux). Below 1,800 f.c. (19 klux) growth is slow and plants will not flower.

Do not overwater plants, because the roots are susceptible to *Rhizoctonia*; however, do not water-stress the plants, or the leaves will burn. A constant liquid fertilizer of 200 ppm nitrogen from a complete fertilizer is recommended. Any substrate with good water-holding capacity, good drainage, and a pH of 6.2 to 7.0 is acceptable.

One rooted cutting is used per 4 in. (10 cm) pots and one or three cuttings is used per 6 in. (15 cm) pot. Plants should be pinched three weeks after final potting, allowing five or six leaves to remain on the plant. Six to seven weeks are required to produce a liner from a rooted cutting and twelve to fourteen weeks are required for production of a finished plant from liners. In warm climates only ten to eleven weeks may be required for plants in 4 in. (10 cm) pots. If three cuttings are used per 6 in. (15 cm) pot, the plants can remain unpinched for a faster crop time.

Diseases

Rhizoctonia and *Thielaviopsis,* or black root rot, can be problems during and after propagation. Liners purchased from specialists should not be planted too deep, because *Rhizoctonia* and *Pythium* can develop.

Disorders

Cold stress occurs at temperatures below 50° F (10° C), and plants will be injured and die. Leaves will turn black and fall off. Lack of flowering can occur if plants are subjected to light levels below 1,800 f.c. (19 klux), low production temperatures, or low nutrition. Premature flowering can be due to high light or insufficient nutrition.

Postharvest

At low temperatures of 40° F (4° C) the leaves turn black.

References

Christensen, O. V. 1975. The influence of low temperature on flowering of *Beloperone, Crossandra, Jacobinia* and *Mackaya. Tidsskrift for Planteavl* 79:459–462. (in Danish)

Daughtrey, M., and A. R. Chase. 1992. Crossandra, p. 49. In: *Ball Field Guide to Diseases of Greenhouse Ornamentals.* Ball Publishing, Batavia, Illinois.

Harthun, E. 1991. Crossandra, pp. 474–475. In: *Ball RedBook,* 15th ed., V. Ball, ed. Ball Publishing, West Chicago, Illinois.

Langefeld, J. 1991. Crossandra, pp. 63–65. In: *GrowerTalks on Crop Culture,* D. Hamrick, ed. Ball Publishing, Batavia, Illinois.

Moes, E. 1976. Temperature for *Crossandra. Gartner Tidende* 11:163–164. (in Danish)

Nell, T. A. 1993. Crossandra, pp. 31–32. In: *Flowering Potted Plants: Prolonging Shelf Performances.* Ball Publishing, Batavia, Illinois.

Paul Ecke Ranch. 2005. Crossandra. *GMPro* 25(10):4.

Cuphea

Common name: Cuphea, Mexican heather, bat-faced cuphea.
Scientific name: *Cuphea hyssopifolia, C. llavea, C. micropetala.*
Family: Lythraceae.

Description, Uses, and Status

Numerous cuphea species are now available; most have small, narrow tubular flowers that flare open at the end. Some species have small attractive glossy elliptical leaves. Two species commonly propagated by cuttings are *C. hyssopifola,* Mexican heather, and *C. llavea,* bat-faced cuphea. Mexican heather has numerous small lavender flowers that cover the 12 to 24 in.

(30 to 60 cm) tall plants. Bat-faced cuphea has green tubular flowers adorned with two scarlet petals and a dark throat on 18 to 24 in. (45 to 60 cm) tall plants. Numerous other species and hybrids are available, many of which are seed propagated, but even those can also be cutting propagated. Most cupheas are tender perennials that are not frost tolerant; they are sold in the spring in pots or hanging baskets.

Flowering Control and Dormancy
The majority of cupheas grown commercially are day-neutral and flower faster in response to high light conditions. *C. micropetala* is a short-day plant.

Stock Plant Management
Maintain good air movement around plants to prevent edema during winter. Do not apply ethephon (Florel) to *C. hyssopifolia* stock plants because they are extremely sensitive to it and will defoliate if sprayed at concentrations as low as 100 ppm.

Cutting Harvest
Terminal cuttings 0.8 to 1.5 in. (2 to 4 cm) long with at least one fully expanded leaf are used.

Propagation
Cuttings rooted in ten to fourteen days at 70° to 75° F (21° to 24° C). Rooting hormones are not required.

Plant Growth Regulators
None are required, but daminozide (B-Nine) sprays at 1,250 to 2,500 ppm or paclobutrazol (Bonzi) at 1 to 5 ppm can be used if needed.

Production and Schedule
Grow cupheas at temperatures of 68° to 75° F (20° to 24° C) during days and 60° to 65° F (16° to 18° C) during nights. Allow plants to dry between irrigations. Use a substrate with a pH of 5.8 to 6.3, and supply 5,000 to 9,000 f.c. (54 to 97 klux) light. Maintain uniform moisture, and do not water-stress the plants, or leaf drop will occur. Fertilize with 100 to 150 ppm nitrogen at every other irrigation. Minimize the amount of ammonium applied because it can produce excessively large leaves prone to marginal necrosis. Since cupheas are sensitive to high soluble salts, leach with clear water periodically to maintain substrate EC.

One rooted cutting and no pinch is used with 4 and 5 in. (10 and 13 cm) pots, one or two rooted cuttings and one pinch with 6 in. (15 cm) pots, and two to four cuttings and one to two pinches with hanging

Cuphea hyssopifolia stock plant.

baskets. Plants are pinched or sheared ten to fourteen days after planting. In the winter 4 in. (10 cm) pots are ready to sell in seven to nine weeks, 5 in. (13 cm) pots in eight to ten weeks, 6 in. (15 cm) pots in nine to ten weeks, 8 in. (20 cm) hanging baskets in ten to twelve weeks, and 10 in. (25 cm) hanging baskets in twelve to fourteen weeks. The crop finishes two to four weeks earlier in the spring.

Diseases
Botrytis, Cylindrocladium, Phytophthora, Pythium, and *Rhizoctonia* can be problems.

Disorders
Plants may collapse suddenly from a variety of causes including root rot, stem canker, overwatering, and high soluble salts. Delayed flowering may be due to excessive ammonia or low light levels, especially in combination with high fertilizer levels or overwatering. *C. llavea* can be especially sensitive to edema during cool production months.

References
Hamrick, D. 2003. *Cuphea,* pp. 323–334. In: *Ball RedBook,* 17th ed., vol. 2, D. Hamrick, ed. Ball Publishing, Batavia, Illinois.

Schoellhorn, R. 2002. Cuphea—the heather that isn't. *GPN* 12(4):88, 90, 92.

Dahlia

Common name: Dahlia.
Scientific name: *Dahlia* hybrids.
Family: Compositae.
Other propagation methods: Seed, division, tissue culture.

'Gallery Art Fair' bedding dahlia.

Description, Uses, and Status
The flowers come in white and shades of yellow, orange, red, and purple in solids as well as bicolored and multicolored patterns. Plants vary in height from 12 in. (30 cm) dwarfs to more than 6 ft. (1.8 m) tall. The stems are hollow; the leaves are opposite and whorled to pinnate. Flower morphology is complex, and flower size varies from larger than 8.25 in. (21 cm) to less than 4 in. (10 cm) in diameter. Dahlias are used as bedding plants, garden specimens, cut flowers, and occasionally potted flowering plants.

Flowering Control and Dormancy
Flowering and tuber formation are both influenced by temperature and photoperiod. If plants are kept under thirteen to fourteen hours of light at 59° F (15° C), they will continuously flower. Most dahlia cultivars flower under a twelve- to fourteen-hour photoperiod. Dahlia is classified as a facultative short-day plant, but note that short days will also cause tuber formation, which is induced by eleven- to twelve-hour days. Once flowers are initiated, floral development is slowed under long photoperiods. The optimal temperature is 61° to 70° F (16° to 21° C).

Stock Plant Management
Stock plants for bedding plant cultivars are typically started from cuttings and maintained under long days to prevent tuber formation. Stock plants for the large-flowered cutting or garden ornamental cultivars can be harvested from disease-free tuberous roots that have been stored at 48° F (9° C) over winter and greenhouse-forced at 55° to 59° F (13° to 15° C) for two to three weeks in February and March. Temperatures are increased to 68° to 79° F (20° to 26° C) for rapid shoot elongation.

Cutting Harvest
Two- to three-node terminal cuttings are used.

Propagation
Stick the cuttings in a well-drained rooting substrate with a pH of 5.8 to 6.2; the substrate temperature should be maintained at 65° F (18° C), and the air temperature at 65° to 70° F (18° to 21° C). Cuttings should be stuck within one or two hours after harvest or arrival; if the cuttings are not stuck within that time frame, they can be held at 42° F (6° C) overnight. Stick ends of the cuttings 0.5 in. (1.3 cm) below the substrate surface so that the leaf canopy touches the substrate. Use 500 to 2,500 ppm IBA to speed rooting and increase uniformity. Provide long days, and mist only enough to keep the cuttings from wilting. Reduce the mist as soon as feasible, usually within four to six days, to prevent diseases. The cuttings should be rooted in three weeks.

Plant Growth Regulators
Numerous chemicals are effective on bedding cultivars, including sprays of ancymidol (A-Rest) at 15 to 26 ppm, daminozide (B-Nine) at 2,500 to 3,500 ppm, paclobutrazol (Bonzi) at 15 to 45 ppm, chlormequat (Cycocel) at 800 to 1,500 ppm, and uniconazole (Sumagic) at 10 to 20 ppm. For potted plants, the following are recommended rates per 6 in. (15 cm) pot: ancymidol at 0.25 to 0.5 mg a.i. (2 to 4 ppm), paclobutrazol at 2 to 4 mg a.i., and uniconazole at 0.25 to 0.5 mg a.i. Day and night temperature difference (DIF) has little to no effect on dahlia.

Production and Schedule
The optimal temperature range for vegetative shoot development is 55° to 77° F (13° to 25° C). Flower initiation and development rates, however, are opti-

mum at 50° to 59° F (10° to 15° C). Cutting-propagated types for potted or bedding plants are grown at 65° to 70° F (18° to 21° C) during days and 63° to 65° F (17° to 18° C) during nights. The shortening days of fall result in tuber formation, and frosts terminate the growth cycle.

Use one rooted cutting per 4 to 6 in. (10 to 15 cm) pot, three cuttings per 10 in. (25 cm) pot or basket, and five cuttings per 12 in. (30 cm) pot or basket. Plants in 4 to 6 in. (10 to 15 cm) pots should be ready to market in six to eight weeks, and those in larger containers in eight to twelve weeks.

Maximum light of 4,500 to 6,000 f.c. (48 to 65 klux) is required during all phases of growth, and fourteen hours of supplemental high intensity discharge (HID) lighting at 400 f.c. (4 klux) may be useful for the first six weeks during winter and early spring. Greenhouse shading should be used only to reduce the temperature in midsummer. Most cultivars flower with a twelve- to fourteen-hour photoperiod. Low light intensities delay the onset of flowering and reduce the number of flowers.

Plants must be kept moist, but not wet. For pot plant production, a standard 200 ppm nitrogen application with each watering is adequate. Any substrate for potted plants should be well drained, have a pH of 7.0, and not contain more than one-third peat.

For potted plants, pinching is usually practiced when one dominant shoot develops. Leave three or four nodes on the shoot so that two to four new axillary shoots will develop. Disbudding the terminal flower should only be done if flowering is too advanced for the planned marketing date. This step will force the axillary flowers to develop.

Diseases

Tomato spotted wilt virus has been reported in dahlias. Plants are also susceptible to *Botrytis,* aster yellows, powdery mildew (*Erysiphe cichoracearum*), bacterial soft rot (*Erwinia carotovora*), and root and stem rots (*Pythium, Rhizoctonia solani, Sclerotinia sclerotiorum*).

Disorders

Flower abortion and blind terminal meristems can occur; they are usually caused by inappropriate temperature or photoperiod for the cultivar.

Postharvest

Cuttings are cold sensitive; temperatures less than 41° F (5° C) can cause cold damage.

References

Brøndum, J. J., and R. D. Heins. 1993. Modeling temperature and photoperiod effects on growth and development of dahlia. *Journal of the American Society for Horticultural Science* 118:36–42.

De Hertogh, A. A. 1996. *Dahlia*—Potted Plants, pp. C47–58. In: *Holland Bulb Forcers' Guide,* 5th ed. International Flower Bulb Centre, Hillegom, The Netherlands.

De Hertogh, A. A., and M. Leonard, 1993. *Dahlia,* pp. 273–283. In: *The Physiology of Flower Bulbs.* Elsevier, Amsterdam.

Horst, R. K. 1990. Dahlia, p. 618. In: *Westcott's Plant Disease Handbook,* 5th ed. Van Nostrand Reinhold, New York.

Humm, B. 1999. Trendy dwarf dahlias. *Grower Talks* 63(6):33–34.

Moser, B. C., and C. E. Hess. 1968. The physiology of tuberous root development in *Dahlia. Proceedings of the American Society for Horticultural Science* 93:595–603.

Rünger, W., and K. E. Cockshull. 1985. *Dahlia,* pp. 414–418. In: *Handbook of Flowering,* vol. II, A.H. Halevy, ed. CRC Press, Boca Raton, Florida.

Warner, R. M., and J. E. Erwin. 2001. Temperature, pp. 10–17. In: *Tips on Regulating Growth of Floriculture Crops,* M. L. Gaston, L. A. Kunkle, P. S. Konjoian, and M. F. Wilt, eds. Ohio Florists' Association Services, Columbus, Ohio.

Whipker, B. E., and P. A. Hammer. 1997. Efficacy of ancymidol, paclobutrazol, and uniconazole on growth of tuberous-rooted dahlias. *HortTechnology* 7:269–273.

Whipker, B. E., R. T. Eddy, and P. A. Hammer. 1995. Chemical growth retardant application to tuberous-rooted dahlias. *HortScience* 30:1007–1008.

Zitter, T. A., M. E. Daughtrey, and J. P. Sanderson. 1989. Tomato spotted wilt virus, pp. 107–112. In: *Vegetable/Horticulture Crops, Fact Sheet P 735.90.* Cornell Cooperative Extension, Ithaca, New York.

Dianthus, Cut

Common name: Carnation, florist carnation.
Scientific name: *Dianthus caryophyllus.*
Family: Caryophyllaceae.
Other propagation methods: Seed, tissue culture.

'Joropo' cut spray carnation.

Description, Uses, and Status

The carnation is one of the world's most popular cut flowers, and hundreds of cultivars are available. The original species has single flowers with five petals and a spice-like fragrance. The miniature, or "spray," carnation is considered to be more similar to the original species' branching habit. Carnations are also grown in a "standard," form with one large flower per stem and no side buds. The most commonly grown cultivars have many petals and come in white, pink, red, purple, yellow, and apricot orange as well as various combinations.

Flowering Control and Dormancy

The modern carnation flowers perpetually under a wide range of photoperiods and climatic conditions. However, the species is classified as a facultative long-day plant because floral induction is more rapid under long-day than short-day conditions. Fewer leaves subtend the flower under long days, while there are more leaves under short days. Floral induction occurs rapidly if the light level is high; if it is low, up to twenty-four to thirty long days are required for floral induction. Shoots become receptive to photoperiod induction when six to eight leaf pairs are formed.

Stock Plant Management

Axillary vegetative shoots differ in the number of leaves that they form prior to floral initiation. Shoots from nodes just below the flower form few leaves prior to flower induction; basipetal shoots form numerous leaves before flowering. This fact is important in selecting cuttings, since basal nodes are superior for producing long stems. Cuttings from stock plants held under short days tend to root better than cuttings harvested from stock plants under long days.

Cutting Harvest

Terminal cuttings that typically have four or five nodes and are 4 to 6 in. (10 to 15 cm) long with a weight of 0.35 oz. (10 g) are harvested. Cuttings can be broken, not cut, from the plant to prevent transfer of pathogens. Until stuck, the cuttings are held in plastic lined boxes, which should remain open to allow air movement.

Sorting of cuttings is important, since thicker shoots grow more slowly after propagation.

Propagation

Cuttings should root in two to four weeks. With plug flats, one cutting is inserted per cell. With the substrate temperature at 60° F (16° C), cuttings will root in approximately three weeks; at 70° F (21° C), they will root in two weeks. NAA speeds rooting. High light is preferred for fast rooting and a high rooting percentage. Cuttings held under long days in propagation tend to root better than cuttings held under short days.

Plant Growth Regulators

None are required.

Production and Schedule

The optimal temperatures for flower production are 55° to 60° F (13° to 16° C) during days and 50° F (10° C) during nights. Flower quality is reduced as temperatures increase above 60° F (16° C) because high temperatures reduce the flower diameter. Cool temperatures and high light levels are a prerequisite for quality cut flowers.

Light intensity determines the rate of floral induction. When light levels are low, floral induction is slow and more leaves are produced; with high light, floral induction is more rapid and stems have fewer leaves at harvest. However, the rate of flower development is not influenced by light irradiance. Low light levels are responsible for weak stems and, consequently, poor quality or low grades, regardless of flower diameter. Greenhouses are never shaded, except to reduce temperatures.

Soluble salts should be checked, since carnation roots are sensitive to high EC; leach the substrate when needed. A fertilizer of 200 ppm nitrogen and potassium is recommended in traditional production. Nitrate nitrogen is favored over ammonium in low light areas to avoid soft winter growth and ammonium toxicity under cold temperatures.

Traditional propagation of carnations uses media suitable for long-term production; they have to have sufficient aeration and drainage because the plants are grown for one to two years. Hydroponic production is more common now, and it uses such substrates as rock wool.

A newly planted rooted cutting can be pinched three to four weeks after the cutting has become established and growth has commenced; four or five pairs of leaves should be left behind. Although four shoots usually develop, some growers allow only three shoots to develop on the inner rows of plants. All or a portion of the resulting shoots can also be pinched five to seven weeks after the first pinch.

With standard carnations, the axillary flower buds are removed as soon as they are large enough to be twisted off. With spray carnations, the apical or dominant flower bud is removed as soon as it is feasible; its removal encourages axillary flower buds to develop uniformly on stems of equal length.

Numerous production schedules have been devised for peak production of flowers for specific holidays. The timing of flower production starts when the rooted cutting is placed on the bench, and the appropriate pinch (or pinches), temperatures, and light intensity and duration are given.

Diseases

Pathogen control starts with purchasing rooted cuttings from a reliable propagator. Systemic diseases such as *Pseudomonas, Corynebacterium,* and *Fusarium* are best controlled by using disease-indexed cuttings, a pasteurized substrate, and strict sanitation.

Alternaria, Botrytis, Phytophthora, Pythium, Rhizoctonia, and various other diseases can be found on the foliage, stems, or flowers. A number of other diseases have been reported, including flower rot (*Sclerotinia sclerotiorum*), root rot (*Armillaria mellea*), southern blight (*Sclerotium rolfsii*), charcoal rot (*Macrophomina phaseolina*), greasy blotch (*Zygophiala jamaicensis*), alternaria blight (*Alternaria dianthi* and *A. dianthicola*), leaf spot (*Septoria dianthi* and *Cladosporium*), powdery mildew (*Oidium dianthi*), downy mildew (*Peronospora dianthicola*), phialophora wilt (*Phialophora cinerescens*), calyx rot (*Stemphylium botryosum*), rust (*Uromyces dianthi*), and viruses.

Disorders

Calyx splitting is the most common nonpathogen prob-lem. The calyx develops under rapid growth conditions, such as high temperatures followed by cool temperatures, which are conducive for optimum petal initiation and development. As a result, the calyx splits under mechanical pressure, and individual petals spill out. Uniform night temperatures and reduced variation between day and night temperatures will aid in lessening this problem. Reducing ammonium, using mainly nitrate nitrogen, and applying sufficient boron will also aid in reducing splitting. Cultivars differ widely in the propensity to split, and proper cultivars should be selected. One solution is to place a rubber band or plastic ring around each calyx, which many producers automatically do when axillary buds are removed.

Postharvest

Cuttings can be stored at 31° F (–1° C)—unrooted ones for six months and rooted for four months—though it may delay rooting. Warmer storage temperatures will increase root initiation but reduce the length of time that the cuttings can be stored. For example, at 34° F (2° C) unrooted cuttings can be stored for one month. Carnation cuttings do not appear to be sensitive to ethylene; however, they are sensitive to blackening, which can occur if too many cuttings are placed in each bag and shipped too warm, especially when the cuttings are lined up. Be sure the cuttings are dry, to prevent disease problems during storage.

References

Bunt, A. C., and K. E. Cockshull. 1985. *Dianthus caryophyllus,* pp. 433–440. In: *Handbook of Flowering,* vol. II, A. H. Halevy, ed. CRC Press, Boca Raton, Florida.

Bunt, A. C., M. C. Powell, and D. O. Chanter. 1981. Effects of shoot size, number of continuous light cycles and solar radiation on flower initiation in carnations. *Scientia Horticulturae* 15:267–276.

Dreistadt, S. H. 2001. *Integrated Pest Management for Floriculture and Nurseries.* University of California Division of Agriculture and Natural Resources Publication 3402. Oakland, California.

Garrido, G., E. A. Cano, M. Acosta, and J. Sánchez-Bravo. 1998. Formation and growth of roots in carnation cuttings: influence of cold storage period and auxin treatment. *Scientia Horticulturae* 74:219–231.

Heins, R. D. and H. F. Wilkins. 1977. Influence of photoperiod on 'Improved White Sim' carnation (*Dianthus caryophyllus* L.) branching and flowering. *Acta Horticulturae* 71:69–74.

Heins, R. D., H. F. Wilkins, and W. E. Healy. 1979. The effect of photoperiod on lateral shoot development in

Dianthus caryophyllus L. cv. Improved White Sim. *Journal of the American Society for Horticultural Science* 104:314–319.

Horst, R. K. 1990. Carnation, pp. 580–581. In: *Westcott's Plant Disease Handbook,* 5th ed. Van Nostrand Reinhold, New York.

Huett, D. O. 1994. Production and quality of Sim carnations grown hydroponically in rockwool substrate with nutrient solutions containing different levels of calcium, potassium and ammonium-nitrogen. *Australian Journal of Experimental Agriculture* 34:691–697.

Langhans, R. W. 1961. *Carnations, A Manual of the Culture, Insects and Diseases, and Economics of Carnation.* New York State and County Agricultural Extension Services; New York State Flower Growers Association, Ithaca, New York.

Laurie, A., D. C. Kiplinger, and K. S. Nelson. 1969. Carnation, pp. 262–282. In: *Commercial Flower Forcing.* McGraw-Hill, New York.

Pokony, F. A., and J. R. Kamp. 1965. Influence of photoperiod on the rooting response of cuttings of carnations. *Proceedings of the American Society Horticulture Society* 86:626–630.

Sparnaaij, L. D., and I. Bos. Genetic variation in dry weight of carnation cuttings: Its causes and consequences. *Euphytica* 90:175–181.

van de Pol, P. A., and J. V. M. Vogelezang. 1983. Accelerated rooting of carnation 'Red Baron' by temperature pretreatment. *Acta Horticulturae* 141:181–188.

Whealy, C. A. 1992. Carnations, pp. 45-65. In: *Introduction to Floriculture,* 2nd ed., R. Larson, ed. Academic Press, San Diego, California.

Dianthus, Pot

'Jade' potted carnation.

Common name: Miniature carnation, pot carnation, dwarf carnation.
Scientific name: *Dianthus carthusianorum.*
Family: Caryophyllaceae.
Other propagation methods: Seed, tissue culture.

Description, Uses, and Status

The well-known carnation has almost single flowers to double flowers that come in white, yellow, pink, red, maroon, lavender, or multicolors. Some cultivars are also scented. The pot carnation is a popular potted flowering plant in Europe and to a lesser extent in North America. Occasionally, pot carnations are grown in hanging baskets and as a garden bedding plant.

Flowering Control and Dormancy

Low temperatures of 54° to 59° F (12° to 15° C) promote lateral shoot development, hasten flower initiation, and increase the number of flowering shoots and the number of flower buds per shoot. However, temperatures at or above 64° F (18° C) hasten flower development. Short photoperiods at low temperatures promote vegetative axillary shoot development but delay flower initiation and visible buds. Long days of fourteen hours or more from incandescent lights at low temperatures hasten flower initiation, decrease the number of days to visible buds, and increase the total number of flowering shoots, but the incandescent light increases internode elongation. Development of flower buds is not controlled by photoperiod, but rather by temperatures of 64° F (18° C) or greater.

Stock Plant Management

Maintain actively growing stock plants to provide fresh cuttings.

Cutting Harvest

Terminal cuttings are harvested. Cuttings can be broken rather than cut from the plant to prevent the transfer of pathogens. Until stuck, the cuttings are held in plastic lined boxes, which should remain open to allow air movement.

Propagation

Cuttings can be propagated at 64° to 68° F (18° to 20° C). Only cuttings from disease-indexed sources must be used because carnations are susceptible to a number of diseases. Supplemental lighting of 290 to 380 f.c. (3 to 4 klux) for eighteen to twenty hours can be provided in low light climates. With plug flats, one cutting is inserted per cell.

Plant Growth Regulators

Many of the vegetatively propagated plants grow only 5 to 6 in. (13 to 15 cm) tall and do not require any plant growth regulators. However, drenches of chlormequat (Cycocel) at 5,000 ppm, uniconizole (Sumagic) at 15 ppm, or paclobutrazol (Bonzi) at 15 ppm are effective.

Production and Schedule

For the first five weeks, cutting-propagated plants should be kept at 54° to 59° F (12° to 16° C) for maximum shoot development and initiation, then at 59° to 64° F (16° to 18° C) for rapid floral development. Stock plants, cuttings, and young plants should be kept under short photoperiods for the first five weeks for maximum shoot development, then finished plants are placed under fourteen-hour or longer photoperiods for rapid floral initiation. Full light of 5,000 to 6,000 f.c. (54 to 65 klux) is used; shade only if excessive temperatures occur or to enhance flower color.

Do not allow the substrate to be continuously moist, or plants will have weak stems and grow taller than necessary. Allow the substrate to dry until roots are visible on the edge of the substrate; excessive watering during this time will greatly increase crop time.

A constant liquid fertilizer of 200 ppm nitrogen and potassium is recommended. A well-drained substrate should be used. The crown should remain above the substrate after planting to prevent disease problems.

Plants are pinched once to promote branching. Twelve to fifteen weeks are required from the time of rooting to flowering.

Diseases

Pathogenic control commences with purchasing rooted cuttings from a reliable propagator. Systemic diseases such as *Pseudomonas, Corynebacterium,* and *Fusarium* can best be controlled by using culture-indexed cuttings, a pasteurized substrate, and strict sanitation. *Alternaria, Botrytis, Heterosporium, Rhizoctonia,* and various other diseases can be found on the foliage, stems, or flowers.

Disorders

Poor branching can be due to low light, low nutrition, high temperatures, or insufficient space. Uneven flowering can be caused by low light or high night temperatures. Leaf tip burn can be due to water stress, high soluble salts, or pesticide phytotoxicity.

Postharvest

Rooted cuttings or plugs can be stored for one to two weeks at 33° to 34° F (0.6° to 1° C). Be sure not to let the cuttings become water-stressed.

References

Goldsberry, K. L. 1997. Dwarf carnation, pp. 47–53. In: *Tips on Growing Specialty Potted Crops,* M. L. Gaston, S. A. Carver, C. A. Irwin, and R. A. Larson, eds. Ohio Florists' Association, Columbus, Ohio.

Hasegawa, M. 1997. Tips for dwarf pot carnations. *Greenhouse Product News* 7(4):8–9.

Horst, R. K. 1990. Carnation, pp. 580–581. In: *Westcott's Plant Disease Handbook,* 5th ed. Van Nostrand Reinhold, New York.

Moe, R. 1983. Temperature and daylight responses in *Dianthus carthusianorum* cv. Napoleon III. *Acta Horticulturae* 141:165–171.

Wandås, F. 1989. *Dianthus carthusianorum,* pp. 30–32. In: *Utplanteringsväxter Trädgrd* 314, Swedish University of Agricultural Sciences, Alnarp, Sweden. (in Swedish)

Diascia

Common name: Diascia.
Scientific name: *Diascia* hybrids.
Family: Scrophulariaceae.
Other propagation methods: Seed.

Description, Uses, and Status

These annuals or tender perennials have numerous red, pink, peach, lavender, or white flowers up to 1 in. (2.5 cm) wide. The plants grow to 18 in. (45 cm) tall and have a mounding or trailing habit. They are marketed in pots, hanging baskets, or mixed containers. A cool-season crop, diascia typically grows best during the late winter and spring in warm climates and in the summer in cool climates. However, newer cultivars are increasingly heat tolerant, extending the season into the summer in warm climates. Plants can tolerate temperatures around 20° F (–7° C) in the landscape.

Flowering Control and Dormancy

Diascia is day-neutral.

Stock Plant Management

Work at Clemson University showed that for maximum cutting numbers the initial pinch on the stock plants should occur after six nodes can be left on the plant, and the resulting side shoots should also be pinched when six nodes can be left on the shoots. By contrast, pinching low and allowing only two or four nodes to remain with both pinches reduces the number of cuttings harvested. For example, pinching to two nodes both times produced 63 cuttings per stock plant over the course of the experiment, while pinching to six nodes produced 154 cutting per stock plant, a 144% increase in cuttings. Thus, building the stock plant scaffold is important to future cutting production.

Cutting Harvest

Terminal cuttings 0.8 to 1.5 in. (2 to 4 cm) long with at least one fully expanded leaf are generally used.

Propagation

Stage 1:
Cutting arrival or harvest and sticking
* Rooting hormones are not required. However, either up to 2,500 ppm IBA alone or IBA with

'Sun Chimes Red' diascia flower.

up to 500 ppm NAA can be used.
* Stick two cuttings per cell when using plug flats.

Stage 2: Callusing
* Maintain a substrate temperature of 68° to 75° F (20° to 24° C).
* Maintain air temperatures of 70° to 80° F (21° to 27° C) during days and 65° to 68° F (18° to 20° C) during nights.
* Keep the substrate sufficiently moist so that water is easily squeezed out of it, but not so much that the cutting base is waterlogged. The base of the cutting needs air for proper rooting.
* Maintain a light intensity of 500 to 1,000 f.c. (5 to 11 klux).
* Begin foliar feeding with 50 to 75 ppm nitrogen from 15-0-15 as soon as leaves begin to show any color loss.
* Maintain a substrate pH of 5.5 to 5.8.
* Transfer the cuttings to Stage 3 after five to seven days, once 50% of the cuttings begin differentiating root initials.

Stage 3: Root development
* Maintain substrate temperatures of 68° to 75° F (20° to 24° C).
* Maintain air temperatures of 70° to 80° F (21° to 27° C) during days and 65° to 68° F (18° to 20° C) during nights.
* Begin drying out the substrate once roots are visible.
* Begin increasing the light intensity to 1,000 to 1,500 f.c. (11 to 16 klux) as the cuttings start to root out.

- Fertilize once a week with 100 to 200 ppm nitrogen, alternating between 15-0-15 and 20-10-20, then maintain fertility at 200 ppm nitrogen.
- Roots should develop in nine to fourteen days.

Stage 4: Toning the rooted cutting

- Maintain air temperatures of 68° to 75° F (20° to 24° C) during days and 62° to 65° F (17° to 18° C) during nights.
- Move the liners from the mist area into an area of lower relative humidity.
- Increase the light intensity to 2,000 to 4,000 f.c. (22 to 43 klux).
- Provide shade during the middle of the day to reduce temperature stress.
- Fertilize once at 150 to 200 ppm nitrogen from 15-0-15.
- The cuttings can be toned for seven days.

Plant Growth Regulators

None is generally required if the plants are grown cool. However, a daminozide (B-Nine) spray at 1,500 to 2,500 ppm or a tank-mixed spray of ancymidol (A-Rest) at 4 to 10 ppm and daminozide at 1,250 to 2,500 ppm can be used fourteen to twenty-four days after sticking unrooted cuttings. During production daminozide sprays at 3,000 to 5,000 ppm or ethephon (Florel) sprays at 500 to 1,000 ppm can also be used to control height and maintain shape. Ethephon applications delay flowering, however.

Production and Schedule

Grow the plants at 65° to 75° F (18° to 24° C) during days and 62° to 65° F (17° to 18° C) during nights. Cooler temperatures below 50° F (10° C) can be used to improve plant quality, but production times will increase greatly. Maintain light levels of 5,000 to 8,000 f.c. (54 to 86 klux).

The substrate pH should be maintained at 5.5 to 5.8. Be sure not to bury the crown below the surface of the substrate, since burial increases the likelihood of crown rot. Apply 200 to 250 ppm nitrogen constant liquid fertilization; as with most cool-season crops, use low-ammonium fertilizers. Extra calcium and magnesium are beneficial, especially early in the crop cycle. An application of micronutrients is also recommended. Plants are susceptible to a high EC. Allow plants to dry well between irrigations, since they are susceptible to overwatering.

Use one plant per 4 in. (10 cm) pot, two per 6 in. (15 cm) pot, and three to four per 10 in. (25 cm) basket. Pinch shoots back to the fifth or sixth leaf pair when the roots reach the edge of the substrate, typically three to four weeks after planting the rooted cuttings. Typically, 4 in. (10 cm) pots are not pinched, 6 in. (15 cm) pots are pinched once, and baskets are pinched twice. Instead of pinching manually, ethephon (Florel) sprays at 500 ppm are often applied at planting. Plants in 4 in. (10 cm) pots are ready to sell in four to six weeks, those in 6 in. (15 cm) pots in five to seven weeks, and those in 10 in. (25 cm) baskets in eight to ten weeks.

Diseases

Root and stem rot from *Botrytis, Pythium,* and *Rhizoctonia* can be a problem.

Disorders

Diascia is especially prone to soft, weak growth, which can be due to a wide variety of factors such as low light, warm production temperatures, and excessive ammonium.

Postharvest

Cuttings are susceptible to stem rot if they receive warm temperatures during shipping and storage.

References

Faust, J. E., and L. W. Grimes. 2005. Pinch height of stock plants during scaffold development affects cutting production. *HortScience* 40:650–653.

Hamrick, D. 2003. *Diascia,* pp. 346–348. In: *Ball Redbook,* 17th ed., vol. 2, D. Hamrick, ed. Ball Publishing, Batavia, Illinois.

Schoellhorn, R. 2003. Nemesia and diascia. *GPN* 13(1):36–38.

Starman, T. W., M. C. Robinson, and K. L. Eixmann. 2004. Efficacy of ethephon on vegetative annuals. *HortTechnology* 14:83–87.

Euphorbia

Common name: Poinsettia, Christmas flower, Christmas star, Mexican flameleaf.
Scientific name: *Euphorbia pulcherrima.*
Family: Euphorbiaceae.
Other propagation methods: Seed.

Description, Uses, and Status

Poinsettia is grown for its clusters of large and striking bracts, the center of each containing the small true flowers, known as cyathia. The cyathia are round to elongate, produce small red stamens, and are subtended by nectaries. Poinsettia foliage is medium to dark green in color and ranges in shape from entire to lobed, even on the same plant. Red is the most important bract color. Other colors and color combinations include white, pink, pink with white margins ("marble"), pink with red flecks, red with pink flecks ("jingle bells"), white with red flecks, purple, and yellow. Several varieties are available with green or gray-green foliage variegated with white or cream. Other varieties have bracts that are curled under or otherwise contorted.

This species is the number one potted flowering crop in the United States and is sold for the Christmas holiday season. It is a major crop in Europe and Australia and a relatively minor one in the rest of the world. Poinsettia is also grown as a hanging basket plant and as a cut flower. The species is also common as a landscape shrub in Zone 11.

Flowering Control and Dormancy

Poinsettia is a short-day plant that initiates flowers when the night lasts at least eleven and three-quarters hours. Flower initiation in most parts of North America occurs naturally around September 25, but it can vary from late September to very early October. Some cultivars initiate flowers early in September; they may have a shorter critical night length than most other cultivars. Flower development, however, requires a longer night length than is required for initiation, and it is usually supplied by naturally lengthening nights in the fall. Night temperatures greater than 70° F (21° C) may delay flower initiation. Weeks to flowering from the start of short days vary from six and a half to ten (response group), depending on the cultivar. However, short days should be provided until pollen is present on the cyathia (anthesis) to ensure proper bract development.

'Monet Twilight' potted poinsettia.

Stock Plant Management

Rooted terminal cuttings for stock plants can arrive anytime from late winter through early summer, depending on the individual stock plant program (see table 1). Factors that determine the arrival date of cuttings include the availability of space (for example, after Easter, Mother's Day, or spring bedding plant sales), the number of cuttings desired per stock plant, the production location, and the dates that cuttings are needed. Stock plants are sometimes flowered and sold; if large plants are desired, cuttings should arrive in March to April, and if small plants are desired, cuttings can arrive as late as early June. In areas of high light and warm temperatures, such as the southern United States, cuttings can arrive later than in cooler, lower light areas and still have the same amount of growth. If cuttings arrive before May 5, be sure to provide long days with incandescent lights to prevent premature flower initiation. If cuttings are going to be harvested in September for a fast late crop, provide long days until all the cuttings are harvested. Cuttings harvested from stock plants in September under artificial long days root faster and have more roots than cuttings from stock plants grown under natural days.

For maximum cutting production, allow the original rooted cutting to develop six to ten nodes before the first pinch. Pinching below six nodes forces axillary shoots to develop from axillary buds, which originally developed under the stress of propagation and thus are slow to grow. Leaving more than twelve nodes on the original plant results in too much axillary shoot growth, competition between the shoots, and weak cuttings. Generally nine to eleven nodes should remain on the main stem for optimum cutting production.

TABLE 1
Sample stock plant production schedules.

PROCEDURE	DATE	COMMENTS
Three-pinch program		
Plant rooted cutting	mid-March	Allow two weeks for establishment. Grow in 12 in. (30 cm) pots, which can be spaced at 18 by 18 in. (45 by 45 cm) when foliage from adjacent plants begins to touch.
Pinch first time	April	Leave six nodes on main shoot.
Pinch second time	May	Leave two or three nodes on axillary shoots.
Pinch third time	June	Leave one or two nodes on shoots. Pinch should occur six weeks prior to first cutting harvest.
Begin harvest	July	Allow five weeks between initial and subsequent harvests. Harvest approximately twenty-five cuttings per plant.
Harvest cuttings	August	Harvest approximately thirty cuttings per plant.
Two-pinch program		
Plant rooted cutting	mid-April	Allow two weeks for establishment. Grow in 10 in. (25 cm) pots, which can be spaced at 15 by 15 in. (38 by 38 cm) when foliage from adjacent plants begins to touch.
Pinch first time	May	Leave six nodes on main shoot.
Pinch second time	June	Leave two or three nodes on axillary shoots. Pinch should occur six weeks prior to first cutting harvest.
Begin harvest	July	Allow five weeks between initial and subsequent harvests. Harvest approximately fifteeen cuttings per plant.
Harvest cuttings	August	Harvest approximately twenty-five cuttings per plant.
One-pinch program		
Plant rooted cutting	May	Allow two to five weeks for establishment and growth. Grow in 6½ in. (17 cm) pots, which can be spaced at 12 by 12 in. (30 by 30 cm) when foliage from adjacent plants begins to touch.
Pinch	June	Leave ten nodes on the main shoot. Pinch should occur six weeks prior to first cutting harvest.
Begin harvest	July	Allow five weeks between initial and subsequent harvests. Harvest approximately ten cuttings per plant.
Harvest cuttings	August	Harvest approximately twenty cuttings per plant.

Adapted from *The Ecke Poinsettia Manual* (2004).

If the plants are mature enough, the first pinch can be used as a cutting for another crop of stock plants. Note, however, that such cuttings may form premature flower buds. If stock plants are immature, use a soft pinch with young leaf removal.

After the first pinch, axillary shoots should be pinched or harvested so that only two to three nodes remain on the axillary shoots. If only one node remains, the number of cuttings harvested will not increase in later harvests. If three or more shoots remain, an excessive number of low-quality shoots or cuttings (with small-diameter stems) will develop, and the timing of successive flushes of cuttings will be less predictable. If weekly harvests are conducted, the cutting harvesters should only be concerned with leaving at least one or two nodes on the remaining shoot. Leaving more than two nodes is not a concern because only the large mature cuttings are harvested, and weak cuttings will continue to develop until they are large enough to be harvested. However, avoid harvesting any cuttings with more than eight leaves, since they may split.

Stock plants can also be grown as treelike, or standard, plants. The axillary shoots, which have to be removed to expose the "trunk," are used as propagation material. This system is less efficient for propagation, but it may result in a more valuable stock plant for retail purposes.

Regardless of the system for producing stock plants, growers must produce a quality plant. Stock plants that are nutritionally deficient, insect infested, or otherwise improperly managed will produce low-quality cuttings. Such cuttings will be slow to root, uneven in development, and produce a poor-quality final crop. Stock plants should be given sufficient space to properly develop. Stock plants can be given a final spacing according to when they were started: those begun in March, 18 by 18 in. (45 by 45 cm); April, 15 by 15 in. (38 by 38 cm); May, 12 by 12 in. (30 by 30 cm); and June, 8 by 8 in. (20 by 20 cm). Plants pinched once will produce ten to twenty cuttings per plant, those pinched twice fifteen to twenty-five cuttings per plant, and those pinched three times twenty-five to thirty cuttings per plant. Closely spaced stock plants will not produce the expected number of cuttings per plant; once a foliar canopy forms, only a set number of cuttings will be produced per week. Growers with limited space would be wise to reduce the number of stock plants because only a set amount of cuttings will be produced.

Optimum production temperatures for stock plants are as follows: substrate temperature of 65° to 70° F (18° to 21° C), and air temperatures of 75° to 80° F (24° to 27° C) during days and 68° to 72° F (20° to 22°

C) during nights. The temperature for the maximum rate of leaf unfolding (the rate of growth) of poinsettia axillary shoots after the pinch is approximately 79° F (26° C), with day and night temperatures equally important. Temperatures should not go above 86° F (30° C), or the cuttings will become thin, and branching may be reduced. Reduced light levels and increased air circulation will allow poinsettia stock plants to tolerate warm temperatures. If needed, night temperatures can be reduced to 64° F (18° C); however, cooler temperatures may increase splitting, leaf mottling, and reduced cutting production.

Stock plants can be flowered as a finish crop. Plants should be trimmed and shaped; thinning is necessary since stock plants often have too many shoots to produce attractive specimens. The final cutting back should occur in early to mid-September for plants flowered under natural day lengths. Any weak or severely misshaped plants should be discarded.

Cutting Harvest

Commercial propagation is by terminal stem cuttings. Cuttings should be vigorous, thick with a minimum stem diameter of 0.16 in. (4 mm), and 1.5 to 3 in. (4 to 8 cm) long early in season. Later in the propagation season longer cuttings can be harvested for a shorter crop time. Cuttings are measured from the base of the cutting to the tip of the apex, not to the end of the leaves. Regardless of length, cuttings should be uniform in size and maturity for a uniform finished crop. Cuttings should also have short internodes; a growth retardant can be applied to the stock plants to reduce internode elongation and prevent stretched cuttings later in production. Remove only enough leaves to allow easy insertion of the cuttings into the substrate; be sure that at least one fully mature leaf remains on the cutting. Try to avoid cuttings with very large leaves, since they are more prone to diseases during propagation. European growers often use shorter cuttings than do North American growers.

Growers need to schedule stock plants as any other crop. First, determine the dates that cuttings are needed. Count back five to seven weeks, depending on the cultivar, to determine the date of the last pinch or cutting harvest. The number of weeks between the last pinch and cutting harvest varies with the cultivar; most require six weeks. When immature cuttings are harvested, rooting is slow and uneven. When large stock plants are grown, the first one to two flushes can be timed for major propagations; subsequent cutting production will not be in flushes. Many growers harvest cuttings weekly.

Propagation

Stage 1:
Cutting arrival or harvest and sticking

- Stick cuttings in a substrate with a pH of 5.8 to 6.3.
- Blocks of foam or rock wool are commonly used in commercial cutting propagation. Cuttings can also be directly propagated into the final pot. With plug flats, one cutting is inserted per cell. Avoid compacting the substrate during propagation or watering with a hose because reduced oxygen in the substrate will delay rooting and increase the potential for diseases.
- Use a rooting hormone on the cutting bases. The hormone can be applied as a powder (2,500 ppm IBA) or as a liquid (1,500 ppm IBA plus 500 ppm NAA) using 50% ethanol or isopropyl alcohol and 50% water. A rooting hormone is not required for rooting, but using one speeds rooting and increases uniformity. Also, the use of hormones may induce rooting higher up on the stem, providing more support for the finished plant than with untreated cuttings.
- Do not space cuttings too close together, since that encourages elongation and increases the potential for disease spread. If possible, provide each cutting with 12 sq. in. (77 cm²) of propagation space. Space per cutting may need to be greater for cultivars with large leaves and less for those with small or curled leaves. After propagating a bench of cuttings, be sure that leaves from one cutting are not shading the shoot tip of an adjacent cutting and causing a delay in rooting.
- Store cuttings at 50° to 60° F (10° to 16° C) for up to twenty-four hours if planting is going to be delayed.

Stage 2: Callusing

- Maintain substrate temperatures of 79° to 83° F (26° to 28° C). Temperatures that are too low, below 68° F (20° C), or too high, above 90° F (32° C), will delay rooting and decrease crop uniformity. Inadequate substrate temperature is a common problem in propagation. Even in warm climates, substrate temperature must be monitored since the evaporation of mist during propagation reduces the temperature. Bottom heating is commonly used and will speed rooting if the substrate temperature is less than 75° F (24° C).
- Maintain air temperatures of 76° to 82° F (24° to 28° C) during days and 70° to 74° F (21° to 23° C) during nights. Temperatures below 80° F (27° C) are thought to reduce moisture stress and the poten-

A strip of rooted poinsettia cuttings.

tial for bacterial soft rot. In particular, lower night temperatures of 68° to 70° F (20° to 21° C) for the first three nights may reduce moisture stress.
- Maintain a light intensity of 500 to 1,000 f.c. (5 to 11 klux).
- Begin foliar feeding with 50 to 75 ppm nitrogen from 14-0-14 or 15-0-15 approximately ten days after sticking. Avoid using 20-10-20, which can cause the immature leaves to become hard and reddish; in addition, the phosphorus will encourage stem elongation.
- Transfer the cuttings to Stage 3 in seven to ten days, once 50% of the cuttings begin differentiating root initials.

Stage 3: Root development

- Maintain substrate temperatures of 72° to 79° F (22° to 26° C). Temperatures that are too low, below 68° F (20° C), or too high, above 90° F (32° C), will delay rooting and decrease crop uniformity.
- Maintain air temperatures of 75° to 80° F (24° to 27° C) during days and 68° to 70° F (20° to 21° C) during nights.
- Increase the light intensity to 1,000 to 1,200 f.c. (11 to 13 klux) as the roots of the cuttings begin to develop.
- Increase fertilization to 100 to 200 ppm nitrogen once a week from 14-0-14 alternating with 20-10-20.
- Maintain a substrate pH of 6.2 and EC of 1.0 to 2.0 mS/cm.
- Apply growth retardants (if not previously applied to stock plants) to cuttings if necessary, to reduce stretching. Typically chlormequat (Cycocel) sprays are used at 2,000 ppm or a tank mix of daminozide (B-Nine) at 1,250 ppm and chlormequat at 1,500 ppm is used. Growth retardants may not be needed with short cultivars or if an application has been previously made to the stock plants prior to propagation. Close spacing, high temperatures, low light, and excessive misting increase the need for growth retardants during propagation.

- Roots should develop in ten to fourteen days.

Stage 4: Toning the rooted cutting

- Maintain an air temperature of 72° to 75° F (22° to 24° C).
- Increase the light intensity to 1,500 to 2,000 f.c. (16 to 22 klux) as the cuttings begin to root out. Overly heavy shade resulting in less than 1,000 f.c. (11 klux) will slow rooting and increase stem elongation. The light intensity can be increased to 4,000 f.c. (43 klux) if the cuttings can be fertilized properly and kept free of moisture stress.
- Fertilize once a week with 150 to 200 ppm nitrogen from 14-0-14.
- If the cuttings are to be shipped, apply a foliar fungicide twenty-four hours prior to shipping to prevent *Botrytis* damage during shipping. Precool cuttings at 48° F (9° C) to remove heat from the boxes.

Success with poinsettia propagation depends on several factors. Poinsettias are susceptible to several diseases during propagation. Clean and sterilize propagation benches, utensils, containers, and hands before starting to propagate cuttings. Maintain sanitary conditions throughout propagation. If diseased cuttings are found, promptly remove them to avoid pathogen spread to healthy cuttings.

Cutting turgidity can be maintained with either propagation tents or a mist or fog system. High-humidity tents are generally preferable to misting systems because of reductions in the leaching of nutrients from the leaves, amount of free moisture on the foliage, and disease incidence. Tenting also eliminates the need for a mist or fog system, which can make propagation directly in the final container more feasible. The major drawbacks of tent propagation are heat buildup and the disposal of the plastic. Tenting may not be feasible in areas with high light intensity or temperatures because of heat buildup under the tent. White plastic is preferable to clear plastic in the summer. High-humidity tents may be needed if water quality is poor, especially if the water EC is over 1.0 mS/cm.

When misting, be sure not to overmist, which can reduce oxygen around the base of the cutting, delay rooting, reduce plant quality, leach nutrients from the foliage, and increase disease. Leaves of overmisted cuttings may appear chlorotic with necrotic edges. Misting may be needed at night during the first few days of propagation if the air is warm and dry. The misting frequency can be reduced during cool, cloudy conditions and when the cuttings begin to root. The mist may be turned off completely if day temperatures can be controlled. Similarly, tents are slowly opened and aeration increased to harden the cuttings. Yellowing from nutrient loss can be prevented by applying fertilizer during propagation. Fertilizer may not be needed if the cuttings are not overmisted and if they were propagated from well-fertilized stock plants.

Cuttings can be directly propagated into the final pot, a procedure known as direct sticking. This propagation method is becoming increasingly popular because it saves labor, reduces production costs, decreases production time by approximately one week, and reduces the potential for foliar disease spread due to greater amount of space around each cutting. Direct sticking, however, requires four to eight times more propagation space than using foam or rock wool blocks. Substrate selection is critical; the substrate must allow sufficient air to prevent root rots, and it must retain enough water to prevent excessive wilting and irrigation without becoming waterlogged. Direct-stuck cuttings perform the best when a dibble hole is created in the substrate to provide air around the base of the cutting and to reduce the chance of diseases.

Cuttings should not be watered until roots begin to form, which normally occurs about seven to ten days after sticking. If cuttings are going to be misted, the preplant starter charge of fertilizer will probably be leached from the substrate within two to three weeks. In such cases, one or two applications of 300 to 400 ppm nitrogen may be required. Finally, the large amount of moist substrate will draw fungus gnats (see chapter 10 for details on managing them).

Plant Growth Regulators

Height control options are numerous for poinsettias, including cultural alterations, day and night temperature difference (DIF), and chemicals. Several growth retardants are effective on poinsettias including chlormequat (Cycocel), daminozide (B-Nine), ancymidol (A-Rest), paclobutrazol (Bonzi), uniconazole (Sumagic), and flurprimidol (Topflor). Growth retardants are most commonly applied as sprays early in the season and as drenches late in the season.

Chlormequat is the most frequently used growth retardant; it is typically used at the rate of 1,000 to 1,500 ppm, although up to 3,000 ppm can be used. Daminozide is often tank-mixed with chlormequat. Typical rates are 750 to 2,500 ppm of daminozide and 1,000 to 1,500 ppm of chlormequat. Spray applications of paclobutrazol are typically at 5 to 30 ppm and uniconazole at 2 to 10 ppm in northern climates. In warm climates the spray rates can be increased to 15 to 45 ppm for paclobutrazol and 5 to 10 ppm for uniconazole. Early-season paclobutrazol drenches of 0.25 to 3 ppm or uniconazole drenches of 0.25 to 1 ppm can be used depending on the cultivar; often they produce more reliable results than spray applications. Late-season paclobutrazol or uniconazole drenches can be applied after the start of short days in cool climates or after October 10 to 25 in warm climates. For drenching, ancymidol is applied at 1 to 2 ppm in cool areas and 2 to 4 ppm in warmer climates. The most recent addition to the list of growth regulators is flurprimidol, which can be applied as a spray 2.5 to 40 ppm for naturally compact plants, 10 to 60 ppm for moderately vigorous plants, and 50 to 80 ppm for vigorous cultivars.

DIF is quite effective on poinsettias for height control. Lowering the temperature in the morning (negative DIF) for two to six hours (the longer the better) starting at sunrise (DROP) is also effective in reducing height, and it's more practical than maintaining a low DIF all day.

Production and Schedule

After propagation, the night temperature used for most poinsettia cultivars is 65° to 68° F (18° to 20° C). Temperatures higher than 70° F (21° C) may delay flower initiation, and ones higher than 75° F (24° C) may delay flower development. Temperatures cooler than 60° F (16° C) will slow plant development and decrease bract size. Those below 55° F (10° C) increase the potential for root rot disease.

Temperature and light intensity are related, and photothermal ratio (light energy to thermal energy) expresses this relationship as moles of light per degree-day. A ratio of high light to low temperature enhances stem strength and increases bract area.

High light is necessary for the best growth. For both stock plants and the finished crop, 3,500 to 4,500 f.c. (38 to 48 klux) is used for cultivars with dark foliage, and 5,000 to 6,000 f.c. (54 to 65 klux) is used for other cultivars if greenhouse temperatures can be maintained below 90° F (32° C). For the finished crop no shading is required in most areas immediately after planting. In warm, high light areas, shading for one to two weeks after planting rooted cuttings results in faster plant establishment. Only a slight reduction of light, 10 to 30%, is required, and the shade should be removed as soon as root growth into the substrate is noted. Light levels can be reduced to 2,000 f.c. (22 klux) after bracts are mature, to reduce bract fading and sunburning.

Long days must be provided before May 5 for stock plants or after September 15 for late-season Christmas crop plants to be marketed after December 10. A minimum of 10 f.c. (108 lux) measured at plant height is needed to prevent flower initiation. For early season crops to be marketed prior to Thanksgiving, plants

Growers can use miniature poinsettias to set themselves apart from their competition. Pictured are miniature single-stemmed 'Winter Rose Dark Red'.

may need to be given short days before September 25.

Water stress is a concern during poinsettia production. Plants should not be allowed to wilt between waterings; wilting will induce lower leaf drop.

Poinsettias have a relatively high nutrient requirement; general recommendations range from 225 to 300 ppm nitrogen for overhead-irrigated plants and 100 to 225 ppm nitrogen for subirrigated plants. Dark-leaf cultivars should generally be grown with a fertilizer rate 25% less than the rate used for cultivars with light green leaves. Poinsettias have a high requirement for calcium, magnesium, and molybdenum; the latter two nutrients can be supplied either by periodic drenches or in the constant liquid fertilization program at 0.1 ppm. Optimum root substrate EC should be 2.8 to 4.1 mS/cm using the PourThru method; 2.0 to 3.5 mS/cm using saturated medium extract; or 0.75 to 1.5 mS/cm using 1:2 substrate:water. Dark-leaf cultivars are more sensitive to high substrate EC than other cultivars and should be grown in a substrate whose EC is at the low end of the optimum range. Substrate EC should be less than 2.7 mS/cm using PourThru; 3.0 mS/cm using saturated medium extract; or 1.0 mS/cm using 1:2 substrate:water from mid-October until flowering.

As with most crops, the growing substrate must be well drained yet retain water to prevent excessive irrigation or postharvest wilting. The pH should be 5.8 to 6.3.

Poinsettias are produced either as unpinched, single-stemmed ("straight up") or pinched, multi-stemmed plants. Most plants are produced as pinched plants. Generally, plants are pinched when sufficient root growth occurs for roots to be visible on the outer edges of the substrate; that occurs within two weeks after planting a rooted cutting in the pot or four to five weeks after direct-sticking a cutting. The number of axillary shoots produced from a pinched plant is usually equal to or one less than the number of nodes or leaves remaining on the plant.

The four types of pinches are soft, medium, hard, and very hard. A soft pinch removes the apex above a young, immature leaf. A medium pinch removes leaves up to 2.75 in. (7 cm) long and associated stem tissue. A hard pinch is made above the first fully expanded mature leaf, and a very hard pinch is made in older stem tissue. A hard pinch is the most common pinch, and it typically produces uniform, vigorous axillary shoots.

Numerous schedules have been developed for potted flowering plants over the years to accommodate a wide range of cultivars, climates, flowering dates, container sizes, and plant styles (single-stemmed, pinched, tubs, trees, and hanging baskets). The most commonly grown type of poinsettia is a single pinched plant in a 6 in. (15 cm) pot. As a general rule, approximately four weeks are required for propagation, one and a half to three weeks from planting a rooted cutting until pinching to allow plants to establish prior to pinching, and another one and a half to three weeks from pinching to the start of short days to allow adequate shoot growth before flower initiation. All other situations are variations of that basic schedule.

For cut flowers, stem length is determined by the time from pinch to the start of short days. For Christmas sales the longest stems are produced by planting rooted cuttings in mid- to late July and pinching one and a half to two weeks later. This allows seven to nine weeks of long days prior to the start of natural short days in late September. Flowering date can be delayed with long-day lighting or accelerated with short-day black cloth.

Diseases

Poinsettias are susceptible to several diseases during propagation, including *Botrytis,* bacterial soft rot (*Erwinia*), and *Rhizopus,* and during finish plant production. *Botrytis cinerea* can occur on any aboveground part of the plant; symptoms include tan to brown water-soaked lesions. During propagation *Botrytis* can rapidly destroy cuttings; during production the symptoms can be stem lesions or spots and blotches on the leaves and bracts; and during postharvest the disease often develops on the nectaries and attacks the cyathia clusters.

Although bacterial rot (*Erwinia caratovora*) is most common during propagation, other bacterial diseases can occur during production, including greasy canker (*Pseudomonas viridiflava*), bacterial canker (*Corynebacterium flaccumfaciens*), bacterial stem rot (*Erwinia chrysanthemi*), and bacterial leaf spot (*Xanthomonas campestris*). Several organisms can cause root and stem rots on poinsettias, including *Pythium, Rhizoctonia solani, Thielaviopsis basicola, Botrytis cinerea, Phytophthora parasitica, Erwinia chrysanthemi,* and *Fusarium. Armillaria mellea* and *Sclerotinia sclerotiorum* have also been reported.

Several other fungal disease organisms are known to attack poinsettias, including powdery mildew (*Erysiphe, Microsphaera euphorbiae,* or *Oidium*), rhizopus blight (*Rhizopus stolonifera*), choanephora wet rot (*Choanephora cucurbitarum*), alternaria blight (*Alternaria euphorbiicola*), poinsettia scab (*Sphaceloma poinsettiae*), leaf spot (*Cercospora*), rusts (*Melampsora* and *Uromyces*), and corynespora bract and leaf spot (*Corynespora cassiicola*).

At least two viruses are known to infect plants: poinsettia mosaic virus (PnMV) and poinsettia cryptic virus (PnCV), but neither shows obvious symptoms in most cases.

Disorders

Poinsettias suffer from a number of disorders during propagation and finished plant production. Finished plants can have problems with bract necrosis (burn), leaf edge burn, stem breakage, premature flower initiation (splitting), cyathia drop, and rabbit tracks. The following problems can occur during cutting handling and propagation.

Premature flower initiation (splitting)

Splitting is the premature initiation and development of terminal flower buds on vegetative or young reproductive plants. The immature flower bud rarely reaches anthesis and is usually surrounded by a whorl of three shoots, each of which is subtended by a leaf. If splitting occurs on vegetative stock plants during long days, the subtending shoots in turn form a terminal flower bud, which is again subtended by a whorl of two to three shoots. The process can continue indefinitely and end cutting production. The entire "inflorescence" should be removed, and normally vegetative shoots will grow from axillary buds. If splitting occurs on young plants to be flowered for Christmas, the terminal flower bud may reach anthesis, but the inflorescence will be malformed, excessively large, and open. Individual bracts may form in the middle of the flower cluster and grow vertically. In addition, if splitting occurs early in the production schedule, vegetative growth will cease and plants may be too short.

The propensity for splitting increases with the age of the shoot (apex), and the potential for splitting can be reduced by frequent pinching of the stock plants. Cultivars vary in their susceptibility to splitting. Splitting can be eliminated by the application of gibberellic acid (GA_3) at 10 to 25 ppm. The application of ethephon (Florel) at 300 to 500 ppm may also reduce splitting if applied within three days of planting rooted cuttings. Splitting can also occur if plants receive short days that are enough to initiate flowers but insufficient for the inflorescence to develop properly. This can especially occur during propagation if long days are not provided.

Yellow leaves

Yellow leaves may occur on cuttings that were exposed to high temperatures during shipping or were not promptly unpacked after receipt. Leaves may also turn yellow in propagation one to four days after sticking. Avoid the problem by unpacking, cooling, and sticking cuttings as soon as possible. Contact the supplier if the cuttings were received in poor condition.

Yellow leaves can also occur later in propagation when nutrients leach from the cuttings during misting. This occurs most frequently when the nutritional status of cuttings is low initially or when cuttings are from cultivars with medium green rather than dark green foliage. High light intensity and high leaf temperatures accentuate the problem. Avoid the problem by applying fertilizers once cuttings begin to root. Also, do not let light levels exceed 1,200 to 1,500 f.c. (13 to 16 klux), and maintain leaf temperatures of 75° to 80° F (24° to 27° C).

Brown callus

As the name suggests, the callus turns dark and brown on the cuttings that are slow to root. Delayed rooting can be due to excessive drying of the cuttings, too much fertilizer, fungicides, disease, or feeding by fungus gnat larvae. Brown callus can also occur on cuttings that are too mature. Prevent the problem from occurring by selecting cuttings of the correct age and providing optimum propagation conditions.

Hard growth

The highest-quality finished plants are produced from robust, actively growing, well-rooted cuttings. Slow-growing cuttings with hard growth result from a variety of causes, including harvesting overly mature or nutrient-deficient cuttings, poor water management (too much or too little mist or humidity), temperature (high or low), or nutritional stress (too much or too little) during propagation. Leaving cuttings under mist too long can also cause hard growth. Any problem that delays cutting development during propagation increases the chances that the cuttings will "stall out."

Leaf distortion

Leaf crippling or distortion can occur either on cuttings just after rooting or on axillary shoots immediately after plants are pinched. The leaves are puckered and often narrow, thickened, curved, and distorted. Symptoms are variable as are the causes of the problem. Frequently, damage to immature leaves from rough handling, thrips, excessive dryness, high temperatuers during propagation, *Botrytis,* and phosphorus fertilizers on the growing point can result in distortion after the leaves mature. In some cases, the original problem may only damage or rupture the cells in a small area, but that area expands and becomes more noticeable as the leaf matures. Although disconcerting at first, plants usually outgrow the problem, and the affected leaves are covered by healthy leaves and bracts.

Chlormequat toxicity

Irregular yellow patches or marginal areas on foliage indicate chlormequat phytotoxicity. Marginal necrosis and leaf dropping may occur with severe damage. If the damage is slight, yellow areas may turn green again.

Postharvest

Cuttings can be stored at 45° to 50° F (7° to 10° C) for up to twenty-four hours if they are kept moist. Cuttings are not sensitive to 1 ppm ethylene for up to twenty hours, but they may be sensitive to higher ethylene levels or exposure to ethylene for a longer time period, resulting in leaf abscission. In addition, nutrient-stressed or stored cuttings may be more susceptible to ethylene damage.

References

Anonymous. 1994. Cutting quality. *The Poinsettia* 9:2.

Barrett, J. 1996. Poinsettia height control. 1996. *Greenhouse Product News* 6(8):12, 13, 14.

Berghage, R. D., and R. D. Heins. 1991. Quantification of temperature effects on stem elongation in poinsettia. *Journal of the American Society for Horticultural Science* 116:14–18.

Berghage, R. D., R. D. Heins, W. H. Carlson, and J. Biernbaum. 1987. *Poinsettia Production*. Michigan State University Extension Bulletin E-1382, East

Lansing, Michigan.

Berghage, R. D., R. D. Heins, and J. E. Erwin. 1990. Quantifying leaf unfolding in the poinsettia. *Acta Horticulturae* 272:243–247.

Berghage, R. D., R. D. Heins, M. Karlsson, and J. E. Erwin. 1989. Pinching technique influences lateral shoot development in the poinsettia. *Journal of the American Society for Horticultural Science* 114:909–914.

Bible, B. B., and R. J. McAvoy. 2000. Calcium-boron regimes effect incidence of postharvest disorders on poinsettia bracts. *HortScience* 35:457. (Abstract)

Bierman, P. M., C. J. Rosen, and H. F. Wilkins. 1990. Leaf edge burn and axillary shoot growth of vegetative poinsettia plants: Influence of calcium, nitrogen form, and molybdenum. *Journal of the American Society for Horticultural Science* 115:73–78.

Cockshull, K. E., F. A. Langton, and C. R. J. Cave. 1995. Differential effects of different DIF treatments on chrysanthemum and poinsettia. *Acta Horticulturae* 378:15–25.

Dole, J. M., J. C. Cole, and S. L. von Broembsen. 1994. Effect of irrigation methods on water use efficiency, nutrient leaching and growth of poinsettias. *HortScience* 29:858–864.

Dreistadt, S. H. 2001. *Integrated Pest Management for Floriculture and Nurseries.* University of California Division of Agriculture and Natural Resources Publication 3402. Oakland, California.

Ecke, P., III., J. E. Faust, J. Williams, and A. Higgins. 2004. *The Ecke Poinsettia Manual.* Ball Publishing, Batavia, Illinois.

Evans, M. R., H. F. Wilkins, and W. P. Hackett. 1992a. Meristem ontogenetic age as the controlling factor in long-day floral initiation in poinsettia. *Journal of the American Society for Horticultural Science* 117:961–965.

Evans, M. R., H. F. Wilkins, and W. P. Hackett. 1992b. Gibberellins and temperature influence long-day floral initiation in poinsettia. *Journal of the American Society for Horticultural Science* 117:966–971.

Faust, J. E., and R. D. Heins. 1996. Axillary bud development of poinsettia 'Eckespoint Lilo' and 'Eckespoint Red Sails' (*Euphorbia pulcherrima* Willd.) is inhibited by high temperatures. *Journal of the American Society for Horticultural Science* 121:920–926.

Faust, J. E., E. Will, X. Duan, and E. T. Graham. 1997. Whole plant and histological analysis of poinsettia stem breakage. *HortScience* 32:509.

(Abstract)

Gapinski, J., and M. Yelanich. 1998. Steps for poinsettia propagation. *Ohio Florists' Association Bulletin* 824:10–11.

Grueber, K. L. 1985. *Control of lateral branching and reproductive development in Euphorbia pulcherrima Willd. ex Klotzsch.* Ph.D. thesis, University of Minnesota.

Hammer, A., and J. Barrett. 2001. Poinsettias, pp. 111–116. In: *Tips on Regulating Growth of Floriculture Crops,* M. L. Gaston, L. A. Kunkle, P. S. Konjoian and M. F. Wilt, eds. Ohio Florists' Association Services, Columbus, Ohio.

Hamrick, D. 1996. Calcium sprays eliminate bract edge burn. *GrowerTalks* 60(7):53.

Hartley, D. 1992. Bract edge burn. *The Poinsettia* 4:2–7.

Konjoian, P. 2000. The effects of florel on the growth and development of poinsettia: a research update. *Ohio Florists' Association Bulletin* 850:12–14.

Kuehny, J. S., and P. Branch. 1997. Poinsettia stem strength. *HortScience* 32:483. (Abstract)

Lawton, K. A., G. L. McDaniel, and E. T. Graham. 1989. Nitrogen source and calcium supplement affect stem strength of poinsettia. *HortScience* 24:463–465.

Miller, S. H. 1984. *Environmental and physiological factors influencing premature cyathia abscission in Euphorbia pulcherrima Willd.* M.S. thesis, Michigan State University, East Lansing, Michigan.

Moe, R., K. Willumsen, I. H. Ihlebekk, A. I. Stupa, N. M. Glomsrud, and L. M. Mortensen. 1995. DIF and temperature DROP responses in SDP and LDP, A comparison. *Acta Horticulturae* 378:27–33.

Nell, T. A., and R. T. Leonard. 1996. Protecting poinsettias from post production losses. *GrowerTalks* 60(3):98, 100, 103, 104.

Roll, M. J., and S. E. Newman. 1997. Photoperiod of poinsettia stock plants influences rooting of cuttings. *HortTechnology* 7:41–43.

Wilkerson, E. G., R. S. Gates, S. Zolnier, S. T. Kester, and R. L. Geneve. 2005. Predicting rooting stages in poinsettia cuttings using root zone temperature-based models. *Journal of the American Society for Horticultural Science* 130:302–307.

Williams, J. E. 1993. Stock plant production from the ground up. *The Poinsettia* 5:2–15.

Woltz, S. S., and B. K. Harbaugh. 1986. Calcium deficiency as the basic cause of marginal bract necrosis of 'Gutbier V-14 Glory' poinsettia. *HortScience* 21:1403–1404.

Evolvulus

Common name: Evolvulus, blue daze.
Scientific name: *Evolvulus glomeratus.*
Family: Convolvulaceae.
Other propagation methods: Seed.

Description, Uses, and Status
This 12 to 14 in. (30 to 35 cm) tall procumbent plant has numerous bright blue flowers with a white eye. The foliage is silvery green. A tender perennial, evolvulus is not frost tolerant and is sold in the spring in pots or hanging baskets.

'Hawaiian Blue Eyes' evolvulus.

Flowering Control and Dormancy
Evolvulus is a long-day plant.

Stock Plant Management
Keep stock plants warm and actively growing to provide fresh cuttings.

Cutting Harvest
Terminal cuttings 0.8 to 1.5 in. (2 to 4 cm) long with at least one fully expanded leaf are used.

Propagation

Stage 1:
Cutting arrival or harvest and sticking
- Store cuttings at 50° to 60° F (10° to 16° C) for up to twenty-four hours if planting is going to be delayed.
- Propagate into plugs or small pots. With plug flats, one cutting is inserted per cell. Interesting, propagating evolvulus cuttings into 2¼ in. (6 cm) pots lined with cupric hydroxide reduced root growth (the root tips stopped growing when they touched the cupric hydroxide) but increased flowering after transplanting.

Stage 2: Callusing
- Maintain a substrate temperature of 68° to 75° F (20° to 24° C).
- Maintain air temperatures of 70° to 80° F (21° to 27° C) during days and 65° to 68° F (18° to 20° C) during nights.
- Keep the substrate fully saturated.
- Maintain a light intensity of 500 to 1,000 f.c. (5 to 11 klux).
- Begin foliar feeding with 50 to 75 ppm nitrogen

from 15-0-15 as soon as leaves begin to show any color loss.
- Maintain a substrate pH of 5.5 to 6.5.
- Transfer the cuttings to Stage 3 after five to seven days, once 50% of the cuttings begin differentiating root initials.

Stage 3: Root development
- Maintain substrate temperatures of 68° to 75° F (20° to 24° C).
- Maintain air temperatures of 70° to 80° F (21° to 27° C) during days and 65° to 68° F (18° to 20° C) during nights.
- Begin drying out the substrate once roots are visible.
- Begin increasing the light intensity to 1,000 to 2,000 f.c. (11 to 22 klux) as the cuttings start to root out.
- Fertilize once a week with 100 to 150 ppm nitrogen, alternating between 15-0-15 and 20-10-20.
- Roots should develop in seven to nine days.

Stage 4: Toning the rooted cutting
- Maintain substrate temperatures of 65° to 70° F (18° to 21° C).
- Maintain air temperatures at 68° to 75° F (20° to 24° C) during days and 62° to 65° F (17° to 18° C) during nights.
- Move the liners from the mist area into an area of lower relative humidity.
- Increase the light intensity to 2,000 to 4,000 f.c. (22 to 43 klux).
- Fertilize twice a week with 150 to 200 ppm nitrogen, alternating between 15-0-15 and 20-10-20.
- The cuttings can be toned for seven days.

Plant Growth Regulators
None are generally required, but paclobutrazol (Bonzi) or chlormequat (Cycocel) can be used.

Production and Schedule
Grow plants at 55° to 60° F (13° to 16° C) during nights and 65° to 75° F (18° to 24° C) during days. The light intensity should be 5,000 to 9,000 f.c. (54 to 97 klux) for this high-light-requiring plant.

Fertilize plants with 150 to 200 ppm nitrogen from 15-0-15 alternating with 20-10-20. Avoid using too much ammonium, which causes soft vegetative growth and stem elongation. The substrate pH should be 6.0 to 6.5. Avoid overwatering, which encourages diseases and soft growth. One rooted cutting is used per 4 in. (10 cm) pot, three per 6 in. (15 cm) pot, and three to four per 8 to 10 in. (20 to 25 cm) hanging basket. Plants grown in pots larger than 4 in. (10 cm) can be pinched once or twice to improve branching and plant shape. As with many trailing plants, pots can become tangled if shoots are not controlled. In the spring cutting-propagated 4 in.

(10 cm) pots are ready to sell in six to eight weeks, 6 in. (15 cm) pots in eight to nine weeks, 8 in. (20 cm) baskets in eight to ten weeks, and 10 in. (25 cm) baskets in ten to twelve weeks. The crop finishes one to two weeks earlier in the summer.

Diseases
Botrytis and *Pythium* can be problems, especially if the plants are grown too wet.

Disorders
Foliage tends to yellow under low temperatures or with overwatering.

References
Hamrick, D. 2003. *Evolvulus,* pp. 383–384. In: *Ball RedBook,* 17th ed., vol. 2, D. Hamrick, ed. Ball Publishing, Batavia, Illinois.

Svenson, S. E., and D. L. Johnston. 1995. Rooting cuttings in cupric hydroxide-treated pots affects root length and number of flowers after transplanting. *HortScience* 30:247–248.

Exacum

Common name: Exacum, German violet, Persian violet.
Scientific name: *Exacum affine.*
Family: Gentianaceae.
Other propagation methods: Seed, tissue culture.

Description, Uses, and Status
Exacum is an annual that grows to 24 in. (60 cm) tall. The plant is heavily branched, commencing at the base, and has ovate glossy dark green leaves 1 to 1.5 in. (2.5 to 4 cm) long. The fragrant flowers, which may be double, are 0.5 to 0.75 in. (1 to 2 cm) wide; they occur in various tints of blue, mauve or white and have golden yellow stamens. Exacum is grown as a potted flowering plant for spring and summer sales.

Flowering Control and Dormancy
Exacum is a day-neutral plant with both vegetative growth rate and rapid reproductive initiation and development dependent on the accumulated light energy.

Close-up of single exacum flowers.

Stock Plant Management
Actively growing plants that are not flowering should be used for propagation. Two to three days prior to the cutting harvest, stock plants can be sprayed with a fungicide to prevent *Botrytis* problems during propagation.

Cutting Harvest

Terminal cuttings with two nodes are used. Any flower buds should be removed. While any of the cultivars can be cutting propagated, the double-flowered cultivars are sterile and must be asexually propagated.

Propagation

Cuttings root easily in two to three weeks in a substrate with a temperature of 72° to 75° F (22° to 24° C). With plug flats, one cutting is inserted per cell.

Plant Growth Regulators

One to three spray applications of daminozide (B-Nine) at 2,500 ppm each can be used. Paclobutrazol (Bonzi) can be used, either as a spray at 75 ppm or as a drench at 0.25 to 0.75 mg a.i. per 6 in. (15 cm) pot.

Production and Schedule

Optimum temperatures are 75° to 80° F (24° to 27° C) during days and 60° to 65° F (16° to 18° C) during nights. Rapid growth and flowering is light dependent. The growth of young rooted cuttings can be stimulated by a sixteen-hour day from fluorescent or high intensity discharge (HID) lights. Full sun is best in the fall, winter, and spring. Shade should be used only to prevent excessive heat buildup in the greenhouse when light levels exceed 4,500 to 6,000 f.c. (48 to 65 klux).

Plants should be grown moist, and not too wet or too dry. Excessive moisture encourages an overabundance of succulent vegetative growth, which is prone to disease. On the other hand, excessive wilting causes premature flower development and small plant size.

A fertilization regime of nitrogen at 150 to 200 ppm, phosphorus at 50 ppm, and potassium at 150 ppm with each irrigation has been recommended. Growers need to exercise caution with fertilization because excessive nutrition can result in soft growth, delayed flowering, and increased susceptibility to disease. The substrate should be well drained with adequate nutrient and water retention and a pH of 6.0 to 7.0.

When plugs are purchased from a specialist, exacum produced in 4 in. (10 cm) pots can be a quick seven-week crop during summer or up to twenty-two weeks during winter.

Diseases

Botrytis has long been a serious problem. Tomato spotted wilt virus, fusarium wilt, basal stem rot (*Nectria haematococca*), and root rot (*Pythium ultimum*) also can be problems.

Disorders

Double-flowered exacum may not completely open or develop a good blue pigment. Delayed flowering can occur with excessive fertilization or irrigation. Premature flowering on too-short plants can occur with excessive wilting.

Postharvest

Cuttings are chilling sensitive and quite susceptible to *Botrytis*.

References

Dreistadt, S. H. 2001. *Integrated Pest Management for Floriculture and Nurseries.* University of California Division of Agriculture and Natural Resources Publication 3402. Oakland, California.

Hasek, R., R. Sciaroni, and G. Hickman. 1986. New growth regulator tested. *Greenhouse Grower* 4(2):52–53.

Hollis, R. J., 1997. Exacum, pp. 64–65. In: *Tips on Growing Specialty Potted Crops,* M. L. Gaston, S. A. Carver, C. A. Irwin, and R. A. Larson, eds. Ohio Florists' Association, Columbus, Ohio.

Irwin, L. 1984. Exacum. *Minnesota State Florists Bulletin* 33(3):8–9.

Sweet, J. 1982. Latest cultural techniques for gloxinias, exacum, streptocarpus, and begonias. *Minnesota State Florists Bulletin* 31(5):11–13.

Wilkins, H. F., and A. H. Halevy. 1989. *Exacum*, pp. 328–330. In: *Handbook of Flowering*, vol. VI, A. H. Halevy, ed. CRC Press, Boca Raton, Florida.

Williams, S., S. Wolf, and E. J. Holcomb. 1983. Growth and flowering of *Exacum* affine at three radiant energy levels. *HortScience* 18:366–367.

Zitter, T. A., M. E. Daughtrey, and J. P. Sanderson. 1989. Tomato spotted wilt virus, pp. 107–112. In: *Vegetable/Horticultural Crops, Fact Sheet* 735.90, Cornell Cooperative Extension, Ithaca, New York.

Fuchsia

Common name: Fuchsia.
Scientific name: *Fuchsia* hybrids.
Family: Onagraceae.
Other propagation methods: Seed.

Fuchsia flower. (B. Whipker)

Description, Uses, and Status

The showy flowers are pendent and colored purple, pink, red, or white. The entire flower may be one color or the sepals and petals may be different colors, resulting in striking color combinations. Double-flowered forms are common. The dark green elliptical leaves are opposite and occasionally variegated. Fuchsias are grown worldwide as perennial garden shrubs in mild climates and as potted flowering plants sold in the spring. Because of the pendulous nature of the plant and flowers, fuchsias are popular hanging basket plants, but some are also sold in pots. Fuchsias also work well as standards. Most fuchsia cultivars perform best in cool climates; however, 'Gartenmeister Bonstadt' and related cultivars are quite heat tolerant and excellent plants for warm climates.

Flowering Control and Dormancy

The apical meristem always remains vegetative; the flowers are axillary. Juvenile plants of most cultivars are obligate long-day plants that flower rapidly with a critical day length of approximately twelve hours. Some cultivars require only five consecutive long days to bloom; however, increasing the number of long days increases the number of reproductive axillary sites. Once flowers are initiated, floral development continues regardless of photoperiod. Old flowering plants are essentially day-neutral.

Stock Plant Management

While long days increase the number and fresh weight of cuttings, stock plants should be kept under short days of ten hours or less to ensure vegetative growth of stock plants and cuttings. Ethephon (Florel) sprays at 500 ppm can be used to increase branching and replace pinching. Hanging basket culture is recommended.

Cutting Harvest

Terminal cuttings 3 in. (8 cm) long are harvested from actively growing plants.

Propagation

Stage 1:
Cutting arrival or harvest and sticking
- Open and unpack boxes as soon as possible when purchasing cuttings.
- Use a rooting hormone (1,000 ppm IBA) on the harder-to-root cultivars.
- Insert one cutting per cell when using plug flats.

Stage 2: Callusing
- Maintain a substrate temperature of 70° to 76° F (21° to 24° C).
- Maintain air temperatures of 75° to 80° F (24° to 27° C) during days and 68° to 72° F (20° to 22° C) during nights.
- Maintain a light intensity of 500 to 1,000 f.c. (5 to 11 klux).
- Misting at night is usually required.
- Begin foliar feeding with 50 to 75 ppm nitrogen from 20-10-20 as soon as leaves begin to show any color loss.
- Maintain a substrate pH of 5.0 to 5.5.
- Transfer the cuttings to Stage 3 after five to seven days, once 50% of the cuttings begin differentiating root initials.

Stage 3: Root development
- Maintain a substrate temperature of 68° to 72° F (20° to 22° C).
- Maintain air temperatures of 75° to 80° F (24° to 27° C) during days and 68° to 70° F (20° to 21° C) during nights.
- Fertilize once a week with 100 to 200 ppm nitrogen, alternating between 15-0-15 and 20-10-20.
- Roots should develop in seven to fourteen days.

Stage 4: Toning the rooted cutting

- Lower the air temperature to 70° to 75° F (21° to 24° C) during the day and 62° to 68° F (17° to 20° C) at night.
- Move the liners from the mist area into an area of lower relative humidity.
- Increase the light intensity to 3,000 to 5,000 f.c. (32 to 54 klux).
- Provide shade during the middle of the day to reduce temperature stress.
- Fertilize twice a week with 150 to 200 ppm nitrogen from 15-0-15 alternating with 20-10-20.
- The cuttings can be toned for seven days.

Plant Growth Regulators

Various plant growth regulators can be used to control internode elongation, including sprays of ancymidol (A-Rest) at 25 to 75 ppm or daminozide (B-Nine) at 1,250 to 2,500 ppm. Drenches of paclobutrazol (Bonzi) at 5 to 10 ppm or uniconizole (Sumagic) at 2 to 5 ppm can be used. Application of ancymidol can promote and hasten floral initiation. Stem elongation can also be controlled by day and night temperature difference (DIF).

Production and Schedule

The optimal temperature range for vegetative growth is 68° to 79° F (20° to 26° C). Little growth occurs below 59° F (15° C) or above 86° F (30° C). Flowering ceases when the average daily temperature rises above 76° F (24° C). Both long days and light intensities of at least 900 f.c. (10 klux) for eighteen hours a day during the winter reduce crop time; however, plants should be shaded in late spring and summer.

A constant liquid fertilization of 200 ppm nitrogen is commonly used. Ammonium should constitute less than 20% of total nitrogen. Spacing varies with the size and type of plant produced; pinched or topiary plants in small 4 in. (10 cm) pots can be produced at 6 by 6 in. (15 by 15 cm). Hanging baskets are spaced sufficiently far enough apart to prevent tangling of the shoots and excessive shading below.

Fuchsia plants respond to pinching, and hanging baskets are commonly pinched two or more times. The first pinch is one to two weeks after planting or when roots have reached the edge of the substrate. Plants are pinched above the fourth or fifth set of leaves.

Three to five cuttings are used in a 10 in. (25 cm) hanging basket. Generally, thirteen to nineteen weeks are required to produce a hanging basket; the timing depends on the season, temperature, and geographic location. Be sure to allow plants to grow to a sufficient size prior to the start of long days.

Diseases

Botrytis, Pythium, Phytophthora, Rhizoctonia, Thielaviopsis, Armillaria, Penicillium, Verticillium, tomato spotted wilt virus, and rusts (*Pucciniastrum epilobii* and *Uredo fuchsiae*) occur.

Stem blight of fuchsia plants.

Disorders

Lack of flowering or delayed flowering can be due to incorrect photoperiod, incorrect temperature, low light, excessive ethephon applications, overfertilization, or overwatering.

Postharvest

Cuttings are ethylene sensitive. Interestingly, immature leaves defoliate before mature leaves.

References

Daughtrey, M., and A. R. Chase. 1992. Fuchsia, pp. 94–96. In: *Ball Field Guide to Diseases of Greenhouse Ornamentals.* Ball Publishing, Batavia, Illinois.

Dreistadt, S. H. 2001. *Integrated Pest Management for Floriculture and Nurseries.* University of California Division of Agriculture and Natural Resources Publication 3402. Oakland, California.

Erwin, J., and B. Kovanda. 1990. Fuchsia production. *Minnesota State Florists Bulletin* 39(5):1–4.

Erwin, J. E., R. D. Heins, and R. Moe. 1991. Temperature and photoperiod effects on *Fuchsia x hybrida* morphology. *Journal of the American Society for Horticultural Science* 116:955–960.

Graves, W. R., and H. Zhang. 1996. Relative water content and rooting subirrigated stems cuttings in four environments without mist. *HortScience* 31:866–868.

Kim, H. Y. 1995. Effects of uniconazole on the growth and flowering of *Fuchsia x hybrida* 'Corallina.' *Acta Horticulturae* 394:331–335.

Maas, F. M., and J. van Hattum. 1998. Thermomorphogenic and photomorphogenic control of stem elongation in *Fuchsia* is not mediated by changes in responsiveness to gibberellins. *Plant Growth Regulation* 17:39–45.

Roberts, R. H., and B. E. Struckmeyer. 1938. The effects of temperature and other environmental factors upon photoperiodic responses of some of the higher plants. *Journal of Agricultural Research* 56:633–677.

Roberts, C. M., G. W. Eaton, and F. M. Seywerd. 1990. Production of *Fuchsia* and *Tibouchina* standards using paclobutrazol and chlormequat. *HortScience* 25:1242–1243.

Sachs, R. M., and C. F. Bretz. 1962. The effect of daylength, temperature, and gibberellic acid upon

flowering in *Fuchsia hybrida*. *Proceedings of the American Society for Horticultural Science* 80:581–588.

Sachs, R. M., A. M. Kofranek, J. DeBie, and J. Kubota. 1972. Reducing height of pot grown fuchsia. *Florists' Review* 150(3883):85–87, 99–101.

von Hentig, W. U., M. Fischer, and K. Köhler. 1985. Influence of daylength on the production and quality of cutting from fuchsia mother plants. *Combined Proceedings of the International Plant Propagators' Society* 34:141-149.

Wilkins, H. F. 1985. *Fuchsia* x *hybrida*, pp. 38–41. In: *Handbook of Flowering*, vol. III, A. H. Halevy, ed. CRC Press, Boca Raton, Florida.

Gardenia

Common name: Gardenia.
Scientific name: *Gardenia augusta*.
Family: Rubiaceae.
Other propagation methods: Tissue culture.

Description, Uses, and Status

This plant is grown for elegant, very fragrant white flowers. The calyx has five elongated stipulelike structures under the pure white multipetaled flower, which can be up to 4 in. (10 cm) in diameter. The plant has opposite thick shiny dark green leaves that are evergreen and lanceolate to ovate in form. Gardenias are sold commercially as garden ornamentals, potted flowering plants, and cut flowers for use in corsages and wedding bouquets. In the United States they are grown mainly in Florida and other warm Gulf states by specialty pot plant producers.

Flowering Control and Dormancy

The duration of the flowering period is largely determined by night temperatures; flowering can be continuous if temperatures remain below 65° F (18° C). In greenhouses, flowering typically starts in December or January and ceases by July; in warm climates outdoors, flowering is in the spring and early summer only. If temperatures remain over 65° F (18° C), the buds abort after several months. While gardenia is a day-neutral plant, short days hasten initiation and early development of flowers, and long days (natural or supplemental) promote rapid development under cool temperatures.

'Radicans' *Gardenia* garden ornamental.

Stock Plant Management

Vegetative stock plants are maintained by holding plants under long days at 70° to 80° F (21° to 27° C).

Cutting Harvest

Terminal or subterminal cuttings 4 to 5 in. (10 to 13 cm) long of six- to eight-week-old half-mature stem tissue are used. Cuttings should have two or three sets of leaves, and they can be harvested from stock plants or from plants in production.

Propagation

Propagation is by terminal vegetative cuttings, which are rooted directly in small pots or plugs filled with a well-aerated substrate. Insert one cutting per cell if using plug flats. Dipping the cutting bases in IBA plus NAA can increase rooting. Gardenia cuttings root at 70° to 75° F (21° to 24° C) and in reduced light; they need high humidity and are commonly propagated under mist, fog, or plastic tunnels. Propagation, which typically occurs from November to February, requires six to eight weeks.

Plant Growth Regulators

Ancymidol (A-Rest), daminozide (B-Nine), paclobutrazol (Bonzi), or flurprimidol (Topflor) can be used to obtain short compact plants. Ancymidol sprays are applied at 50 ppm and drenches at 0.25 mg a.i. (2 ppm) per 6 in. (15 cm) pot. Daminozide sprays are applied at 5,000 ppm, and flurprimodol sprays at 100 to 200 ppm. A drench of paclobutrazol at 12 ppm can also be used.

Production and Schedule

The air temperature should not go below 60° F (16° C); temperatures of 70° F (21° C) during the day and 62° F (7 C) at night are excellent. Keeping the night temperature below 65° F (18° C) is especially important during marketing to maintain the flower buds. The substrate temperature should not go lower than 66° F (19° C) or higher than 79° F (26° C).

High light (full sun) during the vegetative and induction period increases the number of flower buds that develop. Supplementary lighting reduces flower bud abscissions.

Gardenia grows best when the substrate is continuously moist and the humidity is high. Good growth with high plant and flower quality is obtained at low nutritional levels of 100 to 150 ppm nitrogen. No treatment or management step should slow plant growth or flower bud development, and any plant stress may increase flower bud abscission. Pure peat is typically used, and a pH below 6.0 is best, or chlorosis can occur. Chlorosis can also occur if the substrate temperature falls below 60° F (16° C).

For plants in 6 in. (15 cm) pots, pinching occurs eight weeks after rooting. In Denmark the gardenia is a thirty-six- to thirty-eight-week crop using photoperiod control and temperature manipulation. A schedule in warm climates starts with propagation in May and ends with sales the following early spring.

Diseases

Gardenia is susceptible to several diseases, including bud blight (*Botrytis cinerea*), leaf spot (*Phyllosticta, Rhizoctonia, Myrothecium roridum,* and *Xanthomonas campestris* pv. *maculifoliigardeniae*), root and crown rot (*Phytophthora, Rhizoctonia* and *Armillaria*), and powdery mildew (*Erysiphe polygoni*). Stem canker (*Phomopsis gardeniae*) can be prevalent in greenhouse production, but it can be minimized by taking cuttings from the tops of plants and by using resistant cultivars such as 'Veitchii'.

Disorders

Flower bud abscission can occur if night temperatures remain above 65° F (18° C) or light levels are inadequate. Foliar chlorosis and yellowing due to iron deficiency can occur; it is associated with a substrate temperature that is too cool.

References

Baerdemaeker de, C. I., J. M. van Huylenbroeck, and P. C. Debergh. 1994. Influence of paclobutrazol and photoperiod on growth and flowering of *Gardenia jasminoides* Ellis cultivar 'Veitchii'. *Scientia Horticulturae* 58:315–324.

Banko, T. J., and M. A. Stefani. 1995. Cutless and Atrimmec for controlling growth of woody landscape plants in containers. *Journal of Environmental Horticulture* 13:22–26.

Dreistadt, S. H. 2001. *Integrated Pest Management for Floriculture and Nurseries.* University of California Division of Agriculture and Natural Resources Publication 3402. Oakland, California.

Griffith, L. P., Jr. 1998. *Tropical Foliage Plants.* Ball Publishing, Batavia, Illinois.

Horst, R. K. 1990. Gardenia, pp. 651–652. In: *Wescott's Plant Disease Handbook,* 5th ed. Van Nostrand Reinhold, New York.

Kamoutsis, A. P., A. G. Chronopoulou-Sereli, and E. A. Paspatis. 1999. Paclobutrazol affects growth and flower bud production in gardenia under different light regimes. *HortScience* 34:674–675.

Rose, S. A., and R. D. Dickey. 1960–61. The effect of light, plunging medium and fertilization on bud set of *Gardenia jasminoides* 'Veitchii'. *Proceedings of Florida State Horticultural Society* 73:362–363.

Uematsu, L., and H. Tomita. 1981. Studies on gardenia pot plant production. *Bulletin Saitama Horticultural Experimental Station* 10:17–29. (in Japanese)

Whipker, B. E. 2003. Growth regulators for floricultural crops, pp. 439–448. In: 2003 *North Carolina Agricultural Chemicals Manual,* College of Agriculture and Life Science, North Carolina State University, Raleigh, North Carolina.

Wilkins, H. F. 1986. *Gardenia jasminoides,* pp. 127–131. In: *Handbook of Flowering,* vol. V, A. H. Halevy, ed. CRC Press, Boca Raton, Florida.

Gypsophila

Common name: Gypsophila, baby's breath.
Scientific name: *Gypsophila paniculata*.
Family: Caryophyllaceae.
Other propagation methods: Seed, tissue culture, grafting.

'Golan' cut gypsophila.

Description, Uses, and Status

Although a perennial, gypsophila can be grown as an annual; it flowers in late spring to fall, producing two or three harvests of cut flowers each growing season. Plants can reach 40 in. (1 m) tall. The leaves are gray-green, and the flowers are only 0.25 in. (6 mm) wide. Flower colors vary from white to reddish and from single to double. Gypsophila is hardy to Zone 3. *G. paniculata* is the dominant species commercially and is grown worldwide, primarily as a filler cut flower. It is also commonly grown as a garden ornamental and occasionally as a potted flowering plant.

Flowering Control and Dormancy

Gypsophila is a long-day plant, since flowering does not occur under short days unless the plants are vernalized. The critical day length for unvernalized plants is twelve to eighteen hours. In Israel under high ambient light levels, 80% of the plants flowered under short days when rooted cuttings were stored at 32° to 34° F (0° to 1° C) for seven weeks under low levels of fluorescent light (480 f.c., 5 klux) prior to planting. On the other hand, 0% of unvernalized plants flowered under short days. Vernalization also improved the percentage of plants that flowered under long days. However, in Indiana flowering did not occur under short days after vernalization for eight weeks at 41° F (5° C) under low light levels. Plants can be vernalized at 52° F (11° C) when subsequent light levels are high.

Stock Plant Management

In the summer, stock plants for cuttings are kept under short days to keep them vegetative.

Cutting Harvest

Terminal cuttings 1 to 2 in. (2.5 to 5 cm) long with at least one fully expanded leaf are used.

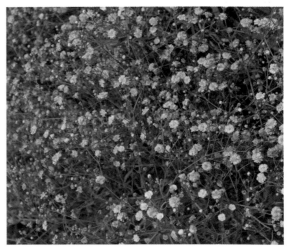
'Festival Pink' gypsophila garden ornamental.

Propagation

Specialty propagators take gypsophila cuttings from disease-free stock and root them under mist in ten to fourteen days. The rooting of terminal gypsophila cuttings was improved with 3,000 to 10,000 ppm IBA dips for five to thirty seconds. Yoder Green Leaf recommended 1,000 ppm KIBA for 'Viette's Dwarf' gypsophila. Insert one cutting per cell when using plug flats. Plugs of rooted cuttings should be transplanted as soon as the root-ball holds together. Holding plugs in the flat too long will slow the growth of plants after transplanting.

Plant Growth Regulators

For cut flower production, none is used. For potted plants use dwarf cultivars or apply paclobutrazol (Bonzi) or uniconazole (Sumagic). Ancymidol (A-Rest) is also effective.

Production and Schedule

For forcing and flowering in greenhouses, 52° F (11° C) is the minimum night temperature. The temperature range for optimal flowering is 61° to 68° F (16° to 20° C); the higher temperature is best at higher light levels, and the lower temperature at lower light levels. At 45° F (7° C) plants remain vegetative even under long days.

The plants, which are most commonly grown outdoors, should be given full light. Sunlight reduction should be used only to control high temperatures. A pH of 6.5 to 7.0 is optimal. Gypsophila is sensitive to high soluble salts. A nutrient solution with nitrogen at 150 ppm can be used with each irrigation; as with most crops, do not overwater. When flowering commences, reduce fertilization to 100 ppm nitrogen. In the field, a wide variety of soil types can be used as long as the pH has been adjusted to 6.5 to 7.0 and drainage is good.

Gypsophila is grown outdoors in Zones 3 to 7; it flowers from late spring through summer if regularly harvested. Plants are primarily field grown but can be produced in the greenhouse. Outdoors after a cold period, plants will flower one to three times from late spring through summer. A plant can be kept in production for up to three years.

Diseases

Many diseases are avoided by using *in vitro*-propagated plants or plants originating from elite disease-free stock plants. The use of clean plant material is critical. *Pythium, Phytophthora, Pellicularia,* and *Rhizoctonia* may result in damping off and death of young plants. Powdery mildew and *Alternaria* leaf spot and flower blight can reduce vigor and quality. *Botrytis* can occur in leaves and flowers during shipping or in a cold moist production environment. Crown gall (*Agrobacterium*), *Sclerotinia sclerotiorum,* bacteria streak (*Erwinia herbicola*), aster yellows, and tomato spotted wilt virus can also occur.

Disorders

Low flower numbers can result from low light levels. Plants may return to vegetative growth if they have been improperly cold treated or placed under long days for an insufficient time period (for example, until plants flower). If temperatures are too low, improper development of flower stems can also occur. Flower browning, which may be due to overmaturity or *Botrytis,* is another possibility.

References

Armitage, A. M., and J. M. Laushman. 2003. *Gypsophila paniculata,* pp. 312–319. In: *Specialty Cut Flowers,* 2nd ed. Timber Press, Portland, Oregon.

Carlson, W. 1986. A cultural guide for gypsophila. *Greenhouse Grower* 4(3):12–13.

Danziger, M. 1993. Potted Gypsophila. *GrowerTalks* 56(10):19.

Danziger, M. 1998. *Gypsophila,* pp. 534–536. In: *Ball RedBook,* 16th ed., V. Ball, ed. Ball Publishing, Batavia, Illinois.

Dreistadt, S. H. 2001. *Integrated Pest Management for Floriculture and Nurseries.* University of California Division of Agriculture and Natural Resources Publication 3402. Oakland, California.

Goto T., Y. Kageyama, and K. Konishi. 2000. Studies on transplant production of *Dianthus caryophyllus* L. and *Gypsophila paniculata* L. using different size cell trays - Effect of cell (root zone) volume and transplanting age on subsequent growth and cut flower quality. *Journal of the Japanese Society for Horticultural Science* 69:749–757.

Kusey, W. E., Jr., and T. C. Weiler. 1980. Propagation of *Gypsophila paniculata* from cuttings. *HortScience* 15:85–86.

Kusey W. E., Jr., T. C. Weiler, P. A. Hammer, B. K. Harbaugh, and G. J. Wilfret. 1981. Seasonal and chemical influences on the flowering of *Gypsophila paniculata* 'Bristol Fairy' selections. *Journal of the American Society for Horticultural Science* 106:84–88.

Shillo, R. 1985. Gypsophila paniculata, pp.83–87. In: *Handbook of Flowering,* vol. III, A. H. Halevy, ed. CRC Press, Boca Raton, Florida.

Yoder Green Leaf Perennials. 2004. *Handling Unrooted Perennials.* www.green-leaf-ent.com/URC_Handling_2004.pdf.

Hedera

Common name: Ivy, English ivy.
Scientific name: *Hedera helix*.
Family: Araliaceae.
Other propagation methods: Seed.

Three cultivars of English ivy.

Description, Uses, and Status

Ivy foliage is evergreen and attractive. The leaf size, shape, and color vary dramatically among cultivars. Depending on the cultivar, plants are used indoors in hanging baskets, pots, topiaries, and dish gardens, or in the landscape as ground, wall, and tree trunk cover. Cut stems also are used as foliage in arrangements.

Flowering Control and Dormancy

Ivy is grown as a foliage plant; flowering and dormancy are not considered. Ivy has a juvenile period, during which cutting propagation is easy. Once the plant matures into the adult form, cutting propagation is typically much more difficult.

Stock Plant Management

Continual selection of superior plants for future stock is essential. The stability of a cultivar may be a problem for the grower; constant selection of stock is required to maintain the desired leaf patterns. Pigmentation or pattern distinction may decrease during winter if shade is too heavy. Maintain adequate magnesium to help keep variegation strong. Hanging basket culture is recommended.

Cutting Harvest

Ivy is propagated by terminal cuttings or by subterminal stem cuttings with one to three nodes. One-node cuttings will take longer to root than cuttings with more nodes. Paul Pilon, Perennial Solutions Consulting, Jenison, Michigan, recommends taking two- or three-node cuttings harvested by cutting just above the top leaf and leaving about 0.25 in. (6 mm) stem remaining. The lower cut should be about 0.50 to 1 in. (1.3 to 2.5 cm) below the bottom node.

Propagation

Cuttings are often directly propagated into the final pot. All ivy cultivars root with ease when juvenile. Adult forms do not root easily. Although not required, 1,000 ppm IBA can be used to speed rooting by one to two days. One to three cuttings can be inserted in each cell of a plug flat. If direct-sticking in larger pots or baskets, six or more cuttings can be used per 6 in. (15 cm) pot, and ten to twelve cuttings per 8 in. (20 cm) basket. The optimum propagation substrate temperature is 70° to 72° F (21° to 22° C). Root-zone heating is a common practice. The cuttings should be rooted and ready for transplanting in three to four weeks. A fine-textured propagation substrate should be used; some propagators add 10% sand to the mix.

Plant Growth Regulators

Ancymidol (A-Rest), chlormequat (Cycocel), and daminozide (B-Nine) are reported to be effective, but they are not required.

Production and Schedule

Production temperature is 65° to 75° F (18° to 24° C). Growth is inhibited at temperatures above 85° to 90° F (29° to 32° C). The solid green landscape cultivars can tolerate full light during part of the day. Most ornamental types grow better under reduced light levels of 1,500 to 2,500 f.c. (16 to 27 klux).

Use 100 ppm nitrogen constant liquid fertilization or controlled-release fertilizers. Peat-lite mixes are commonly used; they should have a pH of 6.0 to 6.5, and should be well aerated yet hold adequate water. No pinching or disbudding is required. Paul Pilon, Perennial Solutions Consulting, notes that 1gal. (4 L) pots direct-stuck with ten cuttings will finish in sixteen weeks, and those with five rooted plugs containing more than one cutting each will finish in ten weeks.

Diseases

Bacterial leaf spot (*Xanthomonas campestris* pv. *hederae*) is the most serious production problem in the greenhouse. *Botrytis, Phytophthora, Pythium, Rhizoctonia, Pseudomonas cichorii,* and tomato spotted wilt virus can also be problems.

Disorders
Outdoors, winter injury may cause browning of the foliage.

Postharvest
Ivy is moderately sensitive to low levels of ethylene, which cause epinasty, twisting and distortion, in the young growth.

References
Adriansen, E. 1985. Kemisk vækstregulering, pp. 142–162. In: *Potteplanter I—Produktion, Metoder, Midler,* O. V. Christensen, A. Klougart, I. S. Pedersen, and K. Wikesjö, eds. GartnerINFO, København, Denmark. (in Danish)

Daughtrey, M., and A. R. Chase. 1992. Hedera, pp. 120–123. In: *Ball Field Guide to Diseases of Greenhouse Ornamentals.* Ball Publishing, Batavia, Illinois.

Dreistadt, S. H. 2001. *Integrated Pest Management for Floriculture and Nurseries.* University of California Division of Agriculture and Natural Resources Publication 3402. Oakland, California.

Hackett, W. P., and C. Srinivasan. 1985. *Hedera helix* and *H. canariensis,* pp. 89–97. In: *Handbook of Flowering,* vol. III, A. H. Halevy, ed. CRC Press, Boca Raton, Florida.

Henney, R. W., A. R. Chase, and L. S. Osborne. 1991. English Ivy. *Foliage Research Note RH-91-15.* Central Florida Research and Education Center, Apopka, Florida.

Horst, R. K. 1990. Ivy, English, p. 693. In: *Westcott's Plant Disease Handbook,* 5th ed. Van Nostrand Reinhold, New York.

Norman, D. J., A. R. Chase, R. E. Stall, and J. B. Jones. 1999. Heterogeneity of *Xanthomonas campestris* pv. *hederae* strains from Araliaceae hosts. *Phytopathology* 89:646–652.

Nowak, J. M., and R. M. Rudnicki. 1990. *Postharvest Handling and Storage of Cut Flowers, Florist Greens, and Potted Plants.* Timber Press, Portland, Oregon.

Pilon, P. 2003. *Hedera helix* 'Duck Foot'. *GPN* 13(10):90, 92–93.

Helichrysum

Common name: Helichrysum, licorice plant, trailing dusty miller.
Scientific name: *Helichrysum microphyllum, H. petiolare, and H. thianschanicum.*
Family: Compositae.
Other propagation methods: Seed.

Helichrysum petiolare 'Petite Licorice'.

Description, Uses, and Status
Several species with silvery foliage are available. *H. petiolare,* licorice plant, is a tender perennial hardy to Zone 10 that grows 12 to 24 in. (30 to 60 cm) tall and has on open mound to trailing habit; it has leaves to 1.5 in. (4 cm) wide. *H. thianschanicum* is a tender perennial hardy to Zone 6; it has narrow leaves and grows in an upright mound. The closely related *Plectostachys serphyllifolia* (formerly known as *H. microphyllum*) has smaller leaves than *H. petiolare* and is hardy to Zone 9. All these species are grown for their silvery gray foliage, but they may produce clusters of small white to yellow flowers.

Flowering Control and Dormancy
Helichrysums are grown for their attractive foliage.

Stock Plant Management
Keep plants actively growing to produce vigorous cuttings. Do not allow stock plants to dry out. Monitor for caterpillars because foliar feeding can greatly impact cutting yield.

Cutting Harvest
Terminal cuttings 0.8 to 2 in. (2 to 5 cm) long with at least one fully expanded leaf are harvested.

Helichrysum thianschanicum 'Icicles'.

Propagation

Stage 1:
Cutting arrival or harvest and sticking
- Stick cuttings within one or two hour after arrival or harvest.
- Use a rooting hormone, 3,000 ppm IBA, on the cutting bases. IBA with up to 500 ppm NAA or 500 to 1,000 KIBA can also be used.
- Insert one cutting per cell if using plug flats.

Stage 2: Callusing
- Maintain a substrate temperature of 68° to 72° F (20° to 22° C).
- Maintain air temperatures of 75° to 80° F (24° to 27° C) during days and 68° to 70° F (20° to 21° C) during nights.
- Maintain a light intensity of 500 to 1,000 f.c. (5 to 11 klux).
- Begin foliar feeding once a week with 50 to 75 ppm nitrogen from 20-10-20 as soon as leaves begin to show any color loss.
- Maintain a substrate pH of 5.5 to 6.3.
- Keep the substrate sufficiently moist so that water is easily squeezed out of it, but not so much that the cutting base is waterlogged. The base of the cutting needs air for proper rooting.
- Transfer the cuttings to Stage 3 after five to seven days, once 50% of the cuttings begin differentiating root initials.

Stage 3: Root development
- Maintain a substrate temperature of 68° to 72° F (20° to 22° C).
- Maintain air temperatures of 75° to 80° F (24° to 26° C) during days and 68° to 70° F (20° to 21° C) during nights.

- Begin drying out the substrate once roots are visible.
- Increase the light intensity to 1,000 to 2,000 f.c. (11 to 22 klux).
- Fertilize once a week with 100 ppm nitrogen, alternating between 15-0-15 and 20-10-20, then increase to 200 ppm.
- Roots should develop in seven to fourteen days.

Stage 4: Toning the rooted cutting
- Maintain substrate temperatures of 68° to 72° F (20° to 22° C).
- Maintain air temperatures at 75° to 80° F (24° to 27° C) during days and 68° to 70° F (20° to 21° C) during nights.
- Move the liners from the mist area into an area of lower relative humidity.
- Increase the light intensity to 2,000 to 4,000 f.c. (22 to 43 klux).
- Fertilize once a week with 150 to 200 ppm nitrogen from 15-0-15 alternating with 20-10-20.
- Apply ethephon (Florel) to increase branching of the finished crop.
- The cuttings can be toned for seven days.

Plant Growth Regulators
Paclobutrazol (Bonzi) drenches to the substrate at 1 to 2 ppm are effective. Up to 8 ppm paclobutrazol can also be applied as a liner drench, but cultivars vary greatly in sensitivity.

Production and Schedule
Grow the plants at temperatures of 65° to 75° F (18° to 24° C) during the day and 50° to 60° F (10° to 15° C) at night. Provide 4,000 to 7,000 f.c. (43 to 75 klux) light.

Use 150 to 200 ppm nitrogen initially, and increase to 200 to 300 ppm nitrogen later when roots reach the edge of the substrate. Supplemental iron applications may be helpful in promoting dark green foliage. The substrate pH should be 5.5 to 6.3. Avoid overwatering, since that may cause the plants to collapse and the foliage to turn black.

Use one plant per 4 in. (10 cm) pot, one to two per 6 in. (15 cm) pot, and three to four per 10 in. (25 cm) basket. Pinch the plants in 4 in. (10 cm) pots as soon as they are established. *H. petiolare* in all container sizes will need periodic pinching and trimming to maintain the plant shape. The last pruning should be three weeks before marketing. *H. petiolare* plants in 4 in. (10 cm) pots are ready to sell in five to seven weeks, those in 6 in. (15 cm) pots in seven to nine weeks, and those in 10 in. (25 cm) baskets in nine to eleven weeks. *H. thianschanicum* plants in 4 in. (10 cm) pots are ready to sell in ten to twelve weeks; those in 6 in. (15 cm) pots and 10 in. (25 cm) baskets are ready in twelve to fourteen weeks.

Diseases
Botrytis on the foliage can be a major problem. *Pythium, Alternaria,* and *Rhizoctonia* can also occur.

Disorders
Growing plants too wet may cause their collapse. Yellowish or reddish older foliage or bleached-out young leaves may be caused by phosphorus toxicity. Too much foliar growth can be due to high nitrogen fertil-

ization or to excessive watering or fertilizing, especially under low light levels. Do not allow pots to dry out.

References
Hamrick, D. 2003. *Helichrysum,* pp. 425–426. In: *Ball RedBook,* 17th ed., vol. 2, D. Hamrick, ed. Ball Publishing, Batavia, Illinois.

Schoellhorn, R., and E. Berghauer. 2002. Helichrysum and vinca. *GPN* 12(8):100, 1001, 113.

Yoder Green Leaf Perennials. 2004. *Handling Unrooted Perennials.* www.green-leaf-ent.com/urc_handling_2004.pdf.

Heliotrope

'Atlantis' heliotrope.

Common name: Heliotrope.
Scientific name: *Heliotropium arborescen.*
Family: Boraginaceae.
Other propagation methods: Seed.

Description, Uses, and Status
Large clusters of small fragrant purple flowers adorn the 8 to 13 in. (20 to 33 cm) plants. A tender perennial, heliotrope is not frost tolerant and is sold in the spring in pots and packs.

Flowering Control and Dormancy
Flowering becomes faster with the longer days, higher light levels, and warmer temperatures of spring.

Stock Plant Management
Provide stock plants with photoperiods of less than ten hours to avoid flowering. Pinch regularly to develop a well-branched canopy.

Cutting Harvest
Terminal cuttings 1 to 2 in. (2.5 to 5 cm) long with at least one fully expanded leaf are harvested from actively growing plants.

Propagation

Stage 1:
Cutting arrival or harvest and sticking
- Stick cuttings within one or two hours after arrival or harvest.
- Rooting hormones are optional with this species.
- Insert one cutting per cell if using plug flats.

Stage 2: Callusing
- Maintain substrate temperatures of 70° to 72° F (21° to 22° C).
- Maintain air temperatures of 70° to 80° F (21° to 27° C) during days and 68° to 70° F (20° to 21° C) during nights.
- Maintain a light intensity of 500 to 1,000 f.c. (5 to 11 klux).
- Begin foliar feeding once a week with 50 to 75 ppm nitrogen from 20-10-20 if there is any loss in foliage color.
- Maintain a substrate pH of 5.8 to 6.2.
- Transfer the cuttings to Stage 3 after six to nine

days, once 50% of the cuttings begin differentiating root initials.

Stage 3: Root development
- Maintain substrate temperatures of 70° to 72° F (21° to 22° C).
- Maintain air temperatures of 70° to 80° (21° to 27° C) during days and 68° to 70° F (20° to 21° C) during nights.
- Increase the light intensity to 1,000 to 2,000 f.c. (11 to 22 klux).
- Fertilize once a week with 100 ppm nitrogen, alternating between 15-0-15 and 20-10-20, then increase to 200 ppm.
- Roots should develop in seven to fourteen days.

Stage 4: Toning the rooted cutting
- Lower the air temperature to 70° to 80° F (21° to 27° C) during the day and 65° to 68° F (18° to 20° C) at night.
- Move the liners from the mist area into an area of lower relative humidity.
- Increase the light intensity to 2,000 to 4,000 f.c. (22 to 43 klux).
- Fertilize once a week with 150 to 200 ppm nitrogen from 15-0-15 alternating with 20-10-20.
- The cuttings can be toned for seven days.

Plant Growth Regulators
Compact cultivars will not need height control, but taller cultivars can be sprayed with chlormequat (Cycocel) at 500 to 1,000 ppm. A tank mix of 1,500 to 3,000 ppm daminozide (B-Nine) and 750 to 1,000 ppm chlormequat can be used if greater control is required.

Production and Schedule
Recommended temperatures are 70° to 75° F (21° to 24° C) during the day and 65° to 68° F (18° to 20° C) at night. After the plants are established, the night temperature can be reduced to 50° to 55° F (10° to 13° C). Provide 4,000 to 7,000 (43 to 75 klux) light.

A rate of 150 to 200 ppm nitrogen is adequate with every other irrigation, increasing to 200 to 300 ppm after plants are established. A light, well-drained substrate at a pH of 5.5 to 6.2 is desired. Monitor the pH level, since heliotrope can reduce it, inducing iron toxicity. Leaf rolling is a symptom of too-low pH. Even, consistent irrigation is also important. Avoid overirrigation, especially after transplanting plugs. Reduce watering, and allow plants to wilt slightly during cool, cloudy weather to prevent root rot.

Heliotrope showing poor growth and necrotic foliage from low EC. (B. Whipker)

Use one plug per 4 in. (10 cm) pot, one to two per 6 in. (15 cm) pot, and three to five per 10 in. (25 cm) pot. Plants should be pinched after they are established and have developed six leaves. Newer, more compact cultivars may not require a pinch. Plants in 4 in. (10 cm) pots are marketable in six to seven weeks, those in 6 in. (15 cm) pots in nine to eleven weeks, and those in 10 in. (25 cm) pots in ten to twelve weeks.

Diseases
Rhizoctonia, Pythium, Botrytis, and powdery mildew can be problems.

Disorders
Leaf edge burn can be due to water stress, high soluble salts, iron toxicity, low substrate pH, or low EC. Light green or yellow foliage can be due to high pH. The foliage is sensitive to rotting in high humidity and when overmisted. Plants may collapse from overwatering, *Botrytis,* or iron toxicity.

Postharvest
Leaf blackening is common on cuttings during shipping.

References
Hamrick, D. 2003. *Heliotropium,* pp. 426–428. In: *Ball RedBook,* 17th ed., vol. 2, D. Hamrick, ed. Ball Publishing, Batavia, Illinois.

Hibiscus

Common name: Tropical hibiscus, Chinese hibiscus, Hawaiian hibiscus.
Scientific name: *Hibiscus rosa-sinensis.*
Family: Malvaceae.
Other propagation methods: Seed, grafting.

Potted hibiscus plants.

Description, Uses, and Status

The flowers of this hibiscus species are up to 5 in. (13 cm) across and come in a variety of colors. The dark green glossy leaves are ovate and normally have a serrated margin. Used as a landscape plant in frost-free areas, the plant can grow to more than 16 ft. (5 m) tall. Outdoors, it is adaptable to hot dry windy areas. Interestingly, the plant also adapts well to the northern home environment and flowers in winter when acclimatized and grown adjacent to a sunny window. Presently, it is grown as a flowering potted plant in 4 to 10 in. (10 to 25 cm) pots in northern Europe and North America. It is also popular as a large patio specimen.

Flowering Control and Dormancy

The flowers are ephemeral, opening in the morning and senescing by evening. Flowering is autonomous, as the flower number depends on the growth rate of the terminal and axillary shoots, which in turn are dependent upon total light energy at the appropriate temperature.

Stock Plant Management

Specialists maintain stock plants for three or more years. Seasonal variations in the ability to root occur with some cultivars. Stock plants that received high intensity discharge (HID) lighting of less than 4,500 f.c. (48 klux) produced cuttings that rooted more rapidly than those receiving higher irradiances. Cuttings are typically harvested from stock plants, but cuttings are sometimes harvested from plants in production. Propagators of unpatented varieties may consider rooting liners in late summer or early fall for sales the following spring; otherwise, plants can be purchased from reputable dealers in warmer climates of the United States.

Cutting Harvest

Hibiscus is commercially propagated by soft wood cuttings with three to four internodes. Cuttings are 3.5 to 5 in. (9 to 13 cm) long with two mature basal leaves. Flowers and buds are usually removed. If the leaves are large, one or two may also be removed to reduce leaf overlapping; removing them will increase air circulation and light penetration as well as reduce disease problems. However, at least one mature leaf should remain on the cuttings.

Unrooted cuttings must be protected from direct sunlight, excessive heat, and water stress until they are planted. When cuttings are allowed to dry prior to sticking or during the early stages of propagation, success is greatly reduced. Most producers buy unrooted cuttings or grow stock plants that are later sold as large patio plants.

Propagation

The optimum substrate temperature is 79° to 86° F (26° to 30° C) for both difficult and easy-to-root cultivars. Supplemental lighting may be beneficial during the propagation of cuttings. The substrate EC should be at least 0.2 mS/cm for optimum root growth. Good subsequent shoot growth is also dependent on adequate nutrition in the substrate. Cultivars vary widely in rapidity of rooting, which ranges from four to eight weeks.

Work in Florida showed that as the substrate temperature increased from 64° to 93° F (18° to 34° C), optimum IBA concentrations for rooting decreased. While no definite recommendations can be made regarding IBA use, the best rooting for most cultivars occurred with 2,500 to 8,000 ppm basal dips for four to ten minutes, depending on the substrate temperature. A typical concentration used is 5,000 ppm. Each cultivar should be individually tested to determine the most favorable rooting hormone regime.

In Sweden, recommended propagation occurs under white plastic tents in the spring and summer and under clear plastic in the fall and winter instead of using mist. In Florida, a similar system maintains 100% relative humidity under polyethylene film. However, mist may be successful in climates with low humidity and high light if humidity control is not available. In Kenya, cuttings rooted best when polyethylene film was laid directly over the cuttings rather than when they were tented or misted. Dead leaves should be removed during propagation to reduce disease spread. In addition, fungicides may need to be applied every two weeks under the tents, starting with sticking.

Cuttings can be rooted in Oasis or similar cubes, or they can be rooted directly in the final pot. With plug flats, one cutting is inserted per cell. When the cuttings are rooted, two to five are transplanted per 4 to 6 in. (10 to 15 cm) pot. Although plants can be held pot-to-pot until growth commences, it is best to give full space and light on the bench immediately.

Plant Growth Regulators

Chlormequat (Cycocel) sprays are commonly used at rates ranging from 200 ppm when applied after the first pinch to 1,000 ppm when the plants reach the desired size. Paclobutrazol (Bonzi) as a spray at 5 ppm or a drench at 0.5 mg a.i. per pot, and uniconazole (Sumagic) as a spray at 10 ppm or a drench 0.025 to 0.2 mg a.i. per pot are also effective.

Production and Schedule

Hibiscus has been successfully grown under a wide variety of temperature regimes from 64° to 102° F (18° to 39° C). The growth rate was linear from 52° to 90° F (11° to 32° C); at higher temperatures, leaf development decreased.

In winter full light is used, whereas shade is used in summer to control temperature. In Mississippi, the highest-quality hibiscus plants were grown under 50% shade in late winter to early spring, reducing light from 4,250 f.c. (46 klux) to 2,100 f.c. (23 klux).

Adequate water is a constant concern, given the large leaf surface and well-developed roots of hibiscus. The plant is a moderate to heavy feeder, requiring 250 ppm nitrogen during the summer and only 150 to 200 ppm nitrogen during the winter. Regular drenches of magnesium sulfate at 8 oz./100 gal. (6.6 g/L) can prevent the interveinal chlorosis of lower leaves typical of magnesium deficiency. Chlorosis of upper leaves may be due to iron deficiency, which can be due to a lack of iron in the substrate or result from a high substrate pH or insufficient root development.

Pinching occurs five to six weeks after propagation, when active growth has commenced. Multiple pinches may be required and can occur every three to four weeks.

In Europe, propagation to flowering required fourteen to nineteen weeks in the spring and twenty-seven weeks in the winter, even with supplemental lighting. In North America, spring and summer production time is twelve to fifteen weeks and up to twenty-four weeks in the winter. The main production period runs from February to April for May to July sales.

Diseases

Two *Pseudomonas* species can occur, one causing an irregular-shaped angular leaf spot (*P. cichorii*) and the other causing small circular lesions (*P. syringae*). *Cercospora* and *Xanthomonas* leaf spot are also observed and similar in appearance. The former has a more distinct yellow halo. Root rot organisms (*Fusarium* and *Phytophthora*) and viruses can occur, especially in stock plants. Other diseases reported include armillaria root rot (*Armillaria mellea*), gray mold (*Botrytis cinerea*), stem rot (*Mycopsphaerella*), nectria canker (*Nectria*), and bacterial leaf spot (*Pseudomonas*).

Disorders

Cold injury can occur at temperatures well above freezing at 50° F (10° C).

Postharvest

The antiethylene agents silver thiosulfate (STS) and 1-MCP (EthylBloc) have been used experimentally to prevent storage-induced leaf yellowing of unrooted cuttings, but they also reduced rooting.

References

Bertram, L. 1991. Vegetative propagation of *Hibiscus rosa-sinensis* L. in relation to nutrient concentration of the propagation medium. *Scientia Horticulturae* 48:131–139.

Carpenter, W. J. 1989. Medium temperature influences the rooting of *Hibiscus rosa-sinensis* L. *Journal of Environmental Horticulture* 7:79–84.

Carpenter, W. J., and J. A. Cornell. 1992. Auxin application duration and concentration govern rooting of hibiscus stem cuttings. *Journal of the American Society for Horticultural Science* 117:68–74.

Daughtrey, M., and A. R. Chase. 1992. Hibiscus, pp. 123–125. In: *Ball Field Guide to Diseases of Greenhouse Ornamentals*. Ball Publishing, Batavia, Illinois.

Dreistadt, S. H., 2001. *Integrated Pest Management for Floriculture and Nurseries.* University of California Division of Agriculture and Natural Resources Publication 3402. Oakland, California.

Faber, W. 1997. Hibiscus, pp. 80–81. In: *Tips on Growing Specialty Potted Crops,* M. L. Gaston, S. A. Carver, C. A. Irwin, and R. A. Larson, eds. Ohio Florists' Association, Columbus, Ohio.

Griffith, L. P., Jr. 1998. *Tropical Foliage Plants.* Ball Publishing, Batavia, Illinois.

Horst, R. K. 1990. Hibiscus, p. 678. In: *Westcott's Plant Disease Handbook,* 5th ed. Van Nostrand Reinhold, New York.

Johnson, C. R., and D. F. Hamilton. 1977. Rooting of *Hibiscus rosa-sinensis* L. cuttings as influenced by light intensity and ethephon. *HortScience* 12:39–40.

Karlsson, M. G., R. D. Heins, J. O. Gerberick, and M. E. Hackmann. 1991. Temperature driven leaf unfolding rate in *Hibiscus rosa-sinensis. Scientia Horticulturae* 45:323–331.

Kelty, M. M. 1984. Container grown hibiscus: Propagation and production. *Proceedings of the International Plant Propagators' Society* 34:480–486.

Lyles, J. L., J. D. MacDonald, and D. W. Burger. 1992. Short- and long-term heat stress effects on phytophthora root rot of *Hibiscus. HortScience* 27:414–416.

Mudge, K. W., V. N. Mwaja, F. M. Itulya, and J. Ochieng. 1995. Comparison of four moisture management systems for cutting propagation of bougainvillea, hibiscus, and kei apple. *Journal of the American Society for Horticultural Science* 120:366–373.

Neumaier, E. E., T. M. Blessington, and J. A. Price. 1987. Effect of light and fertilizer rate and source on flowering, growth, and quality of hibiscus. *HortScience* 22:902–904.

Newman, S. E., S. B. Tenney, and M. W. Follet. 1989. Use of uniconazole to control height of *Hibiscus rosa-sinensis. HortScience* 24:1041.

Serek, M., A. Prabucki, E. C. Sisler and A. S. Andersen. 1998. Inhibitors of ethylene action affect final quality and rooting of cuttings before and after storage. *HortScience* 33:153–155.

Wang, Y. T. 1991. Growth stage and site of application affect efficacy of uniconazole and GA₃ in hibiscus. *HortScience* 26:148–150.

Wang, Q., and A. S. Andersen. 1989. Propagation of *Hibiscus rosa-sinensis*: relations between stock plant cultivar, age, environment and growth regulator treatments. *Acta Horticulturae* 251: 289–309.

Wang, Y. T., and L. L. Gregg. 1989. Uniconazole affects vegetative growth, flowering, and stem anatomy of hibiscus. *Journal of the American Society for Horticultural Science* 114:927–932.

Wikesjö, K. 1981. Odling av *Hibiscus rosa-sinensis. Konsulentavdelningens Rapporter, Tradgård 205,* Swedish University of Agricultural Science, Alnarp, Sweden. (in Swedish)

Wilkins, H. F. 1986. *Hibiscus rosa-sinensis,* pp. 142–143. In: *Handbook of Flowering,* vol. V, A. H. Halevy, ed. CRC Press, Boca Raton, Florida.

Hydrangea

Common name: Hydrangea, French hydrangea.
Scientific name: *Hydrangea macrophylla* ssp. *macrophylla,* var. *macrophylla.*
Family: Hydrangeaceae.
Other propagation methods: Tissue culture.

Description, Uses, and Status

This hydrangea species is a woody perennial growing to 5 ft. (1.5 m) tall. The opposite leaves are rounded to ovate, toothed, and dark green with a surface luster. The terminal inflorescences form a rounded corymb. Flower colors may be white or various shades of pink, blue, purple, or red. The fertile flowers are small, few, and central in the inflorescence. The majority of the inflorescence is sterile, and only the large sepals are showy. Most sales occur at Easter and Mother's Day; however, plants could be forced into flower for Valentine's Day or held in storage longer and forced for Memorial Day. Typically, hydrangeas are grown in 6 in. (15 cm) pots, and they are produced from a cutting with two axillary buds and pinched once, resulting in four inflorescences. Plants with one inflorescence are also produced in 4 to 5 in. (10 to 15 cm) pots. Hydrangea is a common garden ornamental and cut flower too. Numerous other hydrangea species are used as field-grown cut flowers.

Blue potted hydrangea plant.

Flowering Control and Dormancy

Flowering control during commercial production mimics nature. Spring-rooted vegetative cuttings initiate and develop a dormant flower bud by fall under naturally shortening days and cooler temperatures. Plants are defoliated and placed in cold storage and eventually forced into flower in a warm springlike environment.

For summer growth, plants thrive under moderate night temperatures of 65° F (18° C) and fourteen-hour photoperiods and are often grown outdoors. With night temperatures of 55° to 65° F (13° to 18° C), induction commences regardless of photoperiod. However, an eight-hour photoperiod results in rapid flower induction, initiation, and development at night temperatures below 65° F (18° C). Floral induction eventually occurs at temperatures of 66° to 70° F (19° to 21° C), even under fourteen hours of light. At temperatures above 70° F (21° C) induction is inhibited, and above 80° F (27° C) night temperature no flower induction occurs.

Plants require at least six weeks below 65° F (18° C) with leaves present and another six weeks of cold storage with the leaves removed before they can be forced. Prior to defoliation and cold storage, perfect inflorescences with stigmas must have reached G-stage, in that the stigmatic surface must be well indented on all inflorescences. Further floral differentiation and development continue during cold storage.

Plants are moved into dark storage areas. Natural leaf abscission in the dark is aided by using 2-butyne-1,4-diol (7,500 to 12,500 ppm) sprays or ethylene (1:1000 ethylene:air by volume). Defoliation and leaf removal are a major nuisance but must be done, since *Botrytis* may rot the flower buds during cold storage if the leaves are not removed.

The minimum cold treatment is 40° to 45° F (4° to 7° C) for six weeks, or eight weeks at 52° F (11° C). For long-term storage for late forcing production schedules, use 33° to 35° F (1° to 2° C).

Stock Plant Management

Virus contamination and selection of clean stock are issues for the supplier of unrooted cuttings, since a number of viruses can occur. Obviously infected plants should be discarded during production and forcing.

Stock plants should be grown at a minimum temperature of 70° F (21° C) and kept vegetative by twenty-four-hour lighting. Pinch the stem tips every sixty days, and spray the plants with 25 ppm gibberellic acid (GA_3) two to five days after pinching to encourage shoot elongation. Stock plants should be grown in large enough containers to provide rapid, unchecked growth. Replace stock plants every eighteen to thirty months as the plants become old and woody and cutting production decreases. Most producers purchase unrooted cuttings from propagators rather than maintain their own stock plants.

Cutting Harvest

In North America, softwood shoots 5 to 7 in. (13 to 18 cm) long with three or four nodes and a terminal bud are available from propagators in the Pacific Northwest. These shoots are used to make one single terminal cutting with two subtending opposite leaf pairs and one "butterfly" cutting (a cutting with two opposite leaves and axillary buds). Single eye cuttings can also be made by cutting or dividing a butterfly cutting into two single leaf-node pieces. Terminal cuttings root and establish the quickest but require the most propagation space. Butterfly cuttings provide two strong axillary shoots quickly. Single eye cuttings are usually weaker, require a longer propagation and production time, are more susceptible to diseases, and must be pinched two or more times. However, single eye cuttings allow more plants to be propagated from limited cutting material. Terminal cuttings are typically most popular.

The large leaves of hydrangea cuttings can be cut in half to reduce shading of adjacent buds and allow more cuttings to be propagated in a specified area. However, removing too much leaf tissue will slow establishment of the plants after propagation.

Propagation

A variety of propagation media can be used; the prerequisite is that the substrate be well aerated and well drained during the propagation phase. Other requirements are that it be sterilized and have a pH near 6.0. Cuttings can be rooted in propagation beds, flats, or directly into 2½, 3, or 4 in. (6, 8, or 10 cm) pots. With plug flats, insert one cutting per cell. Leaves of the cuttings should not shade adjacent buds, since that may kill the buds. Cuttings can be rooted in the final container if enough propagation space is available. This process begins in April and ends in June. Mist or fog propagation is used.

The substrate should be maintained at a temperature of 70° to 74° F (21° to 23° C). A rooting hormone consisting of either 10,000 ppm IBA in talc or a solution of 500 ppm IBA plus 250 ppm NAA dip is used. During rooting, shade is used to provide an environment of 2,500 to 3,000 f.c. (27 to 32 klux). Rooting occurs within three to four weeks for terminal cuttings, and four to five weeks for butterfly cuttings.

Plant Growth Regulators

Height control is required during both the vegetative and the reproductive forcing phases. One to two sprays of daminozide (B-Nine) at 5,000 to 7,500 ppm, are used during the vegetative phase; the number of sprays depends on the cultivar. Two spray applications of uniconazole (Sumagic) at 62 ppm are also effective.

During forcing, the inflorescence should be no greater than 0.75 in. (2 cm) when applying the plant growth regulator. Two spray applications of daminozide at 2,500 to 5,000 ppm are typically used. Other growth retardants can also be used: ancymidol (A-Rest) drenches at 0.25 mg a.i. (2 ppm) per 6 in. (15 cm) pot, flurprimidol (Topflor) sprays at 100 to 200 ppm, and paclobutrazol (Bonzi) sprays at 50 ppm.

Production and Schedule

A substrate temperature of 60° to 62° F (16° to 17° C) supplied by bottom heat and an air temperature of 58° F (14° C) will allow root growth before shoot growth starts. Forcing temperatures can be increased above or decreased below the recommended 60° to 62° F (16° to 17° C) night temperatures to hasten or slow development. Increase light intensities from 2,500 to 3,000 f.c. (27 to 32 klux) at propagation, to 3,000 to 4,000 f.c. (32 to 43 klux) immediately after rooted cuttings are transplanted, to 5,000 to 7,500 f.c. (54 to 81 klux) during vegetative growth. Shading is normally not used during vegetative growth outdoors in northern latitudes. In more southerly latitudes, light intensity can be reduced up to 50%. During forcing, full light intensity is preferred until the inflorescences begin to open, then shade is used to prevent burning and pigment bleaching. Day temperature control may be lost, so shade may also be required for late spring forcing schedules.

Water loss or stress is of constant concern during hydrangea production and forcing. Hydrangea stomates are reported to never close, and with the large leaf surface abundant amounts of water are required. Marginal leaf and flower necrosis easily occur if the plants are stressed. For this reason, shading is used to reduce temperature and transpiration at high temperatures. However, do not overwater, a common occurrence prior to the start of new root and shoot growth.

Hydrangea fertilizer regimes of 60 to 100 ppm nitrogen are used until flower initiation. During forcing or after dormancy is broken and new root activity has commenced, 100 to 150 ppm nitrogen is adequate.

Controlling pH is essential to obtain the correct flower color. The appropriate pH must be maintained during both the summer vegetative phase and the subsequent forcing phase of the flowering plant. If the pH regimes for pink or blue inflorescences are switched during forcing, a muddy purplish color develops due to a residual effect from the vegetative stage in the floral tissue.

The pH is not actually the cause of pink or blue inflorescences, but a low 5.5 pH influences the availability of specific metal ions, such as aluminum. When aluminum forms a complex with delphinidin-3-glucoside pigment in the sepals, deep blue inflorescences are produced. If no aluminum is present, the pigment remains pink. Phosphorus is in competition with aluminum, so low-phosphorus fertilizers and no phosphoric acid injection must be used in the production of blue hydrangea cultivars. To ensure an adequate supply of aluminum and to maintain an acidic substrate pH of 5.2 to 5.5, aluminum sulfate at 10 to 15 lb./100 gal. (12 to 18 g/L) is used every ten to fourteen days during forcing. Aluminum sulfate is normally applied to blue cultivars one or two times during the summer and at least three times during forcing. However, if plants were not treated with aluminum prior to forcing, aluminum sulfate must be applied within the first five weeks of forcing to produce adequate blue color.

The opposite is true with pink cultivars; superphosphate and ample levels of phosphorus are used, and a pH of 6.0 to 6.2 is maintained. Some cultivars can be either deep blue or pink according to the pH. Pink to red pigment formation can be manipulated if the pH is 6.0 or higher.

The substrate should be pasteurized, have an adequate water-holding capacity, but be well drained and well aerated.

Butterfly cuttings have one pair of axillary buds. After rooting, these buds break dormancy and when three nodes have developed, they are pinched leaving two nodes for a total of four axillary buds. Hopefully, these four buds will break dormancy and will be the site of three to four terminal flower buds. A second pinch can be used to produce plants with a greater number of but smaller inflorescences. Typically, terminal cuttings are sheared to allow three leaf pairs (six buds) to remain, which produce premium-quality plants with five to six inflorescences.

The first pinch is two to three weeks after cuttings have become established. The schedule and timing are based on the type of cutting (terminal, butterfly, or single eye), the date of propagation, and the date of pinching. These three factors are under the control of the producer and are, in turn, based on market demand regarding the desired number of inflorescences per plant and the size of pot being produced for sale. Many growers bypass propagation and purchase dormant plants in 4 to 6 in. (10 to 15 cm) pots or bare-root plants; the dormant plants in 4 in. (10 cm) pots are repotted into 6 in. (15 cm) pots.

Diseases

Powdery mildew (*Ersiphe polygoni*) on leaves is the major problem on outdoor vegetative growth. *Botrytis* during propagation and cold storage is also a concern. Leaf spots (*Cercospora arborescentis, C. hydrangeae, Phyllosticta hydrangeae,* and *Septoria hydrangeae*) can also occur on outdoor-grown plants. Other diseases recorded include root and stem rot (*Pythium* and *Rhizoctonia solani*), southern blight (*Sclerotium rolfsii*), armillaria root rot (*Armillaria mellea*), rust (*Pucciniastrum hydrangeae*), and tomato spotted wilt virus.

Disorders

Weak shoots with or without a flower bud are considered to be the result of insufficient light due to overcrowding during the summer. Premature budding in late summer and autumn results in small flower heads due to inadequate photosynthate/leaf numbers. Total failure to form flower buds can be attributed to temperatures too warm for floral initiation and development, defoliation by mildew or other causes prior to flower formation, or insufficient time for vegetative growth prior to floral induction because of late pinching.

Insufficient cooling (duration or correct temperature) or premature cooling prior to development of G-stage results in slow forcing and an inflorescence that is not morphologically correct and will not form the proper pigment. Various viruses also result in abnormal flower and pigment coloration.

Foliar malformations can also occur (some cultivars are not susceptible) during the summer; the leaves are thickened, leathery, puckered, straplike, and occasionally mottled. These malformations are not due to nutrient deficiencies but occur when temperatures are 91° F (31° C) or higher during the day and 82° F (28° C) or higher during the night. High light levels accentuate the malformations.

Various insects can injure immature leaves and buds, and they can cause malformed leaves. Nutrient deficiencies can occur at a pH below 5.2 or above 6.5. Pigmentation that is not appropriate for the cultivar is the result of a suitable pH not being maintained throughout the production and forcing.

References

Bailey, D. A. 1989a. *Hydrangea Production.* Timber Press, Portland, Oregon.

Bailey, D. A. 1989b. Uniconazole effects on forcing of florists' hydrangeas. *HortScience* 24:518.

Bailey, D. A. 1997. Commercial hydrangea forcing. *Bedding Plants International News* 28(10):1, 6–8.

Bailey, D. A., and B. Clark. 1992. Summer applications of plant growth retardants affect spring forcing of hydrangeas. *HortTechnology* 2:213–216.

Bailey, D. A., and P. A. Hammer. 1988. Evaluation of nutrient deficiency and micronutrient toxicity symptoms in florists' hydrangea. *Journal of the American Society for Horticultural Science* 113:363–367.

Bailey, D. A., and P. A. Hammer. 1990. Possible non-pathogenic origin of hydrangea distortion. *HortScience* 25:808.

Bailey, D. A., and T. C. Weiler. 1984. Control of floral initiation in florists' hydrangea. *Journal of the American Society for Horticultural Science* 109:785–791.

Blom, T. J., and B. D. Piott. 1992. Florists' hydrangea blueing with aluminum sulfate applications during forcing. *HortScience* 27:1084–1087.

Blom, T. J., and R. B. Smith. 1994. Ethylene gas for defoliation of hydrangeas. *HortScience* 29:636–637.

Dreistadt, S. H. 2001. *Integrated Pest Management for Floriculture and Nurseries.* University of California Division of Agriculture and Natural Resources

Publication 3402. Oakland, California.

Litlere, B., and E. Strømme. 1975. The influence of temperature, day length, and light intensity on flowering of *Hydrangea macrophylla* Thumb. Ser. *Acta Horticulturae* 51:285–298.

Okada, M., and K. Okawa. 1974. The quantity of aluminum and phosphorus in plants and its influence on the sepal color of *Hydrangea macrophylla* DC. *Journal of the Japanese Society for Horticultural Science* 42:361–370.

Peters, J. 1975. Flower formation in some cultivars of *Hydrangea macrophylla. Gartenbauwissenschaft* 40:63–65. (in German)

Shanks, J. 1985. *Hydrangea,* pp. 535–558. In: *Ball RedBook,* 14th ed., V. Ball, ed. Reston Press, Reston, Virginia.

Shanks, J. B., and C. B. Link. 1951. Effect of temperature and photoperiod on growth and flower formation in hydrangeas. *Proceedings of the American Society for Horticultural Science* 58:357–366.

Struckmeyer, B. E. 1950. Blossom bud induction and differentiation in *Hydrangea. Proceedings of the American Society for Horticultural Science* 56:410–414.

Impatiens, Bedding

Common name: Bedding impatiens, patience plant.
Scientific name: *Impatiens walleriana.*
Family: Balsaminaceae.
Other propagation methods: Seed.

Description, Uses, and Status
The bedding impatiens is one of the two most important bedding plants in North America; the geranium (*Pelargonium*) is the other. While most bedding impatiens cultivars are seed propagated, there are a growing number of cutting-propagated cultivars with double flowers and/or variegated foliage. Several types of interesting hybrids between *I. walleriana* and other species are also cutting propagated. Plants thrive in open locations to almost deep shade, and they can be grown in packs, pots, hanging baskets, and mixed containers.

Flowering Control and Dormancy
Impatiens is a day-neutral plant. The rate of flowering depends on total light energy accumulated at an appropriate temperature.

Stock Plant Management
Because of the sensitivity of impatiens to thrips and thrips-borne viruses (impatiens necrotic spot virus and tomato spotted wilt virus), much effort must go into ensuring that the stock plants stay thrips free. Monthly ethephon (Florel) can be used on stock plants to keep plants vegetative and to promote branching.

'Fiesta Pink Ruffle' double impatiens flowers.

Cutting Harvest
Terminal cuttings 0.8 to 2 in. (2 to 5 cm) long with at least one fully expanded leaf are harvested.

Propagation

Stage 1:
Cutting arrival or harvest and sticking
- Store cuttings at 50° to 60° F (10° to 16° C) for up to twenty-four hours if planting is going to be delayed.
- Rooting hormones are not required. However, either 2,500 ppm IBA or IBA with up to 500 ppm NAA can be used on cutting bases.
- Stick cuttings so that 0.5 in. (1.3 cm) of the stem is below the substrate surface.
- Insert one cutting per cell if using plug flats.

Stage 2: Callusing

- Maintain substrate temperatures of 70° to 75° F (21° to 24° C).
- Maintain air temperatures of 70° to 75° F (21° to 24° C) during days and 65° to 70° F (18° to 21° C) during nights.
- Keep the substrate sufficiently moist so that water is easily squeezed out of it, but not so much that the cutting base is waterlogged. The base of the cutting needs air for proper rooting.
- Avoid overmisting, which will delay rooting. Bedding impatiens is a good candidate for tenting.
- Maintain a light intensity of 500 to 1,000 f.c. (5 to 11 klux).
- Begin foliar feeding with 50 to 75 ppm nitrogen from 15-0-15 as soon as leaves begin to show any color loss.
- Maintain a substrate pH of 5.5 to 6.0.
- Transfer the cuttings to Stage 3 after five to seven days, once 50% of the cuttings begin differentiating root initials.

Stage 3: Root development

- Reduce the substrate temperature to 68° to 72° F (20° to 22° C).
- Maintain air temperatures of 70° to 75° F (21° to 24° C) during days and 65° to 70° F (18° to 21° C) during nights.
- Increase the light intensity to 1,000 to 2,000 f.c. (11 to 22 klux).
- Fertilize once a week with 100 ppm nitrogen, increasing to 200 ppm; use a fertilizer such as 15-0-15, which is low in ammonium.
- Roots should develop in seven to nine days.

Stage 4: Toning the rooted cutting

- Lower the air temperature to 68° to 75° F (20° to 24° C) during the day and 65° to 68° F (18° to 20° C) at night.
- Move the liners from the mist area into an area of lower relative humidity.
- Increase the light intensity to 1,500 to 2,500 f.c. (16 to 27 klux).
- Fertilize twice a week with150 to 200 ppm nitrogen from 15-0-15 alternating with 20-10-20.
- The cuttings can be toned for seven days.

Plant Growth Regulators

Plant growth regulators can be avoided if plants are not watered or fertilized too much. However, during propagation, paclubutrazol (Bonzi or Piccolo) drenches at 3 to 10 ppm or a tank-mixed spray of ancymidol (A-Rest) at 6 to 12 ppm and daminozide (B-Nine) at 1,250 to 2,500 ppm can be used ten to fourteen days after sticking unrooted cuttings.

During production, 5,000 ppm daminozide sprays can be used. Paclubutrazol is effective at 5 to 18 ppm, but excessive concentrations delay flowering. Sprays of uniconazole (Sumagic) at 5 ppm, flurprimidol (Topflor) at 20 to 60 ppm, or ancymidol at 10 to 44 ppm are also effective. Ethephon (Florel) sprays can also be used at 500 to 1,000 ppm. Plants respond moderately to negative temperature differences (DIF).

Production and Schedule

Recommended day temperatures are 70° to 75° F (21° to 24° C) and night temperatures 60° to 65° F (16° to 18° C). Little or no shade, depending on the season, is used during greenhouse production. Provide 4,000 to 6,000 f.c. (43 to 65 klux) light. Intense sunlight that raises the leaf temperature may reduce growth. However, internode elongation occurs with too much shade.

Internode elongation is maximized when plants are kept continually moist. Moderate water stress results in short plants. When plants reach their final size, more frequent water stress controls growth. Too much water stress, however, results in yellow lower leaves and flower drop.

A rate of 100 to 150 ppm nitrogen is adequate with every second or third irrigation. Wait to begin fertilization until two weeks after transplanting. Excess nitrogen, especially ammonium, results in long internodes, delayed flowering, and numerous leaves. A light, well-drained substrate with a pH 5.8 to 6.2 is desired.

Use one plug per 4 in. (10 cm) pot, one to two per 6 in. (15 cm) pot, and four to five per 10 in. (25 cm) basket. Plants do not need to be pinched; however, plants can be pinched one to two weeks after transplanting. In such a case, pinch back to above the fifth or sixth leaf above the substrate line. Older plants can be trimmed at any time to shape them. Plants in 4 in. (10 cm) pots are marketable in six to nine weeks, those in 6 in. (15 cm) pots in seven to ten weeks, and those in 10 in. (25 cm) hanging baskets in ten to twelve weeks.

Diseases

Unfortunately, impatiens is highly susceptible to its namesake virus, impatiens necrotic spot, and to the tomato spotted wilt virus; impatiens exhibit a variety of symptoms. A number of other diseases, such as stem rot and damping-off (*Rhizoctonia*), leaf spot

(*Pseudomonas syringae*), and gray mold (*Botrytis cinerea*) on the flowers can occur. Other diseases have been reported, including root and crown rot (*Pythium*), verticillium wilt (*Verticillium dahliae*), black root rot (*Thielaviopsis basicola*), southern wilt (*Sclerotium rolfsii*), leaf spots (*Cercospora, Phyllosticta, Ramularia,* or *Septoria*), and soft rot (*Erwinia carotovora*).

Disorders
Ethylene can abort meristems. Delayed or inadequate flowering and excessive height are often due to excessive fertilization (especially high nitrogen and ammonia) and/or irrigation. Leaf yellowing can be due to excessive water stress or low temperatures.

Postharvest
Ethylene causes flower abscission but 0.1 to 1 ppm ethylene for up to twenty hours did not influence leaf abscission or cutting rooting.

References
Barrett, J. E. 1994. Chemical growth regulators, pp. 99–105. In: *Tips on Growing Bedding Plants,* 3rd ed., H. K. Tayama, T. J. Roll, and M. L. Gaston, eds. Ohio Florists Association, Columbus, Ohio.

Barrett, J. E., and J. E. Erwin. 1994. Height control,

pp. 197–213. In: *Bedding Plants IV,* E. J. Holcomb, ed. Ball Publishing, Batavia, Illinois.

Daughtrey, M., and A. R. Chase. 1992. *Impatiens,* pp. 125–131. In: *Ball Field Guide to Diseases of Greenhouse Ornamentals.* Ball Publishing, Batavia, Illinois.

Dreistadt, S. H. 2001. *Integrated Pest Management for Floriculture and Nurseries.* University of California Division of Agriculture and Natural Resources Publication 3402. Oakland, California.

Hamrick, D. 2003. *Impatiens,* pp. 454–463. In: *Ball Redbook,* 17th ed., vol. 2, D. Hamrick, ed. Ball Publishing, Batavia, Illinois.

Kaczperski, M. P., and W. H. Carlson. 1988. Production pointers for Impatiens—#1 bedding plant crop. *Bedding Plants Incorporated* 19(1):6–7.

Nowack, J., and R. M. Rudnicki. 1990. *Postharvest Handling and Storage of Cut Flowers, Florist Greens, and Potted Plants.* Timber Press, Portland, Oregon.

Starman, T. W., M. C. Robinson, and K. L. Eixmann. 2004. Efficacy of ethephon on vegetative annuals. *HortTechnology* 14:83–87.

Whipker, B. E. 2003. Growth regulators for floricultural crops, pp. 439–448. In: *2003 North Carolina Agricultural Chemicals Manual,* College of Agriculture and Life Science, North Carolina State University, Raleigh, North Carolina.

Impatiens, New Guinea

Common name: New Guinea impatiens.
Scientific name: *Impatiens hawkeri.*
Family: Balsaminaceae.
Other propagation methods: Seed.

Description, Uses, and Status
New Guinea impatiens flower colors range from white to pink, red, purple, and salmon. The linear leaves may be green, bronze, or multicolored with a blaze of white, yellow, or orange. The plant can be used in a wide variety of ways; originally considered a spring potted bedding plant and a hanging basket, it is occasionally sold year-round as a potted flowering plant.

Flowering New Guinea impatiens crop in the greenhouse.

TABLE 2

Recommended container sizes and spacing for New Guinea impatiens stock plants.

CROP DURATION	CONTAINER SIZE	OPTIMUM SPACING	MINIMUM SPACING
Less than four months	5½ to 6 in.	1.1 to 1.7 pots/sq. ft.	2.0 pots/sq. ft.
	(14 to 15 cm)	(11.8 to 18.3 pots/m²)	(21.5 pots/m²)
Four to six months	6½ to 7 in.	1.0 to 1.7 pots/sq. ft.	1.3 to 2.0 pots/sq. ft.
	(17 to 18 cm)	(10.8 to 18.3 pots/m²)	(14.0 to 21.5 pots/m²)
Six to eight months	7 to 8 in.	0.7 to 1.0 pots/sq. ft.	1.3 pots/sq. ft.
	(18 to 20 cm)	(7.5 to 10.8 pots/m²)	(14.0 pots/m²)

Adapted from Williams and Ruis, 1995.

Flowering Control and Dormancy

Flowering control is based on total light and temperature as these factors influence total carbohydrates through photosynthesis.

Stock Plant Management

Because of the sensitivity of New Guinea impatiens to thrips and thrips-borne viruses (impatiens necrotic spot virus and tomato spotted wilt virus), much effort must go into ensuring that the stock plants stay insect and disease free. Purchase fresh cuttings for stock plants each season.

Stock plants can be grown in a variety of containers, and plant spacing will depend on the size of the containers used and the duration of the stock plant crop (see table 2). The substrate should maintain its structure for the length of the stock plant crop and provide approximately 50% moisture and 20% air space. The pH should be 5.5 to 6.2, and EC should be maintained at less than 2.0 mS/cm using saturated paste extract or less than 1.2 mS/cm using 1:2 substrate:water dilution. New Guinea impatiens is sensitive to high substrate EC; monitor it regularly and manage it appropriately. Delay fertilizing newly potted stock plants for two to three weeks to allow plants to become established. Thereafter, begin using 125 to 150 ppm nitrogen constant liquid fertilization. Avoid using fertilizers with high levels of minor elements, since New Guinea impatiens is sensitive to minor elements, in particular iron and manganese. Researchers at North Carolina State University reported that shorter cuttings with smaller leaf areas occurred when stock plants were fertilized with nitrogen at 100 ppm; however, the greatest cutting yield, root number, and shoot dry weight were achieved with nitrogen at 300 ppm.

Stock plants should be grown at temperatures up to 85° F (29° C) during the day and 68° to 72° F (20° to 22° C) at night. Flower development is accentuated by a lower temperature of 65° F (18° C), which should be avoided. Flowering is also favored by high light intensity; maintain approximately 3,000 ft. (32 klux).

Stock plants should be regularly pinched, shaped, and thinned. Pinching plants early will provide the structure to support large numbers of cuttings later, and it will reduce flower and bud development. Be sure to pinch secondary shoots if cuttings are not being harvested. This will prevent shoots from getting too mature and will reduce flowering. The last pinch should occur four to five weeks before cuttings need to be harvested. If cuttings are only being harvested lightly, be sure to pinch strong shoots remaining after the cuttings are harvested, to prevent them from getting too old. Plants should also be shaped and thinned periodically to remove weak shoots and excessive foliage. This will open up the plant canopy, increase air circulation, reduce *Botrytis* problems, and allow for easier pest control. Shaping and thinning may be particularly important for overgrown stock plants that have dead foliage within the canopy supporting Botrytis.

Ethephon (Florel) at 250 to 500 ppm aborts flower buds and increases branching of stock plants. Applications can be made every two to four weeks, depending on the cultivar. Some cultivars and intensively harvested plants may not benefit from ethephon. If stock plants are to be sold, treatments should stop eight weeks prior to sales to allow for flower development.

Cutting Harvest

Cuttings comprise one pair of fully expanded leaves, three to four young leaves, and the growing point. The cutting should be 0.75 to 1.2 in. (2 to 4 cm) long with a basal stem that is 0.2 to 0.5 in. (0.5 to 1.3 cm) long. The cutting should not have any flower buds.

Propagation

Stage 1:
Cutting arrival or harvest and sticking

- Store cuttings at 50° to 60° F (10° to 16° C) for up to twenty-four hours if planting is going to be delayed.
- If cuttings are wilted, dip them in 70° F (21° C) water for thirty minutes to rehydrate them prior to sticking.
- Use a rooting hormone, 2,500 ppm IBA, on cutting bases if rooting a number of cultivars together, since this will promote uniformity within the crop. Rooting hormones are not necessary, however.
- Maintain leaf turgidity with mist, fog, or plastic tunnel tents (clear in the winter, white in the summer). Northern growers may have to use tempered water to mist because significant purpling can occur with cold water.
- Root the cuttings in plug trays or directly into the final container. Insert one cutting per cell if using plug flats.

Stage 2: Callusing

- Maintain substrate temperatures of 70° to 75° F (21° to 24° C).
- Maintain air temperatures of 70° to 75° F (21° to 24° C) during days and 65° to 70° F (18° to 21° C) during nights.
- Use as little mist as possible to maintain turgidity without saturating the substrate too much. Keep the substrate sufficiently moist so that water is easily squeezed out of it, but not so much that the cutting base is waterlogged. The base of the cutting needs air for proper rooting.
- Maintain a light intensity of 500 to 1,000 f.c. (5 to 11 klux).
- Begin foliar feeding with 50 to 75 ppm nitrogen from 20-10-20 as soon as leaves begin to show any color loss.
- Maintain a substrate pH of 5.5 to 6.0.
- Transfer the cuttings to Stage 3 after five to seven days, once 50% of the cuttings begin differentiating root initials.

Stage 3: Root development

- Reduce the substrate temperature to 68 ° to 72° F (20° to 22° C).

Increasing ethephon concentration prevents flowering in New Guinea impatiens.

- Maintain air temperatures of 70° to 75° F (21° to 24° C) during days and 65° to 70° F (18° to 21° C) during nights.
- Begin drying out the substrate once roots are visible.
- Begin increasing the light intensity to 1,000 to 1,500 f.c. (11 to 16 klux) as the cuttings start to root out.
- Fertilize with 100 ppm nitrogen, alternating between 15-0-15 and 20-10-20, then increase to 200 ppm.
- Roots should develop in nine to eleven days.

Stage 4: Toning the rooted cutting

- Lower the air temperature to 68° to 75° F (20° to 24° C) during the day and 65° to 68° F (18° to 20° C) at night.
- Move the liners from the mist area into an area of lower relative humidity.
- Increase the light intensity to 1,500 to 2,500 f.c. (16 to 27 klux).
- Provide shade during the middle of the day to reduce temperature stress.
- Fertilize once a week with 150 to 200 ppm nitrogen from 15-0-15 alternating with 20-10-20.
- The cuttings can be toned for seven days.

Plant Growth Regulators

Most cultivars are compact and well branched and require little or no plant growth regulator applications. Height control begins in plug production. Spacing plants properly and growing them on the dry side, but not stressed to the point of wilting, are two steps. High light and zero to negative temperature differences (DIF) or DROP are also important (see chapter 8 for more information). During propagation, paclobutrazol (Bonzi or Piccolo) drenches at 3 to 15 ppm or a tank-mixed spray of ancymidol (A-Rest) at 4 to 10 ppm and daminozide (B-Nine) at 1,250 to 2,500 ppm can be used fourteen to twenty-one days after sticking unrooted cuttings.

During production, all commonly used plant growth regulators are effective as sprays; they include ancymidol at 67 ppm, daminozide at 1,500 ppm, paclobutrazol at 0.5 to 5 ppm, chlormequat (Cycocel) at 500 ppm, uniconazole (Sumagic) at 2 ppm, and flurprimidol (Topflor) at 2.5 to 7.5 ppm.

Production and Schedule

New Guinea impatiens has a very narrow commercially acceptable temperature range of 77° to 80° F (25° to 27° C). Growth is inhibited above 80° F (27° C) and below 63° F (17° C). Light intensity below 3,000 f.c. (32 klux) results in increased internode elongation and increased days to flower. Intensities above 5,000 f.c. (54 klux) can result in reduced growth and leaf rolling.

Once established, New Guinea impatiens transpires large quantities of water, which can be related to its large leaf canopy mass and the warm production temperatures. On the other hand, overwatering newly transplanted plugs can have serious consequences before new roots adequately develop. Roots form better in a moist rather than a wet substrate.

New Guinea impatiens is sensitive to excessive soluble salts; maintain EC at less than 1.5 mS/cm using 1:2 substrate:water dilution. Delay fertilization for two to three weeks after transplanting to the final container. Thereafter, a range of 100 to 200 ppm nitrogen from a balanced fertilizer is adequate for finished plant production. However, be sure not to underfertilize the plants. On the other hand, New Guinea impatiens is also susceptible to iron and manganese toxicity, which are often due to low substrate pH. Symptoms include stunting and twisting or malformations of the upper leaves. Selection of a well-aerated substrate that still retains moisture is critical but challenging. The pH should be 5.8 to 6.5, with 5.9 to 6.1 optimum.

The crop time is ten to fourteen weeks from transplanting a rooted plug. Plants in 6, 8, 10 or 12 in. (15, 20, 25 or 30 cm) pots require two or more weeks longer to produce than those in 5 in. (13 cm) pots.

Diseases

The most serious diseases are impatiens necrotic spot and tomato spotted wilt viruses. The major fungus diseases damping-off and crown rot (*Rhizoctonia*), root rot (*Pythium*), and leaf spot and cutting dieback (*Botrytis*) can be serious. The bacterial disease *Pseudomonas* and fungal pathogen powdery mildew have also plagued production. Other reported diseases include verticillium wilt (*Verticillium dahliae*), black root rot (*Thielaviopsis basicola*), southern wilt (*Sclerotium rolfsii*), leaf spots (*Cercospora, Phyllosticta, Ramularia,* or *Septoria*) and soft rot (*Erwinia carotovora*).

Disorders

Cold damage leading to plant death can occur with extended temperatures of 42° to 47° F (6° to 8° C). Delayed or lack of flowering can be due to light levels less than 2,500 f.c. (27 klux), night temperatures higher than 68° F (20° C), and/or nitrogen levels greater than 200 ppm. Slow root development after planting could be due to root rot, an overly wet substrate, or high substrate EC.

Chlorotic foliage on New Guinea impatiens due to low substrate EC. (B. Whipker)

Postharvest

Ethylene at 0.1 to 1 ppm for 20 hours did not influence leaf abscission or cutting rooting.

References

Daughtrey, M. 1995. Other diseases and their control, pp. 133–140. In: *New Guinea Impatiens,* W. Banner and M. Klopmeyer, eds. Ball Publishing, Batavia, Illinois.

Dreistadt, S. H. 2001. *Integrated Pest Management for Floriculture and Nurseries.* University of California Division of Agriculture and Natural Resources Publication 3402. Oakland, California.

Erwin, J. 1995. Light and temperature, pp. 41–54. In: *New Guinea Impatiens,* W. Banner and M. Klopmeyer, eds. Ball Publishing, Batavia, Illinois.

Erwin, J., M. Ascerno, F. Pfleger, and R. Heins. 1992. New Guinea impatiens production. *Minnesota Commercial Flower Growers Association Bulletin* 41(3):1–15.

Judd, L. K., and D. A. Cox. 1992b. Growth of New Guinea impatiens inhibited by high growth–medium electrical conductivity. *HortScience* 27:1193–1194.

Mikkelsen, E. P. 1995. Rooting, pp. 81–86. In: *New Guinea Impatiens,* W. Banner and M. Klopmeyer, eds. Ball Publishing, Batavia, Illinois.

Mikkelsen Incorporated. 1989. *Cultural information for Mikkel Sunshine New Guinea Impatiens.* Mikkelsens Incorporated Publication, Ashtabula, Ohio.

Pasutti, D. W., and J. L. Weigle. 1980. Growth-regulat-ed effect on New Guinea impatiens hybrids. *Scientia Horticulturae* 12:293–298.

Williamson, J. E., and P. Ruis. 1995. Stock plant production, pp. 65–79. In: *New Guinea Impatiens,* W. Banner and M. Klopmeyer, eds. Ball Publishing, Batavia, Illinois.

Ipomoea

Common name: Ornamental sweet potato.
Scientific name: *Ipomoea batatas.*
Family: Convolvulaceae.
Other propagation methods: None.

'Sweet Caroline Bright Green' and 'Sweet Caroline Purple' ornamental sweet potato in the landscape.

Description, Uses, and Status

This ornamental version of the popular sweet potato is grown for its large leaves that are burgundy, chartreuse, or variegated pink, green, and white. Increasingly variable leaf shapes from heart shaped to palmately lobed are available as new cultivars are released. Flowers can be produced but are usually hidden underneath the foliage. A tender perennial vine grown outdoors in Zones 8 to 10, ornamental sweet potato is not cold tolerant and is sold in the spring in pots and hanging baskets. Some cultivars are quite vigorous. Ornamental sweet potato is one of the best plants for difficult situations outdoors, such as poorly drained soil or hot, dry locations. Shoots arising from overwintered roots should be sprayed with a post-emergence herbicide such as glyphosate to prevent aggressive runners in spring and summer gardens.

Flowering Control and Dormancy

Ornamental sweet potato is a short-day plant. While flowers usually develop below the foliage, this is not a problem because the plants are grown for their foliage. The flowers can be quite attractive, however, and future breeding efforts may develop cultivars used for both flowers and foliage.

Stock Plant Management

Hanging basket culture is recommended. Keep stock plants actively growing for optimum cutting yields. Because of concerns about the sweet potato weevil, some areas are restricted from importing cuttings from states that can host the weevil. In such cases, purchase cuttings from states outside the restricted area.

A sample of the various leaf shapes available on ornamental sweet potato. (B. Whipker)

Ornamental sweet potato flowers. (B. Whipker)

The substrate pH should be maintained at 5.5 to 6.2. Use 100 to 200 ppm nitrogen. The foliage color changes in response to fertilizer levels.

Use one plug per 4 or 6 in. (10 or 15 cm) pot, and two to four per 10 in. (25 cm) basket. Pinching is not required, but plants can be pinched one to two weeks after planting. Older plants in any size container can be trimmed at any time up to two weeks prior to sale to shape them. Generally, 4 in. (10 cm) pots finish in four to five weeks, 6 in. (15 cm) pots in five to six weeks, and 8 to 10 in. (20 to 25 cm) pots or baskets in eight

Edema on an ornamental sweet potato leaf. (B. Whipker)

to ten weeks. Heavily variegated cultivars tend to be slower growing and require an extra week or two.

Cutting Harvest

Terminal cuttings are typically used, but subterminal cuttings can also be used if propagation material is limited.

Propagation

The optimal substrate temperature is 75° to 80° F (24° to 27° C), and bottom heat is encouraged. Maintain a substrate pH of 5.5 to 6.2. Sweet potato cuttings are quite easy to root, usually within four or five days, and they need only enough mist to prevent wilting. A rooting hormone can be used but is not required. Cuttings can be propagated in plugs with one cutting per cell or directly into the final container. Fertilize once with a low rate of nitrogen (50 to 100 ppm) during propagation.

Plant Growth Regulators

Plant size is best controlled culturally with water stress, but uniconazole (Sumagic) sprays at 10 to 25 ppm are effective. Ethephon (Florel) sprays can be used at 500 to 1,000 ppm. A drench of paclobutrazol (Bonzi) can also be used at 8 ppm on plugs prior to transplanting.

Production and Schedule

Grow the plants at 72° to 80° F (22° to 27° C) during days and 60° to 65° F (16° to 18° C) during nights and. Ornamental sweet potato prefers warm temperatures and high light to produce the highest-quality plants. Temperatures below 55° F (13° C) will slow growth significantly. Maintain 4,000 to 7,000 f.c. (43 to 75 klux) light levels. Low light intensities below 1,500 f.c. (16 klux) may reduce leaf coloration.

Diseases

Root rots and viruses can be a problem, but this species is quite durable.

Disorders

Edema may be a problem, but it can be prevented by allowing the substrate to dry between irrigations and by providing good air circulation. Edema, the bursting of cells resulting in corky lesions on the foliage, is accentuated by low light or high humidity.

References

Hamrick, D. 2003. *Ipomoea,* pp. 463–464. In: *Ball RedBook,* 17th ed., vol. 2, D. Hamrick, ed. Ball Publishing, Batavia, Illinois.

Riley, J. 2004. Sweet Carolina ipomoea. *GPN* 14(13):74.

Schoellhorn, R. 2000. Control vegetative plug growth with PGRs. *GMPro* 20(12):53–55.

Starman, T. W., M. C. Robinson, and K. L. Eixmann. 2004. Efficacy of ethephon on vegetative annuals. *HortTechnology* 14:83–87.

Kalanchoe

Common name: Kalanchoe.
Scientific name: *Kalanchoe blossfeldiana.*
Family: Crassulaceae.
Other propagation methods: Seed, tissue culture.

Description, Uses, and Status

Kalanchoe has succulent rounded leaves with scalloped edges and terminal clusters of small flowers. An internationally produced flowering potted plant, kalanchoe is one of the leading potted plants in Europe. The plant is prized for its longevity as a houseplant, and a host of flower colors from white, pink, yellow, and orange to red has increased its popularity. Kalanchoe can also be used in hanging baskets, dish gardens, and the outdoor garden. It is occasionally used for cut flowers.

Flowering Control and Dormancy

Kalanchoe is a short-day plant, requiring only two short days and long nights for the beginning of floral induction. However, increasing the number of short days results in a greater number of individual flowers in the cyme. There can be several hundred flowers per inflorescence. Commercially, plants are typically kept under short-day conditions for induction, initiation, and development until they are sold. Eleven to eleven and a half hours of light and thirteen to twelve and a half hours of dark are recommended for flowering because the critical night length is twelve and a half hours. During the short-day flower induction period, temperatures 80° F (27° C) and higher must be avoided, particularly if this temperature is experienced during the first three hours of dark. Commercially, short days should commence as late as possible during hot summer days to avoid heat buildup, and the black cloth should remain closed as late as possible in the morning until a sufficient dark duration has been reached.

Stock Plant Management

Use artificial long days of at least thirteen hours to maintain vegetative growth of stock plants during the winter. Most growers purchase unrooted or rooted cuttings from specialty propagators.

Cutting Harvest

Cuttings will vary in length from 1.5 to 2.5 in. (4 to 6 cm), since the various cultivars have different

Potted kalanchoe.

internode lengths. Typically, cuttings have two or three nodes and one pair of mature leaves.

Propagation

Terminal cuttings are rooted directly into the final pots. A rooting hormone is not required, since roots form with ease on most cultivars; however, hormones speed rooting of difficult-to-root cultivars. A substrate temperature of 70° to 74° F (21° to 23° C), with 72° F (22° C) optimum, is required for rapid callus formation and rooting within fourteen to twenty-one days. Provide 2,000 to 4,000 f.c. (22 to 43 klux). In winter during propagation, long days must be provided to maintain vegetative growth, and supplemental lighting of 200 f.c. (2 klux) can advance the rate of rooting.

Cuttings can be propagated using mist, syringing, or tents. In Europe, cuttings are covered with clear plastic in the winter and white plastic in the summer for the first ten to fourteen days. This technique can be used in North America, except perhaps in summer, when intermittent mist must be used because of summer heat buildup under the tents. Cuttings can also be covered with cheesecloth or spun-fiber cloths and syringed a couple times a day. If using mist, a minimum amount will be required for this succulent plant; do not oversaturate the substrate.

Begin fertilizing with 50 to 75 ppm nitrogen from 20-10-20 when roots are first visible. Cuttings will be rooted in two to three weeks in the summer, and in three to five weeks in the winter. Continue providing long days as determined by the crop schedule and the desired crop height and flowering time.

Plant Growth Regulators

Daminozide (B-Nine) sprays at 2,500 to 5,000 ppm are used weekly in summer, every ten to fifteen days in fall and spring, and every fourteen to twenty-one days in winter. Ancymidol (A-Rest) sprays at 50 ppm can also be used. Ethephon (Florel) at 250 to 500 ppm, uniconazole (Sumagic), and paclobutrazol (Bonzi) at 2 to 4 ppm are very effective. Day and night temperature difference (DIF) is effective, but DROP is not (see chapter 8 for more information).

Production and Schedule

The optimum temperature for growth is between 64° to 68° F (18° to 20° C). A delay in flowering is observed at temperatures below 61° F (16° C). Above 72° F (22° C), the growth rate increases for some cultivars, while the rate of others may be delayed. At 80° F (27° C) flowering is delayed for all cultivars. Heat delay is caused by high temperatures during the first part of the night (dark period).

A natural day length of eleven and a half or more hours must be present for vegetative growth to be maintained. Lighting is used from September 15 to April 1 in northern latitudes. Incandescent light can be used between 11:00 P.M. and 2:00 A.M., and it can be continuous or cyclic (eight to ten minutes on and twenty-two to twenty minutes off).

Additional supplemental lighting during the winter when plants are under short days has limited influence, particularly if supplemental high intensity discharge (HID) lighting was used during long days. If HID lighting is used during long days, a level of 200 f.c. (2 klux) is beneficial for "summer quality light" during winter. From mid-April to mid-September, however, the light level must be reduced to 5,800 f.c. (62 klux), or leaf anthocyanin dramatically increases and the foliage develops an undesirable red cast.

Do not overirrigate kalanchoe during the rooting process. Excess water enhances root rot problems during growth. Kalanchoe requires an evenly moist substrate with little fluctuation in the moisture level.

The substrate pH should be 5.8 to 6.5. The substrate should consist of at least 50% peat moss and be well aerated because the root system is quite fibrous.

Modern kalanchoe cultivars freely branch and often do not need to be pinched. With 4 in. (10 cm) pot production, plants are typically not pinched. Larger pot sizes are pinched, and only 0.5 to 0.75 in. (1 to 2 cm) of young growth is removed.

Most cultivars require nine or more weeks for flowers to reach anthesis from the beginning of short days. For a typical ten-week-response (time from start of short days to flowering) cultivar, however, this time span can be as long at twelve to thirteen weeks from November to April.

Diseases

The three most prevalent diseases are powdery mildew (*Sphaerotheca fuliginea*), *Botrytis,* and *Phytophthora* crown rot. *Rhizoctonia* stem blight and *Rhizopus* stem canker can also be observed. Other reported diseases include tomato spotted wilt virus, stem rot (*Myrothecium roridum*), black root rot (*Thielaviopsis basicola*), and leaf spots (*Stemphylium* and *Cercospora*).

Disorders

Failure to flower, malformed flowers, or a reduced number of individual flower per inflorescence are frequently related to temperatures that are too high or too low during induction and initiation. High light causes abnormal leaf coloration. Ethylene exposures at any stage of growth can cause a wide range of symptoms.

The unsightly corkiness of edema can disfigure foliage. Edema is caused by the rupture of stomatal cells from excessive water pressure and is accentuated by high humidity, low light, and a wet substrate.

Postharvest

Plants are very sensitive to ethylene; 0.1 ppm was sufficient to produce a response.

References

Anonymous. 1988. *Kalanchoe,* pp. 1–23. Fides Beheer B.V. DeLier, Holland.

Ball, V. 1998. *Kalanchoe,* pp. 586–591. In: *Ball RedBook,* 16th ed., V. Ball, ed. Ball Publishing, Batavia, Illinois.

Carlson, W. H., S. Schnabel, J. Schnabel, and C. Turner. 1977. Concentration and application time of ancymidol for growth regulation of *Kalanchoe blossfeldiana* Poellniz. cv. Mace. *HortScience* 12:568.

Daughtrey, M., and A. R. Chase. 1992. *Kalanchoe,* pp. 135–137. In: *Ball Field Guide to Disease of Greenhouse Ornamentals.* Ball Publishing, Batavia, Illinois.

Dreistadt, S. H. 2001. *Integrated Pest Management for Floriculture and Nurseries.* University of California Division of Agriculture and Natural Resources Publication 3402. Oakland, California.

Hasek, R., R. Sciaroni, and G. Hickman. 1986. New growth regulator tested. *Greenhouse Grower*

4(2):52–53.

Hausbeck, M. K., R. A. Welliver, M. A. Derr, and F. E. Gildow. 1992. Tomato spotted wilt virus survey among greenhouse ornamentals in Pennsylvania. *Plant Disease* 76:795–800.

Miller, R. 1991. New potted plants. *GrowerTalks* 54(11):51, 53, 55.

Mortensen, L.M. and R. Moe. 1992. Effects of CO_2 enrichment and different day/night temperature combinations on growth and flowering of *Rose* L. and *Kalanchoe blossfeldiana* v. Poelln. *Scientia Horticulturae* 51:145–153.

Pertuit, A. J., Jr., 1997. *Kalanchoe,* pp. 94–101. In: *Tips on Growing Specialty Potted Crops,* M. L. Gaston, S. A. Carver, C. A. Irwin, and R. A. Larson, eds. Ohio Florists' Association, Columbus, Ohio.

Schwabe, W. W. 1985. *Kalanchoe blossfeldiana,* pp. 217–235. In: *Handbook of Flowering,* vol. III, A. H. Halevy, ed. CRC Press, Boca Raton, Florida.

Willumsen, K., and T. Fjeld. 1995. Ethylene sensitivity of some flowering potted plants to exogenous ethylene. *Acta Horticulturae* 405:362–371.

Lamium

Common name: Dead nettle.
Scientific name: *Lamium maculatum.*
Family: Labiatae.
Other propagation methods: None.

Description, Uses, and Status

This low-growing perennial has silver and green foliage and short spikes of white, pink, or rose-colored flowers. Dead nettle can spread quickly, especially in moist areas, and it grows to 12 in. (30 cm) tall when in flower in early summer. The species is hardy in Zones 3 to 8 and prefers moderate to heavy shade. Plants are sold in pots and occasionally in hanging baskets.

Flowering Control and Dormancy

Plants will flower in pots but can be sold without flowers, for their variegated foliage.

Stock Plant Management

Maintain stock plants actively growing under high light levels and warm temperatures.

Cutting Harvest

Terminal cuttings 0.8 to 2 in. (2 to 5 cm) long with at least one fully expanded leaf are generally used.

Propagation

Cuttings should be propagated with a substrate temperature of 70° to 75° F (21° to 24° C) using bottom heat. With plug flats, use one cutting per cell. Apply a rooting hormone, 1,000 to 2,500 ppm IBA either alone or with up to 500 ppm NAA. Many cultivars do not require rooting hormone, treat each variety to

'Pink Chablis' dead nettle.

determine those which perform best with rooting hormone. Provide mist for the first six to nine days, and reduce misting as soon as possible to reduce stem elongation during propagation. Rooting should be completed in three to four weeks.

Plant Growth Regulators

Stem elongation is best controlled with high light and cool temperatures. Sprays of uniconazole (Sumagic) at 2 to 5 ppm or paclobutrazol (Bonzi) at 10 to 20 ppm can be used.

Production and Schedule

Grow the plants at temperatures of 60° to 70° F (16° to 21° C) during days and 58° to 65° F (14° to 18° C) during nights. Maintain 3,500 to 7,000 f.c. (38 to 75 klux) light levels. The substrate pH should be maintained at 5.8 to 6.5. Use 200 to 250 ppm nitrogen.

Use one plug per 4 in. (10 cm) pot, two or three per 6 in. (15 cm) pot, and three to five per 10 in. (25 cm) hanging basket. Plants do not need to be pinched. However, older plants can be trimmed at any time to shape them. Plants in 4 in. (10 cm) pots are marketable in six to eight weeks, those in 6 in. (15 cm) pots in eight to ten weeks, and those in 10 in. (25 cm) baskets in ten to twelve weeks.

Diseases
Botrytis and root rots can be problems.

References
Hamrick, D. 2003. *Lamium,* pp. 477–478. In: *Ball RedBook,* 17th ed., vol. 2, D. Hamrick, ed. Ball Publishing, Batavia, Illinois.

Yoder Green Leaf Perennials. 2004. *Handling Unrooted Perennials.* www.green-leaf-ent.com/URC_Handling_2004.pdf.

Lantana

Common name: Lantana, shrub verbena.
Scientific name: *Lantana camara* and *L. montevidensis.*
Family: Verbenaceae.
Other propagation methods: Seed.

Description, Uses, and Status
Lantanas have rounded clusters of small yellow, orange, red, pink, or lavender flowers. Many cultivars have multicolored clusters in which the flowers change color as they age. Lantana foliage is fragrant. *L. camara* tends to grow upright to 36 in. (90 cm) tall in a growing season, while *L. montevidensis* is more horizontal and grows to 18 in. (45 cm) tall. The numerous hybrid cultivars have a variety of growth habits. Lantanas are tender woody perennials that are generally not frost tolerant; they are sold in the spring in pots and hanging baskets. Some cultivars are cold hardier than others and may overwinter in mild climates. All lantanas are heat and drought tolerant and perform well in heat. The plants are invasive in warm climates, and they have become noxious weeds in some tropical and subtropical areas.

Flowering Control and Dormancy
Plants are day-neutral, flowering continuously if provided with high light and warm temperatures.

Stock Plant Management
Cuttings can be harvested from stock plants or from plants in production when they are pinched or trimmed. Ethephon (Florel) at 200 to 300 ppm can be used to prevent flowering. Woody stems will develop over time; therefore, plants should be

'Athens Rose' lantana flower.

trimmed to maintain a dense canopy of herbaceous shoots.

Cutting Harvest
Generally 2 to 3 in. (5 to 8 cm) long softwood cuttings are used.

Propagation

Stage 1:
Cutting arrival or harvest and sticking
- Stick cuttings within one or two hours after arrival or harvest.
- Propagate cuttings into plugs or small pots. Insert one cutting per cell if using plug flats. Interestingly, propagating lantana cuttings into 2¼ in. (6 cm) pots lined with cupric hydroxide reduced root growth because root tips stopped growing when they touched the cupric hydroxide, but it increased flowering after transplanting.

Stage 2: Callusing

- Maintain a substrate temperature of 70° to 76° F (21° to 24° C).
- Maintain air temperatures of 75° to 80° F (24° to 27° C) during days and 68° to 72° F (20° to 22° C) during nights.
- Keep the substrate close to saturation.
- Maintain a light intensity of 500 to 1,000 f.c. (5 to 11 klux).
- Misting at night is usually required.
- Begin foliar feeding with 50 to 75 ppm nitrogen from 20-10-20 as soon as leaves begin to show any color loss.
- Maintain a substrate pH of 5.5 to 6.2.
- Transfer the cuttings to Stage 3 after five to seven days, once 50% of the cuttings begin differentiating root initials.

Stage 3: Root development

- Maintain a substrate temperature of 70° to 76° F (21° to 24° C).
- Maintain air temperatures of 75° to 80° F (24° to 27° C) during days and 68° to 72° F (20° to 22° C) during nights.
- Increase the light intensity to 1,000 to 2,000 f.c. (11 to 22 klux).
- Fertilize once a week with 100 to 200 ppm nitrogen, alternating between 15-0-15 and 20-10-20.
- Roots should develop in seven to nine days.

Stage 4: Toning the rooted cutting

- Maintain air temperatures of 75° to 80° F (24° to 27° C) during days and 68° to 72° F (20° to 22° C) during nights.
- Move the liners from the mist area into an area of lower relative humidity.
- Increase the light intensity to 2,000 to 4,000 f.c. (22 to 43 klux).
- Fertilize twice a week with 150 to 200 ppm nitrogen from 15-0-15 alternating with 20-10-20.
- The cuttings can be toned for seven days.

Plant Growth Regulators

Rooted *L. montevidensis* cuttings in plugs can be drenched with 16 to 32 ppm paclobutrazol (Bonzi). During finished plant production, several chemicals are effective, including sprays of chlormequat (Cycocel) at 3,000 ppm, ethephon at 300 to 1,000 ppm, paclobutrazol at 10 to 40 ppm, and uniconazole (Sumagic) at 5 to 25 ppm. A tank-mixed spray of daminozide (B-Nine) at 2,500 to 7,500 ppm and chlormequat at 1,000 to 1,500 ppm or drenches of paclobutrazol at 2 to 4 ppm can also be used. Ethephon causes floral bud abortion and should not be used after flower buds are visible on the finished crop.

Production and Schedule

Warm production temperatures of 75° to 80° F (24° to 27° C) during the day and 62° to 65° F (17° to 18° C) at night are used. High temperatures, above 95° F (35° C), lead to flower bud abortion. High light of 4,000 to 7,000 f.c. (43 to 75 klux) should be used.

Use 150 ppm nitrogen, and avoid overfertilizing because that will lead to excessive elongation. The substrate pH should be 5.5 to 6.2. Grow plants on the dry side, and avoid overirrigating when transplants are first planted. Water restriction can be used to control growth, but do not allow plants to dry completely because leaf burn will occur.

Use one plant per 4 in. (10 cm) pot, one to two per 6 in. (15 cm) pot, and three to four per 10 in. (25 cm) basket. Pinching one to several times above the fifth or sixth node above the substrate will improve plant shape. Plants in 4 in. (10 cm) pots are ready to sell in six to seven weeks, those in 6 in. (15 cm) pots in seven to eight weeks, and those in 10 in. (25 cm) baskets in ten to twelve weeks.

Diseases

Botrytis and powdery mildew can be problems. Other diseases affecting lantana include *Alternaria, Fusarium, Pythium,* and *Rhizoctonia.*

Disorders

Too much vegetative growth can result from high ammonia levels, excessive fertilizer, or overwatering in combination with low light. Ethephon applied in too-large quantities or too late can also excessively increase shoot mass. Leaf necrosis can result from water stress or high substrate soluble salts. Liners and finished plants will stall if they are grown too cool or if not enough fertility is provided. Insufficient nitrogen will result in light green foliage and possibly a purple color on the foliage.

Postharvest

Cuttings are very sensitive to ethylene, which

Light green foliage and purpling on lantana due to insufficient nitrogen.

results in defoliation.1-MCP (EthylBloc) is effective at preventing ethylene-induced leaf drop.

References

Hamrick, D. 2003. *Lantana,* pp. 479–480. In: *Ball RedBook,* 17th ed., vol. 2, D. Hamrick, ed. Ball Publishing, Batavia, Illinois.

Schoellhorn, R. 2004. Lantana—summer color that's tough as nails. *GPN* 14(3):14–16.

Starman, T. W., M. C. Robinson, and K. L. Eixmann. 2004. Efficacy of ethephon on vegetative annuals. *HortTechnology* 14:83–87.

Svenson, S. E., and D. L. Johnston. 1995. Rooting cuttings in cupric hydroxide-treated pots affects root length and number of flowers after transplanting. *HortScience* 30:247–248.

Lavandula

Common name: English lavender, French lavender, Spanish lavender.
Scientific name: *Lavandula angustifolia, L. dentata, and L. stoechas.*
Family: Labiatae.
Other propagation methods: Seed.

Lavandula stoechus ssp. *pendunculata* 'James Compton'.

Description, Uses, and Status

This well-known herb is valued for its fragrant foliage and flowers. The inflorescence is a short spike of small, tightly packed white to purple flowers. English lavender, *L. angustifolia,* grows 24 to 36 in. (60 to 90 cm) tall, French lavender, *L. dentata,* 12 to 24 in. (30 to 60 cm) tall, and Spanish lavender, *L. stoechas,* 18 to 30 in. (45 to 75 cm) tall. Spanish lavender flowers are topped by several large colorful bracts. Lavender foliage is silver-gray. The species vary in hardiness: English lavender is hardy to Zone 6, French lavender to Zone 8, and Spanish lavender to Zone 7. Plants are typically sold in pots or occasionally in hanging baskets.

Flowering Control and Dormancy

For English lavender, optimum flowering occurs when the species receives a four- to eight-week-long cold treatment at 40° to 45° F (4° to 7° C) for flower initiation. Plants respond best when they have developed forty to fifty leaves. Once initiated, flowering will continue as long as the night temperature remains below 60° F (16° C). Plants may stop flowering during the summer but may flower again in the fall. Spanish lavender is a facultative long-day plant. Other lavender species and hybrids also benefit from long days during production.

Stock Plant Management

Work at Clemson University showed that for maximum cutting numbers the initial pinch on the stock plants should occur after seven nodes can be left on the plant, and the resulting side shoots should also be pinched when seven nodes can be left on the shoots. By contrast, pinching low and allowing only three or five nodes to remain in both pinches reduces the number of cuttings harvested. For example, pinching to three nodes both times produced forty-four cuttings per stock plant over the course of the experiment, while pinching to seven nodes produced seventy-nine cuttings per stock plant, an 80% increase. Thus, building the stock plant scaffold is important to future cutting production.

Cutting Harvest

Terminal cuttings 3 to 4 in. (7 to 10 cm) long are harvested from actively growing plants.

Propagation

Propagate terminal cuttings at 70° to 75° F (21° to 24° C) using bottom heat. Insert one cutting per cell if using plug flats. A rooting hormone, 1,000 to 2,500 ppm IBA or IBA plus NAA, should be used. Provide mist for the first seven to ten days, and reduce misting as soon as possible to prevent delayed rooting. Initial light levels should be 500 to 1,000 f.c. (5 to 11 klux), then increased to 1,000 to 2,000 f.c. (11 to 22 klux). Plants should be pinched in propagation. Rooting should be completed in four to five weeks.

Plant Growth Regulators

None is usually required unless plants are grown as ornamentals in smaller containers, in which case daminozide (B-Nine) sprays at 1,500 to 2,500 ppm can be effective.

Production and Schedules

Recommended day temperatures are 70° to 75° F (21° to 24° C) and night temperatures 65° to 70° F (18° to 21° C). After the plants are established, night temperatures can be reduced to 50° to 55° F (10° to 13° C). Provide 2,000 to 3,000 (22 to 32 klux) initially, which can be increased to 5,000 to 6,000 f.c. (54 to 65 klux) after establishment.

A rate of 150 ppm nitrogen is adequate with every other irrigation. A light, well-drained substrate with a pH 6.5 to 7.0 is desired. Even, consistent irrigation is important. Avoid overirrigation, especially after transplanting plugs. Reduce watering, and allow plants to wilt slightly during cool, cloudy weather to prevent root rot.

Use one plug per 4 in. (10 cm) pot, two per 6 in. (15 cm) pot, and three per 8 in. (20 cm) basket. Plants should be pinched two to three weeks after transplanting. Older plants can be trimmed at any time to shape them. Flowering will generally occur five to six weeks after pinching. Plants in 4 in. (10 cm) pots are marketable in six to eight weeks, those in 6 in. (15 cm) pots in eight to ten weeks, and those in 8 in. (20 cm) baskets in twelve to fifteen weeks.

Diseases

Rhizoctonia, Phytophthora, Botrytis, and powdery mildew can be problems.

Disorders

Lavender foliage is sensitive to rotting in high humidity and when overmisted.

Postharvest

Cuttings are susceptible to foliar blackening during shipping and storage.

References

Hamrick, D. 2003. *Lavandula,* pp. 482–484. In: *Ball RedBook,* 17th ed., vol. 2, D. Hamrick, ed. Ball Publishing, Batavia, Illinois.

Yoder Green Leaf Perennials. 2004. *Handling Unrooted Perennials.* www.green-leaf-ent.com/URC_Handling_2004.pdf.

Lobelia

Common name: Trailing lobelia, edging lobelia.
Scientific name: *Lobelia erinus.*
Family: Campanulaceae.
Other propagation methods: Seed.

Description, Uses, and Status

This trailing species produces masses of small white, lavender, blue, or purple flowers on plants that grow 3 to 6 in. (8 to 15 cm) tall. The color of the blue or purple cultivars can be especially rich and striking in the landscape or in a mixed container. A tender perennial, trailing lobelia is not frost tolerant and is sold in the spring in small pots, hanging baskets, and mixed containers. Cutting-propagated cultivars tend to be more robust and heat tolerant than seed-propagated plants.

Flowering Control and Dormancy

Lobelia is a day-neutral plant.

Stock Plant Management

Stock plants can be grown in pots or hanging baskets. The plants should be kept warm to reduce flowering, and they should be hedged (cut back) to generate a uniform flush of cuttings.

Cutting Harvest

Terminal cuttings 0.8 to 1.2 in. (2 to 3 cm) long with at least one fully expanded leaf are used.

Propagation

Stage 1:
Cutting arrival or harvest and sticking
- Stick cuttings within one or two hour after arrival or harvest.
- Use a rooting hormone of 2,500 ppm IBA on cutting bases. IBA with up to 500 ppm NAA can also be used.
- Insert one cutting per cell if using plug flats.

Stage 2: Callusing
- Maintain a substrate temperature of 68° to 72° F (20° to 22° C).
- Maintain air temperatures of 75° to 80° F (24° to 27° C) during days and 68° to 72° F (20° to 22° C) during nights.

'Periwinkle Blue Improved' trailing lobelia.

- Maintain a light intensity of 500 to 1,000 f.c. (5 to 11 klux).
- Begin foliar feeding once a week with 50 to 75 ppm nitrogen from 20-10-20.
- Maintain a substrate pH of 5.6 to 6.2.
- Transfer the cuttings to Stage 3 after five to seven days, once 50% of the cuttings begin differentiating root initials.

Stage 3: Root development
- Maintain a substrate temperature of 68° to 72° F (20° to 22° C).
- Maintain air temperatures of 75° to 80° F (24° to 27° C) during days and 68° to 72° F (20° to 22° C) during nights.
- Increase the light intensity to 1,000 to 2,000 f.c. (11 to 22 klux).
- Fertilize once a week with 100 to 150 ppm nitrogen, alternating between 15-0-15 and 20-10-20.
- Roots should develop in seven to fourteen days.

Stage 4: Toning the rooted cutting
- Lower the air temperature to 70° to 75° F (21° to 24° C) during the day and 62° to 68° F (16° to 20° C) at night.
- Move the liners from the mist area into an area of lower relative humidity.
- Increase the light intensity to 2,000 to 4,000 f.c. (22 to 43 klux).
- Fertilize once a week with 150 to 200 ppm nitrogen from 15-0-15 alternating with 20-10-20.
- The cuttings can be toned for seven days.

Plant Growth Regulators

None is usually required if plugs and finished plants are grown under high light. However, during propagation daminozide (B-Nine) sprays at 1,500 to 2,500 ppm or a tank-mixed spray of ancymidol (A-Rest) at 4 to 10 ppm and daminozide at 1,250 to 2,500 ppm can be used fourteen to twenty-five days after sticking unrooted cuttings. During production, sprays of paclobutrazol (Bonzi) at 4 ppm, daminozide at 1,500 to 2,500 ppm, or uniconazole (Sumagic) at 1 ppm are effective.

Production and Schedule

Trailing lobelia prefers cool temperatures and high light for the highest quality. Grow the plants at 70° to 75° F (21° to 24° C) during the day and 55° to 60° F (13° to 16° C) at night. After the plants are established, however, they can also be grown at 40° to 45° F (4° to 7° C) for six weeks to promote flowering. If the plants are kept at that temperature, the crop time will be long, so finish at 70° to 75° F (21° to 24° C) during days and 55° to 60° F (13° to 16° C) during nights. Maintain 4,500 to 9,000 f.c. (48 to 97 klux) light levels.

The substrate pH should be maintained at 5.6 to 6.8. Use 200 to 300 ppm nitrogen. Supplemental iron applications may be helpful to promote dark green foliage. Avoid high substrate EC.

Use one plug per 4 in. (10 cm) pot, two per 6 in. (15 cm) pot, and four per 10 in. (25 cm) hanging basket. Although not required, plants can be pinched after rooted cuttings are established. Older plants can be trimmed at any time to shape them. Plants in 4 in. (10 cm) pots are marketable in eight to ten weeks, those in 6 in. (15 cm) pots in nine to eleven weeks, and those in 10 in. (25 cm) hanging baskets in ten to twelve weeks.

Diseases

Botrytis, Pythium and *Rhizoctonia* can cause problems.

Disorders

Growing plants too wet may cause their collapse. *Botrytis* can also cause similar sudden plant death. Leaf necrosis can be caused by water stress or high substrate EC. Too much foliar growth can be due to high nitrogen fertilization, or excessive watering or fertilizing, especially under low light levels.

References

Hamrick, D. 2003. *Lobelia,* pp. 511-512. In: *Ball RedBook,* 17th ed., vol. 2, D. Hamrick, ed. Ball Publishing, Batavia, Illinois.

Lysimachia

Common name: Loosestrife, golden globes, moneywort, creeping jenny.
Scientific name: *Lysimachia congestiflora* and *L. nummularia.*
Family: Primulaceae.
Other propagation methods: Seed.

Description, Uses, and Status

Both species are vines or low groundcovers reaching about 4 in. (10 cm) tall. *L. congestiflora,* loosestrife or golden globes, has green foliage topped with clusters of bright yellow tubular flowers. Cultivars with yellow variegated foliage are especially striking and colorful. Plants are hardy to Zone 9. *L. nummularia,* moneywort or creeping jenny, is covered with small closely spaced round leaves. This species has medium green

Lysimachia congestifolia 'Outback Sunset'.

leaves; cultivars are available with pale green or yellow leaves. Plants are hardy to Zone 4. Both species work especially well in combination baskets and pots or individual pots.

Flowering Control
L. congestiflora flowers more rapidly under long days greater than nine hours. Plants flower above the seventh leaf pair. *L. nummularia* is grown more for its foliage than its small flowers.

Stock Plant Management
Keep plants under short days of nine hours or less to prevent flowering.

Cutting Harvest
Terminal cuttings 2 in. (5 cm) long are harvested from actively growing plants.

Propagation

Lysimachia nummularia **plug flat.**

Stage 1:
Cutting arrival or harvest and sticking
* Store cuttings at 50° to 60° F (10° to 16° C) for up to twenty-four hours if planting is going to be delayed.
* Insert one cutting per cell if using plug flats. Rooting hormone is typically not used.

Stage 2: Callusing
* Maintain substrate temperatures of 68° to 72° F (20° to 22° C); cooler temperatures inhibit rooting.
* Maintain air temperatures of 75° to 80° F (24° to 27° C) during days and 68° to 70° F (20° to 21° C) during nights.
* Maintain a light intensity of 500 to 1,000 f.c. (5 to 11 klux) and short days to inhibit premature flowering.
* Begin foliar feeding with 50 to 75 ppm nitrogen from 20-10-20 if there is any loss in foliage color.
* Maintain a substrate pH of 6.5 to 7.0.
* Transfer the cuttings to Stage 3 after nine to eleven days, once 50% of the cuttings begin differentiating root initials.

Stage 3: Root development
* Maintain substrate temperatures of 68° to 72° F (20° to 22° C).
* Maintain air temperatures of 75° to 80° F (24° to 27° C) during days and 68° to 72° F (20° to

22° C) during nights.
* Increase the light intensity to 1,000 to 2,000 f.c. (11 to 22 klux) and continue short days to inhibit flowering.
* Fertilize once a week with 100 ppm nitrogen, alternating between 15-0-15 and 20-10-20, then increase to 200 ppm.
* Begin drying out the substrate once roots are visible.
* Begin reducing the duration and frequency of mist.
* Roots should develop in seven to fourteen days.

Stage 4: Toning the rooted cutting
* Lower the air temperature to 72° to 75° F (22° to 24° C) during the day and 62° to 68° F (17° to 20° C) at night.
* Move the liners from the mist area into an area of lower relative humidity.
* Increase the light intensity to 2,000 to 4,000 f.c. (22 to 43 klux).
* Fertilize once with 100 to 150 ppm from 15-0-15.
* The cuttings can be toned for seven days.

Plant Growth Regulators
Generally, none are required on these low-mounding or vining plants.

Production and Schedule

Recommended day temperatures are 72° to 75° F (22° to 24° C) and night temperatures 65° to 68° F (18° to 20° C). Although plants are quite heat tolerant after they are established, avoid temperatures over 95° F (35° C). Also avoid cool temperatures below 45° F (7° C). Grow the plants at light levels of at least 5,000 f.c. (54 klux).

Initially, a rate of 100 to 150 ppm nitrogen is adequate with every other irrigation. Monitor the substrate pH regularly; maintain pH 6.5 to 7.0 to prevent excessive uptake of boron or iron from a low pH.

One plug is used per 4 to 6 in. (10 to 15 cm) pot, and three to five per 8 to 10 in. (20 to 25 cm) basket. While plants in 4 in. (10 cm) pots do not need pinching, those in larger containers should be pinched two to three weeks after planting, allowing approximately 1 to 1.5 in. (3 to 4 cm) of stem remaining above the substrate. Large containers may need a second pinch. In the spring 4 in. (10 cm) pots are ready to sell in five to six weeks, 6 in. (15 cm) pots in six to seven weeks, and 8 in. (20 cm) baskets in eight to ten weeks.

Diseases

Botrytis, powdery mildew, *Rhizoctonia, Pythium,* and impatiens necrotic spot and tomato spotted wilt viruses can be problems.

Disorders

Plants may collapse due to cold production temperatures, a wet substrate, or *Botrytis.* Marginal leaf burn can be due to water stress, high soluble salts, viruses, or excessive phosphorus, boron, or iron in the substrate.

References

Hamrick, D. 2003. *Lysimachia,* pp. 518–519. In: *Ball RedBook,* 17th ed., vol. 2, D. Hamrick, ed. Ball Publishing, Batavia, Illinois.

Yoder Green Leaf Perennials. 2004. *Handling Unrooted Perennials.* www.green-leaf-ent.com/URC_Handling_2004.pdf.

Nemesia

Common name: Nemesia.
Scientific name: *Nemesia* hybrids.
Family: Scrophulariaceae.
Other propagation methods: Seed.

Description, Uses, and Status

The clusters of small white, rose, lavender, blue, cream, yellow, or red flowers are produced on plants 8 to 10 in. (20 to 25 cm) tall. Plant habit ranges from weakly upright to trailing. Nemesia is sold in pots, hanging baskets, and mixed containers. A cool-season crop, nemesia typically grows best during the late winter and spring in warm climates and in the summer in cool climates. Plants can sometimes tolerate temperatures around 20° F (–7° C) in the landscape, and some can overwinter to Zone 8.

Flowering Control and Dormancy

Nemesia is day-neutral.

Stock Plant Management

Building the stock plant scaffold is important to

'Compact Pink Innocence' nemesia.

future cutting production. If there is sufficient time after establishment, pinch stock plants up to three times before harvesting cuttings. Increasing the number of pinches from one to three on stock plants before the cutting harvest commences delays the initial harvest but increases the total number of cuttings harvested. Pinching plants only once allowed cuttings to be harvested more quickly after establishment of the stock plants but reduced the total number of cutting produced.

Cutting Harvest

Terminal cuttings 0.8 to 1.2 in. (2 to 3 cm) long with at least one fully expanded leaf are harvested.

Propagation

Maintain a substrate temperature of 70° to 75° F (21° to 24° C) using bottom heat. With plug flats, two cuttings are usually inserted per cell. Rooting hormones are not required, but up to 2,500 ppm IBA alone or IBA with up to 500 ppm NAA can be used. Rooting should be completed in four weeks.

Flats of nemesia cuttings.

Plant Growth Regulators

Plants should not need plant growth regulators if grown cool under high light. However, during propagation daminozide (B-Nine) sprays at 1,500 to 2,500 ppm or a tank-mixed spray of ancymidol (A-Rest) at 4 to 10 ppm and daminozide at 1,250 to 2,500 ppm can be used fourteen to twenty-four days after sticking unrooted cuttings. During production, sprays of daminozide at 2,500 to 3,500 ppm, paclobutrazol (Bonzi) at 30 ppm, ethephon (Florel) at 500 to 1,000 ppm, uniconazole (Sumagic) at 20 to 30 ppm, or flurprimidol (Topflor) at 10 to 15 ppm are effective. Ethephon delays flowering, however.

Production and Schedule

Grow the plants at 65° to 75° F (18° to 24° C) during days and 55° to 60° F (13° to 16° C) during nights. Cooler temperatures, below 50° F (10° C), can be used to improve plant quality, but production times will increase greatly. Maintain light levels of 5,000 (54 klux) or higher.

The substrate pH should be maintained at 5.5 to 6.2. Use 150 to 200 ppm nitrogen, and as with most cool-season crops, apply a low-ammonium fertilizer. Extra calcium and magnesium is beneficial, especially early in the crop cycle. An application of micronutrients is also recommended. Plants are susceptible to a high EC. Allow plants to dry well between irrigations, since they are susceptible to overwatering.

Use one plug per 4 in. (10 cm) pot, two to three per 6 in. (15 cm) pot, and three to five per 10 in. (25 cm) basket. Plants should be pinched after adequate root establishment to maintain their shape and build a strong plant base. Plants in 4 in. (10 cm) pots are ready to sell in four to six weeks, those in 6 in. (15 cm) pots in five to seven weeks, and those in 10 in. (25 cm) baskets in eight to ten weeks.

Diseases

Root rots are common.

Disorders

Nemesia is especially prone to soft weak growth, which can be due to a variety of factors, such as low light, warm production temperatures, and excessive ammonium. Low nutrition can produce thin weak stems; however, excessive fertility can cause undesired stem elongation.

References

Faust, J. E., and L. W. Grimes. 2004. Cutting production is affected by pinch number during scaffold development of stock plants. *HortScience* 39:1691–1694.

Schoellhorn, R. 2003. Nemesia and diascia. *GPN* 13(1):36–38.

Starman, T. W., M. C. Robinson, and K. L. Eixmann. 2004. Efficacy of ethephon on vegetative annuals. *HortTechnology* 14:83–87.

Osteospermum

Common name: African daisy, cape daisy, osteospermum.
Scientific name: *Osteospermum ecklonis.*
Family: Compositae.
Other propagation methods: Seed.

Description, Uses, and Status

This tender perennial produces large numbers of white, pink, rose, violet, yellow, or orange daisy-shaped flowers with either a light or dark center. Some cultivars have bicolored flowers, unusual spoon-shaped petals, or petals with a different color on the top than the underside. Plants grow 12 to 24 in. (30 to 60 cm) tall. Osteospermum is not frost tolerant and is sold in the spring in pots and hanging baskets.

Flowering Control and Dormancy

Osteospermum plants produce more flowers and bloom more uniformly if they receive four weeks of 45° to 55° F (7° to 13 C). Without a cold treatment, flowering is sparse. If plants remain at those temperatures, however, the cold will slow crop development. After the cold treatment, raise the night temperature to 60° to 65° F (16° to 18° C) for faster flowering. Osteospermum is day-neutral.

Stock Plant Management

Building the stock plant scaffold is important to future cutting production. Work at Clemson University showed that for maximum cutting numbers, the initial pinch on the stock plants should occur after fifteen nodes can be left on the plant, and the resulting side shoots should be pinched when ten nodes can be left on the shoots. By contrast, pinching low and allowing only five or ten nodes to remain after the first pinch and two or six nodes after the second pinch reduces the number of cuttings harvested. For example, pinching to five nodes the first pinch and two nodes the second pinch produced 16 cuttings per stock plant over the course of the experiment, while pinching to fifteen nodes first and ten nodes second produced 56 cutting per stock plant, a 250% increase in cuttings. If there is sufficient time after establishment, pinch stock plants up to three times before harvesting cuttings. Increasing the number of pinches from one to three on stock plants before the cutting harvest commences delays the initial harvest but increases the total number of cuttings harvested. Pinching plants only once allowed cuttings to be harvested more quickly after establishment of the stock plants but reduced the total number of cutting produced.

Supplemental high intensity discharge (HID) lighting can increase cutting production of stock plants grown in low light situations. Good air movement through the stock plants to ensure sufficient carbon dioxide will help provide optimum results when using HID lighting.

'Nasinga Pink' osteospermum.

'Peach Symphony' osteospermum.

Cutting Harvest
Terminal cuttings 1.5 to 3 in. (4 to 8 cm) long are harvested.

Propagation
Maintain a substrate temperature of 70° to 75° F (21°° to 24 C) using bottom heat for the first two weeks. Once roots are visible, reduce the temperature to 60° F (15° C) to prevent stem elongation, and also reduce mist frequency and duration. With plug flats, one cutting is inserted per cell. Rooting hormones, either up to 3,000 ppm IBA alone or IBA with up to 500 ppm NAA, should be used. Avoid sticking cuttings too deep because heating mats or closed-system bottom heat units can damage tender cutting bases.

Plant Growth Regulators
During propagation, daminozide (B-Nine) sprays at 1,500 to 2,500 ppm or a tank-mixed spray of ancymidol (A-Rest) at 4 to 10 ppm and daminozide at 1,250 to 2,500 ppm can be used fourteen to twenty-four days after sticking unrooted cuttings. During production sprays of paclobutrazol (Bonzi) at 30 ppm, daminozide at 2,500 ppm, chlormequat (Cycocel) at 750 ppm or flurprimidol (Topflor) at 20 to 60 ppm can be used. Vigorous cultivars respond best to uniconizole (Sumagic) foliar sprays at 8 ppm or substrate drenches of 0.25 to 0.5 mg a.i. per pot.

Production and Schedule
Grow the plants at 65° to 72° F (18° to 22°C) during days and 60° to 65° F (16° to 18°) during nights. Temperatures of less than 70° F (21° C) are required for flowering. Finish at 55° to 65° F (13° to 16° C) during days and 50° to 60° F (10° to 16° C) during nights. Maintain light levels of 5,000 to 6,000 f.c. (54 to 65 klux) or higher.

Substrate pH should be maintained at 5.5 to 6.2. Use 250 ppm nitrogen, and as with most cool-season crops, apply a low-ammonium fertilizer. Plants are susceptible to high EC and high pH. Allow plants to dry well between irrigations, since they are susceptible to overwatering. One plant is used per 4 in. (10 cm) pot, one or two per 5 in. (13 cm) pot, two to three per 6 in. (15 cm) pot, and three to four per 8 to 10 in. (20 to 25 cm) hanging basket. Plants should be pinched three weeks after planting. Generally 4 to 6 in. (10 to 15 cm) pots are ready to sell in fifteen to seventeen weeks, and 8 to 10 in. (20 to 25 cm) baskets in sixteen to eighteen weeks. The crop finishes two to three weeks earlier as spring advances.

Botrytis stem rot on osteospermum. (B. Whipker)

Diseases
Botrytis, Pythium, Phytophthora, powdery mildew, and *Verticillium* can be problems, especially if plants are kept too wet.

Disorders
Delayed flowering or excessive foliar growth can result from either too much nitrogen or low light in conjunction with overfertilizing or with overwatering. Do not allow osteospermum plants to dry out.

Postharvest
Cuttings can be slow to root, and warm shipping and storage temperatures are thought to be factors.

References
Donnelly, C. S., and P. R. Fisher. 2002. High-pressure sodium lighting affects greenhouse production of vegetative cuttings for specialty annuals. *HortScience* 37:623–626.

Faust, J. E., and L. W. Grimes. 2004. Cutting production is affected by pinch number during scaffold development of stock plants. *HortScience* 39:1691–1694.

Faust, J. E., and L. W. Grimes. 2005. Pinch height of stock plants during scaffold development affects cutting production. *HortScience* 40:650–653.

Gibson, J. L., and B. E. Whipker. 2003. Efficacy of plant growth regulators on the growth of vigorous *osteospermum* cultivars. *HortTechnology* 13:132–135.

Hamrick, D. 2003. *Osteospermum,* pp. 539–541. In: *Ball RedBook,* 17th ed., vol. 2, D. Hamrick, ed. Ball Publishing, Batavia, Illinois.

Pelargonium

Common name: Geranium, pelargonium.
Scientific name: *Pelargonium* species and hybrids.
Family: Geraniaceae.
Other propagation methods: Seed, tissue culture.

'Starburst Red' zonal geranium flower.

Description, Uses, and Status

All pelargoniums, or geraniums, in commerce are perennial herbs with hairy leaves that range from slightly lobed to highly dissected. The foliage occurs in various combinations of green, white, ivory, bronze, yellow, and red and is often fragrant. Flowers, which can be single or double and are arranged in umbels, come in shades of red, pink, salmon, or white. The flowers can be solid colored or various combinations of colors. Near-black coloration can occur with regal or Martha Washington geraniums, *P.* x *domesticum.*

Geraniums have been among the most important plants in the bedding plant business for decades. Hybrid seed and zonal geraniums, *P.* x *hortorum*, are the most important types; they are planted primarily in porch or balcony boxes, ground beds, or large pots or tubs. Ivy geranium, *P. peltatum*, and cascade geranium, *P. floribunda*, are used in hanging baskets and porch or balcony boxes, which allow the stems to trail naturally downward.

Unfortunately, the beautiful, showy regal types flower only when temperatures are near 50° F (10° C). Hence, in most areas of the world where they are sold in the spring, flowering ceases in the summer due to high temperatures. Frequently, they are sold as gift or specimen potted flowering plants. They can be planted directly in the garden in cooler climates, such as in coastal areas of western North America.

Scented geraniums are a collection of species with fragrant foliage used most frequently as potted plants or in patio or porch boxes. Most selections are not cold or winter hardy, but they do well in the home during the winter in a sunny southern window.

Flowering Control and Dormancy

All commercial geranium cultivars are considered day-neutral, and the rate of floral initiation and subsequent development are dependent on total light energy received (intensity x duration) at the appropriate temperatures. Many scented geraniums do not readily flower, which is acceptable since they are grown primarily for their fragrant foliage.

Low temperatures are critical with regal geraniums because flower initiation occurs only when temperatures

are less than 62° F (17° C). Initiation requires four weeks. Cold treatment of three to six weeks can occur in the greenhouse or a cooler; the temperature should be 45° to 58° C (7° to 14° C)—54° to 55° F (12° to 13° C) is most commonly used—and the light level greater than 1,950 f.c. (21 klux).

Stock Plant Management

In the past, most greenhouses propagated their own cuttings from stock plants started in July or August of the previous year. Today, cutting-propagated geraniums are primarily grown from unrooted or rooted cuttings received directly from cutting distributors and propagators in early spring. Stock plants grown in an ideal envi-

TABLE 3

Cutting yield relative to that of stock plants established in June. For example, planting stock cuttings in October will provide only 50% of the cutting numbers obtained from planting in June.

MONTH STOCK CUTTING PLANTED	CUTTING YIELD AS % OF JUNE YIELD
June	100
July	90
August	80
September	65
October	50
November	40
December	30
January	20

Adapted from White, 1993.

ronment can produce up to eighty cuttings when planted in August and grown in a 7 in. (18 cm) or larger container. Stock plants of the cascading and ivy types are grown in hanging baskets. Ideally, supplemental lighting should be used in the winter, which increases cutting production 20 to 50%. Shade the plants in the summer and autumn to a maximum light intensity of 5,000 to 6,000 f.c. (54 to 65 klux).

Nutrition affects both stock plant growth and the rooting of cuttings after propagation. For example, at the University of Maryland geranium stock plants were fertilized with deficient, optimal, or excessive nutrient levels of nitrogen, potassium, and phosphorus. The nitrogen level resulted in a more pronounced variation in the rooting of cuttings than either phosphorus or potassium. Deficient and optimal levels of nitrogen resulted in a higher percentage of rooted cuttings (67%) than the excessive level (56%). Although the rooting percentages were lower with the highest level of nitrogen, the number and length of roots were greater.

Stock plants can be trained in a variety of methods. For the "natural bush" method, plants are allowed to branch naturally. When young stock plants are an average of 5 in. (13 cm) tall, they are pinched, leaving at least four nodes. Thereafter, two nodes on each stem are left behind when a cutting is removed. The number of cuttings produced is dependent on when the stock plants were planted (table 3).

For upright-growing geraniums a variation of the natural bush method is to leave the terminal shoot unpinched and to pinch only the side shoots when they are 6 in. (15 cm) long. Thereafter, cuttings are removed. A tall, well-branched stock plant can be grown for sale in May and June but produce a maximum number of cuttings in January and February. Plants are supported with a 3 to 4 ft. (90 to 120 cm) stake. Large older leaves can be removed to allow for light to penetrate the plant's interior, which also helps to prevent *Botrytis* and increase production. Plants can be staked and sold later to retail customers.

Finally, a zonal topiary tree can be formed by gibberellic acid (GA₃) sprays at 250 ppm to quickly elongate single-stemmed cuttings. Four to five applications are made every seven to ten days. When the "trunk" is 24 to 30 in. (60 to 75 cm) tall, pinch the plant and start harvesting cuttings. Plants must be staked. The numbers of cuttings produced by this method are reduced, but the stock plants are of greater retail value.

Axillary branching of stock plants can be stimulated by the use of ethephon (Florel) sprays at 350 to 500 ppm. Cutting production can be increased by 30% when ethephon is sprayed on newly planted stock plants two weeks prior to pinching, when they are 6 to 8 in. (15 to 20 cm) tall. Repeat sprays can be applied to stock plants until midwinter. This ethylene-releasing chemical can cause flower abortion; it has also been used in commercial propagation to reduce the labor needed to remove flowers to control disease and improve sanitation. While ethephon is often used on stock plants to increase branching and prevent flowering, it also controls height.

Chlormequat (Cycocel) sprays at 1,500 ppm are used to improve cutting substance, particularly during winter and low light. Shorter cuttings with thicker and darker green leaves are less prone to wilting. However, some producers spray with GA₃ to encourage internode elongation and facilitate cutting harvest.

Cutting Harvest

Terminal cuttings are generally used for zonal geraniums, but leaf-bud cuttings can be propagated if stock material is limited. Cuttings should have two expanded leaves and a growing point or meristem; flowers and buds should be removed. Cutting stem length can vary from 1.5 to 2.5 in. (4 to 6 cm), depending on internode length. Small cuttings with a minimum of leaf surface require less mist, causing fewer disease and nutrition problems, than cuttings with large leaves that dry out rapidly. Cuttings should be uniform in size, type, and age; they may need to be sorted prior to sticking. A uniform batch of cuttings will root in a similar amount of time. With an inconsistent batch, some cuttings may not root rapidly, leading to overmisting and elongation in the first cuttings that root.

It is especially important never to combine terminal and leaf-bud cuttings, since the terminal cuttings will develop faster. Leaf-bud cuttings are also more susceptible to *Botrytis* during propagation and more responsive to substrate temperature, which should not be less than 70° F (21° C). Leaf-bud cuttings will take up to two more weeks to produce a finished plant than a terminal cutting. When sticking leaf-bud cuttings, be sure the axillary bud is exposed, because planting too deep will delay development.

Cuttings should be snapped or broken from the stock plant, requiring well-grown turgid cuttings. Sharp knives can also be used but must be sterilized frequently to prevent disease spread. Shears or scissors are not recommended, since they will crush the stem. Harvest cuttings in the morning or late afternoon.

For regal geraniums 2 to 2.5 in. (5 to 6 cm) terminal cuttings are used. As with zonal types, the cuttings should be snapped off the stock plant or harvested with sterile knives. Other geraniums types are handled in a similar manner.

Propagation

The following propagation stages are for zonal and ivy geraniums. Information on regal geraniums follows below.

Stage 1:
Cutting arrival or harvest and sticking

- Store the cuttings for at least two hours at 45° F (7° C) to reduce the cutting temperature. Determine how many cuttings can be stuck in one to two hours, and store the remainder in a cool location or a cooler until they can be planted.
- Store the cuttings at 40° to 45° F (5° to 7° C) for up to forty-eight hours if planting is going to be delayed, but note that some leaf yellowing will likely occur.
- Root the cuttings in a variety of media and containers: foam, rock wool, peat-blocks, or plug flats or final pots filled with a well-aerated substrate. Insert one cutting per cell if using plug flats.
- No rooting hormone is needed, but if used, choose a powder formulation because liquid formulations may spread disease among the cuttings.
- Be sure that the leaves of adjacent cuttings do not overlap.
- Use the absolute minimum amount and duration of mist to maintain leaf turgidity. Do not overmist.

Stage 2: Callusing

- Maintain substrate temperatures of 68° to 70° F (20° to 21° C).
- Maintain air temperatures of 68° to 72° F (20° to 22° C) during days and 65° to 70° F (18° to 21° C) during nights.
- Keep the substrate sufficiently moist so that water is easily squeezed out of it, but not so much that the cutting base is waterlogged. The base of the cutting needs air for proper rooting.
- Maintain a light intensity of 1,000 to 2,000 f.c. (11 to 22 klux). Supplemental lighting of 400 to 500 f.c. (4 to 5 klux) may be beneficial in northern or cloudy climates.
- Begin foliar feeding with 50 to 75 ppm nitrogen from 20-10-20 as soon as leaves begin to show any color loss.
- Maintain a substrate pH of 5.5 to 6.0.
- Transfer the cuttings to Stage 3 after seven to ten days, once 50% of the cuttings begin differentiating root initials.

Stage 3: Root development

- Maintain air temperatures of 68° to 72° F (20° to 22° C) during days and 65° to 70° F (18° to 21° C) during nights.
- Begin drying out the substrate once roots are visible.
- Begin increasing the light intensity to 2,000 to 2,500 f.c. (22 to 27 klux) as the cuttings start to root out.
- Fertilize once a week with 100 to 200 ppm nitrogen, alternating between 15-0-15 and 20-10-20, then increase to 200 ppm.
- Raise the substrate pH to 5.8 to 6.0.
- Chlormequat (Cycocel), paclobutrazol (Bonzi), or ancymidol (A-Rest) can be applied to reduce the stretching frequently observed during rooting and shipping.
- Roots should develop in ten to twenty days.

Stage 4: Toning the rooted cutting

- Maintain the air temperatures of 68° to 72° F (20° to 22° C) during days and 65° to 70° F (18° to 21° C) during nights.
- Increase the light intensity to 4,000 f.c. (43 klux).
- Move the liners from the mist area into an area of lower relative humidity.
- Provide shade during the middle of the day to reduce temperature stress.
- Fertilize at 150 to 200 ppm nitrogen from 15-0-15 alternating with 20-10-20.
- The cuttings can be toned for seven days.

Regal geranium cuttings form callus in ten to twelve days when the substrate and day air temperatures are 72° to 77° F (22° to 25° C) and the night air temperature 65° to 67° F (18° to 19° C). A rooting hormone is not needed, but 1,000 ppm IBA can improve the uniformity of rooting. Provide 500 to 1,000 f.c. (5 to 11 klux) light and 50 to 75 ppm nitrogen from 20-10-20 initially. Maintain a substrate pH of 5.5 to 5.8.

After roots begin to develop on the regal geraniums, decrease the air temperature to 68° to 70° F (20° to 21° C) during the day and 62° to 65° F (17° 18° C) at night. Increase the light level to 1,500 to 2,000 f.c. (16 to 22 klux) and the fertilizer to 100 to 200 ppm nitrogen, alternating between 20-10-20 and 15-0-15.

Regal geranium cuttings are hardened off at air temperatures of 58° to 62° F (14° to 17° C) and light levels of 3,500 to 4,000 f.c. (38 to 43 klux). Cuttings will be ready for transplanting within three to four weeks.

Plant Growth Regulators

During the propagation of zonal geraniums, a tank-mixed spray of chlormequat at 750 ppm and daminozide (B-Nine) at 1,500 to 2,500 ppm can be used eighteen to twenty-four days after sticking unrooted cuttings.

During production a chlormequat spray at 750 to 1,500 ppm is commonly used to reduce plant height; multiple applications may be required on vigorous cultivars. Chlormequat at 750 ppm can be tank-mixed with daminozide at 750 to 4,000 ppm to reduce the possibility of phytotoxicity. Chlormequat at 750 ppm can also be tank-mixed with paclobutrazol at 2 to 4 ppm. Ancymidol sprays at 5 to 10 ppm, paclobutrazol sprays at 1 to 4 ppm or drenches at 0.01 to 0.1 ppm, flurprimidol (Topflor) sprays at 15 to 25 ppm, or uniconazole (Sumagic) sprays at 0.5 to 2 ppm or drenches at 0.025 mg a.i. per pot can also be used.

During the propagation of ivy geraniums, a tank-mixed spray of chlormequat at 750 ppm and daminozide at 1,500 to 2,500 ppm can be used eighteen to twenty-four days after sticking unrooted cuttings. During production ivy geraniums can be sprayed with paclobutrazol at 1 to 4 ppm, chlormequat at 750 to 1,500 ppm, or a tank-mixed spray of daminozide at 1,000 ppm and chlormequat at 750 ppm.

Chlormequat sprays at 1,500 to 3,000 ppm or paclobutrazol sprays at 8 ppm can be used on regal geraniums during forcing. Day and night temperature differences (DIF) and DROP are both effective on most types of geraniums (see chapter 8 for more information).

Production and Schedule

For zonal cultivars, a temperature regime of 68° F (20° C) during the day and 63° F (17° C) at night is optimal. For ivy geraniums, an average daily temperature of 68° F (20° C) is best; it can be supplied by a constant temperature for compact growth, or by 75° F (24° C) during the day and 61° F (16° C) at night for greater stem elongation.

Effect of ethephon at 0, 500, and 1,000 ppm (from left to right) on zonal geranium flowers.

Supplemental lighting hastens flowering during periods of low light in winter. It has been found to accelerate floral initiation only when used during the early stages of seedling growth. Consequently, supplemental lighting of at least 350 f.c. (4 klux) for at least four weeks is most important for the first four to six weeks after germination. The best temperature and light combination is a daily mean temperature of 70° F (21° C) and an irradi-ance of 17.3 mol·m⁻²·day⁻¹. In production, zonal geraniums are best grown at 3,500 to 5,000 f.c. (38 to 54 klux). Ivy geraniums are best grown at 2,500 to 3,500 f.c. (27 to 38 klux). Regal geraniums are grown at temperatures of up to 65° F (18° C) during the day and 54° to 58° F (12° to 14° C) at night. Light levels for regal geraniums should be up to 4,000 f.c. (43 klux) until the flower color is first visible, at which time it should be lowered to 2,500 f.c. (27 klux).

While geraniums are genetically adapted to dry conditions and to well-drained soils, their best growth occurs without water stress. Many root rot problems can be traced to excess water, low oxygen, improper leaching, and excess soluble salt accumulation.

After the transplanted rooted cuttings are well rooted, provide 250 ppm nitrogen. When the inflorescence begins to color, decrease the nitrogen concentration to 150 ppm. Reduce nitrogen to 50 ppm during the final weeks prior to shipping when plants are grown at 55° F (13° C). Regal geraniums receive 150 to 300 ppm nitrogen, and ivy geraniums 100 to 150 ppm nitrogen. All geraniums have a high requirement for magnesium and calcium.

Geraniums require a pasteurized, well-drained substrate for adequate root aeration. Optimum pH is 5.6 to 6.0, unless iron or manganese toxicity is a problem, in which case a higher pH, up to 6.2, should be used. Use a slightly lower pH of 5.3 to 5.5 for ivy geraniums. With regal geraniums pH should be 5.6 to 6.0 and EC 0.9 to 1.1 mS/cm.

Zonal geraniums are often pinched during production, more to obtain a cutting than to stimulate axillary branching. Multiple applications of ethephon at 350 ppm can be used on ivy geraniums to encourage branching and reduce elongation. Do not use ethephon within six weeks of shipping cuttings or finished plants.

Generally, in cool climates one rooted cutting in different size pots finish in the following time frames: 4 in. (10 cm) pot in seven to eight weeks, 5 in. (13 cm) pot in nine to ten weeks, 6 in. (15 cm) pot in eleven to twelve weeks, and 7 in. (18 cm) pot in fourteen to fifteen weeks. Plants in warm climates finish one to two weeks sooner.

Ivy geranium propagation and production commence in December, January, and February for April, May, and June hanging basket sales. Use one rooted cutting per 4 to 5 in. (10 to 13 cm) pot, two per 6 to 7 in. (15 to 18 cm) pot, and four to five per 10 in. (25 cm) hanging basket. Generally, in cool climates a 4 in. (10 cm) pot finishes in eleven to twelve weeks, a 5 in. (13 cm) pot or 10 in. (25 cm) basket in thirteen to fourteen weeks, a 6 in. (15 cm) pot in fifteen to sixteen weeks, and a 7 in. (18 cm) pot in seventeen to eighteen weeks. Plants in warm climates finish one to two weeks sooner. Applying ethephon reduces crop time by two to three weeks.

With regal geraniums the four-week cold treatment can commence four weeks after rooted cuttings have become established. Forcing requires seven to ten weeks at 58° to 68° F (14° to 20° C) during midwinter (January to April), and long-day night breaks are used from 10:00 P.M. to 2:00 A.M. using incandescent lamps. Precooled liners with flowers already initiated can be used; they will flower in seven to ten weeks.

Diseases

Xanthomonas campestris pv. *pelargonii* is the most serious disease of geraniums because it is easily spread by propagation or irrigation, often difficult to detect, symptomless for many months after infection, and difficult to control with chemicals. Other systemic diseases include vascular bacterial blights (*Ralstonia solanacearum*), verticillium wilt (*Verticillium albo-atrum*), root and stem rots (*Pythium, Rhizoctonia, Phytophthora, Fusarium,* and *Thielavapsis*), bacterial stem fasciation (*Clavibacter fascians*), and viral diseases. *Ralstonia* is of particular importance because it has a broad host range and one type, known as Race 3, Biovar 2, is cold tolerant and can infect potatoes with the potential to cause serious crop losses if it were to escape the greenhouse. Race 3, Biovar 2 is not normally found in the United States and Canada but occurs in many areas of the world, and consequently its presence is regulated by U.S. federal quarantine. Race 1 already occurs in the southern United States; symptoms include wilting and yellowing of the foliage, but without the foliar spots indicative of *Xanthomonas.*

Foliar and flower diseases include *Botrytis*, bacterial leaf spots and blights (*Pseudomonas cichorii, P. syringae*), fungal leaf spots (*Cercospora brunkii*), and rust (*Puccinia pelargonii-zonalis*). Other reported diseases include bacterial leaf spot (*Pseudomonas cichorii*), leaf spot (*Alternaria alternata*), and armillaria root rot (*Armillaria mellea*).

Disorders

Ivy geranium has a common disorder called edema, in which areas of stomatal cells on the underside of the leaves rupture and form corky abnormalities. This problem is species and cultivar dependent. Rarely has the problem been seen on zonal or seed geraniums. Edema is thought to be related to excessive turgor pressure at night, when the stomates close. Water loss is reduced, but an active, well-developed root system with an adequate water supply and warm substrate temperatures continues to translocate

Botrytis on zonal geranium flowers. (B. Whipker)

water to the leaves. As the disorder progresses, the number of "blisters" increases. Consequently, proper temperatures and possibly reduction of water supply, lower humidity, and cultivar selection can reduce edema.

Geraniums are sensitive to proper pH. Low pH may induce iron or manganese toxicity, especially on zonal geraniums, and high pH may induce foliar chlorosis.

Postharvest

Geranium cuttings have a relatively short postharvest life and low tolerance to long-distance shipping at warm temperatures. Unrooted cuttings can be stored for four to six weeks at 31° F (0.5° C). Rooted cuttings could be stored for up to fifty-six days at 41° F (5° C) and 250 f.c. (2.7 klux) light for nine hours a day.

Leaf yellowing is a common problem with stored or shipped geranium cuttings and may be due to carbohydrate loss, which occurs rapidly under warm temperatures. Ethylene has been assumed to be involved in leaf yellowing, but cuttings exposed to 0.1 or 1 ppm ethylene for twenty hours showed no leaf yellowing or abscission. The antiethylene agents, silver thiosulfate (STS) and 1-MCP (EthylBloc), produced only a modest reduction in leaf yellowing and also reduced rooting in some cases. In fact, the use of anti-ethylene agents actually increased ethylene production by the cuttings. Thus, if ethylene is involved in leaf yellowing, it has either a minor role, or it becomes a problem only when cuttings are stressed from such factors as extended storage durations, warm temperatures, and low nutrient content.

References
Armitage, A. M., and M. J. Tsujita. 1979. The effect of supplemental light source, illumination and quantum

flux density on the flowering of seed-propagated geranium. *Journal of Horticultural Science* 54:195–198.

Arteca, R. N., J. M. Arteca, T. W. Wang, and C. D. Schlagnhaufer. 1996. Physiological, biochemical, and molecular changes in *Pelargonium* cuttings subjected to short-term storage conditions. *Journal of the American Society for Horticultural Science* 121:1063–1068.

Batschke, K. 1999. The regal details. *GrowerTalks* 63(6):57, 58, 60.

Bethke, C. L., and W. H. Carlson. 1985. Seed geraniums—18 years of research. *GrowerTalks* 49(6):58, 60, 62, 64, 66.

Cheng, G. W., S. S. Sargent, and D. J. Huber. 1998. Effects of ethylene scrubber and light on yellowing of geranium transplants. *HortScience* 33:486. (Abstract)

Craig, R. 1986. Regal and ivy leaved geraniums. *Bedding Plant News* 17(6):6–10.

Daughtrey, M., and A. R. Chase. 1992. Geranium, pp. 97–113. In: *Ball Field Guide to Diseases of Greenhouse Ornamentals.* Ball Publishing, Batavia, Illinois.

Dreistadt, S. H. 2001. *Integrated Pest Management for Floriculture and Nurseries.* University of California Division of Agriculture and Natural Resources Publication 3402. Oakland, California.

Eisenberg, B. A., G. L. Staby, and T. A. Fretz. 1978. Low pressure and refrigerated storage of rooted and unrooted ornamental cuttings. *Journal of the American Society for Horticultural Science* 103:732–737.

Erwin, J. 1999. Ivy geranium production. *Ohio Florists' Association Bulletin* 831:1, 15–20.

Erwin, J. and G. Engelen. 1992. Regal geranium production. *Minnesota Commercial Flower Growers Association Bulletin* 41(6):1–9.

Erwin, J. E., and R. D. Heins. 1992. Environmental effects on geranium development. *Minnesota Commercial Flower Growers Association Bulletin* 41(1):1–9.

Erwin, J. E., R. D. Heins, B. J. Kovanda, R. D. Berghage, W. H. Carlson, and J. A. Biernbaum. 1989. Cool mornings control plant height. *GrowerTalks* 52(9):75.

Haun, J. R., and P. W. Cornell. 1951. Rooting response of geranium cuttings as influenced by nitrogen, phosphorus, and potassium nutrition of the stock plant. *Proceedings of the American Society for Horticultural Science* 58:317–323.

Hammer, P. A., and K. Rane. 1999. Southern bacterial wilt found in geraniums. *GrowerTalks* 63(3):80, 82.

Hamrick, D. 2003. *Pelargonium,* pp. 546–560. In: *Ball RedBook,* 17th ed., vol. 2, D. Hamrick, ed. Ball Publishing, Batavia, Illinois.

Jonas, V. M., and K. A. Williams. 2000. Optimum irrigation and fertilization regimes for ivy geranium (*Pelargonium peltatum*). *HortScience* 35:508. (Abstract)

Kaczperski, M. P., R. D. Heins, and W. H. Carlson. 1996. Using temperature, light, and fungicides to prolong the storage life of rooted geraniums cuttings. *HortScience* 31:656. (Abstract)

Kadner, R., and U. Druege. 2004. Role of ethylene action in ethylene production and poststorage leaf senescence and survival of pelargonium cuttings. *Plant Growth Regulation* 43:187–196.

Lang, H., and K. Trellinger. 2001. Geraniums, pp. 88–92. In: *Tips on Regulating Growth of Floriculture Crops,* M. L. Gaston, L. A. Kunkle, P. S. Konjoian, and M. F. Wilt, eds. Ohio Florists' Association Services, Columbus, Ohio.

Langton, F. A., and W. Runger. 1985. *Pelargonium,* pp. 9–21. In: *Handbook of Flowering,* vol. IV, A. H. Halevy, ed. CRC Press, Boca Raton, Florida.

Oglevee, J. R. 1991. Stock plant management, pp. 2–11. In: *Tips on Growing Zonal Geraniums,* 2nd ed., H. K. Tayama, ed. Ohio State University, Ohio Cooperative Extension Service, Columbus, Ohio.

Paton, F., and W. W. Schwabe. 1987. Storage of cuttings of *Pelargonium* x *hortorum* Bailey. *Journal of Horticultural Science* 62:79–87.

Roberts, D. L. 1997. Major geranium diseases. *Professional Plant Growers Association News* 28(1):21–22.

Serek, M., A. Prabucki, E. C. Sisler, and A. S. Andersen. 1998. Inhibitors of ethylene action affect final quality and rooting of cuttings before and after storage. *HortScience* 153–155.

Simone, O. 1997. And now there are four: foliar bacterial diseases of geranium. *Greenhouse Product News* 7(6):38–41.

Trellinger, K. 1997. Top 10 tips for perfect ivy geraniums. *GrowerTalks* 61(8):73, 75.

Tsujita, M. J., and P. M. Harney. 1978. The effects of Florel and supplemental lighting on the production and rooting of geranium cuttings. *Journal of Horticultural Science* 53:349–350.

White, J. W., ed. 1993. *Geraniums IV.* Ball Publishing, Batavia, Illinois.

White, J. W., and S. M. Polys. 1987. Photon flux and leaf temperature effects on flower initiation and early development of 'Red Elite' geraniums. *Journal of the American Society for Horticultural Science* 112:945–950.

Willumsen, K., and T. Fjeld. 1995. The sensitivity of some flowering potted plants to exogenous ethylene. *Acta Horticulturae* 405:362–371.

Pentas

Common name: Pentas, star-cluster, Egyptian star-cluster.
Scientific name: *Pentas lanceolata.*
Family: Rubiaceae.
Other propagation methods: seed.

Description, Uses, and Status

Large clusters of star-shaped white, pink, rose, lavender, or red flowers are produced on 12 to 24 in. (30 to 60 cm) tall upright plants. Cultivars with variegated foliage are available. This tender perennial is not frost tolerant and is sold in the spring in pots or packs. Both seed- and cutting-propagated cultivars are available; those propagated by cuttings are usually taller. Plants are a favorite nectar source for butterflies in the landscape.

Flowering Control

Pentas are facultative long-day plants. High light levels and warm temperatures encourage flowering.

Stock Plant Management

Keep plants under short days and moderate light levels to delay flowering. Pentas should be hedged (cut back) regularly to avoid an irregularly shaped canopy of vegetative and reproductive shoots.

Cutting Harvest

Terminal cuttings 2 in. (5 cm) long are harvested from actively growing plants. Single-node cuttings 2 in. (5 cm) long can also be used.

Propagation

Stage 1: Cutting arrival or harvest and sticking

* Store cuttings at 50° to 60° F (10° to 16° C) for up to twenty-four hours if planting is going to be delayed.
* Use a rooting hormone solution of 1,000 ppm IBA plus 500 ppm NAA.
* Insert one cutting per cell if using plug flats.

Stage 2: Callusing

* Maintain substrate temperatures of 68° to 72° F (20° to 22° C).
* Maintain air temperatures of 75° to 80° F (24° to 27° C) during days and 68° to 70° F (20° to 21° C) during nights.
* Maintain a light intensity of 500 to 1,000 f.c. (5 to 11 klux) and short days to inhibit premature

Pentas flowers. (B. Whipker)

flowering.
* Begin foliar feeding with 50 to 75 ppm nitrogen from 20-10-20 if there is any loss in foliage color.
* Maintain a substrate pH of 6.5 to 7.0.
* Cuttings are prone to slow rooting and extensive development of callus, which is due to insufficient air in the substrate. Callus development in pentas, unlike most other species, is detrimental to rooting and should be avoided.
* Transfer the cuttings to Stage 3 after five to seven days, once 50% of the cuttings begin differentiating root initials.

Stage 3: Root development

* Maintain a substrate temperature of 68° to 72° F (20° to 22° C).
* Maintain air temperatures of 75° to 80° F (24° to 27° C) during days and 68° to 72° F (20° to 22° C) during nights.
* Increase the light intensity to 1,000 to 2,000 f.c. (11 to 22 klux) and continue short days to inhibit flowering.
* Fertilize once a week with 100 ppm nitrogen, alternating between 15-0-15 and 20-10-20, then increase to 200 ppm.
* Begin drying out the substrate once roots are visible.
* Begin reducing the duration and frequency of mist.
* Roots should develop in seven to fourteen days.

Stage 4: Toning the rooted cutting.

* Lower the air temperature to 75° to 80° F (24° to 27° C) during the day and 62° to 68° F (17° to 20° C) at night.
* Move the liners from the mist area into an area of lower relative humidity.

- Increase the light intensity to 2,000 to 4,000 f.c. (22 to 43 klux).
- Fertilize once with 150 to 200 ppm nitrogen from 15-0-15.
- The cuttings can be toned for seven days.

Plant Growth Regulators

Paclobutrazol (Bonzi) sprays up to 45 ppm or drenches of 6 to 10 ppm can be used for vigorous cultivars. Chlormequat (Cycocel) sprays at 800 to 3,000 ppm are also effective.

Production and Schedule

Recommended day temperatures are 72° to 75° F (22° to 24° C) and night temperatures 62° to 65° F (17° to 18° C). Although plants are quite heat tolerant after they are established, avoid temperatures over 100° F (38° C). Avoid overirrigation, especially after transplanting the plugs. Reduce watering, and allow plants to dry slightly during cool, cloudy weather to prevent root rot and foliar diseases.

Initially, a rate of 150 to 200 ppm nitrogen is adequate at every other irrigation. Pentas is one of the species that can reduce the pH of the growing substrate, and it is susceptible to iron toxicity from low pH. Avoid acidic high-ammonium fertilizers and supplemental iron applications. Consequently, monitor pH regularly, and maintain a substrate pH of 6.5 to 7.0. One symptom of iron toxicity is leaf rolling. Plants are also susceptible to magnesium deficiency. Avoid high soluble salts in the substrate.

One plug is used per 4 to 6 in. (10 to 1 cm) pot, and three to five per 8 to 10 in. (20 to 25 cm) pot. Plants should be pinched two to three weeks after planting. Large containers may need a second pinch. In the spring 4 in. (10 cm) pots are ready to sell in five to six weeks, 6 in. (15 cm) pots in six to seven weeks, 8 in. (20 cm) pots in eight to ten weeks, and 10 in. (25 cm) pots in ten to twelve weeks. The crop finishes one to two weeks earlier in the summer.

Diseases

Botrytis, powdery mildew, *Rhizoctonia,* and *Pythium* can be problems. The latter two are especially problems if plants are overwatered.

Disorders

Stunted growth, leaf rolling, and strapped leaves are due to low substrate pH; avoid the problems by keeping the pH higher than 6.5. Marginal leaf burn can be due to water stress, high soluble salts, iron toxicity, or low substrate pH.

References

Hamrick, D. 2003. *Pentas,* pp. 561–563. In: *Ball RedBook,* 17th ed., vol. 2, D. Hamrick, ed. Ball Publishing, Batavia, Illinois.

Harbaugh, B. K. 1995. Getting to the root of pentas. *Greenhouse Grower* 13(4):34, 36.

Petunia

Common name: Petunia.
Scientific name: *Petunia* x *hybrida.*
Family: Solanaceae.
Other propagation methods: Seed.

Description, Uses, and Status

Petunias are grown for their showy white, pink, red, purple, pale yellow, or bicolored flowers, making them a popular summer bedding plant. Plants are sold in pots, hanging baskets, and mixed containers. In warm climates petunias are perennial, but they are used as annuals in temperate zones. Many cultivars can tolerate temperatures below freezing. Petunias are used in mass plantings, porch boxes, tubs, and hanging baskets.

'Suncatcher Coral Prism' petunia flowers.

Flowering Control

Petunias are typically considered to be facultative long-day plants with the critical night length for flowering between thirteen and ten hours. However, many newly released cultivars appear to be day-neutral or short-day plants. High intensity discharge (HID) lighting can overcome photoperiod, in that some cultivars are long-day plants under ambient light and day-neutral under supplemental HID lighting.

Stock Plant Management

Because petunias are vigorous and spreading, stock plants are often grown in hanging baskets for easier management. Supplemental HID lighting can increase cutting production of stock plants grown in low light situations. Good air movement through the stock plants to ensure sufficient carbon dioxide will help provide optimum results when using HID lighting.

Cutting Harvest

Terminal cuttings 0.8 to 2 in. (2 to 5 cm) long with at least one fully expanded leaf are primarily used.

Propagation

Stage 1:
Cutting arrival or harvest and sticking
- Store cuttings at 40° to 45° F (5° to 7° C) for up to twenty-four hours if planting is going to be delayed.
- Rooting hormones are not required. However, either up to 3,000 ppm IBA alone or IBA with up to 500 ppm NAA can be used.
- Insert one cutting per cell if using plug flats.

Stage 2: Callusing.
- Maintain substrate temperatures of 64° to 74° F (18° to 23° C).
- Maintain air temperatures of 70° to 75° F (21° to 24° C) during days and 68° to 74° F (20° to 23° C) during nights.
- Use as little mist as possible to maintain turgidity without saturating the substrate too much. Keep the substrate sufficiently moist so that water is easily squeezed out of it, but not so much that the cutting base is waterlogged. The base of the cutting needs air for proper rooting.
- Maintain a light intensity of 500 to 1,000 f.c. (5 to 11 klux). Supplemental lighting of 400 to 500 f.c. (4 to 5 klux) may be beneficial in northern or cloudy climates.

- Begin foliar feeding with 50 to 75 ppm nitrogen from 15-0-15 as soon as leaves begin to show any color loss.
- Maintain a substrate pH of 5.5 to 6.2.
- Transfer the cuttings to Stage 3 after five to seven days, once 50% of the cuttings begin differentiating root initials.

Stage 3: Root development
- Maintain substrate temperatures of 64° to 74° F (20° to 23° C).
- Maintain air temperatures of 70° to 75° F (21° to 24° C) during days and 68° to 74° F (20° to 23° C) during nights.
- Begin drying out the substrate once roots are visible.
- Begin increasing the light intensity to 1,000 to 2,000 f.c. (11 to 22 klux) as the cuttings start to root out.
- Fertilize once a week at 100 ppm nitrogen, alternating between 15-0-15 and 20-10-20, then increase to 200 ppm.
- Roots should develop in nine to fourteen days.

Stage 4: Toning the rooted cutting
- Lower the air temperatures to 70° to 75° F (21° to 24° C) days and 62° to 68° F (17° to 20° C) at night.
- Move the liners from the mist area into an area of lower relative humidity.
- Increase the light intensity to 2,000 to 4,000 f.c. (22 to 43 klux).
- Provide shade during the middle of the day to reduce temperature stress.
- Fertilize once a week with 150 to 200 ppm nitrogen from 15-0-15 alternating with 20-10-20.
- The cuttings can be toned for seven days.

Plant Growth Regulators

During propagation, daminozide (B-Nine) sprays at 1,500 to 2,500 ppm, paclobutrazol (Bonzi or Piccolo) drenches at 2 to 4 ppm, or a tank-mixed spray of ancymidol (A-Rest) at 6 to 12 ppm and daminozide at 1,250 to 2,500 ppm can be used fifteen to twenty-four days after sticking unrooted cuttings.

During production, a single spray of uniconazole (Sumagic) at 20 to 30 ppm or two sprays, with the first application at 20 ppm and the second at 10 ppm, can be used. Two spray applications of daminozide at 7,500 ppm; single sprays of ancymidol at 10 to 26 ppm or flurprimidol (Topflor) at 15 to 60 ppm, or one paclobutrazol drench at 4 to 5 ppm or spray at 40 to 60 ppm can also be used. Ethephon (Florel) at 500 ppm increases branching and reduces stem length, but it greatly delays flowering.

Use of nitrogen or phosphorus restriction and water stress is effective. Higher nitrogen rates can be applied one to two weeks prior to marketing, to green the foliage. Day and night temperature difference (DIF) is effective but DROP may not be (see chapter 8 for more information).

Production and Schedule

Flowering is rapid at 70° to 79° F (21° to 26° C) and slow at 50° to 59° F (10° to 15° C). Plants are typically grown at temperatures of 65° to 72° F (18° to 22° C) during the day and 62° to 65° F (17° to 18° C) at night. Water restriction is frequently used to slow growth rates and thus prevent rapid flowering, but it may reduce plant quality. Petunias generally require relatively high levels of nitrogen during production, with constant liquid fertilization rates of approximately 250 to 350 ppm for cutting-propagated plants.

Nutrition may be used to control growth rate. Low nitrogen rates can be used to reduce growth. After the plugs were planted, nitrogen rates of 150 ppm produced large plants with light green foliage, while 0 ppm nitrogen was required to control growth. Higher nitrogen rates can be used for one to two weeks prior to marketing to make the foliage greener. Plants can be quite vigorous and readily intertwine, which makes marketing difficult. Provide as much space as possible for pots and baskets. The long vines of many cultivars can be pinched at any time to increase axillary branching and control growth.

Plants in 4 to 6 in. (10 to 15 cm) pots are marketable in five to seven weeks without a pinch; add two more weeks if pinching. Generally, one rooted cutting is used per pot; however, crop time can be reduced by using two cuttings per 6 in. (15 cm) pot. Plant three to four cuttings per hanging basket; the baskets will finish in six to eleven weeks. Winter production takes one to two weeks longer than late spring production due to lower light levels and cooler temperatures.

Diseases

Rhizoctonia and *Schlerotinia* result in basal stem canker and lower leaf collapse and yellowing. *Botrytis* is a common problem on open flowers and can quickly eliminate summer floral displays after a rain or periods of high humidity. Other diseases have been reported, including crown and root rot (*Pythium* and *Phytophthora*), verticillium wilt (*Verticillium dahliae*),

black root rot (*Thielaviopsis basicola*), cottony rot (*Sclerotinia sclerotiorum*), leaf spot (*Mycocentrospora acerina*), powdery mildew (*Oidium*), aster yellows, tobacco mosaic virus, impatiens necrotic spot virus, tomato spotted wilt virus, and numerous other viruses. Tobacco mosaic and tomato mosaic viruses have been documented on cutting-propagated petunias.

Disorders

Chlorosis can occur with iron deficiency (high pH), nitrogen deficiency, or low temperatures. Too much vegetative growth can be due to high ammonium levels or low light, especially in combination with overwatering or overfertilizing. Short days or late applications of plant growth regulators can delay flowering, leading to long crop times.

Postharvest

Ethylene at 0.1 to 1 ppm for twenty hours did not influence leaf abscission or cutting rooting.

References

Armitage, A. M. 1985. *Petunia,* pp. 41–46. In: *Handbook of Flowering,* vol. IV, A. H. Halevy, ed. CRC Press, Boca Raton, Florida.

Cohen, J., N. Sikron, S. Shuval, and A. Gera. 1999. Susceptibility of vegetatively propagated petunia to tobamovirus infection and its possible control. *HortScience* 34:292–293.

Cox, D. 2000. Low phosphorus controls bedding plant growth. *HortScience* 35:457. (Abstract)

Daughtrey, M., and A. R. Chase. 1992. Petunia, pp. 153–154. In: *Ball Field Guide to Diseases of Greenhouse Ornamentals.* Ball Publishing, Batavia, Illinois.

Dole, J. M., B. E. Whipker, and P. V. Nelson. 2002. Producing vegetative petunias and calibrachoa. *GPN* 12(2):30–31, 33, 34.

Donnelly, C. S., and P. R. Fisher. 2002. High-pressure sodium lighting affects greenhouse production of vegetative cuttings for specialty annuals. *HortScience* 37:623–626.

Dreistadt, S. H. 2001. *Integrated Pest Management for Floriculture and Nurseries.* University of California Division of Agriculture and Natural Resources Publication 3402. Oakland, California.

Evans, M. R., and R. H. Stamps. 1996. Growth of bedding plants in sphagnum peat and coir dust-based substrates. *Journal of Environmental Horticulture* 14:187–190.

Flohr, R. C., and C. A Conover. 1994. Production and postproduction watering schedule effects on plant growth, quality and blooming of pansies and petunias. *Proceedings of the Florida State Horticultural Society* 107:414–416.

Hamrick, D. 2003. *Petunia,* pp. 567–574. In: *Ball RedBook,* 17th ed., vol. 2, D. Hamrick, ed. Ball Publishing, Batavia, Illinois.

Horst, R. K. 1990. Petunia, pp. 768–769. In: *Westcott's Plant Disease Handbook,* 5th ed. Van Nostrand Reinhold, New York.

Konjoian, P. 2001. Production pointers for petunias: seed and vegetative. Ohio Florists' Association Bulletin 855:1, 8–10.

Moe, R., K. Willumsen, I. H. Ihlebekk, A. I. Stupa, N. M. Glomsrud, and L. M. Mortensen. 1995. DIF and temperature drop responses in SDP and LDP, a comparison. *Acta Horticulturae* 378:27–33.

van Iersel, M. W., R. B. Beverly, P. A. Thomas, J. G. Latimer, and H. A. Mills. 1998. Fertilizer effects on the growth of impatiens, petunia, salvia, and vinca plug seedlings. *HortScience* 33:678–682.

Wang, S.-Y. 1999. Effects of plant growth regulators on plant size, branching, and flowering in *Petunia* x *hybrida.* HortScience 34:528. (Abstract)

Wilkins, H. F., and H. R. Pemberton. 1981. Interaction of growth regulators and light. *Proceedings of the 14th International Bedding Plant Conference,* Seattle, Washington, 14:182–188.

Plectranthus

Common name: Plectranthus, Swedish ivy.
Scientific name: *Plectranthus* species.
Family: Labiatae.
Other propagation methods: Seed.

Description, Uses, and Status

These trailing to upright plants are grown primarily for their green or variegated foliage but also for loose spikes of flowers. Several commonly grown species are *P. amboinicus,* Cuban oregano, with thick green or variegated leaves; *P. argentatus,* with gray-green or variegated foliage; *P. ciliatus* 'Gold Coin', with pale green to bright yellow foliage; *P. ecklonii,* with deep green leaves and pink or purple flowers; *P. forsteri* 'Marginatus' (also known as 'Variegatus' and often mislabeled as *P. coleoides*), with large bright green white-edged leaves; *P. madagascariensis,* with fragrant green and white hairy foliage; *P. oertendahlii,* with purple and green leaves and silver veins; *P. tomentosus,* with large gray-green leaves; *P. verticillatus* (formerly *P. australis*), with glossy green or green and white leaves; and *P. zuluensis,* with bright green foliage and small spikes of pinkish-white flowers. Other species as well as several hybrids or cultivars of unspecified origin are also available. Most of the species listed here are mounding or trailing, except for *P. amboinicus* and *P. ecklonii,* which are upright. While some species and cultivars have attractive flowers, most are grown for their foliage, which is often fragrant. Plants are grown in pots or hanging baskets.

Plectranthus forsteri 'Marginatus'.

Flowering Control and Dormancy

Most species and cultivars are short-day plants; long days of sixteen hours prevent flowering. For most species, ten- to twelve-hour days induce flowering, which is promoted when plants are grown in cool temperatures.

Stock Plant Management

Stock plants of flowering types should be kept under long days of sixteen hours to prevent flowering, especially when temperatures are cool during the winter. Maintain high light and warm temperatures. Plants should be routinely pinched and trimmed to prevent excessive shoot elongation.

Cutting Harvest

Terminal or subterminal stem cuttings with at least one fully expanded leaf can be used. Cuttings of most species root easily and often have adventitious roots forming on the stems before propagation.

Propagation

Cuttings of most species root rapidly within five to ten days at 70° to 75° F (21° to 24° C) and do not require rooting hormones. One exception is *P. ciliatus* 'Gold Coin', which is slow to root. Use rooting hormones, either up to 3,000 ppm IBA alone or IBA with up to 500 ppm NAA, on the cutting bases of slower-to-root cultivars. The foliage on large-leaved cultivars can be trimmed to reduce *Botrytis* problems. Insert one cutting per cell if using plug flats. Heavy misting rates are usually not required; mist several times a day to avoid wilting. Reduce mist even further after rooting. The substrate pH should be 5.5 to 6.5. Cuttings should be ready to transplant in two and a half to four weeks.

Plant Growth Regulators

Drenches of paclobutrazol (Bonzi) at 0.25 to 1 ppm or uniconazole (Sumagic) at 0.02 to 0.8 mg a.i. per 6 in. (15 cm) pot can be used to control stem length. A tank mix of daminozide (B-Nine) at 1,500 to 2,500 ppm plus chlormequat (Cycocel) at 750 to 1,000 ppm or paclobutrazol foliar sprays at 5 to 20 ppm can also be used to control growth.

Production and Schedule

Grow the plants at 75° to 85° F (24° to 29° C) during the day and 55° F (13° C) at night. Growth slows greatly at temperatures below 50° F (10° C). Plectranthus requires 3,000 to 4,000 f.c. (32 to 43 klux) during production. *P. ciliatus* 'Gold Coin' needs lower light levels than other cultivars. High light levels can results in bleached foliage color and lower plant quality.

Use 150 to 200 ppm nitrogen and a substrate pH of 6 to 7. To prevent a weak root system, avoid overwatering.

Generally, one cutting is used per 4 in. (10 cm) pot, two per 6 in. (15 cm) pot, and three to five per 8 to 10 in. (20 to 25 cm) hanging basket. The 4 in. (10 cm) pot requires about eight weeks from rooted cutting to finish, the 6 in. (15 cm) pot eight to ten weeks, and the hanging basket ten to thirteen weeks.

Diseases

Root rots can be a problem, especially for the slower-growing cultivars. *Botrytis* can also be a problem.

Disorders

Edema (raised, corky growth on the upper surface of the leaf) can occur on some species of plectranthus.

Postharvest

P. forsteri cuttings should not be stored at temperatures lower than 54° F (12° C). Cold damage became apparent after three days at 34° F (1° C) and after six days at 41° F (5° C). Of the cuttings stored at 54° F (12° C) for seven days, 98% rooted. The longer that cuttings were stored, the lower the rooting percentage. Interestingly, cold storage temperature tolerance depended on the growing conditions of the stock plants. Those grown under high light levels, 5,000 f.c. (54 klux) for 12 hours/day, and an average daily temperature of 68° F (20° C) produced cuttings that were chilling sensitive to both 34° F (1° C) and 41° F (5° C) storage temperatures. However, stock plants grown under low light levels, 420 f.c. (4.5 klux) for 10.3 hours/day, and an average daily temperature of 62° F (17° C) produced cuttings that were sensitive to the low 34° F (1° C) and the higher 54° F (12° C) storage temperatures. The former due to chilling sensitivity and the latter due to high respiration reducing carbohydrate content. Note, however, the cuttings grown under low light levels and cool temperatures were less sensitive to chilling than those grown under high light and warm temperatures and tolerated 41° F (5° C) storage.

Ethylene at 0.1 to 1 ppm for twenty hours did not influence leaf abscission or cutting rooting of several plectranthus cultivars.

References

Hamrick, D. 2003. *Plectranthus,* pp. 585–586. In: *Ball RedBook,* 17th ed., vol. 2, D. Hamrick, ed. Ball Publishing, Batavia, Illinois.

Kadner, R. 2002. Storage of cuttings from *Plectranthus coleoides. Gartenbauwissenschaft* 67:190–193.

Kadner, R. 2005. The influenced of stock plant light exposure on optimum storage conditions and rooting behavior of *Plectranthus coleoides* cuttings. *European Journal of Horticultural Science* 70:105-108.

Schoellhorn, R. 2002. Plectranthus—coleus' cousin. *GPN* 12(2):78–80,82.

Schoellhorn, R. 2003. Blooming plectranthus—a study on flowering. *GPN* 13(12):14–16.

Portulaca

Common name: Flowering purslane.
Scientific name: *Portulaca oleracea.*
Family: Portulacaceae.
Other propagation methods: Seed.

Description, Uses, and Status
This low-growing succulent annual produces numerous 1 to 2.5 in. (2.5 to 6 cm) wide flowers. The single or double blooms are available in a broad range of colors including white, pink rose, red, orange, yellow, and bicolors. The leaves are rounded and succulent. Flowering purslane is frost tolerant and is sold in the spring in packs, pots, and hanging baskets. The flattened leaves distinguish this species from the similar moss rose (*P. grandiflora*), which has cylindrical leaves and is seed propagated. Flowering purslane's blossoms close at night and during cloudy and rainy weather. Newer cultivars are more likely to stay open during cloudy weather.

Flowering Control and Dormancy
Portulaca is day-neutral. It flowers more quickly on shoots with fewer leaves under high light.

Stock Plant Management
Stock plants are often grown in hanging baskets for easier management of this spreading species.

Cutting Harvest
Terminal cuttings 0.8 to 1.2 in. (2 to 3 cm) long with at least one fully expanded leaf are used.

Propagation

Stage 1:
Cutting arrival or harvest and sticking
* When purchasing cuttings, open and unpack the boxes as soon as possible, since they are prone to defoliation.
* To decrease *Botrytis* problems, avoid crushing the cuttings when harvesting them.
* Rooting hormones are not required.
* Insert one cutting per cell if using plug flats.

Stage 2: Callusing
* Maintain substrate temperatures of 68° to 72° F (20° to 22° C).
* Maintain air temperatures of 75° to 80° F (24° to 27° C) during days and 68° to 72° F (20° to 22° C)

'Fairy Tales Cinderella' flowering purslane.

during nights.
* Keep the substrate sufficiently moist so that water is easily squeezed out of it, but not so much that the cutting base is waterlogged. The base of the cutting needs air for proper rooting.
* Maintain a light intensity of 500 to 1,000 f.c. (5 to 11 klux).
* Begin foliar feeding once a week with 50 to 75 ppm nitrogen from 20-10-20.
* Maintain a substrate pH of 6.5 to 7.0.
* Transfer the cuttings to Stage 3 after five to seven days, once 50% of the cuttings begin differentiating root initials.

Stage 3: Root development
* Maintain substrate temperatures of 68° to 72° F (20° to 22° C).
* Maintain air temperatures of 75° to 80° F (24° to 27° C) during days and 68° to 72° F (20° to 22° C) during nights.
* Begin drying out the substrate once roots are visible.
* Begin increasing the light intensity to 1,000 to 2,000 f.c. (11 to 22 klux) as the cuttings start to root out.
* Fertilize once a week with 100 ppm nitrogen, alternating between 15-0-15 and 20-10-20, then increase to 200 ppm.
* Roots should develop in nine to eleven days.

Stage 4: Toning the rooted cutting
* Lower the air temperatures to 70° to 75° F (21° to 24° C) during the day and 65° to 68° F (18° to 20° C) at night.
* Move the liners from the mist area into an area of lower relative humidity.
* Increase the light intensity to 2,000 to 4,000 f.c. (22 to 43 klux).

- Fertilize once a week with150 to 200 ppm nitrogen from 15-0-15 alternating with 20-10-20.
- The cuttings can be toned for seven days.

Plant Growth Regulators
None are usually required for this low-growing plant. However, sprays of ancymidol (A-Rest) at 7 to 26 ppm, chlormequat (Cycocel) at 5,000 ppm, or uniconazole (Sumagic) at 15 to 30 ppm are effective. Ethephon (Florel) at 300 to 500 ppm can be used to increase branching, but it should not be applied to stressed plants or less than eight weeks prior to marketing. In addition, test ethephon since it may cause some defoliation at high rates.

Production and Schedule
Grow the plants at 75° to 80° F (24° to 27° C) during the day and 65° to 68° F (18° to 20° C) at night. Cold production temperatures will slow growth greatly. Avoid starting this species early in the spring when temperatures are cool. Crops started later, when temperatures are warm, will often catch up to those started earlier. Light intensity should be 4,500 to 6,000 f.c. (48 to 65 klux).

Fertilize with 200 ppm nitrogen from 15-0-15 alternating with 20-10-20. Avoid using too much ammonium (more than 10 ppm); it causes vegetative growth and reduces flowering. The substrate pH should be 5.8 to 6.2. Avoid overwatering, which encourages diseases and soft growth.

One rooted cutting is used per 4 in. (10 cm) pot, two to three per 6 in. (15 cm) pot, and five to seven per 8 to 10 in. (20 to 25 cm) hanging basket. Plants grown in pots larger than 4 in. (10 cm) can be pinched once or twice to improve branching and plant shape. As with many trailing plants, flowering purslane can become tangled if shoots are not controlled. In the spring cutting-propagated 4 in. (10 cm) pots are ready in five to six weeks, 6 in. (15 cm) pots in six to seven weeks, 8 in. (20 cm) baskets in eight to ten weeks, and 10 in. (25 cm) baskets in ten to twelve weeks. The crop finishes one to two weeks earlier in the summer.

Diseases
Botrytis, Rhizoctonia, Pythium, impatiens necrotic spot virus, and potato Y virus can be problems.

Disorders
Delayed flowering and excessive vegetative growth can be due to high ammonium fertilization or low light, especially in combination with overfertilizing or overwatering. Plants may collapse from overwatering, *Botrytis,* fungus gnats, or oligochaetes.

Postharvest
The cuttings are sensitive to 0.1 to 1 ppm ethylene, which causes defoliation. Storage may accentuate ethylene effects, especially if temperatures are warm.

References
Hamrick, D. 2003. *Portulaca,* pp. 588–589. In: *Ball RedBook,* 17th ed., vol. 2, D. Hamrick, ed. Ball Publishing, Batavia, Illinois.

Rhododendron

Common name: Florist azalea, evergreen azalea, azalea.
Scientific name: *Rhododendron* hybrids.
Family: Ericaceae.
Other propagation methods: Tissue culture.

Description, Uses, and Status
The florist azalea is characterized by small 1.5 in. (4 cm) evergreen glossy leaves, a height of only 12 in. (30 cm), and two or more 1 to 3 in. (2.5 to 8 cm) wide flowers per terminal bud. The individual flowers can be single or double with smooth or ruffled edges; colors vary from pure white through pale to dark pink, rose, orange,

Potted azalea plant.

salmon, and various reds (scarlet, carmine, and crimson). The plants are very well branched, and the stems are thin. Plants are most commonly forced into flower from Christmas to Mother's Day, though they can be programmed to flower year-round by controlling temperature and photoperiod. Historically, the most common pot size was a 6 to 7 in. (15 to 18 cm) azalea pan; now pot sizes of 2, 4, and 5 in. (5, 10, and 13 cm) are used. The florist azalea can also be grown in the standard tree form. Azaleas are known to be expensive plants because of their long-term production cycle.

Flowering Control and Dormancy

The vegetative and reproductive growth cycles used in commerce mimic nature. When plants (shoots or vegetative growth) reach the size required for sale, pinching ceases and flower buds are allowed to form.

Vegetative growth is maintained by long days using night interruption from incandescent lamps. A sixteen- to eighteen-hour total photoperiod (normal day plus night break) is used from fall to spring, after a pinch to maintain or promote vegetative growth. A night temperature of 64° to 72° F (18° to 22° C) with a day temperature that is 10° F (°6 C) or warmer than the night temperature also promotes vegetative growth.

Floral initiation and development are under the control of naturally shortening days or eight hours of short days provided with black cloth. Warm night temperatures of 64° to 72° F (18° to 22° C) also promote rapid and uniform initiation with the greatest number of flower buds formed under short days. Six to eight weeks must be allowed after the last pinch to the beginning of short days.

Plant growth regulators such as daminozide (B-Nine) at 1,500 to 2,500 ppm sprays and chlormequat (Cycocel) at 1,000 to 4,000 ppm sprays are used to reduce internode elongation and synergistically interact with short days to promote earlier floral initiation and development. Plants treated with growth retardants also have more flowers per bud and darker green leaves. Plants given short-day and plant growth regulator treatments force and break dormancy after a cold treatment more uniformly and rapidly than untreated plants.

Dormancy breaking and rapid development of flower buds can be accomplished by several methods. Cold treatments for four to six weeks in the dark at 35° to 40° F (2° to 4° C) or at 40° to 50° F (4° to 10° C) if lighted with 125 f.c. (1,350 lux) for twelve hours are the most common methods.

Stock Plant Management

Azalea cuttings can be harvested from plants dedicated to cutting production or from plants destined to be sold in flower. Finished plants require one or more pinches to produce a well-shaped plant, and cuttings can be harvested at that time. Regardless, young stock plants should be given a soft pinch soon after establishment to build the branching structure for increased cutting production later.

Cutting Harvest

Terminal semihardwood cuttings that are 3 to 4 in. long (8 to 10 cm) are used. Shoots are of the proper maturity if they are brittle enough to break with a snap. Younger shoots are too soft to root well and will bend rather than snap. These shoots wilt excessively when first harvested and are more disease prone during propagation. On the other hand, rooting is slower and less prolific on cuttings that are too old.

Propagation

Azaleas are propagated mainly in the spring using IBA and rooted in peat moss at 70° F (21° C) substrate temperature. The optimum IBA varies from 0.8 to 2.0%, depending on the cultivar. A mixture of 250 ppm NAA and 500 ppm IBA is also effective. Twenty-four-hour misting will probably be required for the first three to four days. The water temperature should be at least 70° F (21° C) to prevent rooting from being delayed. Reduce mist frequency and duration as soon as possible to prevent overmisting, which can also delay rooting. Cuttings should be well rooted in eight to twelve weeks.

Plant Growth Regulators

Foliar sprays of daminozide at 1,500 ppm to 3,500 ppm or chlormequat at 1,000 to 4,000 ppm can be applied. Multiple applications are often used. Ancymidol (A-Rest) sprays at 26 ppm spray, paclobutrazol (Bonzi) sprays at 100 to 200 ppm or drenches at 0.6 to 1.77 mg a.i. per pot, or uniconazole (Sumagic) sprays at 10 to 15 ppm are usually applied only once or twice.

Production and Schedule

Most finished azalea plants are produced from liners that have been grown for several months and pinched one or more times, or they are produced from dormant budded plants, which are full-sized plants ready for flowering after receiving the proper cold treatment. Both the liners and dormant plants are produced by specialists who ship the material to the finished plant producers.

A night temperature of 65° F (18° C) is needed both for optimal vegetative growth and for rapid floral initiation and development. For optimum release of flower bud dormancy, four to six weeks of lighted

40° to 50° F (4° to 10° C) storage is commonly used. For greenhouse forcing into flower, an acceptable temperature is 60° to 65° F (16° to 18° C).

Light intensity is critical during the vegetative growth period. During the summer, light levels are reduced by shading to 3,000 to 4,000 f.c. (32 to 43 klux). In the winter, full light intensity is required for growth or forcing. If temperatures are above 40° F (4° C) during cold storage, light is needed for twelve hours at 125 f.c. (1,350 lux).

Long days of sixteen hours are required during vegetative growth and up to six to eight weeks after the last pinch. Thereafter, eight-hour short days hasten flower initiation.

A peat moss substrate is not easy to water properly. It is easily overwatered, which leads to root rot problems. Conversely, if allowed to become too dry, the peat shrinks away from the pot and rehydration is a problem; the results are plant water stress, root injury, and leaf loss.

Azaleas must be grown in an acid substrate, they have a low requirement for nutrients, and their roots are easily injured by excessive EC. In 1992 R. Larson recommended 315 ppm nitrogen from an acidic 21-7-7 soluble fertilizer in one application every one to two weeks. Azaleas are always grown in 100% peat moss with the pH adjusted at 4.5 to 5.5.

The number of pinches determines the size of the final plant. Azaleas produced in 6 in. (15 cm) or larger pots are often grown from liners. These liners are sheared up to three times to produce a well-branched plant. The time span between shearing is normally six to eight weeks. Generally, three to four nodes are left on the plant, and a 3 to 4 in. (8 to 10 cm) shoot is removed. These shoots can be trimmed and used as cuttings.

Azaleas are available on a year-round basis, which is accomplished by manipulating photoperiod or by long-term storage of budded plants for up to six to eight months at 35° to 37° F (2° to 3° C). The production time from potting a liner to the earliest possible sale of a 6 in. (15 cm) pot is seven months. Small 2 to 3 in. (5 to 8 cm) pots are useful for dish gardens and for color in baskets.

Diseases

Several diseases can cause serious problems during production, cold storage, and forcing. In storage, *Botrytis* can infect flower buds or open flowers. The most important disease is *Cylindrocladium,* which is systemic and causes wilting, root deterioration, and necrotic leaf spotting during any stage of production. *Phytophthora* root rot can be a serious problem, and symptoms are frequently expressed as a slow deterioration of the plant. Other diseases have been reported included leaf rust (*Chrysomyxa*), petal blight (*Ovulinia azaleae*), powdery mildew (*Erysiphe polygoni* and *Microsphaera penicillata*), *Phomopsis,* and *Rhizoctonia.*

Disorders

Chlorotic foliage due to high pH is common. Nonuniform flowering can be the result of placing plants with immature flower buds into cold or another dormancy-breaking treatment. If the dormancy breaking is inadequate, forcing will be slow or flowering won't be uniform. Reduced flower numbers, particularly on lower branches, is the result of growing plants too close together or in inadequate light.

Leaf defoliation can occur if the light intensity is not adequate during 41° to 50° F (5° to 10° C) cold storage. Also, defoliation can be serious, especially during warm, sunny weather, if there is not a careful transition after plants are removed from cold storage until the roots become active and the root-ball is rewarmed to allow for water uptake. Plants should be well misted, temporarily shaded, and held at moderate temperatures to reduce leaf water stress and transpiration.

Bypass shoots are vegetative shoots that develop below the flower buds during floral differentiation. These shoots reduce the quality of the plant by covering up the flowers and possibly causing flower bud abortion if the shoots are especially vigorous. The problem is accentuated forcing late in the season and by cooling for more than six weeks at temperatures greater than 45° F (7° C). It is labor-intensive to remove the shoots manually. To control bypass shoots, paclobutrazol can be applied at 100 ppm six to seven weeks prior to placing the plants in cold storage.

During the summer in warm climates, dormant budded azaleas directly shipped from the supplier should be unpacked and held in the greenhouse for one week prior to placement in the cooler. This process will allow plants to increase carbohydrate levels, and it will reduce foliage loss.

Postharvest

Unrooted cuttings can be held at 31° F (–0.5° C).

References

Aycock, R., and B. I. Daughtry. 1975. Major diseases, pp. 78–88. In: *Growing Azaleas Commercially* (Number 4058). A. M. Kofranek and R. A. Larson, eds. University of California Cooperative Extension

Service, Davis, California.

Ballantyne, D. J., and C. B. Link. 1961. Growth regulators and the flowering of evergreen azaleas (*Rhododendron* cv.) *Proceedings of the American Society for Horticultural Sciences* 78:521–531.

Criley, R. A. 1985. *Rhododendron* and *Azalea*, pp. 180–197. In: *Handbook of Flowering*, vol. IV, A. H. Halevy, ed. CRC Press, Boca Raton, Florida.

Dreistadt, S. H. 2001. *Integrated Pest Management for Floriculture and Nurseries*. University of California Division of Agriculture and Natural Resources Publication 3402. Oakland, California.

Heins, R. D., R. W. Widmer, and H. F. Wilkins. 1978. Growth regulators effective on floricultural crops. *Minnesota State Florists' Bulletin,* August:1–4.

Horst, R. K. 1990. Azalea, pp. 545–546. In: *Westcott's Plant Disease Handbook,* 5th ed. Van Nostrand Reinhold, New York.

Keever, G. J., and W. J. Foster. 1991. Uniconazole suppresses bypass shoot development and alters flowering of two forcing azalea cultivars. *HortScience* 26:875–877.

Kofranek, A. M., and O. R. Lunt. 1975. Mineral nutrition, pp. 36–46. In: *Growing Azaleas Commercially* (Number 4058), A. M. Kofranek and R. A. Larson,

eds. University of California Cooperative Extension Service, Davis, California.

Larson, R. A. 1992. Azaleas, pp. 223–248. In: *Introduction to Floriculture,* R. A. Larson, ed. Academic Press, San Diego, California.

Larson, R. A. 1993. *Production of Florist Azaleas.* Timber Press, Portland, Oregon.

Love, J. 1975. Vegetative growth, pp. 47–51. In: *Growing Azaleas Commercially* (Number 4058), A. M. Kofranek and R. A. Larson, eds. University of California Cooperative Extension Service, Davis, California.

Nell, T. 2001. Azaleas, pp. 48–49. In: *Tips on Regulating Growth of Floriculture Crops,* M. L. Gaston, L. A. Kunkle, P. S. Konjoian, and M. F. Wilt, eds. Ohio Florists' Association Services, Columbus, Ohio.

Pemberton, H. B., and H. F. Wilkins. 1985. Seasonal variation on the influence of low temperature, photoperiod, light source, and GA in floral development of the evergreen azalea. *Journal of the American Society for Horticultural Science* 110:730–737.

Whealy, C. A., T. A. Nell, and J. E. Barrett. 1988. Plant growth regulator reduction of bypass shoot development in azalea. *HortScience* 23:166–167.

Rosa

Common name: Rose.
Scientific name: *Rosa* hybrids.
Family: Rosaceae.
Other propagation methods: Grafting.

Description, Uses, and Status

The rose is one of the world's most popular flowers. All species in the genus are woody and noted for their spines or prickly stems. Plants can be upright, forming a shrub, or they can be trailing or climbing. The leaves, which are alternate, may be deciduous or persistent. Petal colors range from white to pink, yellow, orange, red, green, and even brown with an unbelievable variety of shades and color combinations. Rose fragrance is world renowned, but unfortunately is lacking in many modern cultivars.

Roses are commonly grown as cut flowers, potted plants, and specimen plants in home gardens. Potted plant sizes can range from small plants in 3 in. (8 cm) pots to 36 in. (90 cm) tall topiary tree roses.

Flower of a potted rose plant.

Commercially, three major groups of rose cultivars are recognized: cut flowers, miniature potted flowering plants produced from stem cuttings, and potted garden plants produced from bare-root plants.

Flowering Control and Dormancy

Greenhouse roses are generally day-neutral, and flowering is recurrent and occurs on a year-round basis. Flower initiation is not dependent on environment factors. Floral differentiation occurs shortly after axillary buds are released from apical dominance. Axillary buds from the upper nodes form flower buds sooner and with fewer leaves than lower nodes. The difference in shoot growth based on nodal position must be considered when selecting cuttings for pot roses.

Stock Plant Management

This section on roses focuses primarily on cutting propagation for potted flowering plants. Propagation for cut and garden rose production is accomplished primarily by specialists.

For potted flowering plants, cuttings are generally obtained from plants already in production, but they can also be harvested from stock plants. Production of stock plants may be necessary to provide sufficient cuttings for large crops timed for specific holidays such as Valentine's Day. Stock plants of roses can be especially troublesome because of their susceptibility to spider mites and powdery mildew, both of which can be difficult to control because of the dense foliage that builds up on stock plants.

Cutting Harvest

Miniature flowering potted plants are almost exclusively propagated by single node leaf-bud cuttings. Cutting quality will determine the quality of the potted flowering plant ten to fifteen weeks later. The best cuttings are obtained from shoots that are produced after the second cutback or pinch, which will have three to five nodes. Cuttings are harvested from shoots with a flower bud that is large but not showing petal color. The ideal cutting is harvested from the middle of the shoot and is subtended by a five-leaflet leaf. These single-node five leaflet cuttings root quickly; shoot elongation is rapid and uniform. The single-node cuttings are typically prepared so that there is a 0.75 in. (2 cm) stem above and below the node.

Generally, only one to two suitable cuttings per shoot can be obtained. The upper nodes are not useful for cuttings because they produce weak shoots with few leaves below the flower bud. Flower initiation has already occurred in the axillary buds at the upper nodes of these shoots. These apical nodes frequently have only three-leaflet leaves, which is an indication that they should be discarded. In addition, cuttings will wilt rapidly if harvested when not mature enough. On the other hand, nodes that have already developed axillary shoots should also be discarded. If cuttings are too mature, rooting will be slow, delaying propagation.

Shoots from finished plants are often harvested mechanically and then cut and sorted by hand to the proper size. Regardless of the harvest method, proper selection and sorting of cuttings is critical in providing a rapidly rooting, successful crop. Cuttings should be sorted by stem caliper, shoot age, position on the shoot, and presence of axillary shoots. Cuttings should also be sorted by leaf area, since cuttings with larger leaflets will have more root growth during propagation and more shoot growth after propagation.

Propagation

Four to six cuttings per 4 in. (10 cm) pot and five or more cuttings per pot for larger pot sizes are directly stuck into a the substrate. Cuttings can also be propagated in plug trays and later transplanted to the final pot. The substrate should have a pH of 5.5 to 6.2. The cuttings should be cooled at 34° F (1° C) overnight to remove heat and reestablish turgor. While not required, rooting hormones can be used to improve rooting uniformity; 1,000 ppm IBA plus 500 ppm NAA, 1,000 ppm KIBA or 1,000 ppm KNAA have been used.

Do not allow cuttings to lose turgor. Hand fogging or misting may be needed before a bench is completely planted and ready to be placed into a fog or mist chamber. Prior to this, a fungicide drench can be used. Provide a temperature of 73° to 75° F (23° to 24° C) for rooting. Supplemental or high natural light is essential for rapid rooting in the winter. Maintain 800 to 1,000 f.c. (9 to 11 klux) light. The peat-based substrate must not be kept too moist during rooting, because substrate aeration is essential. A foliar fertilization of 150 ppm nitrogen from 20-10-20 can be applied during propagation to prevent leaf yellowing and speed the rooting process. Interestingly, application of 50 or 100 ppm sodium silicate injected into the mist water increased rooting of cuttings and reduced leaf drop during propagation. Rose cuttings root in seven to ten days, and generally twenty-one to twenty-eight days after propagation shoots are sufficiently tall to cut back.

Plant Growth Regulators

Paclobutrazol (Bonzi) sprays at 16 to 60 ppm are commonly used. A uniconizole (Sumagic) drench of between 0.1 to 0.2 mg a.i. per 5 in. (13 cm) pot can also be used. While a negative temperature difference (DIF) can decrease stem elongation, the effect is not dramatic, and a negative DIF for two hours prior to sunup (DROP) is not effective (see chapter 8 for more information).

Production and Schedule

Roses respond dramatically to temperature. The basic temperature sequence for miniature flowering potted plants is as follows: 73° to 75° F (23° to 24° C) for rooting; 68° to 72° F (20° to 22° C) for seven to ten days after rooting and prior to the first cutback; 68° to 72° F (20° to 22° C) for two to three weeks of growth after cutback; 66° to 72° F (19° to 22° C) for two to three weeks after the second cutback, if practiced; and 64° F (18° C) for the final three to four weeks prior to flowering.

Roses require high light levels. Potted miniature roses for Valentine's Day often receive supplemental lighting with at least 350 to 500 f.c. (4 to 5 klux) during the winter for twelve or more hours a day. Thereafter, supplemental light is not required but can be used. Shade will be needed to control temperatures in the summer.

Overwatering can occur when plants are cut back and the leaf canopy, and consequently transpiration, is reduced. Irrigation should occur one to two days prior to cutback. In addition, the loss of leaf photosynthesis capacity (carbohydrates) may also be responsible for increased root injury after the cutback. Excessive over- or underwatering can cause leaf yellowing, leaf abscission, and root loss.

Few crops can develop and express nutritional problems so quickly and return to normal growth so slowly as the rose. Routine substrate and tissue testing are absolute requirements for stable production. Low EC (1.5 mS/cm) is critical and the N:P:K levels are best at 220:30:195 ppm with a constant liquid fertilizer. A well-drained substrate must be used to facilitate excellent aeration, particularly during rooting of the cuttings. Conversely, 4 in. (10 cm) pots quickly dry during transportation and marketing, and drought stress causes premature leaf drop and flower senescence. Peat-lite mixes with a pH of 5.5 to 6.7 are commonly used.

Two cutbacks are required to produce a well-branched miniature flowering potted plant with numerous flowering stems. The first pinch is seven days after plants are removed from propagation. The second is approximately three weeks later. The height of the first pinch is 1 in. (2.5 cm) above the substrate level; the second pinch is made approximately 0.5 to 0.75 in. (1.3 to 2 cm) above the primary pinch. Be sure that plants are well rooted prior to the pinch, or uneven axillary shoot development will occur.

Scheduling year-round pot plant production is a challenge. Growth rates vary with the season, and minor temperature and light fluctuations can slow or hasten growth. Growth rates also vary with the cultivars; for example, one cultivar may need to be propagated a week earlier than other cultivars to have a color assortment ready for any one marketing date.

Diseases

Mildew (*Sphaerotheca pannosa* pv. *rosae*) and gray mold (*Botrytis cinerea*) are the two major disease problems. *Cylindrocladium scoparium, Pythium, Phytophthora,* and downy mildew (*Peronospora*) may also be problems. *Cylindrocladium* is most common during propagation and can cause significant losses. Sanitation and environmental control are absolute necessities in pot rose production. Diseases must be addressed during all phases, from propagation and production to shipping. Disease problems can be found on both the aerial parts of the plants and the roots. Furthermore, because cuttings are often taken from plants in production, pathogens can be carried from one crop to the next.

Disorders

Blind shoots occur when newly elongating axillary shoots fail to form flower buds. This disorder is due to insufficient light or high temperatures during shoot elongation, causing the flower bud to abort. Both cut flowers and miniature potted plants have a propensity for lower axillary buds to develop into blind shoots.

Postharvest

Cuttings can be stored moist in plastic bags at 36° to 41° F (2° to 5° C) for up to seven days, depending on the cultivar. Some producers believe a twenty-four-hour cold treatment at 34° F (1° C) is beneficial with some cultivars. The use of silver thiosulfate (STS) prevented leaf yellowing of cuttings but inhibited rooting.

References

Blythe, E. K., J. L. Sibley, K. M. Tilt, and J. M. Ruter. 2004. Rooting of rose cuttings in response to foliar applications of auxin and surfactant. *HortTechnology* 14:479–483.

Bredmose, N., and J. Hansen. 1996. Influence of propagation material and method on regeneration, growth and flowering of cut rose cvs. Frisco and Gabriella. *Acta Horticulturae* 424:23–28.

Costa, J. M., and H. Challa. 2002. The effect of original leaf area on growth of softwood cuttings and planting material of rose. *Scientia Horticulturae* 95:111–121.

Dreistadt, S. H. 2001. *Integrated Pest Management for Floriculture and Nurseries.* University of California Division of Agriculture and Natural Resources Publication 3402. Oakland, California.

Gillman, J. H., and D. C. Zlesak. 2000. Mist of applications of sodium silicate to rose (*Rosa* L. H 'Nearly Wild') cuttings decrease leaflet drop and increase rooting. *HortScience* 35:773.

Hamrick, D. 2003. *Rosa*, pp. 601–620. In: *Ball RedBook*, 17th ed., vol. 2, D. Hamrick, ed. Ball Publishing, Batavia, Illinois.

Hasek, R., R. Sciaroni, and G. Hickman. 1986. New growth regulator tested. *Greenhouse Grower* 4:52–53.

Horst, R. K. 1990. Rose, pp. 797–800. In: *Westcott's Plant Disease Handbook*, 5th ed. Van Nostrand Reinhold, New York.

Jørgensen, E. 1992. *Growing Parade-Roses*. Pejoe Trykcenter A/S, Hillreød, Denmark.

Mortensen, L. M., and R. Moe. 1992. Effects of CO_2 enrichment and different day/night temperature combinations on growth and flowering of *Rosa* L. and *Kalanchoe blossfeldiana* v. Poelln. *Scientia Horticulturae* 51:145–153.

Pemberton, H. B., J. W. Kelly, and J. Ferare. 1997. Rose, pp. 112–117. In: *Tips on Growing Specialty Potted Crops,* M. L. Gasten, S. A. Carver, C. A. Irwin, and R. A. Larson, eds. Ohio Florists' Association, Columbus, Ohio.

Sun, W.-Q., and N. L. Bassuk. 1991. Silver thiosulfate application influences rooting and budbreak of 'Royalty' rose cuttings. *HortScience* 26:1288–1290.

Zieslin, N., and R. Moe. 1985. *Rosa*, pp. 214–225. In: *Handbook of Flowering*, vol. IV, A. H. Halevy, ed. CRC Press, Boca Raton, Florida.

Zieslin, N., and T. Byrne. 1981. Plant management of greenhouse roses. Flower cutting procedures. *Scientia Horticulturae* 15:179–186.

Zieslin, N., E. Khayat, and Y. Mor. 1987. The response of rose plants to different night temperature regimes. *Journal of the American Society for Horticultural Science* 112:86–89.

Salvia

Common name: Salvia, sage.
Scientific name: *Salvia* species.
Family: Labiatae.
Other propagation methods: Seed, division.

Description, Uses, and Status
This large genus has many useful species, hybrids, and cultivars including several annual bedding plants and many cut flowers. *S.* x *superba* (or in some cases *S. nemorosa* depending on the source) is one of the more popular perennial species with 6 to 10 in. (15 to 25 cm) spikes of blue, purple, rose, or white tubular flowers on 12 to 30 in. (30 to 75 cm) tall plants. *S. officinalis* is one of the most popular herbs but is also grown for its attractive gray-green or variegated foliage and short spikes of blue flowers. *S. leucantha,* Mexican sage, is a popular cut flower that produces spikes of velvety blue and white flowers late in the fall when days are short. Dozens of other species are grown as garden ornamentals. Many are hardy to Zone 4, but others are quite frost sensitive and grown only as summer annuals. Most species flower in midsummer to fall and prefer full sun. Plants are sold in pots and occasionally in mixed containers.

Salvia officinalis 'Tricolor'.

Flowering Control and Dormancy
Many salvia species are short-day plants, and stock plants must be grown under long days to prevent flowering.

Stock Plant Management
Maintain stock plants under long days, high light, and warm temperatures. Build the plant canopy with pinches every two to three weeks.

Cutting Harvest
Terminal cuttings to 3 in. (8 cm) long are primarily

used, but subterminal cuttings can be taken if propagation material is limited. Cuttings should be vegetative but not woody, since that will slow rooting.

Propagation
Root cuttings in a substrate with a pH of 5.5 to 6.5 and a temperature of 70° to 75° F (21° to 24° C). Mist is usually applied for five to eight days for fast-rooting species and up to eleven days for slower-to-root species. Rooting hormone is generally not required but 500 to 1,000 IBA is recommended for a number of species and cultivars. Insert one cutting per cell if using plug flats. Cuttings are generally well rooted in three to four weeks.

Plant Growth Regulators
Height can be controlled by up to four spray applications of daminozide (B-Nine) at 5,000 ppm each, one spray application of paclobutrazol (Bonzi) at 40 to 60 ppm, or one tank-mixed spray application of daminozide at 5,000 ppm plus chlormequat (Cycocel) at 1,500 ppm. Do not use plant growth regulators on herbal sages that may be eaten by customers.

Production and Schedule
The optimum temperatures depend on the species. Some such as *S. greggi* should be grown cool at 65° to 78° F (18° to 26° C) during the day and 50° to 55° F (10° to 13° C) at night. Other species are grown warm at 70° to 80° F (21° to 27° C) during the day and 62° to 68° F (17° to 20° C) at night. The light intensity should be at least 5,000 f.c. (54 klux) for this sun-loving plant.

Fertilize plants with 100 to 125 ppm nitrogen from 20-10-20. The substrate pH should be 5.6 to 6.0 for most species. Avoid overwatering, which encourages diseases and soft growth.

For most species, one rooted cutting is used per 4 in. (10 cm) pot, two to three per 6 in. (15 cm) pot, and two to five for larger pots. Plants grown in pots larger than 4 in. (10 cm) can be pinched once or twice to improve branching and plant shape. In the spring 4 in. (10 cm) pots are ready to sell in seven to nine weeks, 6 in. (15 cm) pots in seven to ten weeks, and larger pots in ten to twelve weeks. The crop finishes one to two weeks earlier in the summer.

Diseases
Botrytis and root rot are common problems. If propagating under cooler-than-recommended temperatures, a fungicide drench may be beneficial.

Disorders
None are known at this time.

Postharvest
The flowers of many salvia species are sensitive to ethylene, but *S. officinalis* cuttings do not appear to be sensitive to twenty hours of 0.1 to 1 ppm ethylene.

References
Hamrick, D. 2003. *Salvia,* pp. 627–631. In: *Ball RedBook,* 17th ed., vol. 2, D. Hamrick, ed. Ball Publishing, Batavia, Illinois.

Yoder Green Leaf Perennials. 2004. *Handling Unrooted Perennials.* www.green-leaf-ent.com/URC_Handling_2004.pdf.

Sanvitalia

Common name: Sanvitalia.
Scientific name: *Sanvitalia procumbens.*
Family: Compositae.
Other propagation methods: Seed.

Description, Uses, and Status
The small 0.5 to 0.75 in. (1.3 to 2 cm) wide, orange daisylike flowers have a dark brown center and are produced on 8 to 14 in. (20 to 36 cm) tall plants. This annual plant is not frost tolerant and is sold in the spring in packs, pots, or hanging baskets. Plants tolerate heat and drought stress in the landscape.

Flowering Control and Dormancy
Sanvitalia is a facultative short-day plant; short days cause faster flowering on stems with fewer leaves.

Stock Plant Management
Keep stock plants under long days to reduce flowering.

Cutting Harvest
Terminal cuttings 0.8 to 2 in. (2 to 3 cm) long with at least one fully expanded leaf are generally used.

'Sunbini' sanvitalia.

Propagation

Rooting occurs in four to five weeks at 70° to 75° F (21° to 24° C). Stick one cutting per cell if using plug flats. Use rooting hormones on cutting bases; either up to 2,500 ppm IBA alone or IBA with up to 500 ppm NAA should be used. Overmisting delays rooting.

Plant Growth Regulators

Plant growth regulators are generally not required. However, during propagation daminozide (B-Nine) sprays at 2,500 to 3,000 ppm or a tank-mixed spray of ancymidol (A-Rest) at 6 to 12 ppm and daminozide at 1,250 to 2,500 ppm can be used twenty to thirty days after sticking unrooted cuttings.

During production daminozide sprays at 2,500 to 3,000 ppm are effective.

Production and Schedule

Grow plants at 70° to 80° F (21° to 27° C) during days and 55° to 65° F (13° to 18° C) during nights. Maintain light levels of 5,000 (54 klux) or higher. The substrate pH should be maintained at 5.8 to 6.2. Use 200 to 250 ppm nitrogen, and maintain a substrate EC of 0.6 to 0.9 using the 2:1 dilution method.

Use one plant per 4 in. (10 cm) pot, one to two per 6 in. (15 cm) pot, and three to four per 10 in. (25 cm) basket. Pinching can be useful to maintain shape but is often not required. Pinching can be done as often as desired, although it will delay flowering. Plants in 4 in. (10 cm) pots are ready to sell in six to eight weeks, those in 6 in. (15 cm) pots in eight to nine weeks, and those in 10 in. (25 cm) baskets in eleven to twelve weeks.

Diseases

Botrytis and root rots are common. If plants are grown cooler than recommended, root rots will be more prevalent.

References

Mattson, N. S., and J. E. Erwin. 2005. The impact of photoperiod and irradiance on flowering of several herbaceous ornamentals. *Scientia Horticulturae* 104:275–292.

Scaevola

Common name: Scaevola, fan flower.
Scientific name: *Scaevola aemula.*
Family: Goodeniaceae.
Other propagation methods: Seed.

Description, Uses, and Status

This trailing plant has short terminal spikes of white, blue, or purple flowers. It is not frost tolerant and is sold in the spring in packs (rarely), pots, and hanging baskets. The plant is quite heat and drought tolerant, making it ideal for low-maintenance landscapes and hanging baskets, especially in warm climates.

Scaevola can make very attractive hanging baskets.

Flowering Control and Dormancy

Scaevola is day-neutral.

Stock Plant Management

Keep stock plants warm and actively growing to maintain a good cutting supply. Supplemental high intensity discharge (HID) lighting can increase cutting production of stock plants grown in low light situations. Good air movement through the stock plants to ensure sufficient carbon dioxide will help provide optimum results when using HID lighting. Stock plants should be trimmed periodically to prevent old branches from flowering. Research at North Carolina State University reported that trimming stock plants to 6 in. (15 cm) of vegetative growth increased cutting numbers by 151%, total cutting weight by 126%, and shoot length by 10% compared with cutting back more extensively to 3 in. (8 cm). In another experiment at that institution, cuttings were longer when stock plants were treated with ethephon (Florel) foliar sprays of 250 to 1,000 ppm compared with the untreated control. In a third study at the university, stock plants fertilized with nitrogen at 300 ppm produced more cuttings and more roots per cutting than when given nitrogen at 100 ppm.

Cutting Harvest

Terminal cuttings 1 to 2 in. (2.5 to 5 cm) long with at least one fully expanded leaf are generally used.

Propagation

Stage 1:
Cutting arrival or harvest and sticking
- Store cuttings at 48° to 50° F (9° to 10° C) for up to twenty-four hours if planting is going to be delayed.
- A rooting hormone is not required. However, either 2,500 ppm IBA or IBA with up to 500 ppm NAA can be used.
- Insert one cutting per cell if using plug flats.

Stage 2: Callusing
- Maintain substrate temperatures of 68° to 72° F (20° to 22° C).
- Maintain air temperatures of 75° to 80° F (24° to 27° C) during days and 68° to 70° F (20° to 21° C) during nights.
- Keep the substrate sufficiently moist so that water is easily squeezed out of it, but not so much that the cutting base is waterlogged. The base of the cutting needs air for proper rooting.
- Avoid overmisting, and keep cuttings drier than those of most other species.
- Maintain a light intensity of 500 to 1,000 f.c. (5 to 11 klux).
- Begin foliar feeding with 50 to 75 ppm nitrogen from 20-10-20 as soon as leaves begin to show any color loss.
- Maintain a substrate pH of 5.0 to 5.5.
- Transfer the cuttings to Stage 3 after five to seven days, once 50% of the cuttings begin differentiating root initials.

Stage 3: Root development
- Maintain substrate temperatures of 68° to 72° F (20° to 22° C).
- Maintain air temperatures of 75° to 80° F (24° to 27° C) during days and 68° to 70° F (20° to 21° C) during nights.
- Begin drying out the substrate once roots are visible.
- Begin increasing light intensity to 1,000 to 2,000 f.c. (11 to 22 klux) as the cuttings start to root out.
- Fertilize once a week at 100 ppm nitrogen, alternating between 15-0-15 and 20-10-20, then increase to 200 ppm.
- Roots should develop in seven to fourteen days.

Stage 4: Toning the rooted cutting
- Maintain air temperatures of 75° to 80° F (24° to 27° C) during days and 68° to 70° F (20° to 21° C) during nights.
- Move the liners from the mist area into an area of lower relative humidity.
- Increase the light intensity to 2,000 to 4,000 f.c. (22 to 43 klux).
- Provide shade during the middle of the day to reduce temperature stress.
- Fertilize once a week with 150 to 200 ppm nitrogen from 15-0-15 alternating with 20-10-20.
- The cuttings can be toned for seven days.

Plant Growth Regulators

Plant growth regulators are usually not required. However, paclobutrazol (Bonzi) drenches at 1 to 3 ppm or sprays at 20 to 40 ppm are effective. Uniconazole (Sumagic) drenches at 0.125 ppm or sprays at 20 to 30 ppm can be used. Flurprimidol (Topflor) as a 2 to 4 ppm liner dip, a foliar spray of 45 to 60 ppm, or a 0.79 to 2.25 ppm drench is also recommended. Ethephon (Florel) is effective at increasing branching and may replace pinching.

Production and Schedule

Grow scaevola at 75° to 80° F (24° to 27° C) during the day and 65° to 70° F (18° to 21° C) at night. Plants grow best in warm temperatures; do not start them in the greenhouse too early in the spring because they will grow slowly until the weather warms up. Plants can be grown cool after establishment, but flowering will be greatly delayed. Maintain 4,000 to 7,000 ft. (43 to 75 klux) light levels.

The substrate pH should be maintained at 5.5 to 6.0. Plants are susceptible to high pH-induced iron chlorosis, which can be controlled with a lower substrate pH or with applications of iron chelates. Iron sulfate drenches can be used, but be careful not to get it on the foliage. Use 200 to 250 ppm nitrogen from a fertilizer low in phosphorus. As occurs with many Australian natives, moderate to high levels of phosphorus causes yellow-red coloring in older foliage or light yellow bleaching of younger leaves. Of course, a phosphorus level that is too low can also cause purpling of the leaves. Maintain a substrate EC below 2.0 mS/cm using saturated medium extract. Allow plants to dry well between irrigations, since they are susceptible to overwatering.

Use one plant per 4 in. (10 cm) pot, one or two per 6 in. (15 cm) pot, and three to four per 10 in. (25 cm) hanging basket. Plants should be pinched once two to four weeks after the rooted cuttings are planted. Plants in 4 in. (10 cm) pots are marketable in six to eight weeks, those in 6 in. (15 cm) pots in ten to twelve weeks, and those in 10 in. (25 cm) baskets in twelve to fourteen weeks.

Diseases

Botrytis can be a problem on the flowers and foliage. Root and stem rots also occur.

Disorders

Excessive vegetative growth can result from too much nitrogen, low light levels, a wet substrate, or overfertilization under too-low light. Growth will slow significantly if the plants are grown at lower-than-recommended temperatures.

Postharvest

Ethylene at 0.1 to 1 ppm for twenty hours did not influence leaf abscission or cutting rooting.

References

Donnelly, C. S., and P. R. Fisher. 2002. High-pressure sodium lighting affects greenhouse production of vegetative cuttings for specialty annuals. *HortScience* 37:623–626.

Gibson, J. L., and B. E. Whipker. 2004. Ethephon and trimming of *Scaevola aemula* stock plants influence vegetative cutting quantity and quality. *PGRSA Quarterly* 32 (4):119–123.

Gibson, J. L. 2003. *Influence of mineral nutrition on stock plant yield and subsequent rooting of stem cuttings of scaevola, New Guinea impatiens, and vegetative strawflower.* Ph.D. Dissertation, Department of Horticultural Sciences, North Carolina State University, Raleigh, North Carolina.

Hamrick, D. 2003. *Scaevola,* pp. 634–635. In: *Ball RedBook,* 17th ed., vol. 2, D. Hamrick, ed. Ball Publishing, Batavia, Illinois.

McLarney, F. 2003. Scaevola. *GPN* 13(7):136.

Foliar purpling on scaevola due to low phosphorus.

Schlumbergera and *Hatiora*

Schlumbergera **Christmas cactus.**

Common name: Thanksgiving cactus, Christmas cactus, and Easter cactus.
Scientific name: *Schlumbergera truncata* (*Zygocactus truncatus*), *Schlumbergera* x *buckleyi* (*S. bridgesii*), and *Hatiora gaertneri* (*Rhipsalidopsis gaertneri* or *S. gaertneri*).
Family: Cactaceae.
Other propagation methods: Seed.

Description, Uses, and Status

These three holiday cacti are confusing due to frequent taxonomic name changes, interspecific hybrids, and similar appearance. All three species consist of modified stems called phylloclades, which are flat leaflike structures that photosynthesize. *Hatiora* differs from *Schlumbergera* in that the *Hatiora* flower perianth tube is shorter, the stamens are separated, and the stigmatic lobes are spreading. Furthermore, *Hatiora* phylloclades have shallow marginal indentations with obvious bristlelike spines, while those of *Schlumbergera* do not have obvious spines. The main difference between Thanksgiving cactus, *S. truncata,* and Christmas cactus, *S.* x *buckleyi,* is that the former has strongly toothed or pointed edges along the margins of the phylloclades; the latter has smooth-edged margins. Both species have white, rose, white and rose, salmon, salmon pink, or violet flowers; Easter cactus, *H. gaertneri,* has primarily red flowers. Pendulous types of holiday cacti are suitable for hanging baskets, semipendulous types for 4 in. (10 cm) pots, and erect types for 3 in. (8 cm) pots. All three species make colorful potted plants that adapt well in the home and reflower with modest care.

Flowering Control and Dormancy

Schlumbergera

These are considered short-day plants. For rapid floral initiation, the critical night length is between eleven and fourteen hours for plants grown at temperatures of 70° to 72° F (21° to 22° C) during the day and 64° to 65° F (18° C) at night. Commercially, thirteen- to sixteen-hour or naturally long night lengths are used. At 55° F (13° C) flowering will occur at any photoperiod. As the temperature increases, the shorter the photoperiod necessary for flower initiation; at 70° to 75° F (21° to 24° C), no flowering occurs regardless of photoperiod.

During vegetative growth, use temperatures of 63° to 70° F (17° to 21° C) and long days. For floral initiation under short days, use 55° to 59° F (13° to 15° C) night temperatures. Visible buds appear in three to four weeks. After flower initiation, night temperatures can be increased to 65° F (18° C).

Hatiora

H. gaertneri should be thought of as a short-day/long-day plant and flower induction is enhanced by 47° to 55° F (8° to 13° C) night temperatures during the short-day photoperiod. The optimal duration of this cold treatment varies with the cultivar from four to twelve weeks; most cultivars require only four to six weeks. Floral development is enhanced by long days and warm temperatures after the short days and cold treatment. Long days increase the number and uniformity of flowers that will develop. The appropriate temperature for flower development is 65° to 70° F (18° to 21° C).

Stock Plant Management

Stock plants must be grown under long days using night interruptions of light at 5 to 10 f.c. (54 to 108 lux) from 10:00 P.M. to 2:00 A.M. Cuttings can also be harvested from plants in production.

Cutting Harvest

Mature phylloclades are used commercially as cuttings. These single-stem sections are removed from vegetative stock plants by twisting each section 180° and separating it from the mother plant. Avoid using phylloclades from close to the substrate, since they are more likely to be contaminated with soilborne pathogens than phylloclades higher up on the plant. Segments from the upper three tiers are best.

Cuttings should be surface disinfected with a 1:5 chlorine bleach:water solution for five minutes. Strict sanitation should be followed during propagation, because the high humidity and likelihood of substrate overwatering can lead to disease.

Propagation

Two to four cuttings are inserted into each cell in a tray of 60 to 72 cells or in 1½ to 2 in. (4 to 5 cm) pots. When direct-sticking cuttings into the final container, use three segments per 3 to 4 in. (8 to 10 cm) pot, four per 4½ in. (11-cm) pot, and seven per 6 in. (15 cm) pot. Although a rooting hormone is not required, a low rate of IBA, 2 to 200 ppm, will increase cutting survival and decrease the time to rooting. Higher rates of IBA delay production and the number of new phylloclades on the cuttings. A well-drained substrate is a requirement.

The optimum substrate temperature for root growth is 70° to 76° F (21° to 25° C); warmer temperatures promoted axillary bud growth. However, at temperatures below 76° F (25° C) root and bud growth occurred simultaneously.

Supplemental high intensity discharge (HID) lighting of approximately 130 f.c. (1.4 klux), especially if combined with warm temperatures, reduces the time to axillary bud growth and increases the number of phylloclades produced. *Schlumbergera* cuttings should be held under long days during propagation; however, *Hatiora* cuttings do not need to be held under long days.

To maintain stem turgidity, routine fogging by hand or timed intermittent mist can be used. The substrate should be kept moist, but not overwatered. To avoid diseases, allow the phylloclades to dry out slightly during propagation. Use 50 to 75 ppm nitrogen when roots are evident, and increase to 100 ppm nitrogen applied every week when the cuttings are well rooted. Remove new shoots that develop on the cuttings during the first six to eight weeks to encourage more branching later in production.

Plant Growth Regulators

Benzyladenine (BA) sprays can dramatically increase the number of phylloclades when applied after pinching. In addition, a BA spray of 50 to 150 ppm will increase flower bud numbers; it can be applied five to seven days after short days have commenced or after the removal of young immature phylloclades in a process called leveling; see Production and Schedule. No height control is required.

Production and Schedule

Once *Schlumbergera* flowering is induced, a wide range of temperatures can be used, but never over 77° F (24° C). After *Hatiora* flower buds are visible, plants are forced at 65° to 70° F (18° to 21° C) and long days for rapid flower development.

Many cultivars of both genera develop yellow to whitish leaves if exposed to strong sunlight over 3,500 f.c. (38 klux) and/or high temperatures. The optimal light level is between 1,500 and 3,000 f.c. (16 to 32 klux).

Managing the moisture level is the primary control of disease with *Schlumbergera* and *Hatiora*. Allow the phylloclades to dry out slightly during propagation and between irrigations. However, plants should not become severely water stressed.

The nutritional requirements for holiday cacti are modest, and 150 to 200 ppm nitrogen level is adequate. A substrate pH lower than 5.5 may induce iron and manganese toxicity.

During two occasions the phylloclades should be removed. The first is about one month after the end of propagation when new phylloclades are approximately 1.5 in. (4 cm) long. BA sprays can dramatically increase the number of phylloclades when applied after pinching. The second removal occurs five to ten days after the start of short days. The young immature phylloclades are removed, a process known as leveling. Two to three mature phylloclades are left on each plant growing in a 3 in. (8 cm) pot, three to four per plant in a 3½ in. (9 cm) pot, and four to five per plant in a 4 in. (10 cm) pot. A BA spray of 50 to 150 ppm can also be applied five to seven days after short days have commenced or after leveling, to increase flower bud numbers.

Production time is thirty-two to thirty-seven weeks for *Schlumbergera* plants that will be sold from November until March. Propagation commences in December and can continue until March. Rooted cuttings in plugs continue to be potted until April to May. Growth of new phylloclades requires five to six months after leveling. Depending on the cultivar, seven to eight weeks are required for flowering from the beginning of short days.

Hatiora is similar to *Schlumbergera* in regard to timing and scheduling, except the flowering date is more greatly influenced by temperature. Production time is thirty-two to forty-five weeks for sale of 3½ in. (9 cm) pots in March and April.

Diseases

Fusarium is the most common disease and can cause significant losses. *Pythium, Phytophthora, Bipolaris, Botrytis cinerea,* and *Erwinia carotovora* can also be problems. Other reported diseases include stem and root rot (*Rhizoctonia solani*), tomato spotted wilt virus, and cactus virus X.

Disorders

Marginal foliar chlorosis is due to excessive iron levels in the tissue. The long crop cycle for holiday cacti may allow iron accumulation in the tissue, and warm production temperatures may accentuate iron uptake. Increase the substrate pH above 5.5 to reduce iron uptake.

Postharvest

Schlumbergera phyllocades can be stored for twenty-four to forty-eight hours at 40° F (4° C) to enhance rooting; Phylloclades can also be stored for up to three months at 50° to 59° F (10° to 15° C) and at 85 to 95% relative humidity. The segments can be stored in layers up to 1.5 in. (4 cm) deep in open boxes so that air can circulate through the cuttings. *Hatiora* phylloclades can be stored for up to six to eight weeks at 43° to 46° F (6° to 8° C) with constant high humidity.

References

Boyle, T. H. 1990. Flowering of *Rhipsalidopsis rosea* in response to temperature and photoperiod. *HortScience* 25:217–219.

Boyle, T. H. 1991a. Temperature and photoperiodic regulation of flowering in 'Crimson Giant' Easter cactus. *Journal of the American Society for Horticultural Science* 116:618–622.

Boyle, T. H. 1991b. Commercial production of Easter cactus. *Ohio Florists Association Bulletin* 743:5–6.

Boyle, T. H. 1992. Modification of plant architecture in 'Crimson Giant' Easter cactus with benzyladenine. *Journal of the American Society for Horticultural Science* 117:584–589.

Boyle, T. H. 1994. Production of holiday cactus. *Professional Plant Growers Association News* 15(10):15–18.

Boyle, T. H. 1995. BA influences flowering and dry-matter partitioning in shoots of 'Crimson Giant' Easter cactus. *HortScience* 30:289–291.

Boyle, T. H. 1997a. Holiday and Easter Cactus, pp. 82–88. In: *Tips on Growing Specialty Potted Crops,* M. L. Gaston, S. A. Carver, C. A. Irwin, and R. A. Larson, eds. Ohio Florists' Association, Columbus, Ohio.

Boyle, T. H. 1997b. Schlumbergera success tips. *GrowerTalks* 61(5):79, 84.

Boyle, T. H., D. J. Jacques, and D. P. Stimart. 1988. Influence of photoperiod and growth regulators on flowering of *Rhipsalidopsis gaertneri. Journal of the American Society for Horticultural Science* 113:75–78.

Dreistadt, S. H. 2001. *Integrated Pest Management for Floriculture and Nurseries.* University of California Division of Agriculture and Natural Resources Publication 3402. Oakland, California.

Heins, R. D., A. M. Armitage, and W. H. Carlson. 1981. Influence of temperature, water stress and BA on vegetative and reproductive growth of *Schlumbergera truncata. HortScience* 16:679–680.

Kristiansen, K., N. Bredmose, and W. Nielsen. 2005. Influence of propagation temperature, photosynthetic photo flux density, auxin treatment and cutting position on root formation, axillary bud growth and shoot development in *Schlumbergera* 'Russian Dancer'. *Journal of Horticultural Science and Biotechnology* 80:297–302.

Madsen, P., and K. Madsen. 1994. *Production Guide for Rhipsalidopsis/Schlumbergera.* Gartneriet, 207 Slettensvej, Odense N., Denmark 5270.

Rohwer, C. L., and R. D. Heins. 2001. Easter cactus flowering under varied temperature, daylength, and light conditions. *HortScience* 35:591.

Rünger, W., and R. T. Poole. 1985. *Schlumbergera,* pp. 277–282. In: *Handbook of Flowering,* vol. IV, A. H. Halevy, ed. CRC Press, Boca Raton, Florida.

Serek, M., and M. S. Reid. 1993. Anti-ethylene treatments for potted Christmas cactus—Efficacy of inhibitors of ethylene action and biosynthesis. *HortScience* 28:1180–1181.

Wilkins, H. F., and W. Rünger. 1985. *Rhipsalidopsis,* pp. 178–197. In: *Handbook of Flowering,* vol. IV, A. H. Halevy, ed. CRC Press, Boca Raton, Florida.

Solenostemon

Common name: Coleus, painted nettle.
Scientific name: *Solenostemon scutellarioides.*
Family: Labiatae.
Other propagation methods: seed.

Description, Uses, and Status
This sun-loving annual or tender perennial is grown for its colorful foliage. Many cultivars are available in a broad range of color combinations, leaf shapes, and plant heights. Foliage color varies with the light level in the landscape. Plant habit varies from vigorously upright to low and spreading. Vegetatively propagated "sun coleus" cultivars are more tolerant of high temperatures and high light and are slower to flower than seed-propagated cultivars. Coleus is not frost tolerant and is sold in the spring in packs, pots, and hanging baskets. This old-time plant has come back as an important garden ornamental.

Flowering Control and Dormancy
Flowering is accelerated by short days. Coleus is grown for its wonderfully colorful foliage; the small spikes of flowers tend to distract from the display.

Stock Plant Management
Remove flower buds as they appear. However, keeping plants pinched or cuttings harvested should reduce flowering.

Cutting Harvest
Terminal cuttings are generally used, but subterminal cuttings can be harvested if cutting material is limited. The large leaves of some cultivars may need to be trimmed. Cuttings should be sorted, since larger cuttings will root faster than smaller ones.

Propagation
Many cultivars of this fast-rooting species can be easily propagated directly in the final container. Some cultivars are slower growing and should be first propagated in plugs.

Stage 1:
Cutting arrival or harvest and sticking
- Store cuttings at 50° to 60° F (10° to 16° C) for up to twenty-four hours if planting is going to be delayed.
- Rooting hormones are not required.

Bench of coleus plants.

- Insert one cutting per cell if using plug flats.

Stage 2: Callusing
- Maintain substrate temperatures of 68° to 72° F (20° to 22° C).
- Maintain air temperatures of 75° to 84° F (24° to 29° C) during days and 68° to 70° F (20° to 21° C) during nights.
- Maintain a light intensity of 500 to 1,000 f.c. (5 to 11 klux).
- Use as little mist as possible to maintain turgidity without saturating the substrate too much.
- Maintain a substrate pH of 5.8 to 6.0.
- Transfer the cuttings to Stage 3 after five to seven days, once 50% of the cuttings begin differentiating root initials.

Stage 3: Root development
- Maintain substrate temperatures of 68° to 72° F (20° to 22° C).
- Maintain air temperatures of 75° to 80° F (24° to 27° C) during days and 68° to 70° F (20° to 21° C) during nights.
- Begin drying out the substrate once roots are visible.
- Begin increasing light intensity to 1,000 to 2,000 f.c. (11 to 22 klux) as the cuttings start to root out.
- Begin foliar feeding once a week with 100 ppm nitrogen, alternating between 15-0-15 and 20-10-20, then increase to 200 ppm.
- Roots should develop in seven to fourteen days.

Stage 4: Toning the rooted cutting
- Move the liners from the mist area into an area of lower relative humidity and lower temperatures.
- Increase the light intensity to 2,000 to 3,000 f.c. (22 to 32 klux).
- Provide shade during the middle of the day to reduce temperature stress.
- Fertilize with 150 to 200 ppm nitrogen from 15-0-15.
- The cuttings can be toned for seven days.

Plant Growth Regulators
Fast-growing cultivars will probably need a plant growth regulator to control height and maintain plant shape. During propagation, tank-mixed sprays of ancymidol (A-Rest) at 4 to 10 ppm and daminozide (B-Nine) at 1,250 to 2,500 ppm or of chlormequat (Cycocel) at 750 ppm and daminozide at 1,500 to 2,500 ppm can be used ten to twenty-one days after sticking unrooted cuttings.

During production, sprays of paclobutrazol (Bonzi) at 5 to 45 ppm, daminozide at 2,500 to 5,000 ppm, chlormequat at 400 to 3,000 ppm, uniconazole (Sumagic) at 10 or 20 ppm, or flurprimidol (Topflor) at 20 to 40 ppm are effective. A tank-mixed spray of daminozide at 2,500 to 4,000 ppm and chlormequat at 1,000 to 1,500 ppm can also be used.

Production and Schedule
Grow coleus at 70° to 75° F (21° to 24° C) during days and 62° to 65° F (17° to 18° C) during nights. It grows best in warm temperatures; cool temperatures result in slow, excessively compact growth. Maintain 4,000 to 7,000 f.c. (43 to 75 klux) light levels.

The substrate pH should be maintained at 5.6 to 6.0. Use 150 to 200 ppm nitrogen. Maintain a substrate EC of 0.6 to 0.9 mS/cm using 2:1 dilution. Excessive fertility can lead to less vibrant colors. Water stress will cause leaf scorch, since coleus readily wilts when allowed to dry out.

Use one plant per 4 in. (10 cm) or 6 in. (15 cm) pot, and three to four plants per 10 in. (25 cm) hanging basket. Plants should be pinched once two to four weeks after rooted cuttings are planted. Plants in 4 in. (10 cm) pots are marketable in four to five weeks, those in 6 in. (15 cm) pots in five to six weeks, and those in 10 in. (25 cm) baskets in eight to nine weeks.

Diseases
Botrytis, Pythium, and *Alternaria* can be problems.

Disorders
Foliage color changes with the light level. At very high or low light levels one or more colors on the leaves may disappear. Low light also causes excessive stretching. Poor branching can be due to low light levels, cool production temperatures, flowering, or lack of fertilization.

Postharvest
Ethylene at 0.1 to 1 ppm for twenty hours did not influence leaf abscission or cutting rooting.

References
Hamrick, D. 2003. Coleus, pp. 313–315. In: *Ball RedBook,* 17th ed., vol. 2, D. Hamrick, ed. Ball Publishing, Batavia, Illinois.

Solidago

Common name: Goldenrod, solidago.
Scientific name: *Solidago* species.
Family: Compositae.
Other propagation methods: Seed, division, tissue culture.

Description, Uses, and Status
Goldenrods are long-lived plants that grow 2 to 8 ft. (0.6 to 2.4 m) tall with numerous small white to yellow flowers arranged in various types of inflorescences ranging from long slender wands to columnar spikes to loose open plumes. The plants flower from midsummer to late fall. In general, they tolerate heat, drought, and cold and are hardy in Zones 2 to 9. Contrary to popular belief, goldenrods do not cause hay fever (allergic reactions). They produce heavy pollen that requires transportation by insects, whereas hay fever is caused by lightweight, windblown pollen. This misconception has limited the use of goldenrods in the United States. They are used as greenhouse or field-grown cut flowers, both fresh and dried. Goldenrods are also occasionally sold as garden perennials. The plants are especially popular in Europe as cut flowers and garden ornamentals.

Bed of cut goldenrod flowers ready for harvest.

Flowering Control and Dormancy
Although little is known about the flowering of many goldenrod species, most species that have been examined are considered short-day plants. An extended period of short days, however, induces dormancy, and the shorter the day length the more rapid the onset. In nature, the long days of summer stimulate shoot elongation and vegetative growth, whereas the shorter days of late summer induce floral initiation. The continually shortening days of fall induce dormancy in preparation for the onset of winter.

Stock Plant Management
Stock plants of cut flower cultivars should be maintained under long days to prevent flower initiation.

Cutting Harvest
Terminal cuttings 3 to 4 in. (8 to 10 cm) long are harvested in the spring for producing perennial plants.

Propagation
Stem cuttings can be propagated from vegetative shoots. Insert one cutting per cell if using plug flats. Generally, no rooting hormone is needed.

Plant Growth Regulators
Height control of container-grown plants is typically not needed. However, multiple daminozide (B-Nine) sprays at 5,000 ppm, one paclobutrazol (Bonzi) spray at 80 to 100 ppm, or one paclobutrazol drench at 30 ppm is effective. Of course, plant growth regulators are not used on cut flower crops.

Production and Schedule
Young plants can be grown at 65° to 70° F (18° to 21° C) during days and 55° to 65° F (13° to 18° C) during nights. Some goldenrod species tolerate light shade, but most species and hybrids prefer full sunlight. Supplemental lighting of approximately 450 f.c. (5 klux) is recommended.

Avoid overwatering cut flowers when the inflorescences are developing, since that may encourage vegetative side shoots. Plugs and container-grown plants can be fertilized with 50 to 100 ppm nitrogen constant liquid fertilization. A pH of 5.5 to 6.5 is acceptable for container and greenhouse cut flower production, and pH 5.0 to 7.0 is common for field production. For greenhouse production, the substrate EC should be 0.75 to 1.5 mS/cm using 1:2 media:water dilution.

Plants for cut flowers may be grown pinched or unpinched. They are pinched two to three weeks after planting the plugs; three or four leaf pairs per plant should remain. After harvest, the plants should be cut back to the ground and all old tissue removed to stimulate new shoots to develop from the rhizome.

Potted flowering plants are pinched one or two times. As with the plants grown for cut flowers, these plants are pinched two to three weeks after planting the plugs; a second pinch can be done two to three weeks after the first pinch.

Cut flowers should be ready to harvest twelve weeks after planting the plugs if pinched, and ten weeks if not pinched. Plants are pinched three weeks after planting, and long days of sixteen hours are provided for approximately six weeks starting at planting. For unpinched plants, long days of sixteen hours are provided for five weeks after planting. Long-day lighting is discontinued when plants are 12 to 16 in. (30 to 40 cm) tall, and short days are provided for flower initiation. Immediately after harvest, the remaining stems are cut back; the plants will reflower within ten to twelve weeks if supplied with long days for the first five to six weeks and short days thereafter. Each planting can produce up to five flushes of cut flowers, and three or four flushes of cut flowers can be harvested each year.

Total production time for container-grown plants ranges from twenty-nine to forty weeks. The purchase of liners or plugs from specialty propagators can reduce production time to eight to thirteen weeks in 1 gal. (4 L) pots. Plants in 4 to 5½ in. (10 to 14 cm) pots can be produced in ten weeks with one to three cuttings per pot, one pinch, six weeks of long days after planting, and short days to finish.

Diseases
In the greenhouse, goldenrods are sensitive to damping-off and root rots. Outdoors, goldenrods are prone to

rust (*Coleosporium asterum*), which covers the foliage and stems in late summer with rust-colored pustules. Other rust species may also occur, including *Coleosporium delicatulum, Puccinia dioicae, P. virgae-aureae, P. grindeliae, P. stipae, Uromyces perigynius,* and *U. solidaginis.* Powdery mildew (*Ersiphe polygoni*) and numerous leaf spots (*Asteroma solidaginis, Colletotrichum solitarium, Placosphaeria havdeni,* and *Septoria*) can also be problems. Stem blight (*Diaporthe*) has also been reported.

Disorders

Under the low light levels of winter or short days, flower bud abortion can occur in the greenhouse. Supplemental lighting from high intensity discharge (HID) lamps should prevent this problem.

References

Allard, H. A., and Garner, W. W. 1940. *Further observations on the response of various species of plants to length of day.* U.S. Department of Agriculture Technical Bulletin Number 727.

Burrows, R. L. 2002. Goldenrod: Plants with multipurpose potential. *HortTechnology* 12:711–716.

Dreistadt, S. H. 2001. *Integrated Pest Management for Floriculture and Nurseries.* University of California Division of Agriculture and Natural Resources Publication 3402. Oakland, California.

Goodwin, R. H. 1944. The inheritance of flowering time in a short-day species, *Solidago sempervirens* L. *Genetics* 29:503–519.

Horst, R. K. 1990. Goldenrod, p. 661. In: *Wescott's Plant Disease Handbook,* 5th ed. Van Nostrand Reinhold, New York.

Hubert, S. H. 1970. Flower number, flowering time, and reproductive isolation among ten species of *Solidago* (Compositae). *Bulletin of the Torrey Botanical Club* 97:175–189.

Latimer, J. 2001. Herbaceous perennials, pp. 98–110. In: *Tips on Regulating Growth of Floriculture Crops,* M. L. Gaston, L. A. Kunkle, P. S. Konjoian, and M. F. Wilt, eds. Ohio Florists' Association Services, Columbus, Ohio.

McGrew, J. 1998. *Solidago* (goldenrod), pp. 755–757. In: *Ball RedBook,* 15th ed., V. Ball, ed. Geo. J. Ball Publishing, West Chicago, Illinois.

Schwabe, W. W. 1986. *Solidago,* pp. 338–340. In: *The Handbook of Flowering,* vol. V, A. H. Halevy, ed. CRC Press, Boca Raton, Florida.

Yoder Green Leaf Perennials. 2004. Handling Unrooted Perennials. www.green-leaf-ent.com/URC_Handling_2004.pdf.

Sutera and *Jamesbrittania*

Common name: Bacopa.
Scientific name: *Sutera cordata* and *Jamesbrittania* hybrids.
Family: Scrophulariaceae.
Other propagation methods: Seed.

Description, Uses, and Status

Two closely relate genera are called bacopa. *Sutera* has small white to lavender flowers and little rounded leaves. *Jamesbrittania* has small white to dark rose or coppery red flowers and small, more highly dissected leaves. *Jamesbrittania* tends to be a little more upright growing. Both species are tender ground-hugging perennials that perform best in pots, hanging baskets, and mixed containers. The plants are especially well

Sutera 'Abunda Giant White'.

suited to mixed containers since they cascade over the edge. However, newer cultivars are increasingly robust and performing better in the ground in the landscape. The plants are sold in the spring, but they tend to slow down and stop flowering during the middle of the summer in warm climates.

Flowering Control and Dormancy
Sutera is a day-neutral plant that flowers more profusely as the light intensity increases.

Stock Plant Management
Stock plants are often grown in hanging baskets for easier management of these spreading species.

Cutting Harvest
Terminal cuttings 1.5 to 2 in. (4 to 5 cm) long are normally used.

Larger *Sutera* cuttings create taller plugs.

Propagation

Stage 1:
Cutting arrival or harvest and sticking
- Stick cuttings within one or two hour after arrival or harvest of the cuttings.
- Rooting hormones are not required, but 2,500 ppm IBA or IBA with up to 500 ppm NAA can be used on the cutting bases.
- Insert two cuttings per cell if using plug flats.

Stage 2: Callusing
- Maintain substrate temperatures of 65° to 68° F (18° to 20° C).
- Maintain air temperatures of 68° to 72° F (20° to 22° C) during days and 65° to 70° F (18° to 21° C) during nights.
- Use as little mist as possible to maintain turgidity without saturating the substrate too much. Keep the substrate sufficiently moist so that

water is easily squeezed out of it, but not so much that the cutting base is waterlogged.
- Maintain a light intensity of 500 to 1,000 f.c. (5 to 11 klux).
- Begin foliar feeding with 50 to 75 ppm nitrogen from 20-10-20 as soon as leaves begin to show any color loss.
- Maintain a substrate pH of 5.5 to 6.0.
- Transfer the cuttings to Stage 3 after six to eight days, once 50% of the cuttings begin differentiating root initials.

Stage 3: Root development
- Maintain substrate temperatures of 65° to 68° F (18° to 20° C).
- Maintain air temperatures of 68° to 72° F (20° to 22° C) during days and 65° to 70° F (18° to 21° C) during nights.
- Begin drying out the substrate once roots are visible.
- Begin increasing the light intensity to 1,500 to 2,000 f.c. (16 to 22 klux) as the cuttings start to root out.
- Fertilize once a week with 100 ppm nitrogen, alternating between 15-0-15 and 20-10-20, then increase to 200 ppm.
- Roots should develop in eight to ten days.

Stage 4: Toning the rooted cutting
- Lower the air temperatures to 68° to 72° F (20° to 22° C) during the day and 62° to 68° F (17° to 20° C) at night.
- Move the liners from the mist area into an area of lower relative humidity.
- Increase the light intensity to 3,000 to 5,000 f.c. (32 to 54 klux).
- Provide shade during the middle of the day to reduce temperature stress.
- Fertilize twice a week with 150 to 200 ppm nitrogen from 15-0-15 alternating with 20-10-20.
- The cuttings can be toned for seven days.

Plant Growth Regulators
None is usually required, but paclobutrazol (Bonzi) drenches at 3 ppm can be used. Daminozide (B-Nine) sprays at 1,000 to 1,500 ppm can also be used. Ethephon (Florel) sprays at 150 to 200 ppm for *Sutera* and 300 to 500 ppm for *Jamesbrittania* will increase branching and delay flowering.

Sutera plants showing high pH chlorosis. (B. Whipker)

Production and Schedule

Bacopa prefers cool temperatures and high light for the highest quality. Grow the plants at 60° to 70° F (16° to 21°) during the day and 55° to 60° F (13° to 15° C) at night. Warmer night temperatures above 65° F (18° C), however, will produce faster development. Maintain 4,500 to 6,000 f.c. (48 to 65 klux) light levels. Avoid starting *Jamesbrittania* too early in the season, especially in cool or cloudy climates, because of low light levels and cool temperatures.

The substrate pH should be maintained at 5.5 to 6.3. Use 200 to 250 ppm nitrogen. Avoid planting rooted plugs too deep, since that promotes *Pythium*

and *Rhizoctonia* root rots. Also avoid overwatering, which can lead to chlorotic foliage.

Use one plug per 4 in. (10 cm) pot, two to three per 6 in. (15 cm) pot, and four to five per 10 in. (25 cm) hanging basket. Plants should be pinched to the fourth or fifth leaf above the substrate after rooted cuttings are established. Plants in 4 in. (10 cm) pots may not need to be pinched. Older plants in all container sizes can be trimmed at any time to shape the plant. Plants in 4 in. (10 cm) pots are marketable in six to eight weeks, those in 6 in. (15 cm) pots in seven to ten weeks, and those in 10 in. (25 cm) baskets in eight to twelve weeks.

Diseases

Root rots, *Botrytis,* and powdery mildew can be problems.

Disorders

Inadequate flowering can occur from too much nitrogen or from overwatering or fertilizing under low light levels. Yellow foliage can result from overwatering or a high substrate pH leading to iron chlorosis.

References

Hamrick, D. 2003. *Sutera,* pp. 651–653. In: *Ball RedBook,* 17th ed., vol. 2, D. Hamrick, ed. Ball Publishing, Batavia, Illinois.

Torenia

Common name: Wishbone flower, bluewings, torenia.
Scientific name: *Torenia fournieri.*
Family: Scrophulariaceae.
Other propagation methods: Seed.

Description, Uses, and Status

This species has interesting multicolored, slightly tubular flowers with a white to lavender throat edged in pink, rose, blue, or purple and a spot of yellow on the lower petal. The plant grows 6 to 8 in. (15 to 20 cm) tall. It is not frost tolerant and is sold in the spring in packs, pots, hanging baskets, and mixed containers. Both seed- and cutting-propagated cultivars are available. Those propagated by cuttings are much more heat tolerant than those propagated by seed, especially if they are given some shade during the warmest part of the day.

'Pink Moon' torenia.

Flowering Control and Dormancy

Little is known about this free-flowering plant, which may be day-neutral.

Stock Plant Management

Hanging basket culture is preferred. Maintain actively growing stock plants to provide fresh cuttings.

Cutting Harvest

Terminal cuttings 0.8 to 1.2 in. (2 to 3 cm) long with at least one fully expanded leaf are typically used.

Propagation

Maintain a substrate temperature of 70° to 75° F (21° to 24° C) using bottom heat. Apply rooting hormones, up to 2,500 ppm IBA either alone or with up to 500 ppm NAA. Alcohol-based rooting hormones may need to be diluted because they may damage the cutting ends. Insert one cutting per cell if using plug flats. Cuttings will readily elongate in propagation. Daminozide (B-Nine) sprays at 1,500 ppm or chlormequat (Cycocel) sprays at 1,500 ppm can be used beginning one week after sticking and continuing every week thereafter. Rooting should be completed in four weeks.

Plant Growth Regulators

Stem elongation can often be controlled by restricting fertilizer, providing sufficient light, and maintaining moderate, not warm, production temperatures. However, uniconazole (Sumagic) drenches at 15 ppm or daminozide sprays at 1,500 to 2,500 ppm are effective. Do not use ethephon (Florel) on this species because it will significantly delay flowering.

Production and Schedule

Grow the plants at 65° to 70° F (18° to 21° C) during the day and 62° to 65° F (17° to 18° C) at night. Cooler temperatures will slow growth and cause bronze-colored foliage. Maintain light levels of 4,000 to 6,000 (43 to 65 klux) or higher.

The substrate pH should be maintained at 5.8 to 6.0. Use 150 to 200 ppm nitrogen, and avoid high phosphorus levels. Plants are susceptible to a high EC; maintain 2.0 mS/cm, using the saturated paste method. Allow plants to dry well between irrigations, since they are susceptible to overwatering.

Use one plant per 4 in. (10 cm) pot, two to three per 6 in. (15 cm) pot, and four to five per 10 in. (25 cm) basket. Pinch the plants once they are established, approximately one to two weeks after the rooted plugs are planted. Older plants can be trimmed at any time to improve their shape. Plants in 4 in. (10 cm) pots are ready to sell in five to seven weeks, those in 6 in. (15 cm) pots in six to nine weeks, and those in 10 in. (25 cm) baskets in ten to fourteen weeks.

Diseases

Powdery mildew can be a major problem, especially on stock plants. *Botrytis* and root and stem rots can also occur.

Disorders

Excessive fertilization and/or low light levels will lead to soft growth and poor flowering.

Postharvest

Ethylene at 0.1 to 1 ppm for up to twenty hours did not influence leaf abscission or cutting rooting.

References

Hamrick, D. 2003. *Torenia,* pp. 662–663. In: *Ball RedBook,* 17th ed., vol. 2, D. Hamrick, ed. Ball Publishing, Batavia, Illinois.

Tradescantia

Common name: Wandering Jew, inch plant.
Scientific name: *Tradescantia* species.
Family: Commelinaceae.
Other propagation methods: None.

Description, Uses, and Status

These procumbent species are popular hanging basket plants grown for their green, white, red, pink, purple, and silver foliage. One of the most popular is *T. zebrina* (formerly *Zebrina pendula*), which has green and silver stripes on the top of the leaves and purple underneath. Other species grown include *T. cerinthoides,* with leaves smooth and green above and purplish and hairy below; *T. fluminensis,* with green or green and white striped foliage; *T. pallida* (purple heart, formerly *Setcreasea purpurea*), with long purplish red leaves; *T. sillamontana,* with long leaves covered in gray hairs; and *T. spathacea,* with long leaves that are dark green above and purple below. Numerous cultivars are available for several of the species. As this genus is once again getting industry attention, more cultivars are likely to be released in

Tradescantia pallida variegated form.

the future. These popular plants also perform well in shady outdoor mixed containers and ground beds. They are typically sold in hanging baskets but also occasionally in pots and mixed containers. *T. pallida* is a noteworthy perennial because it is drought tolerant, sun or shade adapted, and moderately cold hardy to Zone 7.

Tradescantia sillamontana flowers.

Flowering Control and Dormancy

Most species are grown for their foliage and not their flowers, which tend to be small and short-lived. *T. pallida* flowers in the fall or spring and may be a short-day plant.

Stock Plant Management

Stock plants are often grown in hanging baskets for easier management of these vigorous, spreading species. Keep stock plants actively growing, since cuttings from hardened or flowering plants are slow to root. Some producers of finished plants use trimmings from plants in production to propagate future crops.

Tradescantia zebrina (formerly *Zebrina pendula*) pots.

Cutting Harvest

Terminal cuttings are generally taken for quickest establishment, but subterminal cuttings can also be taken. Cuttings can be harvested with a knife, but some are brittle enough when turgid to be harvested by hand. Terminal cuttings and subterminal cuttings should be 3 to 4 in. (8 to 10 cm) long with at least one mature leaf. One or more leaves can be removed to allow for easier insertion into the substrate. For some of the species with small foliage and thin stems, clumps of shoots, each with multiple nodes, can be harvested and propagated directly in the final pot.

Propagation

Most species are so easy to propagate that cuttings are readily direct-stuck in the final pot or hanging basket. Misting is not required if the humidity is high enough to prevent water stress. If mist is used, avoid overmisting because that will encourage diseases. For most species, fertilize with 100 to 150 ppm nitrogen when roots appear; use a higher rate, 200 ppm nitrogen, for *T. pallida*.

Plant Growth Regulators

Ancymidol (A-Rest) sprays at 25 to 132 ppm can be used to control height. Paclobutrazol (Bonzi) drenches at 0.5 mg a.i. per 6 in. (15 cm) pot may also be effective.

Tradescantia pallida (formerly *Setcreasea purpurea*) **plug flats.**

Production and Schedule

Grow the plants at 75 to 80° F (24° to 27° C) during days and 65° to 70° F (18° to 21° C) during nights. They grow best in warm temperatures. Maintain 3,500 to 4,500 f.c. (38 to 48 klux) light levels.

The substrate pH should be maintained at 5.6 to 6.0. Use 100 to 150 ppm nitrogen, which can be increased to 200 to 250 ppm nitrogen later in production. Water stress will cause leaf scorch, since these plants readily wilt when allowed to dry out.

For larger species such as *T. pallida*, use one plant per 4 in. (10 cm) pot, two to three per 6 in. (15 cm) pot, and five to seven per 10 in. (25 cm) hanging basket. For smaller species, such as *T. zebrina*, use three or more cuttings per 4 in. (10 cm) pot, and ten or more in larger containers. Plants can be pinched once two to four weeks after the rooted cuttings are planted, but it is often not necessary, especially if enough cuttings are inserted into each container. Older plants can be trimmed at any time to shape the plant or provide cuttings. Plants in 4 in. (10 cm) pots are marketable in four to five weeks, those in 6 in. (15 cm) pots in five to six weeks, and those in 10 in. (25 cm) baskets in eight to nine weeks.

Diseases

Botrytis can occur.

Disorders

Foliar tip burn is common and can be due to high soluble salts, low humidity, fluoride, or water stress. Water stress will also hasten the dieback that often occurs in the center of older hanging basket plants.

Postharvest

Ethylene at 0.1 to 1 ppm for twenty hours did not influence leaf abscission or cutting rooting of several species tested.

References

Hamrick, D. 2003. *Setcreasea,* pp. 642–643, *Zebrina,* pp. 689. In: *Ball RedBook,* 17th ed., vol. 2, D. Hamrick, ed. Ball Publishing, Batavia, Illinois.

Verbena

Common name: Common garden verbena, florist's verbena.
Scientific name: *Verbena canadensis, V.* x *hybrida, V. rigida, V. tenera,* and *V. tenuisecta.*
Family: Verbenaceae.
Other propagation methods: Seed.

Description, Uses, and Status

These medium to low-growing plants have rounded clusters of small tubular white, pink, rose, red, lavender, or apricot flowers. The blossoms of some cultivars have a white eye, white stripes, or darker flecks. The species are quite attractive and range in height and habit from a very prostrate 6 in. (15 cm) for *V. tenuisecta* to an upright 12 to 24 in. (30 to 60 cm) for

'Lanai Lavender Star' verbena.

V. canadensis and *V. rigida.* Modern hybrids tend to be low growing, averaging 6 to 10 in. (15 to 30 cm) high and up to 24 in. (60 cm) across. *V. canadensis* is hardy to Zone 5, but most species and cultivars are best treated as tender perennials that can take temperatures around 20° F (–7° C) in the landscape and may overwinter to Zone 8. The various species and hybrids are sold in the spring in packs, pots, and hanging baskets. Species such as *V. tenuisecta* can be quite heat and drought tolerant in the landscape. The hybrids often stop flowering in the middle of summer in hot climates, but newer hybrids are increasingly heat tolerant.

Flowering Control and Dormancy

Verbenas are day-neutral but tend to flower more rapidly under warm temperatures and the long days of late spring.

Stock Plant Management

Stock plants are often grown in hanging baskets for easier management of these spreading species. Building the stock plant scaffold is important to future cutting production. Work at Clemson University showed that for maximum cutting numbers, the initial pinch on the stock plants should occur after six nodes can be left on the plant, and the resulting side shoots should also be pinched when six nodes can be left on the shoots. By contrast, pinching low and allowing only two or four nodes to remain reduces the number of cuttings harvested. For example, pinching to two nodes both times produced 153 cuttings per stock plant over the course of the experiment, while pinching to six nodes produced 220 cutting per stock plant, a 44% increase in cuttings. If there is sufficient time after establishment, stock plants should be pinched up to three times before cuttings are harvested. Increasing the number of pinches from one to three on stock plants before the cutting harvest commences delays the initial harvest but increases the total number of cuttings harvested. Pinching plants only once allowed cuttings to be harvested more quickly after establishment of the stock plants but reduced the total number of cutting produced.

Supplemental high intensity discharge (HID) lighting can increase cutting production of stock plants grown in low light situations. Good air movement through the stock plants to ensure sufficient carbon dioxide will help provide optimum results when using HID lighting.

Cutting Harvest

Terminal cuttings 2 to 3 in. (5 to 8 cm) long are harvested. Be sure to grade and sort cuttings well to provide a uniform crop.

Propagation

Stage 1:
Cutting arrival or harvest and sticking
- Store cuttings at 48° to 50° F (9° to 10° C) for up to twenty-four hours if planting is going to be delayed.
- Rooting hormones are not required, but 750 to 2,500 ppm IBA can be used.
- Insert one cutting per cell if using plug flats.

Stage 2: Callusing
- Maintain substrate temperatures of 68° to 72° F (20° to 22° C).
- Maintain air temperatures of 75° to 80° F (24° to 27° C) during days and 68° to 70° F (20° to 21° C) during nights.
- Keep the substrate sufficiently moist so that water is easily squeezed out of it, but not so much that the cutting base is waterlogged. The base of the cutting needs air for proper rooting.
- Maintain a light intensity of 500 to 1,000 f.c. (5 to 11 klux).
- Begin foliar feeding with 50 to 75 ppm nitrogen from 20-10-20 as soon as leaves begin to show any color loss.
- Maintain a substrate pH of 6.2 to 6.5.
- Transfer the cuttings to Stage 3 after five to seven days, once 50% of the cuttings begin differentiating root initials.

Stage 3: Root development
- Maintain substrate temperatures of 68° to 72° F (20° to 22° C).
- Maintain air temperatures of 75° to 80° F (24° to 27° C) during days and 68° to 70° F (20° to 21° C) during nights.
- Begin drying out the substrate once roots are visible.
- Begin increasing the light intensity to 1,000 to 2,000 f.c. (11 to 22 klux) as the cuttings start to root out.
- Fertilize with 100 to 150 ppm nitrogen, alternating between 15-0-15 and 20-10-20.
- Roots should develop in seven to fourteen days.

Stage 4: Toning the rooted cutting
- Lower the air temperature to 70° to 75° F (21° to 24° C) during the day and 62° to 68° F (17° to 20° C) at night.
- Move the liners from the mist area into an area of lower relative humidity.

- Increase the light intensity to 2,000 to 4,000 f.c. (22 to 43 klux).
- Provide shade during the middle of the day to reduce temperature stress.
- Fertilize twice a week with 150 to 200 ppm nitrogen from 15-0-15 alternating with 20-10-20.
- The cuttings can be toned for seven days.

Plant Growth Regulators

During propagation, daminozide (B-Nine) sprays at 1,500 to 2,500 ppm or a tank-mixed spray of ancymidol (A-Rest) at 4 to 10 ppm and daminozide at 1,250 to 2,500 ppm can be used fifteen to twenty days after sticking unrooted cuttings. During production, sprays of paclobutrazol (Bonzi) at 5 to 30 ppm, daminozide at 1,500 to 2,500 ppm, chlormequat (Cycocel) at 800 to 1,500 ppm, or uniconazole (Sumagic) at 10 ppm are effective. A tank-mixed spray of daminozide at 2,500 to 3,500 ppm plus chlormequat at 750 to 1,000 ppm can also be used.

Ethephon (Florel) sprays at 300 to 500 ppm can be used to increase the number of axillary shoots and decrease stem elongation; however, discontinue use eight weeks prior to marketing. Benzylaminopurine (BA) sprays of 30 ppm applied immediately after planting increased number of roots and axillary shoot development.

Production and Schedule

Verbena prefers cool temperatures and high light. Grow the plants at 68° to 75° F (20° to 24° C) during the day and 62° to 65° F (17° to 18° C) at night. Maintain 4,500 to 6,000 f.c. (48 to 65 klux) light levels.

The substrate pH should be maintained at 5.8 to 6.2. Use 150 to 200 ppm nitrogen, which can be increased to 200 to 300 ppm later in production. Watering is critical for verbena. Water stress causes leaf scorch, but overwatering accentuates root and crown rots.

Use one plant per 4 in. (10 cm) pot, one to two per 6 in. (15 cm) pot, and three to five per 10 in. (25 cm) hanging basket. Plants should be pinched to the fourth or fifth leaf above the substrate after the rooted cuttings are established. Older plants can be trimmed at any time to shape the plant. Plants in 4 in. (10 cm) pots are marketable in six to eight weeks, those in 6 in. (15 cm) pots in eight to ten weeks, and those in 10 in. (25 cm) baskets in ten to twelve weeks.

Diseases

Powdery mildew, *Botrytis,* root and crown rots, and viruses can be problems.

Disorders

Yellowing of the foliage can occur due to iron chlorosis from high substrate pH or too-cool production temperatures. Necrotic leaf edges can be due to water stress, high soluble salts, excessive temperatures or light, or powdery mildew. Delayed flowering and too much vegetative growth can be due to overfertilizing, especially in combination with too much ammonium or low light, or to overwatering.

Postharvest

Ethylene exposure at 0.1 to 1 ppm for twenty hours did not influence leaf abscission or cutting rooting.

References

Donnelly, C. S. and P. R. Fisher. 2002. High-pressure sodium lighting affects greenhouse production of vegetative cuttings for specialty annuals. *HortScience* 37:623–626.

Faust, J. E., and L. W. Grimes. 2004. Cutting production is affected by pinch number during scaffold development of stock plants. *HortScience* 39:1691–1694.

Faust, J. E., and L. W. Grimes. 2005. Pinch height of stock plants during scaffold development affects cutting production. *HortScience* 40:650–653.

Hamrick, D. 2003. *Verbena,* pp. 672–674. In: *Ball RedBook,* 17th ed., vol. 2, D. Hamrick, ed. Ball Publishing, Batavia, Illinois.

Svenson, S. E. 1991. Rooting and lateral shoot elongation of verbena following benzylaminopurine application. *HortScience* 26:391–392.

Vinca

Common name: Vinca vine, periwinkle.
Scientific name: *Vinca minor* and *Vinca major.*
Family: Apocynaceae.
Other propagation methods: Division.

Vinca minor 'Illumination'.

Description, Uses, and Status
Both species are well-known vines grown primarily for their decorative foliage. *V. major* has large leaves, 1 to 3 in. (2.5 to 8 cm) long, and 2 in. (5 cm) wide purple flowers. *V. minor* has smaller 0.5 to 1.5 in. (1.3 to 4 cm) long leaves and 1 in. (2.5 cm) wide flowers, which can be white, blue, or purple and either double or single. Flowers are produced during the spring and summer. Both species have a number of cultivars with variegated foliage; however, flowering is quite sparse on some of the *V. minor* cultivars with variegated leaves. *V. minor* is more cold hardy, to Zone 4, than *V. major,* which is hardy only to Zone 7. Plants are typically sold in pots, hanging baskets, and mixed containers. Both species can be aggressive in some regions or in some parts of the landscape, where they should not be used.

Flowering Control and Dormancy
High light levels encourage flowering.

Stock Plant Management
Stock plants can be grown in pots or hanging baskets. Low light levels reduce flowering. Ethephon (Florel) sprays at 500 ppm are an essential treatment two to four weeks before harvest.

Cutting Harvest
Terminal cuttings 2.5 in. (6 cm) long are harvested from actively growing plants. Two-node cuttings are preferred.

Propagation

Stage 1:
Cutting arrival or harvest and sticking
- Insert two cuttings per cell if using plug flats.
- Use a rooting hormone, 1,000 ppm IBA, on the cuttings bases.

Stage 2: Callusing
- Maintain substrate temperatures of 68° to 72° F (20° to 22° C).

- Maintain air temperatures of 75° to 80° F (24° to 27° C) during days and 68° to 70° F (20° to 21° C) during nights.
- Maintain a light intensity of 500 to 1,000 f.c. (5 to 11 klux).
- Begin foliar feeding with 50 to 75 ppm nitrogen from 20-10-20 if there is any loss in foliage color.
- Maintain a substrate pH of 5.6 to 6.2.
- Transfer the cuttings to Stage 3 after five to seven days, once 50% of the cuttings begin differentiating root initials.

Stage 3: Root development
- Maintain substrate temperatures of 68° to 72° F (20° to 22° C).
- Maintain air temperatures of 75° to 80° F (24° to 27° C) during days and 68° to 72° F (20° to 22° C) during nights.
- Increase the light intensity to 1,000 to 1,500 f.c. (11 to 16 klux).
- Fertilize once a week with 100 to 150 ppm nitrogen, alternating between 15-0-15 and 20-10-20.
- Reduce and then eliminate misting as soon as possible.
- Roots should develop in fourteen to twenty-one days.

Stage 4: Toning the rooted cutting
- Lower the air temperature to 70° to 75° F (21° to 24° C) during the day and 62° to 68° F (17° to 20° C) at night.
- Move the liners from the mist area into an area of lower relative humidity.
- Increase the light intensity to 1,500 to 2,000 f.c. (16 to 22 klux).

- Fertilize once a week with 100 to 150 ppm nitrogen from 15-0-15 alternating with 20-10-20.
- The cuttings can be toned for seven days.

Plant Growth Regulators

Ethephon (Florel) sprays can be used at 500 to 1,000 ppm. Be careful to avoid applying too much because plants may take a long time to grow out of it in the landscape.

Production and Schedule

Recommended temperatures are 70° to 75° F (21° to 24° C) during the day and 62° to 65° F (17° to 18° C) at night. Avoid temperatures over 95° F (35° C). Provide 1,000 to 2,500 (11 to 27 klux) for both species initially. After *V. minor* is established, it can be grown at light levels of 4,000 to 9,000 f.c. (43 to 97 klux).

Initially, a rate of 150 ppm nitrogen is adequate at every other irrigation; increase to 200 to 300 ppm after plants are established. A light, well-drained substrate with a pH 5.6 to 6.2 is desired. Avoid high soluble salts in the substrate.

Use one plug per 4 in. (10cm) pot, three per 6 in. (15 cm) pot, and three to five per 10 in. (20 cm) basket. Both species have strong apical dominance, and plants should be pinched two to three weeks after transplanting. Older plants can be trimmed at any time to shape them. Older plants will also produce new shoots from below the substrate. Plants in 4 in. (10 cm) pots are marketable in six to eight weeks, those in 6 in. (15 cm) pots in seven to eight weeks, and those in 8 in. (20 cm) baskets in nine to eleven weeks.

Diseases

Rhizoctonia, Phytophthora, and impatiens necrotic spot virus, and tomato spotted wilt virus can be problems.

Disorders

Slow growth and poor shoot elongation can be due to too much ethephon, low production temperatures, or insufficient fertilizer, especially ammonium.

References

Hamrick, D. 2003. *Vinca,* pp. 676–677. In: *Ball RedBook,* 17th ed., vol. 2, D. Hamrick, ed. Ball Publishing, Batavia, Illinois.

Starman, T. W., M. C. Robinson, and K. L. Eixmann. 2004. Efficacy of ethephon on vegetative annuals. *HortTechnology* 14:83–87.

Yoder Green Leaf Perennials. 2004. *Handling Unrooted Perennials.* www.green-leaf-ent.com/URC_Handling_2004.pdf.

Index